reload

reload

rethinking women + cyberculture

edited by
Mary Flanagan and Austin Booth

The MIT Press Cambridge, Massachusetts London, England

This book was set in Janson and Rotis by Graphic Composition, Inc.
Printed and bound in the United States of America.

Library of Congress Cataloging-in-Publication Data

reload : rethinking women + cyberculture / edited by Mary Flanagan and Austin Booth.
  p. cm.
  Includes bibliographical references and index.
  ISBN 0-262-06227-5 (hc. : alk. paper) — ISBN 0-262-56150-6 (pbk. : alk. paper)
  1. American fiction—Women authors—History and criticism. 2. Women and literature—United States—History—20th century. 3. Computers and women—United States—History—20th century. 4. American fiction—20th century—History and criticism. 5. Computers and civilization—Fiction. 6. American fiction—Women authors. 7. Computers and women—Fiction. 8. Computers and civilization. 9. Computers in literature. I. Flanagan, Mary, 1969– II. Booth, Austin.

PS151 .R45 2002
813/.50809287 21   2001056235

Contents

Contents

Acknowledgments

Octavia E. Butler, "Speech Sounds" first appeared in *Isaac Asimov's Science Fiction Magazine*, December 1983. Copyright © 1983 by Davis Publication, Inc. Reprinted with the kind permission of the author.

Candas Jane Dorsey, "(Learning About) Machine Sex" first appeared in *Machine Sex and Other Stories*, 1988. Copyright © 1988. Reprinted by permission of Wooden Door & Associates Press.

Veronica Hollinger, "(Re)reading Queerly: Science Fiction, Feminism, and the Defamiliarization of Gender" first appeared in *Science-Fiction Studies* #77, Volume 26, Part 1, March 1999. Copyright © 1999. Reprinted with the kind permission of the author and *Science-Fiction Studies*.

Shariann Lewitt, "A Real Girl," from *Bending the Landscape: Original Gay and Lesbian Writing*, Vol. 1: Science Fiction, edited by Nicola Griffith and Stephen Pagel. Copyright © 1998 by Nicola Griffith and Stephen Pagel. Reprinted by permission of The Overlook Press.

Anne McCaffrey, "The Ship Who Sang" first appeared in *The Magazine of Fantasy and Science Fiction*; Copyright © 1961, 1989 by Anne McCaffrey. From *The Ship Who Sang*. Reprinted by permission of the author and the author's agents, the Virginia Kidd Agency, Inc.

Laura J. Mixon, *Proxies* [excerpt] first appeared in novel form from Tor Press. Copyright © 1998. Reprinted with the kind permission of the author and Trident Media Group, LLC.

C. L. Moore, "No Woman Born" first appeared in *Astounding Science Fiction*. Copyright © 1944 by Street and Smith Publications, renewed 1972 by C. L. Moore. Reprinted by permission of Don Congdon Associates.

Mary Rosenblum, "Entrada" first appeared in *Isaac Asimov's Science Fiction Magazine*, February 1993. Copyright © 1993, Bantam Doubleday Dell Magazines for Asimov's Science fiction. Reprinted with the kind permission of the author.

Melissa Scott, *Trouble and Her Friends* [excerpt] first appeared in novel form from Tor Press. Copyright © 1994 by Melissa Scott. Reprinted by permission of the publisher.

Sue Thomas, *Correspondence* [excerpt] first appeared in novel form from Overlook Press, Woodstock, New York. Copyright © 1991 by Sue Thomas. Reprinted by permission of The Overlook Press.

Amy Thomson, *Virtual Girl* [excerpt] first appeared in novel form from Tor Press, 1993; reprinted with the kind permission of P.P.I., New York.

James Tiptree Jr., "The Girl Who Was Plugged In" first appeared in *New Dimensions 3*. Copyright © 1973, 2001 by the Estate of Alice B. Sheldon. From *Her Smoke Rose Up Forever*. Reprinted by permission of the author's Estate and the Estate's agents, the Virginia Kidd Agency, Inc.

Thanks

The editors of the volume would like to deeply thank Jeanne Ellgar, Mark Booth, and Franklin Miller, who were indispensable in bringing this project to completion.

We would also like to thank our friends, mentors, and heroes, those who have had an influence on the creation of this work: Deidre Lynch, Patricia Mellencamp, Cecelia Condit, J. Leighton Pierce, Valley Export, Lauren Rabinovitz, Christopher Egert, Royal Roussel, Deborah Walters, Lloyd Walker, Brian Brantner, Rae Staseson, Kimberly Sawchuck, Franklin Miller III, and Timothy Lenoir; Brenda Battleson, Judy Adams-Volpe, Don Hartman, Gemma DeVinney, Karen Senglaup, and, of course, James Tiptree, Jr.

We especially are grateful to our authors for writing such thought-provoking essays and being patient during the process of editing and proofing the book.

Finally, thanks to the staff at The MIT Press for working so diligently to help us follow our rather unorthodox brand of bookmaking; Douglas Sery and Kathy Caruso deserve extra thanks.

Illustration Credits

Part opening pages: Image on p. 42 courtesy of VNS Matrix; image on p. 234 courtesy of VNS Matrix; image on p. 456 courtesy of Shu Lea Chang from the Brandon Teena online exhibit.

Images in chapter 12 courtesy of Suzanne Treister (CD-ROM and accompanying book published by Black Dog Publishing Limited, UK. ISBN: 190103366X email: info@ bdp.demon.co.uk) and VNS Matrix.

Images in chapter 13 are reproduced with the kind permission of Shu Lea Chang, SUMMIT—Stanford University, and The Wellcome Trust. Visible Human Project (VHP) hosted by the NLM—National Library of Medicine © 1999 (http:// www.nim.nih.gov/research/visible/).

Images in chapter 22 courtesy of Eidos Interactive, Char Davies, and Mary Flanagan.

Images from *Osmose* and *Ephémère* © 2000 Char Davies/Immersence Inc. and Soft-image, Inc./ (http://www.immersence.com/); images of "Spaces of Form" © 1999 L. Vigdor (http://www.paraspace.com/).

Editors and Contributors

About the Editors

Austin Booth   is the Humanities Specialist for the University Libraries at the University of Buffalo (SUNY). She holds graduate degrees in English and Women's Studies from the University of Michigan, undergraduate degrees in English and Economics from Cornell University, and an MIS from the University of California at Berkeley. Her recent publications include studies of users and information gateway sites, as well as work on gender and cyberculture.

Mary Flanagan   is an experimental media maker, multimedia designer, and teacher interested in exploring gender implications at the intersection of art and science. Her article, "Mobile Identities, Digital Stars, and Post-Cinematic Selves," is included in Fall 2000's *Wide Angle*. She has also produced her own online educational game for girls ages 9–11 <http://www.josietrue.com> and received a prestigious National Science Foundation grant for the project. Recent creative work includes the interactive VRML environment [recovery] (1998), the internationally shown VRML performance [The Perpetual Bed] (1998–1999), and the creative computer virus [phage] (2000), which creates a feminist map of the machine. Installations include *Career Moves*, a computer-controlled board game (2000) and *Corporate Ladder* (1999). Recent virtual performances and installations have been exhibited at the Central Fine Arts Gallery in Soho, the Guggenheim Gallery Online at Chapman University, and the Whitney 2002 Biennial. <http://www.maryflanagan.com>

Notes on Contributors

Alison Adam   is a senior lecturer at the Information System Institute, University of Salford, United Kingdom, where she teaches AI, ethics, and social science to computing students. Her main research interest is in gender and ICTs. Her book, *Artificial Knowing: Gender and the Thinking Machine*, was published by Routledge in 1998.

Octavia E. Butler has been writing science fiction since the early 1970s. Her work includes the Patternist series, about an elite group of mentally linked telepaths ruled by Doro, a 4,000-year-old immortal African, *Kindred*, the Xenogenesis trilogy, and other novels and short stories. In 1995 Butler was awarded a MacArthur Foundation Genius Grant.

Sharon Cumberland is an Associate Professor of English at Seattle University. She is working on a book about African American slave narratives, as well as articles on Hispanic stereotypes in American film and on fan fiction on the Internet. Her most recent article, in *Links and Letters*, is "North American Desire for the Spanish Other: Three Film Versions of Blasco-Ibaoez' Blood and Sand."

Dianne Currier completed her Ph.D. in Critical Theory at the Centre for Comparative Literature and Cultural Studies at Monash University Australia. Her research concerns the theoretical frameworks that Deleuze and Guattari offer for feminists theorizing technology, cyberspace, and transformation. She is currently teaching in media studies at Monash.

Candas Jane Dorsey lives in Edmonton, Alberta, Canada and is both a publisher and an author of science-fiction novels and short stories including *Black Wine* (1997). She is a founding member and past president of SF Canada, the Canadian association of professional science-fiction writers.

Julie Doyle and Kate O'Riordan are doctoral students based at the universities of Sussex and Brighton (UK), respectively. Julie Doyle is researching histories of gendered embodiment within the discourse of surgical science, while Kate O'Riordan is exploring the representations and relations of gender through the Internet. Both teach and study in the fields of English and Media Studies.

Thomas Foster is an Associate Professor of English at Indiana University and Director of the Cultural Studies Program there. He has published several articles on cyberpunk fiction and technoculture topics, and he has a book forthcoming from the University of Minnesota Press entitled *The Souls of Cyber-Folk*, focusing on gender, sexuality, and race in popular narratives about cyborgs and cyberspace.

Heather Hicks is Assistant Professor of English at Villanova University, where she teaches courses on postmodern American fiction and feminist theory. She has published on William Gibson and Joanna Russ and is currently writing a book on how American authors have depicted transformations in the meaning of public, paid work since World War II.

Veronica Hollinger is Associate Professor of Cultural Studies at Trent University in Peterborough, Ontario, Canada. She has published widely on speculative fiction and is co-editor of *Science Fiction Studies*. She is also co-editor of two critical collections, *Blood Read: The Vampire as Metaphor in Contemporary Culture* (University of Pennsylvania Press, 1997) and *Edging into the Future: Science Fiction and Contemporary Cultural Transformation* (University of Pennsylvania Press, forthcoming).

Shariann Lewitt (S. N. Lewitt, Nancy Zaroulis), a science-fiction writer, is author of the 1997 novel *Interface Masque, Songs of Chaos* (1993), and many other science-fiction novels. She also has written with Susan Shwartz under the joint name Gordon Kendall.

Anne McCaffrey's first story was published by Sam Moskowitz in *Science Fiction + Magazine*, and her first novel was published by Ballantine Books in 1967. She has published fifty-four books, including collaborations and small press editions, and fifty-four short stories—garnering seventeen awards for her writing.

Laura J. Mixon is a chemical engineer by training and an environmental engineer by profession, a former Peace Corps volunteer, an occasional computer and multimedia designer, and a progeny development manager (a mom). A native New Mexican, she is an unregenerate green chile–eater and coffee lover. Her writing explores the social impacts of technological change (on family and gender roles, for example), the effect of technology on the environment and vice versa, the nature of consciousness, and genetic experimentation. She sold her first novel in 1985, and since has published a number of books and shorter works, including *Burning the Ice* (2001), *Proxies* (1998), and *Glass Houses* (1992).

C. L. Moore (1911–1987) (Catherine L. Moore) was science-fiction author who was given the 1981 World Fantasy Award for Lifetime Achievement and a 1998 inductee into the Science Fiction and Fantasy Hall of Fame. Moore was one of the few women writing science fiction fantasy in the 1930s and 1940s.

Lisa Nakamura is Assistant Professor of English at Sonoma State University, where she teaches postcolonial literature and critical theory. She is co-editor of *Race and Cyberspace* (Routledge 2000), and is also working on a book tentatively entitled *Cybertypes: Race, Ethnicity, and Identity on the Internet*. Her recent work on race and the Internet appears in *CyberReader, Cyberculture*, and *Race in Cyberspace*.

Catherine S. Ramírez is a recent graduate of the Ph.D. program in Ethnic Studies at UC Berkeley. She is an Assistant Professor in the Department of English at the University of New Mexico, where she teaches courses on Chicana/o literature and culture, feminist theory, science fiction, and cultural studies. She is currently writing a book on the participation of Mexican American women in the zoot subculture of the 1940s.

Mary Rosenblum (Mary Freeman) is the author of many short stories and fiction, including *Chimera* (1993) and *The Stone Garden* (1995). "Mary makes a terrific goat cheese. She'll merrily hunt, prep, cook, and serve wild game in exactly the same way Martha Stewart cannot." She was the winner of the Compton Crook Award in 1994 and the Asimov Reader Award in 1997. Rosenblum lives in Oregon.

Melissa Scott has been writing science fiction since 1984. She earned her Ph.D. in Comparative History at Brandeis University. She was the 1986 winner of the John W. Campbell Award for Best New Writer and won the 1996 Lambda Literary Award for Gay/Lesbian Science Fiction.

Theresa M. Senft (janedoe@echonyc.com) is a graduate student in the Department of Performance Studies at New York University focusing on gender and technology. She is currently completing a dissertation, to be published in 2001 by Peter Lang, on the female Web-camera "stars" who have inspired films like *The Truman Show*. Theresa is a co-author of *History of the Internet, 1843–Present* (ABC-Clio Press) and co-editor of a special issue of the journal *Women & Performance*, entitled "Sexuality & Cyberspace."

Jyanni Steffensen is an ARC Postdoctoral Research Fellow in the Department for Social Inquiry at the University of Adelaide, Australia. She is currently working on a project titled "Queer Machines: Narratives of the Subject in Technoculture," which examines the ways in which the body, gender and sexuality are imaginatively and narratively (re)constructed in various artistic and scientific discourses.

Sarah Stein is an Assistant Professor in Communication Media at North Carolina State University in Raleigh, teaching media theory and production, with research interests in discourses of gender, visual culture, and popular representations of new technologies. Her former life was as a documentary filmmaker in New York City; two of the films she edited won Academy Awards.

Rajani Sudan is Associate Professor of English at Southern Methodist University. She has published many articles on popular film and eighteenth- and nineteenth-century British literature and is the author of *Enlightened Xenophobia*.

Sue Thomas is the Director of the trAce Online Writing Community <http://trace.ntu.ac.uk/> and has written widely about technology. She has published two novels, *Correspondence* and *Water*, and her fifth book, recently completed, is set in a virtual community.

Amy Thomson is a full-time writer. She is the John W. Campbell award-winning author of *Virtual Girl* and *The Color of Distance*. She lives with her husband in the Pacific Northwest.

James Tiptree Jr., a.k.a. Dr. Alice Sheldon, was born in 1915 in Chicago, Illinois. A graphic artist, painter, C.I.A. agent, and science-fiction author, Sheldon wrote numerous novels and short stories from 1973, when she was fifty-three, until her death in 1987. The James Tiptree Jr. Award for science-fiction writing is offered in her memory.

Bernadette Wegenstein, a linguist, semiotician, and specialist in Romance Languages and Cultures, received her doctorate from Vienna University in 1997. She is currently an Assistant Professor in the Department of Media Study at the University at Buffalo, where she is researching her current project, "New Bodies—New Worlds: Corporeal Narratives at the Turn of the Millennium." Her study of the representation of AIDS in the European Media, *Die Darstellung von AIDS in den Medien*, appeared in 1998.

INTRODUCTION

Austin Booth and Mary Flanagan

In 1998 the editors of this collection wanted to find an anthology of women's cyberpunk fiction for use in a cybertheory course and could not find one, despite the increasing number of women writing what can loosely be called cyberfiction—writing that explores the relationship between people and virtual technologies. We wished to show students that our technoculture, imagined so creatively by writers such as William Gibson, Bruce Sterling, Rudy Rucker, and Neal Stephenson (and reimagined by popular Hollywood cinema), is actively being reshaped by women's voices. As teachers, we wanted to make available to students the feminist voices challenging the two existing visions of cyberspace: that of the almost exclusively male cyberpunk writers and technoculture aficionados (the *Wired/Mondo* generation) and that of cyberfeminist theorists.

This book fills two problematic gaps—the absence of a volume that introduces women's cyberfiction and the absence of a volume that considers gender and technology issues from fictional and theoretical viewpoints with and against each other. This collection brings together women's fictional representations of cyberculture with feminist theoretical and critical investigations of gender and technoculture. No anthology of women's cyberfiction exists; science-fiction anthologies that do focus on women are typically either fantasy or utopia collections, and cyberpunk anthologies have almost totally excluded women.[1] Women writers such as Melissa Scott, Nicola Griffith, Laura J. Mixon, and Lisa Mason, however, are utilizing the feel, ethos, and themes of cyberpunk in their work.[2] We want to bring critical attention to this literature as well as to investigate the relationship between women's popular and theoretical conceptions of cyberspace; we believe that the fiction and theory gathered here inform each other in subtle and complex ways.

Within this collection, the practice of theory drives the exploration of fictional narratives and vice versa. Rather than collapsing fiction and criticism or sharply separating practice and theory, this collection provides a variety of viewpoints from which to consider a similar set of concerns—the effects of profound and rapid technological change on culture, particularly on women's lives. By examining a range of works, we can come to a larger understanding of both the revolutionary and reactionary effects of cyberculture on women. We hope that the inclusion of both fiction and theory in this volume bridges the conceptual and institutional rift between theory and fiction—the tension between high and popular culture, like that between theory and fiction, can be described as inherent to cyberculture and its representations: culturally and aesthetically, it is a hybrid merging of "lowbrow" street culture with "highbrow" intellectual and academic interests.

Science fiction is a vital source of narratives through which we understand and represent our relationships to technology. Studying these stories can help us examine how we conceive our present. In fact, the stories we tell ourselves about our relationship to machines have the potential to shape our material relationships to machines in the near future.[3] We believe that women's fictional representations of cyberspace and cyberculture, largely ignored in cyberculture/cyberpunk studies, are crucial to an informed understanding of our present technoculture: First, women's science fiction, despite its limited-run editions, is a popular literature with a significant and vocal fan base. Science fiction is no longer a subculture dominated by male writers and readers; the increasing presence of women in science-fiction culture as authors, readers, and fans has meant that science fiction itself pays more attention to issues of gender. Second, women's cyberfiction can be read productively against what has been an all-male canon of cyberpunk literature. Women writers are appropriating the cyberpunk aesthetic—metaphors of jacking in, figures of outlaws and outsiders, and film-noir rhetoric—for their own ends. Third, reading women's cyberfiction can illuminate studies of technology and postmodernism, particularly work focusing on anxieties about the decentering and fragmentation of the subject and studies concerned with the status of the body. Fourth, women's cyberfiction may be read productively against feminist postmodern critical theory and practices, particularly claims about the liberatory nature of the transcendence of gender and the body, and the destabilizing cultural effects of the hybridity of the female cyborg. Women's cyberfiction rewrites the familiar cultural narratives of cyberpunk literature and the Hollywood cyborg film, offering an alternative set of visions while at the same time challenging the critical and theoretical trends of utopian cyberfeminism.

The stories and critical/theoretical pieces gathered in this volume offer multiple alternatives to narratives of the hacker console cowboy, narratives of the feminist cyborg, and the myths of a "gender-free" cyberculture. Cyberculture and its figures of cyborgs and cyberspace emerge here as neither solely the purview of masculine authority and representation nor as a wholly liberating set of metaphors and practices for women. Rather, a picture of cyberspace as contradictory and complex develops: a space in which there is oppression as well as room for tactical and oppositional maneuvers.

In this introduction, we briefly outline contexts within which to understand the women's cyberfiction and critical/theoretical accounts of gender and cyberspace gathered here: feminist science fiction, the cyberpunk movement of the 1980s, feminist studies of technology and science, and cyberfeminism. Readers will also find an overview of women's cyberfiction in chapter 2.

Feminist Science Fiction

Feminist science fiction is crucial to understanding recent cyberfiction writing by women; it has a rich tradition of posing significant questions about the relationships among gender, technology, and culture. In her influential essay "What Can a Heroine Do? Or Why Women Can't Write," Joanna Russ claims that science fiction has the potential to be a "liberating" genre for women because it allows for the imagining of oppositional social and sexual categories—in particular, for the imagining of alternative notions of gender and gender roles.[4] Feminist science fiction, like feminist theory, pays special attention to the cultural construction of gender, the gendering of the Cartesian divide between mind and body, the maintenance of social and sexual hierarchies under patriarchy, and multiple challenges to notions of unified, stable subjectivity.[5] Feminist science fiction exists in a complex relationship to popular genres, both drawing from and opposing the conventions of mainstream science fiction and fantasy in order to imagine new representations of gender and gender relations that challenge conventional science fiction. As Sarah Lefanu comments, "Feminist SF, then, is part of science fiction while struggling against it."[6] Indeed, several historians of women's science fiction have claimed that feminist appropriation of science fiction, ostensibly a masculine genre, can serve as a model for feminist strategies of opposition and resistance in larger cultural contexts.

Science fiction has long been thought of as a "masculine" genre, as a genre written by male authors for male readers. But even during the 1930s and 1940s, when science-fiction magazines were at their height of popularity, female writers such as C. L. Moore and Leigh Brackett established themselves within the genre.[7] Robin Roberts's *A New Species: Gender and Science in Science Fiction*, for example, reads pulp science fiction as a protofeminist "forerunner" to contemporary feminist utopias and science fiction and argues that science fiction offers women writers the "opportunity for radical revision and reclamation," especially in narratives about science.[8] *Reload* includes an example of such a protofeminist work, C. L. Moore's "No Woman Born" (1944), an early account of a female cyborg (see chapter 14).

Women's science fiction came into its own in the 1960s and 1970s. Science fiction was a form in which women writers could tease out the implications of second-wave feminism, with a particular focus on manipulating cultural structures and hierarchies. Novels such as Joanna Russ's *The Female Man* (1975), Naomi Mitchison's *Solution Three* (1975), and Marge Piercy's *Woman on the Edge of Time* (1979) were grounded in second-wave feminist politics and theories, just as earlier feminist science fiction was based on the tenets of nineteenth-century feminism.[9] These novels exposed gender and sexuality as cultural constructs rather than as "natural" phenomena. The metaphors and conventions of science fiction—aliens, time travel, alternate realities, relativism—proved to be rich material through which to examine gender and sexual politics. Writers such as Suzy McKee Charnas, Sally Miller Gearhart, Mitchison, Piercy, and Russ were able to expose the sexist assumptions not only of much science fiction, but also of the world in which they lived.

Important concerns of women's science fiction have been incorporated into women's cyberfiction and into cyberfeminist criticism. Here, we take a look at some common features of women's science fiction: utopias, dystopias, the figure of the alien, and fragmented subjectivity, in order to better understand the historical context of cyberfeminism, cyberpunk, and women's cyberfiction.

Utopias and Separatists

Women science-fiction writers in the latter half of the twentieth century depicted strong female characters in roles usually reserved for men such as scientists, political leaders, spaceship captains, inventors, explorers, and warriors. The works of Anne McCaffrey, Ursula K. Le Guin, Marion Zimmer Bradley, Octavia E. Butler, and Vonda McIntyre contain skilled, smart, and highly resourceful heroines. Many of these authors portray imaginary cultures in which women are politically or socially dominant, alternative familial and social structures, such as matriarchy, developed, and a marked emphasis was placed on women's feelings, particularly female desire. The post-apocalyptic conventions so often used in science fiction were refashioned into a critique of patriarchy; in fact, as several critics have pointed out, in much women's science fiction of the 1970s and 1980s the apocalypse or cataclysm that has ravaged humanity or has led to the need for a new social order is sexism or "patriarchy itself."[10] The work of many women science-fiction writers in the 1970s and 1980s including Suzy McKee Charnas's *Motherlines* (1978), *Walk to the End of the World* (1978), *The Furies* (1995);

Pamela Sargent's *The Shore of Women* (1986); and Sally Miller Gearhart's *The Wander-ground: Stories of the Hill Women* (1980) are utopian narratives of self-sufficient, all-female societies. Separatism in these works is invoked as a necessary precondition for cultural and social change. These fictional new social orders mount a critique of the un-equal power hierarchies maintained by patriarchy and demonstrate how the cultural constructions of gender difference serve to maintain those hierarchies.

Many examples of utopian science fiction imagined the potential consequences of the erasure of gender difference. In Ursula K. Le Guin's *The Left Hand of Darkness* (1978), human sexuality is on a cycle; during "kemmer," humans can choose to become male or female. The Concord World presented in Melissa Scott's post-apocalyptic *Shadow Man* (1995) recognizes nine different sexual preferences and five different bio-logical sex categories; Emma Bull's *Bone Dance* (1991) and Kelley Eskridge's "And Sa-lome Danced" (1995) also explore the complex relationship among gender, sex, and sexuality.

Dystopias and Systems

In the 1980s and 1990s, feminist science-fiction writers turned to producing dystopic visions of the future. If feminist utopias of the 1970s and 1980s emphasized women's freedom and autonomy, the dystopias of the 1980s and 1990s accentuated the social and political consequences of the denial of that autonomy. Dystopias such as Suzette Haden Elgin's *Native Tongue* (1984); Margaret Atwood's *The Handmaid's Tale* (1986); Octavia E. Butler's *Mind of My Mind* (1977), *Patternmaster* (1976), and the *Xenogenesis* trilogy: *Dawn* (1987), *Adulthood Rites* (1988), and *Imago* (1989); Zoë Fairbairns's *Benefits* (1988); and Nicola Griffith's *Slow River* (1995) depict worlds in which the feminist movement has failed, and women are positioned as sexual and reproductive objects rather than as subjects.[11] These dystopias are set largely in highly technologized urban centers, con-trolled by totalitarian governments. As opposed to women's utopias, which were largely antitechnological, or nontechnological in nature, women's dystopias are highly engaged with questions of technology, and explore both the possibilities and problems techno-culture poses for women in particular. See chapter 2 for a further analysis of the tech-nologies within recent feminist dystopias.

Aliens

Women science-fiction writers have made particular use of the science-fiction trope of the alien in order to explore the creation and maintenance of hierarchies of cultural dif-ference, and the categories of self and other.[12] After all, women writers have themselves been aliens in the field of science-fiction writing. As outsiders in a male tradition, women writers have been able to explore the status of marginality, providing a different "alien" viewpoint on the construction of cultural categories. Science fiction has long used the figure of the alien to invoke anxieties about cultural differences such as man/woman, white/black, upper class/lower class; however, much science fiction invokes these anxieties precisely to bolster these differences, rather than break them down. Women's science fiction, in contrast, uses the figure of the alien to expose the ways in which racial and gendered boundaries are constructed and the ways in which those boundaries maintain hierarchies of domination and power (indeed to expose the very anxiety over boundary collapse itself as xenophobic and sexist). Octavia E. Butler, for example, reworks slave narratives through the figure of the alien (in *Wild Seed*, *Mind of My Mind*, and *Clay's Ark*) in order to demonstrate the implausibility of fixed racial categories.

Subjectivities

Dystopias by Rebecca Ore, Melissa Scott, and Judith Moffett, offer narratives that contain fragmented, multiple subjectivities and experiment frequently with postmodern, decentered narrative forms, including *Gaia's Toys* (1997), *Shadow Man* (1995) and *Dreaming Metal* (1997), and *The Ragged World: A Novel of the Hefn on Earth* (1991). Feminist science fiction has challenged transcendental concepts of the self, knowledge, and rationality, and it has exposed those very notions as conceptually revolving around and supporting dominance of a Western white male subject. Feminist science-fiction narratives mount a challenge to the notion of a unified self, and, like feminist theory, have worked to expose the notion of a "universal" self as reifying a male self. In addition, women science-fiction writers frequently use fragmented narratives and split/multiple narrators to examine conceptions of the self. Joanna Russ's *The Female Man*, for example, tells the story of four women—Joanna, Janet, Jael, and Jeannine—who are fragments of a female subject that refuses to become unified or fixed. Both cyberfeminism and cyberfiction expand on the notion of the split subject by imagining consciousness as a network, and identity as inescapably multiple.

Building on a foundation of women's writing that has centered on utopias, dystopias, the figure of the alien, and the importance of the subject, important recent women's science fiction has further focused on female subjects and subjectivity, providing images of women as strong main characters in space and other-world settings (Kay Kenyon, Vonda McIntyre, Connie Willis, Mary Rosenblum). Chapter 2 explores in depth women's treatment of the subject in women's cyberfiction, exemplifying a new set of anxieties and contradictions around female subjectivity.

"Classic" Cyberpunk

Veronica Hollinger writes, "Cyberpunk is not the only mode in which science fiction has demonstrated an anti-humanist sensibility."[13] As noted earlier in this chapter, anti-humanism was a powerful tool in feminist science fiction. While women's science fiction has a tradition of writers who use fragmented narratives to examine the maintenance of fixed conceptions of the self and of power relations in patriarchal society, the tradition of cyberpunk uses the fragmentary, decentered aesthetic to culminate in an entirely different, quite masculine genre. Several critics have argued that 1980s cyberpunk was influenced by 1970s feminist science fiction. In fact, Samuel R. Delany contends that canonical cyberpunk itself is indebted to feminist science fiction as an "absent mother," that feminist science fiction gave cyberpunk a conceptual framework "without which we wouldn't be able to read it," and, in fact, that without feminist science fiction, "there wouldn't *be* any cyberpunk."[14]

A subgenre of science fiction, cyberpunk emerged in the mid-1980s as a movement sparked by William Gibson's novels.[15] Cyberpunk writers, including Bruce Sterling, Rudy Rucker, and Neal Stephenson, have examined the implications of Western technology–driven culture—"not from shopworn formulas of robots, spaceships and atomic energy, but from cybernetics, biotech and the communications web."[16] Cyberpunk prepares readers for life in the postindustrial, media-saturated late-twentieth and early-twenty-first centuries by depicting a world of biotechnology, genetic enhancement, artificial intelligence, and networked, mediated consciousness. Bruce Sterling calls cyberpunk "an unholy alliance of the technical world . . . and the underground world of pop culture, visionary fluidity and street-level anarchy."[17] Cyberpunk literature focuses on a believable near future, where rebels live at the margins of a technologically enhanced society rife with "systems"—corporate conglomerates, religions, and strict governments—all of which incorporate the use of high-tech surveillance or information systems. Cyberpunk tends to be characterized as a subculture (in both fiction and in "real life") populated by young male outlaws who hack and crack computer networks to steal, manipulate, or erase the information they find.[18] *Reload* offers several pieces of fiction that show another side to a hacking subculture and the role of the outsider—see, for example, Melissa Scott's *Trouble and Her Friends* (excerpted in chapter 4) and Candas Jane Dorsey's "(Learning About) Machine Sex" (chapter 3).

Cyberpunk has been hailed as the quintessential postmodern genre. It explores the construction of the body (usually the sign of a stable unified self) and challenges the humanistic conception of the real as opposed to the artificial or the virtual. Although much science fiction has explored and even questioned the boundaries between humans and machines, and between the natural and the artificial, cyberpunk is particularly interested in the relationships among cultural binaries such as nature/science, body/mind, human/machine, female/male, and, particularly, real/unreal. The most popular examples of cyberpunk fiction (and resulting Hollywood film adaptations) are particularly interested in the human/machine hybrid, the cyborg: a figure that "is not only a physical amalgam of human and machine, but represents a radical shift in subjectivity. The cyborg combines a humanly incorporated personal consciousness with a technologically incorporated machine consciousness."[19] Indeed, the work of the prominent figures in the genre is obsessed with permeable minds and bodies, with what Bruce Sterling describes as "the theme of body invasion: prosthetic limbs, implanted circuitry, cosmetic surgery, genetic alteration. The even more powerful theme of mind invasion: brain-computer interfaces, artificial intelligence, neurochemistry—techniques radically redefining the nature of humanity, the nature of the self."[20] The women's cyberfiction gathered in *reload* advances these themes in works that explore alternate bodies (Shariann Lewitt's "A Real Girl," chapter 25; James Tiptree Jr.'s "The Girl Who Was Plugged In," chapter 28; and Anne McCaffrey's "The Ship Who Sang," chapter 6) as well as multiple consciousnesses (Laura J. Mixon's *Proxies*, excerpted in chapter 23).

Cyberpunk's attitude toward technoculture and its concomitant breakdown of accepted boundaries is both enthusiastic and anxious. Although cyberpunk explores the potential destabilization of identity through virtual reality, cybernetics, and biotech, "traditional" gender identities and relations are reinscribed. Whether cyberpunk texts with their antihumanist claims decenter or merely reinstate a particular gendered, raced, located self has been a question of debate. Cyberpunk has successfully questioned humanist dichotomies such as mind/body and human/machine but has not offered a new form for exploring the other; it has not lived up to the challenge of rewriting gender roles. Indeed, "cyberpunk narrates the pleasurable crisis in white masculinity within the body-marked postmodern age"[21]; in other words, it explores the particular crisis of white masculinity in a postmodern culture.[22] Scott Bukatman (1993) concludes, for example, that the fantasies of cyberpunk are ultimately about empowering masculinity. Cyberpunk's revolutionary claims must be carefully scrutinized; its heady style and upfront radical stance conceal its ultimate conservatism when it comes to reconceptualizing class, gender, and race.

Despite similar challenges to humanism and subjectivity, much feminist science fiction offers a very different agenda than cyberpunk: whereas feminist science fiction, like cyberpunk, challenges transcendental concepts of the self, knowledge, and rationality, feminist science fiction exposes and questions those very notions as conceptually revolving around and supporting dominance of a Western white male subject. Cyberpunk, however, celebrates this dominance; perhaps cyberpunk's interrogation of the mind/body split is simply a reinforcement of seventeenth-century Cartesian thinking. Cyberpunk, like other science fiction, is about "transcendence" through technology; yet these offers of transcendence "point cyberpunk back to the romantic trappings of the genre at its most conventional, as does the valorization of the (usually male) loner rebel/hacker/punk who appears so frequently as its central character."[23] Even if male cyberpunk texts are not feminist, however, or do not deconstruct the relationship between gender and technology, cyberpunk itself—in its exploration of subjectivity and technology, its deconstruction and fragmentation of the subject via representations of technoculture, and its attention to the discursive and the material body and to the effects of embodiment—is ripe for feminist investigations and intervention.

Feminist Studies of Technology and Science

Any discussion of women and digital culture, cyberculture, and virtual technologies needs to be placed within the context of feminist studies of technology and science. The 1980s and 1990s saw the emergence of feminist studies of the relationship of gender and technology that included not only examinations of technological artifacts, but of technological practices, systems of knowledge, institutions, and competencies as well. These studies focus on three general areas: (1) the position of women in technological disciplines, including the sexual division of labor within technological fields; (2) women's experience of technology, including the effects of domestic, industrial, information, and medical technologies on women's lives; and (3) the gendering of technology—that is, the feminization or eroticization of certain technologies.

Traditional histories of technology have ignored both women's contributions to technological innovation and women's experience of new technologies. Feminist accounts of technology combat the myths that technology creates better working conditions, improves the quality of domestic life, and diminishes gender divisions at home and work. Histories of women, automation, and technology such as *Women, Technology, and Innovation* edited by Joan Rothschild (1982) or *The Technological Woman* edited by Jan Zimmerman (1983) emphasize that like domestic technologies, "labor-saving" office technologies such as typewriters and computers, far from liberating women, increase women's work and confine women to low-level jobs. *Mechanical Brides* (1993), the companion volume to an exhibition of the same name at the Smithsonian, documents ways in which advertisements for modern appliances and office machinery represent a passive relationship between women and mechanical devices. In these historical, popular representations, ideal domestic and office arrangements have been represented as one in which the female body is a mere extension of a machine: both woman and machine in service as mechanical brides to the men for whom they work.[24] Examining the role of women during times of technological change highlights the ways in which women have been conceptually and institutionally tied to technology.

Feminist studies of science have greatly influenced both feminist philosophy and feminist studies of technology, taking the cultural study of technology one step further into scientific disciplines themselves. This feminist "invasion" of science opened up debates about epistemology and the mind/body split, and called for a rethinking of conceptions of the subject and space. These questions led to innovations in other fields, including cyberfeminism and cyberfiction. Feminist studies of science have focused on how science understands gender and women, and how gender constructions affect science.[25] It is this latter area that has produced the most controversial literature in feminist science studies, which show that science is affected by social relations including gender assumptions, attitudes, language, and metaphors. These works argue that science is not "objective"; what science takes as its object and how it understands its object are socially constructed.

Feminist studies of science have greatly influenced both fictional and theoretical treatments of technoscience and cyberculture. The work of Evelyn Fox Keller, a mathematical biologist, is among the best of such research. In *Reflections on Gender and Science* (1996), Keller looks at how knowledge develops according to gendered "attitudes" of research communities. Keller, looking at the content and rhetoric of scientific knowledge, argues that scientific inquiries and conclusions are profoundly affected by gender. In her work, for example, Keller has shown how scientists favor dictatorial or controlling models rather than interactive models—such as computer networks—to explain scientific phenomena.[26] Like other feminist scientists, Keller pays particular attention to the construction of objectivity and reason as gendered concepts and argues for an alternative notion of scientific practice.[27] Epistemology is also a central concern for feminist science—writers like Sandra Harding arguing that what we call "knowledge" is itself culturally situated and might appear differently if viewed from the standpoint of women or other socially marginal groups.[28] Harding is in favor of standpoint theory, arguing that the critical perspectives of those who have traditionally been excluded can make better science by including a perspective that acknowledges standpoint, or cultural context, rather than one that claims objectivity. These epistemological concerns are reflected in feminist science fiction as well, for writers disengaging and splitting the subject do so with political consciousness. Also, epistemologies concern the body; long have women been tied to the body and ways of knowing grounded in the body. Feminist science fiction and theoretical cyberfeminist writing both play with such relations. In her book *Artificial Knowing* (1998), Alison Adam examines the ways in which gender is inscribed in artificial-intelligence systems. Adam argues that it is especially important to put AI systems in a cultural context because, unlike other computer systems, AI "claims to model aspects of human intelligence," yet such knowledge is based on a model of a male knowing subject.

Donna Haraway, trained as a biologist and perhaps the "original" cyberfeminist (though not self-proclaimed), is one of the most well known feminist critics of the ideologies and epistemologies of science. She treats science as a set of narratives: In *Primate Visions* (1989), Haraway examines the studies of primatology and interprets them as stories that attempt to define human nature and human origins. To Haraway, reading these accounts also means reading the institutional contexts of their creation, distribution, and reception. In other words, Haraway does not read primatology for what it tells us about primates, or human origins, but for what it tells us about our culture. She suggests we read our stories of cyberculture in the same critical way.

Cyberfeminism

Probably the most often cited and reprinted piece in cyberculture and cyberfeminist studies is Donna Haraway's essay "A Cyborg Manifesto: Science, Technology, and Socialist Feminism in the Late Twentieth Century."[29] Unlike many postmodern theorists, Haraway is optimistic, even utopian, about the potential of the machine/human combination, the cyborg. Haraway's essay argues that the figure of the cyborg is not a figure of horror, but a figure of empowerment. While noting that the means of production of technology is rarely beneficial for women, ultimately she suggests we should celebrate the cyborg because it signifies the breaking down or subversion of dichotomies associated with domination and inequity.[30]

Grounded in both practice and theory, cyberfeminism can be thought of as a new wave of feminist theory and practice that is united in challenging the "coding" of technology and in investigating the complex relationships between gender and digital culture. Cyberfeminism is concerned with the ways in which cybertechnologies affect women's lives in particular. Women software developers, hackers, online chat enthusiasts, performance artists, cyberpunk writers, technosex participants, game designers, and digital artists create narratives that explore both the pleasures and pitfalls of digital culture for women, creating complex positions for themselves in a digital world that potentially allows for new types of relations among women, men, and machines.

Cyberfeminists write about a digital world that goes beyond work culture: Cyberculture in these texts is a revolutionary social experiment with the potential to create new identities, relationships, and cultures. The style of many cyberfeminist works and Web sites, like the style of the Internet or digital culture itself, is not linear, but is a collage, an assembly, of stories, facts, theories, drawings, quotes, and parenthetical comments. Sadie Plant's *Zeros + Ones* (1997) is one of the best examples of such works: it both enacts and describes the spirit of exhilaration and unregulated movement within cyberculture. As a nonlinear work it reflects, through its unfolding, the networked nature of digital culture and argues that women are the unsung heroines of the digital revolution (beginning with Ada Lovelace and her experiences with Charles Babbage's difference engine). Plant further implies, through an emphasis on interconnections and intersections, that women's histories, cultures, biologies, and sexualities make them the quintessential wired posthumans—a position that some find liberating and others find to be essentialist. This debate exemplifies the tensions within cyberfeminism itself, for part of the cyberfeminist goal of rethinking women's relationship to technology is to undo the pairing of women with nature.[31] The task at hand, while critiquing old stereotypes, must be to avoid a new kind of essentialism: that is, an essentialism that posits women as "naturally" akin to multitasking, fluidity, and networks.

Comprised of a diverse range of interventions and experiments, cyberfeminism is not a focused, unified political movement, but a sporadic, tactical, contradictory set of theories, debates, and practices. While divided in their beliefs about the role of technology in culture, theorists and practitioners are united through their experimentation with technology and their investigation of the ways women are working with technology. From writers such as Sadie Plant and Donna Haraway to cultural groups such as webgrrls to artists like Lynn Hershman Leeson, cyberfeminists believe new technologies open radical possibilities for women's politics, for exploring ideas of agency and subjectivity, and for creating a uniquely female space.[32] Other feminists, such as Lisa Nakamura, Rosi Braidotti, Faith Wilding, and Chela Sandoval are wary of such liberatory claims and note that new technologies reproduce problematic issues within culture, including the familiar power dynamics of sexism and of racial and gender inequity. Wilding notes, "New media exist within a social framework that is already established in its practices and embedded in economic, political and cultural environments which are still deeply sexist, and racist."[33] These internal contradictions are inherent to cyberfeminism itself and are significant precisely because there is so much at stake with the integration of new technologies into everyday life—issues such as who has access, who is represented by and within technology and how, and the ways in which the technologies are used. Women increasingly use, produce, and consume complex technologies. But what does this increased presence mean? Are women merely becoming more efficient consumers and workers? Has feminism changed how technologies are created, and for whom?

According to "classic" cyberpunk fiction, high-tech advertising, *Wired* magazine, cultural events such as Burning Man, and lingering cyberculture personalities such as Timothy Leary, cyberspace is free of the constraints and prejudices of our "actual" social and physical spaces.[34] The two most powerful myths about the Internet are that, first, it is an "identity-free" space (because users can create alternative identities on the Net, identity becomes completely detached from the body, and from sociocultural categories such as gender, class, race, or age) and, second, that because the Internet allows for "free" exchange of information, cyberspace is free also of class and cultural hierarchies. Writers such as like Laurel Sutton, Stephanie Brail, and Dale Spender, however, express ambivalence about whether cyberspace really does lead to the breakdown of the social barriers of the material world, especially when it comes to gender and the treatment of women. For along with tales of women's empowerment and success with the Internet, there are accounts of inequality of access and use, as well as documented online sexism and harassment.[35] Further, reports such as Julian Dibbell's 1993 *Village Voice* article document "virtual" rape.[36] Many observers and participants suspect that cyberculture will simply duplicate the social and gendered hierarchies of material culture, and fear that the notion of a new egalitarian world in cyberspace is merely a utopian fantasy.[37]

Any discussion of women and technology needs to be placed in the context of women's access to technology within the international labor economy. Feminist accounts of technology work to dissolve the myth that computerized and electronic technologies will break down gendered hierarchies and segregation in the workplace or improve working conditions for women. Women enter most frequently into technology networks as workers rather than as users or creative producers of high-end technology. Melanie Millar (1998) calls attention to the uneven effects of cybertechnology on diverse groups of women—the cyberfeminist, the computer-chip factory worker, and the pizza delivery phone operator who punches orders into a database have very different relations to cyberculture. Behind the scenes of the digital economy, low-skilled women work in manufacturing and service industries such as microchip production. Instead of easing the oppression of Third World women, the technological revolution has merely perpetuated their oppression in a new workplace. As Rosi Braidotti says, "Hyper-reality does not wipe out class relations: it just intensifies them."[38] Despite the vision of global access that digital technology seems to offer—a utopian world that transcends gender, class, nationality, and race—the gap between those who have access to technological resources and those who do not is growing. The writings in *Reload*, however, explore women as authors, creators, and workers equally; they also look at what the product of that work will be. The work of Sue Thomas, Melissa Scott,

Candas Jane Dorsey, Anne McCaffrey, James Tiptree Jr., and Mary Rosenblum included in *reload*, for example, all interrogate the effects of technology on women's working lives.

The status of identity within cyberspace is one of the most widely contested questions within cyberfeminism. In a virtual world, our traditional conception of the self as individual, stable, unique, and grounded in a (gendered) body is brought into question; identity can be multiple and malleable, a "signifier" without a clear referent. In *The War of Desire and Technology at the Close of the Mechanical Age* (1995), Sandy Stone argues that we are moving toward a "transgendered" culture—that is, one in which identity will not be connected to bodies or physical attributes, and in which "multiple personality" will cease to be pathological. A virtual culture, Stone argues, is one in which digital phenomena such as online identities are also legitimized and real. Other important work on identity that has been incorporated by cyberfeminists includes Judith Butler's *Gender Trouble* (1990). Butler argues that femininity is a performance and contends that subversive performances of femininity reveal "that the original identity after which gender fashions itself is an imitation without an origin."[39] In her *Life on the Screen* (1995), Sherry Turkle looks at the ability of the computer to transform identity and relationships. She argues that assuming alternate online identities can have positive psychological and social effects, loosening personal and social repressive boundaries. As Turkle writes, "Computer screens are the new location for our fantasies, both erotic and intellectual," and as such, they can be very liberating for women who can play out aspects of themselves they might otherwise repress or ignore.[40]

Cyberfeminist works tie questions of identity to issues of the body and performance. In her discussions of online communication, Lisa Nakamura envisions the following: "A diversification of the roles which get played, which are permitted to be played, can enable a thought provoking detachment of race from the body, and an accompanying questioning of the essentialness of race as a category. Performing alternative versions of self and race jams the ideology-machine, and facilitates a desirable opening up of what Judith Butler calls 'the difficult future terrain of community' in cyberspace."[41] Nakamura explores the ways in which cyberspace allows for raced performances such as passing or blackface. Sandy Stone also writes about the relationships between bodies, identity, and performance and explores the relationships among virtual bodies and feminist theories of performance. According to Stone, virtual technologies allow us to see the operations of the mapping of cultural identity onto material bodies.[42] Writers such as Teresa M. Senft, however, take issue with performative transgressions by cyberfeminists and examine the ways that such performance has its critical limits.

These questions of identity are clearly bound up with questions of the body in both the material and virtual worlds. Just as cyberculture forces us to ask what constitutes identity, it forces us to ask what constitutes a body. Writing by Anne Balsamo and N. Katherine Hayles, for example, interrogates the boundary between body and machine; in *Technologies of the Gendered Body* (1996), Anne Balsamo argues that the body is a hybrid construction of the physical and the discursive and calls attention to the effacement of women's material labor by electronic technology. By showing how technologies of the body create cyborgs that retain traditional gender roles and attributes, she demonstrates that technology reproduces rather than rewrites gender constructions. In *How We Became Posthuman* (1999), N. Katherine Hayles takes up the question of the relationship between the body as discursive effect and the body as lived phenomenological experience in cyberspace. Tracing the trope of disembodiment through the history of computer theory, Hayles criticizes cybertheorists who ignore the material body, and she argues for an approach to the body in cyberspace that treats the body as mutually determined by the discursive and the material.[43]

Indeed, one could argue that while bodies are refashioned in cyberspace, gender and racial categories are kept remarkably intact—the body that emerges is a particularly white body. As Braidotti notes, digital culture does not eradicate racism but "intensifies it and it brings it to implosion." Posthuman bodies are marked by race and gender, or default to a "white" body.[44] Not only are particular bodies privileged, but disembodiment and body modifications are only available on gendered, racial terms. Braidotti believes that "the last thing we need at this point in Western history is a renewal of the old myth of transcendence as flight from the body. Transcendence as disembodiment would just repeat the classical patriarchal model, which consolidated masculinity as abstraction, thereby essentialising social categories of 'embodied others.'"[45]

Hayles, Balsamo, and Braidotti all examine issues around the body by exploring the cyborg as a metaphor in feminist theory and within popular narratives. As Balsamo points out, the cyborg as metaphor is fraught with difficulties precisely because it is already such a ubiquitous image in popular culture, an image that, unfortunately, replicates traditional ways of thinking about gender. She cautions that the cyborg is not radical or utopian per se, but that the "dominant representation of cyborgs reinserts us into dominant ideology by reaffirming bourgeois notions of human, machine, and femininity."[46] She argues that Haraway has "failed to consider how the cyborg has already been fashioned in our cultural imagination."[47] What interests Balsamo, and most of *reload*'s contributors, is the way that the cyborg metaphor and its meaning have become an important cultural site of contestation, "a site of feminist politics in this postmodern age."[48] If the cyborg expresses new types of subjectivity, those new types do not necessarily upset gender dichotomies but represent instead an "emerging" subjectivity that consists of "amalgams of old and new."[49]

loading . . .

reload's collection of fiction and critical writing should be read as a set of responses to feminist theories of cyberspace and of the cyborg. Together, the fiction and criticism create a new space between a utopian cyberculture of endless possibilities for multiple subjectivities/embodiments on one hand, and nostalgia for (or fantasies of) a pretechnological/antitechnological utopia on the other.

Beyond cyberfeminism and writings by feminist cyberfiction authors (further explored in chapter 2), women are intervening in other aspects of digital culture: digital art and installation, performance, interactive media, and hypertext/hyperfiction. Women artists are rewriting the arts using interactive media, performance, and texts to examine relationships among gender, cultural divisions (high art, low art), and theories of representation. The editors hope to explore women's digital art and digital texts in a future volume.

Notes

1. There are, however, a few women's science-fiction collections that contain cyberfiction; the best of these is the *Women of Wonder* series, edited by Pamela Sargent.
2. "Classic" cyberpunk collections such as *Mirrorshades* (Sterling 1988) and *Crystal Express* (Sterling 1989) include only one female author, Pat Cadigan. Cadigan's groundbreaking works include short stories such "Pretty Boy Crossover" (1989), "Rock On, Rock On" (1989), and her 1991 novel *Synners*, which has received much critical attention.
3. Many software developers have read cyberpunk fiction to get ideas for "perfect products"; Mark Pesce, one of the creators of the Virtual Reality Modeling Language (VRML), notes the importance of Neil Stephenson's work as a model in the technological development of VRML.
4. Joanna Russ, "What Can A Heroine Do? Or Why Women Can't Write," in *Images of Women in Fiction: Feminist Perspectives*, ed. Susan Koppelman Cornillon (Bowling Green, OH: Bowling Green State University Popular Press, 1972), 18.
5. On women's science fiction, see Lefanu (1988), Roberts (1993), Barr (1987), Wolmark (1994), and Donawerth (1997).
6. Sarah Lefanu, *In the Chinks of the World Machine: Feminism and Science Fiction* (London: The Women's Press, 1988), 5.
7. Pamela Sargent's *Women of Wonder* anthologies have helped bring these writers to both popular and critical attention.
8. Robin Roberts, *A New Species: Gender and Science in Science Fiction* (Urbana, IL: Illinois University Press, 1993). Joan Rothschild, ed., *Women, Technology, and Innovation* (New York: Pergammon, 1982), 40. Also Jane Donawerth's "Science Fiction by Women in the Early Pulps, 1926–1930," in *Utopian and Science Fiction by Women: Worlds of Differ-*

ence, ed. J. Donawerth and C. A. Kolmerten (Liverpool: Liverpool University Press, 1994) also documents the surprisingly large number of women writers who wrote for science-fiction pulp magazines.

9. See *Utopian and Science Fiction by Women: Worlds of Difference*, ed. J. Donawerth and C. A. Kolmerten (Liverpool: Liverpool University Press, 1994), for an account of women's utopian science fiction.

10. See Wolmark (1994) and Lefanu (1997).

11. Lefanu (1988) argues that dystopian science fiction by women "contain[s] an element of hopefulness that rests on a belief in the power and efficacy of women's speech" (75).

12. In *Frankenstein's Daughters: Women Writing Science Fiction*, Donawerth (1997) describes four types of aliens who frequent women's science fiction: the humanoid woman as alien, the woman as animal, the minority woman as alien, and the woman as machine.

13. Veronica Hollinger, "Cybernetic Deconstructions: Cyberpunk and Postmodernism," in *Storming the Reality Studio: A Casebook of Cyberpunk and Postmodern Science Fiction*, ed. L. McCaffery (Durham, NC: Duke University Press, 1991).

14. Tatsumi Takayuki, "Some Real Mothers: An Interview with Samuel R. Delany," *Science Fiction Eye* 1 (March 1988): 9.

15. N. Katherine Hayles, *How We Became Posthuman: Virtual Bodies in Cybernetics, Literature, and Informatics* (Chicago: University of Chicago Press, 1999), 36.

16. Bruce Sterling, *Mirrorshades: The Cyberpunk Anthology* (New York: Ace, 1986), x–xi.

17. Sterling, *Mirrorshades*, x.

18. On the Japanese, see Lauraine Leblanc, "Razor Girls: Genre and Gender in Cyberpunk Fiction," *Women and Language* 20 (1997): 71.

19. Istvan Csicsery-Ronay, "Postmodernism's SF/SF's Postmodernism," *Science Fiction Studies: Science Fiction and Postmodernism* 55 (1991): 191.

20. Sterling, *Mirrorshades*, xiii.

21. Thomas Foster, "Incurably Informed: The Pleasures and Dangers of Cyberpunk," *Genders* 18 (1993): 4.

22. Foster, "Incurably Informed," 4.

23. Veronica Hollinger, "Cybernetic Deconstructions."

24. See, for example, Ruth Cowan's study, *More Work for Mother* (1983), which argues that the introduction of "labor-saving" household appliances (such as the washing machine, the vacuum, and the dishwasher)—far from freeing women from the drudgery of housework—actually led to housewives working harder than ever. Standards of cleanliness became more stringent, thereby creating less, not more, free time. These histories include *Women, Technology, and Innovation*, edited by Joan Rothschild (1982); *The Technological Woman*, edited by Jan Zimmerman (1983); and the collection *Technology and Women's Voices*, edited by Cheris Kramarae (1988). The Kramarae collection exam-

ines technology's effect on women's communication. Judy Wajcman's *Feminism Confronts Technology* (1991) looks at a range of technologies, including the remote control, in vitro fertilization, and office automation, and argues that these technologies maintain unequal gender and class relations. Her material on word processing and the "deskilling" of woman's work is particularly convincing. Wajcman includes an important critique of antitechnology arguments that are based on an assumption that there is such a thing as "women's values," and that those "values" are inherently antitechnology.

25. Exemplary works that explore this question include Emily Martin's *The Woman in the Body* (1987); *Body/Politics*, edited by Mary Jacobus, Evelyn Fox Keller, and Sally Shuttleworth (1990); Ruth Hubbard's *The Politics of Women's Biology* (1990); and Sue Vilhauer Rosser's *Biology and Feminism* (1993).

26. Keller's discussion of Alan Turing is also likely to be of interest to scholars of cyberculture.

27. For additional explorations of the politics of scientific and technological knowledge, see the essays collected in *Sex and Scientific Inquiry*, edited by Sandra Harding and Jean O'Barr (1987); *Feminism and Science*, edited by Evelyn Fox Keller and Helen Longino (1996); *Cultural Studies of Science and Technology*, edited by Anne Balsamo (1998); and *The Science Studies Reader*, edited by Mario Biagioli (1999). For an excellent selection of recent European work on gender/technology relations, see *Between Monsters, Goddesses and Cyborgs*, edited by Nina Lykke and Rosi Braidotti (1996).

28. Harding's work includes *Discovering Reality* (with Merrill B. Hintikka, 1983), *The Science Question in Feminism* (1986), *Whose Science? Whose Knowledge?* (1991), and *Is Science Multicultural?* (1998).

29. In *Simians, Cyborgs, and Women* (1991). A version of the chapter first appeared in the *Socialist Review*.

30. For Haraway, the figure of the cyborg also becomes a metaphor for coalition politics, the joining together of diverse political groups to fight a specific political battle. Haraway's later work *Modest-Witness, Second-Millennium: Femaleman Meets OncoMouse* (1996) again looks into the relationship between feminism and science, exploring issues such as reproductive freedom and biological approaches to race in an attempt to imagine a feminist, multicultural account of technoscience. Certainly Haraway's manifesto argues for the productive use of the cyborg metaphor in feminist theory.

31. The pairing of women/nature has been studied in the works of countless scholars (Haraway, Keller, Plant, etc.) and is seen as an attack on feminine subjectivity and cultural autonomy.

32. See Plant's *Zeros + Ones*, Haraway's essay "A Cyborg Manifesto," and Lynn Hershman Leeson in artist statements available at <http://www.art-tech.org/html/virtual/hershman.html>.

33. Faith Wilding, "Where Is the Feminism in Cyberfeminism?" 1998. Online. Available at <http://www.obn.org/cfundef/faith_def.htmlpar 10>.

34. See, for example, Larry Harvey's speech at the Burning Man "Be-In" in January 1997, which touts cyberspace as a site for liberation.

35. See especially the collection *Wired Women: Gender and New Realities in Cyberspace*, ed. Lynn Cherny and Elizabeth Reba Weise (Seattle, WA: Seal Press, 1996); also Dale Spender's *Nattering on the Net: Women, Power, and Cyberspace* (North Melbourne: Spinifex Press, 1996).

36. "A Rape in Cyberspace," which describes rape in a Multi User Domain (MUD), was also published in *Flame Wars* (Dery 1994). See Dibbel's "A Rape in Cyberspace or How an Evil Clown, a Haitian Trickster Spirit, Two Wizards, and a Cast of Dozens Turned a Database into a Society," *The Village Voice*, December 21, 1993, S. 36–42.

37. *Wired Women*, edited by Lynn Cherny and Elizabeth Weise (1996), documents such notions; the volume is a collection of insiders' accounts of digital culture from women computer experts, artists, and journalists. It includes personal narratives and ethnographic explorations of the culture of *Wired* magazine, abuse of women within the hacker culture, sexist marketing of software and computers, erotic encounters on the Internet, and the way gender is played out in e-mail, newsgroups, MUDs and MOOs, and computer games.

38. Available at <http://www.let.ruu.nl/womens_studies/rosi/cyberfem.htm>. See also *Scattered Hegemonies: Postmodernity and Transnational Feminist Practices*, ed. Caren Kaplan and Inderpal Grewal (Minneapolis: University of Minnesota Press, 1994).

39. Judith Butler, *Gender Trouble: Feminism and the Subversion of Identity* (New York: Routledge, 1990), 138. See also Butler's *Bodies That Matter: On the Discursive Limits of "Sex"* (New York: Routledge, 1993).

40. Cleo Odzer, an anthropologist, in *Virtual Spaces: Sex and the Cyber Citizen* (1997) also argues that assumptions of online identities and erotic interactions in graphical, audio, and text environments make women freer to explore their sexuality than they are in the real world.

41. Lisa Nakamura, "Race in/for Cyberspace: Identity Tourism and Racial Passing on the Internet." 1995. Online. Available at <http://acom.grove.iup.edu/en/workdays/Nakamura.html>.

42. On gender performativity and virtual embodiment, see Theresa Senft and Stacy Horn, eds., *Sexuality and Cyberspace: Performing the Digital Body*. Special issue of *Women and Performance* 9.1 (1996), and Sue-Ellen Case, *The Domain-Matrix: Performing Lesbian at the End of Print Culture* (Bloomington: Indiana University Press, 1996). On performing race in cyberspace, see Nakamura (1995).

43. For critiques of the convention of disembodiment in cyberpunk narratives and representations of cyberspace, see Nixon (1992), Springer (1996), and Dery (1996).

44. Here we refer to Richard Dyer's *White* (1997), which documents the creation of whiteness; this study is quite useful in cybercultural studies.

45. Available at <http://www.let.ruu.nl/womens_studies/rosi/cyberfem.htm>.

46. Anne Balsamo, "Reading Cyborgs Writing Feminism," *Communication* 10 (1988): 343.

47. Balsamo, "Reading Cyborgs Writing Feminism," 343.

48. Balsamo, "Reading Cyborgs Writing Feminism," 345.

49. N. Katherine Hayles, "The Life Cycle of Cyborgs: Writing the Posthuman," in *A Question of Identity*, ed. M. Benjamin (New Brunswick, NJ: Rutgers University Press, 1993), 154.

Works Cited

Adam, Alison. *Artificial Knowing: Gender and the Thinking Machine*. New York: Routledge, 1998.

Atwood, Margaret. *The Handmaid's Tale*. Boston: Houghton Mifflin, 1986.

Balsamo, Anne. "Reading Cyborgs Writing Feminism." *Communication* 10 (1988): 331–345.

Balsamo, Anne. "Feminism for the Incurably Informed." *South Atlantic Quarterly* 92 (1993): 681–712.

Balsamo, Anne. *Technologies of the Gendered Body: Reading Cyborg Women*. Durham, NC, and London: Duke University Press, 1996.

Balsamo, Anne, ed. *Cultural Studies of Science and Technology*. New York: Routledge, 1998.

Barr, Marleen S. *Alien to Femininity: Speculative Fiction and Feminist Theory*. Westport, CT: Greenwood Press, 1987.

Biagioli, Mario, ed. *The Science Studies Reader*. New York: Routledge, 1999.

Braidotti, Rosi. "Cyberfeminism with a Difference." 1996. Online. Available at <http://www.let.uu.nl/womens_studies/rosi/cyberfem.htm>.

Bukatman, Scott. *Terminal Identity: The Virtual Subject In Postmodern Science Fiction*. Durham, NC, and London: Duke University Press, 1993.

Bull, Emma. *Bone Dance*. New York: Ace, 1991.

Butler, Judith. *Gender Trouble: Feminism and the Subversion of Identity*. New York: Routledge, 1990.

Butler, Judith. *Bodies That Matter: On the Discursive Limits of "Sex."* New York: Routledge, 1993.

Butler, Octavia E. *Patternmaster*. New York: Warner, 1976.

Butler, Octavia E. *Mind of My Mind*. New York: Warner, 1977.

Butler, Octavia E. *Wild Seed*. New York: Pocket Books, 1981.

Butler, Octavia E. *Dawn*. New York: Warner, 1987.

Butler, Octavia E. *Adulthood Rites*. New York: Warner, 1988.

Butler, Octavia E. *Imago*. New York: Warner, 1989.

Butler, Octavia E. *Clay's Ark*. New York: Warner Books, 1996.

Cadigan, Pat. *MindPlayers*. New York: Bantam, 1987.

Cadigan, Pat. "Pretty Boy Crossover." *Patterns*. New York: Bantam, 1989.

Cadigan, Pat. "Rock On, Rock On." *Patterns*. New York: Bantam, 1989.

Cadigan, Pat. *Synners*. New York: Bantam, 1991.

Case, Sue-Ellen. *The Domain-Matrix: Performing Lesbian at the End of Print Culture.* Bloomington: Indiana University Press, 1996.

Charnas, Suzy McKee. *Walk to the End of the World.* New York, Berkley, 1978.

Charnas, Suzy McKee. *Motherlines.* New York: Berkley, 1978.

Charnas, Suzy McKee. *The Furies.* London: The Women's Press, 1995.

Cherny, Lynn, and Elizabeth Reba Weise, eds., *Wired Women: Gender and New Realities in Cyberspace.* Seattle, WA: Seal Press, 1996.

Cowan, Ruth. *More Work for Mother.* New York: Basic, 1983.

Csicsery-Ronay, Istvan. "Postmodernism's SF/SF's Postmodernism." *Science Fiction Studies: Science Fiction and Postmodernism* 55 (1991).

Dery, Mark. *Flame Wars.* Durham, NC: Duke University Press, 1994.

Dery, Mark. *Escape Velocity: Cyberculture at the End of the Century.* New York: Grove Press, 1996.

Dibbel, Julian. "A Rape in Cyberspace or How an Evil Clown, a Haitian Trickster Spirit, Two Wizards, and a Cast of Dozens Turned a Database into a Society." *The Village Voice*, December 21, 1993, S. 36–42

Donawerth, Jane. *Frankenstein's Daughters: Women Writing Science Fiction.* New York: Syracuse University Press, 1997.

Donawerth, Jane, and Carole A. Kolmerten, eds. *Utopian and Science Fiction by Women: Worlds of Difference.* Liverpool: Liverpool University Press, 1994.

Dyer, Richard. *White.* London and New York: Routledge, 1997.

Elgin, Suzette Haden. *Native Tongue.* New York: Daw, 1984.

Fairbairns, Zoë. *Benefits.* London: The Women's Press, 1988.

Foster, Thomas. "Incurably Informed: The Pleasures and Dangers of Cyberpunk." *Genders* 18 (1993): 1–10.

Foster, Thomas. "'Trapped by the Body'? Telepresence Technologies and Transgendered Performance in Feminist and Lesbian Rewritings of Cyberpunk Fiction." *Modern Fiction Studies* 43 (1997): 708–743.

Gearhart, Sally Miller. *The Wanderground: Stories of the Hill Women.* London: The Women's Press, 1980.

Griffith, Nicola. *Slow River.* London: HarperCollins, 1995.

Haraway, Donna. *Primate Visions: Gender, Race, and Nature in the World of Modern Science.* New York: Routledge, 1989.

Haraway, Donna. "A Cyborg Manifesto: Science, Technology, and Socialist Feminism in the Late Twentieth Century." In *Simians, Cyborgs, and Women: The Reinvention of Nature,* 149–181. London and New York: Routledge, 1991.

Haraway, Donna. *Modest-Witness, Second-Millennium: Femaleman Meets OncoMouse.* London and New York: Routledge, 1996.

Harding, Sandra. *The Science Question in Feminism.* Ithaca, NY: Cornell University Press, 1986.

Harding, Sandra. *Whose Science? Whose Knowledge?* Ithaca, NY: Cornell University Press, 1991.

Harding, Sandra. *Is Science Multicultural?* Bloomington: Indiana University Press, 1998.

Harding, Sandra, and Merrill B. Hintikka. *Discovering Reality*. Boston: Kluwer, 1983.

Harding, Sandra, and Jean O'Barr, ed. *Sex and Scientific Inquiry*. Chicago: University of Chicago Press, 1987.

Hayles, N. Katherine. "The Life Cycle of Cyborgs: Writing the Posthuman," in *A Question of Identity*, ed. M. Benjamin. New Brunswick, NJ: Rutgers University Press, 1993.

Hayles, N. Katherine. *How We Became Posthuman: Virtual Bodies in Cybernetics, Literature, and Informatics*. Chicago: University of Chicago Press, 1999.

Hollinger, Veronica. "Cybernetic Deconstructions: Cyberpunk and Postmodernism," *Mosaic* 23 (1990): 29–44.

Hubbard, Ruth. *The Politics of Women's Biology*. New Brunswick, NJ: Rutgers University Press, 1990.

Jacobus, Mary, Keller, Evelyn Fox, and Shuttleworth Sally, eds. *Body/Politics*. New York: Routledge, 1990.

Kaplan, Caren, and Inderpal Grewal, eds. *Scattered Hegemonies: Postmodernity and Transnational Feminist Practices*. Minneapolis: University of Minnesota Press, 1994.

Keller, Evelyn Fox. *Reflections and Gender and Science*. New Haven: Yale University Press, 1996.

Keller, Evelyn Fox, and Helen E. Longino, eds. *Feminism and Science*, 187–202. New York: Oxford University Press, 1996.

Kramarae, Cheris, ed. *Technology and Women's Voices*. New York: Routledge, 1988.

Leblanc, Lauraine. "Razor Girls: Genre and Gender in Cyberpunk Fiction." *Women and Language* 20 (1997): 71–80.

Lefanu, Sarah. *In the Chinks of the World Machine: Feminism and Science Fiction*. London: The Women's Press, 1988.

Le Guin, Ursula K. *The Left Hand of Darkness*. London: Granada, 1978.

Lykke, Nina, and Rosi Braidotti, eds. *Between Monsters, Goddesses and Cyborgs*. London: ZED, 1996.

Martin, Emily. *The Woman in the Body*. Boston: Beacon, 1987.

McCaffery, Larry, ed. *Storming The Reality Studio. A Casebook of Cyberpunk and Postmodern Science Fiction*. Durham: Duke University Press, 1991.

Millar, Melanie. *Cracking the Gender Code: Who Rules the Wired World?* Toronto: Second Story Press, 1998.

Mitchison, Naomi. *Solution Three*. New York: The Feminist Press, 1975.

Moffett, Judith. *The Ragged World: A Novel of the Hefn on Earth*. New York: Ballantine Books, 1991.

Nakamura, Lisa. "Race in/for Cyberspace: Identity Tourism and Racial Passing on the Internet." 1995. Online. Available at <http://acom.grove.iup.edu/en/workdays/Nakamura.html>.

Nixon, Nicola. "Cyberpunk: Preparing the Ground for Revolution or Keeping the Boys Satisfied," *Science Fiction Studies* 19 (1992): 219–235.

Odzer, Cleo. *Virtual Spaces: Sex and the Cyber Citizen.* New York: Berkley, 1997.

Ore, Rebecca. *Gaia's Toys.* New York: Tor, 1997.

Piercy, Marge. *Woman on the Edge of Time.* London: The Women's Press, 1979.

Plant, Sadie. *Zeros + Ones: Digital Women and the New Technoculture.* New York: Bantam, 1997.

Roberts, Robin. *A New Species: Gender and Science in Science Fiction.* Urbana, IL: Illinois University Press, 1993.

Rosser, Sue Vilhauer. *Biology and Feminism.* New York: Twayne, 1993.

Rothschild, Joan, ed. *Women, Technology, and Innovation.* New York: Pergamon, 1982.

Rucker, Rudy, ed. *Mondo 2000 : A User's Guide to the New Edge: Cyberpunk, Virtual Reality, Wetware, Designer Aphrodisiacs, Artificial Life, Techno-Erotic Paganism, and More.* New York: Harper Perennial, 1992.

Russ, Joanna. "What Can a Heroine Do? Or Why Women Can't Write." In *Images of Women in Fiction; Feminist Perspectives,* ed. Susan Koppelman Cornillon, 3–20. Bowling Green, OH: Bowling Green State University Popular Press, 1972.

Russ, Joanna. *The Female Man.* Boston: Beacon, 1975.

Sargent, Pamela. *The Shore of Women.* New York: Bantam, 1986.

Sargent, Pamela, ed. *Women of Wonder: SF Stories by Women about Women.* Harmondsworth: Penguin, 1978.

Sargent, Pamela, ed. *The New Women of Wonder: Recent Science Fiction stories by Women about Women.* New York: Vintage, 1978.

Sargent, Pamela, ed. *More Women of Wonder: Science Fiction Novelettes by Women about Women.* Harmondsworth: Penguin, 1979.

Sargent, Pamela, ed. *Women of Wonder, The Classic Years: Science Fiction by Women from the 1940s to the 1970s.* New York: Harcourt Brace, 1995.

Sargent, Pamela, ed. *Women of Wonder, The Contemporary Years: Science Fiction by Women from the 1970s to the 1990s.* New York: Harcourt Brace, 1995.

Scott, Melissa. *Shadow Man.* New York: Tor, 1995.

Scott, Melissa. *Dreaming Metal.* New York: Tor, 1997.

Senft, Theresa, and Stacy Horn, eds. *Sexuality and Cyberspace: Performing the Digital Body.* Special issue of *Women and Performance* 9.1 (1996).

Spender, Dale. *Nattering on the Net: Women, Power, and Cyberspace.* North Melbourne: Spinifex Press, 1996.

Springer, Claudia. *Electronic Eros: Bodies and Desire in the Postindustrial Age.* Austin: University of Texas Press, 1996.

Stephenson, Neal. *Snow Crash.* New York: Bantam Books, 1992.

Sterling, Bruce. *Mirrorshades: The Cyberpunk Anthology.* New York: Ace, 1986.

Sterling, Bruce. *Crystal Express.* New York: Ace Books, 1989.

Stone, Allucquère Rosanne. *The War of Desire and Technology at the Close of the Mechanical Age.* Cambridge, MA: MIT Press, 1995.

Takayuki, Tatsumi. "Some Real Mothers: An Interview with Samuel R. Delany." *Science Fiction Eye* 1 (March 1988): 9.

Turkle, Sherry. *Life on the Screen: Identity in the Age of Internet.* New York: Simon & Schuster, 1995.

Wajcman, Judy. *Feminism Confronts Technology.* University Park: Pennsylvania State University Press, 1991.

Wilding, Faith. "Where Is the Feminism in Cyberfeminism?" 1998. Online. Available at <http://www.obn.org/cfundef/faith_def.html>.

Wolmark, Jenny. *Aliens and Others: Science Fiction, Feminism and Postmodernism.* Iowa City: University of Iowa Press, 1994.

Zimmerman, Jan, ed. *The Technological Woman.* London: Pandora, 1983.

2

WOMEN'S CYBERFICTION: AN INTRODUCTION

Austin Booth

This chapter provides an overview of authors and themes associated with what we are calling women's cyberfiction—fiction by women that focuses on technoculture. Chapter 1 outlines several contexts within which to understand women's cyberfiction: feminist science fiction, the cyberpunk movement of the 1980s, and feminist-cyborg theory. As chapter 1 states, we want not only to bring attention to this tremendously valuable, rich literature, which has been largely ignored by critics, but also to raise questions about the relationship between women's popular and theoretical accounts of cyberspace. Women's cyberfiction may be productively read against cyberculture theory, particularly claims about the liberatory nature of the figure of the cyborg and the potential transcendence of gender and the body in cyberspace. Women's cyberfiction exposes cyberspace to be a much more treacherous and vulnerable terrain than previously imagined, and places questions of embodiment and subjectivity in a more complex cultural context of race, history, sexuality, nation, and class.

Women's cyberfiction predates the almost exclusively male cyberpunk movement of the mid-1980s. C. L. Moore was writing about the relationships between humans and machines as early as the 1940s, and Anne McCaffrey and Alice B. Sheldon (writing as James Tiptree Jr.) were writing about cyborgs in the 1970s. As noted in the introduction (chapter 1), Samuel Delany argues that the existing cyberpunk itself is indebted to feminist science fiction as an "absent mother."[1] Most science-fiction readers know of Pat Cadigan as the sole woman identified with the cyberpunk movement, but there are many other women science-fiction writers who write what could be called post-cyberpunk—science fiction that borrows heavily from cyberpunk technology and theory. Contemporary women writers such as Melissa Scott, Laura J. Mixon, Raphael Carter, Lisa Mason, and others are appropriating the style and setting of cyberpunk in order to articulate women's views of technoculture. Women's cyberfiction functions as both part of and resistant to the larger cyberpunk culture of which it is a part—in other words, these authors use cyberpunk's own terms to challenge its depictions of the near future.

Many critics have argued that the cyberpunk of the 1980s did not live up to its potential in reconfiguring cultural categories such as gender, race, nation, and class.[2] Similarly, popular culture's depictions of cyborgs also do not seem to reflect the breakdown of stable cultural identities, a breakdown that cultural theorists argue produced the figure of the cyborg in the first place. As film theorist Claudia Springer (1996) has pointed out, cyborgs in popular fiction and film possess exaggerated masculine and feminine characteristics, thus reinforcing the boundary between genders even as those same narratives rely on the cyborg's transgression of other boundaries (such as that between the human and machine) for much of their narrative interest and energy. Like the cyberpunk authors of the 1980s, today's women cyberfiction writers examine the pleasures and anxieties that accompany the dissolution of the boundaries between human and machine and between reality and virtuality. Unlike their male counterparts, however, women cyberfiction authors have articulated structures of power and domination: these women are both rewriting our conception of cyberspace as male, and rewriting the male conception of cyberspace. Women's cyberfiction exposes cyberpunk's treatment of the anxiety over disembodiment and the dissolution of stable, unified identity as a particularly white male anxiety, an anxiety that might be figured and experienced differently, although not necessarily beneficially, by women. In addition, unlike many male cyberpunk authors, women writers do not feminize cyberspace, nor do they figure jacking in to digital networks as heterosexual coupling. In Pat Cadigan's *Synners*, for example, men who wish to enter cyberspace are implanted with sockets, which are characterized as "the female . . . the receiver . . ."—the male characters are the receptors, rather than the "jack" that plugs into a feminized cyberspace.[3]

Technologies

In our introduction to *reload* we discuss the increasing presence of women in science-fiction culture as authors, readers, and fans; this has meant that science fiction itself pays more attention to issues of gender. Nevertheless, much of the feminist science fiction of the 1970s described utopias that had little to do with the high-tech world of modern culture. Women's cyberfiction, however, combines feminist science fiction's examination of gender and gendered relations with cyberpunk's exploration of what it means to live in a technoculture. Like much cyberpunk, women's cyberfiction portrays a dystopic future—a world of extreme economic extremes and class antagonism, pervasive violence, and environmental disaster ruled over by multinational corporations via global information and communication networks. Pleasure within this culture can increasingly be found only through virtual-reality technologies, technologies that themselves are frequently controlled by the same corporate and bureaucratic powers that control everyday life. Women's cyberfiction documents how women and other marginalized groups can maneuver for survival within this technodystopia. In this fiction there is no "outside" position from which to critique technology, just as there is no "outside" position from which to critique gender. This writing avoids the extremes of the antitechnological utopianism of much earlier women's science fiction and the utopianism of much recent cyberfeminism, or what Carol Stabile (1994) characterizes as the "technophilia" and "technomainia" present in many feminist theories of technology. It also avoids the tendency either to embrace or to vilify the technology itself, tendencies that appear in many theoretical and popular accounts of the pervasive nature of information and communication technologies. In these narratives, technology is itself neither a means for domination nor a means of resistance.

Near-future visions of technoculture are harsh worlds for women. Novels like Melissa Scott's *Trouble and Her Friends* (excerpted in chapter 4) and Mary Rosenblum's *Chimera* depict worlds in which women are kept in an underclass that is denied the benefits of technology. Social position is dictated by one's access to advanced technologies, and women, people of color, lesbians and gay men, and the elderly are routinely denied access to these technologies by those in power. The future is marked by a distribution of resources more uneven than our own. Twenty-first century Toronto, as described in Afro-Caribbean Canadian Nalo Hopkinson's *Brown Girl in the Ring*, is typical of the urban landscapes imagined in women's cyberfiction. The main character, a young woman named Ti-Jeanne, her new baby, and her Voudoun-practicing herbalist grandmother live in "the Burn," the dangerous, ruined central urban core of Toronto evacuated by the rich and walled in by corporations and those who have fled to live in the high-tech, elite, safe suburbs. In the Burn, even simple technologies such as basic household utilities are no longer functioning. Marge Piercy's *He, She and It* also describes a world in which the vast majority of people live in poverty in toxic slums, while the elite work for (and are owned by) "multis" (multinational corporations), which have absolute control over their lives. In Laura J. Mixon's *Proxies*, resources are so scarce and environmental disaster so extreme, most of the characters try to remain ensconced in virtual reality, rather than venture out into their "real" world.

And yet the heroines of these novels show amazing fortitude—they are extremely creative and resourceful in adopting and adapting the technologies they need to survive. Women's cyberfiction is replete with cyborgs, but equally important are its representations of women as technology users (whether they have machine parts or not—that is, whether they are cyborgs or not). Like hackers, and as hackers, these heroines work the systems that control their worlds. As Sam, the teenage hacker heroine of Pat Cadigan's *Synners* says, "[I]f you couldn't walk on the floor, you walked on the ceiling. If you couldn't walk on the ceiling, you walked on the walls and if you couldn't walk *on* the walls, you walked *in* them, encrypted. Pure hacking."[4] Sam barters her labor (hacking) and stolen data in exchange for discarded equipment and living essentials. The agoraphobic lesbian heroine of Laura J. Mixon's *Glass Houses*, Ruby, uses waldoes—cyborgs she has made from discarded machine parts—to work as a salvage rescuer, providing subsistence-level income not only for her, but for her girlfriend/roommate as well, who otherwise is forced to work as a prostitute.

Although the heroines of women's cyberfiction show far-ranging technical expertise and dazzling ingenuity, they are stuck in dead-end, dangerous, and low-paying jobs.[5] In works like "Steelcollar Worker," *Seeds of Time*, and *Chimera*, women form a subclass of workers, positioned by a global labor market as the lowest of technoworkers. *Glass Houses*'s Ruby works as a salvage rescuer in places so dangerous others refuse to work them. Helva, the heroine of *The Ship Who Sang*, has the machine body of a spaceship, but works as a feminized servant-bride for her captains rather than as a captain herself. Jewel Martina, the Hispanic heroine of *Chimera*, works as a medical aide who wants to become an Internet investment broker but cannot because she does not have the money to afford the proper access to the Net. The protagonist of Raphael Carter's *The Fortunate Fall*, Maya Tatyanichna Adreyeva, is a "camera"—a television journalist outfitted with microchips that interface directly with her senses so that all of her thoughts and feelings can be transmitted, felt, and thought by viewers who possess "moistdisks." Her ex-girlfriend works as a screener, censoring data Maya transmits. Neither is a pleasant occupation: As Maya says, "When I got into the business, you could either be a camera or a screener, never both; when they wired you, you were tracked for life . . . the bastard . . . who invented this technology. It's his plotline we're forced to repeat. For the camera, a stranger with the key to all your secrets. For the screener, feeling closer than a sister to someone who does nothing but push you away."[6] Women's cyberfiction thus deromanticizes the hacker ethos of much cyberpunk fiction and utopian cyberfeminism—after all, even in our present technoculture most women who work with technology are assemblers or processors rather than programmers or producers. In Gwyneth Jones's *Escape Plans*, women are recognized as being better than men at work on the interface, but a discriminatory gap (similar to our own) exists between the elite who control the networks and those that are plugged in (the SUbs). In *Escape Plans*, it is precisely those who interface with the central networks via brain sockets who are the *least* powerful.

Within these fictional technocultures, the female protagonists only have access to older or less sophisticated technologies. Lesser technologies are used both to mark and to maintain their users as lower class. In many of these novels, systems of social differentiation are based on which type of technology one uses. In Marion Zimmer Bradley's *Darkover* novels, for example, only the aristocrats possess the telepathic skills needed to access the matrix technology. The AIs in Lisa Mason's *Arachne* are clearly ranked: the mainframes, controbots, and industrialbots with their "elegant rows of little recessed lights along [their] shoulder ridges and thigh tubes [and] fully articulated arm and leg pieces" are on the top, and the traffic controllers, copbots, knockoffs, "chippy mechanicals," semisentient shopping carts, and roving ATMs are on the bottom. Pr. Spinner, the female AI in *Arachne*, is always worried about the state of her equipment, complaining to another AI that "my rollers have been jamming lately at the least little thing. I can't get up the wheelchair ramps half the time. And my arms are a wreck. . . . Any day these arms are going to fall right off. . . . I can just see it. I'll be rolling down Telegraph Avenue, and my whole breastplate will fall right off. Bot! The embarrassment! I exist in constant fear of it."[7] Maya, the camera in *The Fortunate Fall*, is also marked by her aging technological implants, complaining to her electronic car that she has "more nanobugs in my head than a corpse has worms. They're the *old kind*."[8] Thus the method one uses to access cyberspace becomes a means of social differentiation. Maya cannot afford a private jack but must use public jacks "crusted with reddish-brown spots . . . [and] greasy with someone's hair oil" to access certain parts of the Net.[9] In *Chimera* Jewel Martina is too poor to be "netted" (that is, internally wired) and therefore has to use "skinthins" (external public networking nodes) to enter virtual reality. In Melissa Scott's *Trouble and Her Friends*, hackers are differentiated according to how they connect to the network. Some hackers connect using a keyboard, but Trouble and her friends connect through neural brainworms. Their neural brainworms, though the most effective and involving way to experience virtual reality (VR), mark Trouble and her friends as doubly other: as lesbians and as lower-class hackers. In other words, even in a culture where everyone is wired, all wires are not created equally. These novels and short stories stress the importance, often overlooked in cyberculture studies, of distinguishing between particular types of digital technologies; these fictions demonstrate that each technology carries with it a culturally and historically specific meaning or resonance (rather than simply an abstract value or meaning as "technology").

The heroines of women's cyberfiction typically use technology not only to survive but also to challenge evils of various sorts—information control; environmental destruction; reactionary governments and military organizations; global corporatization, etc. Indeed, stories of women using technology to effect social change are a driving plot force in many of these novels. (The question of what a feminist social and technological agenda should be is, of course, as frequently debated in these texts as it is in feminist theory.) Their existence on the literal margins of the city spaces and planets that make up the postmodern landscape of their worlds gives many of these heroines room to maneuver in order to perform subversive, oppositional tasks alongside their more legitimate functions. Most of the women are hackers, women who exist on the margins of respectability, are able to cross the boundaries between legitimate and illegitimate work, and are part of underground communities producing both the technologies that support the dominant culture and the anxieties that surround those technologies. Piercy's *He, She and It* describes a family of female hackers: Piercy's Malkah is a computer programmer who works both to keep the Jewish town of Tikva safe from attacks from corporations and to create programs that the town sells to ensure its economic survival. Her daughter, Riva, is a computer pirate who steals information from the corporations to give to the people, and her granddaughter, Shira, is a computer scientist who challenges the multinational corporations that control their world in a battle for custody of her son. In Mary Gentle's *Left to His Own Devices*, Valentine Branwen, a hacker who previously worked for the military writing "landscapes for wars," releases a virus that will corrupt global databases in order to create "open government [and] information flood,"[10] and in *The Fortunate Fall*, Maya reveals that the Net does not fulfill its potential to be "the most democratic form of communication that the world has even known . . . the poor bumblings of human compassion with perfect electronic sympathy" but is instead an "official version of humanity," a "slickly post-produced," fake version of multiculturalism, one that excludes any real difference.[11]

Many of the female protagonists in these works appropriate digital technologies designed for military and industrial purposes for other uses. In Ursula Le Guin's *Always Coming Home*, for example, the post-holocaust Kesh culture uses computer technologies almost solely for creative and aesthetic purposes, and in *Chimera*, virtual-reality technologies are also used to create art. In Misha's *Red Spider White Web*, Kumo makes holograms that she uses to enact revenge on her rapist, and, in a nice twist, in Pat Murphy's *The City, Not Long After*, community artists band together to use cybertechnologies to produce cyberart to fight off the military in a postapocalyptic Bay Area. In fact, much women's cyberfiction examines and challenges the very definition of technology, exposing the stories we tell about technology, what technology is for, and even what constitutes technology, as just that—stories. These works expose definitions of technology as constructions that work to exclude what women do and redefine technology to include communication, emotion, and magic. Jewelle Gomez's "Lynx and Strand" and James Tiptree Jr.'s *Up the Walls of the World*, for example, describe women who are able to merge or cross subjective boundaries. Marion Zimmer Bradley's *Darkover* novels and many of Pat Cadigan's works also portray characters who possess a technology-enhanced sense of empathy.[12] These works draw connections between technology, magic, and spiritualism. Emma Bull's *Bone Dance* and Nalo Hopkinson's *Midnight Robber* combine artificial intelligence, cyborgs, and Voudon. And both Le Guin's *Always Coming Home* and Misha's *Red Spider White Web* show intersections between Native American mysticism and technoculture. In these works information technology is an integrated part of the natural world, not set in opposition to it.

Identities

Women writers of cyberfiction tend to focus on the socially and economically marginal: Unlike classic cyberpunk tales of "hacker cowboy" outsiders, these novels are populated by women of color, illegal workers, handicapped characters, lesbians, the poor, and the homeless. Technology has not erased sexism, racism, and heterosexism in these works, so much as it has exaggerated them and given them new forms—new frontiers to which to send undesirables (*Seeds of Time*), new low-paying jobs (*Glass Houses*), and new ways to erase identities and memories (*The Fortunate Fall*). Many women science-fiction writers have used science fiction to talk about structures and systems of difference and domination; specifically, they have used the figure of the alien to talk about gendered and raced "others," using one type of alienation to talk about the other, using the mapping of self/other onto human/alien to talk about the mapping of self/other onto man/woman or white/nonwhite.[13] Women's science fiction is also known for its exploration of ways in which systems of discrimination such as sexism and racism reinforce each other. Building on this earlier work, women's cyberfiction describes the creation and maintenance of systems of difference and discrimination within technocultures. *Bending the Landscape*, a collection of science-fiction stories edited by Nicola Griffith and Steve Pagel, contains many cyberfiction stories in which the alien or the "other" is a lesbian or gay man. Mary Rosenblum's work explores a variety of types of cultural difference—the main characters in *Chimera* include not only Jewel Martina, but also David Chen, a gay virtual-reality artist who uses virtual reality to explore themes of difference.

Just as earlier women's science fiction used the figure of the alien to describe systems of difference and domination, women's cyberfiction uses the figures of the robot and the cyborg to show how difference and domination function in technocultures. Piercy's *He, She and It* parallels the treatment of cyborgs in technocultures with the treatment of Jews in Renaissance Prague. Depictions of female robots and cyborgs in women's cyberfiction continue the work of earlier women's science fiction in figuring woman as alien to explore the ways in which women are alienated within our everyday culture, the way women are always already figured as "others." In women's cyberfiction, the woman as technoproduct—cyborg, robot, program—becomes the figure through which objectification is explored (and not, as much feminist cyberculture theory would predict, always overcome). In other words, women's cyberfiction uses the depiction of how female cyborgs, robots, and programs are constructed and dehumanized to expose the way women in general are constructed and dehumanized. Female characters frequently acquire mechanical bodies as a means of becoming more pleasurable and useful to men. In "The Girl Who Was Plugged In" (chapter 28), for example, P. Burke is given a cyborg body that she controls via "eccentric projection or sensory reference" because her physical body is deformed. Similarly, Helva, the heroine of "The Ship Who Sang," is forced to become a "shell person," permanently wired into and surrounded by a spaceship body. Several works, such as C. L. Moore's "No Woman Born" (chapter 14) and Tanith Lee's *Electric Forest*, depict female cyborg performers as a means of exposing femininity and even heterosexual desire as a performance.

Historically, science fiction has represented female cyborgs and robots as objects, as sex toys for their creators. The most famous of these is perhaps Lester del Rey's "Helen O'Loy," a rewriting of Pygmalion (another story of a man creating a perfect woman). In "Helen O'Loy," not only is the robot woman an object, an other, but gender remains mapped onto the mind body distinction—that is, women are aligned with the body and men are aligned with the mind—even when the body is a mechanical one. Women's cyberfiction rewrites both *Pygmalion* and "Helen O'Loy" by telling stories of women who take male robots and cyborgs as their lovers—stories such as *He, She, and It*, Tanith Lee's *The Silver Metal Lover*, and Rebecca Ore's *The Illegal Rebirth of Billy the Kid*—as well as by telling stories of manmade female cyborgs and robots who claim their own, separate subjectivity. In stories like "The Girl Who Was Plugged In" and "No Woman Born," female cyborgs, originally designed for male pleasure, rebel. As Deirdre, the heroine of "No Woman Born" asserts, she is "superhuman," "not sub-human" (287). Amy Thomson's novel *Virtual Girl* rewrites the Pygmalion myth, telling a tale of a male hacker who creates a female cyborg that misunderstands the command/programming input "you are the most important thing to me" as "you are the most important thing," and goes on to reprogram herself accordingly. In Elisabeth Vonarburg's *The Silent City*, the cyborg Elisa goes so far as to kill her maker.[14]

Women's cyberfiction explores the tension between the cyborg as a figure of oppression and the cyborg as a figure of emancipation that one can observe in the cyberculture theory described in chapter 1. Female cyborgs in women's cyberfiction represent *both* the final triumph of a male technological culture (the machine-woman as object) and the triumphant emergence of the female technology user of the future who upsets the alignment of masculinity with technology. Indeed, the cyborg in women's cyberfiction serves as an image for this contest over the meanings or implications of technoculture for women. In chapter 5, Heather Hicks points out that *He, She and It* reveals these contradictory aspects of the cyborg through the novel's comparison of Yod, the "metaphor of the cyborg as product of controlling cybernetic processes," with Nili, the "metaphor of the cyborg as embodying resistance to that control." If female cyborgs prove to be useful figures for women cyberfiction writers to think through the effects of technology and the formation of cultural boundaries, they also prove useful as a way of thinking through the disruption of cultural boundaries. Cyborgs, after all, are not simply an "other," but are a hybrid of self and other, human and machine; cyborg hybridity calls attention to the constructed nature of categories such as "human" and "machine" and exposes the permeability of the boundary between them. Like most cyberpunk, women's cyberfiction uses the figure of the cyborg to interrogate notions of the unified, stable self, and to investigate the condition of the multiplicity and provisionality of the postmodern subject. As Mary Rosenblum's character Jewel puts it, "We are all so many people . . . a patchwork."[15] The female cyborg becomes a way of talking about the multiple ways women are positioned in a postmodern technoculture. As Anne Balsamo points out, the cyborg becomes a figure through which "to reflect on the ways in which, historically, women have experienced fragmented subjectivies and identities."[16] That is to say, if the cyborg is the ultimate representation of the fragmented postmodern self, it is especially so for women, who already experience themselves as such.

The figure of the female cyborg is ubiquitous in women's cyberfiction. Laura J. Mixon's Ruby Kubick is typical of the fragmented, cyborg heroines of women's cyberfiction: she is able to download her consciousness via a neural implant into her many waldoes, occupying their bodies and their perspectives simultaneously while remaining in / keeping her own. In the passage that follows, one of Ruby's waldoes, Golem, is carrying Ruby's physical body. Here, Ruby achieves a literally hyphenated subjectivity, crossing the border between subject and object, self and other, as well as human and machine: "I-Golem looked down at the woman in my arms. It was Ruby-me, of course, and her-my eyes closed, fluttering a little. She-I curled with her-my cheek against Golem's chassis. She-I looked so young and vulnerable from the outside, not ugly and scrawny like me. I was terrified that I wouldn't be able to keep her from harm; I wished she were back home, safe, right this very minute."[17] Mixon provides us with a model not only of the fractured and multiple subject, but of fractured and multiple viewpoints as well. Ruby sees herself both from the outside as "she / I" and from the inside as "me." Fragmented characters like Ruby call into question both familiar dichotomies such as human / machine, male/female, and subject/object as well as the structures of power those dichotomies they maintain. In Pat Cadigan's *Mindplayers* the central character, Allie, is a "pathosfinder," whose work "mindplaying" consists of helping others "move past irrelevant and superficial mental trash to the real feeling, the real soul"[18] Allie meshes her mind with her clients' minds via a computer to which both she and her client are connected via plugs in their eye sockets. When Allie "mindplays," not only does she enter into and clear out her clients' minds, but they enter hers, and become permanent parts of her own identity. Many of the characters in women's cyberfiction are biracial, calling attention to the constructed nature of racial boundaries as well. These characters provide a valuable perspective, one that exists neither wholly outside nor inside a given cultural group, a perspective from which an understanding and critique of cultural operations of difference can be made.

Although some of the cyborgs in women's cyberfiction experience their gender identity as split or multiple (Ruby's multiple bodies are frequently referred to, for example, as "my-his" body or "my-hers" body), perhaps surprisingly, many cyborgs in women cyberfiction retain their identity as females.[19] Gender identity is fairly stable in this fiction (even as femininity itself is reconfigured or redefined via women performing "masculine" tasks, and having "masculine" relationships with technology). The stability of gender in these texts calls into question the relationship between pairs of cultural binaries, such as human/machine, man/female, and self/other. Women's cyberfiction is careful to point out that a cyborgian human/machine identity does not necessarily lead to the breakdown or erasure of all other cultural binaries. It seems careful not to collapse or equate the challenge that biracial characters pose to systems of racial difference to the challenge that cyborg characters pose to systems of human/machine difference. So, in women's cyberfiction, the hybridity of the cyborg is not subversive per se. By refusing to present the hybridity of the female cyborg as automatically subversive, these texts also ask us to pay closer attention to the ways in which we are "all cyborgs." In their specific accounts of differently configured female cyborgs, these texts challenge readers to ask of cyberculture theory a series of questions: are all women cyborgs because women have mechanical body parts, or because women participate in technology-based economies as workers, or because women have historically experienced fragmented or multiple identities? How do we characterize different women's very different relationships to their cyborgian nature, both in terms of their relationship to technology and to various, multiple systems of difference? Women's cyberfiction provides detailed accounts of the lives of female cyborgs that can help us answer these questions.

Bodies

Male cyberpunk authors have tended to privilege disembodiment over embodiment, their male characters yearning to reach what Mark Dery (1996) calls "escape velocity," to escape the body through technological transcendence. As several critics have noted, by equating the mind with cyberspace and the body with "real" space and by treating the realms as discreet, separable spaces, cyberpunk of the 1980s reinstates the mind / body split. Critics have noted as well that 1980s cyberpunk figures the mind / body split and the virtual / reality split as a gendered one, treating the real and the "meat" of the body as female and the virtual and the mind as male. In women's cyberfiction too, male characters frequently yearn to leave their bodies, to transcend embodiment through technology. In *Chimera*, David's male lover, Flander, desires nothing more than to "lose the flesh"[20] and become fully immersed in the electronic network, and in *Synners*, Visual Mark, too, dreams of escaping his body. These texts call attention to the fact that the dream of giving up the body has nothing to do with eradicating gender or, more important, gender discrimination, but precisely the opposite. The separation of mind and body in cyberpunk, as several critics have pointed out, leaves masculinity undisturbed and unthreatened.

Just as many female protagonists in women's cyberfiction do not want to give up female identity, they do not want to give up the female body. Many women's cyberpunk stories depict women rejecting the lure of disembodied projection into cyberspace. As Gina in *Synners* says, "Only the embodied can really boogie all night."[21] Women have a different relationship than men do to cyberspace. Many female characters conceive of cyberspace not as an escape from or transcendence of embodiment, but precisely the opposite: as a means of enhancing or multiplying embodied experiences. In *Synners*, for example, the two women hackers, Sam and Gina, use cyberspace as a space in which to communicate or connect with others; the two male hackers, Gabe and Visual Mark, however, use cyberspace to escape connections, especially embodied ones, and produce video dreams. Embodiment is integral to the female characters: Sam hacks in via a terminal that actually draws its power from her body, an insulin-pump chip reader that is connected to her belly (and in the end, Sam's is the only access point in the novel that remains uninfected by a massive virus in the network); in *The Fortunate Fall*, Maya's lover, who downloaded herself into the network to avoid detection as a lesbian, wants nothing more than to become reembodied. Similarly, Trouble and her friends choose an embodied interface—a brainworm, a neural implant that creates a direct interface between their nervous systems and information networks, allowing information and physical sensations to be translated into each other. Just as the protagonists in women's cyberfiction do not want to give up female identity or subjectivity, but would rather reclaim or rewrite it, so they want to reclaim or rewrite embodiment precisely because the body has been the site of being marked or written.[22] As Trouble speculates, the very people whose bodies have been made most vulnerable through being marked as "other" are those who opt to relate to cyberspace in an embodied fashion, choosing the brainworm that "let[s] you use the full range of your senses, not just sight and sound, to interpret the virtual world"[23] despite the dangers involved:

Maybe that was why the serious netwalkers, the original inhabitants of the nets, hated the brainworm. Not so much because it gave a different value, a new meaning, to the skills of the body, but because it meant taking that risk, over and above the risk of the worm itself. Maybe that was why it was almost always the underclasses, the women, the people of color, the gay people, the ones who were already stigmatized as being vulnerable, available, trapped by the body, who took the risk of the wire.[24]

Anne Balsamo, in her reading of *Synners*, claims that the novel "offers an alternative narrative of cyberpunk identity that begins with the assumption that bodies are always gendered and always marked by race."[25] Women characters tend to conceive of the body as mediated, by culture as well as by technology, rejecting what Haraway calls the notion of the "body in isolation" as a false one. Many of the male characters in women's cyberfiction, however, do not see bodies as "marked" or mediated. As Gina, the black female hacker in *Synners* puts it, "she could have told them who was *really* fucking *marked*."[26] In other words, the male characters see their bodies as simply unmarked, rather than as mediated by gender and race, or marked as white and male. In emphasizing the importance of the materiality of the body, and the importance of the body to the construction of subjectivity, women's cyberfiction echoes feminist theoretical efforts to "reclaim" embodiment as crucial to an understanding of postmodern culture.[27] As Balsamo points out, although *Synners* "reassert[s] . . . gender and race as defining elements of post-human identity," it treats whiteness, finally, as the male characters treat masculinity—as the absence of a mark.[28] That is to say, even though the novel illuminates the way in which the men read gender as a marker only for women, the novel itself treats race as a marker only for people of color.

The refusal to give up the body also reflects these authors' understanding of the complexity of the relationship between embodiment and cyberspace. In women's cyberfiction the virtual body is not imagined as completely separate or separable from the physical / material body.[29] Characters in *Glass Houses, Proxies,* and *He, She and It* have multiple bodies and multiple forms of embodiment, rather than simple embodiment or disembodiment. Not only do many of these novels explore both the pleasure and the pain that can accompany embodiment in both the real and the virtual worlds, but they also depict the real and the virtual spaces as integrated and mutually influencing spaces, spaces in which embodiment in one has consequences for embodiment in the other. In *Chimera*, for example, David, the virtual-reality artist, has chosen a fully embodied relationship to cyberspace. He is "netted"—his body is wired so that he is fully embodied in virtual reality, and in embodied contact with the virtual world at all times. What happens to David's body in one world happens to David's body in the other. Women's cyberfiction rejects the tendency, found in both cyberpunk fiction and contemporary popular rhetoric about the Internet, to represent cyberspace as an alternative to or escape from the physical world. In other words, along with rejecting the mind / body dualism, these novels reject the mapping of that dualism onto the virtual / real.

Although I have outlined some of the central themes of women's cyberfiction, many more questions remain to be asked, questions that can only be touched on here. One of the questions that is raised by women's cyberfiction is the relationship of technological culture to rape. Rape is a pervasive part of lives of many of the female characters in women's cyberfiction. How does rape figure into the way women writers depict embodiment for women? How does rape function as part of a technoculture's gendering of women? Is rape one of the ways that the female body is marked?

Second, more investigation needs to be done into how nation and nationality function in women's cyberfiction. Some women's cyberfiction, for example, reproduces American anti-Japanese paranoia, frequently figured as panic over global corporatism and the ubiquity of information and communication technologies. How do these fictions leave popular understandings of nation, ethnic identity, and the relationship between sexuality and race intact?

Third, the representation of information itself in this fiction needs to be explored in much more detail. How is information embodied or disembodied in these texts? What is the relationship between the politics of secrecy, the commodification of information, and sexuality in these novels? How, for example, is interiority figured in these novels? Is there an epistemology of the closet in cyberspace? And finally, how does print technology figure into these narratives, especially as these fictions are print artifacts themselves?

Notes

1. Takayuki Tatsumi, "Some Real Mothers: An Interview with Samuel F. Delany," *Science Fiction Eye* 1 (March 1988): 9.
2. Nicola Nixon (1992), for example, argues that despite cyberpunk's claim to be "radical" or "revolutionary," it is complicit with the conservatism and antifeminist backlash of 1980s Reagan America. Moreover, Thomas Foster (1993) points out that while cyberpunk "calls into question the privilege of the white male individual and therefore may enable the recognition of other forms of historical experience . . . at the same time the generalization of this crisis may reinstitute the white male experience of postmodernity as a new norm" (15).

3. Pat Cadigan, Pat, *Synners* (New York: Bantam Books, 1991), 63.

4. Cadigan, *Synners*, 351.

5. Even those women like Carly Nolan, *Arachne*'s genetically engineered female junior associate for a legal megafirm, who do have decent-paying jobs, can lose their jobs in a nanosecond if they do not keep up production. Carly must link into a shared electronic network where she can conduct work at one hundred times normal speed. Indeed *Arachne* (Mason 1990) is all about the precariousness of job security in a technoculture labor market.

6. Raphael Carter, *The Fortunate Fall* (New York: Tor, 1996), 30.

7. Lisa Mason, *Arachne* (New York: William Morrow, 1990), 19–20.

8. Carter, *The Fortunate Fall*, 21.

9. Carter, *The Fortunate Fall*, 38.

10. Mary Gentle, *Left to His Own Devices* (London: Orbit, 1994), 141.

11. Carter, *The Fortunate Fall*, 236.

12. See Robin Roberts (1993) on female science-fiction writers' use of theories of psi.

13. Octavia Butler's works, for example, have long focused on the ways that gender and race difference create outsiders and how different kinds of alienation are developed and maintained.

14. See Jenny Wolmark (1995) for a discussion of how female cyborgs become the subject, the "desiring I" in such "postmodern romances" as *Bone Dance*, *Winterlong*, *Aestival Tide*, *White Queen*, and *Escape Plans*.

15. Mary Rosenblum, *Chimera* (New York: Del Rey, 1993), 321.

16. Anne Balsamo, "Reading Cyborgs Writing Feminism," *Communication* 10 (1988): 343.

17. Laura J. Mixon, *Glass Houses* (New York: Tor, 1992), 60–61.

18. Pat Cadigan, *Mindplayers* (New York: Bantam Books, 1987), 20.

19. There are, of course, exceptions—in several of these fictions, gender is fluid or multiple. Frequently this changeable gender is linked to, or the result of, cyborg status. In *Bone Dance*, the main character, Sparrow, is neutral, while in Elisabeth Vonarburg's *The Silent City*, the cyborg Elisa can become any gender.

20. Rosenblum, *Chimera*, 296.

21. Cadigan, *Synners*, 433.

22. For further reading on the question of embodiment within women's cyberfiction, see Thomas Foster, "'Trapped by the Body?' Telepresence Technologies and Transgendered Performance in Feminist and Lesbian Rewritings of Cyberpunk Fiction," *Modern Fiction Studies* 43 (1997): 708–742.

23. Melissa Scott, *Trouble and Her Friends* (New York: Tor, 1994), 29.

24. Scott, *Trouble and Her Friends*, 128.

25. Anne Balsamo, "Feminism for the Incurably Informed," *South Atlantic Quarterly* 92 (1993): 692.

26. Cadigan, *Synners*, 390.
27. See, for example, Elizabeth Grosz's *Volatile Bodies: Toward a Corporeal Feminism* and Judith Butler's *Bodies That Matter: On the Discursive Limits of "Sex."*
28. Anne Balsamo, "Feminism for the Incurably Informed," 693.
29. See chapter 24 for a discussion of these novels' representation of the ways physical and virtual bodies are imbricated in one another as well as how "the doubling of embodiment" in virtual reality often has the critical function of liberalizing or making visible the cultural limitations that structure how we imagine bodies.

Works Cited

Balsamo, Anne. "Reading Cyborgs Writing Feminism." *Communication* 10 (1988): 331–345.

Balsamo, Anne. "Feminism for the Incurably Informed." *South Atlantic Quarterly* 92 (1993): 681–712.

Butler, Judith. *Bodies That Matter: On the Discursive Limits of "Sex."* New York: Routledge, 1992.

Dery, Mark. *Escape Velocity: Cyberculture at the End of the Century.* New York: Grove Press, 1996.

Foster, Thomas. "Meat Puppets or Robopaths?: Cyberpunk and the Question of Embodiment." *Genders* 18 (1993): 11–31.

Foster, Thomas. "'Trapped by the Body?' Telepresence Technologies and Transgendered Performance in Feminist and Lesbian Rewritings of Cyberpunk Fiction." *Modern Fiction Studies* 43 (1997): 708–742.

Grosz, Elizabeth. *Volatile Bodies: Toward a Corporeal Feminism.* Bloomington: Indiana University Press.

Nixon, Nicola. "Cyberpunk: Preparing the Ground for Revolution or Keeping the Boys Satisfied?" *Science-Fiction Studies* 19 (1992): 219–235.

Springer, Claudia. *Electronic Eros: Bodies and Desire in the Postindustrial Age.* Austin: University of Texas Press, 1996.

Stabile, Carol A. *Feminism and the Technological Fix.* Manchester: Manchester University Press, 1994.

Roberts, Robin. *A New Species: Gender and Science in Science Fiction.* Urbana: University of Illinois Press, 1993.

Wolmark, Jenny. "The Postmodern Romances of Feminist Science Fiction." In *Romance Revisited*, ed. Lynne Pearce and Jackie Stacey, 158–168. London: Lawrence & Wishart, 1995.

Fiction

Bradley, Marion Zimmer. *Darkover Landfall.* New York: Daw, 1972.

Bull, Emma. *Bone Dance.* New York: Ace Books, 1991.

Cadigan, Pat. *Mindplayers.* New York: Bantam Books, 1987.

Cadigan, Pat. *Synners.* New York: Bantam Books, 1991.

Carter, Raphael. *The Fortunate Fall.* New York: Tor, 1996.

del Ray, Lester. "Helen O'Loy." *Astounding Science Fiction* 22 (1938): n.p.

Gentle, Mary. *Left to His Own Devices.* London: Orbit, 1994.

Gomez, Jewelle. "Lynx and Strand." In *Don't Explain: Short Fiction.* Ithaca, NY: Firebrand Books, 1998.

Griffith, Nicola, and Steve Pagel, eds. *Bending the Landscape: Science Fiction.* Woodstock, NY: Overlook Press, 1998.

Hopkinson, Nalo. *Brown Girl in the Ring.* New York: Warner Books, 1998.

Hopkinson, Nalo. *Midnight Robber.* New York: Warner Books, 2000.

Jones, Gwyneth. *Escape Plans.* London: Unwin/Orion, 1986.

Kenyon, Kay. *Seeds of Time.* New York: Bantam Spectra, 1997.

Lee, Tanith. *Electric Forest.* Garden City, NY: Nelson Doubleday, 1979.

Lee, Tanith. *The Silver Metal Lover.* New York: Daw Books, 1981.

Le Guin, Ursula K. *Always Coming Home.* New York: Harper & Row, 1985.

Mason, Lisa. *Arachne.* New York: William Morrow, 1990.

McCaffrey, Anne. *The Ship Who Sang.* [1969] 1979. New York: Ballantine.

McIntyre, Vonda. "Steelcollar Worker." *Analog Science Fiction and Fact,* 112 (November 1992): n.p.

Misha. *Red Spider White Web.* Scotforth, Lancaster: Morrigan Publications, 1990.

Mixon, Laura J. *Glass Houses.* New York: Tor, 1992.

Mixon, Laura J. *Proxies.* New York: Tor, 1998.

Murphy, Pat. *The City, Not Long After.* New York: Doubleday, 1989.

Ore, Rebecca. *The Illegal Rebirth of Billy the Kid.* New York: Tor, 1991.

Piercy, Marge. *He, She and It.* New York: Fawcett Crest, 1991.

Rosenblum, Mary. *Chimera.* New York: Del Rey, 1993.

Scott, Melissa. *Trouble and Her Friends.* New York: Tor, 1994.

Thomson, Amy. *Virtual Girl.* New York: Ace, 1993.

Tiptree, James Jr. (Alice Bradley Sheldon). *Up the Walls of the World.* New York: Berkley, 1978.

Vonarburg, Elisabeth. *The Silent City.* New York: Bantam/Spectra, 1992.

Women's Cyberfiction

Women Using Technology

From information technology to interactive media, nanotechnology to neural networks, and video games to virtual reality, cyberculture has become everyday culture. Women are taking to the Net in droves, for communication, community building, and professional and creative work. The number of women using the Internet in 1999 nearly quadrupled since 1996, and World Wide Web sites designed and maintained by women are continually increasing.[1]

The fiction, theory, and criticism gathered in part I examine how digital technologies enter into women's personal, social, and work lives. Each piece articulates the complex relationship with technology women experience in their production and consumption of cybertechnologies. These stories and essays examine the tension between the liberatory potential and the frequently quite oppressive realities of women's experience of digital technologies. Many of the pieces included here, for example, remark on the importance of digital technologies to the maintenance of the economies of corporate capitalism and patriarchal sexual economies. The pieces are also united in calling attention to women as technology users, rather than as female cyborgs. As chapter 1 points out, feminist accounts of technology combat the myths that technology creates better working conditions, improves the quality of domestic life, and diminishes gender divisions at home and work. However, technology does not emerge here as solely the tool of the dominant (masculine) culture or as having a predetermined meaning; these works suggest ways in which the meaning of technology is reconstructed within specific historical and cultural contexts.

Candas Jane Dorsey's Tiptree award–winning short story "(Learning About) Machine Sex" (1988) (chapter 3) focuses on women's position in both sexual and techno-cultural economies. The narrative tells the story of Angel, a young, brilliant computer programmer who determines that orgasm is binary—and therefore programmable. Angel creates an orgasm machine that eradicates a sexual economy in which women exchange sex for money. The story examines the role of women as machines or mechanical brides, and the status of sex as a commodity in a machine culture. Melissa Scott's novel *Trouble and Her Friends* (1994) also chronicles the lives of female computer experts. Scott's work, which won the 1995 Lambda Literary Award for Gay/Lesbian Science Fiction and the John W. Campbell Award, is an example of a queer critique of male cyberpunk literature—the story parodies, for example, the "cowboy" plots and metaphors of much cyberpunk literature. The novel focuses on a group of gay and lesbian computer hackers who connect to digital networks through illegal "brainworms," neural implants that create a direct interface between their nervous systems and the network; "brainworms" transform data into bodily sensations, meaning that the queer hackers in Scott's novel experience the Net as embodied beings. The novel opens with the passage of the Evans-Tindale Bill, a bill that allows the government to regulate cyberspace and makes hacking illegal. Scott's work goes on to make connections between the status of the group of hackers as technological outlaws and their status as sexual outlaws.[2] The epistemology of cyberspace, in other words, is linked to the epistemology of the closet. *Trouble and Her Friends* also raises interesting questions about the relationship between queer performance, embodiment, technology, and gender/sexual identity. The excerpt included here (chapter 4) is from the beginning of the novel and describes the passage of the Evans-Tindale Bill and the breakup of two female hacking partners, Trouble and Cerise.

Both "(Learning About) Machine Sex" and *Trouble and Her Friends* are about women who make their living using computer technologies. In "Striking Cyborgs: Reworking the 'Human' in Marge Piercy's *He, She and It*" (chapter 5), Heather Hicks argues that concepts of work, frequently overlooked by theorists of cyberculture, are crucial to an understanding of technoculture and its representations. In her reading of Marge Piercy's 1991 cyberfictional novel, *He, She and It*, Hicks reads the cyborg as a "human form penetrated and co-opted by a distinctively late-capitalist work ethic." In Hicks's account, Piercy claims that we are all cyborgs, *not* because of our relationship to technological systems, but because of our relationship to *work*. Hicks reads cyborgian theory and other fictional texts alongside Piercy's novel in order to discuss the economic contexts of cyborgs and the worker in postindustrial technoculture.

Anne McCaffrey is a tremendously popular science-fiction author. We've included her story "The Ship Who Sang," (chapter 6), which first appeared in *The Magazine of Fantasy and Science Fiction* in 1961; it was later developed into a novel, which in turn spawned a series of new works by McCaffrey and other writers. "The Ship Who Sang" tells the story of Helva, a "shell person," who functions as the encapsulated brain or guiding mechanism for a spaceship. The narrative raises interesting questions about female cyborgian desire and sexuality. Because she is permanently encased in a titanium shell, Helva cannot experience physical sex. She does, however, have intimate relationships with "brawns," or human partners, who can be women or men; these relationships are quite intimate and follow traditional romantic conventions of courtship and marriage. The story also raises questions about the body and transcendence of the body; because Helva becomes a cyborg when she is very young, she has no real experience of losing her human body. Despite her lack of a human body, however, Helva is quite clearly female; indeed, she is quite traditionally "feminine." Most interestingly for a cyborgs, Helva is never violent, and her protective shell and networked consciousness are never used as a weapon. Rather, it is her lifelong training for her career as the "brain" of a ship that shapes her identity.

Mary Rosenblum's 1993 short story "Entrada" (chapter 7) also depicts the day-to-day life of a female technoworker. Rosenblum's story, however, draws particular attention to issues of class, and differences among women in terms of access to and relationships with technology. Mila Aguilar works as a caregiver for a rich old woman named Amelia Connor-Vanek to earn her way out of the nightmarish, water-deprived, and crime-infested suburbs. Mila attends "HarvardNet" to get a college degree, while Amelia dreams in a drug-induced VR program. Mila's story challenges those who see the potential for computers to break down class and ethnic barriers in women's lives; the story reminds us that most women are only involved with computers as word processors, assembly-line workers, or medical technicians, and are unlikely to reap the benefits of the cyberrevolution. It also calls attention to the ways in which the labor of women of color using technology supports the maintenance of class systems and the more profitable and pleasurable use of technology by the privileged.

Another exploration of a woman's "lived experience" in a computer-mediated world, Sarah Stein's essay "A CyberRoom of One's Own" (chapter 8) focuses on the utopian claims of technology firsthand and relates her own interactions with technology as a worker and creator. Arguing that multitasking is not a newfound joy for women using technology but a constant state of affairs for women who fulfill many roles, Stein focuses on women's space, subjectivity, and creativity from the point of view of a woman filmmaker, mother, and academic in the United States. Stein works to bring cyberfeminist claims to a personal level, looking at her own lifelong relationship with film-making technologies.

Alison Adam's "The Ethical Dimension of Cyberfeminism" (chapter 9) provides an analysis and critique of cyberfeminist philosophy. She notes that the heady writings of cyberfeminists often forget the fact that women's relationship to technology is not always positive. She looks to the "mood of the moment," the mid-1990s when cyberfeminism developed, as a time when "women discovered the enrichment and empowerment that advanced communications and information technologies promised."

Adam, a computer scientist, now calls instead for a reinsertion of politics into cyber-feminism, noting that "the political side of cyberfeminism has yet to coalesce into a meaningful political voice." Adam looks to feminist ethics to rethink aspects of traditional ethics in an attempt to bring the political back into cyberfeminist discourse. Adam concludes that only if political and ethical aspects are brought to cyberfeminism can it deliver its early promise.

One example of ways in which women are using the Internet for building "utopic" cyberfeminist enclaves is interactive and collaborative writing. Sharon Cumberland's essay "The Five Wives of Ibn Fadhlan: Collaborative Fiction Writing on Antonio Banderas Web Sites" (chapter 10) looks at the uses of cyberspace for women's fan fiction writing. Fan fiction itself works as a model of cultural appropriation; women are rewriting pop culture for their own ends, and the Internet allows this to be a very feasible and networkable activity. To Cumberland, *The Five Wives of Ibn Fadlan* and other fan fiction like it also typifies "one of the most rapidly developing areas of women's writing today." Women are using the Internet to develop their own voices, writing skills, and technical prowess as well as to create important communities along the way. The essay asks important questions about fandom, women's communities, and communication.

Sue Thomas's novel *Correspondence* (1991) is also an account of women writing women. It is a narrative experiment itself about narrative (and technological) experiments. The novel tells several interrelated stories: one a science-fiction tale told in the second person in which a female computer programmer, who works as a "compositor" of virtual-reality fantasies/role-playing games, is in the process of replacing her body parts with cybernetic prostheses. The virtual realities that this character creates function as metaphors for the novel writing itself. We meet the compositor as she is working to create another story in a virtual-reality experience, a story of two women, Shirley and Rosa, and their romantic relationship with each other. Both stories are interrupted by a "mouthpiece" (an omniscient narrator) who gives instructions about how to operate the role-playing game. The novel is interspliced with a fourth "story": quotations from the works of Marvin Minsky, the Toshiba Professor of Media Arts and Sciences at MIT, and Douglas Hofstadter, College Professor of Cognitive Science and Computer Science at Indiana University. Interspersed throughout the novel are "infodumps," short passages that contain the author's musings and manifestos on potential relationships between people and machines (e.g., "Machine Religion" or "Machine as Friend"). The novel itself exists as a hypertext without hypertext, drawing connections between the machine and fiction, virtual reality and narrative, creating other women and creating narratives, creating bodies and creating narratives, and, of course, woman and machine. We have included an excerpt from the beginning of the novel (see chapter 11).

Correspondence is a metafictional story, calling attention to its own status as a fictional artifact. Jyanni Steffensen's study of the world of Rosalind Brodsky also presents us with central computer-using narrator protagonists and women artists "building" women. Artist Suzanne Treister created another persona, Rosalind Brodsky, in 1995, both in a book and in her more recent CD-ROM, *No Other Symptoms—Time Traveling with Rosalind Brodsky.*[3] Treister creates a space in which fetishism and sexuality, subjectivity and technology, are negotiated in relation to personal histories/fictions and histories of the twentieth century. Brodsky time-travels to undergo psychoanalysis with Sigmund Freud, Carl Jung, Melanie Klein, Jacques Lacan, and Julia Kristeva. Through these analytic sessions—financed from the manufacture and sale of her unique line of luxury-feature vibrators—Brodsky/Treister performs significant critical interventions into psychoanalytic theories about female sexuality, ventriloquizing and deuniversalizing Lacanian theory. In her essay "Doing It Digitally: Rosalind Brodsky and the Art of Virtual Female Subjectivity" (chapter 12), Jyanni Steffensen analyzes Rosalind Brodsky from a cyberfeminist, queer perspective. According to Steffensen, the virtual subject Rosalind Brodsky, like VNS Matrix's ALL NEW GEN and the DNA Sluts before her, is transforming the ways in which identities are articulated in narrative. The collapse of narrative account, fiction, and theory Steffensen creates in her essay is reflective of Treister's narrative strategy; both collapse fiction, theory, VR, and RL in their work as tactics for rereading psychoanalytic theory and male cyberpunk narratives.

Notes

1. Helen Dancer, "Modems are a Grrrl's Best Friend," *The Bulletin with Newsweek* 117 (Nov. 16, 1999): 85.
2. The Evans-Tindale Bill Scott depicts is eerily similar to recent legislation labeling cybercrimes as terrorist acts.
3. Available at <http://www.ensemble.va.com.au/tableau/suzy/>.

(LEARNING ABOUT) MACHINE SEX

Candas Jane Dorsey

A naked woman working at a computer. Which attracts you most? It was a measure of Whitman that, as he entered the room, his eyes went first to the unfolded machine gleaming small and awkward in the light of the long-armed desk lamp; he'd seen the woman before.

Angel was the woman. Thin and pale-skinned, with dark nipples and black pubic hair, and her face hidden by a dark unkempt mane of long hair as she leaned over her work.

A woman complete with her work. It was a measure of Angel that she never acted naked, even when she was. Perhaps especially when she was.

So she has a new board, thought Whitman, and felt his guts stir the way they stirred when he first contemplated taking her to bed. That was a long time ago. And she knew it, felt without turning her head the desire, and behind the screen of her straight dark hair, uncombed and tumbled in front of her eyes, she smiled her anger down.

"Where have you been?" he asked, and she shook her hair back, leaned backward to ease her tense neck.

"What is that thing?" he went on insistently, and Angel turned her face to him, half-scowling. The board on the desk had thin irregular wings spreading from a small central module. Her fingers didn't slow their keyboard dance.

"None of your business," she said.

She saved the input, and he watched her fold the board into a smaller and smaller rectangle. Finally she shook her hair back from her face.

"I've got the option on your bioware," he said.

"Pay as you go," she said. "New house rule."

And found herself on her ass on the floor from his reflexive, furious blow. And his hand in her hair, pulling her up and against the wall. Hard. Astonishing her with how quickly she could hurt how much. Then she hurt too much to analyse it.

"You are a bitch," he said.

"So what?" she said. "When I was nicer, you were still an asshole."

Her head back against the wall, crack. Ouch.

Breathless, Angel: "Once more and you never see this bioware." And Whitman slowly draws breath, draws back, and looks at her the way she knew he always felt.

"Get out," she said. "I'll bring it to Kozyk's office when it's ready."

So he went. She slumped back in the chair, and tears began to blur her vision, but hate cleared them up fast enough, as she unfolded the board again, so that despite the pain she hardly missed a moment of programming time.

Assault only a distraction now, betrayal only a detail: Angel was on a roll. She had her revenge well in hand, though it took a subtle mind to recognise it.

Again: "I have the option on any of your bioware." This time, in the office, Whitman wore the nostalgic denims he now affected, and Angel her street-silks and leather.

"This is mine, but I made one for you." She pulled it out of the bag. Where her board looked jerry-built, this one was sleek. Her board looked interesting; this one packaged. "I made it before you sold our company," she said. "I put my best into it. You may as well have it. I suppose you own the option anyway, eh?"

She stood. Whitman was unconsciously restless before her.

"When you pay me for this," she said, "make it in MannComp stock." She tossed him the board. "But be careful. If you take it apart wrong, you'll break it. Then you'll have to ask me to fix it, and from now on, my tech rate goes up."

As she walked by him, he reached for her, hooked one arm around her waist. She looked at him, totally expressionless. "Max," she said, "it's like I told you last night. From now on, if you want it, you pay. Just like everyone else." He let her go. She pulled the soft dirty white silk shirt on over the black leather jacket. The complete rebel now.

"It's a little going away present. When you're a big shot in MannComp, remember that I made it. And that you couldn't even take it apart right. I guarantee."

He wasn't going to watch her leave. He was already studying the board. Hardly listening, either.

"Call it the Mannboard," she said. "It gets big if you stroke it." She shut the door quietly behind herself.

It would be easier if this were a story about sex, or about machines. It is true that the subject is Angel, a woman who builds computers like they have never been built before outside the human skull. Angel, like everyone else, comes from somewhere and goes somewhere else. She lives in that linear and binary universe. However, like everyone else, she lives concurrently in another universe less simple. Trivalent, quadrivalent, multivalent. World without end, with no amen. And so, on.

They say a hacker's burned out before he's twenty-one. Note the pronoun: he. Not many young women in that heady realm of the chip.

Before Angel was twenty-one—long before—she had taken the cybernetic chip out of a Wm Kuhns fantasy and patented it; she had written the program for the self-taught AI the Bronfmanns had bought and used to gain world prominence for their MannComp lapboard; somewhere in there, she'd lost innocence, and when her clever additions to that AI turned it into something the military wanted, she dropped out of sight in Toronto and went back to Rocky Mountain House, Alberta, on a Greyhound bus.

It was while she was thinking about something else—cash, and how to get some— that she had looked out of the bus window in Winnipeg into the display window of a sex shop. Garter belts, sleazy magazines on cheap coated paper with Day-Glo orange stickers over the genitals of bored sex kings and queens, a variety of ornamental vibrators. She had too many memories of Max to take it lightly, though she heard the laughter of the roughnecks in the back of the bus as they topped each others' dirty jokes, and thought perhaps their humour was worth emulating. If only she could.

She passed her twentieth birthday in a hotel in Regina, where she stopped to take a shower and tap into the phone lines, checking for pursuit. Armed with the money she got through automatic transfer from a dummy account in Medicine Hat, she rode the bus the rest of the way ignoring the rolling of beer bottles under the seats, the acrid stink of the onboard toilet. She was thinking about sex.

As the bus roared across the long flat prairie she kept one hand on the roll of bills in her pocket, but with the other she made the first notes on the program that would eventually make her famous.

She made the notes on an antique NEC lapboard which had been her aunt's, in old-fashioned BASIC—all the machine would support—but she unravelled it and knitted it into that artificial trivalent language when she got to the place at Rocky and plugged the idea into her Mannboard. She had it written in a little over four hours on-time, but that counted an hour and a half she took to write a new loop into the AI. (She would patent that loop later the same year and put the royalties into a blind trust for her brother, Brian, brain damaged from birth. He was in Michener Centre in Red Deer, not educable; no one at Bronfmann knew about her family, and she kept it that way.)

She called it Machine Sex; working title.

Working title for a life: born in Innisfail General Hospital, father a rodeo cowboy who raised rodeo horses, did enough mixed farming out near Caroline to build his young second wife a big log house facing the mountain view. The first baby came within a year, ending her mother's tenure as teller at the local bank. Her aunt was a programmer for the University of Lethbridge, chemical molecular model analysis on the University of Calgary mainframe through a modem link.

From her aunt she learned BASIC, Pascal, COBOL and C; in school she played the usual turtle games on the Apple IIe; when she was fourteen she took a bus to Toronto, changed her name to Angel, affected a punk hairstyle and the insolent all-white costume of that year's youth, and eventually walked into Northern Systems, the company struggling most successfully with bionics at the time, with the perfected biochip, grinning at the proper young men in their grey three-piece suits as they tried to find a bug in it anywhere. For the first million she let them open it up; for the next five she told them how she did it. Eighteen years old by the phony records she'd cooked on her arrival in Toronto, she was free to negotiate her own contracts.

But no one got her away from Northern until Bronfmann bought Northern lock, stock and climate-controlled workshop. She had been sleeping with Northern's boy-wonder president by then for about a year, had yet to have an orgasm though she'd learned a lot about kinky sex toys. Figured she'd been screwed by him for the last time when he sold the company without telling her; spent the next two weeks doing a lot of drugs and having a lot of cheap sex in the degenerate punk underground; came up with the AI education program.

Came up indeed, came swaggering into Ted Kozyk's office, president of Bronfmann's MannComp subsidiary, with that jury-rigged Mann-board tied into two black-box add-ons no bigger than a bar of soap, and said, "Watch this."

Took out the power supply first, wiped the memory, plugged into a wall outlet and turned it on.

The bootstrap greeting sounded a lot like Goo.

"Okay," she said, "it's ready."

"Ready for what?"

"Anything you want," she said. By then he knew her, knew her rep, knew that the sweaty-smelling, disheveled, anorectic-booking waif in the filthy, oversized silk shirt (the rebels had affected natural fabrics the year she left home, and she always did after that, even later when the silk was cleaner, more upmarket, and black instead of white) had something.

Candas Jane Dorsey

Two weeks ago he'd bought a company on the strength of that something, and the board Whitman had brought him yesterday, even without the software to run on it, had been enough to convince him he'd been right.

He sat down to work, and hours later he was playing Go with an AI he'd taught to talk back, play games, and predict horse races and the stock market.

He sat back, flicked the power switch and pulled the plug, and stared at her.

"Congratulations," she said.

"What for?" he said. "You're the genius."

"No, congratulations, you just murdered your first baby," she said, and plugged it back in. "Want to try for two?"

"Goo," said the deck. "Dada."

It was her little joke. It was never a feature on the MannComp A-One they sold across every MannComp counter in the world.

But now she's all grown up, she's sitting in a log house near Rocky Mountain house, watching the late summer sunset from the big front windows, while the computer runs Machine Sex to its logical conclusion, orgasm.

She had her first orgasm at nineteen. According to her false identity, she was twenty-three. Her lover was a delegate to MannComp's annual sales convention; she picked him up after the speech she gave on the ethics of selling AIs to high school students in Thailand. Or whatever, she didn't care. Kozyk used to write her speeches but she usually changed them to suit her mood. This night she'd been circumspect, only a few expletives, enough to amuse the younger sales representatives and reassure the older ones.

The one she chose was smooth in his approach and she thought, well, we'll see. They went up to the suite MannComp provided, all mod cons and king-size bed, and as she undressed she looked at him and thought, he's ambitious, this boy, better not give him an inch.

He surprised her in bed. Ambitious maybe, but he paid a lot of attention to detail.

After he spread her across the universe in a way she had never felt before, he turned to her and said, "That was pretty good, eh, baby?" and smiled a smooth little grin. "Sure," she said, "it was okay," and was glad she hadn't said more while she was out in the ozone.

By then she thought she was over what Whitman had done to her. And after all, it had been simple enough, what he did. Back in that loft she had in Hull, upstairs of a shop, where she covered the windows with opaque mylar and worked night and day in that twilight. That night as she worked he stood behind her, hands on her shoulders, massaging her into further tenseness.

"Hey, Max, you know I don't like it when people look over my shoulder when I'm working."

"Sorry, baby." He moved away, and she felt her shoulders relax just to have his hands fall away.

"Come on to bed," he said. "You know you can pick that up whenever."

She had to admit he was being pleasant tonight. Maybe he too was tired of the constant scrapping, disguised as jokes, that wore at her nerves so much. All his efforts to make her stop working, slow her down so he could stay up. The sharp edges that couldn't be disguised. Her bravado made her answer in the same vein, but in the mornings, when he was gone to Northern, she paced and muttered to herself, reworking the previous day until it was done with, enough that she could go on. And after all what was missing? She had no idea how to debug it.

Tonight he'd even made some dinner, and touched her kindly. Should she be grateful? Maybe the conversations, such as they were, where she tried to work it out, had just made it worse—

"Ah, shit," she said, and pushed the board away. "You're right, I'm too tired for this. *Demain.*" She was learning French in her spare time.

He began with hugging her, and stroking the long line along her back, something he knew she liked, like a cat likes it, arches its back at the end of the stroke. He knew she got turned on by it. And she did. When they had sex at her house he was without the paraphernalia he preferred, but he seemed to manage, buoyed up by some mood she couldn't share; nor could she share his release.

Afterward, she lay beside him, tense and dissatisfied in the big bed, not admitting it, or she'd have to admit she didn't know what would help. He seemed to be okay, stretched, relaxed and smiling.

"Had a big day," he said.

"Yeah?"

"Big deal went through."

"Yeah?"

"Yeah, I sold the company."

"You what?" Reflexively moving herself so that none of her body touched his.

"Northern. I put it to Bronfmann. Megabucks."

"Are you joking?" but she saw he was not. "You didn't, I didn't. . . . Northern's *our* company."

"My company. I started it."

"I made it big for you."

"Oh, and I paid you well for every bit of that."

She got up. He was smiling a little, trying on the little-boy grin. No, baby, she thought, not tonight.

"Well," she said, "I know for sure that this is my bed. Get out of it."

"Now, I knew you might take this badly. But it really was the best thing. The R&D costs were killing us. Bronfmann can eat them for breakfast."

R&D costs meant her. "Maybe. Your clothes are here." She tossed them on the bed, went into the other room.

As well as sex, she hadn't figured out betrayal yet either; on the street, she thought, people fucked you over openly, not in secret.

This, even as she said it to herself, she recognised as romantic and certainly not based on experience. She was street-wise in every way but one: Max had been her first lover.

She unfolded the new board. It had taken her some time to figure out how to make it expand like that, to fit the program it was going to run. This idea of shaping the hardware to the software had been with her since she made the biochip, and thus made it possible and much more interesting than the other way around. But making the hardware to fit her new idea had involved a great deal of study and technique, and so far she had had limited success.

This reminded her again of sex, and, she supposed, relationships, although it seemed to her that before sex everything had been on surfaces, very easy. Now she had sex, she had had Max, and now she had no way to realize the results of any of that. Especially now, when Northern had just vanished into Bronfmann's computer empire, putting her in the position again of having to prove herself. What had Max used to make Bronfmann take the bait? She knew very clearly: Angel, the Northern Angel, would now become the MannComp Angel. The rest of the bait would have been the AI; she was making more of it every day, but couldn't yet bring it together. Could it be done at all? Bronfmann had paid high for an affirmative answer.

Certainly this time the bioware was working together. She began to smile a little to herself, almost unaware of it, as she saw how she could interconnect the loops to make a solid net to support the program's full and growing weight. Because, of course, it would have to learn as it went along—that was basic.

Angel as metaphor; she had to laugh at herself when she woke from programming hours later, Max still sleeping in her bed, ignoring her eviction notice. He'll have to get up to piss anyway, she thought; that's when I'll get him out. She went herself to the bathroom in the half-dawn light, stretching her cramped back muscles and thinking remotely, well, I got some satisfaction out of last night after all: the beginnings of the idea that might break this impasse. While it's still inside my head, this one is mine. How can I keep it that way?

New fiscal controls, she thought grimly. New contracts, now that Northern doesn't exist any more. Max can't have this, whatever it turns into, for my dowry to MannComp.

When she put on her white silks—leather jacket underneath, against the skin as street fashion would have it—she hardly knew herself what she would do. The little board went into her bag with the boxes of pills the pharmaceutical tailor had made for her. If there was nothing there to suit, she'd buy something new. In the end, she left Max sleeping in her bed; so what? she thought as she reached the highway. The first ride she hitched took her to Toronto, not without a little tariff, but she no longer gave a damn about any of that.

By then the drugs in her system had lifted her out of a body that could be betrayed, and she didn't return to it for two weeks, two weeks of floating in a soup of disjointed noise, and always the program running, unfolding, running again, unfolding inside her relentless mind. She kept it running to drown anything she might remember about trust or the dream of happiness.

When she came home two weeks later, on a hot day in summer with the Ottawa Valley humidity unbearable and her body tired, sore and bruised, and very dirty, she stepped out of her filthy silks in a room messy with Whitman's continued inhabitation; furious, she popped a system cleanser and unfolded the board on her desk. When he came back in she was there, naked, angry, working.

A naked woman working at a computer. What good were cover-ups? Watching Max after she took the new AI up to Kozyk, she was only triumphant because she'd done something Max could never do, however much he might be able to sell her out. Watching them fit it to the bioboard, the strange unfolding machine she had made to fit the ideas only she could have, she began to be afraid. The system cleanser she'd taken made the clarity inescapable. Over the next few months, as she kept adding clever loops and twists, she watched their glee and she looked at what telephone numbers were in the top ten on their modem memories and she began to realise that it was not only business and science that would pay high for a truly thinking machine.

She knew that ten years before there had been Pentagon programmers working to model predatory behaviour in AIs using Prolog and its like. That was old hat. None of them, however, knew what they needed to know to write for her bioware yet. No one but Angel could do that. So, by the end of her nineteenth year, that made Angel one of the most sought-after, endangered ex-anorectics on the block.

She went to conferences and talked about the ethics of selling AIs to teenagers in Nepal. Or something. And took a smooth salesman to bed, and thought all the time about when they were going to make their approach. It would be Whitman again, not Kozyk, she thought; Ted wouldn't get his hands dirty, while Max was born with grime under his nails.

She thought also about metaphors. How, even in the new street slang which she could speak as easily as her native tongue, being screwed, knocked, fucked over, jossed, dragged all meant the same thing: hurt to the core. And this was what people sought out, what they spent their time seeking in pick-up joints, to the beat of bad old headbanger bands, that nostalgia shit. Now, as well as the biochip, Max, the AI breakthrough, and all the tailored drugs she could eat, she'd had orgasm too.

Well, she supposed it passed the time.

What interested her intellectually about orgasm was not the lovely illusion of transcendence it brought, but the absolute binary predictability of it. "When you learn what to do to the nerve endings, and they are in a receptive state, the program runs like kismet. Warm boot. She'd known a hacker once who'd altered his bootstrap messages to read 'Warm pussy.'" She knew where most hackers were at; they played with their computers more than they played with themselves. She was the same, otherwise why would it have taken a pretty-boy salesman in a three-piece to show her the simple answer? All the others, just like trying to use an old MS-DOS disc to boot up one of her Mann lapboards with crystal RO/RAM.

Angel forgets she's only twenty. Genius is uneven. There's no substitute for time, that relentless shaper of understanding. Etc. Etc. Angel paces with the knowledge that everything is a phase, even this. Life is hard and then you die, and so on. And so, on.

One day it occurred to her that she could simply run away.

This should have seemed elementary but to Angel it was a revelation. She spent her life fatalistically; her only successful escape had been from the people she loved. Her lovely, crazy grandfather; her generous and slightly avaricious aunt; and her beloved imbecile brother: they were buried deep in a carefully forgotten past. But she kept coming back to Whitman, to Kozyk and Bronfmann, as if she liked them.

As if, like a shocked dog in a learned helplessness experiment, she could not believe that the cage had a door, and the door was open.

She went out the door. For old times' sake, it was the bus she chose; the steamy chill of an air-conditioned Greyhound hadn't changed at all. Bottles—pop and beer—rolling under the seats and the stench of chemicals filling the air whenever someone sneaked down to smoke a cigarette or a reef in the toilet. Did anyone ever use it to piss in? She liked the triple seat near the back, but the combined smells forced her to the front, behind the driver, where she was joined, across the country, by an endless succession of old women, immaculate in their fortrels, who started conversations and shared peppermints and gum.

She didn't get stoned once.

The country unrolled strangely: sex shop in Winnipeg, bank machine in Regina, and hours of programming alternating with polite responses to the old women, until eventually she arrived, creased and exhausted, in Rocky Mountain House.

Rocky Mountain House: a comfortable model of a small town, from which no self-respecting hacker should originate. But these days, the world a net of wire and wireless, it doesn't matter where you are, as long as you have the information people want. Luckily for Angel's secret past, however, this was not a place she would be expected to live—or to go—or to come from.

An atavism she hadn't controlled had brought her this far. A rented car took her the rest of the way to the ranch. She thought only to look around, but when she found the tenants packing for a month's holiday, she couldn't resist the opportunity. She carried her leather satchel into their crocheted, frilled guest room—it had been her room fifteen years before—with a remote kind of satisfaction.

That night, she slept like the dead—except for some dreams. But there was nothing she could do about them.

Lightning and thunder. I should stop now, she thought, wary of power surges through the new board which she was charging as she worked. She saved her file, unplugged the power, stood, stretched, and walked to the window to look at the mountains.

The storm illuminated the closer slopes erratically, the rain hid the distances. She felt some heaviness lift. The cool wind through the window refreshed her. She heard the program stop, and turned off the machine. Sliding out the backup capsule, she smiled her angry smile unconsciously. When I get back to the Ottawa Valley, she thought, where weather never comes from the west like it's supposed to, I'll make those fuckers eat this.

Out in the corrals where the tenants kept their rodeo horses, there was animal noise, and she turned off the light to go and look out the side window. A young man was leaning his weight against the reins-length pull of a rearing, terrified horse. Angel watched as flashes of lightning strobed the hackneyed scene. This was where she came from. She remembered her father in the same struggle. And her mother at this window with her, both of them watching the man. Her mother's anger she never understood until now.

———

Her father's abandonment of all that was in the house, including her brother, Brian, inert and restless in his oversized crib.

Angel walked back through the house, furnished now in the kitschy western style of every trailer and bungalow in this countryside. She was lucky to stay, invited on a generous impulse, while all but their son were away. She felt vaguely guilty at her implicit criticism.

Angel invited the young rancher into the house only because this is what her mother and her grandmother would have done. Even Angel's great-grandmother, whose father kept the stopping house, which meant she kept the travellers fed, even her spirit infused in Angel the unwilling act. She watched him almost sullenly as he left his rain gear in the wide porch.

He was big, sitting in the big farm kitchen. His hair was wet, and he swore almost as much as she did. He told her how he had put a trailer on the north forty, and lived there now, instead of in the little room where she'd been invited to sleep. He told her about the stock he'd accumulated riding the rodeo. They drank Glenfiddich. She told him her father had been a rodeo cowboy. He told her about his university degree in agriculture. She told him she'd never been to university. They drank more whiskey and he told her he couldn't drink that other rot gut any more since he tasted real Scotch. He invited her to see his computer. She went with him across the yard and through the trees in the rain, her bag over her shoulder, board hidden in it, and he showed her his computer. It turned out to be the first machine she designed for Northern—archaic now, compared with the one she'd just invented.

Fair is fair, she thought drunkenly, and she pulled out her board and unfolded it.

"You showed me yours, I'll show you mine," she said.

He liked the board. He was amazed that she had made it. They finished the Scotch.

"I like you," she said. "Let me show you something. You can be the first." And she ran Machine Sex for him.

He was the first to see it: before Whitman and Kozyk who bought it to sell to people who already have had and done everything; before David and Jonathan, the Hardware Twins in MannComp's Gulf Islands shop, who made the touchpad devices necessary to run it properly; before a world market hungry for the kind of glossy degradation Machine Sex could give them bought it in droves from a hastily created—MannComp-subsidiary—numbered company. She ran it for him with just the automouse on her board, and a description of what it would do when the hardware was upgraded to fit.

It was very simple, really. If orgasm was binary, it could be programmed. Feed back the sensation through one or more touchpads to program the body. The other thing she knew about human sex was that it was as much cortical as genital, or more so: touch is optional for the turn-on. Also easy, then, to produce cortical stimuli by programmed input. The rest was a cosmetic elaboration of the premise.

At first it did turn him on, then off, then it made his blood run cold. She was pleased by that: her work had chilled her too.

"You can't market that thing!" he said.

"Why not. It's a fucking good program. Hey, get it? Fucking good."

"It's not real."

"Of course it isn't. So what?"

"So, people don't need that kind of stuff to get turned on."

She told him about people. More people than he'd known were in the world. People who made her those designer drugs, given in return for favours she never granted until after Whitman sold her like a used car. People like Whitman, teaching her about sexual equipment while dealing with the Pentagon and CSIS to sell them Angel's sharp angry mind, as if she'd work on killing others as eagerly as she was trying to kill herself. People who would hire a woman on the street, as they had her during that two-week nightmare almost a year before, and use her as casually as their own hand, without giving a damn.

"One night," she said, "just to see, I told all the johns I was fourteen. I was skinny enough, even then, to get away with it. And they all loved it. Every single one gave me a bonus, and took me anyway."

The whiskey fog was wearing a little thin. More time had passed than she thought, and more had been said than she had intended. She went to her bag, rummaged, but she'd left her drugs in Toronto, some dim idea at the time that she should clean up her act. All that had happened was that she had spent the days so tight with rage that she couldn't eat, and she'd already cured herself of that once; for the record, she thought, she'd rather be stoned.

"Do you have any more booze?" she said, and he went to look. She followed him around his kitchen.

"Furthermore," she said, "I rolled every one of them that I could, and all but one had pictures of his kids in his wallet, and all of them were teenagers. Boys and girls together. And their saintly dads out fucking someone who looked just like them. Just like them."

Luckily, he had another bottle. Not quite the same quality, but she wasn't fussy.

"So I figure," she finished, "that they don't care who they fuck. Why not the computer in the den? Or the office system at lunch hour?"

———

"It's not like that," he said. "It's nothing like that. People deserve better." He had the neck of the bottle in his big hand, was seriously, carefully pouring himself another shot. He gestured with both bottle and glass. "People deserve to have—love."

"Love?"

"Yeah, love. You think I'm stupid, you think I watched too much TV as a kid, but I know it's out there. Somewhere. Other people think so too. Don't you? Didn't you, even if you won't admit it now, fall in love with that guy Max at first? You never said what he did at the beginning, how he talked you into being his lover. Something must have happened. Well, that's what I mean: love."

"Let me tell you about love. Love is a guy who talks real smooth taking me out to the woods and telling me he just loves my smile. And then taking me home and putting me in leather handcuffs so he can come. And if I hurt he likes it, because he likes it to hurt a little and he thinks I must like it like he does. And if I moan he thinks I'm coming. And if I cry he thinks it's love. And so do I. Until one evening—not too long after my *last* birthday, as I recall—he tells me that he has sold me to another company. And this only after he fucks me one last time. Even though I don't belong to him any more. After all, he had the option on all my bioware."

"All that is just politics." He was sharp, she had to grant him that.

"Politics," she said, "give me a break. Was it politics made Max able to sell me with the stock: hardware, software, liveware?"

"I've met guys like that. Women too. You have to understand that it wasn't personal to him, it was just politics." Also stubborn. "Sure, you were naive, but you weren't wrong. You just didn't understand company politics."

"Oh, sure I did. I always have. Why do you think I changed my name? Why do you think I dress in natural fibres and go through all the rest of this bullshit? I know how to set up power blocs. Except in mine there is only one party—me. And that's the way it's going to stay. Me against them from now on."

"It's not always like that. There are assholes in the world, and there are other people too. Everyone around here still remembers your grandfather, even though he's been retired in Camrose for fifteen years. They still talk about the way he and his wife used to waltz at the Legion Hall. What about him? There are more people like him than there are Whitmans."

"Charlotte doesn't waltz much since her stroke."

"That's a cheap shot. You can't get away with cheap shots. Speaking of shots, have another."

"Don't mind if I do. Okay, I give you Eric and Charlotte. But one half-happy ending doesn't balance out the people who go through their lives with their teeth clenched, trying to make it come out the same as a True Romance comic, and always wondering what's missing. They read those bodice-ripper novels, and make that do for the love you believe in so naively." Call her naive, would he? Two could play at that game. "That's why they'll all go crazy for Machine Sex. So simple. So linear. So fast. So uncomplicated."

"You underestimate people's ability to be happy. People are better at loving than you think."

"You think so? Wait until you have your own little piece of land and some sweetheart takes you out in the trees on a moonlit night and gives you head until you think your heart will break. So you marry her and have some kids. She furnishes the trailer in a five-room sale grouping. You have to quit drinking Glenfiddich because she hates it when you talk too loud. She gets an allowance every month and crochets a cozy for the TV. You work all day out in the rain and all evening in the back room making the books balance on the outdated computer. After the kids come she gains weight and sells real estate if you're lucky. If not she makes things out of recycled bleach bottles and hangs them in the yard. Pretty soon she wears a nightgown to bed and turns her back when you slip in after a hard night at the keyboard. So you take up drinking again and teach the kids about the rodeo. And you find some square-dancing chick who gives you head out behind the bleachers one night in Trochu, so sweet you think your heart will break. What you gonna do then, mountain man?"

"Okay, we can tell stories until the sun comes up. Which won't be too long, look at the time; but no matter how many stories you tell, you can't make me forget about that thing." He pointed to the computer with loathing.

"It's just a machine."

"You know what I mean. That thing in it. And besides, I'm gay. Your little scenario wouldn't work."

She laughed and laughed. "So that's why you haven't made a pass at me yet," she said archly, knowing it wasn't that simple, and he grinned. She wondered coldly how gay he was, but she was tired, so tired of proving power. His virtue was safe with her; so, she thought suddenly, strangely, was hers with him. It was unsettling and comforting at once.

"Maybe," he said. "Or maybe I'm just a liar like you think everyone is. Eh? You think everyone strings everyone else a line? Crap. Who has the time for that shit?"

Perhaps they were drinking beer now. Or was it vodka? She found it hard to tell after a while.

"You know what I mean," she said. "You should know. The sweet young thing who has AIDS and doesn't tell you. Or me. I'm lucky so far. Are you? Or who sucks you for your money. Or josses you 'cause he's into denim and Nordic looks."

"Okay, okay. I give up. Everybody's a creep but you and me."

"And I'm not so sure about you."

"Likewise, I'm sure. Have another. So, if you're so pure, what about the ethics of it?"

"What *about* the ethics of it?" she asked. "Do you think I went through all that sex without paying attention? I had nothing else to do but watch other people come. I saw that old cult movie, where the aliens feed on heroin addiction and orgasm, and the woman's not allowed orgasm so she has to O.D. on smack. Orgasm's more decadent than shooting heroin? I can't buy that, but there's something about a world that sells it over and over again. Sells the thought of pleasure as a commodity, sells the getting of it as if it were the getting of wisdom. And all these times I told you about, I saw other people get it through me. Even when someone finally made me come, it was just a feather in his cap, an accomplishment, nothing personal. Like you said. All I was was a program, they plugged into me and went through the motions and got their result. Nobody cares if the AI finds fulfillment running their damned data analyses. Nobody thinks about depressed and angry Mannboard ROMs. They just think about getting theirs.

"So why not get mine?" She was pacing now, angry, leaning that thin body as if the wind were against her. "Let me be the one who runs the program."

"But you won't be there. You told me how you were going to hide out, all that spy stuff."

She leaned against the wall, smiling a new smile she thought of as predatory. And maybe it was. "Oh, yes," she said. "I'll be there the first time. When Max and Kozyk run this thing and it turns them on. I'll be there. That's all I care to see."

He put his big hands on the wall on either side of her and leaned in. He smelled of sweat and liquor and his face was earnest with intoxication.

"I'll tell you something," he said. "As long as there's the real thing, it won't sell. They'll never buy it."

Angel thought so too. Secretly, because she wouldn't give him the satisfaction of agreement, she too thought they would not go that low. *That's right*, she told herself, *trying to sell it is all right—because they will never buy it.*

But they did.

A woman and a computer. Which attracts you most? Now you don't have to choose. Angel has made the choice irrelevant.

In Kozyk's office, he and Max go over the ad campaign. They've already tested the program themselves quite a lot; Angel knows this because it's company gossip, heard over the cubicle walls in the wash-rooms. The two men are so absorbed that they don't notice her arrival.

"Why is a woman better than a sheep? Because sheep can't cook. Why is a woman better than a Mannboard? Because you haven't bought your sensory add-on." Max laughs.

"And what's better than a man?" Angel says; they jump slightly. "Why, your Mann-Comp touchpads, with two-way input. I bet you'll be able to have them personally fitted."

"Good idea," says Kozyk, and Whitman makes a note on his lapboard. Angel, still stunned though she's had weeks to get used to this, looks at them, then reaches across the desk and picks up her prototype board. "This one's mine," she says. "You play with yourselves and your touch-pads all you want."

"Well, you wrote it, baby," said Max. "If you can't come with your own program. . . ."

Kozyk hiccoughs a short laugh before he shakes his head. "Shut up, Whitman," he says. "You're talking to a very rich and famous woman."

Whitman looks up from the simulations of his advertising storyboards, smiling a little, anticipating his joke. "Yeah. It's just too bad she finally burned herself out with this one. They always did say it gives you brain damage."

But Angel hadn't waited for the punch line. She was gone.

4

TROUBLE AND HER FRIENDS (EXCERPT)

Melissa Scott

Trouble was gone. Cerise had known it from the moment she entered the strangely neat apartment, the inevitable clutter—disks, books, and papers, here a sweater, there a pair of shoes—all missing along with Trouble. She went through the two rooms in the greyed light of the winter afternoon, checked the single closet and the battered trunks that held the rest of their clothes, not looking at the computers until the last, already sure of what she would find. Half the system was gone, Trouble's half, the portable holomultex drive and the brainbox and the braid of cables and biojacks that carried signals to the implanted processors in their brains. There was no paper note.

A light was flashing on the media console, and she touched the code keys to retrieve the single message. The voice that broke from the speaker was familiar, but not Trouble—Carlie, babbling on about something she couldn't be bothered to hear right now—and she killed the message, not bothering to save it for later. She turned away from the wall of blank screens and cubbies filled with data decks and players, the ugly oyster-grey carpet squeaking underfoot, and looked around the little room as though she was seeing it for the first time. Outside the single window, the sun was setting beyond the buildings on the far side of the little park, throwing a last cold light across the grey stone and concrete. A reflection like a spark flared from the highest side windows of the Lomaro Building half a mile away—three-quarters of a kilometer, she corrected automatically—and faded as she stared. The sun dropped into a bank of dirty clouds, and the light went out as though someone had flicked a switch. On the horizon, beyond the five- and six-story buildings of the local neighborhood, neon flickered to life, running like light along the edges of the buildings.

She shivered, and reached overhead into the web of invisible control beams that crisscrossed the apartment, waved her hand twice to bring on the main lights. A yellow light flashed on the display by the door instead, warning her that she hadn't replaced the main battery. She swore under her breath—that had been Trouble's chore—and went to the panel herself, switched lights and heat to full and touched the button that brought the opaque screen down over the window. It was sheer indulgence, this system, costing at least two months' rent to install, but once the security—black security, black-market and blackest-night effective, run off an illegal direct-line power tap—had been in place, it had seemed a shame not to install the convenience systems as well. She remembered Trouble balancing on an uneven chair beside the door, drill-driver in hand, bolting the last of the extra control boxes into place. That had been their indulgence for a job well done, right before the hearings began, three months before David Terrel was actually convicted of armed robbery because of a particularly brutal icebreaker he carried in his toolkit. The last good times, she thought, feeling at the moment only the cold, and turned back to the dismantled machines.

Seeing the system broken, the empty spaces where Trouble's machines had been, made her shiver again, something like fear or rage or sorrow threatening to break through the numbness, but she shoved the feelings down again, and went back into the bedroom for the things she needed to repair the gaps. She had spares of everything that Trouble had taken, machines she had used before she'd met Trouble, and she hauled their cases out from under the bed, brushing dust from the lids. The wind moaned through the rungs of the fire escape that slanted down past the bedroom window; she glanced at it, hearing loose bolts rattle on the landing one story above, and went back into the outer room.

It didn't take long to rebuild the system. Trouble had worked with her usual precision, taking nothing that wasn't hers, leaving the backup disks stacked prominently in front of the dusty keyboard. There was a hollyblock there, too, holographic storage, and Cerise moved it impatiently aside to plug her own holodrive into the multiple sockets. She replaced Trouble's dedicated brainbox with her own—an older model, but still serviceable, still fast enough to let her run the nets without danger—and found a length of cable to reconnect the various components. She looked at the hollyblock, but did not pick it up, turned instead to the rarely used keyboard and began methodically to recreate her machine.

The screen lit and windowed as she worked, giving her a schematic view of the reconstructed system; she touched keys, reestablishing virtual links that had been broken when the physical links were removed, and watched the schematic shift, rotating in the uppermost window to show her the new links outlined in red. A string of text asked for confirmation. She gave it the code it wanted, and watched as the red lines slowly turned to yellow and then to green, blending in with the rest of the design. When she was sure it was complete, she dismissed that image, and sorted through the directories until she found her private mailbox. It took two keys to open it, one a name—she made a mental note to change that—the other a meaningless string of letters, but she found nothing new in the lists of files. That was as she'd expected, and she dosed the program, reaching instead for the hollyblock. If Trouble had left her anything, any explanation, it would be there.

She fitted the box carefully into the replacement multex drive, and touched the keys that initiated the test sequence. Everything came back green, and she pressed a second set of keys to access the drive. A dozen files, each indicated by an individual symbol, an icon, bloomed on her screen. She frowned then—she had expected more, some message, some more useful labels, something—but touched the first icon. The file blossomed in front of her, filling the screen with a peculiar half-squashed, half-stretched image that she recognized once as the two-dimensional representation of a network file—of their network map, she realized suddenly, of the map she and Trouble had painstakingly built over the four years of their partnership. It was one of their more useful tools: there were no commercial maps available—not covering all the nets—and the ones that did exist were deliberately flawed, deliberately distorted to hide the control areas from people who had no business having access. And there were plenty of corporate spaces, privately owned systems that nonetheless also existed in the unreal "space" of the myriad networked computers that was the nets; all of those preferred to be invisible, at least to an outside eye.

On the net itself, of course, things were different. Once you plugged yourself into the system—either via the implanted dollie-box and dollie-slot, the direct-on-line-image processor system, which gave a text-speech-and-symbol interface, or through the full-sense brainworm, with its molecular wires running directly into the brain that let you experience virtuality as though it were real—it was easy enough to find your way around the nets. There were signposts, vivid neon images, and the swirling rivers and lines of light that were the virtual reflection of the data itself, which anyone who'd been on the nets for any length of time could read like a tracker read spoor. But the map was useful for planning a job, when you had to enter the nets from the safest point, so that the security programs, watchdogs and trackers and callback systems, and all the panoply of IC(E)—Intrusion Countermeasures (Electronic)—would either lose your trail in the confusion of conflicting data or never have the chance to track you down. Remotely, Cerise was surprised that Trouble had taken the copy with her, though she supposed it was possible that Trouble had made two copies out of the network files, their own secure space. But then, Trouble had said it was time to give up cracking.

It was very quiet in the apartment, too quiet, just the distant sound of wind and the occasional rattle of the fire escape in the other room. Cerise winced, and reached for the main remote, jabbed at buttons until the media center lit. Trouble had left the main screen tuned to the news channel, and the blare of the announcer's voice filled the room.

"—top story, the Senate today voted to override the presidential veto of the Evans-Tindale Bill, joining the House in handing the president a resounding defeat. Marjorie Albuez in Washington has more on the story."

"Thank you, Jim. By accepting the compromise bill sponsored by Charles Evans and Alexander Tindale, Congress today seems to have ensured that the United States will remain the only industrial nation that is not a signatory to the Amsterdam Network Conventions."

The voice droned on, but Cerise was no longer listening. She swung back to face the linked computers, the remaining files forgotten, and reached for the dollie-cord snugged into its housing at the base of the dedicated brainbox. She tilted her head to fit the cord into the dollie-slot behind her right ear, but did not launch herself directly onto the nets. This was why Trouble had left. She had been talking for months about what would happen if the U.S. rejected the Amsterdam Conventions, about how even the supposedly benign Evans-Tindale Bill would destroy the cracker community, bring them all finally under an alien, ill-conceived, ill-fitting law. For a moment, Cerise almost believed those prophecies of doom. No one had believed that Congress would buy Evans-Tindale, it bore no relation to virtuality . . .

"—completes what the so-called Nunberg Act—the Industrial Espionage Act, as it is more properly known—attempted to provide two years ago." That was a new voice, but Cerise didn't turn to identify the speaker. "The Evans-Tindale Bill codifies the various provisions of the Nunberg Act, and creates a new entity within the Treasury Department that will have enforcement responsibility on the nets, replacing the patchwork system currently in place. In a nutshell, Evans-Tindale, like the Nunberg Act before it, redefines so-called cyberspace as a particular legal jurisdiction, and establishes a code of law governing these electronic transactions."

Which means, Cerise thought, that we're all screwed. She sat for a long moment, staring at her screen, at the distorted image displayed in its central window. That map no longer mattered, because now there was no reason to keep those secrets, at least not in the legal world of the bright lights: there was a new law out there, and one that could be enforced the real world. And for the shadows—the illegal worlds crackers and grey- and black-market dealers, the world where she had lived ever since she'd run away from her home, her true name, and the secretarial school that had been her second home— it meant the end of an era. It would longer be possible to dodge the law in one jurisdiction by claiming that you, or your machines, or your target, were located elsewhere; it would no longer be possible to argue that there was no theft where there was no real property. All that had been decided, and by fiat, not the net's own powerful consensus. And Evans-Tindale also meant that there was no longer any possibility of legalizing the brainworm. The old-style crackers and the legal netwalkers had proclaimed their innocence by blaming everything on the brainworm and its users, and no one in authority seemed to know enough to know that they were lying.

She reached for the safety, cupped it in her left hand, hesitated, and wound the cord twice around her wrist, just in case. If she pressed that button, or its virtual analogue, the system would shut down instantly and automatically, dumping her back in the safety of her own home system, her own body. She took a deep breath, fighting back despair, and used her right hand to touch the sequence that opened a net gateway. The brainworm responded perfectly, its impulses overriding the merely physical input of the apartment, and she flung herself out into the glittering perpetual night that was the net.

Alice in Wonderland, Alice down the rabbit hole, Alice out in cyberspace, flung among the lines of data, flying across fields of light, the night cities that live only behind her eyes. Power rides fingers, she moves from datashell to datashell, walking the nets the ghost of a shadow, her trail vanishing behind her as she goes. She carries power in the dark behind her eyes.

And she needs it, tonight, in the chaos that whirls between islands of the corporate spaces, their boundaries marked by heaps and new whorls of glittering IC(E). The bulletin boards, the great sink of the BBS where all the lines of data eventually meet and merge and pool into a sink of slow transfer, limited nodes, and low-budget users, are in upheaval. The familiar icons and signpost-symbols that guide the unwary are gone completely, erased by their owners or remade in new and somehow threatening form. Icons whirl past her, some representing people she knows, has worked with. She smells fear sharp as sweat, hears the constant rustling murmur of the transactions that surround her as the brainworm translates what is truly only electrons, data transferred from computer to computer, to sensation in her brain. She glimpses a familiar shape, a hint of flowing robes that move against the current of the datastream that enfolds them, and tries to follow. But the crowding icons—balled advertising, jostling users, once a virtual pickpocket, groping for useful programs in other people's toolkits—block her way and she loses the robed icon at the main exchange node, where the data flows down from the outer nets like a waterfall of lights.

She turns back toward the center of the maze that is the BBS, following the shape of the underlying structural spiral rather than the illusion of shops and storefronts and tented stalls— unfamiliar shop-icons, old names and symbols blanked or greyed or simply missing—heading for a node where someone will surely know where Trouble has gone. Trouble will have left a message there, if she left anything at all. This is free space, unprotected, and the air stinks of it, the salt sea-smell the brainworm gives to undefended bits of data. At any other time, she would stop to taste, to savor, to see what news is drifting in the wind—and maybe especially tonight she should stop, listen to the whispers and shouts and read the posts that fill the message walls, but Trouble is gone, and that matters more than any law. She can hear voices, snatches of conversation, names repeated, not her own, but familiar nonetheless: the netgods have spoken, the oldsters who built and managed the first nets, and they've thrown their weight behind Evans-Tindale. Cerise sneers at that, and doesn't care that the brainworm broadcasts that emotion. The old netwalkers are out of touch with the new conditions, with the better, faster, and wider-band dollie-slots and especially with the brainworm; of course they'd support this law as a way to keep their own power supreme.

In a blank mirror that was once the center of a pair of swinging doors, she sees herself reflected, her icon blond-girl-in-blue-dress-and-pinnie, the child she never should have been, and then the mirror empties, and she puts her hand through it just like Alice and walks, her feet barely touching the illusion of a floor, into a temporary space.

Inside the mirror is a cave of ice, not the warm wood saloon she had expected, lined in IC(E) to keep out the intruders; the cowboys and the piano player are all missing, vanished into chill white silence, and a personal icon stands in the center where the bar had been, a woman-shape dressed like a dance-hall girl in snow-white velvet and silver fringe and silver-spangled stockings, the cloth drawn back into a bustle, cut down at the bodice to reveal breasts like hills of snow. Cerise feels the chill of the IC(E) on her skin, tingling down her spine like danger; she smells a tracker program, sharp as burned cloves, can almost taste the candy-sweet data that lies like shards of glass below the illusory floor. Miss Kitty deals in that data, stolen, borrowed, invented, even imagined, and in the commerce of messages passed unread.

I'm looking for Trouble, Cerise says, and waits.

She gets no answer, Miss Kitty's icon stands still and silent, and Cerise frowns and takes a step forward. And then she smells it, the scent of rotten meat, the corpse-smell the brainworm uses to signal absolute disaster. Even as she turns to run, the walls fold inward, IC(E) spiking downward. She feels its cold driving at her, lifts a hand to ward off the nearest spine, and its jagged tip scores a deep line along her arm. The brainworm reflects its touch as searing pain and the thin trace of blood ghostly along her icon-arm. There's no reason far this attack, she's no danger to Miss Kitty, never has been, has been in fact a good supplier, but there's no time to form a protest. No time even to reach for an icebreaker, or any of the other programs she carries in her toolkit; this is serious IC(E), deadly serious, and she closes her hand convulsively, triggering the safety. The world dissolves around her, the spikes of the IC(E) fading to static as they touch her skin

—and she leaned back in her chair, untangling her fingers from the cord of the safety. The screen in front of her flashed a bright-red icon, and a text message below it SESSION ABORT. She glared at that—it was an admission of defeat to trigger to the safety, to run away from danger—and then, belatedly, became aware of the faint scent of hot metal rising from the linked machines. She frowned then, and touched the brain-box. The casing was warm, warmer than it should have been. Her frown deepened, and she set the safety aside, touched keys to call up a diagnostic program. The session-abort icon vanished, replaced by a spinning clock-face; a moment later, it, too, disappeared, and the program presented her with a list of the various components and their conditions. Two of the five fuses had tripped in the brainbox, and one had gone in the bio-translator as well. Cerise shivered, even though she'd expected it, and reached for her box of spares. Miss Kitty's IC(E) had been set to kill—and what the hell the woman thought she was doing, Cerise added silently, transmuting fear to anger, I don't know. The whole nets have gone crazy—they must have, if anybody's actually supporting Evans-Tindale. And if Miss Kitty tried to kill me. Though that probably wasn't personal. She closed her eyes for an instant, remembering the frozen icon and the sudden smell of death. No, probably not personal at all, she decided. If I were abandoning a grey-market space—and I think she must've done just that—that's the way I'd play it. A striking icon to catch people's attention, and then hair-trigger IC(E) to go after whoever tried to follow me. Or, like Miss Kitty did, whoever showed up first.

She rubbed her arm where the IC(E) had touched her—there were no marks on her skin, just the tingling reminder of a near miss in her nerves—and then began methodically to shut down the system. She couldn't replace the fuses with the machines running, and she couldn't go back out onto the nets until the fuses were replaced: no choice, she thought, and swung away from the system. The media wall was still talking at her, the screen now showing a panel of suits discussing the implications of the change. She scowled at them, worked the remote to mute the sound, and only then recognized one of the suited figures as George Aferiat, who had written software for the first dollie-slots and their associated implants, and who had also run a shadow space in the BBS before he'd gotten law. There was nothing more zealous than a convert. She lifted her middle finger to the screen, and turned back to the message board.

It didn't take a lot of work to retrieve Carlie's message from the trash—even cheap machines had the option these days, and her system was far from cheap. She glanced at the linked machines—everything was shut down and saved; all she had to do was wait for the chips to cool and trigger the playback. Carlie Held's voice poured from the little speaker, as perfect as though he himself stood beside her.

"Cerise, Trouble, if either of you's there, pick up, we're in deep shit." There was a pause, and Cerise pictured him standing in the tiny office that served his storefront surgery, the privacy handset swamped in his huge hand. "OK, you're not there. OK. If you haven't heard, Evans-Tindale passed—goddamn Congress overrode the veto—which means the worm stays illegal, and Treasury gets to make the law on the nets. I need to talk to you—we all need to talk. Call me as soon as you can."

Cerise heard the click of the connection breaking, and a red light flashed on the tiny status screen: end of message. She swore under her breath, and reached for her own handset, touched the codes that would connect her with Carlie's surgery. She heard the beeps as the system routed her call—a local, twelve sharp musical tones, seven for location, three for payment, two for privacy—and then waited as the ring pulsed in her ear. She counted six, and knew Carlie wasn't answering—wasn't there—but let it ring a dozen more times, staring at the posturing suits in the media screen, before she finally hung up. Carlie was gone, too.

And that was ridiculous, she told herself. She jabbed buttons again, punching in another number—Arabesque, Rachelle Sirvain in the real world: another local call, just in the next ward, five minutes away by the subway. The phone rang, rang again; she counted ten before she hung up, fighting sudden panic. It was almost as if she was the last one of them left, the last survivor—She shoved that thought away, and punched a third number. This time, the answering machine picked up on the third ring.

"Hi, you've reached five-five—"

Cerise broke the connection—Dewildah was gone, too—and punched a final set of codes. In the media screen, the talking suits had disappeared, to be replaced by a head, a serious-looking woman who wore secretarial goggles. The phone rang, rang again, and then a sharply accented voice said, "Hello?"

Cerise let out breath she hadn't realized she was holding. "Butch. Thank God you're home."

"Cerise? Are you all right?"

She could hear the concern in Butch van Liesvelt's voice, and managed a shaky smile. "Yeah—well, no, Trouble's gone and there's all this with Evans-Tindale—"

"Yeah." There was a little pause, and Cerise could hear in the background the indistinct sounds of someone talking—television, probably, she thought. In the screen, the image changed again, became a pair of lists showing the differences between the Amsterdam Conventions and Evans-Tindale. In one corner of the screen, a much smaller talking head—male this time—babbled away, mouth moving without sound.

"Look," van Liesvelt said abruptly, "I'm heading over to Marco Polo's. Carlie called from there, he said he and Max were there already, and that Arabesque was on her way. I was just going to call you and Trouble, I talked to Dewildah already—"

"Trouble's gone," Cerise said again.

"Gone? What do you mean, gone?"

"I mean she's gone. She packed up her stuff and left. I don't know where she is." Cerise took another deep breath, fought back the baffled anger. "Or why, exactly, but I think I can guess. I'll meet you at Marco Polo's. We can talk there." "You sure?" van Liesvelt asked, and Cerise felt her eyes fill with tears. Of all their oddball group—a half-dozen or so crackers who had dared both the brainworm and the risks of real-world contact—it was van Liesvelt, shambling, physically graceless Butch, who'd done the most to take care of all of them.

"Yeah, I'm sure. I'll see you at Marco Polo's."

She cut the connection before van Liesvelt could ask anything more. She set the handset back on its hook, taking ridiculous care with the placement, waiting until the tears were gone again before she turned her mind to business. She worked the remote again, shutting down the media wall, and grabbed her leather coat off the hook by the door before she could change her mind.

The wind had risen since the afternoon, curled in as she opened the door, bringing the smell of the wet streets and driving a handful of tattered leaves around her ankles. Cerise shivered, tucking her chin down into the coat's high collar, then had to reach back to pull the door shut behind her. She jammed her hands into her pockets, wishing she'd remembered gloves, and tore the lining again where she'd cut the pocket for a borrowed gun. This wasn't a particularly bad part of town, no more than most, and better than some, but there had been times when she needed a gun's threat to balance the odds. Or to get them out of whatever Trouble had talked them into. It hadn't happened often— Trouble was generally reasonable, cautious—but every now and then she'd accept a challenge, even one that hadn't been meant, and they would all have to live with the consequences. Like now.

Cerise shook the thought away, the memory of Trouble furious and confident, facing down a pair of local boys with knives. She had downplayed it later, always pointed out that the kids had been maybe thirteen, fourteen years old and obviously trying their first mugging. But Cerise had never forgotten the crazy grin, the sheer, black-hearted determination, and had been, herself, more than a little afraid. She had caught the look again four months ago, when Evans-Tinsdale passed the first time, and had done her best not to see it. Trouble had said then that she was quitting, that they couldn't go on if the bill passed, and she had obviously meant it.

It was almost dark out now, and all the streetlights were on, swaying gently in the cold wind. Cerise shrugged herself deeper into her heavy coat, stepping more quickly across the moving shadows, heading for the nearest subway station at the corner of Elm and Cass. Not that it was all that far to Marco Polo's, less than a dozen blocks, but it was cold, and dark already, and the secretary gangs, the dollie-girls, tended to lurk on the fringes of New Century Square. As she came out into the brighter light of the intersection, however, she saw the lines waiting beyond the ticket booths, men and women huddled into drab, windproof coats, here and there the brighter cloth of a student uniform, and she muttered a curse under her breath. The system was backed up again—it had never been built to handle the current loads—and she could easily walk to the Square before she even made it town onto the platform. She lengthened her step, heading up Cass into the teeth of the wind.

Once she had passed the intersection, with its bright lights and the low-standing brick station, foot traffic thinned out. This was mostly small shops and offices, all of which closed promptly at five to let their people get out of the city-center before full dark, and the doors and ground-floor windows were barred, steel shutters or heavy grills drawn tight over their vulnerabilities. Security lights showed like blue pinpoints in the corners of a few windows, and there were metal mesh sleeves across the swaying streetlights, casting webbed shadows over the pooled light A few of the lights were broken anyway, leaving patches of greater dark, and she crossed them warily, wondering if she'd been stupid after all. But she was already past the bus lines at Stadium Road—not that they were running, it wasn't a game night—and it would take longer to walk back to the station than it would to keep going. She could see the lights of the Square in the distance, the haze of gold neon bright at the end of the street, the gold-and-red bars of the Camberwell Beer sign just visible between a pair of buildings: only another four or five blocks to go and she'd be in the relative safety of the crowded Square. She kept walking, not hurrying, glad of her soft-soled shoes and the dark coat that helped her pass unobserved, and reached the end of Cass without encountering another pedestrian.

New Century Square was as busy as ever, lights glaring from the subway kiosk at the center of the circle, more light, red and gold and green neon, flashing from the signs and display boards that ringed the Square, and from the signs that glowed and flickered over the myriad doorways. The gaudy lights helped to disguise buildings that hadn't been new eighty years ago, when the century turned and the Square had been rechristened in hopes of attracting a new clientele for the new years. Maybe half a dozen suits were standing outside the station, staring up at the news board and its displays—currently a pretty dark-skinned actress showing teeth and tits and a new shampoo. There were more suits inside the ticket booths, men and women alike looking tired and irritable, and Cerise guessed that the system still wasn't running properly. A handful of dollie-girls were hanging out under the awning outside the discount store watching the suits. The youngest looked twelve or so, the oldest maybe sixteen, and each of them wore a parody of corporate suit—the skirts too short, slit thigh-high, the jackets too tight and sexy, their faces layered with clown-bright makeup. Their shoes, bright neon-satin pumps, had three- and four-inch heels sheathed in steel, and there would be flip-knives and maybe a gun or two in the sequinned hand bags. They belonged to the secretarial so-called college over on Market Street, Cerise knew, kids who had indentured themselves to the school and its placement service to get the implants, dollie-box and dollie-slot, that could eventually win them a decent job with a corporation. They had found out too late, they always found out too late, that they didn't automatically get the training or the bioware that would let them walk the nets, or even use the systems to their full capacity. It was no wonder they took to the streets to get a little of their own back. She had been one of them, eight years ago before she'd figured out how to get into the BBS and found the grey-market dealers there, and she gave them a wide berth, knowing what they, what she, were capable of doing. She was aware of their stares as she passed, the anger buried under the troweled-on color, and ignored it, knowing better than to meet someone's eyes and trigger a confrontation. Trouble would have laughed—if she was in one of her difficult moods, she would have said something, anything, earned her name yet again. But then, Trouble had somehow never learned to lose. How she'd managed that, Cerise didn't know, even after four years together working the nets, and three years as lovers: she wasn't corporate, and besides, the corporations taught you early to lose to them. But she sure wasn't city-trash, either.

She heard the click of heels behind her, steel on stone, and then a second set of footsteps, the same sharp almost musical clink not quite in synch with the first, and did not turn. The wall of a store rose to her right, solid brick banded with neon: no place to run, except into the street and the traffic, and that would mean losing anyway. The skin between her shoulder blades tingled, an electric touch at the center of her spine. She had played the game before, knew exactly what was happening and then she heard the voices, rising shrill to be certain she, and all the others, heard.

"—that hair."

"Pull it out, girl."

Cerise turned then, the fury rising in her, caught the dollie-girl by the lapel of her too-tight jacket, swung her sideways into the brick of the wall. The girl staggered, losing her balance on the high heels, and Cerise hauled her up bodily, using both lapels this time, and slammed her back against the bricks, narrowing missing a light tube. She caught a glimpse of the second girl, mouth open in shock, falling back a step or two at the sheer craziness, and looked down at the girl in her hands. She hung dazed, one button torn loose, her eyes unfocused and filled with reflex tears. Cerise shook her, not caring that her head bounced off the bricks, felt her scrabble without result for safer footing.

"You touch me," Cerise said, "and I'll fucking kill you."

She hadn't spoken loudly, sounded calmer than she felt, but the girl heard, eyes widening so that a tear ran down her painted face, drawing a long line of scarlet from her mascara. Cerise lifted her, barely feeling the effort, and let her go again, saw her slide gracelessly to the bottom of the wall and sit for an instant, long legs sprawling, before the other girl moved to help her up. Cerise turned her back on them, not caring, daring them, even, to follow her. There was nothing, not even a catcall, last defiance, and she felt the sharp sting of regret before the reaction set in.

She was still shaking a little, adrenaline-anger and fear mixed, when she turned down the narrow street that led to Marco Polo's and pushed open the door badged with a neon cactus and pagodas, wincing as the twanging steel-string music hit her like a blow. The downstairs room was filled with a mix of suits and lower-level tech-types and a fair number of secretaries and temps of both sexes on the hustle. Most of them were standing four-deep at the bar, bellowing indistinguishable orders at the sweating bartenders, or crowded in groups of six or seven around the tiny tables. A few, maybe a dozen or so, were already on the little dance floor, arms linked across each others' shoulders, feet moving in approximate coordination. Twin television monitors hung at the ends of the bar, and the news anchor beamed down like a benevolent deity. His words were inaudible through the music and the shouted conversations, but the logo beside his head was the familiar computer-chip-and-gavel that had come to stand for Evans-Tindale. Cerise made a face, seeing that, and began to work her way through the crowd toward the stairs that led to the upper bar.

It was a jovial crowd, this early, everybody loose but not yet drunk enough to think of trouble, and it wasn't difficult to get through the mob, no need to resort to elbows or stepping on toes. She smiled mechanically at suits, and they edged smiling away, letting her worm through the spaces. She fetched up at the foot of the stairs in a sudden pocket of silence as the song ended, and stood there for a moment catching her breath, looking back toward the monitors. The Evans-Tindale logo was still in place, though the image behind it had changed: the screen was filled with protesters, all waving placards that called for the U.S. to sign the Amsterdam Conventions. The camera focused on one sign, carried by a black woman who looked young and serious enough to be a student at a real college; it read, in bright red letters, A: U.S. AND LIBERIA. Q: WHO HASN'T SIGNED? That wasn't quite true, Cerise thought—she vaguely remembered that there were a couple of Asian nations that hadn't yet agreed to the Conventions—but it was close enough. At her side, a tallish suit, good-looking, broad bones and a not-too-neat mustache, shook his head.

"I don't get it," he said, to no one in particular. "What's the problem?"

Cerise looked at him in disbelief, wanting to say something but not knowing where to begin. Evans-Tindale was going to change everything, was going to destroy the nets as they were, and offered nothing to replace them—A suited woman edged up to the man, handed him one of the two beers she carried, holding them well away from her body.

"Technies," she said. "If they can't have their toys—"

The music started again, with a wail of synthetic brass, drowning out her words. Cerise shook herself—there was nothing you could say to some people, nothing that would make any difference—and started up the stairs.

The upstairs room—it had never had another name, wasn't even officially reserved for a netwalker clientele, though the occasional suit or temp who wandered in from downstairs usually left quickly enough—was much quieter, and she let the heavy door thump shut again behind her with a sigh of relief. There was no music here, just the occasional murmur of voices and the overlapping noise of five or six television monitors, each tuned to a different channel. Most of the little tables scattered across the dimly lit room were occupied by netwalkers who sat alone or in twos and threes, muttering together or with their eyes fixed on the monitors mounted from the ceiling. She recognized some of the faces—Johnny Winchester, for one, scrawny and greying, who had been on the nets since the invention of the dollie-slot, and was syscop, the on-line legal authority, for one of the official public spaces. He'd been to D.C. four times to testify, supporting the Amsterdam Conventions, had argued at the last that Evans-Tindale was better than nothing. I hope you're satisfied, Cerise thought, and headed for the bar, giving his table a wide berth.

The bar itself was mechanical, which meant a limited selection of drinks, but Marco didn't have to pay a fifth bartender. Cerise fed a couple of slips of citiscrip into the machine, and it whirred to itself for a moment before filling a plastic cup with wine. In the dim light it looked more like water, and she sniffed it to be sure before she turned away. There were a few other faces she knew, not many: netwalkers didn't as a rule congregate in the real world. It took something like this to bring them together, and even then most of them weren't talking to each other, just sitting and listening to the monitors. She recognized a pair of women from the Arts Round Table, sitting together with a man she didn't know. All three looked grim, and they had their heads close together; as she made her way past the table, she saw that they had a portable machine set up, and were staring avidly at its screen. Neither of the women were on-line, and the man didn't even seem to have a dollie-slot; what good they thought they could do, she didn't know. There was another familiar shape at a table at the back of the room, a rangy man, bearded and scowling, a flashing pin in the shape of his red-hand icon fastened to the lapel of his neat suit-jacket, and Cerise looked hastily away. Bran-Boru, or whatever his real name was, had a reputation for being chancy, and she had no desire to attract his attention.

Then at last she saw van Liesvelt, skinny and blonde and rumpled, even sitting down taller than the others at the corner table. He lifted his hand in greeting, beckoning her over; Cerise waved back, not trying to hide her relief, and came to join them. The others were there, too: Carlie Held still in working whites under his grubby jacket, Arabesque slowly crumpling the fingers of a VR glove—the old-fashioned virtual-reality interface, not good for anything but games and blunt-instrument science anymore—into an ungainly fist, Max Helling with his partner Jannick Aledort at his back, Aledort listening, not quite part of the group, while Helling talked. Max was always talking, Cerise thought, and took the last chair, next to Dewildah Mason, who looked up at her with a wry smile and a nod of greeting.

"So where's your other half?"

"Trouble's gone," Cerise said, and to her horror heard her voice crack. She took a sip of the wine to cover it, swallowed wrong, and choked. Mason reached over to pound her on the back, brown eyes wide with concern.

"That's what you said," van Liesvelt said.

Giving me time to pull myself together, Cerise thought, and nodded her thanks, setting the wine down again.

"Yeah." Her voice was still strained, and her throat hurt, but at least she didn't sound as though she were going to cry.

"Evans-Tindale?" Helling asked. He was a thin, feral-looking man, a little older than the rest of them. He'd been on the net for years, had more business connections in the shadows, knew more about buying or selling black-market programs and data than any of the others. Cerise sometimes thought he only stayed friends with them because they were all queer, and the old-style netwalkers still didn't approve of him, wouldn't approve of him no matter how good he was because of it. She suspected he'd taken the risk of the brainworm for the same reason: the old-style netwalkers wouldn't respect his work once he'd gotten it, but then, they hadn't ever respected him. The brainworm did give you an advantage on the nets, let you use the full range of your senses, not just sight and sound, to interpret the virtual world. The old-style netwalkers claimed to hold it in contempt, said that it was a crutch, something for second-raters, but Cerise suspected, had always suspected, that they were just afraid. The worm entailed risks: implantation and direct-to-brain wiring was always tricky, could leave you a mental cripple if the operation went wrong, and the oldsters had never quite been able to face that possibility. The dollie-slots and the associated implants didn't touch the brain, ran along existing nerves—less of a risk, and more of a challenge to use, or so the oldsters said.

"Trouble wouldn't just run away," Arabesque said. She set the VR glove down on the dented tabletop, curled her own hand over it, matching finger to finger. Her skin was only a little lighter than the black plastic, and both were like shadows in the indirect light.

"She said she would," Held said. He shook his head, laid his huge hands flat on the tabletop. It was hard, seeing them, to believe that he was as good a cybermedic as he actually was; harder still to believe that he was qualified to install and modify brainworms. Or at least he was qualified in the EC, where he'd trained: the worm was still illegal here, and there wasn't any chance of legalizing it now that Evans-Tindale had passed. "She said from the beginning she wasn't going to stick around if Congress overrode the veto." He shook his head, and pushed himself back from the table. "Anybody else want another drink?"

Van Liesvelt shook his head, and Mason said, "Yeah, thanks, Carlie." She held out a glittering strip of foil, and Held took it, turned away toward the bar.

"That wasn't all she was bitching about," Arabesque said, and gave Cerise a hard look. "Last time I talked to her, she said you two'd had a disagreement over a job."

Cerise made a face. This was the part she hadn't wanted to think about, the part she hadn't wanted to remember: she'd been warned, and she'd miscalculated badly. "There's a new corporate space, with new IC(E). I didn't recognize the system, but I thought we could crack it. Trouble doesn't—didn't agree. But it's interesting IC(E)." She could almost see it, taste it, in memory, a massive cylinder of glass, light spiraling slowly up its side, to drift down again in a faint haze, hiding the codes that make up the real security. She had never seen IC(E) that tight before, could hardly wait to try to crack it. . . .

"What was the company?" That was Aledort, leaning forward a little further over the back of his own chair and Helling's shoulder.

"I don't know yet," Cerise answered. "I told you, it's a new space to me."

"Better hold off a while," Helling said. "You don't know what's going to happen under Evans-Tindale."

Van Liesvelt nodded agreement, for once unsmiling. His mustache looked more ragged than ever, as though he'd been chewing on it.

"I can't believe Trouble just left," Mason said.

"Neither can I," Arabesque said, and Cerise glared at her.

"I told you what happened. We'd been talking about the job—"

"You can't call it a job," Helling objected. "If you don't know who made the IC(E) or what's behind it, it's not a job." Cerise ignored him. "And she said she wasn't going to do it, It was crazy with the second vote coming up. She said if Evans-Tindale passed, if they overrode the veto, she wasn't going to stay on the nets. And when I came home this afternoon, she was gone, and all her equipment with her."

"Jesus," van Liesvelt said.

"I called about three," Held said, reappearing with two glasses. He handed one to Mason, along with a couple of plastic slugs, and reseated himself next to van Liesvelt. "So I guess she was gone then. I'd just got out of surgery, heard from a guy in the waiting room." He shook his head. "Man, I couldn't believe it. They won't sign the Conventions, and then they turn around and pass this shit."

"I was on my way back from campus," Mason said unexpectedly. She had been a student at a real college, still held an extension card from the university. "I was waiting for the commuter train, there must've been twenty of us, and this guy—I hardly know him, his name's Bill something, or maybe Paul. Anyway, he comes up to me and says, 'You're on the nets, right? Did you hear they overrode the veto?' And looked at him— I still can't believe I did this—and I said, 'You got to be kidding. That can't be right, you must've got it wrong.' And he says, 'No, they've got the monitors on in the pizza place'—there's a pizza place right next to the train station—'and they broke into the soaps to make the announcement.' So I went over there, and sure enough, the monitor's on, and the screen's showing the vote count. And I just stood there. I thought for a minute he'd gotten the story backward that we'd won, because the numbers were so high for Evans-Tindale, but he hadn't. They'd overridden it, no question. No appeal, no nothing. I damn near didn't bother getting on the train."

"I was on the net," Helling said. "I—" He stopped, glancing over his shoulder at Aledort, who was scowling, and began again. "I'd just drifted back into the BBS, riding the stream, and I thought—I don't know what I thought. It felt like an earthquake, everybody trying to log on or off or to do something, all at once. I mean, the ground shook." He waved his hands in the air, miming the motion. "Literally. I couldn't keep my balance for a minute. And then everybody starting talking, shouting, and I ran for the nearest node and got the hell off the system." He shook his head. "It's still crazy out there. I got back on before I came over here. I thought maybe somebody would be talking sense out there, but it's insane. Half the old spaces are shut down, the BBS is clogged solid with traffic, there's new IC(E) in half the corporate spots I looked at. It's just crazy."

"Miss Kitty shut down the saloon," Cerise said. "And left some very nasty IC(E) behind her." She didn't need to add any more to it: they all knew Miss Kitty, did business with her, and knew Cerise as well.

"Well, she was in a really bad position," Helling said. "Under the new laws, my God, everything she traded in was felony material."

"Wonderful," van Liesvelt said. "I have to admit, Trouble's got a point. It's not exactly going to be safe, staying in the shadows."

"Only if you're not careful," Cerise said.

Arabesque nodded. "Yeah. It changes how we do business, ups the risks and the stakes. My God, you know what we can charge now?"

"Yeah, and end up like Terrel," Mason muttered. "Serving three-to-ten for a so-called armed robbery—you just better be careful what you carry in your toolkit now."

There was a little silence, and then van Liesvelt said, "I was over on the Euronets when the news came through. I'd told a couple of old friends there was no way the override would happen. It took me twenty minutes, realtime, to work my way back to home node. I thought I'd have to hit the safety before I found a way through the traffic."

Cerise whistled under her breath. Twenty minutes in realtime, not the subjective time of the nets, was ridiculously long. Usually one could make one's way from one side of the nets the other—traveling twice around the world in the process—in that time.

"What in the world," Mason said, "are we going to do now?"

"Do?" Arabesque fixed her with an angry stare. "Pretty much what we've always done, that's what we're going to. Cracking was always illegal, don't kid yourself, 'Wildah. We'll just have to be more careful—and that's all."

"I don't know," Held said. "I think it's different." He shook his head. "Very different."

Van Liesvelt nodded in morose agreement, and wiped beer out of his mustache. "I was wondering about Europe, heading there, I mean."

"The real business—most of the real targets, real data, data worth money—is still in U.S. jurisdiction," Helling said. "Or can claim it is. And they've explicitly overruled appealing to Amsterdam Conventions. It's in the law."

"Fuck," van Liesvelt muttered, and took another swallow of his beer.

Cerise said, "I'm with Arabesque. We got to stick with it. What else can we do?"

"Go straight?" Helling murmured, with a curl of his lip. Held laughed without humor, and Arabesque shook her head. Van Liesvelt said, "Not likely."

Cerise allowed herself a sour smile, acknowledging the pun—the one thing they all had in common, besides the brainworm, was being gay—but it faded quickly. Going straight, moving out of the shadows into the bright lights of the legal world, the legal nets, would be difficult: they, none of them, had the corporate connections to become the sort of consultant that would let them go on paying their bills, and none of the other jobs that were open to freelancers were particularly challenging, or particularly well-paid. And corporate employment. . . . Unconsciously her mouth twisted again as she tried to imagine herself, any of them, fitting into the polite, restrained world of the corporations. If any of them had been suited to the corporate life, he or she would already be part of it. The perks of a corporate job were too good, despite the risk of layoffs, to be passed up lightly.

The noise from the monitors changed, flared briefly, and then settled to a single voice. Cerise turned in surprise to see that the three monitors in her line of sight were now tuned the same channel—so were they all, from the way Jerry Singlar's voice coalesced out of the hubbub. Singlar was one her least favorite anchors, an ex-cracker gone to the bright lights with a vengeance, a man who pretended to know and love the nets even as he proved he didn't understand an thing about them. She made a face, but did not look away. The others were looking at the monitors, too, not just at their table but all across the room, and the talk faded quickly, leaving only Singlar's voice crackling out of the half-dozen speakers.

"—commentary. The override of the presidential veto Evans-Tindale has brought consternation to the nets, a result not unexpected among those of us who have walked the nets for the past decade. Despite attempts at self-policing, the nets have long been a lawless place, a haven for a criminal minority as well as for the law-abiding majority. This situation has become impossible to tolerate, as the depredations of the so-called crackers, descendants of the criminal hackers of the twentieth century, have become the center of a criminal economy that rivals the Mafia in scope and enterprise."

Arabesque made a rude noise, half laughter, half spitting, and Mason waved her to silence. Helling muttered something under his breath that sounded like, "I wish," and Aledort laid a hand on his shoulder.

"This economy, which thrived only by the absence of law, has spawned a number of subcultures, all dangerous in their own right. But the most dangerous of these, the one that has caused the most talk and the one that the Evans-Tindale will do most to control, is that of the brainworm. These untested and potentially deadly implants—far more dangerous than the common dollie-slots, because the brainworm requires placing hardware in the brain itself—have contributed to the spread of the cracker culture by giving these hard-line criminals access to a new technology that is unbeatable by people equipped with only ordinary, and legal, implants."

"Oh, bullshit," Cerise said.

Held said, in the voice of a man making an old, and losing, argument, "The brainworm is legal in Europe and there's no more cracking from the Euronets. And people don't die from installation there, either."

"It figures," Arabesque said, with suppressed fury, "it just figures they'd try to blame the worm."

"It's easier than writing intelligent laws," Helling said.

"They have laws that make sense," van Liesvelt said. "All they had to do was sign the Amsterdam Conventions. . . ."

"Oh, shut up." That was Johnny Winchester, weaving to his feet at the center of the room. He stumbled slightly nearly overturning his table and tipping his beer so that it slopped over the edge of the glass to form a slowly spreading puddle on the tabletop. "Jerry's right, if you people hadn't brought in the worm, gone cracking with it, none of this would've happened."

"Bullshit," Cerise said again.

Arabesque said, "Dream on. They've been looking for an excuse to crack down for a hundred years."

"Yeah, and you people gave it to them." Winchester stared at them. Behind him, the spilled beer began to drip off the edge of his table.

"Fucking wireheads," someone else said, from the dark behind him.

"Hey people," Held said, voice dropping into his best street-doc register. "This hurts all of us."

"And there are plenty of people cracking without the worm," van Liesvelt said, not quite quietly enough.

There was an ambiguous murmur from the rest of the room, not agreement, not rejection, an undirected anger that made the back of Cerise's neck prickle with sudden fear. She had heard that note before, on the streets when she was fifteen, running with the gangs, the sound of a group looking for a scapegoat; she had never thought to hear it here, among the people of the net, and never directed at herself. She looked around the room as though for the first time, seeing the majority of pale faces, male faces, sitting for the most part alone or in twos and threes: nothing like her own group, none of the easy realworld friendship. She had never before seen so many of the others together off-line.

She looked back at the others, and saw Aledort leaning back a little, eyes narrowed. He had heard the same thing she had, and Aledort usually went armed.

Helling said, "Nobody's going to wipe out cracking anyway. The multinationals pay too damn well."

He had said the right thing, Cerise realized. There was little ripple of scornful laughter, and, underneath it, the release of tension like a sigh. She took a deep breath, reached for her wine, and took a long drink without really tasting it. In the background, Singlar droned on, his voice alternately reproving and paternal by turns, but she determinedly ignored it, concentrating on the wine. She set the glass carefully back in its wet circle, wondering what she was going to do. Whatever else Evans-Tindale had done, it had broken the old community of the net, divided the old-style crackers, the ones who relied on the dollie-boxes, from the ones who use the brainworm—and was that the intention? she wondered suddenly. It would be more subtle than she would have expected from people who didn't know the net—and conspiracy theories are usually wrong, she told herself sternly. The only certainty is that the nets have changed irrevocably. And Trouble is gone, my life changed with that as much as with the new law. The only question is, what to do now.

She took another deep breath, still looking at the glass of wine in its wet circle. Singlar's voice rumbled on behind her, but she didn't turn to look again at the monitors.

"—establish a new enforcement agency—something like the Texas Rangers, if you will, bringing law to the virtual frontier—"

Arabesque was right about one thing, though: it was going be a lot harder to make a living cracking without ending up in a real jail. She would need new equipment, top-of-the-line machines to replace the old systems she and Trouble had owned, maybe new bioware to bring her brainworm up to speed, and that meant a trip to Seahaven—the real one, she amended, with an inward smile, not the virtual town that went by the same name. The seacoast town was the East Coast's greatest source for black- and grey-market netware, hard and soft alike. But it was correspondingly expensive: she would have to crack that IC(E), the IC(E) Trouble had refused to face with her. Anything with that big a fence around it had to be valuable, and there would be a grace period before Treasury got itself together. She could take what she needed, sell it, and be on the road to Seahaven, the real Seahaven, before anyone knew what had happened. And it would serve Trouble right, prove she'd been wrong to leave—

"Cerise?" Van Liesvelt was leaning forward slightly, both elbows on the tilting tabletop.

"Hey, careful," Held said, and Arabesque pressed down on her side of the table, steadying it.

"You all right, Cerise?" van Liesvelt asked.

Cerise nodded. "Yeah, I'm all right," she said, and thought she meant it. She smiled, calculating the effect. "I'll be going Seahaven. After I've done some—work."

Helling said, "That was serious IC(E), Trouble said. And you don't know what's behind it."

"If there's that much IC(E)," Cerise said, "it has to be worth something. And I want to do some shopping."

"Your credit's good with me," Held said. He had done her other implants, from the original dollie-slot and box to the brainworm. Cerise nodded her thanks.

"I appreciate it, Carlie, but I don't take charity." She looked around the table. "Anyone interested in coming in on this with me?"

Mason shook her head. "I'm—I think I'm going to lie low for a while," she said, and Cerise was suddenly certain that was not what the other woman had meant to say. "You're quitting," Arabesque said, the words an accusation, and Mason glared at her.

"I don't know yet, but I'm damn sure it's the smart thing do."

"Butch?" Cerise said.

Van Liesvelt looked down at his beer. "I think Dewildah's right. I'm going to lie low, see how things shape up before I take on anything else."

Cerise nodded. "Arabesque?"

The other woman hesitated, made a face. "I know the job you mean, and I'm not taking on that IC(E) with what I got right now. You wait a month, let me get my new bioware tuned in, and I'll go in with you."

"I'm not waiting," Cerise said flatly. If I wait, she thought, if I wait, Trouble may come back and try to talk me out of it again—or worse still, maybe she won't come back; and I'll be left truly on my own. She shook the thought away. "Max, you interested?"

"I've plenty of work of my own, thanks," Helling answered.

"Fine."

Held said again, "Cerise, I do give credit—"

"And I don't take charity." Cerise shook her head, shaking away temptation. "Thanks, Carlie, but I can't." I don't care what Trouble says, what any of them say, she thought. I'm not going to let things change.

5

STRIKING CYBORGS: REWORKING THE "HUMAN" IN MARGE PIERCY'S HE, SHE AND IT

Heather Hicks

In the annals of texts that have sought to imagine Western civilization's step from the human-centered perspective that has been our legacy since the Renaissance to a society that understands itself as "posthuman," few contemporary novels are more often discussed than Marge Piercy's *He, She and It* (1991). Subsequently published in Great Britain under the title *Body of Glass* (1992), Piercy's eleventh novel has drawn the attention of those concerned with the posthuman for two reasons. First, by conceiving her novel as two interwoven narratives, one highlighting the oppression of Jews in Prague at the height of the Renaissance and the other exploring the near-future development of a breakthrough cybernetic "man," Piercy seems to invite us to read her cyborg, Yod, as the endpoint of the often divisive man-centered philosophies that have flourished since the 1500s. Second, Piercy does nothing to hide her profound debt to either the fictional bastion of the posthuman, the postmodern science fiction known as "cyberpunk," or the theoretical guru of this epistemology, Donna Haraway. "We're all cyborgs," insists Shira, the female protagonist and lover of Yod in *He, She and It*, unmistakably echoing Haraway's landmark paean to posthumanism, "A Cyborg Manifesto."[1]

To date, however, those who have explicated Piercy's novel have neglected her most distinctive contribution to the body of thought that poses the "cyborg" as the inevitable replacement for the time-honored but troubled concept of the "human." For if the essence of Haraway's cyborg is its mixture of human and machine parts, Piercy's cyborg has less to do with machine *parts* than machine *process*. Indeed, I'll argue here that Piercy presents her archetypal cyborg not as the conventional hybrid of the "human" and the "machine," but instead as the human form penetrated and co-opted by a distinctively late-capitalist work ethic. In this reading, Piercy's array of noncybernetic characters are all "cyborgs," not because they, like Yod, are profoundly integrated with technological systems, but because they "work" as a machine works, not as an occupation, but as the defining term for their state of animation in the world they inhabit.

"Cyborg Life"

Those of us who think and write about contemporary literature and culture may at times begin to feel that we have reached "cyborg" saturation. The cyborg surfaces as a touchstone concept in virtually every discussion of cultural manifestations of technological change. Haraway can claim the patent on this heuristic assemblage, and her place at the head of the cyborg intellectual trade has been given due homage in every subsequent exchange. This has not stopped the proliferation of modified cyborg models, however. Indeed, giving Haraway's cyborg one makeover after another has been crucial in keeping its stock up in the intellectual market where new formulations of the state of Western culture are the dominant currency. Yet however faddish the regular recycling of this trope may begin to appear, its staying power suggests its usefulness as an intellectual rallying point for all of us who find contemporary cultural transformations too astonishing and dramatic to warrant anything less than the special effect that is the cyborg metaphor.

For Haraway, of course, cyborgs are "theorized and fabricated hybrids of machine and organism."[2] Although she acknowledges the military origins of these high-tech confabulations, Haraway treats them/us as potentially utopian. "[M]y cyborg myth," she writes, "is about transgressed boundaries, potent fusions, and dangerous possibilities which progressive people might explore as one part of needed political work"(154). For my purposes, however, it is important to note that these potent fusions take place in a specifically economic context in her manifesto; Haraway's socialist principles, evident in her commitment to praxis as well as theory, make her especially conscious of the interface between postindustrial technologies and *workers*. In the two sections of her essay titled "The Informatics of Domination," and "The 'Homework Economy' Outside 'The Home,'" she critically assesses the disempowered condition of the contemporary working class. Careful to attend to "the 'multinational' material organization of the production and reproduction of daily life" as well as "the symbolic organization of the production and reproduction of culture and imagination" (165), Haraway nuances her theoretical formulations with discussions of the daily stress that both male and female workers are experiencing in the United States as well as in the countries Western businesses casually term "off-shore": "The success of the attack on relatively privileged, mostly white, men's unionized jobs is tied to the power of the new communications technologies to integrate and control labor despite extensive dispersion and decentralization. The consequences of the new technologies are felt by women both in the loss of the family (male) wage (if they ever had access to this white privilege) and in the character of their own jobs, which are becoming capital-intensive; e.g., office work and nursing" (166–167).

Our awareness of female workers' anxieties and pain is particularly honed by Haraway's fine-grained depiction of their daily lives. High-tech multinational capitalism is made real and immediate in her references to female electronics workers' difficulties: "In the prototypical Silicon Valley, many women's lives have been structured around employment in electronics-dependent jobs, and their intimate realities include serial heterosexual monogamy, negotiating childcare, distance from extended kin or most other forms of traditional community, a high likelihood of loneliness and extreme economic vulnerability as they age" (166).

Earlier sections of Haraway's essay, which produce magic-realist marriages of fantasy and philosophy reminiscent of a Hieronymous Bosch painting, might make us doubt her concern with or awareness of such tedious matters as work. In the above passages, however, the "intimate realities" of workers' lives emerge as a central component of Haraway's understanding of technology's place in the contemporary world.

It is workers, then, who Haraway hopes to liberate from the "integrated circuit" in which they find themselves, by reimagining what technology and the human are. In these terms, the cyborg becomes the surrogate myth to which we might entrust our futures: "One important route for reconstructing socialist-feminist politics is through theory and practice addressed to the social relations of science and technology, including crucially the systems of myth and meanings structuring our imaginations. The cyborg is a kind of disassembled and reassembled, postmodern, collective and personal self" (163). The cyborg identity is the springboard for a historical transformation in which workers' encounters with technology would be entirely free of the current, negative effects that she has diagnosed in her manifesto.

While a comprehensive review of the variations on Haraway's cyborg that other scholars have subsequently masterminded is beyond the scope of this essay, I believe that it is safe to say that very few have retained Haraway's preoccupation with the demands of work as the crucial relay between the human and machine. A number of critics, including John R. R. Christie, Thomas Foster, Mary Catherine Harper, and Sharon Stockton, have foregrounded the ontology of fragmentation and hybridity that Haraway celebrates, then explored the lurking unities (or, alternatively, Cartesian dualisms) that continue to haunt contemporary cyborg identities.[3] Others, including Chela Sandoval and Joseba Gabilondo, have broadened the signifying power of the cyborg, understanding it, respectively, as a centuries-old figure of subaltern resistance and as a marker of Western technological hegemony. While both Sandoval and Gabilondo produce fascinating revisions of the cyborg in a multinational context, the daily lives of postcolonial cyborgs—virtually all of which are constituted by work and the search for work—are not in evidence.[4] While in their attempt to define the principles of "cyborgology" Chris

Hables Gray, Steven Mentor, and Heidi J. Figueroa-Sarriera refer to work as one of several origins for contemporary conceptions of the cyborg, they ultimately strive for a flexible definition of this rubric that, in its preoccupation with the place of cyborgs in "systems," extends from individuals who interact with technology to whole corporations, and even whole national governments.[5] Even more abstract is David Porush's redefinition of the cyborg as the merging of the human and the utopian. "Every utopian inscription onto the human," Porush writes, "produces a new and improved vision of a cyborg."[6] In this formulation, Porush seems to distill the pure optimism of Haraway's account and locate in it the essence of the cyborg.

Indeed, among the second-generation cyborg theories spawned since Haraway's manifesto first appeared in 1985, it is only David Brande's that seems, like Haraway's, to invite readers to regard work as elemental to any discussion of the contemporary interface between humans and machines. In the "Business of Cyberpunk," Brande defines the cyborg as "an effect of advanced capitalism's restructuring of modes and relations of production and its corresponding transformations in ideological production."[7] He proceeds to critique most discussions of the cyborg and of its natural habitat, cyberpunk science fiction, as imprecise in their formulations of the economic context that has made us the cyborgs we are today:

With some exceptions (including commentary by Pam Rosenthal, Andrew Ross, and Larry McCaffery), critics often situate [William] Gibson's work within the context of "postindustrialism" and occasionally praise it for its depictions of "late capitalism," without defining these terms or saying exactly how his work embodies or works through them. While it is, perhaps, out of a healthy skepticism of "vulgar" base/superstructure models of economics and culture that leftist critics are wary of making deterministic claims about the connections between macroeconomic transformations and the appearance of the cyborgs, the social and economic conditions of the production of cyborg life nonetheless remain to be articulated.[8]

Brande moves from this point of departure to offer a useful characterization of "the social and economic conditions of the production of cyborg life," which focuses on large dynamics and "coercive laws" of capitalist markets.[9] Brande finally reads Gibson, the maestro of cyborgs, as producing a generative "ideological fantasy that structures reality," in which capitalist flows render the "rationalist citizen subject" a consumer-cyborg devoid of any trace of interiority.[10] Yet, while Brande maps out the economic imperatives that determine our existence as cyborgs—and even the depthless nature those imperatives impart to us—the daily processes by which we function as cyborgs remain largely unaddressed in his discussion.

For that, we need to turn to one of Brande's sources. En route to his theoretically rich, post-Marxist reading, Brande points to the matter-of-fact depiction of contemporary labor that Pam Rosenthal offers in her meditation on cyberpunk and post-Fordism. Rosenthal's straightforward assertion that "the contemporary transformation of production and consumption is changing the way in which we experience our everyday lives," though less theoretical, seems to bridge the gap that other cyborg theorists, including Brande, erect between themselves and those they inadvertently portray as somehow more obliviously awash in capitalism.[11] That bridge is constituted by our shared experience as workers, a point that Rosenthal makes in an account of post-Fordism that encompasses blue- and white-collar work alike:

Post-Fordism . . . poses a whole new approach to time on and off the job: the hyped-up, insecure syncopations of workaholism and unemployment, the increasing employment of part-time and contract workers, and more layoffs as flexible transnationals decamp to avail themselves of cheaper labor overseas, or as they retrofit their plants with computerized automation technologies at home. What until fairly recently had seemed a reasonably self-evident positive dynamic within a well-defined arena now seems at best a set of mixed messages within an environment of shifting boundaries and rapidly transmutating rules.[12]

While Brande moves quickly from this vision of work experience articulated by Rosenthal to a more abstract domain of cyborg subjectivity, I would like to dwell longer in the quotidian exigencies of post-Fordist work.

Admittedly, in academic essays such as this one, writing about the demands and rewards of working for a living is not commonplace. As Andrew Hoberek recently observed, while work is often the defining "experiential and ideological matrix through which . . . model[s] of late capitalist/postmodern culture get . . . channeled," one can detect "a larger inability within contemporary cultural studies to imagine work, and the working class, outside the context of manual labor."[13] This limitation, as Hoberek points out, is a grave one in a society in which non-manual-service work has become normative. One might argue that, contrary to Hoberek's assessment, work is no longer a crucial means by which individuals make sense of their own existence within capitalism. Donald Lowe, for example, suggests that consumption has displaced labor's defining role in the American popular consciousness. "The visual construction and presentation of self in terms of consumption relations," he observes, "has by now overshadowed the class relations of production in the workplace."[14] Yet a number of cultural arenas, particularly television, where representations of work and its conflicts abound, suggest that cultural critics are too quick to dismiss the centrality of work to contemporary social and cultural dynamics.[15]

Perhaps new labor questions are not being raised by academics as often as they could because the diminishing gap between other forms of service work and academia makes such discussions painfully self-reflexive. One need only to look at the "Final Report" of the MLA Committee on Professional Employment to sense deeply the realities of downsizing and work speed-up in our own profession.[16] Or perhaps the differences that still remain between the flexible but diffuse nature of an academic's regimen of teaching and research and the ostensibly more contained and externally motivated work of others in the service arena leaves many scholars with some doubt about what it is the "average" American does at work. Where are all of those people going on their long commutes? What activities do they undertake when they get to the unthinkably vast number of workplaces to which we do not, cannot, have access?

Although such questions may seem to divide us, Juliet Schor's economic study, *The Overworked American*, suggests that American workers of every description are sharing in a profound immersion in chronic work. Schor's study, which struck such a chord with its readers when it was first published in 1992 that it quickly became a bestseller, demonstrates that the number of hours Americans work has risen dramatically since the late 1940s. Schor's throrough and measured research suggests that this trend toward constant work is a phenomenon of both the working and professional classes. Among America's lowest paid workers, Schor reports, the pressure to work multiple jobs has become epidemic.[17] Among professional workers, on the other hand, single salaried jobs have expanded to fill evening and weekend hours once understood as personal time.[18] Overall, Schor's research establishes that the average American worked 163 hours more per year in 1987 than she or he did in 1969—over an extra month of work per year.[19] Such overwork translates into a misery that is telegraphed to readers in the many personal testimonials her text includes. Her study confirms what we as academics seem to forget too often in our attempts to articulate the "postmodern condition": in a society in which the average adult enjoys only sixteen-and-a-half hours of waking leisure time per week, our relationship to work is crucial to understanding our "cyborg" subjectivity.[20]

Indeed, although Schor does not speak the cyborg idiom, she understands the centrality of the mythologies of technology to our lived experiences as well as Haraway. Speaking of the surprising lack of dialogue concerning overwork and job stress that inspired her to undertake her study, Schor characterizes technology as a mystifying national obsession:

The experts were unable to predict or even see these trends. I suspect they were blinded by the power of technology—seduced by futurist visions of automated factories effortlessly churning out products. After all, they say, if we can build robots to do humans' work, what sense is there in doing it ourselves? Appealing as this optimism may be, it misses a central point about technology: the context is all important. Machines can just as easily be used to harness human labor as to free it. To understand why forty years of increasing productivity have failed to liberate us from work, I found that I had to abandon a naive faith in technological potential and analyze the social, economic, and political context in which technology is put to use. Only then was I able to see that the experts' vision of our economic system is both analytically mistaken in ignoring powerful economic incentives to maintain long working hours, and historically inadequate, owing to a selective misreading of the past.[21]

Her suggestion that technology has been used to "harness human labor" is reinforced by the coincidence of the increase in work hours with the introduction of cybernetics into work processes after World War II. From Schor's vantage point, filling our lives with technology has meant acquiescing to longer and more onerous days (and nights) of work. To remedy this situation, Schor seems to call for a new collective narrative of our intimate lives with cybernetic technology, one that reflects the historically specific nature of that encounter as a suffusion of the demands of work into the architecture of our being.

In what follows, I will suggest that Marge Piercy provides such a narrative in *He, She and It*, a text that allows us to rethink the attention given to the technological components of the cyborg as a chimera—to borrow from Piercy's own lexicon—a false surface behind which a distinctively contemporary epistemology of work resides as the essence of the cyborg.[22] Locating in *He, She and It* a complicating, liberal feminist impulse to empower women through access to public work, I also want to reintroduce questions of gender as central to an understanding of the cyborg as an icon of contemporary labor. Finally, I'll conclude with a review of other contemporary "cyborg texts" in which the transformation of the "human" into the "cyborg" can be reread as a symbolic sacrifice of the individuality and free will historically associated with humanism on behalf of an internalization of unprecedented contemporary work imperatives.

"My Work, My Life"

The central plot of *He, She and It* concerns the efforts of Shira, a gifted computer scientist, to provide Yod, a cyborg of revolutionary technical sophistication, with sufficient understanding of human motives and behaviors for him to "pass" as a biologically conceived man. Shira has fled her corporate employers after they granted custody of her son to her estranged husband and returned to her home town, Tikva, a noncorporate "free town." Yod has been designed to protect Tikva from the many corporate and non-corporate aggressors that threaten its existence in the violent, dystopic future that Piercy has imagined for this novel, a future with the trademark cyberpunk elements of wrenching class strife, environmental collapse, and global reliance on an Internet en-hanced by ever more convincing virtual-reality technologies.

The question around which Piercy makes all of this revolve is whether Yod can truly become human. The text approaches this issue from several angles; by borrowing heav-ily from romance novel formulas to portray a love affair between Shira and Yod, for ex-ample, Piercy explores sexuality as a gateway through which we embrace the "other" as ourselves. Struggling with her choice to become sexually involved with Yod, Shira imagines women in the first human civilizations turning to men for companionship: "Such a woman sought comfort in the embrace of a being like and unlike herself, as men were unlike women, intimate strangers surely just as exotic and peculiar to Shira as this machine in the form of a man who knelt before her, wanting at least to please" (239). Why not fit machines, Piercy asks us here, within the already unstable rubric of the "hu-man" that men and women have uneasily cohabitated for centuries? More interestingly, still, Piercy parallels the history of anti-Semitism with the Luddite hostilities Yod in-spires, inviting us to regard his technology as simply another ethnicity. Again, she cap-italizes on the flexibility evident in the history of humanism—a flexibility that has meant the delineations of the human have constantly been in flux in response to chang-ing cultural mores regarding race and ethnicity—in order to signal that its meaning could be altered to accommodate the machinic.

Given the logic that this latter comparison sets in motion, however, it may surprise many readers that at the conclusion of the novel, Yod is sent on a suicide mission from which he does not return, and that the possibility of making others like him is resound-ingly condemned. What overrides the enthusiasm for alterity with which the text ini-tially approaches its portrait of Yod? I would suggest that it is the problem of Yod's identity as a worker that exposes him to the critical gaze of the community of Tikva and turns his supporters into critics of the larger plan under which he was conceived. "The creation of a conscious being as any kind of tool—supposed to exist only to fill our needs—is a disaster," concludes Malkah at the end of the text, though an ardent friend and admirer of Yod (412). Shira repeats a nearly identical perspective, as does Yod in a communiqué released after his final act of self-sacrifice. Though most of Piercy's text appears designed to lull us into complacent acceptance of Yod's posthuman inevitability, it finally rejects its own program on the grounds that Yod can never transcend an existence conceived as pure labor.

To fully grasp the implications of this, we need to step back and consider what precipitated Yod's downfall in the text. Yod succeeds in "passing" as human for the better part of the text until, near its conclusion, Shira's jealous ex-lover, Gadi, mischievously registers a complaint to the Tikva town council that Yod is receiving no wage for the highly visible security services he is providing the town. This act is the outcome of an earlier discussion between Shira, Avram, who is Yod's creator, and Gadi concerning Yod's status as an unpaid worker. In these earlier debates, Gadi suggests that Yod's life is currently one of "slave labor," and Shira agrees, insisting to Avram, "If you want him to pass as human, you must establish his economic identity" (212). These concerns that Yod's entire existence is defined by unrewarded labor are reinforced when Yod reports that Gadi's is not the only complaint about his apparent exploitation: "Several people noticed that I patrol the Base during the day and the perimeter at night," he announces. "They put in a complaint of overwork on my behalf" (364).

It is this perceived injustice—all work and no pay/play—that is expressed in slightly more abstract terms in the repeated justifications for discontinuing this sort of research in robotics and cybernetics at the conclusion of the text. Yet hasn't Piercy foreclosed on one or two alternative endings that would permit her posthuman, so appealingly compared to other oppressed minorities, to live on and flourish rather than being "terminated" or permanently "retired" to borrow the language of two classic cyborg films? The answer must certainly be yes. Piercy could, for instance, have resolved the crisis of Yod's identity as "slave labor" by staging a climax in which the town, after heated debate, assents to paying Yod, thus defining his life as only in part economically motivated and implicitly agreeing to provide Yod with time off the job—time for him to be human within the logic of this text.

It is clear after a moment's reflection, however, what a dilemma such a possibility would create for Piercy. A well-established Leftist with deep and abiding loyalty to the working class from which she herself emerged, could she really promote the idea of giving paid work to machines?[23] The outset of the text suggests that such an eventuality is conceivable to her, certainly. The very moment at which she introduces the parallel between the experience of Jews and future cybernetic beings is the one in which their twin threats as job seekers is first acknowledged. Of the Jews, Malkah, Shira's grandmother reflects: "For centuries we had occupied a small, dishonorable but necessary role, because we were the bankers, the pawnbrokers, the exchanges, the source of loans; it was the work permitted us. But once Chistians became bankers, Jews began trying to do the same work as everybody else, even though most trades were officially forbidden us. We had to make a living, and we couldn't just take in each other's washing" (20).

Thirty pages later she characterizes hatred toward robots in these terms: "When robots were created with sufficient artificial intelligence to carry out complex tasks, a movement started in opposition, . . . circa 2040. . . . [P]eople found the first humanoid robots cute, fascinating and then quickly disturbing. Riots and Luddite outbreaks of machine bashing occurred. People were afraid that machines would replace them, not in dangerous jobs but in well-paid and comfortable jobs. Robots were sabotaged, and destructive riots broke out even in corporate enclaves—"(48).

By inviting this particular comparison between Jews and machines, Piercy appears immediately to force the readers' hand. It seems that we must concede the injustice of depriving machines of their jobs, when we are confronted with a narrative that makes denying them work appear every bit as semiotically contingent, and thus arbitrary, as the decisions that left Jews in ghettoes. From this beginning, Piercy develops her parallel narratives of the creation of a Golem in Renaissance Prague and of the contemporary struggle of Yod to enjoy human status in terms that return us again and again to a sense that machines' relegation to the category of the subhuman is no more just than Jews' mistreatment at the hands of Christians. Since she could never condone the bigotry of denying Jews access to equal pay for equal work, for obvious reasons only incidentally related to her own Judaism, it appears throughout much of the text that Piercy is prepared to extend the same rights to Yod and his kind.

Yet she cannot, finally. Born in 1936, Piercy is a member of the first generation of Americans to face adulthood in an era in which manufacturing work was made almost entirely off-limits to humans by their robotic counterparts. This reallocation of work had a particularly negative impact on inner-city communities like the one in Detroit where Piercy herself was born and raised.[24] Ultimately, Piercy's political allegiance to working men and women apparently dispels the force of her theoretical musings on economic justice for the posthuman. Perhaps realizing she had strayed into political territory that she wanted no part of, Piercy never really entertains the possibility of Yod being paid in the final pages of her text.

She does, however, open another possible route to the salvation of Yod. If the wrongness of the prototype Yod lies in his identity as a worker with no personal identity, why not create a cyborg that is not a worker at all but, instead, just a lover for Shira? Shira considers this possibility in the final chapter: "Yod had said it himself: it was immoral to create a conscious weapon. She vehemently agreed. No, she would not create a cyborg to suffer from Yod's dilemma. She was not intending to build a golem; she was going to build a mate. It might take her two years, it might take her five, but then she would have her lover. She would have Yod, but not a Yod who belonged to Avram: no, a Yod who belonged only to her. He would look just like Yod; he would be just like Yod, minus all those problems with violence" (426).

Shira imagines a being that will serve only her emotional needs, rather than any larger economic interests. Yet it is precisely this role of emotional servant that stymies Shira's enthusiasm for the new plan. She quickly realizes that "she could not manufacture a being to serve her, even in love," and, braced by this newfound conviction, destroys the last remains of Yod's circuitry (428). It is unimaginable for Shira that a machine could transcend its essential capacity to perform tasks. Piercy's text implicitly maintains here that technology is nothing less than labor concretized in material form—labor embodied—and that every piece of machinery can only work if it exists, can only exist if it works. Such a being, if it takes human form, is a slave, she concludes, and the symbolic rejection of such beings is unmistakable and definitive: Piercy kills off her cyborg, once and for all.

This insight seems an important one to introduce into our current attempts to theorize the cyborg as our most compelling contemporary icon of the posthuman. Piercy's text opens the way for an understanding of the cyborg not as a "myth" of the merging of technology with a passive, idealized human body, but instead as a metaphor for an intensification of exertion on the part of actual people produced by our truck with machines. In so doing, it begins, I think, to illuminate the daily dimensions of our cyborg lives in terms that more abstract discussions of the cyborg do not. As Schor's study demonstrates, there is much evidence to suggest that, in America at least, new technological developments, such as home computers, faxes, mobile phones, and the omnipresent Internet, have produced a citizenry engulfed by the demands of their work lives. A host of other recent publications with titles like *The Time Bind* and *When Work Doesn't Work Anymore* reinforce the sense of crisis.[25]

By dramatizing cyborg identity as a nightmare of overwork, Piercy's text raises the question of whether the common embrace of the cyborg as a promising exit from the vexed era of humanism is really a surrender of a longstanding fiction of the human self for an even more confining ontology. In this reading, the "human" residue in cyborg life is that part not disciplined by a rationalized work regime. As Christie has pointed out in his reading of Piercy's novel, the repeated rejections of Yod as our cyborgian future—that no being's existence should be determined exclusively by the functions she or he performs for others—is a reiteration of Kant's "categorical imperative." This famous ground rule of humanism states that each human must "[a]ct so that you treat humanity, whether in your own person or in that of another, always as an end and never as a means only."[26] While the tangle of philosophies that constitute what we call "humanism" has its shortcomings, this does not seem to be one of them. Shouldn't the new self, the un-self we're seeking, be able to exist apart from the demands of work? If so, is the cyborg truly the escape hatch we're looking for? In Piercy's gradual exposure of Yod's existence as a being defined entirely by the tasks and goals he must accomplish, we seem to see a rejection of such a life as permissibly posthuman.

What is perhaps most perplexing and remarkable about Piercy's text, however, is that killing Yod does not solve the problem of the rest of the characters who, as Shira notes, are also "all cyborgs." Near the end of the novel Malkah attempts to articulate the distinction between Yod and these human-born cyborgs. "It's better to make people into partial machines," she muses, "than to create machines that feel and yet are still controlled like cleaning robots" (412). Yet, Piercy more generally represents Yod as simply the extreme point of a continuum across which contemporary humans are stretching. At the key moment in which Shira identifies herself and the others of her world as cyborgs, she insists to Yod, "You're just a purer form of what we're all tending toward" (150). And, indeed, I maintain that, like Yod, Piercy's other cyborgs are machines less in terms of technological components than in terms of an essential, unflagging commitment to work. In other words, while Piercy symbolically annihilates the talismanic figure of total work in the text, the condition itself persists in Yod's absence. What are we to make of the fact that all around the cyborg Yod are characters who avow their work lives as entirely central to their existence?

Most emblematic of this apparent paradox in the text is Malkah, Shira's grandmother. In conversations in which Malkah counsels others in the text, we are invited to perceive her as the novel's moral center, a sage whose perspectives on large ethical and philosophical questions have been honed by her long, daring life. Her advice to Shira constitutes a particularly substantial portion of the novel, and much of that advice concerns giving work the highest possible priority. Perceiving Shira as excessively preoccupied with her emotional attachments to others, Malkah pleads with her granddaughter to "work in the center and love to the side" (55). Indeed, Malkah's dependence on her own identity as a worker is dramatized when, midway through the text, she is attacked while at her virtual workstation. Traumatized by this on-the-job assault, Malkah cannot at first return to work and sinks into a deep depression: "If only they had sent an assassin after me on the street," she laments, "if only they had sent a fake message robot to blow up in my face. But to attack me in my work, that was a stroke of true genius. Now I fear my own creativity" (158). When at last she is able to recommence her work as a computer programmer, it is as though her lifeless form has been reanimated, the cyborg has been reactivated: "I [am] free," she reflects, "to reenter my work, my life."

Such avowals, of course, make Yod's extermination a puzzling resolution to Piercy's flirtation with the posthuman. Why, if Malkah lives to work, can't Yod? Piercy parades past us an array of other characters, from Yod's "workaholic" creator, Avram, to Riva, a tireless data pirate, to Chava, a central figure in her Renaissance narrative—all of whom choose to "make work the center." It is ostensibly Yod's lack of freedom to change employment or employer that marks his work experience as unique in the workaholic culture that Piercy portrays. The many other workaholics that people her text are driven by conviction, by loyalty, by ambition to work constantly, rather than programming. Yet at other moments, including this passage in which Shira comforts Yod, Piercy invites us to disregard that distinction—to regard Yod as simply the most extreme expression of a society that treats work as the essence of one's identity:

"You were created to protect a vulnerable and endangered community."
"What were you created to do?"
"I see your point. But once we grow up, we all have purposes, goals, functions in a society."
"Set by yourself."
Shira hefted a quartz paperweight, put it down. "Not necessarily. When I worked for Y-S, I governed little in my life. I certainly didn't set my own goals at work, and I wasn't in control at home. And now? Avram set up this project, and he's my boss as much as he's yours." (150–151)

While this debate seems at first a sort of rhetorical flourish on the part of Shira, its validity is borne out in Piercy's portrait of the near future. To a remarkable extent, "purposes, goals, fuctions" are the essence of the human lives (now posthuman?) that she depicts.

In some sense, Piercy's termination of Yod could be read as a symbolic rejection of the larger social context that is generating this work culture. The future Piercy imagines for the capitalist order is one in which the middle-class leisure introduced by reforms in working hours and secured by increased productivity after World War II has long been eclipsed by an imperative to work spurred by stark extremes of wealth and poverty. As Piercy explains early in the text, nine-tenths of the world she imagines lives in enormous slums where the daily struggle for survival translates into constant toil. At the other extreme are the "multis"—multinational corporations that dictate every aspect of their employees lives. These companies bid for their employees in auctions meant to evoke the slave trade; to be employed by a multi is to be "owned" by it (166).

It is the citizens of Tikva's desperation to remain free from the multis without sinking into the economic ruin of the "Glop" that motivates Avram's creation of Yod. Yet Piercy's most apparent critique of these economic and social relations is her gesture toward the possibility of dramatic change within both the corporations and the slums. At the end of her novel, the corporation, Y-S, is violently fractured by a strategic assault by Tikva, and the subjugated citizens of the "Glop" stage a massive strike. Such narrative twists communicate Piercy's desire to hint at a global future unencumbered by the panorama of endlessly laboring cyborgs that people this text.[27]

To grasp fully Piercy's variation on cyborg identity, however, we need to weigh her condemnation of exploitative overwork against her liberal feminist faith that women can be empowered by lives wholly committed to paid, public work. When Malkah describes her work, it is impossible not to hear echoes of liberal feminist paeans to work running back to Betty Friedan:

I have been a defender of my people. I am a small woman who has stood tall. I have been independent. I have relished my own company, and when I let a man into my bed, it was for my enjoyment only and the pleasure of his company—not because I needed any more from him than that mutual zest and exploration that used to be my best means of recreation. I have been protected by others, certainly, excused guard duty; my town has revered and celebrated me because I helped us all to stay free. . . .

I have indeed been a proud creature, running in the wind of my own mind, free and driven at once. . . .

In the image world, I am the power of my thought, of my capacity to create. There is no sex in the Base or the Net, but there is sexuality, there is joining, there is the play of minds like the play of dolphins in surf. In a world parceled out by multis, it is one of the only empowered and sublimely personal activities remaining. I have always known I was exceptionally blessed to be able to revel in my work. (160–161)

Malkah's work in the Internet, although performed for economic ends, is, paradoxically, a "sublimely personal" act. This fusion of Malkah's personal life with her work life makes her ontologically akin to Yod. Yet, in Malkah's case, she feels empowered by this saturation in work. She is "free and driven at once," while Yod's drives prevent him from being free. What distinguishes the work ethic of the machine from that of the liberal feminist here is the thin tissue of "selfhood" that contemporary humanism permits women such as Malkah to assume.

Like so many feminists before her, Piercy represents work as an escape from the conception of women as weak bodies, designed only for reproduction. When Malkah is attacked in her work, she perceives the assault as a rape, thinking, "I am a magician of chimeras, and now my magic is penetrated, undone" (160). This attack removes her from the realm of her mind to that of her body: "Now I am reduced to my aging body in my room, which is luxurious but insufficient as a world. At seventy-two, I knock against my limits constantly in the flesh. I cannot walk as far as I used to. My knees give way. I don't sleep soundly. My body creaks and groans" (161). In a remarkable knotting together of images of taking away a woman's work and raping her, Piercy makes work the ultimate marker of female empowerment and its loss the ultimate disempowerment.

This reading is amplified by Piercy's inclusion of the character Chava in her narrative thread about the Renaissance. Piercy's depiction of Chava seems inspired by the lengthy list of protofeminist literary heroines who defy the pressures of domesticity to pursue lives of public work. Chava explains that she gave up care of her son after being widowed in order to pursue work as a midwife and as secretary to the famous rabbi, the Maharal. She reflects that during the years she was a wife and mother, her life was a strictly embodied one: "For those four years, my life was what will we eat, is his shirt clean, feelings of the bed, pregnancy, then my son, Aaron, colic, dirt, feeding, seeing him grow and unfold. The flesh closed over me, and I drowned" (290). Having escaped this life of the flesh, she revels in her life of work: "I can read and write, not just one language but seven languages. . . . Are there twenty women in all of Europe with whom I could converse about the matters that interest me? I like midwifery. I like to try my hand now and then at cooking and making nice. But my real life is going back and forth between women's business of birthing and what men have made their business, the life of the mind, my studies" (290).

Between Malkah and Chava, then, Piercy creates an extended historical meditation on women's struggle to achieve empowerment through paid public work. And, indeed, the conclusion of the text continues this sociopolitical thread still further. We are told that Shira has embraced the work patterns that Malkah has to this point in the text typified: "As soon as Malkah took an extended leave, Shira had been asked by the council to fill her grandmother's seat as a Base Overseer. She found in herself a swelling power, an intensifying concentrated energy for work" (423). Shira joins the long, celebrated line of women in Piercy's text who embrace lives of public work.

Perceiving the feminist impulse behind Piercy's portrait of the intense work lives of Malkah, Chava, and other women in the text requires us to return again to the status of the cyborg as an icon of late-capitalist labor in *He, She and It*. By combining representations of women workers transcendentally committed to lives of work with a bleak portrait of the cyborg as inescapably bound to work, Piercy captures the historical conflicts that inhere in postindustrial economic relations. Yod's unsuccessful struggle to transcend the essential identity of laborer that his technological components signify can be read as an ungendered resistance to the expanding requirements of all forms of rationalized work. Piercy's attention to the work of women, on the other hand, brings additional specificity to her vision of technology and work. Women's struggle to escape private, unpaid and underpaid, embodied forms of domestic labor reminds us that women have a history of subsisting as working bodies, unprotected by the rights given to those understood as humanist "selves." In these terms, Yod becomes an ominous reminder that cyborg identity could become the postindustrialist's answer to the exploited "others" of the industrial era.

My Body, My Workplace

A survey of other major contemporary representations of the cyborg suggests that Piercy's is far from the only text that invites us to understand this figure as one rendered "posthuman" by essential functionality that its technological components connote. In Greg Bear's *Blood Music*, for example, the body of ambitious scientist Vergil Ulam is overrun by engineered "biochips." These "microscopic logic circuits," which quickly spread from Vergil to others, subsume individual selves within an enormous, visionary act of labor. The cells themselves explain this process in the following terms: "Information is passed between clusters sharing in assigned tasks, including instruction and memory. Mentality is thus divided between clusters performing a function. Important memory may be *diffused* through all clusters. What you think of as INDIVIDUAL may be spread throughout the *totality*."[28]

Although in some sense the cells that "speak" here are behaving according to biological mandates that existed before Vergil's experiment, it is only when they are mechanized—transformed into "the world's tiniest machines"—that their work regime subjugates their human host.[29] While prior to the revolution Vergil triggers, the human body "worked" because of cell functions that human consciousness could not perceive; the modified cells that Vergil engineers adapt that consciousness, reducing it to a mere medium for their labor.

William Gibson's novels are full of cyborgs whose technological components have transformed their lives into pure work. Or, rather, by incorporating machine parts into themselves, voluntarily or involuntarily, they have passed from an existence in which they live, to one in which they function—in which they *work*. Molly, the infamous "razor girl" of the Matrix trilogy, has taken on the role of street heavy by submitting to a variety of cybernetic implants. Molly's work identity, signified by the implants, exists to the exclusion of some other, private self. "Anybody any good at what they do, that's what they *are*, right?" she remarks to the data "cowboy," Case. "You gotta jack, I gotta tussle."[30]

In Molly's case, her utilitarian, work-centered view of human existence seems to have precipitated her incorporation of highly visible technological parts. Those machine elements simply realize her commitment to *be* what she *does*. The character of Angie, who appears in the latter two texts of the trilogy, *Count Zero* and *Mona Lisa Overdrive*, is involuntarily transformed into a global celebrity by the circuitry her father has implanted in her head. This technology makes existence as a "sim-star" inevitable, inescapable. The technology performs a certain function, and her "self" becomes ancillary to the work capacity that inhabits her, or which she inhabits.[31]

In Neal Stephenson's *Snow Crash*, perhaps the most graphic instance of the cyborg phenomenon as the interface of the self and the inescapable compulsion to labor appears not in human but in animal form. Stephenson's baroque, ingenious "rat things"—part machine, part pit bull—represent the concretization of work protocols within the realm of the animal. Of the rat-thing, Stephenson writes, "[H]is job is to keep bad strangers out of his yard. He does not do anything else."[32] This translation of the uncertain impulses of an animal into an utterly consistent, rationalized work ethic is accomplished by the transformation of the dog into a cyborg. Doing one's job and nothing else is the implicit credo of all of the cyborgs of Stephenson's machine-saturated future. Its hero and heroine, a "free-lance hacker" and skateboard-riding courier, are merely caricatures of the new flexible work force whose willing embrace of advanced communication technologies means they are always on the job; as with the other cyborgs, their bodies are their workplaces.

Finally, as I mentioned earlier, several films concerned with the posthuman have invited us to understand the cyborg as an icon of contemporary work patterns. The very euphemisms for cyborg death in *Bladerunner* and the *Terminator* films imply living is the equivalent of working in the ontology of the cyborg. If to be "retired" or "terminated" is to die, must not working be the entire extent of life? In *Bladerunner*, which invites elaborate parallels with American slave narratives, the replicants struggle toward a life beyond relentless work; yet the technologically penetrated lives of their ostensibly "human" counterparts are no less circumscribed. As Sarah Connor points out in *T2*, the Terminators never stop working. They are what they do, and they are the result, as we perceive when we meet the workaholic Miles Dyson in the director's cut of the film, of similarly exhaustive human industry.[33]

Finally, all of these texts require that we shift our attention from what machines *are*, to what they *do*. Meeting their challenge, we are confronted with a picture of tireless industry in which we may already see an unsettling reflection of ourselves. The question we must ask ourselves is, Can the cyborg metaphor lead us to an imaginative domain where we are more free than we are today? Perhaps Marge Piercy's first novel about humans and their machines, in retrospect, answers the questions a later text of hers raised. In *Woman on the Edge of Time*, human freedom is facilitated by quiet, unseen machines. It is only in the sections of her novel where she seeks to frighten her readers that those work activities coded in machine parts suffuse the human body, and the results are humans not liberated but under control. Far from the penetrations our contemporary technologies seem to symbolize, the automated technologies that generate her "postwork" society in Mattapoisett go about their business of pure work without getting under our skin.

At the conclusion of her discussion of cyberpunk science fiction, Pam Rosenthal identifies what she regards as that genre's chief lesson: "that the ideal of a final/original uncontaminated humanness is, at bottom, what is most clumsy, old-fashioned, and naive about outmoded images of technological society."[34] Such a warning bears repeating here because I do not wish to offer this reading of the cyborg as a symbol of the penetration of a stringent, late-capitalist work ethic into the "human" as a way of recuperating "uncontaminated humanness"—a self purified of all traces of the demands of labor. The "human," as Piercy's novel illustrates, is what we make of it; search as we may, there is no "natural" state of perfect humanness from which we have strayed or to which we can retreat.

Embracing the concept of the posthuman is, of course, one way to reject the common presumption that to be "human"—in any of the this term's ever-changing senses—is our destiny. Yet the texts I have discussed here also demonstrate that the posthuman may be as destructive a category as its predecessor. To transgress the boundaries of the human by working like a machine, they imply, is not a victory. And, in spite of Piercy's flattering portrait of it, the liberal "triumph" of working for selfhood hardly seems a better solution. Although they never clearly delineate a viable posthuman ontology, these contemporary texts illustrate that to achieve such an ontology will require a new understanding of work itself—an understanding that puts the cyborg in all of us on strike.

Notes

1. Marge Piercy, *He, She and It* (New York: Fawcett Crest, 1991), 150. Subsequent references are cited parenthetically. Haraway's declaration in the opening section of her manifesto that "we are cyborgs" initiated an intense and ongoing debate about the degree to which cybernetic technologies have transformed or even eclipsed contemporary assumptions about the "human" (150).
2. Donna J. Haraway, "A Cyborg Manifesto: Science, Technology, and Socialist-Feminism in the Late Twentieth Century," in *Simians, Cyborgs, and Women: The Re-*

invention of Women, ed. Donna J. Haraway (New York: Routledge, 1991), 150. Subsequent references are cited parenthetically.

3. John R. R. Christie, "A Tragedy for Cyborgs," *Configurations* 1 (1992): 171–196; Thomas Foster, "Meat Puppets or Robopaths?: Cyberpunk and the Question of Embodiment," *Genders* 18 (1993): 11–31; Mary Catherine Harper, "Incurably Alien Other: A Case for Feminist Cyborg Writers," *Science-Fiction Studies* 22 (1995): 399–420; Sharon Stockton, "'The Self Regained': Cyberpunk's Retreat to the Imperium," *Contemporary Literature* 36 (1995): 588–612.

4. Joseba Gabilondo, "Postcolonial Cyborgs: Subjectivity in the Age of Cybernetic Reproduction," in *The Cyborg Handbook*, ed. Chris Hables Gray, Steven Mentor, and Heidi J. Figueroa-Sarriera (New York: Routledge, 1995), 423–432; Chela Sandoval, "New Sciences: Cyborg Feminism and the Methodology of the Oppressed," in *The Cyborg Handbook*, ed. Chris Hables Gray, Steven Mentor, and Heidi J. Figueroa-Sarriera (New York: Routledge, 1995) 407–421.

5. Chris Hables Gray, Steven Mentor, and Heidi J. Figueroa-Sarriera, "Cyborgology: Constructing the Knowledge of Cybernetic Organisms," in *The Cyborg Handbook*, ed. Chris Hables Gray, Steven Mentor, and Heidi J. Figueroa-Sarriera (New York: Routledge, 1995) 1–14.

6. David Porush, "Hacking the Brainstem: Postmodern Metaphysics and Stephenson's *Snow Crash*," in *Virtual Realities and Their Discontents*, ed. Robert Markley (Baltimore: Johns Hopkins University Press, 1996), 122.

7. David Brande, "The Business of Cyberpunk: Symbolic Economy and Ideology in William Gibson," in *Virtual Realities and Their Discontents*, ed. Robert Markley (Baltimore: Johns Hopkins University Press, 1996), 79.

8. Brande, "The Business of Cyberpunk," 79–80.

9. Brande, "The Business of Cyberpunk," 88.

10. Brande, "The Business of Cyberpunk," 96, 99.

11. Pam Rosenthal, "Jacked In: Fordism, Cyberpunk, Marxism," *Socialist Review* 21 (1991): 81.

12. Rosenthal, "Jacked In," 89.

13. Andrew P. Hoberek, "The 'Work' of Science Fiction: Philip K. Dick and Occupational Masculinity in the Post-World War II United States," *Modern Fiction Studies* 43 (1997): 375, 376. Nicholas K. Bromell has leveled a similar critique at contemporary literary criticism of the nineteenth century in his article, "'The Bloody Hand' of Labor: Work, Class, and Gender in Three Stories by Hawthorne," *American Quarterly* 42 (1990): 542–564.

14. Donald Lowe, *The Body in Late-Capitalist USA* (Durham: Duke University Press, 1995), 67.

15. Indeed, the workplace seems to be the normative setting for both situation comedies and dramas on American television. Turn to any major network on any night of the

week, and you will see representations of Americans' work lives constructed to inspire laughter, tears, or both. Why American television programming focuses on our work lives so much more consistently than American literature is a question that remains to be explored.

16. MLA Committee on Professional Employment, "Final Report," December 1997.

17. Juliet B. Schor, *The Overworked American: The Unexpected Decline of Leisure* (New York: Basic Books, 1992), 21–22.

18. Schor, *The Overworked American*, 17–19.

19. Schor, *The Overworked American*, 29.

20. This statistic comes from Schor, *The Overworked American*, 1.

21. Schor, *The Overworked American*, 5–6.

22. While Haraway also uses the term *chimera* when characterizing her cyborg as a "theorized and fabricated hybrid of machine and organism" (150), I prefer Piercy's specific use of this term to describe the illusory images programmers create in cyberspace to mask and distract from real and vulnerable systems.

23. For an autobiographical account of Piercy's working-class origins and history of political activism, see "Marge Piercy," *Contemporary Authors Autobiography Series*, vol. 1, ed. Dedria Bryphonski (Detroit: Gale, 1984), 267–281.

24. For a discussion of the impact of automation on America's inner cities, see Cornel West, *Race Matters* (New York: Vintage, 1993).

25. Arlie Hochschild, *The Time Bind: When Work Becomes Home, and Home Becomes Work* (New York: Holt, 1997); Elizabeth Perle McKenna, *When Work Doesn't Work Anymore: Women, Work, and Identity* (New York: Delacorte Press, 1997).

26. This translation comes from Ernst Cassirer, *Kant's Life and Thought*, trans. James Haden (New Haven: Yale, [1918] 1981) 248, and is quoted from Tony Davies, *Humanism* (New York: Routledge, 1997), 120.

27. Piercy's particularly intense awareness of the changing social and economic relations of the late twentieth century is evident in the transformation her thinking about work and technology has undergone from her first full-scale treatment of this topic in *Woman on the Edge of Time* (New York: Fawcett Crest, 1976), where she optimistically anticipates a fully automated, postwork society engendered by a national shift toward egalitarian socialist politics. *He, She and It* updates the possibilities and threats of automation in the context of the contemporary realities of multinational corporate capitalism—capitalism of a scale that Piercy could only imagine fleetingly, in a brief, nightmarish dystopic sequence, in 1976.

28. Greg Bear, *Blood Music* (New York: Ace, [1985] 1996), 164.

29. Bear, *Blood Music*, 13.

30. William Gibson, *Neuromancer* (New York: Ace, 1984), 50.

31. William Gibson, *Count Zero* (New York: Ace, [1986] 1987) and *Mona Lisa Overdrive* (New York, Ace Books, 1988).

32. Neal Stephenson, *Snow Crash* (New York: Bantam, 1992), 444.
33. See Ridley Scott's *Blade Runner* (1982) and James Cameron's *Terminator 2* (1991).
34. Rosenthal, "Jacked In," 99.

Works Cited

Bear, Greg. *Blood Music.* New York: Ace, 1996.

Brande, David. "The Business of Cyberpunk: Symbolic Economy and Ideology in William Gibson." In *Virtual Realities and Their Discontents,* ed. Robert Markley, 79–106. Baltimore: Johns Hopkins University Press.

Bromell, Nicholas K. "'The Bloody Hand' of Labor: Work, Class, and Gender in Three Stories by Hawthorne." *American Quarterly* 42 (1990): 542–564.

Christie, John R. R. "A Tragedy for Cyborgs." *Configurations* 1 (1992): 171–196.

Davies, Tony. *Humanism.* New York: Routledge, 1997.

Foster, Thomas. "Meat Puppets or Robopaths?: Cyberpunk and the Question of Embodiment." Cyberpunk: Technologies of Cultural Identity. Special issue of *Genders* 18 (1993): 11–31.

Gabilondo, Joseba. "Postcolonial Cyborgs: Subjectivity in the Age of Cybernetic Reproduction." In *The Cyborg Handbook,* ed. Chris Hables Gray, Steven Mentor, and Heidi J. Figueroa-Sarriera. 423–432. New York: Routledge, 1995.

Gibson, William. *Count Zero.* New York: Ace, 1987.

Gibson, William. *Mona Lisa Overdrive.* New York: Bantam Books, 1988.

Gibson, William. *Neuromancer.* New York: Ace Books, 1984.

Gray, Chris Hables, Steven Mentor, and Heidi J. Figueroa-Sarriera, eds. *The Cyborg Handbook.* New York: Routledge, 1995.

Gray, Chris Hables, Steven Mentor, and Heidi J. Figueroa-Sarriera. "Cyborgology: Constructing the Knowledge of Cybernetic Organisms." In *The Cyborg Handbook,* ed. Chris Hables Gray, Steven Mentor, and Heidi J. Figueroa-Sarriera. 1–14. New York: Routledge, 1995.

Haraway, Donna J. "A Cyborg Manifesto: Science, Technology, and Socialist-Feminism in the Late Twentieth Century." In *Simians, Cyborgs, and Women: The Reinvention of Women,* ed. Donna J. Haraway, 149–181. New York: Routledge, 1991.

Harper, Mary Catherine. "Incurably Alien Other: A Case for Feminist Cyborg Writers." *Science-Fiction Studies* 22 (1995): 399–420.

Hoberek, Andrew P. "The 'Work' of Science Fiction: Philip K. Dick and Occupational Masculinity in the Post-World War II United States." *Modern Fiction Studies* 43 (1997): 374–404.

Hochschild, Arlie. *The Time Bind: When Work Becomes Home, and Home Becomes Work.* New York: Holt, 1997.

Lowe, Donald. *The Body in Late-Capitalist USA.* Durham: Duke University Press, 1995.

McKenna, Elizabeth Perle. *When Work Doesn't Work Anymore: Women, Work, and Identity* New York: Delacorte Press, 1997.

"Marge Piercy." *Contemporary Authors Autobiography Series.* vol. 1, ed. Dedria Bryphonski. Detroit: Gale, 1984.

Markley, Robert, ed. *Virtual Realities and Their Discontents.* Baltimore: Johns Hopkins University Press, 1996.

MLA Committee on Professional Employment. "Final Report." December 1997.

Piercy, Marge. *He, She and It.* New York: Fawcett Crest, 1991.

Piercy, Marge. *Woman on the Edge of Time.* New York: Fawcett Crest, 1976.

Porush, David. "Hacking the Brainstem: Postmodern Metaphysics and Stephenson's *Snow Crash.*" In *Virtual Realities and Their Discontents*, ed. Robert Markley, 107–141. Baltimore: Johns Hopkins University Press.

Rosenthal, Pam. "Jacked In: Fordism, Cyberpunk, Marxism." *Socialist Review* 21 (1991): 79–103.

Sandoval, Chela. "New Sciences: Cyborg Feminism and the Methodology of the Oppressed." In *The Cyborg Handbook*, ed. Chris Hables Gray, Steven Mentor, and Heidi J. Figueroa-Sarriera, 407–421. New York: Routledge, 1995.

Schor, Juliet B. *The Overworked American: The Unexpected Decline of Leisure.* New York: Basic Books, 1992.

Stephenson, Neal. *Snow Crash.* New York: Bantam, 1992.

Stockton, Sharon. "'The Self Regained': Cyberpunk's Retreat to the Imperium." *Contemporary Literature* 36 (1995): 588–612.

West, Cornel. *Race Matters.* New York: Vintage, 1993.

Films Cited
Cameron, James. *Terminator 2.* 1991.

Scott, Ridley. *Blade Runner.* 1982.

6

THE SHIP WHO SANG

Anne McCaffrey

She was born a thing and as such would be condemned if she failed to pass the encephalograph test required of all newborn babies. There was always the possibility that though the limbs were twisted, the mind was not, that though the ears would hear only dimly, the eyes see vaguely, the mind behind them was receptive and alert.

The electroencephalogram was entirely favorable, unexpectedly so, and the news was brought to the waiting, grieving parents. There was the final, harsh decision: to give their child euthanasia or permit it to become an encapsulated "brain," a guiding mechanism in any one of a number of curious professions. As such, their offspring would suffer no pain, live a comfortable existence in a metal shell for several centuries, performing unusual service to Central Worlds.

She lived and was given a name, Helva. For her first three vegetable months she waved her crabbed claws, kicked weakly with her clubbed feet and enjoyed the usual routine of the infant. She was not alone, for there were three other such children in the big city's special nursery. Soon they all were removed to Central Laboratory School, where their delicate transformation began.

One of the babies died in the initial transferral, but of Helva's "class," seventeen thrived in the metal shells. Instead of kicking feet, Helva's neural responses started her wheels; instead of grabbing with hands, she manipulated mechanical extensions. As she matured, more and more neural synapses would be adjusted to operate other mechanisms that went into the maintenance and running of a spaceship. For Helva was destined to be the "brain" half of a scout ship, partnered with a man or a woman, whichever she chose, as the mobile half. She would be among the elite of her kind. Her initial intelligence tests registered above normal and her adaptation index was unusually high. As long as her development within her shell lived up to expectations, and there were no side-effects from the pituitary tinkering, Helva would live a rewarding, rich, and unusual life, a far cry from what she would have faced as an ordinary, "normal" being.

However, no diagram of her brain patterns, no early IQ tests recorded certain essential facts about Helva that Central must eventually learn. They would have to bide their official time and see, trusting that the massive doses of shell-psychology would suffice her, too, as the necessary bulwark against her unusual confinement and the pressures of her profession. A ship run by a human brain could not run rogue or insane with the power and resources Central had to build into their scout ships. Brain ships were, of course, long past the experimental stages. Most babies survived the perfected techniques of pituitary manipulation that kept their bodies small, eliminating the necessity of transfers from smaller to larger shells. And very, very few were lost when the final connection was made to the control panels of ship or industrial combine. Shell-people resembled mature dwarfs in size whatever their natal deformities were, but the well-oriented brain would not have changed places with the most perfect body in the Universe.

So, for happy years, Helva scooted around in her shell with her classmates, playing such games as Stall, Power-Seek, studying her lessons in trajectory, propulsion techniques, computation, logistics, mental hygiene, basic alien psychology, philology, space history, law, traffic, codes: all the et ceteras that eventually became compounded into a reasoning, logical, informed citizen. Not so obvious to her, but of more importance to her teachers, Helva ingested the precepts of her conditioning as easily as she absorbed her nutrient fluid. She would one day be grateful to the patient drone of the subconscious-level instruction.

Helva's civilization was not without busy, do-good associations, exploring possible inhumanities to terrestrial as well as extraterrestrial citizens. One such group—Society for the Preservation of the Rights of Intelligent Minorities—got all incensed over shelled "children" when Helva was just turning fourteen. When they were forced to, Central Worlds shrugged its shoulders, arranged a tour of the Laboratory Schools, and set the tour off to a big start by showing the members case histories, complete with photographs. Very few committees ever looked past the first few photos. Most of their original objections about "shells" were overridden by the relief that these hideous (to them) bodies *were* mercifully concealed.

Helva's class was doing fine arts, a selective subject in her crowded program. She had activated one of her microscopic tools, which she would later use for minute repairs to various parts of her control panel. Her subject was large—a copy of *The Last Supper*—*and* her canvas, small—the head of a tiny screw. She had tuned her sight to the proper degree. As she worked she absentmindedly crooned, producing a curious sound. Shell-people used their own vocal cords and diaphragms, but sound issued through microphones rather than mouths. Helva's hum, then, had a curious vibrancy, a warm, dulcet quality even in its aimless chromatic wanderings.

"Why, what a lovely voice you have," said one of the female visitors.

Helva "looked" up and caught a fascinating panorama of regular, dirty craters on a flaky pink surface. Her hum became a gurgle of surprise. She instinctively regulated her "sight" until the skin lost its cratered look and the pores assumed normal proportions.

"Yes, we have quite a few years of voice training, madam," remarked Helva calmly. "Vocal peculiarities often become excessively irritating during prolonged interstellar distances and must be eliminated. I enjoyed my lessons."

Although this was the first time that Helva had seen unshelled people, she took this experience calmly. Any other reaction would have been reported instantly.

"I meant that you have a nice singing voice . . . dear," the lady said.

"Thank you. Would you like to see my work?" Helva asked politely. She instinctively sheered away from personal discussions, but she filed the comment away for further meditation.

"Work?" asked the lady.

"I am currently reproducing *The Last Supper* on the head of a screw."

"Oh, I say," the lady twittered.

Helva turned her vision back to magnification and surveyed her copy critically. "Of course, some of my color values do not match the old Master's and the perspective is faulty, but I believe it to be a fair copy."

The lady's eyes, unmagnified, bugged out.

"Oh, I forget," and Helva's voice was really contrite. If she could have blushed, she would have. "You people don't have adjustable vision."

The monitor of this discourse grinned with pride and amusement as Helva's tone indicated pity for the unfortunate.

"Here, this will help," said Helva, substituting a magnifying device in one extension and holding it over the picture.

In a kind of shock, the ladies and gentlemen of the committee bent to observe the incredibly copied and brilliantly executed *Last Supper* on the head of a screw.

"Well," remarked one gentleman who had been forced to accompany his wife, "the good Lord can eat where angels fear to tread."

"Are you referring, sir," asked Helva politely, "to the Dark Age discussions of the number of angels who could stand on the head of a pin?"

"I had that in mind."

"If you substitute 'atom' for 'angel,' the problem is not insoluble, given the metallic content of the pin in question."

"Which you are programmed to compute?"

"Of course."

"Did they remember to program a sense of humor, as well, young lady?"

"We are directed to develop a sense of proportion, sir, which contributes the same effect."

The good man chortled appreciatively and decided the trip was worth his time.

If the investigation committee spent months digesting the thoughtful food served them at the Laboratory School, they left Helva with a morsel as well.

"Singing" as applicable to herself required research. She had, of course, been exposed to and enjoyed a music-appreciation course that had included the better-known classical works, such as *Tristan und Isolde, Candide, Oklahoma!*, and *Le nozze di Figaro*, along with the atomic-age singers, Birgit Nilsson, Bob Dylan, and Geraldine Todd, as well as the curious rhythmic progressions of the Venusians, Capellan visual chromatics, the sonic concerti of the Altairians and Reticulan croons. But "singing" for any shell-person posed considerable technical difficulties. Shell-people were schooled to examine every aspect of a problem or situation before making a prognosis. Balanced properly between optimism and practicality, the nondefeatist attitude of the shell-people led them to extricate themselves, their ships, and personnel, from bizarre situations. Therefore to Helva, the problem that she couldn't open her mouth to sing, among other restrictions, did not bother her. She would work out a method, bypassing her limitations, whereby she could sing.

She approached the problem by investigating the methods of sound reproduction through the centuries, human and instrumental. Her own sound-production equipment was essentially more instrumental than vocal. Breath control and the proper enunciation of vowel sounds within the oral cavity appeared to require the most development and practice. Shell-people did not, strictly speaking, breathe. For their purposes, oxygen and other gases were not drawn from the surrounding atmosphere through the medium of lungs but sustained artificially by solution in their shells. After experimentation, Helva discovered that she could manipulate her diaphragmic unit to sustain tone. By relaxing the throat muscles and expanding the oral cavity well into the frontal sinuses, she could direct the vowel sounds into the most felicitous position for proper reproduction through her throat microphone. She compared the results with tape recordings of modern singers and was not unpleased, although her own tapes had a peculiar quality about them, not at all unharmonious, merely unique. Acquiring a repertoire from the Laboratory library was no problem to one trained to perfect recall. She found herself able to sing any role and any song which struck her fancy. It would not have occurred to her that it was curious for a female to sing bass, baritone, tenor, mezzo, soprano, and coloratura as she pleased. It was, to Helva, only a matter of the correct reproduction and diaphragmatic control required by the music attempted.

If the authorities remarked on her curious avocation, they did so among themselves. Shell-people were encouraged to develop a hobby so long as they maintained proficiency in their technical work.

On the anniversary of her sixteenth year, Helva was unconditionally graduated and installed in her ship, the XH-834. Her permanent titanium shell was recessed behind an even more indestructible barrier in the central shaft of the scout ship. The neural, audio, visual, and sensory connections were made and sealed. Her extendibles were diverted, connected, or augmented, and the final, delicate-beyond-description brain taps were completed while Helva remained anesthetically unaware of the proceedings. When she woke, she *was* the ship. Her brain and intelligence controlled every function from navigation to such loading as a scout ship of her class needed. She could take care of herself and her ambulatory half in any situation already recorded in the annals of Central Worlds and any situation its most fertile minds could imagine.

Her first actual flight, for she and her kind had made mock flights on dummy panels since she was eight, showed her to be a complete master of the techniques of her profession. She was ready for her great adventures and the arrival of her mobile partner.

There were nine qualified scouts sitting around collecting base pay the day Helva reported for active duty. There were several missions that demanded instant attention, but Helva had been of interest to several department heads in Central for some time and each bureau chief was determined to have her assigned to *his* section. No one had remembered to introduce Helva to the prospective partners. The ship always chose its own partner. Had there been another "brain" ship at the base at the moment, Helva would have been guided to make the first move. As it was, while Central wrangled among itself, Robert Tanner sneaked out of the pilots' barracks, out to the field, and over to Helva's slim metal hull.

"Hello, anyone at home?" Tanner said.

"Of course," replied Helva, activating her outside scanners. "Are you my partner?" she asked hopefully, as she recognized the Scout Service uniform.

"All you have to do is ask," he retorted in a wistful tone.

"No one has come. I thought perhaps there were no partners available and I've had no directives from Central."

Even to herself Helva sounded a little self-pitying, but the truth was she was lonely, sitting on the darkened field. She had always had the company of other shells and more recently, technicians by the score. The sudden solitude had lost its momentary charm and become oppressive.

"No directives from Central is scarcely a cause for regret, but there happen to be eight other guys biting their fingernails to the quick just waiting for an invitation to board you, you beautiful thing."

Tanner was inside the central cabin as he said this, running appreciative fingers over her panel, the scout's gravity-chair, poking his head into the cabins, the galley, the head, the pressured-storage compartments.

"Now, if you want to goose Central and do *us* a favor all in one, call up the barracks and let's have a ship-warming partner-picking party. Hmmmm?"

Helva chuckled to herself. He was so completely different from the occasional visitors or the various Laboratory technicians she had encountered. He was so gay, so assured, and she was delighted by his suggestion of a partner-picking party. Certainly it was not against anything in her understanding of regulations.

"Cencom, this is XH-834. Connect me with Pilot Barracks."

"Visual?"

"Please."

A picture of lounging men in various attitudes of boredom came on her screen.

"This is XH-834. Would the unassigned scouts do me the favor of coming aboard?"

Eight figures were galvanized into action, grabbing pieces of wearing apparel, disengaging tape mechanisms, disentangling themselves from bedsheets and towels.

Helva dissolved the connection while Tanner chuckled gleefully and settled down to await their arrival.

Helva was engulfed in an unshell-like flurry of anticipation. No actress on her opening night could have been more apprehensive, fearful, or breathless. Unlike the actress, she could throw no hysterics, china objets d'art, or greasepaint to relieve her tension. She could, of course, check her stores for edibles and drinks, which she did, serving Tanner from the virgin selection of her commissary.

Scouts were colloquially known as "brawns" as opposed to their ship "brains." They had to pass as rigorous a training program as the brains and only the top 1 percent of each contributory world's highest scholars were admitted to Central Worlds Scout Training Program. Consequently the eight young men who came pounding up the gantry into Helva's hospitable lock were unusually fine-looking, intelligent, well-coordinated, and well-adjusted young men, looking forward to a slightly drunken evening, Helva permitting, and all quite willing to do each other dirt to get possession of her.

Such a human invasion left Helva mentally breathless, a luxury she thoroughly enjoyed for the brief time she felt she should permit it.

She sorted out the young men. Tanner's opportunism amused but did not specifically attract her; the blond Nordsen seemed too simple; dark-haired Alatpay had a kind of obstinacy for which she felt no compassion; Mir-Ahnin's bitterness hinted an inner darkness she did not wish to lighten, although he made the biggest outward play for her attention. Hers was a curious courtship—this would be only the first of several marriages for her, for brawns retired after seventy-five years of service, or earlier if they were unlucky. Brains, their bodies safe from any deterioration, were indestructible. In theory, once a shell-person had paid off the massive debt of early care, surgical adaptation, and maintenance charges, he or she was free to seek employment elsewhere. In practice, shell-people remained in the Service until they chose to self-destruct or died in line of duty. Helva had actually spoken to one shell-person 322 years old. She had been so awed by the contact she hadn't presumed to ask the personal questions she had wanted to.

Her choice of a brawn did not stand out from the others until Tanner started to sing a scout ditty recounting the misadventures of the bold, dense, painfully inept Billy Brawn. An attempt at harmony resulted in cacophony and Tanner wagged his arms wildly for silence.

"What we need is a roaring good lead tenor. Jennan, besides palming aces, what do you sing?"

"Sharp," Jennan replied with easy good humor.

"If a tenor is absolutely necessary, I'll attempt it," Helva volunteered.

"My good *woman*," Tanner protested.

"Sound your A," said Jennan, laughing.

Into the stunned silence that followed the rich, clear, high A, Jennan remarked quietly, "Such an A Caruso would have given the rest of his notes to sing."

It did not take them long to discover her full range.

"All Tanner asked for was one roaring good lead tenor," Jennan said jokingly, "and our sweet mistress supplied us an entire repertory company. The boy who gets this ship will go far, far, far."

"To the Horsehead Nebula?" asked Nordsen, quoting an old Central saying.

"To the Horsehead Nebula and back, we shall make beautiful music," said Helva, chuckling.

"Together," Jennan said. "Only you'd better make the music and, with my voice, I'd better listen."

"I rather imagined it would be I who listened," suggested Helva.

Jennan executed a stately bow with an intricate flourish of his crush-brimmed hat. He directed his bow toward the central control pillar where Helva *was*. Her own personal preference crystallized at that precise moment and for that particular reason: Jennan, alone of the men, had addressed his remarks directly at her physical presence, regardless of the fact that he knew she could pick up his image wherever he was in the ship and regardless of the fact that her body was behind massive metal walls. Throughout their partnership, Jennan never failed to turn his head in her direction no matter where he was in relation to her. In response to this personalization, Helva at that moment and from then on always spoke to Jennan only through her central mike, even though that was not always the most efficient method.

Helva didn't know that she fell in love with Jennan that evening. As she had never been exposed to love or affection, only the drier cousins, respect and admiration, she could scarcely have recognized her reaction to the warmth of his personality and thoughtfulness. As a shell-person, she considered herself remote from emotions largely connected with physical desires.

"Well, Helva, it's been swell meeting you," said Tanner suddenly as she and Jennan were arguing about the baroque quality of "Come All Ye Sons of Art." "See you in space sometime, you lucky dog, Jennan. Thanks for the party, Helva."

"You don't have to go so soon?" asked Helva, realizing belatedly that she and Jennan had been excluding the others from this discussion.

"Best man won," Tanner said wryly. "Guess I'd better go get a tape on love ditties. Might need 'em for the next ship, if there're any more at home like you."

Helva and Jennan watched them leave, both a little confused.

"Perhaps Tanner's jumping to conclusions?" Jennan asked.

Helva regarded him as he slouched against the console, facing her shell directly. His arms were crossed on his chest and the glass he held had been empty for some time. He was handsome—they all were—but his watchful eyes were unwary, his mouth assumed a smile easily, his voice (to which Helva was particularly drawn) was resonant, deep, and without unpleasant overtones or accent.

"Sleep on it, at any rate, Helva. Call me in the morning if it's your opt."

She called him at breakfast, after she had checked her choice through Central. Jennan moved his things aboard, received their joint commission, had his personality and experience file locked into her reviewer, gave her the coordinates of their first mission. The XH-834 officially became the JH-834.

Their first mission was a dull but necessary crash priority (Medical got Helva), rushing a vaccine to a distant system plagued with a virulent spore disease. They had only to get to Spica as fast as possible.

After the initial, thrilling forward surge at her maximum speed, Helva realized her muscles were to be given less of a workout than her brawn on this tedious mission. But they did have plenty of time for exploring each other's personalities. Jennan, of course, knew what Helva was capable of as a ship and partner, just as she knew what she could expect from him. But these were only facts, and Helva looked forward eagerly to learning that human side of her partner which could not be reduced to a series of symbols. Nor could the give-and-take of two personalities be learned from a book. It had to be experienced.

"My father was a scout, too, or is that programmed?" began Jennan their third day out.

"Naturally."

"Unfair, you know. You've got all my family history and I don't know one blamed thing about yours."

"I've never known either," Helva said. "Until I read yours, it hadn't occurred to me I must have one, too, someplace in Central's files."

Jennan snorted. "Shell psychology!"

Helva laughed. "Yes, and I'm even programmed against curiosity about it. You'd better be, too."

Jennan ordered a drink, slouched into the gravity couch opposite her, put his feet on the bumpers, turning himself idly from side to side on the gimbals.

"Helva—a made-up name . . ."

"With a Scandinavian sound."

"You aren't blond," Jennan said positively.

"Well, then, there're dark Swedes."

"And blond Turks and this one's harem is limited to one."

"Your woman in purdah, yes, but you can comb the pleasure houses—" Helva found herself aghast at the edge to her carefully trained voice.

"You know," Jennan interrupted her, deep in some thought of his own, "my father gave me the impression he was a lot more married to his ship, the Silvia, than to my mother. I know I used to think Silvia was my grandmother. She was a low number, so she must have been a great-great-grandmother at least. I used to talk to her for hours."

"Her registry?" asked Helva, unwittingly jealous of everyone and anyone who had shared his hours.

"422. I think she's TS now. I ran into Tom Burgess once."

Jennan's father had died of a planetary disease, the vaccine for which his ship had used up in curing the local citizens.

"Tom said she'd got mighty tough and salty. You lose your sweetness and I'll come back and haunt you, girl," Jennan threatened.

Helva laughed. He startled her by stamping up to the column panel, touching it with light, tender fingers.

"I *wonder* what you look like," he said softly, wistfully.

Helva had been briefed about this natural curiosity of scouts. She didn't know any-thing about herself and neither of them ever would or could.

"Pick any form, shape, and shade and I'll be yours obliging," she countered, as train-ing suggested.

"Iron Maiden, I fancy blondes with long tresses," and Jennan pantomimed Lady Godiva–like tresses. "Since you're immolated in titanium, I'll call you Brunehilde, my dear," and he made his bow.

With a chortle, Helva launched into the appropriate aria just as Spica made contact.

"What'n'ell's that yelling about? Who are you? And unless you're Central Worlds Medical, go away. We've got a plague. No visiting privileges."

"My ship is singing, we're the JH-834 of Worlds, and we've got your vaccine. What are our landing coordinates?"

"Your *ship* is singing?"

"The greatest SATB in organized space. Any request?"

The JH-834 delivered the vaccine but no more arias and received immediate orders to proceed to Leviticus IV. By the time they got there, Jennan found a reputation await-ing him and was forced to defend the 834's virgin honor.

"I'll stop singing," murmured Helva contritely as she ordered up poultices for his third black eye in a week.

"You will not," Jennan said through gritted teeth. "If I have to black eyes from here to the Horsehead to keep the snicker out of the title, we'll be the ship who sings."

After the "ship who sings" tangled with a minor but vicious narcotic ring in the Lesser Magellanics, the title became definitely respectful. Central was aware of each episode and punched out a "special interest" key on JH-834's file. A first-rate team was shaking down well.

Jennan and Helva considered themselves a first-rate team, too, after their tidy arrest.

"Of all the vices in the universe, I *hate* drug addiction," Jennan remarked as they headed back to Central Base. "People can go to hell quick enough without that kind of help."

"Is that why you volunteered for Scout Service? To redirect traffic?"

"I'll bet my official answer's on your review."

"In far too flowery wording. 'Carrying on the traditions of my family, which has been proud of four generations in Service,' if I may quote you your own words."

Jennan groaned. "I was *very* young when I wrote that. I certainly hadn't been through Final Training. And once I was in Final Training, my pride wouldn't let me fail . . .

"As I mentioned, I used to visit Dad on board the Silvia and I've a very good idea she might have had her eye on me as a replacement for my father because I had had massive doses of scout-oriented propaganda. It took. From the time I was seven, I was going to be a scout or else." He shrugged as if deprecating a youthful determination that had taken a great deal of mature application to bring to fruition.

"Ah, so? Scout Sahir Silan on the JS-422 penetrating into the Horse-head Nebula?" Jennan chose to ignore her sarcasm.

"With *you*, I may even get that far. But even with Silvia's nudging *I* never daydreamed myself *that* kind of glory in my wildest flights of fancy. I'll leave the whoppers to your agile brain henceforth. I have in mind a smaller contribution to space history."

"So modest?"

"No. Practical. We also serve, et cetera." He placed a dramatic hand on his heart.

"Glory hound!" scoffed Helva.

"Look who's talking, my Nebula-bound friend. At least I'm not greedy. There'll only be one hero like my dad at Parsaea, but I *would* like to be remembered for some kudos. Everyone does. Why else do or die?"

"Your father died on his way back from Parsaea, if I may point out a few cogent facts. So he could never have known he was a hero for damming the flood with his ship. Which kept the Parsaean colony from being abandoned. Which gave them a chance to discover the antiparalytic qualities of Parsaea. Which *he* never knew."

"I know," said Jennan softly.

Helva was immediately sorry for the tone of her rebuttal. She knew very well how deep Jennan's attachment to his father had been. On his review a note was made that he had rationalized his father's loss with the unexpected and welcome outcome of the Affair at Parsaea.

"Facts are not human, Helva. My father was and so am I. And *basically*, so are you. Check over your dial, 834. Amid all the wires attached to you is a heart, an underdeveloped human heart. Obviously!"

"I apologize, Jennan," she said.

Jennan hesitated a moment, threw out his hands in acceptance, and then tapped her shell affectionately.

"If they ever take us off the milk runs, we'll make a stab at the Nebula, huh?"

As so frequently happened in the Scout Service, within the next hour they had orders to change course, not to the Nebula, but to a recently colonized system with two habitable planets, one tropical, one glacial. The sun, named Ravel, had become unstable; the spectrum was that of a rapidly expanding shell, with absorption lines rapidly displacing toward violet. The augmented heat of the primary had already forced evacuation of the nearer world, Daphnis. The pattern of spectral emissions gave indication that the sun would sear Chloe as well. All ships in the immediate spatial vicinity were to report to Disaster Headquarters on Chloe to effect removal of the remaining colonists.

The JH-834 obediently presented itself and was sent to outlying areas on Chloe to pick up scattered settlers who did not appear to appreciate the urgency of the situation. Chloe, indeed, was enjoying the first temperatures above freezing since it had been flung out of its parent. Since many of the colonists were religious fanatics who had settled on rigorous Chloe to fit themselves for a life of pious reflection, Chloe's abrupt thaw was attributed to sources other than a rampaging sun.

Jennan had to spend so much time countering specious arguments that he and Helva were behind schedule on their way to the fourth and last settlement.

Helva jumped over the high range of jagged peaks that surrounded and sheltered the valley from the former raging snows as well as the present heat. The violent sun with its flaring corona was just beginning to brighten the deep valley as Helva dropped down to a landing.

"They'd better grab their toothbrushes and hop aboard," Helva said. "HQ says speed it up."

"All women," remarked Jennan in surprise as he walked down to meet them. "Unless the men on Chloe wear furred skirts."

"Charm 'em but pare the routine to the bare essentials. And turn on your two-way private."

Jennan advanced smiling, but his explanation of his mission was met with absolute incredulity and considerable doubt as to his authenticity. He groaned inwardly as the matriarch paraphrased previous explanations of the warming sun.

"Revered mother, there's been an overload on that prayer circuit and the sun is blowing itself up in one obliging burst. I'm here to take you to the spaceport at Rosary—"

"That Sodom?" The worthy woman glowered and shuddered disdainfully at his suggestion. "We thank you for your warning but we have no wish to leave our cloister for the rude world. We must go about our morning meditation, which has been interrupted—"

"It'll be permanently interrupted when that sun starts broiling you. You must come now," Jennan said firmly.

"Madame," said Helva, realizing that perhaps a female voice might carry more weight in this instance than Jennan's very masculine charm.

"Who spoke?" cried the nun, startled by the bodiless voice.

"I, Helva, the ship. Under my protection you and your sisters-in-faith may enter safely and be unprofaned by association with a male. I will guard you and take you safely to a place prepared for you."

The matriarch peered cautiously into the ship's open port. "Since only Central Worlds is permitted the use of such ships, I acknowledge that you are not trifling with us, young man. However, we are in no danger here."

"The temperature at Rosary is now ninety-nine degrees," said Helva. "As soon as the sun's rays penetrate directly into this valley, it will also be ninety-nine degrees, and it is due to climb to approximately one hundred eighty degrees today. I notice your buildings are made of wood with moss chinking. Dry moss. It should fire around noontime."

The sunlight was beginning to slant into the valley through the peaks, and the fierce rays warmed the restless group behind the matriarch. Several opened the throats of their furry parkas.

"Jennan," said Helva privately to him, "our time is very short."

"I can't leave them, Helva. Some of those girls are barely out of their teens."

"Pretty, too. No wonder the matriarch doesn't want to get in."

"Helva."

"It will be the Lord's will," said the matriarch stoutly and turned her back squarely on rescue.

"To burn to death?" shouted Jennan as she threaded her way through her murmuring disciples.

"They want to be martyrs? Their opt, Jennan," said Helva dispassionately. "We must leave and that is no longer a matter of option."

"How can I leave, Helva?"

"Parsaea?" Helva asked tauntingly as he stepped forward to grab one of the women. "You can't drag them *all* aboard and we don't have time to fight it out. Get on board, Jennan, or I'll have you on report."

"They'll die," muttered Jennan dejectedly as he reluctantly turned to climb on board.

"You can risk only so much." Helva said sympathetically. "As it is we'll just have time to make a rendezvous. Lab reports a critical speedup in spectral evolution."

Jennan was already in the air lock when one of the younger women, screaming, rushed to squeeze in the closing port. Her action set off the others. They stampeded through the narrow opening. Even crammed back to breast, there was not enough room inside for all the women. Jennan broke out space suits for the three who would have to remain with him in the air lock. He wasted valuable time explaining to the matriarch that she must put on the suit because the air lock had no independent oxygen or cooling units.

"We'll be caught," said Helva in a grim tone to Jennan on their private connection. "We've lost eighteen minutes in this last-minute rush. I am now overloaded for maximum speed and I must attain maximum speed to outrun the heat wave."

"Can you lift? We're suited."

"Lift? Yes," she said, doing so. "Run? I stagger."

Jennan, bracing himself and the women, could feel her sluggishness as she blasted upward. Heartlessly, Helva applied thrust as long as she could, despite the fact that the gravitational force mashed her cabin passengers brutally and crushed two fatally. It was a question of saving as many as possible. The only one for whom she had any concern was Jennan and she was in desperate terror about his safety. Airless and uncooled, protected by only one layer of metal, not three, the air lock was not going to be safe for the four trapped there, despite their space suits. These were only the standard models, not built to withstand the excessive heat to which the ship would be subjected.

Helva ran as fast as she could but the incredible wave of heat from the explosive sun caught them halfway to cold safety.

She paid no heed to the cries, moans, pleas, and prayers in her cabin. She listened only to Jennan's tortured breathing, to the missing throb in his suit's purifying system and the sucking of the overloaded cooling unit. Helpless, she heard the hysterical screams of his three companions as they writhed in the awful heat. Vainly, Jennan tried to calm them, tried to explain they would soon be safe and cool if they could be still and endure the heat. Undisciplined by their terror and torment, they tried to strike out at him despite the close quarters. One flailing arm became entangled in the leads to his power pack and the damage was quickly done. A connection, weakened by heat and the dead weight of the arm, broke.

For all the power at her disposal, Helva was helpless. She watched as Jennan fought for his breath, as he turned his head beseechingly toward *her*, and died.

Only the iron conditioning of her training prevented Helva from swinging around and plunging back into the cleansing heart of the exploding sun. Numbly she made rendezvous with the refugee convoy. She obediently transferred her burned, heat-prostrated passengers to the assigned transport.

"I will retain the body of my scout and proceed to the nearest base for burial," she informed Central dully.

"You will be provided escort," was the reply.

"I have no need of escort."

"Escort is provided, XH-834," she was told curtly. The shock of hearing Jennan's initial severed from her call number cut off her half-formed protest. Stunned, she waited by the transport until her screens showed the arrival of two other slim brain ships. The cortege proceeded homeward at unfunereal speeds.

"834? The ship who sings?"

"I have no more songs."

"Your scout was Jennan."

"I do not wish to communicate."

"I'm 422."

"Silvia?"

"Silvia died a long time ago. I'm 422. Currently MS," the ship rejoined curtly. "AH-640 is our other friend, but Henry's not listening in. Just as well—he wouldn't understand it if you wanted to turn rogue. But I'd stop *him* if he tried to deter you."

"Rogue?" The term snapped Helva out of her apathy.

"Sure. You're young. You've got power for years. Skip. Others have done it. 732 went rogue twenty years ago after she lost her scout on a mission to that white dwarf. Hasn't been seen since."

"I never heard about rogues."

"As it's exactly the thing we're conditioned against, you sure wouldn't hear about it in school, my dear," 422 said.

"Break conditioning?" cried Helva, anguished, thinking longingly of the white, white furious hot heart of the sun she had just left.

"For you I don't think it would be hard at the moment," 422 said quietly, her voice devoid of her earlier cynicism. "The stars are out there, winking."

"Alone?" cried Helva from her heart.

"Alone!" 422 confirmed bleakly.

Alone with all of space and time. Even the Horsehead Nebula would not be far enough away to daunt her. Alone with a hundred years to live with her memories and nothing . . . nothing more.

"Was Parsaea worth it?" she asked 422 softly.

"Parsaea?" 422 repeated, surprised. "With his father? Yes. We were there, at Parsaea when we were needed. Just as you . . . and his son . . . were at Chloe. When you were needed. The crime is not knowing where need is and not being there."

"But *I* need *him*. Who will supply my need?" said Helva bitterly.

"834," said 422 after a day's silent speeding, "Central wishes your report. A replacement awaits your opt at Regulus Base. Change course accordingly."

"A replacement?" That was certainly not what she needed, a reminder inadequately filling the void Jennan left. Why, her hull was barely cool of Chloe's heat. Atavistically, Helva wanted time to mourn Jennan.

"Oh, none of them are impossible if *you're* a good ship," 422 remarked philosophically. "And it is just what you need. The sooner the better."

"You told them I wouldn't go rogue, didn't you?" Helva said.

"The moment passed you even as it passed me after Parsaea, and before that, after Glen Arthur, and Betelgeuse."

"We're conditioned to go on, aren't we? We *can't* go rogue. You were testing."

"Had to. Orders. Not even Psych knows why a rogue occurs. Central's very worried, and so, daughter, are your sister ships. I asked to be your escort. I . . . don't want to lose you both."

In her emotional nadir, Helva could feel a flood of gratitude for Silvia's rough sympathy.

"We've all known this grief, Helva. It's no consolation, but if we couldn't feel with our scouts, we'd only be machines wired for sound."

Helva looked at Jennan's still form stretched before her in its shroud and heard the echo of his rich voice in the quiet cabin.

"Silvia! I *couldn't* help him," she cried from her soul.

"Yes, dear, I know," 422 murmured gently and then was quiet.

The three ships sped on, wordless, to the great Central Worlds base at Regulus. Helva broke silence to acknowledge landing instructions and the officially tendered regrets.

The three ships set down simultaneously at the wooded edge where Regulus's gigantic blue trees stood sentinel over the sleeping dead in the small Service cemetery. The entire Base complement approached with measured step and formed an aisle from Helva to the burial ground. The honor detail, out of step, walked slowly into her cabin. Reverently they placed the body of her dead love on the wheeled bier, covered it honorably with the deep-blue, star-splashed flag of the Service. She watched as it was driven slowly down the living aisle, which closed in behind the bier in last escort.

Then, as the simple words of interment were spoken, as the atmosphere planes dipped in tribute over the open grave, Helva found voice for her lonely farewell.

Softly, barely audible at first, the strains of the ancient song of evening and requiem swelled to the final poignant measure until black space itself echoed back the sound of the song the ship sang.

7

ENTRADA

Mary Rosenblum

The rail was half empty, this early in the morning. Head aching, Mila Aguilar stared through the smeared window. Tract houses slid past below the concrete span—*los burbios*, acres of dust and junk, blotched with green wherever people could afford the water for crops. No gang on the rail today, thank God. Just techs on their way in to shifts at the Fed-Med clinics, child-care workers and service personnel. Asians. Latinos. A few blacks. No one looked at her. You didn't look—not unless you were asking for trouble.

The air smelled like sweat and urine and old plastic, as if it had been shut up in this car for weeks, breathed over and over again. It choked her suddenly, filled her with a squeezing claustrophobia that made the headache worse. Trapped. Every day of her working life she had taken this ride. She would do so until the end of her days, unless she found a way out. She clutched the grimy seat-back as they roller-coastered through the east hills. Little Cambodia slid by beneath the concrete track; a green patchwork of expensively watered vegetable plots. A flash of bright color caught her eye. Painted onto a crumbling highway overpass, Asian men and women fought strangling vines beneath tranquil blossoms.

Samuel Lujan had painted that mural. She had leaned over the crumbling wall in the middle of a hot night, watching those painted faces come to life beneath his hissing brush. They had made love afterward—right there on the overpass, cushioned by their tangled clothes. His long hair had showered down around her, and on that night, in that time and place, it had seemed that they would be together forever. There could be no other way for them to live.

But Sam had wanted out, too; out of the barrio. He had chosen his door and had walked through it. She had not followed. Mila's stomach clenched as the mural slid backward out of sight. The rail arched up and over the river, and the city towers rose to swallow them; so clean and bright after *los burbios*, surrounded by their well-watered park-blocks. Their shadows swallowed the rail, and hunger stirred in Mila's belly. It was not food that she craved. Those towers meant freedom. They meant escape. There were doors in those towers—for her, for Mila Aguilar. All you needed was an *entrada*; a way inside.

And she had found one. Mila slung her uniform bag over her shoulder and pushed her way down the aisle as the rail whispered to a stop. Orange plastic seats, grimy graffiti-covered walls, a crumpled condom wrapper on the gray composite floor; these were the images of morning, of hurry, of another precious step away from the barrio and *los burbios*. Put your card in the slot, touch in your number and run, because you're going to be late. A transit cop stared at her. Cops always stared if you were running and you weren't white. Lots of cops *here*, public and private. No gangs. No blades. Amelia Connor-Vanek's tower rose like a snowy mountain from its garden. She lived at the top, the old *bruja*. At the very top, where no one could look down on her except God.

Invisible security opened the door for Mila and closed it after her. It let her cross the carpeted lobby and opened the door of the lift. Mila combed her fingers through her short hair as the lift rose upward, shifting her bag to her other shoulder. By the time she got into her uniform, she would be late after all. But you didn't wear any kind of medical uniform on the street.

Ginger was waiting in the apartment anteroom, already dressed in her street clothes. "Rail running late again? The old girl's still asleep." She tossed her blonde head. "Bloodchem and biostats are normal. She was a case, last night. I had to call in a massage therapist at two AM. How do you *stand* her on days?" Ginger rolled her eyes. "If she puts her hand on my ass one more time, I'm quitting." She scooped up her uniform bag and a palmtop reader. "See you tonight."

"See you, Ginger." Mila went on into the apartment and peeked into the old *bruja's* bedroom.

Still asleep, and the monitor displays were okay. Mila stripped in the enormous living room, slowly and without haste. The handwoven carpet tickled her bare feet as she pulled on her uniform coverall. These were the symbols of escape: silk upholstery, wool carpet, the breathtaking view from this tower room. The headache had faded at last, but the hunger was always there. Always.

Are you there? Amelia's voice came over the comm on Mila's belt, shrill and querulous. *I've called you twice, damn it. I don't pay you to be late.*

"I'm sorry, Señora," Mila called out. Bullshit, on that *twice*. She quickly sealed the front of her coverall. "The rail was late. I'm coming right away."

"How many times do I have to tell you that if you want to say more than 'Yes, Señora' to me, you do it in person?" Leaning back in her reclining bed, Amelia Connor-

Vanek glared as Mila came through the door. "I pay you for your physical presence, my dear. I already have a monitor."

The old *bruja* was in one of those moods. "Yes, Señora," Mila murmured. "I'm sorry, Señora." She looked like something dead, all wrinkled and ugly, no cosmetic work at all, and she could afford plenty. "I forgot." Mila kept her eyes on the white fold of sheet across Amelia's lap. The old *bruja* wore sexy see-through nightgowns, as if she was a fourteen-year-old *puta*. "I didn't sleep well last night, and I guess I'm tired."

"A new lover?" Amelia leered up at her as Mila came around the bed to read the monitor. "I hope you picked a pretty one, this time."

"I don't have a lover." Mila bit off the words as she uncapped the sampler. "I need to do your morning bloodwork."

"Touchy, dear?" Amelia chuckled deep in her throat. "You still miss him? The boy who went into the Army?"

"He was not a boy, Señora." Mila pressed her lips together as she slipped the sampling catheter into the port in Amelia's arm. "It was over long ago."

Sam had thought that the Army would be a door for him. Maybe it was, but it was not one she had wanted to take. They had parted in anger, and there had been no word from him since. What was there to say? The old *bruja* liked to mention Sam, to play her little hurting games. She knew everything. That was her trade—information. They made the big money, the information brokers. She was a *bruja* with the spell to turn rumor into gold. It scared Mila, how much she knew. And it excited her.

The monitor hummed, sipping its microliters of blood, testing for signs of death, so that it could be expensively postponed for another day or week or year. Death came to everyone, but it came to the rich later and with greater difficulty.

Mila snapped the tubing out of the port and dropped it back into the machine. "What would you like for breakfast, Señora?"

"Coffee."

"If you don't eat, Ginger will have to run IVs again tonight."

"So let her. I don't care what she does to my body when I'm asleep."

Mila flinched as Amelia's withered hand closed around her wrist. Head averted, she stood very still as Amelia Connor-Vanek began to stroke her face. The old woman's fingers felt like rat feet on her skin, dry and furtive. Mila closed her eyes as the rat-feet fingers wandered lower; touching, caressing, lifting the weight of Mila's breasts with unhurried sensuality. It had made her sick at first, the dry scaly touch of this woman's hands. She bit her lip. Think of how many licensed medical aides are on the agency waiting list. Think of the three years she had waited for this job, any job. It could be worse, somewhere else.

Even if it wasn't, she would stay.

Amelia laughed softly, possessively, as if she had been reading Mila's thoughts. "Such lovely skin—it's your Spanish heritage. You keep me alive, child," she said. "You're honest, or perhaps honestly dishonest is more accurate, since no one can afford to be completely honest in this world of ours." She laughed again, a brittle sound, like breaking glass. "I've come to appreciate the value of honesty, in all its guises. One of these days, I'll give you a bonus, my child. A little gift."

"Yes, Señora." Mila shivered beneath those fingers—couldn't help herself. The old *bruja* had felt her shudder and was smiling. You don't own me, Mila thought fiercely. This is a trade, *bruja*. Nothing more. Her head had started to hurt again, throbbing with the beat of her pulse. It always got worse when the old *bruja* touched her. Mila lifted her chin, fighting sudden dizziness. "I need to do my log," she said, too brightly. "After, I will take you down to the fountain court. There are otters in the pool. Señora Anderson's aide told me."

"Don't patronize me." Amelia pushed Mila's hand roughly away. "I'm not impressed by holographic otters. Real ones might be interesting, but they'd never use real animals. They'd shit in the fountain. I see no reason to parade my decaying flesh in front of all those plastic parodies of youth."

There was a shadow in Amelia's eyes that Mila had never seen before—pain, perhaps? But the bloodwork had been normal. "What does it matter?" Mila asked with a sweet twinge of malice. "Do you care what they think, downstairs?"

"Cabin fever, child? Has the novelty of all this luxury worn off?" Amelia's withered lips twisted. "I don't need a mirror. I look at your face and I see my reflection. Why should I torture myself with the fountain court?"

"Oh, you're mistaken, Señora. You are a handsome lady. . . ."

"Stop the flustered Mex servant routine." Amelia seized Mila by the arms, pulling her close so that Mila had to look into her pale eyes. "I'm not going to fire you just because you see an old hag when you look at me, and by now you know it. Don't pretend that you don't; or I'll think that you *are* stupid and I *will* fire you."

The old *bruja's* nails hurt, and her breath was sour in Mila's face. "I am Guatemalan, not Mexican," she said softly. "If you don't like the way people look at your body, why don't you get it fixed?"

For a long moment, Amelia stared into her face. Then she laughed, a deep booming laugh that seemed impossible for such a shriveled, wasted woman. As abruptly as she had started, she fell silent. "I am afraid." Her pale eyes pinned Mila. "Now you are the only person in this shitty world who knows that I am afraid of anything." She released Mila and reached for the raw-silk robe beside the bed. "I own you, child, and you hate me for it."

"You do not own me." Mila met Amelia's shadowed eyes. "No one owns me."

"You have ambitions, don't you?" Amelia's voice was a dry whisper. "Ambitions as large as my own once were. I respect that. I have decided that I want breakfast after all. Call Antonio's and have them send me smoked turkey and provolone cheese on a sour-dough roll. With fresh dirt-grown asparagus. And then I want you to set up my dreams."

Mila opened her mouth to protest, closed it without speaking. "Yes, Señora." She looked away from those cold, shadowed eyes. "Right away."

Mila sat beside the monitor, eyes on the bright numbers that tracked Amelia Connor-Vanek's cheating of death. On the clean white bed, Amelia fell into dreams beneath her VR mask. The breakfast dishes lay piled on a tray beside the bed. That meal—real meat, real cheese, and vegetables grown in irrigated soil instead of a tank—had probably cost more than Mila made in a week. The old *bruja* had barely touched anything. Mila caught a rich whiff of turkey and her stomach growled. She could eat the leftovers if she wanted, but the thought of eating food that Amelia's fingers had touched made her ill.

She checked the monitor once more and got to her feet, too restless to sit still. The blinds were open on the inside wall. In this tower, the rooms ringed a central court that was roofed with a clear composite, so that you could sit under real trees and look up at real sky. All climate-controlled, of course. The recycled air and water were tested hourly. You didn't have to worry about what might be seeping into the river this week or which factory had "accidentally" released what into the atmosphere yesterday. Far below, the fountain leaped into the air, shimmering with light. The holoed otters would be sliding down a holoed mud bank, playing and splashing. Were otters extinct? Mila tried to remember.

On the bed, Amelia made a soft noise. A sob. She did that sometimes—cried. Crazy to pay all that money to a VR designer for something that made you cry. Amelia's hands twitched, and she sobbed again. It was an innocent sound, somehow. Like a child crying for a lost treasure. It sounded strange, coming from those pale withered lips. Mila checked the monitor. All normal—as normal as it could be. Some drugs were illegal—even for the Amelias of this world. Rev was one of them. But without Rev, VR was just VR, no matter how good a designer you hired. Shoot Rev into your veins and you *lived* it.

Get some, Amelia had ordered when Mila had first started working for her. She had assumed that Mila would have connections. Because she was Latina, from the barrio. Mila's lip curled. She had done it—for the same reason that she stood still beneath

Amelia's hands. "Not because you own me," she whispered. The words hung in the cool, clean air.

Mila prowled to the far wall. At her touch, the tissue-thin strips of the blinds contracted into fine threads, letting in a flood of noontime sun. The river was a dirty brown trickle in the bottom of its bed. The green smear was Little Cambodia. Out there, in *los burbios*, your soul was up for sale. The government owned you for its subsidy dollars, or an employer who could claim your flesh as a bonus, because the only alternative was unemployment and the brand of full-subsidy on your personal file. Or the Army owned you. Sam had called it a contract. A way out, for a price. A choice between owners was no choice at all. Only up here, in the towers, could you truly choose.

Mila slapped the blinds closed. The monitor said that Amelia was dreaming, that she was healthy, in spite of the drug in her veins. *La Señora* had set the timer for three hours. It was time. Mila sat down at the main terminal in the living room. "Log on," she said. "Password *entrada*."

Harvard Equivalency Curriculum, the terminal intoned softly. *Marketing Theory, 202. Do you wish to continue from your place of exit?*

"Yes." Text blinked onto the screen; assigned reading for the quarter. International Marketing Theory. How to figure out what needed to be sold, how to find the people to make it and the people to sell it to. Mila listened to the soft hum of the apartment's silence and began to read, struggling a little, because her mother had only been able to afford a public high school-equivalency and a decent vocational training program for her daughter. Words and comprehension came slowly at times—but HarvardNet had accepted her and that was something.

This was why she put up with Amelia's hands, why she risked supplying her with her drugs; this was the trade. HarvardNet was the best university-equivalency on-line, and she would never be able to afford it on her salary. A HarvardNet degree was her admission to the city. She could land a job with one of the smaller firms, maybe go freelance someday. This was her *entrada;* this was her escape.

If Amelia didn't find out about it. If she didn't look over her Net expenses and discover the tuition charges. It was a risk. So far, the accounting program hadn't flagged it, and the old *bruja* never bothered to look. God, the woman had money.

The global enterprise webs eliminate middle-level managers and push authority for product development and sales down to independent engineers and marketers whose compensation is directly linked to the unit's profits. Brokers at the web's center provide financial and logistical aid, but give the unit discretion over spending, up to a point. Sony-Matohito, for example, is comprised of 287 autonomous companies.

Line by line, Mila read, breathless with the sense of future that the words gave her. The headache was back again. She clenched her teeth and fought it.

In the most decentralized webs, brokers identify marketing potential and contract with independent businesses to fill production needs. Thus production moves to the cheapest labor market and does so at the wink of the stock market. Nationalism has become nothing more than an emotionally loaded mythology with no real connection to the international nature of commerce.

Adrenaline rushed through Mila's veins as fingers seemed to touch her neck. Blurred memory broke in her head; fright, the dry touch of fingers on her throat and Amelia's soft voice, whispering, whispering . . . then it was gone. A dream? Mila looked over her shoulder, but the room was quiet. Empty. She shivered. Nerves, she told herself, and turned her attention back to the screen.

A beeper went off, shrill enough to make her ears hurt. Mila jerked upright, groggy, vaguely aware that she must have fallen asleep in front of the screen. Her belt alarm! Amelia! She bolted to her feet and ran for the bedroom, adrenaline crashing through her system, the shrill electronic pulse trumpeting *death* throughout the apartment.

Mila had the Justice Center cell to herself. She sat on the narrow bed, staring vaguely at the dull-green wall beyond the expanded mesh of the cell. Overcrowding wasn't a problem anymore. You got the death penalty for so many things. Without appeals, cells emptied fast. You could get the death penalty for negligence if you were a licensed aide. The juries were always city people, and so many city people were old. They could afford to be old. Too many of those jurors would have aides at home. They would see themselves in Amelia Connor-Vanek.

But I didn't kill her, Mila told herself one more time. I gave her the usual dose. It was the same stuff, and there was no reason for her to die. The words carried no comfort. It *was* her fault. Rev was illegal, and she had administered it. Never mind that the old *bruja* would have fired her if she had refused.

If she had remained sitting beside Amelia's bed, Amelia would not have died. She had died from an overdose of Rev.

Which meant that she had to have done it to herself, but there had been no note. The cops on the scene hadn't even bothered to record Mila's hysterical claim of suicide. The bored court-appointed lawyer had fed her case into LegalNet and had advised her to plead guilty. *Without a suicide note, you're dead, sweetheart. If you didn't do it, you'd better agree to full questioning*, he had told her. *Psychotropes, the whole nine yards. If you help them nail your connection, we can probably cut a deal with the DA.*

Her connection had been Sam. He'd gotten the stuff for her through his friend Salgado, because Amelia had offered twice street price and Sam had needed the money. So she'd told the lawyer to go to hell.

Have it your way, sweetheart, he had said. She hadn't seen him in the two weeks since her arrest.

Mila stared down at her hands, limp in her lap. How many days had she been here, waiting for her trial? Three? Ten? She had lost count. Mesh walls, concrete floor and ceiling, one bed, one toilet/sink combination, a table and a chair. No privacy. If you wanted to piss, the guards got to watch. And they did. Everything was painted the same dull green as the walls and bolted to the floor.

When she was nine, some of the boys on the street had snared a coyote in the scrubby field beyond the development. They had kept it in an old plastic airline kennel. She remembered how it had crouched in the tiny cage, yellow eyes empty of hope or fear, skinny and crawling with lice. It didn't snarl or bite at the sticks that the boys poked through the bars. It just crouched there. It had finally died.

A guard marched down the corridor. "You, Aguilar. On your feet."

Mila stood slowly, heart contracting in her chest. Her trial? Would her lawyer even *be* there? Would it matter if he was?

"You got a visitor. Turn around." The guard—a man—opened the cell and cuffed her hands behind her. He also put his hand between her legs.

Mila pressed her lips together, remembering Amelia's rat-feet fingers on her breasts. A visitor? Who was going to visit her here? Prison was contagious. Especially when the cops were looking for a drug connection. She stumbled as the guard shoved her forward. The visiting cubicles were just this side of the thick door at the end of the corridor. The guard pushed her inside, and the lock clicked. A video screen was set into the green wall. A battered plastic stool stood in front of it. The air smelled like mildew and fear.

"Sam?" Mila's eyes widened as the screen shimmered to life. No. It could not be. "What are *you* doing here?"

"I had some leave. I heard, when I got home." His face was anguished. "Mila, what *happened?*"

How many times had they asked her that question, over and over until her head pounded with the rhythm of the words? "I don't know," she whispered, and struggled with the tears that were trying to come. She hadn't shed a tear, not since they'd taken her from Amelia's apartment. If she started crying now, she'd never stop. She'd cry until there was nothing left of her but a shriveled husk on the floor, until her soul and her mind were empty. "Never mind," she said. "I don't want to talk about it, Sam, do you hear me? There's nothing you can do." Tell me how you are, she wanted to say. Tell me that you're fine, that your choice was a good one for you, at least. Please, *querido*.

She didn't say it. She could read the answer in his face, in spite of the grainy video. His hair was Army-short and his face looked skeletal, as if he'd lost weight. He had new muscles; stringy, lean muscles. He seemed harder, older. Changed.

"They sent us to Indonesia," he said. "For the UN—to stop this revolution, I guess. It was so damned easy. We only lost a few people—they might as well have been using sticks against what we had. We didn't even make the US NewsNet."

Mila had to look away. His eyes were the coyote's eyes. If she looked into the mirror, she would see the same eyes in her own face. We were human once, she thought bitterly. At least I think we were.

"*Cairña?* I love you." He stretched out his arms, as if he could reach through the video, through the concrete wall, could put his arms around her and hold her tight.

His face was full of grief. He was afraid for her, and his fear ate at the hard wall that she'd built around herself these past days. She could see her death reflected in his face. In a moment, that wall would crack apart and the terror would rush in to drown her. "Go away," she whispered. "Don't come here again, Sam. Not ever, do you hear me? I don't want to see you. I don't want to hear from you." She threw herself against the locked door, tugging at the cuffs, wanting to pound on it with her fists. "Turn it off!" she yelled to the invisible eavesdroppers. "I want to go back to my cell."

No one answered, but when she looked over her shoulder, the screen was blank again; a flat gray square of nothingness in the green wall. Trembling, she limped back to the stool and sat down. Her shoulder ached where she had slammed it into the door. I love you, *querido*. She held the words inside herself, like a charm, clenched in a fist. I love you. But it was too late. In her mind, she opened the fist and her palm was empty.

The door lock clicked behind her. Mila waited without turning for the guard to yank her off the stool and hustle her back to her cell.

"Ms. Aguilar?"

A woman's voice, much too polite to be a guard's. Reluctantly, Mila looked. The stranger stood just outside the door, flanked by a guard. She had dark red hair, cut short and stylish, and a strong bony face. She was dressed in a sleek tunic suit. The suit looked too expensive for a court-appointed lawyer. Mila waited.

"Ms. Aguilar, I'm Rebecca Connor. You've been released into my custody."

She stepped aside, obviously expecting Mila to hop to her feet and trot along at her heels. Mila sat coyote-still, waiting for the stick. "Why am I released?"

The guard started forward, but the woman put out a hand.

"Ms. Aguilar, I am Amelia Connor-Vanek's daughter. I had my lawyer post bail for you." She was tapping her foot impatiently. "Could we discuss this in private, please?"

That made Mila blink. The bail figure had been astronomical. It always was, if you weren't an Anglo. Making bail was a pretty dream, like finding a pot of gold under a rainbow or winning the national lottery. Not applicable personally to Mila Aguilar. "Yes," Mila said with a cold glance at the guard. "I would prefer to discuss this in private."

The guard took her back to her cell and gave her the clothes she'd been wearing on the day they arrested her. The day Amelia died. He cuffed her again and wouldn't take the cuffs off until they reached the front door of the Justice Center. He had given the rest of the things they had seized—her uniform bag and its contents—to the woman. As if Mila was a stray dog being claimed by its owner. Mila stalked through the door and out into the sunshine, half-blinded by the harsh, welcome light, resisting the urge to shake herself all over like a dog. Or a coyote.

"My car is over here." The woman put a hand on her elbow.

"You don't have to hold on to me." Mila touched the thin band of the parole collar around her neck. "It would be foolish to run away.

"I'm sorry." The woman took her hand away abruptly. "Were they all as bad as that jerk?"

Mostly they had been worse. Mila shrugged and watched the woman's lips tighten. She didn't like having her friendly overture rejected. You want something from me, Mila thought. You paid a lot for it, and I don't know what it is, yet. I do not think you are my friend. She climbed into the woman's car. It was a private vehicle, licensed for alcofuel. She revised the cost of the woman's suit upward. The old *bruja* had never spoken of a daughter. Not once. I should worry, Mila thought. I should be afraid. She merely felt numb. She kept seeing Sam's face in her mind; the new hard line of his jaw and the coyote-shadows in his eyes.

The woman drove silently, threading the manicured park-blocks that surrounded the big residential towers and their retail clusters. She was going to Amelia's tower. Mila recognized the neighborhood. The woman parked in the subsurface garage. Security's invisible eyes stared down from ceiling and walls. Mila felt the first stir of apprehension as the lift carried them upward. Some kind of trap? The lift door opened to Amelia's private anteroom. "Why did you pay my bail?" Mila asked.

"I need your help." The woman stepped out.

Sure. Mila followed her reluctantly through the anteroom and into the carpeted living room. In prison, her pre-arrest past had become brittle and unreal, fragile as old-fashioned movie film that could crumble at the touch. The familiar scent of Amelia's rooms brought it back to her in a staggering rush; Sam and the barrio and Amelia's dead, gray face.

"You look as if you're going to faint." The woman started to reach for her, caught herself and pushed a silk-upholstered chair toward her. "I think you'd better sit down."

"I'm fine, Señora Connor." Mila held on tightly to the chair back. "I told the police everything I know. There's nothing else to tell. I can't help you." Mila had escaped the kennel, now. She could be afraid again. "Who are you, and what is it that you want?"

"I told you who I am. I want a file." Rebecca Connor paced across the enormous carpeted space that Amelia had rarely used. "My mother bought and sold . . . information. I suspect you know that." She paused by the transparent inner wall, staring down into the upper branches of the fountain-court trees. "She had retired, but she would have kept some special information. As . . . insurance. I can't find it."

"I didn't steal it."

"I didn't say you did. Do I see otters down there?" Connor's shoulders moved, as if she had sighed. "What I did find was obsolete. Useless. And it was easy to find. That makes me think that there is more and that it isn't obsolete. I'm hoping that you can find it for me."

"Why me?" Mila lifted her chin. "I'm just an aide, Señora. A dumb Latina from the barrio. What would I know about a file? *La Señora* didn't tell me anything."

Connor turned away from the wall at last. Her eyes were cold. "Are you a dumb Latina? My mother is . . . *was* . . . very creative at hiding things in plain sight. What I want is your intuition. I want you to find her hiding place. The information has to be in hard-data form. It's not in her Netspace." Connor laughed coldly. "I'm better at that than she ever was, and she knew it."

"I can't help you." Mila crossed her arms, aware of the thin parole collar, heavy as a stone around her neck.

"You're going to try." Rebecca's eyes were a brilliant augmented green, cold as sea ice. "I bought you for the price of your bail and the leverage it took to get you off the DA's weekly conviction list. My mother kept a record of your course hours, you know. We could add theft to your negligence charge. We'll make a trade." She smiled thinly. "You cooperate, and I'll edit Amelia's financial records to hide your theft. If you find the file for me, I'll lean on the DA to drop the negligence charge."

So the old *bruja* had known about the courses all along. *Honestly dishonest*, she had called Mila, with her hands on her breasts. It had truly been a trade; the hands for the credit hours. "I have to help you." Mila didn't try to keep the bitterness out of her voice. "I have no choice, do I?"

"You have a choice," Connor said gently. "You know, you did quite well in your course work, for someone with a public education from the Net."

Mila turned away, hating this woman, hating her more than she had ever hated anyone in her life. Because she had all the power and Mila had none and had never really had any. Her *entrada* had been an illusion only, and this woman had flung it in her face. "Tell me what you want me to do," she said.

This woman's method of looking for something was a strange one, Mila decided. She wanted Mila to touch, taste, smell, examine, and listen to every single item in the entire apartment. They started in the bedroom because that was where Amelia had spent most of her time. By evening, Mila decided that she would grow old before they finished.

"Nothing happens." She scowled at the holocube she was holding. "What do you expect? Trumpets? A sign from God?"

"You're not done with that yet. Taste it. Lick it. Just *do* it." Sitting cross-legged on the floor, Connor ran a hand through her rumpled hair. "Something will happen. I don't know what."

"I told you . . .

". . . *La Señora* never told me anything," Connor finished for her. "I think she was playing a game with you and me. She knew that I'd come looking. I think you're the key."

"Why should you come looking? Why not just give it to you?" Mila touched the tip of her tongue to the black base of the holocube and grimaced. A man smiled at her from the center of the cube. He had a long face and warm green eyes, and his hair hung down in a dozen red-gold braids. "And why should I have some kind of key?" she asked.

"Amelia knew I'd come looking because she taught me this business and I knew her . . . methods. She didn't give anything away to *anyone*, honey, and certainly not to me. We are—were—competitors." Connor took the cube from Mila's hand. "It would be her little joke, to make you the key. She knew how I felt about her Mex girls."

"I am Guatemalan."

Connor shrugged and put the cube back on its shelf, straightening it carefully.

"Who is that?" Mila asked.

"He was Aaron Connor. My father—the only man she ever bothered to marry. I don't know why she did that. Maybe because he actually loved her. More the fool, he." She picked up a laptop reader. "Try this," she said coldly.

Was. So he was dead? Such bitterness in this woman. Mila took the reader. It was an old one—not the slick holomodel that Amelia had used, when she bothered to use a reader. Mila nearly dropped it as the screen brightened. You're getting warmer, Mila. The words glowed briefly and vanished.

Connor hissed softly through her teeth and snatched the reader from Mila's hands. "See this?" She pried a tiny silver disk from the reader's edge. "It was matched to your skin chemistry. It would only activate the message if you picked it up. I knew she was playing games." She threw the reader across the room.

Mila flinched as it hit the wall and cracked. "So she *did* this." Like a child's game— warmer, colder, you're getting hot. Hope and anger burned like twin flames in her heart. She had thought that the old *bruja* might have left a suicide message in her Netspace, that some Latino-hating cop had erased it. "She hid it," Mila whispered. "The note."

"What note?"

"The suicide note." Mila bent to pick up the broken reader. "She *hid* it. For me to find." A game, and the stakes were Mila's life. A *bruja* for real.

"Forget it, dear." Connor's voice was cold. "Amelia Connor-Vanek didn't suicide. Your connection sold you some bad drugs, and you didn't watch the monitor long enough to catch it. Who are you trying to protect, anyway?" Connor picked up a musicube and held it up to the light. "Negligence is no big feather for a DA's cap. I checked on your case. They'd pull your license and let you walk, for your connection." She tossed the cube to Mila.

Not that trade. Not now, not ever. "I don't remember who it was." Mila cupped her palms around the cube, touched it with her tongue, held it to her ear.

"It was your boyfriend, wasn't it? Yes, he's in my mother's file on you." Connor shrugged. "Poor judgment, honey. No full-sub Army bait is worth your life—no matter how good he is in bed."

"He was an artist." *Was.* She had put it in the past tense, as if he was dead—as if that part of him was dead.

"An artist?" The woman's lip curled. "I suppose you can call yourself anything you want, on a full subsidy."

"Do you think it is a pleasant life?" Mila hissed. "Living in the suburbs with enough to eat and drink—almost—and nothing ahead of you but another empty day? It was not his choice, Señora Connor. His mother was a hooker, okay? Her implant failed, and there he was." She touched the red-and-blue licensed-aide patch on her shoulder. "I could get this, only because my mother was never on full subsidy. Sam grew up on full subsidy. For him, there was only the Army."

This was what he had told *her*, so angry on that last day. And she had argued with him, yelled at him, wept. Mila laid her clenched fists gently on her thighs. "He saw what was all around him on the streets," she said. "He saw rage, fear, despair, and hope. He saw the things that we have stopped seeing because they are always there and it hurts too much. He took that hurt, and he painted it on the walls and the overpasses and the rail. He gave it life, all that hurt, but no one gave him a choice. Do you understand?"

"Are you telling me that you love him?" Connor's face was still, without emotion. "Love is a luxury of your class, Mila—a charming myth, like winning the lottery. In my game, you know better. Love is nothing more than a pretty type of loyalty, and loyalty is something that you sell for a very good price. My mother could have told you that. She never let loyalty get in her way—not to a lover, not to her daughter."

"Sam is not part of this, and he was not my connection." Mila threw the musicube back into its bin. "It was suicide."

"It was not suicide." Connor stood up, glaring down at her, fists clenched at her sides as if she wanted to hit Mila. "Tell me about your mother. Did she want you to have a better life than she? That's a part of your suburban culture too, isn't it? The kids have a chance at the future that didn't quite work out for Mom and Dad? Did you make your mother proud of you when you got your license? Or wasn't it enough for her? Is that why you stole course time from Amelia?"

"My mother died when I was twelve." Mila picked up the next cube. "She got cancer." The grief was so old that she barely felt it anymore. Her mother had worked nights at the Bon, playing dress-up with the wealthy. She had slept during the day while Mila did her lessons on the Net. Maybe it had been the leukemia that had made her sleep so much. Or maybe, when you finally realized that your life wasn't going to go anywhere else, that you had everything you were ever going to get, there was nothing else to do but sleep. Mila wanted to touch her forehead, to probe for the echo of the so-frequent headache. With an effort, she kept her hand still. "At forty-two, at her skill level, she didn't qualify for viral therapy under Fed-Med."

"I'm sorry."

"You're not. Why should you be?" Mila tossed the last of the musicubes back into the bin.

"Yes, you're Amelia's type. You'd react to her little cruelties, and she'd like that. But she'd break you, in the end." Conner got to her feet and yanked her tunic straight. "She taught me the business, but not enough to be better than she. Oh no. She was the queen. The one who could sell you anything, for the right price. Who was going where, with what product line, and why. The Cartel's top-secret plans for a better mousetrap. Who was in bed with whom and when. And how they did it, if you really wanted to know. That's the coin of the realm, these days. Information. And I'm better than she ever was." Connor stared down at Mila. "Much better, do you understand? She'll never forgive me for that."

"She is dead," Mila said softly. "It's late. Can I go home, please?" *Home.* An empty word for four walls and an empty bed.

"No." Connor looked around the room as if she expected something to leap at her out of the shadows. "You stay here until we're finished."

Mila shrugged. A cell was a cell. This one didn't smell as bad as the one at the Justice Center.

Mila woke to darkness and silence, head aching, hands clutching reflexively at the blanket tangled around her waist as she tried to remember where she was. Amelia's apartment. Memory returned, borne on the feel of the cushions beneath her shoulders. She was asleep on the floor, on the silk-covered cushions that no one ever used. Mila sat up, pushing hair back from her sweaty face. A sibilant whisper of breathing was Señora Connor, asleep on the sofa. Neither of them had wanted to sleep in Amelia's bed.

The darkness pressed in around her, thick and heavy, as if the air-conditioning had failed. She could feel the blood pounding in her brain, as if her skull might burst any second. Unwinding the blanket from her legs, Mila got silently to her feet. She had never been here in the dark. Faint light seeped in through the fountain-court wall. It stretched the room into vast unexplored dimensions. Mila longed suddenly for her small, neat bedroom. It was crowded, the crummy tract house where she lived. But in the darkness, it was always familiar. Angelina's baby would cry and wake Roberto up. Guillermo would get home from his shift at the clinic, making the pipes bang as he ran water in the kitchen. He would leave it on too long, and Angelina would come out to scold him for using up their water ration. They were landmarks, those baby cries and hissing whispers. Landmarks of safety.

Safety was a chain. It could tether you to the barrio forever. Here, it could bind her to this red-haired woman. You had to take risks, or be the coyote trapped in its kennel. Mila took a deep breath and tiptoed into Amelia's bedroom. In the doorway, she hesitated. The bed was in shadow, and for a terrible moment she thought Amelia was there, that she would reach out and seize Mila's arm with her rat-feet fingers. But it was empty, the bed; sheeted and white. Mila sat down on the edge and reached for the VR mask on the table. There *was* a suicide note. Mila was sure of it, never mind what Señora Connor said. It was here, for her to find. And somewhere, the old *bruja* was laughing at her.

The mask covered her face like thick pliable skin, made her breathless with claustrophobia, even though it stopped at her lips. Amelia had worn this. It had soaked up the feel of her ancient skin. Mila shuddered violently as she smoothed it down around her neck. The lenses in the mask made the room appear distorted and strange, like looking through the bottom of a glass. In a reality parlor, you paid to put on skinthins that

covered your whole body, jumped up and down in some little room, while you pretended to be Spiderman or a ninja or an eagle. For all her money and custom-designed
VR fantasies, the old *bruja* had only bothered with a mask. No gloves, even.

Mila hesitated. I am afraid, she thought. I am afraid she is here, waiting for me in
the darkness; waiting to swallow me up. A small noise from the other room made her
jump. Señora Connor, who held all the cards and would take whatever Mila found. Mila
froze, hearing nothing but a hum of silence. "Log on," Mila said. Her voice sounded
high and breathy, and nothing happened. Coded for Amelia's voice only? Relieved in
spite of herself, Mila reached for the mask. Then she caught her breath as the lenses in
the mask blurred with sudden light and color.

The Net must have recognized the VR connect and started to run a file automatically. Mila clutched the edge of the bed as the light brightened. A beach. She was on a
beach of black sand with an endless blue horizon in front of her. Waves curled and broke
into white foam with a low roar, and seagulls shrieked overhead. Mila caught her breath.
It looked so *real*, but she felt the sheets beneath her palms. When she glanced down, she
had no body, saw nothing but the black sand beneath her and a tuft of tough-looking
grass that whipped in a wind she didn't feel—as if she was invisible, or a ghost.

Very strange.

A man and a child were running through the surf, laughing. His damp hair trailed
over his shoulders in red-gold tangles. The girl's hair was even redder than his. She
squealed with delight as the man caught her and tossed her into the air. A woman had
joined them. She was young too, like the man. Mila's age. They held hands, as in one of
those slick ads for the vacation packages that you couldn't really afford, but paid for
anyway, because it looked so damn good in VR.

Now they were walking across the black sand, walking toward Mila and laughing.
The man and the woman were looking at each other over the little girl's head. Sam had
looked at her like that. Before the anger and the Army. Mila swallowed, her throat tight.
They walked past her. Invisible observer, Mila watched them climb the low dune beyond the beach. They were picking up clothes and a cooler that would be full of food,
laughing and talking to each other about little things—about how the girl needed a nap
and maybe they would take a nap, too, only you could tell that it wasn't sleep they were
thinking about from the look in their eyes and the way they touched each other.

Mila raised a hand to her mouth, felt the soft thickness of the mask beneath her fingers. She recognized him now—the man in the holocube. Rebecca's father, the one man
Amelia had married. So the red-haired child was Rebecca Connor? Mila looked again
at the woman, at the line of cheek and jaw beneath the smooth young flesh. "Amelia,"
she whispered. As the trio disappeared over the crest of the dune, a gusty unfelt wind

———

whipped up a plume of sand. The sand twisted into a whirling column. Mila recoiled as it solidified and took on human shape.

"I've been waiting for you." Amelia leered at her, shriveled and pale in a blue bikini. "You are ambitious, child. I knew that you would come looking for your bonus. You're not one to wait politely to be handed a bone, are you?" Her grin widened. "Well, it's yours. Almost. Just tell me my name."

"Amelia," Mila said. She was moving. Mila stared down and discovered that she had a body now. It looked like her own body, brown skin marred by the birthmark on her hip. Sam would kiss that small spot when they made love—would bite it gently. She was walking toward Amelia. In a rush of panic, Mila tried to stop, but she was only wearing a mask and she had no control over her VR body. "Amelia," she cried. "Your name is Amelia Connor-Vanek."

Still grinning, Amelia reached for her.

"Exit!" Mila tore the mask from her face, blinking in the sudden darkness.

"What's going on? Light!" Connor stood in the doorway, eyes puffy with sleep. "I heard you yell," she said as the room lights brightened. "What were you doing?" Her eyes narrowed as she noticed the VR mask clutched in Mila's hand.

"I thought that the file might be here." Mila dropped the mask back onto the bed-side table. "I don't like VR. It scares me."

"I told you that the file isn't in her Netspace." Connor's tone was cold. "I checked. My mother never liked the Net." Her lip curled. "But she needed a good Net operator, so she made me into one. To serve her needs. I didn't hire you to check her VR files."

"You didn't hire me." Mila stood up. "You bought me, remember?" The file *was* in the virtual. The old *bruja* had said so. She must have fixed it, like she had fixed the reader—so that only Mila would summon her shriveled ghost. Mila shivered. "That was you," she said. "On the beach."

"You figured that out, did you?" Connor turned to stare down into the fountain court. "It was a vacation, on some island she rented. I'd forgotten about it," she said softly. "Lovers are a liability in this business. If they care about you, they make you too vulnerable. So you buy yourself ones who don't care, and if they're stupid enough to fall in love with you, you dump them. Your father died before you were born, but your DNA record makes you his. Is that why your mother named you Milagra? It means *miracle* in Spanish, doesn't it?"

"He had a heart attack. He smoked when he was younger, and it was on his medical record. So the ambulance wouldn't take him to the hospital. My mother didn't know she was pregnant when he died. She had to pay for the DNA match to prove I was his, or they would have cut our subsidy. Don't tell me that you're sorry, Anglo."

"No federal funds for illegitimate pregnancies. No federally funded treatment for self-induced illness." Connor turned slowly to face her. "Amelia divorced Aaron about a month after that vacation. She kept me, because she could turn me into something useful. Oh, she was generous. She gave him a lot of money. He used it to kill himself. Jet skiing. Hang gliding off Everest. High-altitude sky diving. It took him a couple of years. She didn't care. He didn't matter to her, and I only mattered because I was useful. What do you want from life, Milagra Aguilar? Tell me."

The soft light cast shadows beneath her cheeks, made her look old in spite of her smooth skin and bright hair. It had to have been a long time ago, that beach. If she ever gave up the cosmetic work and the fetal-cell implants, she'd look like Amelia.

"I do not want to be a coyote," Mila said softly. "I paid for the courses I took. I paid for them in full. I am going home now, because I do not want to sleep in this place. I will come back tomorrow to help you look for your treasure."

"That's the only VR file she had." Connor looked past Mila, as if she had forgotten that she was there. "What a crazy thing to keep."

Mila walked past her and out to the lift, heart beating fast enough to make her breathless. She knew where the file was, never mind what Señora Connor said about the VR. The treasure would be information. It would be valuable, and it would be hers. All she needed was the old *bruja's* name. A riddle. More of her little games. The lift doors whispered open. Mila thought that Señora Connor might try to stop her, but the apartment was silent. As if it was empty.

It wasn't empty. It was full of ghosts. Mila shivered and stepped quickly into the lift.

She went to Salgado.

He didn't live in the barrio, but out on the fringe of the suburbs in a large house that must have belonged to someone very rich, once. He was what Amelia had been, but on a smaller scale; a local *brujo*. In the old times, he would have sold charms against the evil eye, love potions, and cures for warts. Now he sold fake kids for the subsidy role, news of a job that was going to open up, and the name of the person to bribe for the interview. Salgado was small, but he would know the right connections. She needed Salgado. It didn't matter that it was the middle of the night. Salgado worked at night.

His guards let her in; young punks with braided hair who undressed her with their eyes—and would do it with their hands if Salgado threw her out. Head high, Mila shouldered past them. The house took her breath away. Outside, it was shabby, a sagging ruin in a landscape of dead shrubbery. Inside, walls and ceiling glowed with real wood. Soft yellow light made the grain shine like satin. White carpet covered the floor, and tall porcelain vases held fresh-cut flowers.

"I am very impressed, Señorita." Salgado bowed her formally onto a coral-colored sofa, dark eyes glittering with laughter. "You are out of jail. That is quite an achievement."

"I am." Mila smiled back coldly, unwilling to be charmed. He was like Señora Connor; sexy on the surface, but old underneath. His eyes calculated, always. "I have come to talk to you about a deal."

"What kind of deal?" The calculating eyes pinned her, shrewd and without warmth above his smile. "Your employer is dead. What do you have to offer me? Beyond your body, that is?"

Mila ignored his leer. "I am employed by her daughter. She believes that there is a file of very valuable information to be found. She has hired me to find it." Mila allowed herself a faint smile. "I have found it and she has not."

Salgado steepled his fingers and stared at the ceiling.

A waiting game. He knew who she worked for. It was his business to know. He wanted her to tell him, and then he would score points. Points mattered. Mila waited.

Salgado sighed at last, a concessionary sigh. "It is possible that information from that quarter might have value. If it is any good, I will give you something for it."

"If it is as good as I believe, I will want a lot," Mila said softly. They stared at each other silently for a long moment. "I will need to download it from a VR without anyone knowing."

Salgado smiled, but this time his smile was thoughtful, and he played gently with his perfect black hair. "I'll give you what you need," he said. "Come back to me if you get something, and we will discuss it."

All she needed was the name, the answer to the riddle. Her *entrada*. It was almost dawn. In the gray light the neighborhood looked pale and colorless, as if all life had drained away during the night. The dead trees and rusting cars had always been there, but in this cold light they made the streets look like a ghost town, as if everyone had died overnight. This street was mostly Bangladeshi, the last refugees admitted before the borders closed to everyone except rich Anglos. The flea market on the corner was as drab and lifeless as the rest of the street, all color gone from the woven rag mats that divided the empty lot into stalls.

A bent sexless figure was sweeping dust with a frayed broom. A bundle of cloth beside the cracked sidewalk was a woman. Dead or just sleeping? Mila hesitated, saw the gentle rise of the woman's chest. Sleeping, with her arm tucked around a knotted-string bag of onions. Waiting for the market to open.

Almost to the barrrio, almost home. Think of a name, think of the answer, the ticket inside, the *entrada*. Her headache was back, worse than ever. Mila sat down on the front steps of a tall house with arched windows and a circular driveway. The windows had been broken and mended with plastic. Black strands of electrified wire fenced in rows of carrots in the front yard. The adrenaline-rush of her find had faded, and fatigue made the muscles in her legs quiver.

Why did the old *bruja* do Rev and watch herself run on a long-ago beach? Mila blinked, eyes full of sand, too tired, almost, to think. She had spent hours dreaming. Every day. Mila had always assumed that she had a library of custom-designed diversions to play in.

But the beach had been the only VR. So her daughter had said. Crazy *bruja*. Crazy *vieja*. Movement caught Mila's eye—a shadow creeping along the house wall behind her. Danger? Awake in an instant, skin tingling with adrenaline, Mila stood. It wasn't stalking *her*. Mila almost slipped away—always the safe thing to do—but a thin hissing halted her. She knew the sound. An airbrush. She'd heard it too many times not to know it. Cautiously, Mila tiptoed closer to the house. No sign of life behind the sheeted windows. She edged around the corner, screened by the leafless skeletons of dead shrubbery.

It was a kid, thirteen maybe. He crouched in front of a bare stretch of wall, working on a picture. The hissing brush shaded in a human figure with sweeps of brown and gold.

Goose bumps rose on Mila's arms. He reminded her of Sam—the same hunched concentration, the same braid hanging forward over his shoulder. She must have made a sound because the kid looked up, eyes wide and darkly startled. "Wait," Mila said, but he was already running, back bent, scurrying across the dusty yard. He vaulted one-handed over a battered chain-link fence at the back of the property and vanished.

He didn't look at all like Sam. The picture would be good, though, when he finished it. Mila touched a painted straggle of black hair, stared at the smear of wet color on her fingertip. I do not think of Sam anymore, she thought, and felt a quick pain in her chest. A deal with Salgado—a *deal*, and not just a sale—would include his bed. They both knew it. There would be no place for Sam in her life, even if he wanted to be there, even if the Army didn't own him.

Love is a pretty type of loyalty, Señora Connor had said. *And loyalty is something that you sell for a very good price*. It was the truth, Mila thought bitterly. She was already thinking of how to use Salgado, how to learn the way into that invisible labyrinth that hid wealth and power at its center. Someone tweaked the striped sheet that curtained the house's front window, and Mila hurried on down the street.

A lover who cared about you was a liability. The *bruja's* daughter had said that too, in her bright, bitter voice. She had been right, and suddenly Mila knew why the old *bruja* watched her young self run down the beach over and over again with the man whose name she had kept, and their child.

Because she had loved him once, no matter what Señora Connor said. Because that time had been *hers*, not an item to be sold or traded, but a random moment that had no value to anyone except Amelia Connor-Vanek. Mila shook her head. The old *bruja* could have had her VR designer make that family see her, welcome her, forgive her—whatever she wanted. Rev would have made it *real.* But she had chosen to remain a ghost. An outsider forever, unseen and untouchable. To punish herself? To remind herself of what she had traded away? Or to remind herself of what she must be? *"Siempre solo,"* Mila whispered. "Alone."

I had faith in you, child.

Mila froze in the middle of the buckled sidewalk, skin going hot and cold in waves. The old *bruja's* voice. Inside her head! The street faded to a blur, overlaid by an image of the terminal screen in front of her, of meaningless words frozen still. Now, she remembered her terror as Amelia touched her, *caught!* Then the rat-feet fingers had stroked her throat, and she had felt the soft roughness of a drug patch before fear and surprise faded away to a dream of voices whispering, whispering in her ears. . . .

"What have you done to me?" Mila whispered, struggling with terror.

There are some very specialized hypnotropes available on tile drug market. Back in my early years, when I still operated in the flesh, I became quite skilled at implanting and blocking information. You can bury all kinds of things in the human brain—there is a lot of useful storage space there. When I am finished, you won't remember a thing, child. Until it's time.

Rebecca Connor had been right. Mila smothered hysterical laughter. The file wasn't in the VR. It had been in Mila's head all this time.

I told you I admired your honest dishonesty. I had a daughter once. Perhaps you find that hard to believe, but I did. I taught her everything that I knew, and I taught her too well. When she had learned everything I could give her, she walked away from me. She disdained me. I had entertained a dream that we would work together, that we would be the best. A youthful dream. In this business, you work best alone.

She is better than me.

It's funny. I thought about calling her the other day—just to speak to her again. It's too late for that. Never have children, Milagra Aguilar. You cannot afford to look behind you in this business, and children tether you to the past. They tempt you to look over your shoulder, to remember who you were and compare that person to yourself. Never look back. Keep your eyes on tomorrow, or you will turn into a pillar of salt. You will slow down, and the competition will take the world away from you. Remember that, child. So here is your bonus. Your gift. You will fig-ure out how to use it. You know where you want to go, and you are willing to pay what it costs to get there. I predict that you will go far. Nothing is certain in this world, but I have made you my heir. Because you are like me.

And now, I'm going to go lie down. I have quit this game, and there is salt in my veins. I don't plan to spend the rest of my life hiding from boredom, and I am tired of bribing Death. By the time you wake up, it will be too late for you to intervene.

Mila staggered as the street solidified around her, bright with morning sun. The old *bruja* had killed herself and left her suicide note in Mila's brain. Mila moaned with the pain in her head. A man shuffled past her, brown-skinned, with a wispy black beard, dressed all in white. He watched her nervously from the corner of his eyes, crowding the curb. Mila stared at him blankly.

Names, numbers, words without meaning, filled her brain. They pressed against the walls of her skull until she thought her head would explode. She had to record them, right now. She had to release them.

She ran all the way back to the house, burst through the door and past a startled An-gelina. Not on a terminal, not when Salgado knew about the file—she was still thinking clearly enough to know better than that. Guillermo had paper, because he wrote poetry after his shift some nights and he said that the Net killed poetry. Mila hammered on his door until he woke. Angelina was babbling questions at her, clutching at her arm, but the words had no meaning, were lost in the jumble of syllables / numbers / names that filled her pounding head. Mila shook her off, snatched the dog-eared pad from the surprised and bleary Guillermo, and fled to her room, slamming the door in Angelina's face.

She wrote all morning. Sitting cross-legged on the bed, hunched over the pad, she filled page after page with her clumsy script. The words, dates, numbers, came to her one after another, without meaning, without control. As she wrote each one down, it vanished from her mind, popping like a soap bubble. She, Mila, watched from a small corner of her mind as her fingers scurried across the page. She had no control over them. She was merely a vehicle for the old *bruja's* ghost, the skin of her hands a glove for those rat-feet fingers. How many times had the old *bruja* crept up behind her as she studied, with her drugs and her whispers?

Sometime in the afternoon, the words ran out. Mila dropped the pen onto the bed and straightened her fingers. An angry red groove marked the side of her finger where she had clutched the pen, and she smothered a cry as her hand cramped viciously. Her body ached, as if it had taken the effort of every muscle to get those words down onto the paper. One by one, she picked up the sheets, numbering them carefully. She recognized some of the names. They were on the NewsNet; politicians, and corporate names that *everyone* knew. Vilchek-Wasabe. EuroSynco. Sony-Matohito. The connections would be in the dates and account codes. In time, she would understand them. Mila folded the pages neatly. This was a ball of platinum string that she and Salgado could unravel for a long time. Each new thread would lead to others, would lead her deeper into the labyrinth of the old *bruja's* world. This was, indeed, a treasure. This was her *entrada*.

She sat on the bed in the afternoon heat, pages in her hand, remembering black sand and a young woman laughing. In her mind, she heard the echo of Amelia's whispering. It made her feel unclean, as if those rat-feet fingers had groped across her soul. *You are like me*, the old *bruja* had said. Mila shuddered, folded the sheets of paper, and shoved them into her pocket.

Rebecca was asleep on the sofa when Mila let herself into the apartment. Her eyelids fluttered and she made a small sound in her sleep, like a sob. Like Amelia, dreaming of her lost beach. For a moment, Mila stood silent, looking down at her, then she bent and touched her shoulder lightly. Rebecca's eyes flew open, and she stood up in one swift motion.

"You came back." She thrust her fingers through her hair. "I didn't expect you to come back. You had the file when you left, didn't you?"

Mila nodded.

"I am not as good as my mother," Rebecca said with quiet bitterness. She looked out at the treetops beyond the interior wall. "She despised me for that—for being less than she was. That's why I finally split."

"She said you were better than she ever was."

"Ha." Rebecca's lip twitched. "So what do you want for it?"

"Everything in this life is a trade, is it not?" Mila pulled the folded sheets of paper from beneath her shirt and handed them to Rebecca. "This is the only copy," she said.

Rebecca took them without a word, her eyes on Mila's face.

"I will not trade," Mila said softly. "But I will ask you for two favors. I do not want to go back to jail. You said you can do that. And I want Samuel Lujan discharged from the Army. I will give you his ID number."

Still silent, Rebecca turned the crumpled pages one by one. Finally, she looked up. Her face was a mask of stillness. The green eyes were ice, but there were shadows in their depths. "You know what you have in this file." Her voice was cold. "You are too bright not to know, too bright not to guess how much you could get for it, from me or elsewhere. Why did you give this to me, Mila?" She waited one heartbeat. Two. "There are people I can hire to dig the truth out of you."

Mila felt goose bumps rise at the cold promise in this woman's tone. She could not trade, she could not sell this file. If she did, part of her soul would go with it, tangled in that ball of platinum string. It would consume her, as it had consumed this woman and her mother. It would own her in a way that Amelia Connor-Vanek never had. She would spend her life following that string, until she became a shriveled gray husk in a golden kennel. It still tempted her; that *entrada*, that ticket *out* and *up*, her entrance into) the world of the towers. *You are like me*, Amelia Connor-Vanek had said, and it was true. Part of her longed to snatch those crumpled pages back from Rebecca, to run headlong into that labyrinth and find the center.

"It is not mine." With an effort, she met Rebecca's sea-ice stare. "Your mother meant this file for you, not for me. I do not want it. What matters to you?" she asked softly. "What is important to *you*, Señora Connor?"

"To be the best." Rebecca's eyes flickered. "But Amelia will never know, will she? I believe you." Her shoulders lifted slightly, as if she had sighed. "My mother would laugh, but I do. Keeping you out of jail is no problem, but it will take a little finesse to get your license reinstated."

"And Sam?"

"Your boyfriend." Rebecca stuffed the folded paper into the pocket of her tunic. "He can reenlist, you know. Unless you want me to stick him with a dishonorable?"

The city had painted out the Little Cambodia mural. She had seen the gray blotch of new paint from the rail. If she had opened that kennel, so many years ago, would the coyote have bolted? Perhaps. Perhaps not—if there was nowhere else to go. She had not opened it. "If he wants to reenlist, it is his choice," Mila whispered. "I will not come back here again."

"I was right about one thing." Rebecca's voice halted Mila in the doorway. "There was no suicide note."

Mila turned slowly. Was there a shadow of the coyote's stare in those ice-green eyes, too? What did Amelia's death mean to this woman? Would she blame herself, or would she see her own future in that empty bed? "There was no note," Mila said softly. "*La Señora* would never kill herself. It was an accident—a bad batch of the drug."

She went into the anteroom to wait for the lift. Some things you could not trade. Some things you had to give away. The lift whispered open to take her down and out of this tower world. Not forever. She would find her *entrada*. She would come back. Someday.

"Milagra?" Rebecca stood in the anteroom doorway. "I have this place in Antarctica. Near McMurdo, in the U.S. reservation. The very big fish in this little global pond of ours live there. They pay their employees exorbitantly well. You should be able to pay for the rest of your degree with what you make." She pulled a small card from her pocket. "You have enough money to get there. I paid you for your time." She tossed the card to Mila.

Mila caught it. A key-card, with an address on it. She turned it over in her palm, mouth open to say no, wanting no obligations, no ties to this woman and her world.

"I wish," Rebecca said quietly, "that I had tried to forgive my mother."

She knew. Mila curled her fingers around the hard edges of the card, suddenly and intensely sorry for this woman. *Siempre solo.* Some things, perhaps, you had to accept as gifts.

"*Gracias*," she said softly.

8

A CYBERROOM OF ONE'S OWN

Sarah Stein

When asked in 1929 to address two women's colleges on women and the arts, Virginia Woolf (1957) noted the lamentably few published women writers in history and took her listeners on a discursive—and circuitous—exploration of this absence. She came to the conclusion that it was a function of a patriarchal societal structure that excluded women from the financial means and the physical and mental space—a "room of one's own"—needed for creative production.

With a new century's beginning and with sweeping changes in communication networks, women still suffer under similar conditions. Women have gained legal control of their own money, and greater numbers than could have been imagined in 1929 now work outside the home. But they continue to work inside the home when they finish their paid jobs, and women still earn far less and occupy far lower status in every field dominated by men.

With many of the old obstacles still resonant, new challenges have been brought by digital culture. The growing ubiquity of communication technologies, connecting people at vast distances with remarkable speed through a wide range of modalities, are also colonizing ever greater parts of daily life. In our evolving information society, the sheer volume of information takes on an increasingly frantic and deafening quality. Silence—essential to the germination of any creative expression—has become harder to achieve. Time and space are needed to give room to the sinking down into the material at hand, and to the rising up of insight and imaginative urges. How can we find that room for reflection, for listening, inwardly and outwardly?

To Woolf's call for a room of one's own, I would add another. But what should such a space be named? Room to breathe, deeply? Room to sink down into the embodiedness of everyday life? That checking back in through awareness of the breath into stillness, is, in my experience, crucial to the creative process, whether that is writing or any other production. In this brief rumination, I relate two interactions with technology that touch on the lived experience in these early days of a computer-mediated world. In doing so, my focus is on the question of women's creativity and what is needed for its health and well-being, from the point of view of a woman filmmaker and academic in America at the beginning of a new century.

It was at a small academic conference that I first began focusing on certain assumptions behind the celebratory claims made for simultaneous communication channels. The conference topic was on narrative and virtuality with a strong literary theorist flavor, and the invitation to explore the university's new media lab was appealing if only to walk outside to another building.

We were led to terminals in a computer lab and instructed in logging on to a MOO. I was eager, having read a lot about such virtual environments. The notion of the textual evocation of space was particularly intriguing; it had seemed an opportunity for imaginative and literary expression to blossom. I had one prior experience with a MOO in the course of an online seminar. It had not gone well: the commands and the online instructions were baffling, and I failed to "meet" the people who had arranged to log on at the same time. I considered it a problem of technical literacy and was anticipating a very different journey, given the physical presence of a seasoned MOO traveler as a guide.

Logged on, we were assigned names for our avatars; I was Melon. Then came a lesson in the curious third-person functionality of these sites: "Melon waves hello." The world of this MOO was entirely constructed by textual description; thus, physical gestures and visual images had to be conveyed by words alone.

Our leader in this venture was a faculty participant in the conference. His enthusiasm for the medium was contagious. He promised a stimulating experience, one marked by the heady pleasures of simultaneous, scintillating threads of conversation, as many as people wished to engage in. He started us off with a dense lead-in: Ilya Prigorgine, Deleuze, hypertext theory.

I was still floundering with "Melon nods in agreement" by the time the conversation seemed to have come unglued. Our leader, still engaged with his theorists' take on virtual narrative, was to all appearances engaged in a collective monologue. Much of the other strands of conversation were devoted to the recitation of several drunken revels that had taken place the night before. The delay due to typing speed and transmission backups meant responses to the theory thread emerged often separated by three or four exchanges about who had downed more shots. Not quite the thrill of intellectual exchange I'd anticipated. Another participant sent some instructions on moving to a different cyberlocation, a yacht site where others had logged on. But the textual evocation of the yacht was uninspired and read like a prime-time soap opera: "The moon shines bright on the water off the side of the deck. The tinkle of champagne glasses mingles with the mellow sounds of a jazz trio, and the muffled call of seagulls." I moved back to the first "room," where Prigorgine seemed to be in danger of drowning in virtual beer, and I quit.

Back in our conference room, my MOO colleague held forth. "Eight threads of conversation!" he cried. "What a thrill, to be able to jump from one discussion to another, and to juggle them all simultaneously."

The word *juggle* clicked for me. The unappealing nature of the MOO world was less, because of the banalities that founded it, than a splendidly opposed set of desires. My days are spent attempting to meet apparently insatiable demands of a professional, domestic, and personal nature. They fragment my attention and leave me drained. Juggling is all I do. Teaching, advising, writing, committee work, childcare, housework, domestic arrangements, social network maintenance, caring for aging parents—to name just a few multitasking acts of my distributed subjectivities. To me, a thrilling, scintillating time is to be given the chance to do just one thing.

I don't know if this is a gendered perspective. I do know that the MOO enthusiast had few of the roles I perform. To him, fractured attention was a novelty. To me, it was commonplace. For him, participation in the MOO felt like an expansion of his intellectual powers, a test of his capacity to track multiple cognitive strands simultaneously. To me, it was a repeat of the usual order of things, a grind I had happily left behind for the two days of the conference.

Significantly, the conference mentioned above and most academic conferences in this country each year take place in the flesh, in a dedicated space. Huge numbers of people travel to them, often at substantial cost to themselves. They relish the experience of being away from the daily demands on their bodies and minds, and they value the time and location devoted just to the business—whether social or intellectual—at hand. They also prefer the multiple dimensions of communicating in the body with other bodies in proximate space at these events. At an intensive workshop held on our campus for a teaching, learning, and technology system-wide roundtable, no attendees took us up on the offer to attend via video conferencing, despite the four-hour travel time for some participants and despite the subject of the gathering, online distance education.

My MOO experience has left me pondering, amid the trumpeting of the great gains computer-mediated communication is bringing to our individual and societal lives, the space available in which to be generative. What is fertile ground for contemplation, for insight, for deciphering, for awareness? These musings were fueled by a remark made later in the day by another participant. Wealth in the future, he said, will be measured to the degree to which you can be unplugged. That struck a chord, though in part what the statement evoked for me was likely quite different from what it meant to the speaker.

For me there arose images of the legions of women—secretaries and assistants—who would make that unplugged status possible, as they read and responded to the barrage of e-mail messages and faxes, as they linked through the URLs, and as they culled and condensed the endless flood of new data.

This is of course not an activity new to an information society. These are the same ranks of women who have been making a sacred space of the inner office since they joined the work force at the turn of the century, and who often perform the same function in the home, dexterously steering children and intrusive telephone callers away from the doors of a home office or den.[1]

Behind all this shepherding and buffering activity by women on behalf of men's work, particularly that of white middle- and upper-class males, is some notion of dedicated space. Creativity and productivity require concentration and focus—thus, few distractions and interruptions.

Women still carry 80 percent of the domestic responsibilities when they work outside the home. Online distance education promoters often cite the mother at home, unable to leave small children for the traditional classroom. A recent *Chronicle of Higher Education* story featured a cover image of a woman seated at a computer attending to her young child's request for attention; the caption read, "A student at North Lake College juggles distance education and child care" (Carr 2000). The story detailed the problems of retaining online students. Curiously, it did not remark further on what the cover picture so vividly communicated: Women distance education students have special problems related to their roles as domestic caretakers. A space dedicated to learning—such as a traditional classroom or a library—can seem in contrast a rare privilege, a luxury of space and time relegated to doing just one thing. *In the future, the poor will have computers and the rich will have teachers.*

Information overload is present and accelerating. In many ways the deluge of ubiquitous communication—anytime, anywhere—coupled with the implicit demand to do more in less time and at the same time, seems to mirror the rhythm of many women's lives. As documented by Ruth Schwartz Cowan (1983), among others, the revolution in domestic technologies in the first half of the twentieth century never brought the leisure time promised by the commercial forces targeting women. Instead, the bar was raised on the standards of hygiene as each new machine was incorporated into the home, and women's workdays lengthened rather than shortened. In a parallel fashion, as computing functions become increasingly mobile, one of the most far-reaching consequences appears to be that ever more work is expected throughout ever more hours of the day.

For creativity to flourish, there needs to be time carved out of the flow and there needs to be stillness. Walter Benjamin ([1936] 1968) remarked on the germinative power of *boredom* in the creative process: "Boredom is the dream bird that hatches the egg of experience. A rustling in the leaves drives him away. His nesting places—the activities that are intimately associated with boredom—are already extinct in the cities and are declining in the country as well. With this the gift for listening is lost and community of listeners disappears" (91). Benjamin's prescription for the nurturance of storytelling echoes in the meditation practices many spiritual paths advocate to still what the Buddhists refer to as the "drunken monkey mind," the internal chatter so terribly difficult to bring under control. These practices aim at the gradual cessation of inner noise, to allow in the inner silence the ability to hear what surrounds us and is within.

The Internet currently bears some resemblance to the drunken monkey mind—a never-ceasing, never-exhausted stream of chatter, at times informative, less frequently a conduit for knowledge. The economic imperatives driving much of the technological development are strengthened by the exponential growth of the noise. The ad banners proliferate and, similar to television, users skim past the escalating clutter of the new media landscape, so accustomed as we are to the constancy of impersonally produced personal address.

If, as I am suggesting, there needs to be another kind of room for women's productive and creative relationship to old and new media, where can we look for pointers? What is needed as the Internet and our use of it matures, to support, for instance, the nuance and suggestiveness Woolf found in the writing of women and not elsewhere?

In edging toward some possibilities, I turn to another technology, motion picture editing systems, in both their old and their new incarnations. Several principles involved with this artistic form may hold some clues as to where development in communication technologies needs to focus.

In the early days of editing, film was threaded onto an upright Movieola, a compact machine that looked something like a robot. There was a feed and a takeup arm for both picture and sound. The film advanced through the gate, projecting the image into a small monitor, and the soundtrack was pulled across an audio head, feeding into a small speaker. A foot pedal, similar to that on a sewing machine, ran the motor. There was an automatic switch to run the sound and picture together or separately, but when you were making cuts, you only used the foot pedal.

My first experience as a film editor was on this machine. I had been given a silent sequence to edit and was equally thrilled and terrified. How to create a dramatic order of these random shots, with no narration or script to structure it, nor music track to pace it? Worse, how to decide *where* to mark the cut in or out? How long should each shot last—and on what basis would I know?

I was rescued from near panic by the machine itself. I discovered that the motor pulsed. If I listened carefully while watching the silent image flow by, it gave me the perfect cut point each time—beat, beat, beat, cut. Shot after shot worked this way, one moving rhythmically into the next. The narrative logic of the footage revealed itself to me, and the scene came into sharp focus.

This happened many years ago—more than thirty now. So I can't say whether it was on day three or four of this magical symbiosis, this perfect dialogue that had opened itself between me and the machine, that I became aware of the connection between the pulse of the motor and my foot. The motor ran when my foot trod on the foot pedal. Beat, beat, beat, cut. Press, press, press, lift. I was alternately pressing my foot harder and softer on the pedal. When I saw the cut points, I lifted my foot. My body generated the rhythm of the cuts, bypassing the mind's attempts to figure them out based on principles that could be translated into words and formulas.

The question of how I could have missed so obvious a connectedness gets us to epistemology. How do we know what we know? Cultural constructions of masculine subjectivity have long held hostage the realm of the mind, identifying feminine subjectivity with embodiment, the material realm. Debased together, the feminine and the body/earth are assigned the arcane, the night, those human functions not subject to the light of cognition, nor to formula-revealing keyword searches. The movement and rhythm of film, the plastic visual arts set in motion, are based on human sensory-perceptual responses. Breath, blood flow, heartbeat—the intelligence of the body and the tempo of film, twenty-four frames a second. No masculinized notion of the transcendent mind here—the film must "work," in large part, based on a rhythm that is experienced viscerally.

From the upright Movieola, I went to flatbed editing, where the film is wound onto plastic cores that lay on their sides on metal plates. On this machine I had a lever that, when pushed to the right, would pull the film forward; to the left, backward. I transferred my pulsing rhythm from my foot to my hand, and once again would beat out the tempo of the cuts.

When I teach editing nowadays, I teach only on computerized nonlinear editing systems. The film or video footage is digitized into electronic bits, and all the editing takes place through a keyboard. The screen is the same as a computer monitor and the same distance away. Digital editing lends extraordinary advantages to the cutting process, allowing instant special effects, all the retrieval power of a high-speed microprocessor, and endless duplications with no loss of quality.

But there are problems that arise with digital editing that were not present with earlier systems. The keyboard stroke is of a different order of tactile connection than the foot pedal or hand lever. One can mark the cuts but without the rhythmic pulsing accompaniment. With film editing, the smallest picture unit you could cut was a frame, one twenty-fourth of a second long. Those of us with long experience could sense when a cut was too long even by that amount and improve it. Now, nonlinear systems allow cutting inside the frame, deleting or transforming the equivalent of slivers of image or sound. In addition, the editor is seated much closer to the image than on the flatbed editing system, thus diminishing the perceptual—and metaphoric—distance so critical to constructing a film.

We have been given machines that operate in nanoseconds, but those responses dependent on the human body move at a slower pace. The upshot of this is that much cutting on digital systems is so tight as to be airless. When viewed later one finds there are no breathing spaces, just a relentless, fast-paced forward thrust. Those who have edited feature films for theatrical release on nonlinear systems often conform the actual 35mm film print to the digital version and project it to get a realistic sense of the editing pace. In many cases, they must add back to the end of shots extra frames that feel like dead space on the computerized systems.[2]

All of which brings us back to the physical body. Issues of disembodiment, of what constitutes a "real" versus a "virtual" body, with debates about the viability of binary categories such as real and virtual, will occupy some of us as we move further into digitization and virtualization. As Kate Hayles warns in "Embodied Virtuality: Or How to Put Bodies Back in the Picture": "The virtual body partakes of both of the ephemerality of information and the solidity of physicality or, depending on one's viewpoint, the solidity of information and the ephemerality of flesh. I believe that those who nostalgically try to deny the importance of information in understanding the virtual body are as misguided as those who . . . try to reduce the body only to information. Either position misses the complexities of the crossings and interpenetrations that constitute the virtual body at this cultural moment" (1996, 12). But nevertheless, the human body will remain the canvas onto which image, text, form and sound are projected. The body breathes in and breathes out, the heart pumps, all at a tempo not subject to the breakneck pace of computer speed or Internet time.

Moore's Law states that computer power (and therefore speed) doubles every eighteen months. There is no equivalent to Moore's Law at work in the human body. We view and process moving images more quickly than we used to, especially with the advent of MTV and the ten-to-fifteen-second commercial time slot. But these wash over the human perceptual framework like water, impressionistic, pure sensation, not intended to touch at depth or invoke sustained thought (indeed, as with commercials, the opposite is desired).

There are two movements that I can identify as particular to the process of editing film. One is a sinking *down and inward*, what I think of as immersion in the material to be worked with. With film footage, that involves screening it over and over many times, until it has penetrated the memory and the senses. Out of that immersion new associations and juxtapositions arise. This process gives weight to the intuitive, the imaginative, that which sidesteps conscious, verbal expression.

The second movement is the first's opposite. It requires a perceptual stepping back from the worked material, one that translates best into an *actual* distancing from what is being shaped. When teaching, I instruct my production students to get up from the chair in front of the monitor and stand at the back of the room. Sitting at a computer monitor is too close. There is a need for a view of the whole picture—metaphorically, in film parlance, the extreme wide shot or establishing shot. The structure has to be made visible, and this distance is critical. One must move back and forth between these two poles of immersion and detachment or the full potentiality of the footage cannot be realized.

Many artists—female and male alike—have spoken of the need to enter into a dialogue with the medium with which they are working. This receptive stance—culturally ascribed to the feminine—is crucial. It realizes the aspect of communion at the root of communication. Before and throughout the process of manipulating any medium, there needs to be recognition of this dialogic, communicative give-and-take; it brings balance to what is popularly perceived as imposing one's mind and will on the material in any creative production.

From all of these experiences I draw out a couple of implications that may serve to orient journeys further into the production of art in the culture of cyberspace. The foremost of these is the presence of the physical body. Far from the status of meat accorded it by the early (and primarily male) cyberpunk writers, it provides a navigational anchor that can continue to guide us in making and responding to new forms of cyberart.

With that, I look to women to become more involved in developing new communication modalities for digital forms. Virtual spaces promise something akin to the immersion I spoke of earlier; Brenda Laurel's work in Banff, *Placeholder*, created smart critter avatars in virtual reality as an attempt to explore the immersive rather than spectator position of users.[3]

Hypertext, with its alinear, decentered, polyvocal, relational, and mutable qualities often identified by traditional masculine regimes with feminine subjectivity, has been both hailed and challenged as a subversive form able to undermine and destabilize traditional narrative's authoritative claims (Page 1996; Greco 1996; Palatella 1995). One of the most interesting of these is Shelley Jackson's (1995) *Patchwork Girl by Mary/Shelley and Herself.* In it, Jackson stitches together fragments to create a monstrous female body—a Frankensteinian construction—in ways not so dissimilar to the act of film editing, with its intersections and juxtapositions that yield something otherwise inexpressible. What I find most interestingly related to filmmaking is a remark by Jackson (quoted in Hayles 2000), in which she reflects on the status of the female body in relation to writing: "'The banished body is not female, necessarily, but it is feminine,' Jackson remarks in 'Stitch Bitch.' 'That is, it is amorphous, indirect, impure, diffuse, multiple, evasive. So is what we learned to call bad writing. Good writing is direct, effective, clean as a bleached bone. Bad writing is all flesh, and dirty flesh at that. . . . Hypertext is everything that for centuries has been damned by its association with the feminine'" (534). Structuring a film through editing—both fictional and nonfictional—is essentially a form of "writing" the film. And a significant difference between film and digital images is that film is dirty. Those of us who grew up consuming media for much of the twentieth century have been conditioned to judge the authenticity of images based on the look of film. The sensitivity of film stock enables it to re-present the textures and blemishes of material reality; the cinematic look has in turn informed what we have come to judge as authentic. In addition, we view film prints that are scratched, particles of dust adhering to the surface of the celluloid, and we see past them, accustomed as we are to looking through eyes that have minute motes dancing in the air in front of us. Electronic media—video and digital—are much too *clean*—sterile, really—to look "real." Perhaps this points to a direction we need to explore further, the "dirty flesh" of the feminine arts, and what form and manner in which to birth them in the digitized arena.

Hardware developments are needed as well: something akin to the foot pedal or hand lever that allows the breath and the heartbeat to intermingle with computer generation. Equally, recognition of the deafening effect of the onslaught of information is needed. It does indeed "inform" our sensibilities and warrants a discernment that honors the other side of our natures—that which needs silence and breathing space for germinative power.

Notes

1. For a historical perspective on women's entry into the corporate work force via the typewriter, see Davies 1988; and on women and the telephone, see Rakow 1988. Also of interest is Gray 1992 on the gendering of television watching and control of the VCR, especially as it relates to the need expressed by her female subjects to perform domestic tasks while watching television.

2. The speed with which edits can be made and special effects rendered has also resulted in greatly reduced editing time allotted in budgets (Ansen and Sawhill 1996). This

curtails the process of engagement with the film footage and diminishes the "dialogic" encounters with the material being shaped.

3. An anthology edited by Mary Anne Moser and Douglas MacLeod (1996) includes several essays on artistic forays into the virtual that seek, like Laurel's *Placeholder*, to integrate the body both as cultural construction and as lived experience in material form.

Works Cited

Ansen, D., and R. Sawhill. The new jump cut. *Newsweek* (September 2, 1996), 64–66.

Benjamin, W. The storyteller. In *Illuminations*, trans. H. Arendt, 83–109. New York: Schocken Books, [1936] 1968.

Carr, S. As distance education comes of age, the challenge is keeping the students. *The Chronicle of Higher Education* 46, no. 23 (February 11, 2000): A39–41.

Cowan, R. S. *More Work for Mother.* New York: Basic Books, 1983.

Davies, M. W. Women clerical workers and the typewriter: The writing machine. In *Technology and Women's Voices: Keeping in Touch*, ed. C. Kramarae, 29–40. London and New York: Routledge and Kegan Paul, 1988.

Gray, A. *Video Playtime: The Gendering of a Leisure Technology.* London and New York: Routledge, 1992.

Greco, D. Hypertext with consequences: Recovering a politics of hypertext. In *Hypertext '96: The Seventh ACM Conference on Hypertext*, 85–92. New York: ACM, 1996.

Hayles, N. K. Embodied virtuality: Or how to put bodies back in the picture. In *Immersed in Technology: Art and Virtual Environment*, ed. M. A. Moser and D. Macleod, 1–28. Cambridge, MA: MIT Press, 1996.

Hayles, N. K. Flickering connectivities in Shelley Jackson's *Patchwork Girl:* The importance of media-specific analysis. *Postmodern Culture* 10, no. 2 (2000): 13. Available at <http://jefferson.village.virginia.edu/ pmc /current.issue/10.2hayles.html>.

Jackson, S. *Patchwork Girl by Mary/Shelley and Herself.* Watertown, MA: Eastgate Systems, Electronic, 1995. Available at <http://www.eastgate.com>.

Moser, M. A, and D. MacLeod, eds. *Immersed in Technology: Art and Virtual Environments.* Cambridge, MA: MIT Press, 1996.

Page, B. Women writers and the restive text: Feminism, experimental writing and hypertext. *Postmodern Culture* 6, no. 2 (January 1996). Available at <http://www.iath.virginia.edu/ pmc /text-only/ issue.196/>.

Palattella, J. Formatting patrimony: The rhetoric of hypertext. *Afterimage* (August 1995).

Rakow, L. P. Women and the telelphone: The gendering of a communications technology. In *Technology and Women's Voices: Keeping in Touch*, ed. C. Kramarae, 207–228. London and New York: Routledge and Kegan Paul, 1988.

Woolf, Virginia. *A Room of One's Own.* San Diego: Harcourt, Brace, Jovanovich, [1929] 1957.

9

THE ETHICAL DIMENSION OF CYBERFEMINISM

Alison Adam

The term "cyberfeminism" captured the mood of the moment for many women in the mid-1990s who were discovering the enrichment and empowerment that advanced communications and information technologies promised. The term seems to have sprung up simultaneously in several parts of the world, notably with VNS Matrix[1] in Australia and with Sadie Plant's[2] writing in the United Kingdom. Yet even from its birth, cyberfeminism seems to have been something of a problem child. This chapter identifies and explores those problems and goes on to question the continuing relevance of cyberfeminism in the twenty-first century. I conclude that only if the political and especially the ethical dimensions are thoroughly interwoven into cyberfeminism's somewhat hesitant theoretical roots can it deliver its early promise.

Cyberculture

If, as I claim, cyberfeminism has proved a somewhat unruly child, then perhaps we need to look to its parents to understand its roots.

One parent is *cyberculture*, the term used to describe the explosion of interest in cultures developing around virtual reality (VR), the Internet, and artificial intelligence (AI) and artificial life (the modeling of populations using digital technology)—much of which speaks in a markedly futuristic voice. Few cultural commentators can fail to marvel at the extraordinary efflorescence of cyberculture—a burgeoning interest in the social sciences has quickly spawned a number of anthologies.[3] Cyberculture has a number of interesting features, not least of all its relationship to feminism.

First of all, in its popular form it is a youth culture. At first sight it appears to go against the grain of a more general worldview that is skeptical about the progress of science and technology. The "anti-science" view came to prominence in the 1960s with worries over nuclear power and warfare, and it lives on in various guises in concerns over animal testing, ecological destruction, cloning and genetic testing, genetically modified foods, and so on. If not exactly "anti-science" today, one can at least characterize this broad sweep of viewpoints as critical of technoscience and strongly aware of political and ethical concerns. Whether or not one agrees with a particular position, remembering that some activities such as destroying genetically modified crops may lie outside the law, there is no doubt that politics and ethics are overwhelmingly the drivers of this movement. One should also note that although it might be difficult to argue that this movement cuts across class barriers, it certainly appeals to a wide range of ages and to both genders.

Cyberculture presents an interesting contrast in its appeal to youth, particularly young men. Clearly it engages their interest in the technical gadgetry of computer technology, and in this it has been strongly influenced by the cyberpunk genre of science fiction, which although offering a distinctly dystopian vision of the future, at least offers alternative heroes in the form of the macho "console cowboys." To "jack in" to "cyberspace" appears to offer a way of transcending the mere "meat" of the body, signaling a male retreat from bodies and places where bodies exist.

Jacking in, cyberspace, meat are metonymic cyberpunk terms that have entered the lexicography of cyberculture, many of them from William Gibson's *Neuromancer,* the first cyberpunk novel.[4] In *Neuromancer,* the hero, Case, logs onto or jacks into cyberspace through a special socket implanted in his brain. Cyberspace is a shared virtual reality, a "consensual hallucination" where the body that one chooses to enter into within cyberspace has bodily sensations and can travel in the virtual reality. Meat-free, but sinister artificial intelligences inhabit cyberspace, having finally downloaded themselves and having left their obsolete, merely meat, bodies behind. But these images are a far cry from contemporary cyberspace and the current mundanities of logging onto a computer, of experiencing the Internet, often rather slowly, through the interface of screen and keyboard.

A Meat-Free Existence

It is interesting to note the contrast between the bodily involvement of anti-science protesters in their protest and the shunning of the somatic by cyberculture's console cowboys. Physical protest and demonstration has long been the tactic of those opposing nuclear weaponry. Genetically modified crops are destroyed by organized groups of protesters; some animal rights protesters have even died for their cause. Contrast this with the way that cyberculture's aficionados often appear to have forgotten that they have bodies at all. However, the ultimate inevitability of one's "meat" is demonstrated by Stone's observation: "The discourse of visionary virtual world builders is rife with images of imaginal bodies freed from the constraints that flesh imposes. Cyberspace developers foresee a time when they will be able to forget about the body. But it is important to remember that virtual community originates in, and must return to the physical. No refigured virtual body, no matter how beautiful, will slow the death of a cyberpunk with AIDS. Even in the age of the technosocial subject, life is lived through bodies."[5]

One wonders what sort of bodies virtual-reality developers will have in store for us. For instance, Thalmann and Thalmann[6] picture a perfect, blond, red-lipped Marilyn Monroe lookalike seemingly without irony. And writing as a prominent mainstream AI roboticist, apparently quite separately from and rather earlier than cybercultural influences, Hans Moravec has proposed the idea of *Mind Children*.[7] Moravec's opinions belong more to the realm of the science-fiction writers than to hard-nosed engineering based roboticists, for he envisions a "postbiological" world where the human race has been swept away by its artificial children, the robots. Our DNA, he suggests, will find itself out of a job when the machines take over, robots with human intelligence will be common within fifty years.

There are at least two important issues at stake in projecting this curiously meat-free existence. The first concerns birth. Moravec sees his robots as his progeny and this has strong parallels with Stefan Helmreich's[8] research on an artificial life (A-life) laboratory where the scientists involved were strongly motivated by metaphors of birth. Feminists might question *why* they feel the need to have artificial or robot children. But if the roboticists are not creating weapons of destruction, like all parents they may not be able to control the actions of their offspring. Sue Jansen[9] has pointed to the way in which several AI scientists express their dream of creating their own robots, of "becoming father of oneself."[10]

Helmreich argues that A-life researchers take this view one step further in their creations of "worlds" or "universes." He asked a researcher how he felt in building his simulations. The reply was, "I feel like God. In fact I am God to the universes I create."[11]

The options then are (1) to create an artificial world and become God, (2) to download the mind into a robot, or (3) to enter the realm of pure intellect in cyberspace. All these views involve both the assumption that it is possible to leave the body behind and the masculinist desire to transcend the body. This, of course, leads to the idea of escape.

Cyberspace as Escape

The idea of transcendence and escape is important in the rhetoric of cyberculture. Indeed some authors[12] suggest that therein lies cyberculture's appeal as a means of producing new forms of expression, new psychic experiences that transcend mundane uses of technology, in a fusion of technology and art with cyberspace as the medium of this transformation. This offers an alternative to drug culture where virtual reality and re-lated information technologies offer a seemingly endless supply of new experiences but without the toxic risks of drugs. Ralph Schroeder[13] analyzes the tension between the technical problems that have yet to be solved and the worldview of human wish fulfill-ment that has been projected onto the technology. In popular form probably the most available form of cyberculture is the cyberpunk nightclub and cybercafe, which spring up in the middle of U.K. and U.S. cities. In addition, a number of North American mag-azines or fanzines (zines, for short) proclaim themselves the denizens of cybercultures. In upholding the traditionally macho values of cyberpunk, they are unlikely to find a mass audience among feminists. Anne Balsamo[14] sums up their style: "Interspersed throughout the pages of *Mondo 2000* and conference announcements, a tension of sorts emerges in the attempt to discursively negotiate a corporate commodity system while upholding oppositional notions of countercultural iconoclasm, individual genius, and artistic creativity. The result is the formation of a postmodern schizo-culture that is unselfconsciously elitist and often disingenuous in offering its hacker's version of the American dream."

Cyberculture for Feminists

It seems unlikely that the cyberpunk version of cyberculture, in its masculine attempts to transcend the "meat," holds much appeal for women and especially for feminists, par-ticularly as feminist analysis has gained so much momentum in recent years, in so many areas—not least of all within science and technology. The problem is that cyberculture, at least in its popular form, lacks a critical edge. The lack of critique manifests itself in several different ways. First, popular cyberculture is in danger of becoming ensnared in the nets of technological determinism, a determinism against which both modern sci-ence and technology studies and gender and technology research have long wrestled to be free. Broadly speaking, for cyberculture, technological determinism offers a view that takes technological development as inevitable, as having its own inner logic and where society dances to technology's tune rather than, possibly, the other way round. In cyberculture, determinist views are given voice in predictive statements about what sort of technology we will have ten, twenty, or fifty years hence. Such predictions are always subject to revision; if they are long enough in the future the perpetrator will be long gone, and so the owners of the predictions need never really be called to account.

Such technological predictions also carry predictions of how the technology will be used. For instance, the prediction that the widespread availability of teleshopping means that we will sit at home making purchases denies the complex physical and emo-tional pleasures of shopping in a world where we are often reminded that a visit to the mall is the most popular leisure pursuit for the middle classes in developed countries. Some of us may not wish to lose the pleasures of the meat; indeed many of us may believe that we are not "us" without our meat. The high priests and priestesses of cyberculture are expert in such futurespeak, in blending an almost mystical way of writing with a view that the advances on which they depend may be just around the corner.

Given that cyberculture draws so much from the rhetoric of cyberpunk fiction there are interesting tensions. Cyberpunk's future world is dystopian; there are no communities, only dangerous, alienating urban sprawls. Yet cyberculture looks to a future utopia where communities will spring up (and already have done) on the Internet, somehow to replace the old communities that people feel they have lost. Kevin Robins[15] sees a tension between the utopian desire to recreate the world afresh, in a virtual culture that is heavily dependent on a rhetoric of technological progress on the one hand, and a dissatisfaction and rejection of the old world on the other. Part of this hope manifests itself in the promise of a digital voice for groups traditionally far removed from political and economic power.[16] For instance, Jennifer Light[17] argues that computer-mediated communications on the Internet, as they escape centralized political and legal control, may diversify and offer alternative courses of action for women.

But if there is a determinism at work in the utopian view of the future that such utterances seem to suggest, there is also a determinism in the uncritical acclaim with which future advances in the technology are hailed. Truly intelligent robots, shared virtual realities, and cyberspace rest on technological advances that have not yet and may never happen. This means we need to keep a cool head when thinking about virtual reality and cybertechnology.

The Comfort of Cyborgs

If popular cyberculture offers little comfort for feminists, then it may be that we should look elsewhere within the groves of cyberculture, to the writings of academic theorists and to studies of women's use of the internet and VR, in chatrooms and in Usenet groups. If cyberculture is cyberfeminism's wayward father, then her mother is surely to be found in cyborg feminism.

While sociological studies of cyberculture are proliferating, one of the most potent images to emerge is that of the cyborg, or cybernetic organism. The idea of the cyborg hails from cyberpunk fiction and film but also predates it in older images of the fusion of human and machine. The cyborg is not a feminist invention; indeed in its manifestation in films such as *Terminator* and *Robocop* it is the epitome of masculine destruction, yet it has been appropriated as a feminist icon, most famously in Haraway's *A Cyborg*

Manifesto[18] which John Christie describes as having "attained a status as near canonical as anything gets for the left/feminist academy."[19]

In Haraway's hands the cyborg works as an ironic political myth initially for the 1980s but stretching into and finding its full force in the next decade and well beyond, a blurring, a transgression and deliberate confusion of boundaries of the self, a concern with what makes us human and how we define humanity. Her vision, coming before the upsurge of interest in virtual reality and the specific identification of cyberculture as a cultural entity, sees modern war as a cyborg orgy, coded by C^3I, command-control-communication-intelligence. In our reliance on spectacles, hearing aids, heart pacemakers, dentures, dental crowns, and artificial joints, not to mention, computers, faxes, modems, and networks, we are all cyborgs, "fabricated hybrids of machine and organism."[20]

The cyborg is to be a creature of a postgendered world. As the boundary between human and animal has been thoroughly breached, so too has the boundary between human and machine. The transgression of boundaries and shifting of perspective signals a lessening of the dualisms that have troubled feminist writers, and this means that we do not necessarily have to seek domination of the technology. This is a move away from earlier feminist theories toward a thoroughly postmodern feminism, which has since become a more mainstream part of feminist theory in the ten to fifteen years since the original writing of Haraway's essay. Her cyborg imagery contains two fundamental messages:

First, the production of universal, totalizing theory is a major mistake that misses most of the reality. . . ; and second, taking responsibility for the social relations of science and technology means refusing an anti-science metaphysics, a demonology of technology, and so means embracing the skilful task of reconstructing the boundaries of daily life. It is not just that science and technology are possible means of great human satisfaction, as well as a matrix of complex dominations. Cyborg imagery can suggest a way out of the maze of dualisms in which we have explained our bodies and our tools to ourselves. This is a dream not of a common language, but of a powerful infidel heteroglossia.[21]

Why has Haraway's essay held such an appeal for feminists? It is partly the language she uses, the mixture of poetry and politics. Christie notes "its ability to move with a kind of seamless rapidity from empirically grounded political recognition of the profound and deadly military-industrial technologies to a cyborg empyrean."[22] All this has heralded an upsurge of academic interest in the program of cyborg feminism, which in terms of gender, sexuality, and the body is found most notably in the work of Sandy Stone especially on boundary transgressions,[23] and Anne Balsamo on virtual reality and bodies.[24]

Cyberfeminism

If Haraway's "A Cyborg Manifesto" has played so vital a role in spawning a feminist cyborg postmodernism, feminists may be disappointed in some of its offspring. For instance, in looking to the lure of cyberculture, Judith Squires argues: "whilst there *may* be potential for an alliance between cyborg imagery and a materialist-feminism, this potential has been largely submerged beneath a sea of technophoric cyberdrool. If we are to salvage the image of the cyborg we would do well to insist that cyberfeminism be seen as a metaphor for addressing the inter-relation between technology and the body, not as a means of using the former to transcend the latter."[25]

It seems as if Squires is arguing that cyberfeminism, if indeed there is such a thing, is in danger of falling into the same trap with regard to the body, as cyberculture in general, which is a particularly masculine connotation of the new continuity of mind and machine. As I shall discuss below, although there are some feminist approaches to cyberculture that do not suffer from the same problems, it is with the writings of Sadie Plant, self-declared cyberfeminist, that Squires takes issue. Plant's writing has done much, at least in the United Kingdom, to bring issues of women and cybernetic futures to a more popular audience.[26] Squires describes Plant's style as one that "shares the apoliticism of the cyberpunks but also invokes a kind of mystical utopianism of the eco-feminist earth-godesses."[27]

In addition, Plant's writing has a universalizing tendency against which Haraway and many other feminist writers have fought a long battle, arguing that women's experiences are *not* all of a piece. This manifests itself in statements such as the following: "Women . . . have always found ways of circumventing the dominant systems of communication"[28]; "they (women) are . . . discovering new possibilities for work, play and communication of all kinds in the spaces emergent from the telecoms revolution"[29]; "Women are accessing the circuits on which they were once exchanged."[30] But who are these women? Allowing for the way in which some of this material was written for a more popular audience, it does not seem quite enough to say that "facts and figures are as hard to ascertain as gender itself in the virtual world."[31] At least by the time of Plant's most recent writing a number of empirical studies of women's use of the Internet exist as well as many more on women and computing in general, some of which offer facts and figures.[32] The lack of reference to these or any studies like them makes it difficult to know who are the women about which Plant is talking. This is a pity, given the rather pleasing image that she creates of women subverting the Internet toward their own ends.

There is evidence to show that women are still in the minority in Internet usage, even in the United States, the most wired country in the world.[33] There is a tension between the way that some women clearly find the Internet a potent means of communication with one another, as witnessed by the proliferation of women's newsgroups, and at the same time the negative effects of stories about sexual harassment. It is this tension that prompts Kira Hall to talk of two forms of cyberfeminism.[34] First, what she terms *liberal cyberfeminism* sees computer technology as a means toward the liberation of women. On the other hand *radical cyberfeminism* manifests itself in the "women only" groups on the Internet that have sprung up in response to male harassment.

Susan Herring's well-researched study of discourse on the Internet shows that computer-mediated communication does not appear to neutralize gender.[35] As a group she found women more likely to use attenuated and supportive behaviour while men were more likely to favor adversarial postings. These she linked to men favoring individual freedom, while women favor harmonious interpersonal interaction. And these behaviors and values can be seen as instrumental in reproducing male dominance and female submission.

The view also exists that interactions in cyberspace can magnify and accelerate inequalities and harassment found elsewhere, which is broadly the conclusion of Carol Adams's study of cyberpornography: "Multiple examples—including overt computer-based pornography and a careful analysis of male privilege in cyberspace—powerfully confirm feminist analyses of society and pornography. Indeed, it appears that certain features of cyberspace can accelerate and expand the male dominance and exploitation of women already familiar to us 'in real life'" (IRL).[36]

In case one imagines that all one has to do is literally to pull the plug, one should take heed of Stephanie Brail's story of the harassment she received by way of anonymous, threatening, obscene e-mail messages that she was unable to trace. These came in the wake of a "flame war" in a newsgroup on alternative magazines, where she and others wished to talk about "Riot Grrls," a postfeminist political group. "At the mention of Riot Grrls, some of the men on the group started posting violently in protest. . . . I . . . had no idea how much anti-female sentiment was running, seemingly unchecked, on many Usenet forums."[37] So fearful did she become that she made sure the doors in her house were always locked and she practiced self-defense. Brail adds that the real result is that she never gives out home phone numbers and addresses now and has stopped participating in Usenet newsgroups. She says, "And that is the true fallout: I've censored myself out of fear."[38]

If it is difficult to recognize the women in Plant's writing, it is also difficult to recognize the technology. There is a mystical, reverential tone with which she treats "complex dynamics, self-organizing systems, nanotechnology, machine intelligence."[39] The "connectionist machine is an indeterminate process, rather than a definite entity. . . . Parallel distributed processing defies all attempts to pin it down, and can only ever be contingently defined. It also turns the computer into a complex thinking machine which converges with the operations of the human brain."[40]

But it is the loss of the political project, originally so important in Haraway's cyborg feminism, which is most problematic in Plant's elaboration of cyberfeminism. Some of the reason for the loss is possibly because Irigaray is the only feminist writer to which Plant relates her work, and of all the French feminist writers, Irigaray exhibits the greatest sense of their being little point in attacking the structures of patriarchy. More important, the problem may also relate to the coupling of cyberfeminism to cyberpunk and cyberculture, which deliberately sets itself apart from politics. Squires finds this the most disquieting aspect of cyberfeminism;[41] for although cyberpunk offers no hope of a better world, Plant is claiming that cyberfeminism offers women a better future, but with no political basis to back this up.

Cyberfeminism in the Twenty-First Century

In its cynicism over traditional political structures and its enthusiasm for information and communications technologies, cyberfeminism forgets that women's relationship to technology is not always positive. However, much other research can be used to paint a more balanced picture, which shows what use women *are* making of the new cybertechnologies and which can be used to preserve at least some sense of political project, even if there is no consensus as to what the politics should be. Indeed it is interesting to note that a number of more recently published works make use of cyberfeminism in their titles.

Susan Hawthorne and Renate Klein's, *CyberFeminism* is the first anthology specifically devoted to the topic.[42] The editors of this book are similarly uninspired by the type of cyberfeminism of which Squires is critical, interpreting the topic in a more practical way in a range of upbeat though critical projects. This also ties in with other authors' interpretations of cyberfeminism as a practical project of getting women online and keeping them online.[43]

Lyn Cherny and Elizabeth Reba Weise's,[44] *wired_women* collection paints a fascinating picture of some women's actual uses of Internet technology. As Howard Rheingold suggests on the back cover, these are "women who know their net culture from the inside," so they could well be candidates for Plant's cyberfeminists, subverting the pathways of the Internet for their own ends. It is no criticism to point out that the writers in this collection are highly educated North American women, doctoral students and computer professionals, confidently enjoying and at home with their technology, with jobs and positions that not only provide the necessary technical equipment but also permit them access and the time to use it. They are among the elite of technically confident women, yet amid the cheerful humor and their easy natural use of the new jargon are many tales of male harassment on the newsgroups and bulletin boards.

Hence the vector of recent writing on cyberfeminism is more practical and less speculative than earlier writing, and it remains positive in tone while retaining a balance between positive and negative experiences. However the political side of cyberfeminism has yet to coalesce into a meaningful political voice. Significantly the ethical dimension of cyberfeminism remains almost completely unexplored. The remainder of the chapter marks a beginning to the process of such an exploration.

Ethics and Cyberfeminism—Feminist Ethics

There are (at least) two aspects to the relationship of ethics and cyberfeminism. The first aspect involves the appropriation of relevant ethical theory; the second involves applying that theory to significant examples and drawing out implications for the development of further policy and even legislation. The relevant ethical theory may be found among the burgeoning collection of writings of feminist ethicists.

Feminist ethics involves rethinking and revising aspects of traditional ethics that devalue the moral experience of women.[45] Arguing that traditional ethics fails women in that it regards their experiences as uninteresting, one observes that at the same time it places an emphasis on traditional masculine ways of ethical reasoning that are based on individual, rationalistic, rule-based ethical models. The overall aim of feminist ethics is "to create a gender-equal ethics, a moral theory that generates non-sexist moral principles, policies and practices."[46]

Feminist ethics can help expose the power inequalities that case studies often reveal and that traditional computer and Internet ethics renders invisible in its pursuit of mainstream ethical views and its lack of critique of professional roles and structures. It is this critical edge that has proved appealing to many feminist authors. The challenge then is to harness this energy into positive applications in cyberfeminism.

Applying Feminist Ethics to Cyberfeminism

It is not an easy task to see how feminist ethics might be applied to cyberfeminism. The best place to start lies in a somewhat different direction from cyberfeminism's more usual job of discussing ways that women have appropriated digital technology for their own ends. Instead we should look to some perennial ethical problems of the Internet, uncover the ways in which these can be viewed as gendered problems, and enter into a thorough analysis of their gendered nature that incorporates the concepts of feminist ethics. Cyberstalking, Internet pornography (particularly pedophilia), and hacking are all contenders. Most cyberstalkers are male, their victims female.[47] Most Internet pedophiles are male, their victims children and their families.[48] Although it does not make sense to talk about one category of victim in the same way for hacking, it is clear that hacking itself is a predominantly masculine activity; indeed the absence of women hackers has often been a source of comment in the hacking fraternity.[49]

What draws some men to such antisocial, even criminal activity, perpetrated through digital technologies? Carol Gilligan's ethic of care,[50] Annette Baier's second-person knowing,[51] and Sara Ruddick's maternal ethics[52] all emphasize the web of connectedness of moral agents in contrast to the rugged moral individualism of traditional ethical theory, particularly Kantian theory.[53] The pathology of the perpetrators of all three varieties of cyberproblem leans toward the masculine social outcast, with few friends and little sense of community or empathy. Indeed although we might be revolted by his abusive crimes, one member of an Internet pedophile ring in a U.K. documentary explicitly alludes to the sense of community that he felt on the Internet.[54] The challenge then for a cyberfeminist ethics is to develop further the argument that shows how the masculine individualism of traditional ethics is damaging in extreme circumstances, particularly when coupled with the dystopian, apolitical stance of cyberculture that allows individuals somehow to justify to themselves that their activities are not wrong.

Conclusion

The aim of this chapter has been to form a critique of cyberfeminism that concurs with other authors in arguing that cyberfeminism's apparently apolitical stance is problematic, not least of all in its avoidance of ethical questions. Although practical examples of cyberfeminist activities offer a much more promising direction for the cyberfeminist project, the ethical dimension still tends to remain in the background. The way forward would seem to lie in a much more explicit attack on ethical problems concerning digital technology from feminist ethics, particularly in acting as a pointer to future policy and ultimately legislation. Whether cyberfeminism will go down in the annals of feminist history as purely a late-twentieth-century phenomenon, or whether it can be rescued for the twenty-first century by developing a new political and ethical consciousness, remains to be seen.

Acknowledgment

An earlier version of part of this chapter was published in Alison Adam, *Artificial Knowing: Gender and the Thinking Machine* (New York and London: Routledge, 1998).

Notes

1. Suniti Namjoshi, *Building Babel* (Melbourne: Spinifex, 1996).

2. Sadie Plant, "On the Matrix: Cyberfeminist Simulations," in *Cultures of the Internet: Virtual Spaces, Real Histories, Living Bodies*, ed. Rob Shields (London, Thousand Oaks, CA, and New Delhi: Sage, 1996), 170–183.

3. Stanley Aronowitz, Barbara Martinson, and Michael Menser with Jennifer Rich, eds., *Technoscience and Cyberculture* (New York and London: Routledge, 1996); Michael Benedikt, ed., *Cyberspace: First Steps* (Cambridge, MA, and London: MIT Press, 1994); Jon Dovey, ed., *Fractal Dreams: New Media in Social Context* (London: Lawrence & Wishart, 1996); Charles Ess, ed., *Philosophical Perspectives on Computer-Mediated Communication* (Albany: State University of New York Press, 1996); Mike Featherstone, Mike Hepworth, and Bryan S. Turner, eds., *The Body: Social Process and Cultural Theory* (London, Thousand Oaks, CA, and New Delhi: Sage, 1991); Chris Hables Gray, ed., *The Cyborg Handbook* (London and New York: Routledge, 1995); Rob Shields, ed., *Cultures of the Internet: Virtual Spaces, Real Histories, Living Bodies* (London, Thousand Oaks, CA, and New Delhi: Sage, 1996).

4. William Gibson, *Neuromancer* (New York: Ace Books, 1984).

5. Allucquère Rosanne Stone, "Will the Real Body Please Stand Up?: Boundary Stories about Virtual Cultures," in *Cyberspace: First Steps*, ed. Michael Benedikt (Cambridge, MA, and London: MIT Press, 1994), 113.

6. Nadia M. Thalmann and Daniel Thalmann, eds., *Artificial Life and Virtual Reality*, (Chichister, UK: Wiley, 1994).

7. Hans Moravec, *Mind Children: The Future of Robot and Human Intelligence* (Cambridge, MA, and London: Harvard University Press, 1988).

8. Stefan Helmreich, "Anthropology Inside and Outside the Looking-Glass Worlds of Artificial Life." Unpublished paper, Department of Anthropology, Stanford University, Stanford, CA, 1994.

9. Sue C. Jansen, "The Ghost in the Machine: Artificial Intelligence and Gendered Thought Patterns," *Resources for Feminist Research* 17 (1988): 4–7; Sue C. Jansen, "Making Minds: Sexual and Reproductive Metaphors in the Discourses of the Artificial Intelligence Movement." Paper presented at the Electronic Salon: Feminism Meets Infotech in connection with the 11th Annual Gender Studies Symposium, Lewis and Clark College, March 1992.

10. Jansen, "The Ghost in the Machine," 6.

11. Helmreich, "Anthropology Inside and Outside the Looking-Glass Worlds of Artificial Life," 5.

12. Ralph Schroeder, "Cyberculture, Cyborg Post-Modernism and the Sociology of Virtual Reality Technologies: Surfing the Soul in the Information Age," *Futures* 26, no. 5 (1994): 519–528.

13. Schroeder, "Cyberculture, Cyborg Post-Modernism," 525.

14. Anne Balsamo, *Technologies of the Gendered Body: Reading Cyborg Women* (Durham, NC, and London: Duke University Press, 1996), 131–132.

15. Kevin Robins, "Cyberspace and the World We Live In," *Fractal Dreams: New Media in Social Context*, ed. John Dovey (London: Lawrence and Wishart, 1996), 25.

16. Ailsa Barry, "Who Gets to Play? Access and the Margin," in *Fractal Dreams: New Media in Social Context*, ed. John Dovey (London: Lawrence and Wishart, 1996), 137.

17. Jennifer Light, "The Digital Landscape: New Space for Women?," *Gender, Place and Culture* 2, no. 2 (1995): 133–146.

18. Donna Haraway, "A Cyborg Manifesto: Science, Technology and Socialist-Feminism in the Late Twentieth Century," in *Simians, Cyborgs and Women: The Reinvention of Nature* (London: Free Association Books, 1991), 149–181.

19. John R. R. Christie, "A Tragedy for Cyborgs," *Configurations* 1 (1993): 172.

20. Haraway, "A Cyborg Manifesto," 150.

21. Haraway, "A Cyborg Manifesto," 181.

22. Christie, "A Tragedy for Cyborgs," 175.

23. Allucquère Rosanne Stone, "Violation and Virtuality: Two Cases of Physical and Psychological boundary Transgression and Their Implications. Unpublished manuscript, 1993; Stone "Will the Real Body Please Stand Up?," 81–118; Allucquère Rosanne Stone, *The War of Desire and Technology at the Close of the Mechanical Age* (Cambridge, MA, and London: MIT Press, 1995).

24. Balsamo, *Technologies of the Gendered Body*.

25. Judith Squires, "Fabulous Feminist Futures and the Lure of Cyberculture," in *Fractal Dreams: New Media in Social Context*, ed. Jon Dovey (London: Lawrence and Wishart, 1996), 195.

26. Sadie Plant, "Beyond the Screens: Film, Cyberpunk and Cyberfeminism," *Variant* 14 (1993): 12–17.

27. Squires, "Fabulous Feminist Futures," 204.

28. Plant, "Beyond the Screens," 13.

29. Sadie Plant, "Babes in the Net," *New Statesman & Society* (January 27, 1995), 28.

30. Plant, "On the Matrix," 170.

31. Plant, "Babes in the Net," 28.

32. Alison Adam, Judy Emms, Eileen Green, and Jenny Owen, eds., *IFIP Transactions A-57, Women, Work and Computerization: Breaking Old Boundaries-Building New Forms*,

(Amsterdam: Elsevier/ North-Holland, 1994); Carol Adams, "'This Is Not Our Fathers' Pornography': Sex, Lies and Computers," in *Philosophical Perspectives on Computer-Mediated Communication*, ed. Charles Ess (Albany: State University of New York Press, 1996), 147–170; Frances Grundy, *Women and Computers* (Exeter, UK: Intellect Books, 1996); Susan Herring, "Posting in a Different Voice: Gender and Ethics in CMC," in *Philosophical Perspectives on Computer-Mediated Communication*, ed. Charles Ess (Albany: State University of New York Press, 1996), 115–145; Jennifer Light, "The Digital landscape"; Lesley Regan Shade, ed., "Special Issue on Gender and Networking," *Electronic Journal of Virtual Culture* 2, no. 3 (1994); Lesley Regan Shade, "Is There Free Speech on the Net? Censorship in the Global Information Infrastructure," in *Cultures of the Internet: Virtual Spaces, Real Histories, Living Bodies*, ed. Rob Shields (London, Thousand Oaks, CA, and New Delhi: Sage, 1996), 11–32.

33. James E. Pitkow and Colleen M. Kehoe, "Emerging Trends in the WWW User Population," *Communications of the ACM* 39, no. 6 (1996): 106–108.

34. Kira Hall, "Cyberfeminism," in *Computer-Mediated Communication: Linguistic, Social and Cross-Cultural Perspectives*, ed. Susan C. Herring (Amsterdam and Philadelphia: John Benjamins Publishing, 1996), 147–170.

35. Herring, "Posting in a Different Voice."

36. Adams, "'This Is Not Our Fathers' Pornography,'"148.

37. Stephanie Brail, "The Price of Admission: Harassment and Free Speech in the Wild, Wild West," in *wired_women: Gender and New Realities in Cyberspace*, ed. Lynn Cherny and Elizabeth Reba Weise (Seattle, WA: Seal Press, 1996), 157.

38. Brail, "The Price of Admission," 157.

39. Plant, "Babes in the Net."

40. Plant, "Beyond the Screens," 174–175.

41. Squires, "Fabulous Feminist Futures," 208.

42. Susan Hawthorne and Renate Klein, eds., *CyberFeminism: Connectivity, Critique, and Creativity* (Melbourne: Spinifex, 1999).

43. Christine Ann Nguyen Fredrick, "Feminist Rhetoric in Cyberspace: The *Ethos* of Feminist Usenet Groups," *The Information Society* 15 (1999): 187–197; Sibylle Gruber, "Communication Gone Wired: Working Toward a 'Practiced' Cyberfeminism," *The Information Society* 15 (1999): 199–208.

44. Lyn Cherny and Elizabeth Reba Weise, eds., *wired_women: Gender and New Realities in Cyberspace* (Seattle, WA: Seal Press, 1996).

45. Rosemarie Tong, "Feminist Ethics," in *The Stanford Encyclopedia of Philosophy*, ed. E. Zalta (Fall 1999 Edition).

46. Tong, "Feminist Ethics."

47. Alison Adam, "The Ethics of Cyberstalking," in *Virtual Gender*, ed. Eileen Green and Alison Adam (London and New York: Routledge, 2001).

48. BBC News/Panorama, "Paedophile Ring Exposed." Available online at <http://news.bbc.co.uk/hi/english/audiovideo/programmes/panorama/newsid_/1162880.st>. 12 February 2001.

49. Paul Taylor, *Hackers: Crime in the Digital Sublime* (London & New York: Routledge, 1990).

50. Carol Gilligan, *In a Different Voice: Psychological Theory and Women's Development* (Cambridge, MA: Harvard University Press, 1982).

51. Annette Baier, *Postures of the Mind: Essays on Mind and Morals* (Minneapolis, MN: University of Minnesota Press, 1985).

52. Sara Ruddick, *Maternal Thinking: Toward a Politics of Peace* (Boston: Beacon, 1989).

53. Rosemarie Tong, *Feminine and Feminist Ethics* (Belmont, CA: Wadsworth, 1993).

54. BBC News/Panorama, "Paedophile Ring Exposed."

Works Cited

Adam, Alison. "The Ethics of Cyberstalking." In *Virtual Gender*, ed. Eileen Green and Alison Adam. London and New York: Routledge, 2001.

Adam, Alison, Judy Emms, Eileen Green, and Jenny Owen, eds. *IFIP Transactions A–57, Women, Work and Computerization: Breaking Old Boundaries–Building New Forms.* Amsterdam: Elsevier/North-Holland, 1994.

Adams, Carol. "'This Is Not Our Fathers' Pornography': Sex, Lies and Computers." In *Philosophical Perspectives on Computer-Mediated Communication*, ed. Charles Ess, 147–170. Albany: State University of New York Press, 1996.

Aronowitz, Stanley. Barbara Martinson, and Michael Menser with Jennifer Rich, eds. *Technoscience and Cyberculture.* New York and London: Routledge, 1996.

Baier, Annette. *Postures of the Mind: Essays on Mind and Morals.* Minneapolis: University of Minnesota Press, 1985.

Balsamo, Anne. *Technologies of the Gendered Body: Reading Cyborg Women.* Durham, NC, and London: Duke University Press, 1996.

Barry, Ailsa. "Who Gets to Play? Access and the Margin." In *Fractal Dreams: New Media in Social Context*, ed. Jon Dovey, 22–44. London: Lawrence and Wishart, 1996.

BBC News/Panorama. "Paedophile Ring Exposed." Available online at <http://news.bbc.co.uk/hi/english/audiovideo/programmes/panorama/newsid_/1162880.st>. 12 February 2001.

Benedikt, Michael, ed., *Cyberspace: First Steps.* Cambridge, MA: MIT Press, 1994.

Brail, Stephanie. "The Price of Admission: Harassment and Free Speech in the Wild, Wild West." In *wired_women: Gender and New Realities in Cyberspace*, ed. Lynn Cherny and Elizabeth Reba Weise, 141–157. Seattle, WA: Seal Press, 1996.

Cherny, Lyn, and Elizabeth Reba Weise, eds. *wired_women: Gender and New Realities in Cyberspace.* Seattle, WA: Seal Press, 1996.

Christie, John R. R. "A Tragedy for Cyborgs." *Configurations* 1 (1993): 171–196.

Dovey, Jon, ed., *Fractal Dreams: New Media in Social Context.* London: Lawrence and Wishart, 1996.

Ess, Charles, ed., *Philosophical Perspectives on Computer-Mediated Communication.* Albany: State University of New York Press, 1996.

Featherstone, Mike, Mike Hepworth, and Bryan S. Turner, eds. *The Body: Social Process and Cultural Theory.* London, Thousand Oaks, CA, and New Delhi: Sage, 1991.

Fredrick, Christine Ann Nguyen. "Feminist Rhetoric in Cyberspace: The *Ethos* of Feminist Usenet Groups." *The Information Society* 15 (1999): 187–197.

Gibson, William. *Neuromancer.* New York: Ace Books, 1984.

Gilligan, Carol. *In a Different Voice: Psychological Theory and Women's Development.* Cambridge, MA: Harvard University Press, 1982.

Gray, Chris Hables, ed., *The Cyborg Handbook.* London and New York: Routledge, 1995.

Gruber, Sibylle. "Communication Gone Wired: Working Toward a 'Practiced' Cyberfeminism." *The Information Society* 15 (1999): 199–208.

Grundy, Frances. *Women and Computers.* Exeter, UK: Intellect Books, 1996.

Hall, Kira. "Cyberfeminism." In *Computer-Mediated Communication: Linguistic, Social and Cross-Cultural Perspectives*, ed. Susan C. Herring, 147–170. Amsterdam and Philadelphia: John Benjamins Publishing, 1996.

Haraway, Donna. "A Cyborg Manifesto: Science, Technology and Socialist-Feminism in the Late Twentieth Century." In *Simians, Cyborgs and Women: The Reinvention of Nature*, 149–181. London: Free Association Books, 1991.

Hawthorne, Susan, and Renate Klein, eds. *CyberFeminism: Connectivity, Critique, and Creativity.* Melbourne: Spinifex, 1999.

Helmreich, Stefan. "Anthropology Inside and Outside the Looking-Glass Worlds of Artificial Life." Unpublished paper, Department of Anthropology, Stanford University, Stanford, CA., 1994. (Available from the author at <stefang@leland.stanford.edu>).

Herring, Susan. "Posting in a Different Voice: Gender and Ethics in CMC." In *Philosophical Perspectives on Computer-Mediated Communication*, ed. Charles Ess, 115–145. Albany: State University of New York Press, 1996.

Jansen, Sue C. "The Ghost in the Machine: Artificial Intelligence and Gendered Thought Patterns." *Resources for Feminist Research* 17 (1988): 4–7.

Jansen, Sue C. "Making Minds: Sexual and Reproductive Metaphors in the Discourses of the Artificial Intelligence Movement." Paper presented at the Electronic Salon: Feminism Meets Infotech in connection with the 11th Annual Gender Studies Symposium, Lewis and Clark College, March 1992.

Light, Jennifer. "The Digital Landscape: New Space for Women?" *Gender, Place and Culture* 2, no. 2 (1995): 133–146.

Moravec, Hans. *Mind Children: The Future of Robot and Human Intelligence.* Cambridge, MA, and London: Harvard University Press, 1988.

Namjoshi, Suniti. *Building Babel.* Melbourne: Spinifex, 1996.

Pitkow, James E., and Colleen M. Kehoe. "Emerging Trends in the WWW User Population." *Communications of the ACM* 39, no. 6 (1996): 106–108.

Plant, Sadie. "Beyond the Screens: Film, Cyberpunk and Cyberfeminism." *Variant* 14 (1993): 12–17.

Plant, Sadie. "Babes in the Net." *New Statesman & Society* (January 27, 1995): 28.

Plant, Sadie. "On the Matrix: Cyberfeminist Simulations." In *Cultures of the Internet: Virtual Spaces, Real Histories, Living Bodies*, ed. Rob Shields, 170–183. London, Thousand Oaks, CA, and New Delhi: Sage, 1996.

Robins, Kevin. "Cyberspace and the World We Live In." In *Fractal Dreams: New Media in Social Context*, ed. Jon Dovey. London: Lawrence & Wishart, 1996.

Ruddick, Sara. *Maternal Thinking: Toward a Politics of Peace*. Boston: Beacon Press, 1989.

Schroeder, Ralph. "Cyberculture, Cyborg Post-Modernism and the Sociology of Virtual Reality Technologies: Surfing the Soul in the Information Age." *Futures* 26, no. 5 (1994): 519–528.

Shade, Lesley Regan. "Is There Free Speech on the Net? Censorship in the Global Information Infrastructure." In *Cultures of the Internet: Virtual Spaces, Real Histories, Living Bodies*, ed. Rob Shields, 11–32. London, Thousand Oaks, CA, and New Delhi: Sage, 1996.

Shade, Lesley Regan. ed. "Special Issue on Gender and Networking." *Electronic Journal of Virtual Culture* 2, no. 3 (1994). (To retrieve electronically send command GET EJVCV2N2 PACKAGE to <LISTSERV@KENTVM.KENT.EDU>.)

Shields, Rob, ed. *Cultures of the Internet: Virtual Spaces, Real Histories, Living Bodies*. London, Thousand Oaks, CA, and New Delhi: Sage, 1996.

Squires, Judith. "Fabulous Feminist Futures and the Lure of Cyberculture." In *Fractal Dreams: New Media in Social Context*, ed. Jon Dovey, 194–216. London: Lawrence and Wishart, 1996.

Stone, Allucquère Rosanne. "Violation and Virtuality: Two Cases of Physical and Psychological Boundary Transgression and Their Implications." Unpublished manuscript, 1993. (Available in electronic form from <sandy@actlab.rtf.utexas.edu>.)

Stone, Allucquère Rosanne. "Will the Real Body Please Stand Up?: Boundary Stories about Virtual Cultures." In *Cyberspace: First Steps*, ed. Michael Benedikt, 81–118. Cambridge, MA: MIT Press, 1994.

Stone, Allucquère Rosanne. *The War of Desire and Technology at the Close of the Mechanical Age*. Cambridge, MA: MIT Press, 1995.

Taylor, Paul. *Hackers: Crime in the Digital Sublime*. London and New York: Routledge, 1990.

Thalmann, Nadia M., and Daniel Thalmann, eds. *Artificial Life and Virtual Reality*. Chichester, UK: Wiley, 1994.

Tong, Rosemarie. *Feminine and Feminist Ethics*. Belmont, CA: Wadsworth, 1993.

Tong, Rosemarie. "Feminist Ethics." In *The Stanford Encyclopedia of Philosophy*, ed. E. Zalta (Fall 1999 Edition). Available online at <http://plato.stanford.edu/archives/fall1999/entries/feminism-ethics>. 24 November 1999.

10

THE FIVE WIVES OF IBN FADLAN: WOMEN'S COLLABORATIVE FICTION ON ANTONIO BANDERAS WEB SITES

Sharon Cumberland

When I first came up with the idea for this series, I was not thinking of Antonio at the time, but of the friendship I share with these ladies. I was driving home from the grocery store and the thought occurred to me, "We care about each other so much, I bet we could even be in a harem, all married to the same man, and still get along great!"

—*JoAnn K. Prater, "Johanna of Bavaria"*

The Five Wives of Ibn Fadlan is a sequence of related stories set in the ninth century CE, in which each wife of an Arab sheik tells the tale of how she was kidnapped from a distant country and brought to Baghdad to be married to Ahmad Ibn Fadlan, a character who is also the protagonist of Michael Crichton's novel *Eaters of the Dead* (1976). The five women authors are fans of Spanish actor Antonio Banderas, who starred in the film version of Crichton's novel, *The 13th Warrior*. They used the universe of the film to insert themselves into the romantic world of an imaginary harem. While Crichton's novel tells a buddy story about an Arab diplomat who falls in with Vikings and goes with them to a far kingdom to kill monsters (a revisioning of *Beowulf*), the five fan writers tell a story about the protagonist that *they* want to hear: A mysterious sheik accepts virgins from a villainous kidnapper as repayment of a debt, then marries each in turn, showing them his kindness, generosity, and, of course, his sexual prowess. Over the course of the five stories, the wives and their offspring become as devoted to one another as they are to their dashing husband, forming a community that unites their disparate cultures.

While *The 13th Warrior* is an adventure saga, focused on the action film demographics of 18- to 25-year-old men, *The Five Wives of Ibn Fadlan* is a romance that capitalizes on the exotic (and erotic) themes of desert romances from *The Sheik* to *The English Patient*. Unlike the novel and the movie, which exist in commercialized media,

The Five Wives of Ibn Fadlan was written to be posted on the Internet for the Antonio Banderas fan community. With only themselves and their specialized audience to please—female authors write for a predominantly female audience—the authors could express themselves freely.

The Five Wives of Ibn Fadlan, and thousands of stories like it, typify one of the most rapidly developing areas of women's writing today: fan fiction on the Internet. Women who frequent celebrity Web sites are engaged in collaborative storytelling about their iconic heroes, creating screenplays, short stories, and novels for an audience of enthusiastic fans.[1] Although fan fiction is not a new phenomenon, it has been, and continues to be, a genre dominated by women, both as writers and as readers (Jenkins 1992, 6; Bacon-Smith 2000, 115). In some modes of fan fiction, authors appropriate established characters from film or television in order to create transformations of familiar narratives such as *Star Trek, The X Files,* or *Xena: Warrior Princess.* Other modes appropriate real-life actors, rock stars, country singers, or music groups and make them characters in fictional stories.

What is remarkable about this phenomenon is that women—who in the past might have limited their participation in fan culture to reading fan romances or movie magazines—are now using the Internet to develop their own voices and writing skills. Furthermore, the Internet's properties of anonymity and direct access to interested readers are enabling women to form friendships with one another that eventually become more important than their original attraction to the celebrity icons themselves. Collaborative writing, either through the contribution of individual stories to a Web anthology or by group storytelling, is a tool of community building. I suggest that for writers of fan fiction the de facto function of the celebrity icon is to embody a site where networks of friendship can be formed. Just as the fictional wives of Ibn Fadlan form a harem of shared interest and support around their common husband, so fan fiction writers form a community of shared interest and support around the celebrity who drew them to the communal Web site in the first place.

Scholarship is in the early stages of understanding friendship formation on the Internet in general and on women's fan sites in particular, so it isn't yet clear whether community building is a typical characteristic of fan sites. But as this discussion will show, fan fiction is closely related to another predominantly female form of writing, the popular romance—a genre that also creates community around celebrity writers and that inspires women to form community with one another. The Internet has taken popular romance writing to the populace itself by permitting women to write fiction without passing through the gauntlet of editorial evaluation, to express themselves sexually without fear of exposure or embarrassment, and to find an enthusiastic audience without the barrier of money exchange. Women who were formally content to be readers are now using the Internet to become writers and to form community through writing collectives.

Internet Access and Usage for Women

I bought my first home computer because I wanted to get to know [Antonio's] Internet fans. My interest in Antonio has prompted me to learn more about computers than I would have ever thought I wanted to know. I know how to design and implement a web page. I have developed skills with the manipulation of pictures with graphics programs.

—*Christine Hillhouse, "Christine of Scotland"*

Many of the Banderas fans who are collaborating on fan fiction met at the Antonio Banderas Web Mall created in 1995 by Kathleen Grant, a Banderas fan and professional Web developer. This sophisticated site contains a chatroom, two threaded discussion boards, extensive photo archives, the weekly "Antonio Admirers Newsletter," film clips, a filmography and biography, as well as links to related film and fan sites. The Web Mall is maintained by volunteers who have formed a community around the site and who have educated each other in the technology required to keep the site current. Fans meet and form the friendships that have developed into fiction-writing collectives such as the *Antonio Banderas Kiss Book*, created in 1998 by three fans and maintained on a Web site of the same name. The *Kiss Book* is an anthology site that contains hundreds of individual and linked stories based on the characters Antonio Banderas has portrayed in films. In addition, the Web Mall also supports specific story sites such as *Zorro Returns*, a collaborative sequel to the film *The Mask of Zorro* by a group of sixteen fan writers, and an original novel, *Torero*, by a group of three fan writers. These fan sites have motivated women to learn Internet skills, with the more experienced women coaching the less experienced, enabling participation at the level each individual chooses, from simple chatting and e-mailing to Web design and site administration.

For instance, Susan Jaime ("Susanna of Spain" in *The Five Wives of Ibn Fadlan*), says of her computer literacy, "I've learned a little bit from my job, but mostly from friends at work and the 'chicas' at the Banderas Mall site."[2] Some of the participants in these sites work in the computer industry or in computer-intensive jobs, as do K. C. McMinn ("Keliana the Gypsy" in *The Five Wives of Ibn Fadlan*), who is an applications trainer and consultant, and Sandie Sledge (editor of the "Antonio Admirers Newsletter"), who in her capacity as a high school librarian maintains computerized catalogues and runs computer and multimedia labs for her students. Others, like fan-author Susan Hughes (*Torero*), are almost completely self-taught yet have acquired so much skill in the process of working on Banderas-related fiction and Web sites that their expertise melds smoothly into their working lives.

Since participation in collaborative fan fiction requires some degree of access and willingness to learn computing, it isn't surprising that shared technical knowledge goes along with shared heroes. But many other kinds of Web sites devoted to women's interests—Oxygen: A Woman's View of the World, the Association for Women in Computing (AWC), and Webgrrls International—address the need for women to overcome their computer phobias by offering encouragement and internet how-to's. Rachel Adelson (2000), in a series of articles on the AWC Web site called "Introducing Live Wire: Computer Confidence for Women," explains why special focus is needed to support women in technology: "Simply put, we need it more. We use computers less than men, work in the industry in much smaller numbers, are far less educated technically and are less visible on line." Graphic interfaces and other mediations have made the "feel" of computers and the Internet less technical, but they do not completely disguise the fact that these technologies were developed by men for the use of other men. Thus the pervasive context for women's efforts in cyberspace, regardless of expertise, is what Lee Quinby (1999) refers to as "Virile-Reality"—a term that not only references the masculine history and style of the digital world, but which targets the false promises of gender and race equality in the unembodied world of cyberspace. "Too many of these promises equate consumer hype and biotech hookups with social equality and have been formulated as desirable without sufficient input from feminists," Quinby states. "Virile-reality cultivates the virago and undermines the feminist," which is to say that women must either enter the world of technology by adapting to the masculinist mindset, the *vir* (Latin for "man") of *vir*tual reality, or stay out of it (1082). The "Internet anxiety" that many women experience is grounded in an intuitive, and often experienced, sense that the digital world is perpetuating the same gender, race, and class discrimination that characterizes the real world.

Even sophisticated women users, the "geek chicks" who work in highly technical fields with their male "geek" counterparts, are subject to the social pressures that limit their access to the elite realms of "ultra-proficient programming" or "hacking." Kirilly Robert, a woman working in the open source community, discusses issues of "nature" and "nurture" that keep women from entering the "hard" dimensions of the computer industry. In her online article, "Geek Chicks: Second Thoughts," Robert (2000) writes that more women are needed in this male-dominated profession to "bring a different perspective and generate new ideas." She notes that women in the computer industry are found more commonly in "soft" areas such as "user interface and psychology, written and verbal communications, group interactions (both electronic and face to face)," and she proposes that these skills be included in the definition of hacking to give them more prestige and to open up the rarified world of computer languages to broader, more holistic ideas.

Predictably, male responders in the threaded discussion that follows chastise Robert for being both a misogynist and a feminist. One calls Robert's ideas "dangerous and regressive," interpreting her suggestions to mean that "women should be content to take a backseat to men" instead of making the sacrifices required to do programming like male hackers. Another responder rejects the idea that women can be hackers at all, saying, "Please try to understand your nature. If you don't fly, it may be because you haven't been encouraged to do so; but that's unlikely. It also may be that you don't have wings." This hostility to the "different perspectives" and "new ideas" that geek chicks would bring to the fundamentals of programming makes cyberspace more hostile to female users in general.

Furthermore, if a woman does try to participate as an equal in male-dominated settings, she may be required to adopt a masculine style or identity in order to succeed, as Lori Kendall observes in her article about gender performance on male-dominated social MUDs (multiuser dungeon/discussion groups): "The male bias of many online spaces requires performances of masculinity from both male and female participants" (1998, 133). Geek chicks like Kirrily Robert, who attempt to bring their holistic and social intuition into the very structure of programming meet with the perennial "nature" argument that is trundled out whenever women try to enter the social debate by voting, leaving the home to take jobs, moving beyond the corporate "glass ceiling," or helping to build an Internet that is communal and user-friendly.

Yet as more women overcome their aversion to the male-dominated world of computing and learn to create environments—both professional and recreational—where other women feel comfortable, the Internet will begin to feel more like home to the millions of women who venture online every year. Popular romance provides an apt metaphor for this process since the typical romance begins with conflict between the heroine and the patriarchal lover—whether a contemporary boss, a Regency rogue, a Barbary pirate, or a desert sheik—and ends with the heroine insisting upon acknowledgment of her uniqueness: in effect, a sensitization and "feminization" of the hero before the happy ending can be accomplished. The masculine nature of the Internet can be compared to a romantic hero like Fadlan, the hero of *The Five Wives of Ibn Fadlan*. Though the heroines are brought to his kingdom kicking and screaming, they find love and remain willingly, making his kingdom their own. Fan fiction writers like Christine Hillhouse, who are motivated by their attraction to an iconic hero to overcome their reluctance and "learn more about computers than I would have ever thought I wanted to know," are part of a force that is changing the computer environment from the masculinist "virile reality" to a place that enables women to find a voice and a community. They are using their powers of storytelling to make the kingdom their own.

Popular Romance and the Desert Fabula

For me it's a release from everyday life. It's a lot of fun to have "sisters" in an imaginary way. As for collaborating with the others, it makes it more of an adventure to "bounce" ideas off one another and by doing this the story comes out more powerful and more fun to read.

—*Susan Jaime, "Susanna of Spain"*

One of the fields of popular culture where women have found community and voice is the romance novel, often identified as the "Harlequin novel" after the publishing company that perfected the form and dominates a crowded field. These novels are also called "formulas" because the reader is assured a lively female protagonist in conflict with a patriarchal/romantic male, often a boss or other authority, and an optimistic ending, usually marriage. In "Romance in the Age of Electronics: Harlequin Enterprises," Leslie W. Rabine tracks the evolution of the romance formula from the 1970s through the "profound changes in both [women's] domestic and paid labor situations" (1985, 250), of the mid-1980s. As women left the home for the work force, the Harlequin heroine was transformed from a housewife to an employee. However, the fictional heroines confront the patriarchy by engaging in often violent conflict with the male authority figure, forcing him to deal with the heroine as a human being. Rabine observes that the love the heroine feels for her hero/antagonist is also the mechanism that will give her what she wants: "recognition of herself as a unique, exceptional individual. In addition to acknowledging her sexual attraction and her professional competence, [the hero] must also recognize her as a subject, or recognize her from her own point of view" (250). Thus, in spite of its formulaic plotting, popular romance is the only mass-market genre that guarantees the female reader a female protagonist who is neither a victim nor an object. As Jennifer Cruise Smith says of her discovery of the world of romance: "For the first time I was reading fiction about women who had sex and then didn't eat arsenic or throw themselves under trains or swim out to the embrace of the sea" (1999, 82).

Nevertheless, popular romance also incorporates conventional patriarchal values that may seem antithetical to most constructions of feminism: strict adherence to gender roles, the resolution of conflict in marriage, and the fundamental idea that women are completed by men. This last value often leads to sex scenes in which the heroine initially resists the hero but then succumbs gladly to his force. And there are other aspects of romance novels that give some readers pause. Why, for instance, does the independent heroine still expect the hero to treat her like a "lady"? Why does love always flower out of conflict? Why are romance novels so oblivious to race and class issues? Why are so many women ashamed to admit that they read popular romance? These contradictions are hardly surprising when one considers that only a generation ago the majority of middle-class American women could choose to stay home or to work (though job selection was narrow and job equity was poor). Now, at the start of the twenty-first century, staying at home to raise children seems like a luxury only the rich can afford. Though progress has been made in admitting women to higher education and the professions, little progress has been made in establishing those support systems for the family that will guarantee children the same security they enjoyed when their mothers were at home, or that will free a working woman from the domestic responsibilities she had as a housewife. Nostalgia for a time when women were "treated like ladies" or had family servants is understandable, as is the hostility toward men, who earn more, have freer access to education and technology, have less responsibility for the upkeep of home and family, and whose sexual demands—no matter how buffered by love and marriage— objectify women in terms of sexual and reproductive function. Small wonder that popular romance novels, authored by women for women, portray the heroine as ambivalent and hostile toward the hero, while at the same time harboring a desire for his love. In the fantasy universe of the popular romance, these tensions are acted out and resolved in the sexual and emotional bodies of the heroine/protagonist and hero/antagonist.

While there are many subgenres within the popular romance form, the desert fabula is one of the earliest, invented in 1919 by Edith M. Hull, author of *The Sheik*. Subject of a popular silent film starring Rudolph Valentino, *The Sheik* established the now-familiar themes of a Western woman on a journey, the mysterious Arab who kidnaps her, and the plot of resistance, passion, capitulation, and marriage. The heroine is forced to rely on her own resources, transforming a desperate situation into a triumph of love and marriage. This requires both her own commitment to self-sufficiency and a conversion of the hero from his ultra-male ways to a more vulnerable and sympathetic stance. *The Five Wives of Ibn Fadlan* is a development of the desert fabula that takes the form beyond the happiness of the individual heroine by using a harem theme as a metaphor for fan community and friendship.

It is strange, then, considering the positive subtext found in all versions of romance, that women are ashamed to admit they read them. "I found myself overwhelmingly self-conscious to be purchasing [a romance novel]," says Maria Bianca Rhodes, "and afraid that I might even get caught by someone I know" (qtd. in Person 1988, 362). Feelings of shame and embarrassment stem in part from the fact that the problems of sentimental love are, as Ethel Spector Person notes, "relegated almost exclusively to private concerns and popular culture" (1988, 18). The divide between high and low culture presumably makes a distinction between those with educated taste, appealing to the intellect, and those with uneducated taste, appealing to the emotions. Any devotion to popular narra-tive—soap operas, fandom, "trashy" novels—forces women to defend themselves from assumptions of laziness, pathetic longings, empty lives, and even insanity.

This is where the Internet has made a difference in the way women approach their self-expression through popular media. The Internet offers women both privacy and access to like-minded people. Women can take the romance genre one step further by becoming their own authors. While Harlequin and other publishers have always invited readers with a penchant for writing to become published writers themselves, they only hire those who can master the formulas. In many cases the aspiring romance writer is overly accomplished, her stories too complex or ideologies too realistic to sell to ro-mance publishers, who have accustomed a mass audience to predictable narratives. On the Internet, however, there is an eager and focused audience for romance of all kinds, including fan romance such as *The Five Wives of Ibn Fadlan* and the thousands of stories written with popular culture heroes and heroines.

Just as the Harlequin romance formula guarantees characters that will engage with each other in predictable ways that satisfy the emotional needs of the readers, so fiction that reproduces a known "universe," such as *Star Trek* or *The 13th Warrior,* offers pre-dictable settings and characters to the fan readers, who know that their favorite charac-ters will act out emotional needs that were not addressed in the original film or TV show. By appropriating desirable characters to enact original stories, fan authors are ad-dressing the same issues as the popular romance novels—patriarchy versus the inde-pendent woman—but they are doing it, in a sense, with the man (or woman) of their choice. Issues of control and domination are cast in another light entirely if the desired hero is a chosen subject, if the story is told to a community of sister fans, and if the very act of telling the story makes the woman an independent narrator rather than a passive consumer. The issue of shame evaporates in a fan collective. As Deena Glass says of her experience writing fiction with the other "wives" of Ibn Fadlan: "Knowing that I am not alone in my appreciation of Antonio Banderas as an actor gives my 'obsession' with him approval and validates it" (see Glass et al. 2000).

Friendship Formation on the Internet

Sharon Cumberland

I would say that Antonio's influence is to have been the catalyst for some of the best friendships I've ever experienced. We constantly learn from each other and help one another grow. It's as if we all live in the same neighborhood, and meet for coffee every day, the way our mothers would have—except we're in cyberspace.

—*K. C. McMinn, "Keliana the Gypsy"*

Ever since the emergence of the Internet as a social force in the early 1980s, social scientists and communication theorists have engaged in hot debate about whether or not authentic friendships can be formed in virtual communities. One group argues that intimate relationships are impossible where eye contact and physical contact are absent, and that virtual reality isolates people from the real world. Another group argues the opposite, based upon studies such as Parks and Floyd (1996), whose analysis of a large Usenet group establishes the claim for authentic friendship formation in cyberspace. Their strategy was to select large random samples of virtual reality Usenet groups and to compare the results with real-life friendship studies. One such friendship study analyzes the development of what are called "weak ties" and "strong ties" in social relations—those networks of friendships that give people the support they need in various aspects of their lives. Adelman, Parks, and Albrecht have defined "weak ties" as "a wide range of potential supporters who lie beyond the primary network of family and friends" (1995, 126). They are relationships with friendly but not intimate acquaintances, like the pharmacist, the mailman, the bartender, and other familiar folk one encounters daily. Though not intimates, these individuals can have a powerful influence, can "dramatically extend the individual's access to information, goods, and services" in addition to offering support when stronger ties are disrupted, as when moving or coping with death or illness in the family. Furthermore, these ties can be formed with both animals and with "those portrayed in the mass media." As the authors note, "people may derive support or guidance from fictional characters in the media. They often attribute a sort of fantasy-level intimacy or friendship in their 'parasocial relationships' with media characters" (146). Thus fans can form "weak ties" with the media figures—fictional and nonfictional—to whom they feel attraction and from whom they feel a benevolent force. For anyone who has spent time in a fan community, these "weak ties" formed with iconic figures is experientially and intuitively obvious. When asked what role Antonio Banderas plays in their lives, the women interviewed for this project gave a broad range of responses that supply evidence of "weak ties:" "I call him my muse," reports one fan.

"The depth, the feeling, the passion in his work, helps me unlock those same things inside myself." Many fans report that they have acquired newfound interest in foreign films, Spanish culture, foreign travel, and language studies in addition to using the computer and honing their writing skills. In addition to inspiring his fans to expand their interests, Antonio Banderas the person—as apart from his onscreen persona—seems to have personal reality for his fans. By reading interviews, articles, and biographies, a certain sense of the individual emerges, which gives some fans a strong sense of friendship with him. "The role Antonio plays in my life is one of companion," says Chrissy. "He escorts me through my day. He is there with me through good times and bad." Says Susan, "I enjoy him as an actor, as an attractive man, as someone who lives a fascinating life, and I admire him for his substantial accomplishments."

Social science and communication theorists are beginning to understand that relationships can be actual even when formed in a single direction. What is lacking in the interpersonal dimension can be supplied by imagination, research, and study—what has been called "expertise" or "competence" in terms of a fan's level of knowledge about the star, his/her history, and the characters he/she plays. By sharing fan expertise with other fan experts—at conventions and through fan sites—the groups embody their iconic figures by making them vividly present in conversation and other acts of celebration. Henry Jenkins's groundbreaking study on fan culture and television, *Textual Poachers: Television Fans and Participatory Culture* (1992) was the first to identify fans as an empowered group who appropriate media creations for their own social, creative, and emotional purposes. A more recent study, Nancy K. Baym's *Tune In, Log On: Soaps, Fandom, and Online Community*, examines the world of soap operas and the service they have performed for generations of women. Like popular romance novels, the characters in soap operas "have the potential to empower women," but unlike romance novels "soaps create a social space, enhancing women's social bonds to one another" (2000, 16). By forming "weak ties" with media characters, similar (and often stronger) ties are formed with the fan community.

P. David Marshall in *Celebrity and Power: Fame in Contemporary Culture*, defines the exchange between the "celebrity sign" and the audience as a process of "making sense of the social world," a process that is "simultaneously an activity of the members of the dominant culture, who are instrumental in the procreation of the celebrity sign, and of the members of subordinate cultures, who are, for the most part the audience that remakes the sign"(1997, 51). In other words, movie stars are cultural products marketed and remunerated by the commercial creators for their "star power" or ability to attract loyal fans into the movie theaters, but it is the fans who remake the star into an iconic figure with whom they can form a weak tie. This process is easier if the celebrity conducts his offscreen life in a way that causes his fans to admire him. For instance, the fact that Antonio Banderas has a stable family life in spite of his "Latin lover" screen persona is a reinforcing characteristic for the mostly middle-aged, middle-class women who are his fans.[3]

Forming weak ties with the iconic figure is the prelude for fans to form strong ties with one another. Adelman, Parks, and Albright describe "strong ties" as relationships with the "intimacy and frequency of interaction characteristic of stronger ties to family and close friends" (1995, 126). Parks and Floyd found that "on-line relationships are genuine personal relationships in the eyes of the participants," and that two-thirds of users responding to their questionnaires "migrate" from friendship on the Internet to other forms of contact, including telephone calls, gift exchanges, meetings in person—even marriage (82). Although Antonio Banderas Web sites form a small cultural field, they do provide additional evidence that cyberfriendships have a strong tendency to migrate into real-life friendships. On the questionnaires I sent out, I asked respondents what the other "chicas" meant to them, and if they had ever met or contacted any other fans they had met on a Banderas Web site. Though my number of informants is small (23 fan fiction writers), the proportions conform to Parks and Floyd's finding: Two-thirds of my respondents have sought out other fans in person and have developed what they characterize as extremely close and supportive relationships with one another. For instance, the "Chica Convention" for Antonio Banderas fans convened in 1999 and 2000, promising to become an annual event. I myself traveled to Chicago in 1998 to meet fans from the Web Mall with whom I had been enjoying cyberfriendship for three years. I felt a strong determination to translate the mental images I had of my cyberfriends into a real-world experience. It is this determination that Parks and Floyd discovered and quantified with their much larger Usenet survey. Consistent with that survey, the balance of my informants who have not met other fans face-to-face still "migrate" in terms of telephone calls, letters, and exchanges of books, videos, magazines, and collectibles. They refer to their Banderas-site cyberfriends as "best friends," and sources of "essential" support. "I would be bereft without them," reports one fan. Says another, " We are kindred spirits. We are soul mates." Ultimately, it is this sense of kinship that seems to matter the most to Banderas fans. As Susan Hughes reports, "I have developed a few very close friends through the Web Mall—people with whom I have a lot in common—and I find we discuss our personal lives far more than we discuss Antonio."

This statement points to one of the complex transformations that occur on Banderas fan sites via communal storytelling. The iconic figure becomes a reflective surface that redirects the affection flowing toward him back onto the community that generates the affection. To use the terms that surface frequently among the fans, the Banderas persona acts as a "muse," an "inspiration," and a field upon which to locate soulmates. Once this rechanneling of affection is accomplished, the centrality of the icon is diminished, and personal friendship takes precedence.

Zorro Returns: Secondary Orality and the Banderas Hero

Finding Antonio enabled me to find a group of wonderful women with whom I have shared creativity, happiness, triumph, sorrow and tragedy . . . and also the appreciation for a fine actor, human being, and . . . a damn good butt!

—*Deena Glass, "Deena of Judea"*

Though the Internet is constantly shifting, at the time of this writing there are three different Web sites (out of the 30 or so devoted to Banderas) that support over six hundred works of collaborative fiction, in various genres, based on the characters Banderas has played. But the original collaborative narrative written by Banderas fans is *Zorro Returns*, a fantasy sequel to the 1998 film *The Mask of Zorro*, in which Antonio Banderas played the title role. The narrative, which was open to all who wished to participate, has twenty-four scenes written by a total of sixteen people, with as many as three collaborators for a single scene. It tells the story of Alejandro Murrieta, a bandit who was transformed into El Zorro in the film *The Mask of Zorro* and who, in the fan sequel, fights an array of variously motivated villains while having lots of sex. Although the moderator attempted to limit the number of new characters and plot twists and to encourage writers to advance existing story lines, *Zorro Returns* enjoys the kind of wild plot swings, narrative cul-de-sacs, improbable characters, and unmotivated sex scenes that one would expect from a group of enthusiastic amateurs whose relish in telling their fantasies supercedes their interest in shaping them into the confines of the novelistic form.

Thus *Zorro Returns* not only stands as a monument to communal inclusivity but suggests a relationship to folk legend—episodic scenes in which a community describes the adventures of a folk hero—in this case, three different aspects of what we might call the Banderas-hero woven in with the older tale of El Zorro. The project was highly successful in that it achieved its goal of providing Banderas fans with entertainment that amused and satisfied them. As I watched this storytelling phenomenon unfold over the course of about three months in the winter of 1998—and even wrote a chapter myself—it was as though there were a crowd of people sitting around an electronic campfire listening as some members of the community took turns building a picaresque legend around their shared hero.

In this sense, *Zorro Returns* offers an illustration of Walter J. Ong's theory of "secondary orality," which posits that virtual storytelling, though dependent upon writing, has a "striking resemblances to [primary orality] in its participatory mystique, its fostering of a communal sense, its concentration on the present moment, and even its use of formulas . . . for groups immeasurably larger than those of primary oral culture—McLuhan's global village" (1982, 136). The inclusiveness of *Zorro Returns* fostered just this communal sense in that it encouraged people to tell stories who might never have attempted to do so in the face of the rigidity of the print media and the less immediate interest of the general public in their celebrity hero. There is also a formulaic quality that emerges in fan constructs of the Banderas-hero that is reminiscent of oral epic heroes in their large, outwardly directed gestures and personality traits, as opposed to what Ong describes as the literate hero/antihero whose personality is self-reflective and psychological. In primary oral cultures, all characters had to be large and memorable or they would be forgotten. Although Banderas himself has played many emotionally complex and nuanced characters, the fans' transformations of the Banderas-hero are memorable—large, dramatic, vivid—like characters in oral epics. The predominant traits of the Banderas-hero, extrapolated from the fan fiction must always have (1) *ojos negros* (deep brown eyes) and an elegant, graceful figure; (2) an androgynous combination of physical masculinity and emotional sensitivity; (3) redeeming qualities no matter how transgressive the original character is on film; and (4) an understanding of and appreciation for women. He is fundamentally romantic but never objectifying.

While the acceptable range of behavior for the Banderas-hero seems to prevail on all the fan sites devoted to him, an ongoing collection of short stories at the *Antonio Banderas Kiss Book* site contains a proliferating anthology of stories that demonstrate his qualities. Also known as the *Kiss Page*, this site provides a place for all fans of Antonio Banderas to expand their favorite characters with new stories. According to K. C. McMinn, the editor, an average of four new stories per week are being submitted by fans who write about Banderas film characters that cover the spectrum from Miguel Bain, an amoral hit man in the action film *Assassins*, to Francisco Leal, the freedom fighter in the film version of Isabel Allende's novel *Of Love and Shadows*. Nevertheless, these stories remain within the understood range of rhetoric and behavior that are consistent with the group understanding of who their hero can and cannot be.

A dramatic example of this is a collaborative serial entitled *The Revenge of Miguel Bain*—a fantasy sequel to the 1995 film *Assassins*—written by the same fan collective who wrote *The Five Wives of Ibn Fadlan*. In the film, the character played by Antonio Banderas is a maniacal murderer who tracks down and kills young lovers and aimlessly shoots passersby—a despicable character who is a departure from characters Banderas has played, and who, except in his physical appearance, does not conform to the traits of the Banderas-hero. Though he dies in the film, Bain is resurrected by fans in *The Revenge of Miguel Bain* to the requirements of the Banderas-hero: No longer a murderous hit man, he becomes a feisty lover for the beautiful heroine. In other words, even if Hollywood is ignorant of who the Banderas-hero is meant to be, and even if the actor himself experiments with nonheroic roles, the fans will reconceive the character in their own writing, investing him with the necessary heroic traits.

The Five Wives of Ibn Fadlan: Storytelling in the Harem

Historically, harem life was sometimes not warm and friendly, so our characters' eventual acceptance of one another and resulting friendships may not be accurate—but that acceptance acts as a symbol of our real-life relationships with one another.

—*K. C. McMinn, "Keliana the Gypsy"*

The ideal exotic and sexual role for the Banderas-hero is the sheik who presides over a harem of loving women—a metaphor that seems intuitively correct because the actor himself commands a following of devoted female fans. Yet the desert fabulae from which this image comes are not based on historical constructions of harem life but on Western fantasies dating from the sixteenth century, when explorers began returning with reports from the Ottoman Empire of the sultan presiding over a household of as many a three hundred wives and concubines, all living exclusively for his sexual pleasure. Leslie P. Pierce, in *The Imperial Harem: Women and Sovereignty in the Ottoman Empire*, says that "[w]e in the West are heir to an ancient but still robust tradition of obsession with the sexuality of Islamic society"—a sexuality that appeared to institutionalize the exciting taboos of multiple sex partners and the superman who could satisfy so many.

Yet, as Pierce describes, the harem was in fact a sacred place, taboo only in the sense of being holy, inviolable ground. "The word *harem* is a term of respect, redolent of religious purity and honor," and Mecca is the most revered *harem* in Islam. The term "is gender specific only in its reference to the women of a family," which implies a deep respect for the role of women in the social construct (Pierce 1993, 5). The Western concept of the harem as a sort of royal brothel in which women vie for the sexual favors of one man is a projection of European concerns with Christian religion and governance. So while McMinn posits that "life in the harem was not warm and friendly," she is drawing on the Western concept of "harem," assuming that women were in competition with one another for the attentions of their sheik.

In fact, Pierce points out, the reproductive life of an Islamic sultan was carefully regulated for political purposes: "Sexual relations between the sultan and chosen women of the harem were embedded in a complex politics of dynastic reproduction. This fact belies the simplistic but indefatigable notion that harem women acquired power by imprisoning sultans in the thrall of heir seductiveness" (1993, 3). Clearly the romantic notion of the sultan and his harem that gave rise to the desert fabulae is based only superficially on the institution itself. Yet McMinn has intuited through her collaborative fan writing a central characteristic of the Islamic harem—that women form familial relationships with one another on the strength of their shared interests, and that these relationships are based on respect for the family rather than competition for the sultan. Thus, while *The Five Wives of Ibn Fadlan* is framed in terms of Western constructs of harem life, as opposed to the historical Islamic harems themselves, a certain sympathy resonates in the formation of friendship communities among women on the Internet and the Islamic concept of *harem* as sacred, rather than the Western concept of "harem" as sex slavery. It is this Western concept that is redeemed by the fan writers, who use their romantic narrative to transform sexual bondage into love and freedom.

The Five Wives of Ibn Fadlan begins with "Johanna of Bavaria" describing in a flashback how she was kidnapped from her merchant father at the age of seventeen as she traveled with him through the mountains. The evil kidnapper, Renauld, murders her father and enslaves Johanna on a ship that takes her to the exotic and mysterious land that will be her home. Johanna is given to Fadlan in partial payment of a debt that Renauld owes the sheik. She is bathed and perfumed by the household women and presented to the twenty-year-old Fadlan who explains that he intends to marry her the next day. She struggles and protests until, alone and with no other recourse, she succumbs and goes through with the ceremony. That night, when the sheik consummates the marriage with the right combination of kindness and passion, she falls in love with him and becomes the chief wife of his harem. She bears him many children over the next eighteen years, including Ahmed, the first son and heir.

In each successive story the continuing character, Renauld, kidnaps another virgin to pay his debt to Fadlan. Deena is part of a caravan traveling from Judea to Spain where she is to be married to a merchant in Toledo when Renauld overcomes her protectors and steals her away to the desert. Christine of Scotland is kidnapped by Vikings from her Highland home and sold to Renauld who, by this time, has lost some of his murderous qualities and become a businesslike escort. By the fourth story, when Susanna of

Spain leaves her home in Madrid with her mother's blessing to avoid being married to the man of her father's choice, Renauld is an avuncular presence who comes to admire his captive, complimenting her on her dashing qualities and functioning more as an ambassador than a kidnapper when he delivers her to Fadlan. In the final story, Renauld is a fully developed older man who struggles to get the gypsy girl, Keliana, to the sheikdom in good health since she will be the final payment of his debt and, readers sense, because Renauld knows that the impoverished Romany will have a much better life with the loving sheik and her sister wives. Renauld is a dynamic character, emerging over the course of the tales as a sympathetic agent who delivers each of the wives into the unexpected source of their happiness.

Ahmad Ibn Fadlan, on the other hand, is not a dynamic character. He is always passionate, always intense, always good-hearted, humorous, and affectionate. In other words, he is another manifestation of the Banderas-hero: physically beautiful, androgynous in his combination of male sexuality and female sensitivity to feelings, redeemed from the transgressive qualities that would make his character problematic for the reader. Though he accepts and virtually enslaves innocent girls in a harem, the crime of kidnapping is displaced onto Renauld, while the issue of enslavement is rendered moot (in the context of the narrative) by marriage. Thus the Banderas-hero departs from the romance formula in that he is in no need of transformation from patriarchal cruelty. He only needs to dispel the ghost of Western patriarchy by showing the fearful protagonists that the harem is a utopia of equality, in which every wife will be honored for her unique qualities.

Though a collaborative collection of stories, *The Five Wives of Ibn Fadlan* is really one master narrative told in five variations. Each heroine is in the transitional moment that separates her from her father; she is helpless in the face of the reifying world, represented by Renauld; she is forced to live in a harem, enslaved by her gender. But she is redeemed to live a full and satisfying life by the good-hearted sheik who insists upon legitimizing her through marriage and by the sister-wives who provide the community in which each member receives recognition and support. The subtext of resistance, in which the heroine's father is murdered, left behind as the heroine embarks on her journey, or openly defied, intensifies as she struggles with Renauld, who reinstates the patriarchal force. Yet the final man in this succession of captors, Fadlan, is willing to let her go, as he assures Deena in words that would apply to all: "You shall be ransomed, nay, I shall send you to your betrothed with your dower intact and your honor unblemished." This is because the ideal hero is not interested in possession but in partnership. He would rather send the heroine back to her father's house, that is, to the dependency of her childhood, rather than have her dependent upon him for anything other than love—the agent that transforms bondage into freedom. In their discussion of the desert fabula, Bettinotti and Truel describe this trope of transformation as key to the genre: "What originally appeared to be a story of captivity and enslavement turns out to be a story of resistance and female liberation" (1997, 192). As Fadlan says in the final story to Keliana, "You are a treasure, my treasure, always . . . and you are bound to me, but only with love."

The authors of *The Five Wives of Ibn Fadlan* use the metaphor of a harem to represent a friendship that owes its existence to their shared interest in Antonio Banderas. Using the Western construct of the harem, it is an elegant metaphor in that the vehicle (harem) addresses all points of the tenor (community, sexuality, exoticism) while observing the romantic tropes of the desert fabula. Yet the metaphor raises questions about the reinscription of patriarchal gender roles. To what extent are these stories empowering if the heroine sees herself as part of a harem? Can women be said to be liberated if they insist on returning to metaphors of subordination and enslavement? Why, for instance, could the Banderas-hero not be imagined as the lover to five powerful queens, diplomats, or woman warriors? Put another way, what aspect of male dominance is essential to the pleasure of these collaborative narratives?

As Edward Said notes in his famous discussion of orientalism, "the Orient seems to suggest [to the Western imagination] not only fecundity but sexual promise (and threat), untiring sensuality, unlimited desire, deep generative energies" (1978, 188). This description identifies the Oriental stereotype as essentially female—as opposed to Western stereotypes of masculinity. The dominant male figure is always the elegant, exotic sheik, whose habits and procedures stand in direct opposition to Western conventions of power. A recurring theme in *The 13th Warrior*, for instance, is Fadlan's fastidious cleanliness and elegant manners, his disgust with the Vikings who never bathe, who eat like pigs, and who manifest a love of gore and adventure that forms a principle signifier in Western inscriptions of masculinity. With his flowing robes, kohl-lined eyes, and slight build, he seems like a woman compared to the huge, hairy Northmen, who tease and mistrust him until he proves his dexterity with weapons and demonstrates his loyalty in battle. The sheik, then, can be read as a feminized man or a masculinized woman—an androgynous figure who has the best of both genders—the civility and beauty of a woman together with the aggression and courage of a man.

This construction of the sheik as androgynous or feminized is partially grounded in Western interpretations of Islamic society—what Pierce described as the Islamic social distinctions between the privileged and common "that cut across the dichotomy of gender." Western travelers who expected extreme signifiers of Western masculinity in those who could satisfy hundreds of wives and concubines were met instead with figures whose authority was signified by the number of social layers between himself and the public eye. The sultan, surrounded by his enormous entourage, seemed as pampered and protected as any member of the female harem. Given that many of these protectors were eunuchs, whose proximity to the sultan and promotion to higher duties depended, in part, upon the removal of sexual threat to the harem (Pierce 1993, 12), it is no wonder that the tension between the apparent effeminacy of the sultan and his entourage, and the erotic implications of multiple wives and concubines, defined the exotic extremes of harem fantasy. One has only to conjure the image of Rudolph Valentino, who epitomized the exotic, erotic, somewhat effeminate sheik in the famous silent film version of Hull's novel, to understand how thoroughly Hollywood institutionalized the oppositional tension of the androgynous sex god—a role to which Banderas is often declared the heir.

Whether seated in Western fantasies of Islamic society or amplified by Hollywood's love of the exotic, however, the androgyny of the Banderas-hero is ideally mirrored in the sheik of *The Five Wives of Ibn Fadlan*. In the transition from the West to the imaginary East, each heroine is forced to act out the male-imposed rape fantasies of Western culture, only to arrive in a utopia where the patriarch has been transformed into the ideal androgynous human—a passionate man in the bedroom, loyal and violent on the battlefield, and yet as sensible and affectionate as an ideal woman everywhere else. Thus the only aspect of male dominance essential to the pleasure of these narratives is sexual—and even then Fadlan is as courteous in bed as he is elsewhere, his sexual prowess undiminished by his kindliness. Remembering that the polarities of male power and female sensitivity are stereotypes, within these broadly drawn heroic characteristics, the sheik figure can be said to integrate male and female identity.

Popular culture has the imaginative authority to integrate these stereotypes in more than one way. For example Xena, the warrior princess, integrates the masculine and feminine into the feminine body, while Dax, an alien on *Star Trek: Deep Space Nine* incorporates a nongendered being into both male and female bodies. For those fans who seek gender integration into the male body, the sheik provides a solution to the gender divide. In Western thought, of course, the harem is a male fantasy of female availability and subjection. But for the authors of *The Five Wives of Ibn Fadlan*, the harem is a symbol of community with one another and the male muse who brought them together, one that McMinn refers to as "a symbol of our real-life relationships with one another."

The Five Wives of Ibn Fadlan exists at the intersection of an array of social and literary movements critical to women at this moment in history: access to technology, the formation of online communities, the revisioning of gender relationships through popular romance, and the collaboration on fan fiction writing that valorizes communal friendship as much as the iconic figure who prompted the activity in the first place. Out of the hundreds of stories available to illustrate these issues, *The Five Wives of Ibn Fadlan* is especially revealing for its use of a classic romance genre, the desert fabula, to reconceptualize the patriarch as an idealized, feminized man and the harem as a community bound by love rather than power. Reading the tropes of this story against the Internet itself, one can speculate that the "virile-reality" of Internet technology will, like Ahmed Ibn Fadlan, retain the best of its masculine qualities while acquiring more and more of the approachability, the "intuitive and clear interfaces" that women can bring to the enterprise. Through collaborative storytelling on fan Web sites, women are appropriating twenty-first-century technology in the process of creating supportive female communities.

Notes

1. By "collaborative fiction" I mean (1) works that are written on the Internet by multiple authors or (2) Internet anthologies of single-authored stories that refer to the larger aims of related stories (such as *The Five Wives of Ibn Fadlan*).
2. This and the following quotations from fan fiction writers are taken from interviews, e-mails, and questionnaires I have collected from the authors of Antonio Banderas fiction found on the Antonio Banderas Web Mall and the *Antonio Banderas Kiss Book*.
3. The connection between actors' private lives and fan loyalty is embedded in Hollywood history by way of the famous Production Code designed to ensure purity on screen, with concomitant pressure on actors to avoid scandal offscreen. See my article "North American Desire for the Spanish Other: Three Film Versions of Blasco Ibáñez's *Blood and Sand*" (Cumberland 1999).

Works Cited

Adelman, Mara, Malcom R. Parks, and Terrence Albrecht. "Beyond Close Relationships: Support in Weak Ties." In *Cybersociety*, ed. Steven Jones, 31–42. New York: Sage, 1995.

Adelson, Rachel K. "Introducing Live Wire: Computer Confidence for Women." Association of Women in Computing. Online. Available at <http://awchq.org/ livewire/ index.html>. October 10, 2000.

Bacon-Smith, Camille. *Science Fiction Culture*. Philadelphia: University of Philadelphia Press, 2000.

Baym, Nancy K. *Tune In, Log On: Soaps, Fandom, and Online Community*. Thousand Oaks, CA: Sage, 2000.

Bettinotti, Julia, and Marie-Francoise Truel. "Lust and Dust: Desert Fabula in Romances and Media." *Paradoxa* 3, nos. 1–2 (1997): 184–194.

Crichton, Michael. *Eaters of the Dead*. New York: Ballantine, 1976.

Cumberland, Sharon. "North American Desire for the Spanish Other: Three Film Versions of Blasco Ibáñez's *Blood and Sand.*" *Links & Letters* 6, (1999): 43–59.

Cumberland, Sharon. "Private Uses of Cyberspace: Women, Desire, and Fan Culture." *Media in Transition.* Online. Available at <http://media-in-transition.mit.edu/articles/index_cumberland.html>. July 8, 2000.

Glass, Deena, Christine Hillhouse, Susanna Jaime, K. C. McMinn, and JoAnn K. Prater. "The Five Wives of Ibn Fadan." Banderas Kiss Book II." Online. Available at <http://members.tripod.com/banderas_kisses/index.html>. July 8, 2000. Also available online at <http://fac-staff.seattleu.edu/slc/index.html>. October 10, 2000.

Jenkins, Henry. *Textual Poachers: Television Fans and Participatory Culture.* New York and London: Routledge, 1992.

Kendall, Lori. "'Are You Male or Female?' Gender Performances on Muds." In *Everyday Inequalities: Critical Inquiries,* ed. Jodi O'Brien and Judith A. Howard, 131–154. Malden, MA, and Oxford: Blackwell, 1998.

Marshall, P. David. *Celebrity and Power: Fame in Contemporary Culture.* Minneapolis: University of Minnesota Press, 1997.

McMinn, K. C. "Banderas Kiss Book II." Online. Available at <http://members.tripod.com/banderas_kisses/main.html>. July 14, 2000.

Ong, Walter J. *Orality and Literacy: The Technologizing of the Word.* London and New York: Methuen, 1982.

Parks, Malcom R., and Kory Floyd. "Making Friends in Cyberspace." *Journal of Communication* 46, no. 1 (1996): 80–97.

Person, Ethel Spector. *Dreams of Love and Fateful Encounters: The Power of Romantic Passion.* New York: Norton, 1988.

Pierce, Leslie P. *The Imperial Harem: Women and Sovereignty in the Ottoman Empire.* New York: Oxford University Press, 1993.

Quinby, Lee. "Virile-Reality: From Armageddon to Viagra." *Signs: Journal of Women in Culture and Society* 24, no. 4 (1999): 1079–1087.

Rabine, Leslie W. "Romance in the Age of Electronics: Harlequin Enterprises." In *Feminist Criticism and Social Change,* ed. Judith Newton and Deborah Rosenfelt. New York: Methuen, 1985.

Robert, Kirrily "Skud." "Geek Chicks: Second Thoughts." *Freshmeat.Net.* Online. Available at <http://freshmeat.net/news/2000/02/05/949813140.html>.

Said, Edward. *Orientalism.* New York: Vintage: 1978.

Smith, Jennifer Cruise. "This Is Not Your Mother's Cindarella: the Romance Novel as Feminist Fairy Tale." In *Romantic Conventions,* ed. Anne K. Kaler and Rosemary E. Johnson-Kurck. Bowling Green, OH: Bowling Green State University Popular Press, 1999.

11

CORRESPONDENCE **(EXCERPT)**

Sue Thomas

When people ask, 'Could a machine ever be conscious?' I'm often tempted to ask back, "Could a person ever be conscious?" I mean this as a serious reply, because we seem so ill equipped to understand ourselves. Long before we became concerned with understanding how we work, our evolution had already constrained the architecture of our brains. However, we can design our new machines as we wish, and provide them with better ways to keep and examine records of their own activities—and this means that machines are potentially capable of far more consciousness than we are. To be sure, simply providing machines with such information would not automatically enable them to use it to promote their own development, and until we can design more sensible machines, such knowledge might only help them find more ways to fail: the easier to change themselves, the easier to wreck themselves—until they learn to train themselves. Fortunately, we can leave this problem to the designers of the future, who surely would not build such things unless they found good reasons to.

—*Marvin Minsky, from* The Society of Mind

WHO ARE YOU?

People often turn away from you in the street, but you can understand that. You find them pretty scary too, and of course you know that you're both frightened by the same thing—you see a little bit of yourself in them, and they see you likewise. The only difference is that you understand, and they don't. You've heard them whisper, when they think you're too far away to hear:

'There's something odd about that woman, but I can't quite figure out what it is. She's just not quite the same as us . . .'

Oh, but you are! There's a trace of you in every one of them, but they just can't see it.

It's like the story about the man who is killed in a road accident. His son is rushed to hospital seriously injured, but in the operating theatre the surgeon declares, 'I cannot operate on this patient. He is my son.' It's unbelievable how many people just can't work that one out. It's necessary to have a certain mind-set to appreciate the obvious, and the same applies when they look at you. The aspects of your difference are incomprehensible to them, despite the fact that they are really very apparent.

Anyway, you make people feel uncomfortable. Because of that, you've developed the habit of going out very little. Most of your requirements can be delivered to your house, for which you must thank your Regis 3000 terminal. It was worth every penny—you can do all of your online shopping and banking with it, although of course you can't live entirely on electronic money, and you do need to go to the cash-card machine occasionally to get something for incidentals.

You look forward to the creature comforts of the cash-card. It provides an affectionate familiarity in a world which offers very little in that direction to people such as yourself (although you don't actually know whether there are any others like you anyway). You go to the bank in the dead of night when everyone else is safely tucked up in bed. You always drive there, and you spend as little time as possible out of the car.

You used to walk around the streets in the dark quite often, until you had an unpleasant encounter which brought home to you very forcefully the extent to which you invoke dislike in people. Now these days you're careful to drive, and if you should meet anyone, even while waiting at traffic lights, you make sure that you avoid their stares. They don't like the look in your eyes, it seems—it incites them to violence, or at the very least, a glowering hostility.

But the cash-card machine is your friend. Every time you insert your card you feel a thrill as the welcome window slides up:

Please enter your personal number

Most certainly you will! Only too happy to oblige! You tap in your code and the machine hums in greeting. It has a special tone for you—in fact you suspect that you have developed your own discreet mutual admiration society. You like to stand in front of it for as long as you dare, bathing in the orange glow of the screen. It's not quite like the machines at home—no doubt that's something to do with the type of work it does. It interacts with people twenty-four hours a day, whereas your machines have only you. But whatever the reason, a trip to the bank does wonders . . .

BREAK

Hi! My name's Marie, and I'm here to guide you through the story. Sorry I wasn't here to greet you, but I hope you're finding your way okay.

Now, I don't want you to worry too much about me—I'll just plod along in the background, bringing you the facts when you need them. I'm only a mouthpiece really. If you have any questions, please don't hesitate to ask. Otherwise, I'll just point out the people and places of interest as we go along, and all you have to do is sit back and enjoy. I will, of course, be giving you information from time to time to help you keep up as the scenario develops.

Oh, and naturally it's my legal duty to warn you that this is a role-play. Wasn't that mentioned in your brochures? Oh dear. Well, it should have been. Someone must have slipped up down at the office. I'll explain again. You've been allotted a character to play and I'm just here to fill you in on the background details. You've already become acquainted? Great!

Now, if you look under your seats you should find a starter pack containing guilt, loneliness and desire. It's there? Oh good, at least someone has been doing their job properly. Now on this trip we are also fortunate to have been given a free sample of wish-fulfillment, although I must warn you to use it in single doses only. Lifetime supplies are available from Regis, although to be honest they're extremely expensive. In fact, just between you and me I don't think they've sold any at all yet. But I shouldn't be telling you that really, should I? Anyway, I hope you enjoy your small free sample.

Okay. If everyone's ready we'd better get on. I'll be up here at the front should anyone need me. Before you tune in your headsets, please register the following infodump. You will receive more information as we proceed.

Regis Tours / infodump 1

MACHINE MYSTICISM

Before the Renaissance, there was no distinction between philosophy and science, and the old magicke worked alongside new discoveries. Paracelsus, for example, left us an invaluable legacy of knowledge in the pharmaceutical field, but he also devised a recipe for constructing a homunculus out of human sperm, horse manure and blood.

The Renaissance insisted on defining the machine as a phenomenon separate to humanity, but automata continued to represent the bridge between imagination and empiricism.

Descartes concluded that mind and body are two different states—the rational and the mechanical. The latter could be reproduced by automata and animals. The former, comprising Judgment, Will and Choice, only by humanity.

The connection, or interface between the two, was said to be the Third Eye, or pineal gland.

. . . does wonders for your isolation problem.

You weren't always such a recluse. That has in fact been rather forced upon you, and there are times when you regret the whole thing and wish you'd never taken it on. But most of the time you're quite happy, and of course your work takes up a great proportion of your thoughts.

You are a compositor of fantasies. A grand title which doesn't hint at the day-to-day grind of the job. Often you're so overwhelmed by the amount of source material that you just stop altogether and take a week off. You're lucky because you can switch off completely and take a well-earned rest, then begin work again feeling fresh and ready to go.

The project you're working on right now is quite complex. You got it because of your seniority, but even so you can't help wondering whether Alan is testing you out in some way. Sometimes you imagine him sitting in his big black swivel chair, racking his brains trying to think of a job he can give you which will finally prove impossible. Then he can justify throwing you on the scrapheap. Well, let him try. You know you're the best in the business, and when you get this latest one sorted out it will be stunning.

YOU DREAM

You had a dream last night. That's pretty unusual for you—a busman's holiday, you might say.

You were with your family again. You were travelling somewhere in an aeroplane, and you were nervous. You've never liked flying but always strained to hide your fear from the children. You wouldn't like to think you'd passed on such a silly bad habit. Anyway, in the dream you were sitting next to John and the kids sat across the aisle playing some sort of noisy card game. Suddenly one of them, you remember it was Charlie, threw the cards into the air in a fury, and they fluttered down all over the place. You bent to pick them up before the steward saw them, but when you straightened up again you found that everyone had disappeared, including the plane itself, and you were standing alone on a high cliff-top. The sea was dark and the sky full of rain clouds. Big white birds wheeled above your head. You still held the pack of cards, but you couldn't make the patterns any more. Somehow you knew that John and the children were hidden in the suits—a king and two knaves. As you stood there, panic-stricken, trying to decode the patterns, you found yourself awake and sobbing with fear and loneliness.

You don't like to dream. Memories that are best hidden seem to bubble up and spoil things. Therefore you have arranged not to sleep for the next seven days, just in case there might be a repetition of last night.

It's a facet of your new personality that you can schedule your past life and file it to the back of your mind. This sort of auto-amnesia makes day-to-day living so much more pleasant. It means that in effect your consciousness is permanently keyed in to Real Time. If you want to recall a memory, you can select it in the same way that other people choose a video, and when you've finished with it, it's filed away, and to all intents and purposes forgotten.

Regretfully, though, some malfunction of your psyche allows memories to be recalled at random and played through your subconscious without your knowledge. In fact, you suspect that this happens quite often, but the only time you can be sure is when you have a dream like the one featuring the aeroplane.

You are worried that these malfunctions will hinder your work, so you try to refrain from sleep as much as possible. It's just as well, because today you had the most enormous delivery of mail.

You've ordered a long list of research material. Sorting it all out is going to be a mammoth task, so you've decided just to take on board whatever comes in the morning post plus any new faxes et cetera that come through during the day. Running through the new material takes up most of the daylight hours, then you meditate upon it during the evening before building the next block. It can be very tiring work, and today's input has rather daunted you. Perhaps you never will finish this piece or, worse still, perhaps Alan will take it away from you and give it to some young high-flier.

Don't panic! It will be finished, and it will be damn good. Of course, not 'good' in the sense of 'pleasant.' It is an unfortunate fact that composited fantasies can all too often turn out to be nightmares. However, you have a positive feeling about this one. You think it'll work out in ways that will initially disorientate people, maybe even shock them, but in the end it will get to them because you're sure you're on the right track now. You reckon you know what it is they're all after, even if they don't know it themselves.

When you were a real woman, you always knew instinctively what it was that people needed. If someone was hungry, or lonely, or in need of a cuddle, you could always tell, and nine times out of ten you could give them exactly what they wanted. Right on the button.

It's no surprise that this talent led you straight towards being the perfect wife/ mother/daughter/neighbour/friend/ and finally/ mistress. Although you have to confess that there was a slight hiccup on the mistress side. You became the lover of a man who needed you desperately—but, and here's the rub—you discovered to your horror that you needed him just as much. In fact, your desire for him exceeded his for you. Now that had not been in your imaginings. You were thrown into confusion for a time, and your talent for pleasing people began to atrophy through disuse.

For almost a year subsequent to your disastrous affair, you were impervious to the feelings of others, and thought only of yourself. It was a miserable time, and when the scales finally fell from your eyes you found before you a family deprived for the last twelve months of all the care and attention so necessary for them to thrive. It was not easy, but you put everyone back on the right track and atoned for your carelessness at letting them drift, uncared for, for so long. After a couple of years you were your old self again.

Later on, you wished that you'd remained closed off and impervious, because then it would have been easier to cope with the loneliness that followed.

Regis Tours / infodump2

MACHINE AS FRIEND

Machines make good friends. Although at present computer systems cannot be given the capacity for free will and emotion, we are content to attribute them anyway, just as if they were dogs and cats. We say 'this toaster/calculator/car *won't* work'. Not 'can't' or 'is not programmed to', but *won't*. Our machines have nervous breakdowns, they are stupid. We assault them with our lists to make them work.

Sometimes we are entranced by them. Sometimes they make us laugh. We talk to them even when they have no voice recognition capability. We think that they have no character—so we give them one. The philosopher Descartes is reputed to have owned an automaton which was a simulacrum of his estranged daughter, Francine. He took it everywhere with him until it was thrown overboard by an angry ship's captain who thought it was evil.

Perhaps in the future we will have Francines who are perfect in every detail and identical to their originals.

We may not like the idea at the moment, but we've always cherished pictures of our loved ones, so why not simulations?

Sue Thomas

YOU GO OUT

You have resolved never to visit the cash-card machine again. You'll find another way to draw money from your account.

Last night you had a very narrow escape. You drove down to the bank quite early—at about ten o'clock. You were anxious to log in—maybe you had a premonition that you'd never meet the machine again.

There is a wide forecourt in front of the bank, and as you waited in the queue, eyes downcast as usual, a group of disco roller-skaters arrived. They had with them a portable cassette player which blasted out the music for their street dance. Carrying the hefty machine, they took it in turns to skate up and down the forecourt. Every time the skater passed you, however, the music disappeared in a crackle of interference.

By the time that the queue had gone and you were the only one standing at the machine, it had become obvious that there was some connection between your presence and the roar of static. You do, of course, have the same problem at home, but for the most part you manage to reduce it with a system of dampers.

You stayed a while in front of the machine, watching the lights flicker and wishing that you could talk to each other better. You felt very lonely.

Reluctantly turning to go, you came face to face with one of the skaters. He had obviously been drinking. Caught so unawares, you quickly dropped your gaze and began to walk past him, but he wheeled round to bar your way, then grasped your jaw and forced your face up again until you were staring straight into his eyes. You tried to defocus, but it was too late.

Like so many others in the past, he didn't comprehend what he saw, and he was scared. But his status as leader meant that he must straight away translate his fear into violence. Wordlessly, he tightened his grip on your neck. His eyes held yours for a second before he broke away and spat.

'Look at this, lads! Look at this slag's eyes! Weird, en't they?'

The others crowded nearer to stare and jeer, but instead they fell silent. You stood there together in a speechless huddle, while they shuffled their feet in embarrassment.

You stayed calm, clutched your money, and walked to the car. You could feel by the prickles on the back of your neck that they were watching you, and even as you turned the ignition you could see them in the rear-view mirror. They advanced curiously, skating slowly across the forecourt behind their leader, and accompanied by music drowned in a growing cloud of static.

Pressing hard on the gas you drove off fast, leaving them clustering goggle-eyed by the side of the road and followed by a parting jet of spittle.

Well, that must be the end of your little outings. You daren't risk any further attention. Now that even your physical presence singles you out, it's just too dangerous. And
apart from anything else, you simply couldn't afford the repair bills.

Regis Tours / infodump 3

MACHINE RELIGION

Pre-Christian mythology contains many stories of mechanical devices which reputedly
mimicked human and animal form. Even the mediaeval Christian Church made use of
religious statues which were mechanically animated in order to make them appear more
realistic and awe-inspiring. It was believed that the Holy Spirit entered into these statues and brought them to life, imbuing them with religious mystery.

The computer is yet one more blasphemous refinement of the pseudo-human
machine.

YOUR LONELINESS

You have a double bed, and on it beats a single heart.

For a long time you kept them both at the ready in case of visitors, but now you've
lost the habit. You don't change the sheets so often these days, and it's ages since you
sprayed the pillows with perfume. Your heart, too, is crumpled and stained—to be honest it's something of an embarrassment to you. One of your deepest fears is that you may
be knocked over by a bus in the High Street, and have to have emergency open-heart
surgery. They would find some pretty strange organs there, but apart from that, what
would they say, those suave knife-men, when they opened you up and found this
wretched blotched organ?

'Ugh, it's disgusting. You would have thought that she'd keep herself tidy.'

'Look at that wound. It's obviously been suppurating for years. It's a wonder that
the whole thing hasn't gone rotten.'

Well, not to worry. It will never come to that. When the end comes, if it ever does,
your secret shame will go safely to the grave. But of course, by that time your old heart
will be long gone anyway. Sometimes it's hard for you to imagine how things will be.
But it's certainly easier than remembering how things were.

You used to enjoy going to bed. It was a great pleasure to roll around between the
sheets with John, sucking and sweating. Every now and then he'd stop, and look at you
with such serious eroticism that you'd shudder along the whole length of your body. You
used to like that.

But you also used to like just as much the other nights when he was away, and you went to bed alone.

You would have a bath with a drop of almond oil in it to glaze the surface of the water. You liked to gently lift one leg out of the water and watch the sheen as the oil clung to it. Then you'd pat yourself dry all over, like they tell you to do in ladies' magazines, and slip under the covers. Your limbs felt like warm plastic. The first thing would be his faint scent on the sheets, and you would smile to yourself. You'd say out loud, 'That was lovely, last night. It really was!' Then you'd say it again, looking in the mirror this time to capture a sensual flicker of the memory. You'd slide your smooth oiled body around on the soft sheets, caressing yourself in the ways that he'd touched you the night before. Life was wonderful then, when your bed held the perfume of love. Now, it just smells of cigarette ash and paper.

You sleep surrounded by paper. Recently you moved to the centre of the mattress because things were getting into a mess. Now you have the data you're currently working with on the left side, and magazines and newspapers on the right. You usually keep your notebook under the pillow.

Your notebook is blue and green on the outside, and white, blue and smudgy on the inside. It's a bit messy because you use it to catch the overflow of your life. It's rather like a sink-tidy in that respect. Those pieces of debris which just won't go down the plughole you chuck into the notebook and leave there until they've passed even the smelly stage, and have decomposed to nothing. You never take the notebook out of the house, for the same reason that you fear open-heart surgery.

Beside your bed you have a digital clock radio. You find it useful because you like to know what time it is when you wake up in the middle of the night. The police like to know details like the time when they're interviewing victims. You haven't been burgled yet, although sometimes the idea seems quite attractive. It could be quite nice to wake up in the night and know that someone is there. As he leans over you, and in the second before he presses his thumbs to your throat, you could fantasise that he'd brought you a nice cup of tea and the morning paper. You could keep your eyes closed and pucker up your lips for a good-morning kiss.

You'd have to keep your eyes closed.

Regis Tours / infodump 4

Correspondence [excerpt] (fiction)

MACHINE RELIGION

Thou shall not make unto thee any graven image or any likeness of any thing that is in Heaven above or that is in the earth beneath, or that is in the water under the earth; thou shalt not bow down thyself to them nor serve them, for I the Lord thy God am a jealous God.

—*The Second Commandment*

BREAK

Um—if I could just interrupt for a moment—it's time to give you all some input about your role. Just a little bit of background to help you, and then you can proceed. Could you all retune to the Guidetron frequency . . . I'm switching you in now . . .

Being a compositor means that you must keep your receptors open twenty-four hours a day. It's the only way to do the job properly. Of course, you're all highly sensitive to other people's needs already, but that empathy needs to be fed endlessly with data if it's to be productive. You will find that your enhanced Regis system will prevent exhaustion and depression.

Women make the best compositors, although there are a few men who make a living at it. Bereaved mothers are the best candidates of all. This is because although they have no demands on their imaginative resources their faculties are well developed and in need of an outlet.

Compositing is really no more than a sophisticated development of the baser arts of painting, music, drama and writing. Artists of all sorts throughout the ages have tried to capture human dreams, desires and fears, and they were successful on a limited scale. Bosch was the master of nightmare, Rubens and Goya portrayed erotic desire, et cetera, et cetera. But each artist was informed by only a minuscule area of human experience— his/her own, plus a few snippets read or seen—and could therefore only deal within a very restricted field.

Compositors take their data from every possible source, but it's extremely important that out of all this research there arises at least one central character. Usually this character is the focus—through it the client is able to experience the sensations depicted in the fantasy.

The method used is the old tool of deconstruction. When it was first developed, its only purpose was to facilitate understanding—beyond that it seemed to have little creative use. Practitioners would dismantle a piece of writing, like a child taking apart a transistor radio, and then proudly survey the pieces scattered on the ground saying Now We Know How It Works. But they found that once it was disassembled they could not put it back together. The radio would never play again, the mystique of the poem would dissolve. Having achieved this remarkable negation the practitioner was then able to declare that since this object was evidently constructed of no more than selected groups of words supported by a fragile animus which crumbled when touched, then the original maker had lost control and become disassociated from it. 'For the reader to be born, the author must die,' declaimed Roland Barthes.

Naturally, electronics led the way when it was time to progress beyond this cul-de-sac. In fact it was Regis who designed the very first compatible systems. The transistor gave way to the microchip, and soon we had systems that could play 'Rock Around the Clock' while at the same time computing accounts, recording messages, printing hard copy, etc, etc. The technicalities were less of a problem than achieving the mind-set of realising it could be done.

And that's what compositors do too. They take up the old expressions and allow them to speak to each other all at the same time, in parallel. And as with any complex system, this means that we must first break them down into their component parts. Then we sort and reclassify them and then allow them to grow back together as hybrids. Enhanced meaning, enhanced beauty, enhanced mystique.

Compositors spend years researching and absorbing every facet of human experience and perception relating to their current brief.

For example, a typical project might be to build a fantasy of warmth, for sale to geriatric hospitals. The compositor will spend twelve months absorbing every different physical sensation of warmth. They will read descriptions of the ways in which people visualise being warm, and learn the associated colours, smells, and musical tones. Then they construct a multisensory experience which could be used to revive patients who had been admitted suffering from hypothermia.

One of the most important features of Regis fantasies is that they are built using holistic principles which encapsulate the essence of the subject as it has been experienced by people throughout the ages, or at least since the advent of record-keeping. They are designed in a multisensory package to cover every eventuality. This means that the artistic part of our work entails the translation of the entirety of human perception into a function which is meaningful to everyone, regardless of age, creed or colour.

It can, of course, be tricky, because the ultimate end of human desire is often refused admittance by the fantasist and is therefore relegated to the subconscious mind. Your job entails digging it up again, in order to realise that final goal into a tangible illusion—no matter how distasteful it may prove to be. Regis trains you in the precise skill of finding out exactly what it is that people want, and that end result is not always very pleasant.

You are warned that this can lead to a degradation of the art if indelicately handled. In respectable tech-entertainment companies like Regis the clientele demand a certain sophistication and finesse, but for compositors with fewer moral scruples there is a fortune to be made from salacious and violent fantasies.

You have been allotted a difficult and intriguing role to play, but your guide will be available at all times.

Please note that as a compositor your role-character is enhanced with authentic Regis augmentation software. This is designed to facilitate the creative process, and has no other function. RE-PROGRAMMING OF ANY KIND, EITHER OF OR BY THE COMPOSITOR, IS STRICTLY FORBIDDEN.

Datablock A is now on-line, but first please tune to info-dump 5.

Regis Tours / infodump 5

THE MACHINE AS BODY

Those of us who have operated a supermarket checkout till, or a word processor, or who have even just driven a car, have experienced themselves as an extension of a machine. We are used to thinking of our machines as extensions of our limbs and minds, but have we considered that we too are extensions of the machine's capabilities?

Working with a machine the operator becomes most efficient when she stops thinking about what she's doing, and begins to operate in a semi-automatic mode.

This feels good.

It can be quite exhilarating, almost like deep meditation.

It is this melding of mind and machine which turns small boys with inadequate social skills into computer addicts.

Marvin Minsky has described the brain as a meat machine—a construction composed of organic microchips. Extending the organic analogy, he sees the functioning of a computer as based not on the electronic activation of switches in a linear progression, but rather as a society of elements. It has been difficult to design a computational model of human psychology because human responses happen extremely fast and synchronistically. Although, of course, computers are very fast too, they are still unable to do more than one thing at a time, and for this reason the human brain remains, for the moment at least, technically superior.

But it won't be long before computers catch up, and soon we will have systems which operate through a series of differing interactive relationships.

Add to this the capacity for learning, which many computers already have, and perhaps we are on the way to creating a functioning pseudo-human being.

Regis Tours / infodump 6

> Making variations on a theme is the crux of creativity. But it is not some magical, mysterious process that occurs when two indivisible concepts collide; it is a consequence of the divisibility of concepts into already significant subconceptual elements.
>
> —*Douglas Hofstadter, from* Metamagical Themas

FROM YOUR GIVEN DATA YOU CREATE ROSA

The piece is beginning to come together now. It will be about a woman, and her name will be Rosa. Rosa Lee. Gipsy Rose. Rose of Tralee. Your Rosa. You love her already. In your mind's eye you can see her. She has dark hair, thick and wavy. Bobbed around her neck, with a heavy fringe which falls over her eyes when she talks. She speaketh through a veil of darkness. Her eyes are a chestnut brown, the sort of eyes that are bright with knowing, like a Quaker lady's.

You have seen them, coming out of the Friends' Meeting House on a Sunday morning, those lovely Quaker ladies. Usually elderly, short grey hair, sensible clothes and sturdy shoes. Sensible souls. They hold up their heads as they walk, and they walk straight in a determined but slow manner. Although not always slow—some are brisk. Late on a Sunday morning, refreshed by silence, they pass into the cold winter sun. And Rosa has eyes like theirs.

She has no religion though. She is not a deliberate worshipper. Instead, her whole presence acknowledges the source of worship without requiring the act.

All these words, and you've only got as far as her eyes! There's more to come. You see her as ruddy-skinned with full lips, a small dark mole on her left cheek. She could have freckles on her nose which darken in the summer. She's about five-six or -seven and sturdily built. In fact, plump. Let her be plump with strong wide calves and a rounded belly. The tops of her arms are fleshy and powerful, and she is freckled there too. Her breasts are heavy and full and her back is short in length but broad from shoulder to shoulder. This is your Rosa, and she will walk the path for you and find the answer. But let's not rush things—she's not yet properly sentient. She's only a composite built of data, and although you're excited by the prospect of her journey, she herself is not yet even aware of it, She lives and breathes in your imagination and it's not yet time for you to meet her. But she'll be here soon, and her story will unfold itself.

Meanwhile, someone else keeps trying to butt in. You can't keep her out. She's a pain. Yesterday when you logged in, her profile popped up on the screen, so you reset. You only need one person in this fantasy—two would make it complicated.

But after you reset, there she was again, trying to squeeze in next to Rosa. You look at her—she's hopeless. Not Rosa's type at all. She's very much a designer lady. Travels a lot without getting anywhere. Has no soul, no philosophy. She's not right, and you want her out of it. Now.

The trouble is, there's not much you can do about it. Once it's got to this stage, the programme runs itself. You're only an input facility, one of many, and you can't control the neural data which pass into the system. There's a reason for that, of course—it's to stop you from consciously interfering with the processing—which is what you'd do now if you could, just to keep that woman out. You were happy with Rosa on her own. She's yours. She's the best thing you've had for a long time.

Anyway, you'd better not let it worry you or you'll end up inputting even more of her and she'll ruin it completely . . .

Hang on . . . she's got a name now . . . Shirley. Not a very pretty name. Boring. But . . . , oh . . . she's pushing in . . . you can't keep her out . . . get away! . . . she's messing it up . . . oh no . . . you can't stop her . . .

12

DOING IT DIGITALLY: ROSALIND BRODSKY AND
THE ART OF VIRTUAL FEMALE SUBJECTIVITY

Jyanni Steffensen

This chapter is an exploration of digital female subjects, cyberfeminisms, fembots, and Freud. It is broadly an intervention in the debate(s) about women and cyberculture. In it, I analyze, from a cyberfeminist, queer, poststructural, and psychoanalytic perspective, a virtual, time-traveling subject called Rosalind Brodsky. Brodsky (RB) is an evolving fictional construction of Australian Anglo/Polish/Jewish painter and digital artist Suzanne Treister. The most sophisticated manifestation of Brodsky to date, one central to my investigation, is a CD-ROM titled . . . *No Other Symptoms: Time Travelling with Rosalind Brodsky* (1999).[1] This hypermedia text was launched, appropriately, at the Freud Museum (Freud's last home), in Hampstead, North London, in January 2000. The artist's work—rendered in her characteristically baroque visual and hypertext style—creates a space in which issues of "insanity" and humor, fetishism and sexuality, subjectivity and technology are negotiated in relation to personal histories/fictions and histories of the twentieth century. My reading suggests ways of approaching this work that might be useful for feminist theorists.

Apart from the extraordinary density and complexity of its multimedia format (text, film, video, sound, music, Treister's painting), *No Other Symptoms* is composed, postmodernly, almost entirely of intertexts. The matrix engineered by Treister appropriates thematic concerns from cyberpunk fiction (the fiction of a culture saturated by electronic technology), science fiction (with its emphasis on time and space traveling), psychoanalytic discourses on gender, sexuality, and the Oedipal family, political histories and revolutions, and Holocaust narratives of dispossession and genocide. The female cybersubject configured by Treister as agentic, mobile, and polysignified differs significantly from the traditional male-produced female technosubjects in that she is not reproduced as an object of male sexual desire.

Since 1995, Treister has been working on the digitalized Brodsky through whom the artist has, in part, reconfigured the classic Oedipal scenario in intertextual (art, psychoanalysis, technology) and intercultural (Anglo-Christian/Eastern European–Jewish) terms. According to Treister's artist's statement: "Brodsky fetishises history. She is a necrophiliac invader of spaces containing the deaths of her ancestors, through the privileged violence of technology. She dresses up like her ancestors, how she thinks they would dress." Brodsky says: "Sometimes I look for my ancestors in VR. I dress up like them, how I think they dressed. It's like a form of cross-dressing, I guess." In contradistinction to traditional masculinist (and most feminist) cyberheroines, Brodsky is Jewish.

I will begin by providing a brief outline of Brodsky and her virtual world, before providing some theoretical frameworks in which this character might be understood, and finally moving into a more detailed psychoanalytic reading of how the subject is signified. Treister provides the reader with a biography for her subject that, from Brodsky's birth in 1970, is intimately interwoven with narratives of psychoanalysis and fictions of technoscience. According to the author, RB was born at University College Hospital in central London, the same hospital to which the child psychoanalyst Melanie Klein was taken in her last illness. In fact, Brodsky claims that as a child, her family lived opposite Klein in Bracknell Gardens in Hampstead. The young Rosalind used to watch Klein in her front garden, fascinated that the older woman resembled images of her paternal grandmother, Rosalind Blum, who had been killed in the Holocaust.

The older Rosalind was educated at St. Martin's College, where she also had a part-time job in the New Technologies and Multimedia department just before her death in 2058. At some time in her career(s) she worked as a technoscientific researcher at the Institute of Militronics and Advanced Time Interventionality (IMATI). This fictional Institute is working with virtual technologies that render users' bodies invisible in their own time and space. The main function of the institute is to develop virtual simulations of key moments in history so that researchers can carry out experimental interventions within these virtual times/worlds. In conservative academic circles, considerable resistance to this form of "anthropological" research exists. At times Brodsky suffered from high levels of work-related stress and was widely thought to harbor delusions of actual time traveling. However, many of her colleagues at IMATI believed that her virtual travels were authentic, and that she had discovered a methodology for temporal and spatial displacement of her body—namely, that she time-traveled. Unfortunately, according to Treister's narrative, her body displacement codes are indecipherable today.

Narratology

Narratologically, the CD text can most usefully be understood as hypertext fiction, rather than cybertext fiction, in that its narrative nodes, while multilinear, are not open, technically, to user programming. Characteristic of hypertexts in that it is composed of bodies of electronically linked multimedia components with no primary axis of organization, the CD nevertheless offers interactive reading(s) in the Derridean sense. The hypertext system permits individual readers to choose his or her center of investigation from a menu of nodes. The individual reader might configure both RB and the text according to which, and how many, narrative nodes are explored and in which order.

The virtual world of Rosalind Brodsky offers up numerous nodal possibilities that might accord with the provisional points of focus of different readers in that RB is a successful technoscientist who carried out major historical research (and experimental interventions) in film, psychoanalysis, music, the Russian Revolution, the 1960s, and Eastern European history. Her virtual place of residence is a medieval castle based on Konigsschloß Neuschwanstein in Bavaria, a dwelling once occupied by King Ludwig. She hosted the *Rosalind Brodsky Time Travelling Cookery Show* for Introscan TV Corporations Network where, in one memorable episode, she disassembled a German Black Forest cake and remade the ingredients into Polish pierogi with chocolate and cherry filling. Wearing her electronic time-traveling costume to rescue her grandparents from the Holocaust, Brodsky made several attempts to locate her grandparents, on one attempt ending up mistakenly (a systems error occurred) on the film set of *Schindler's List* (1994). At some time in history (possibly the late 1960s and early 1970s), RB fronted a successful rock band called the Satellites of Lvov. While traveling in the future, she developed an intense interventionist interest in genetically altered food, for instance, Clono Chutney and other products manufactured by Nutragenitica.

Epistemologically, this reconfiguration of a female technosubject as an open set of nodal possibilities assembled between writer and reader resembles poststructural theories of decentered subjectivity. In relation to new media practices, the hypertextual construction of the CD-ROM—its interactive user mode of multiple narrative pathways and its extratextual dimensions of multimedia integrated forms—constitute a set of postmodern feminist signifying practices. There is no narratalogical, linear goal, no narrative closure that is characteristic of much masculinist cyberdiscourses. Unlike popular cyberheroines such as Lara Croft, Brodsky is not a "good action hero, unafraid to use an Uzi or throw a grenade when the need arises—that is, all the time."[2] She does not appear in a "nightie" as a reward for the (assumed male) player who finishes the game, as does Croft in *Tomb Raider 2*. Neither is there any authentic "woman" up ahead, no essential woman to be reclaimed by feminists from a lost past, and no unified Cartesian self to be constructed in the present. In psychoanalytic terms, *No Other Symptoms* constitutes a complex matrix of symbolic positions for women other than "mother," "phallic woman," "object of male desire," or "lack"—that is, the only positions designated to women in the narrative constructions of the (assumed) male subject.

Psychoanalysis

This multidimensionality of the hypertext resonates with the complexity of the desiring economy of the female technosubject constructed by Treister. *No Other Symptoms* constitutes a virtual space in which female subjectivity *is* signified as phallic—Brodsky's "weapon" of choice is a set of luxury feature vibrators—but only as part of a polymorphously signified symbolic. Treister mobilizes her digital protagonist's vibrators as a point of entry to traditional psychoanalytic technologies of female sexuality in order to parody and decenter their phallocentric construction.

I will concentrate my reading on Treister's construction of Brodsky's sexed subjectivity as it emerges from her interventionist encounters with the psychoanalysts Sigmund Freud, Melanie Klein, and Jacques Lacan. RB financed her time-traveling psychoanalytic excursions through the design, manufacture, and sale of her line of unique, luxury, feature vibrators. The fictional case histories of these sessions are included in the text of *No Other Symptoms*. Although the author states that Brodsky's psychoanalysis "failed," my own analysis of the text(s) suggests that it is difficult to determine conclusively whether RB, on the one hand, or the psychoanalysts, on the other, failed the analysis. All of the analysts become increasingly anxious when confronted by the significance of Brodsky's technological, female masturbatory devices.

There are several options for a player to penetrate to the case histories of Brodsky's sessions with the analysts. For instance, from *Rosalind Brodsky's Perpetual Electronic Time Travelling Diary* one can >select>A day in 1928 when Brodsky time-traveled for a session with Freud in Vienna > select Time Travel> A subsequent visit to Freud in London in 1938 when she finds her feature vibrators have been placed on his desk >select Time Travel> A bar in London, 1964, where Brodsky has gone to recover from her therapy session. One of the other hypertext pathways to the psychoanalysts' clinics is via the closet behind Rosalind's desk at IMATI. From the wardrobe, the CD-ROM interactor can virtually enter Freud's study at Maresfield Gardens, Hampstead eavesdropping on a conversation between the ghosts of Freud and the ghost of his daughter Anna Freud, also a psychoanalyst. They are discussing the time-travelling analysand. Freud's ghost dematerializes, leaving behind a book >select Book> This volume contains Freud's case history of his analysis with Brodsky.

The technoproficient Brodsky will be read queerly as a cyberfeminist parody on the phallocentric signification of both masculinist cyberpunk texts and the classic narratives of psychoanalytic theory. One of the classic psychoanalytically related scenarios of the cyberpunk construction of masculine subjectivity is the anxiety/desire model enacted in relation to the fantasy of the nonpermeability of body boundaries. In cyberpunk texts, organs are replaced, and various technologies are implanted into bodies and perceptual

| Figure 12.1 |
Vibrators from the house of Brodsky displayed in sex shop window, Soho, London, 1988. (Warhol, Lacan, and Schloss Neuschwanstein vibrators are featured.)

organs; male cyberpunk characters are penetrated. The fears and desires that Freud located in the unconscious continue to haunt classic cyberpunk characters. In this cyberfeminist reversal, they also queerly haunt Freud whose carefully technologized body of writing on "feminine" sexuality is metaphorically "penetrated" by the intrepid cybertraveler from his technologically unimaginable future.

Genre

Generically and thematically, *No Other Symptoms* might be assimilated by, or categorized as, a part of the body of cyberpunk fiction that has emerged since the 1980s. Cyberpunk is the fiction of a culture saturated by electronic technology. Its vocabulary is the language of cybernetics, biotechnology, corporational greed, and urban subcultures. Cyberpunk has emerged as more than a term for writers and print text. It is now

| Figure 12.2 |
Ghosts of Maresfield Gardens' video still. (Ghosts of Sigmund and Anna Freud played by June and
Maximiliam Treister, parents of the artist.)

employed across a range of media and cultural practices. The term is generally understood as a framework for conceptualizing a set of relationships to new technologies. In
psychoanalytic terms, this would include an understanding of the complex relationships
between shifts in cultural effects under the impact of new technologies and concomitant shifts in subjectivities.

Thomas Foster in "Incurably Informed: The Pleasures and Dangers of Cyberpunk" identifies three, sometimes overlapping analytic approaches to cyberpunk fiction.[3] He states that cyberpunk has been studied as a science-fiction genre, as a variety
of postmodern fiction, and as a site of analysis for cultural studies. He alerts us to the
fact that one of the most significant, and overlooked, writers of cyberpunk texts was also
a woman—Pat Cadigan. According to Foster, Cadigan's novel *Synners* (1991) raises the
question of the relations between new technologies, their impact on gendered identi-

ties and the cultural logic of postmodernism. Foster points out that the postmodern crisis of universality implied by cyberpunk fiction tends paradoxically to universality (i.e., assumes that the postmodern crisis affects all social subjects equally and in the same fashion). Of the postmodern "crisis" in general and the questions raised by Cadigan's novel, Foster writes: "The postmodern condition of forced signification or being incurably informed is an effect of the postmodern critique of universality—that is, a critique of the unmarked and therefore normative subject position of the middle-class, white male individual" (1993, 2).

The social situation constructed in cyberpunk fiction is, for Foster, one in which all subjects signify for others, in which all bodies function as signifying surfaces. The usually universally signifying (unmarked) male body and phallic (disembodied, transcendent) subjectivity, in other words, finds itself in crisis. In cyberpunk texts, this situation is usually represented as one of fragmentation or balkanization. Cyberpunk fiction poses a world in which cultural diversity and the formation of specific cultural identities is an explicit problem. Foster raises the question of whether this realignment of the global village constructed by cyberpunk writers offer women and men opportunities to rethink categories of gender and their relation to sexual identities. He also claims that there has been very little specifically feminist cultural criticism on the topic. I would argue that the way in which Treister constructs Brodsky transculturally, as Anglo/ Eastern European/ Jewish constitutes a significant intervention into the realm of cyberpunk characters from a culturally critical position. The construction of this cyberheroine's vibrator-signified sexuality also suggests a point at which gender and sexuality might be rethought in terms of contemporary technologies. One might also argue that there has also been too little attention paid to the specific sexualities of male cyberpunk characters from male theorists.

One such exception is Andrew Ross, who suggests that possibly no anthology so effectively betrays the masculinist values of cyberpunk as the collection titled *Semiotext(e) SF*.[4] According to Ross, the editors, Rudy Rucker and Peter Lamborn Wilson, commissioned material from contributors whose work had been rejected by more mainstream publications. Although the editors clearly assembled a range of formerly rejected material, they also produced a volume that loudly proclaimed the gender, ethnic, and racial conservatism of new cyberpunk writers. Penetrating penises figure prominently on every page in the form of a flip book illustration of the "High Performance Waldo," a penis modeled on "the Biomorph human penis rarely seen beyond the best sex professionals" (Ross 1991, 27). Ross argues that this form of cyberpunk fiction offers fully delineated urban fantasies of white male folklore. He also describes the logic underpinning the fantasies embodied in VR applications where chic French women are made available as flirting partners to help you, the ideal male interactor, perfect your French language skills. In contemporary cyberpunk narratives, as in VR applications, cyberspace heroes are usually men, whose ethnic and /or racial identity, although rarely made explicit, is contextually Western, Anglo, heterosexual, Christian, white.

Cyberfeminism

In analyzing this phenomenon, Anne Balsamo suggests that cyberspace offers such men an enticing retreat from the burdens of their cultural identities.[5] In this sense, it is apparent that although cyberspace appears to represent a territory free from the burdens of history, it will, in effect, serve as another site for the technological and no less conventional inscription of the gendered, racially marked body. Despite the fact that VR technologies offer a new stage for the construction and performance of body-based identities, it is likely that old identities will continue to be more comfortable, and thus more frequently reproduced. In other words, the fact that virtual realities and cyberspace offer new information environments does not guarantee that people will use the information in better ways. It is just as likely that these new technologies will be primarily utilized to tell old stories—stories that reproduce, in high-tech guise, traditional narratives of the subject.

In thinking about the rearticulation of old identities to new technologies, Balsamo concludes that the virtual body is neither simply a surface upon which are written the dominant narratives of Western culture nor a *representation* of cultural ideals. She argues that the virtual body has been transformed into the very medium of cultural expression itself, manipulated, digitalized, and technologically constructed in virtual environments. She continues:

Enhanced visualisation technologies make it difficult to continue to think about the material body as a bounded entity, or to continue to distinguish its inside from its outside, its surface from its depth, its aura from its projection. As the virtual body is deployed as a medium of information and encryption, the structural integrity of the material body as a bounded physical object is technologically deconstructed. If we think of the body not as a product, but rather as a process and embodiment as an effect—we can begin to ask questions about how the body is staged differently in different realities. Virtual environments offer a new arena for the staging of the body—what dramas will be played out in these virtual worlds. (Balsamo 1996, 131).

Treister's work, like that of her predecessors, VNS Matrix and their cybergirls ALL NEW GEN and the DNA Sluts,[6] can be read as a concerted effort on the part of cyberfeminist digital artists to transform the masculinist reproduction of female-sexed subjectivity. In these feminist-inspired virtual worlds, the female body is staged as active, intelligent, polymorphously sexual. This constitutes a significant shift from the cyberpunk signification of female subjects as passive objects of male desire (the cyberbimbo), or as a metaphor for technology as "female," threatening, and out of control (the fembot/vamp). In the postfeminist, posthuman virtual worlds suggested by Balsamo, the female body is significantly refigured, visually and metaphorically, to present the reader/user with different ways of thinking about women. The cyberpunk characters and worlds articulated by VNS and Treister can be relocated in a short history of cyberfeminist theoretical and critical interventions.

Alice Jardine, writing in "Of Bodies and Technologies," states that the fields of theories and practices covered by the words "the body" and "technology" are enormous.[7] For Jardine there are questions of gender and women, especially to the extent that both are frequently absent from discussions of technology and the body—as if men's and women's bodies had been represented in the same way throughout Western philosophies and histories, as if women (as historically constructed bodies) had had control over the technology. In Jardine's account, technology always has to do with the body and thus with gender and women in some form. She asserts that sexual difference is present when we investigate technology at the level of male fantasy as with the virgin and the vamp, where technology is represented as an asexual virgin mother—neutral, obedient, and subservient to man—or as a vamp, castrating phallic woman, issuing threats, and acting out of control.

Vamps have a long history in the technofictional milieu of literary and cinematic production, appearing in various guises as fembots, as feminine sexualized metaphors for mechanical, industrial, and electronic technology. These figures include automata, robots, androids, replicants, and the more recent cyborg hybrids of the technotronic age. Claudia Springer notes that with the historical transition from automata (the mechanical) to robots (the industrial) in technocultural production, the significance assigned to artificial beings changed.[8] "Robots were no longer evaluated as charming mechanical novelties; rather they were evaluated on the basis of what they were capable of doing, either for humans or to humans. In the late twentieth century, machines have been replaced by intricate systems of microelectronic circuitry"(90). Within particular masculinist discourses—including cinematic ones—technocultural production becomes associated with fantasies of excessive female sexuality. Fembots become metaphors for technology run amok, imagined as something like gigantic domestic appliances without a "fuckin' off-switch."[9]

Metropolis inaugurates the tradition of urban dystopias in the cinema, associating technology with women's bodies to represent the threat of unleashed female sexuality/robotics. This tradition is appropriated postmodernly in the intertexts of *Blade Runner* and *Eve of Destruction*. Springer argues that even when a film incorporates feminine metaphors for electronic technology, it can still enunciate a misogynistic position. *Eve* combines electronic imagery from the late twentieth century with the industrial imagery of *Metropolis* to condemn female sexuality. The body of Eve 8, the fembot, represents both steely industrial strength and the mysteries of microelectronic circuitry. She is constructed as a fetishized phallic woman with dangerous internal workings—the Defense Department has installed a nuclear device at the end of a tunnel inside her vagina. Female sexuality is linked to destruction in the tradition of *Metropolis*, and both are associated with the inner workings of electronic technology.

As a critical intervention in the historically ubiquitous cultural fantasy of the fembot, the cyberfeminist collective VNS Matrix spurns the "big Hoover sucking up/off mere mortal men" option and imaginatively enters the big body of technology via the micro-option. In the computer game *Game Girl*, the player is invited to identify with (among other things) a virus that penetrates and disorders the data banks of Big Daddy Mainframe. This virus is one manifestation of All New Gen (an omnipotent intelligence). One might join the DNA Sluts (another manifestation of ANG) in the Alpha bar for a cocktail of G-Slime, served by a male robot, to lubricate the process.

Cyberfeminist theorists, such as Donna Haraway, Sadie Plant, and Zoë Sophia/Sofoulis, also imagine and articulate a different relation between body and machine and between women and technology. This trajectory is based on a transgressive strategy and politics that imagines a perverse alliance between women and machines. Taking Jardine's observation that women and machines have come alive and have come to identity at approximately the same time, Sophia's observation that women and computers are structurally equivalent—that is, user-friendly—and Plant's tale of a paranoid man on television who thundered that "women and robots are taking our jobs," cyberfeminism simply points out the subversive alliance between women and all nonhuman intelligent activity. Further, they observe the extent to which these connections have always been in place. Plant writes in "Cybernetic Hookers" that women and machines have become disloyal: They have begun to think for themselves. She defines a cyberfeminist end of the millennium as the "Empire of the Senseless" whose replicunts say: "Fuck him, he was only a man. Men, especially straight men, aren't worth anything. Anymore. In this city, women are just what they always were, prostitutes. They live together and they do whatever they want to do."[10] Plant defines woman as neither manmade with the dialecticians, biologically fixed with the essentialists, nor wholly absent with the Lacanians. She is, for Plant, in the process "turned on with the machines" (5).

Speaking of contemporary digital arts practice in her essay "On the Matrix: Cyberfeminist Simulations," Plant also suggests that "the activities which have been monopolized by male conceptions of creativity and artistic genius now extend into the new multi-media and interactive spaces of the digital arts, women are at the cutting edge of experimentation in these zones."[11] She lists Beth Stryker's *Cyberqueer* and Ingrid Bachmann and Barbara Layne's *Faultline* (North America), Linda Dement's *Typhoid Mary* (Australia), and the French artist Orlan's technobody as instances in which "construct cunts access the controls"(181). In many ways VNS Matrix, the cyberfeminists, and Treister remain critical of the masculinist rationales of cyberculture, while often appropriating the languages of this culture, and they continue rewriting the female technobody in terms more appropriate for contemporary women.

Some cyberfeminist theorists began to rethink "the female body" (understood here as the "maternal body") as a metaphor in relation to cyberculture. Cathryn Vasseleu writes in "Virtual Bodies/Virtual Worlds" that in virtual reality, the site of reproduction is relocated from the maternal body to the matrix of cyberspace.[12] One of the questions asked by the Australian psychoanalytic cyberfeminist Zoë Sophia in "Virtual Corporeality" is: "What place does the female body have in cyber-space?"[13] Initially, she answers this question in the negative: "Femininity and maternity are present, but displaced onto masculine and corporate technological fertility." Sophia is not simply conflating the biological (female) and the sociological category of gender (woman) with "femininity" and "maternity." What Sophia is specifying is a masculine excess that finds expression in feminine and technomaternal figures, for instance, in the "womby red brain-womb" of the computer HAL from *2001: A Space Odyssey* or the womby computer mother in *Alien*. Instead of a female-identified woman, Sophia suggests, we find an Athenoid (daddy's girl), or an emotionally remote machine-woman. Women in these masculinist scenarios are represented as signs or objects, but not usually as the possessors or subjects of knowledge. If women and computers are structurally equivalent in a masculinist imaginary, then cyberspace can be imagined within the male computer hacker's imagination as a maternal or a feminine body—a matrix—to be penetrated, cut up, and manipulated in quests to appropriate and control resources. However, on the other hand, argues Sophia, from a feminist perspective the prospect exists for adopting more dialogical and negotiated styles of interacting with computers and other material semiotic actors. One possible source of fascination with artificial intelligence and technobodies for feminists, women science-fiction writers and technoartists, suggests Sophia, is that "if these artificial second selves can be loved and accepted as powerful, resistant, speaking subjects, so too might women, long acclaimed as monstrous to conventional categories of self and other"(16).

In psychoanalytic terms, Sofoulis mobilizes Brodsky's childhood neighbor Melanie Klein's theories of part-objects (e.g., breast, penis); Klein's relocation of primary castration as the loss of the breast (for which the penis might then be a substitute); the "epistemophilic phase" (imaginary research into the mother's body for good objects—children, feces, the father's penis); and the "femininity complex" of boys as a framework for reading masculinist technoart mythical productions such as "womb-brains."[14] Sofoulis asserts that whereas phallocentric explanations focus on the boy's discovery of woman's lack, equally decisive for subsequent cultural production is the mother-identified pre-Oedipal boy's discovery of his own lack of maternal organs—of breasts, vagina, and womb. In Klein's narrative of the femininity complex of boys, maternal/female organs are targets of envy and appropriation. But, Sofoulis adds, following Klein, this maternal identification and envy is denied and compensated for by an overvaluation of the phallus and Oedipal identification with the father.[15] Sofoulis continues that the disavowed elements of maternal identification and organ envy are sublimated into "cultural activities in which men play out fantasies of intellectual and technological productions as forms of reproduction, where inventions are brainchildren of 'fertile' minds and men can unite with technologies to produce monsters without the aid of women" (91). What Sofoulis is driving toward with Klein here is the formulation of a realm of the mythic along with those of the imaginary and the symbolic. What Sofoulis suggests is that within the context of the idea that maternal identification and envy is repressed from the symbolic order, it is not repressed from cultural production generally but rather sublimated into the mythic. This domain of the mythic includes, for Sofoulis, both technology and art. From this perspective, she reasons, the Oedipus complex provides a partial resolution of the boy's femininity complex. It eases the boy's journey into male-dominated spheres of cultural production where pre-Oedipal fantasies are legitimated as culturally valued activities conducted in the Name-of-the-Father and signified as phallic. Sofoulis asserts that on closer scrutiny these cultural productions of art and technology bear the marks of a more polymorphous system of significations and fantasies (e.g., anal, oral, maternal) (92). If, as Sofoulis points out, the imaginary femininity complex of the boy (i.e., his envy of and fantasmatic appropriation of maternal/female organs) is sublimated in the cultural production of mythic womb-brain configurations, then one might speculate as a corollary that in a feminine mythic the appropriation of missing male organs might apply. In "Slime in the Matrix," Sofoulis suggests just that: "If masculine sublimation in technoculture has been about acquiring the missing feminine organs (e.g., to make magical brain-wombs), then VNS Matrix images mythically develop the slogan 'Give a girl a spanner' and suggests that feminine sublimation might involve the appropriation of the phallus as a magical symbol" (100).

While I do not disagree with Sofoulis's development of a theory of cybergirl appropriation of the phallus as an imaginary (and powerful) symbol—after all, Brodsky manufactures vibrators—one might have reached the same theoretical conclusion by reexamining Freud's theory of lesbian subjectivity. By rereading Freud's theory of masculinity complexes in women, rather than Klein's theory of femininity complexes in boys, one can also avoid falling into the trap of conflating "woman" with "maternity"— that is, assuming the "female body" to be synonymous with the "maternal body." Reading Freud queerly also permits "clitoris" rather than "womb" into the mythical order as a primary signifier. If the reverse of masculine cybercultural appropriation of "womb" (as matrix) is the appropriation by female cybercultural producers of the "phallus," then the mythical dimension of heterosexual procreative sexuality is also reproduced. My readings of VNS Matrix in "Slippery Metaphors for Technology," and Treister's *No other Symptoms* here suggest a more queer spin on the ways in which female cyberartists construct a mythical order and virtually refigure female bodies.

In Freud's theories, girls who refuse to give up the wish for, or fantasy of, acquiring the missing organ (their already castrated penis) are marked by him as suffering from a "masculinity complex." In his view they tend toward feminism and homosexuality. In 1924 Freud added to the *Three Essays* a "phallic" stage of infantile genital organization in which its difference from adult genital organizations is marked by the primacy of the phallus.[16] In the symbolic order of adult sexuality, for both sexes, only two genitals, the penis and the vagina, come into account.[17] The clitoris as a primary signifier of adult female sexuality is repressed in the symbolic organization of adult sexuality. However, on the Freudian path to female homosexuality there is a disavowal of women's castration, a refusal to acknowledge the symbolic meaning of sexual difference. For Freud, female homosexuals refuse the normal path to femininity via acceptance of castration and the transfer of libidinal cathexis from mother to father (via penis envy). They retain their pre-Oedipal phallic (active) sexuality and retain the maternal figure as a model for later object attachments. In other words, the lesbian subject retains the clitoris as her primary sexual organ and continues to love feminine figures. In this fantasmatic scenario, both mother and daughter could be said to be signified as phallic (powerful), and the clitoris is dragged into the symbolic order as a primary signifier. Insofar as this scenario could be said to endow female subjects with the magical phallus as well as retain the clitoral signifier, then the female subject could be said to be signified in Sofoulis/Kleinian terms as a cunt-prick.[18]

VNS Matrix call a cunt a cunt frequently and explicitly: "We are the modern cunt." This cyberart collective deploys "pussy" as a form of greeting as in "Salutations, pussy." Bodily organs and technical processes including cultural and technological production are resignified by this witty foursome—proclaiming themselves as "mercenaries of slime," as "cybercunts"—as extremely slippery metaphors. References to female genitals and bodily secretions figure significantly in this context both metaphorically in the feminine sublimations in technoculture ("we make art with our cunts") and in the re-writing of female libidinal investments as queer ("I slide into her"). The cunt-signified scenarios are not deployed as sites for the production or reproduction of maternity or symbolically inscribed motherhood for women. They are redeployed as a site for the construction of libidinal pleasures—in sex, in horizontal rather than Oedipal (vertical) relationships, in technological production, in sexy technology—a feminized and post-feminist erotics of technocultural production.

The name of the game, in VNS appropriations of future languages, is "infiltration and remapping the possible futures outside the (chromo)phallic patriarchal code" (VNS Matrix). In this imaginative game of infiltration and subversion, of Big Daddy Main-frame, of masculine technoproduction and its discourses, VNS Matrix appropriates paternal organs, spermatic metaphors, and metaphors of viral infection as well as those references on female genitals and bodily processes. The DNA Sluts are imaged, pumped-up Barbie dolls ("muscular hybrids") with laser beams shooting from their clitori. These may be read as fantasy phalluses. Spermatic and penetrative metaphors are utilized in imaging the mutating female subject as a virus that infiltrates/penetrates the technobody of Big Daddy's imperialistically and militaristically deployed data banks, also a "queer" proposition.

The time-traveling Brodsky utilizes her briefcase (her attaché case) of *Vibrators from the House of Brodsky* to penetrate and disorder psychoanalytic thinking. These objects can also be said to operate in the text as signifiers in a post-Freudian/Lacanian mythical order of female technocultural production as well as a remetaphorization of the female body in a technological age. These magical phalluses (female fetishes) are also signifiers of infiltration into, and appropriation and remapping of, masculinist codes. They are objects for penetrating and disrupting the body of psychoanalytic tech-nologies and the narratives of cyberculture. At no point is the female body metaphorized or mythologized as a maternal body. Brodsky is constructed as an agen-tic heroine who penetrates the male-dominated body of history in which gender and sexuality have been traditionally constituted and commits her own havoc. Treister's ability to simulate (and humorously reorder) the thinking of individual psychoanalytic theorists in relation to Brodsky's technoscientific knowledges and practices could only be described as uncanny. The case histories are written in the "voices" of Freud, Klein, and others, and appear, within this virtual world, as cannily "authentic."

Brodsky's analysis began on May 7, 1886, but was suspended until 1928 since there had been a programming malfunction in relation to dates, and Brodsky promised to return when Freud had had time to develop his ideas further. This time lapse also gave Freud time to recover from the trauma of his first encounter with this twenty-first-century female subject. He admits that he hid his notes lest anyone think he was neurotic for believing his analysand's time-traveling capabilities—which is why, apparently, they do not appear in his published writings on female subjectivity and sexuality. In his notes, Freud records his extreme disturbance in the *umheimlich/heimlich* moment of discovering that a highly successful female scientific researcher and business entrepreneur would finance her travels and analysis from the manufacture and sale of mechanical objects designed for female sexual pleasure:

Further into the analysis Rosalind arrived one day with some strange objects in her briefcase which she told me she had made herself. When I realised their function I was at first struck down with horror and revulsion for they were mechanical devices for the purpose of masturbation. Not only this, but at the end of each device was either a human head or a small architectural model.

The most disturbing moment came when I recognised myself in one of these objects. (Freud 1928) (qtd. in Treister 1999)

At this moment he tells Rosalind that she is depraved and his horror increases when she admits that it was the profits from the sale of these "contraptions" that had paid for her analysis with him. She then offers him a set as a gift. In attempting to formulate a theory of female subjectivity, Freud tentatively suggests that her motive for constructing these "unfortunate devices" might be a "perverted" means of dealing with her repressed fears of her father's castration (i.e., his loss of place, Poland, and objects including his murdered mother). The vibrators then are screens superimposed over the father's losses that "in turn conceal Rosalind's repressed fear of her father's castration, the possibility of the actuality of which, if time were reversed, would result in his inability to give birth to her" (Freud 1928) (qtd. in Treister 1999, 420).

Brodsky flatly denies this hypothesis, informing Freud that in the 1960s there had been a sexual revolution and that these vibrators would not be considered "depraved" objects. Venturing to ask his strange analysand if she made use of the vibrators for her own pleasure, Freud learned that she did indeed make use of some of them, but not others. She refuses to divulge her reasons for these choices. During an earlier session in

1928, Brodsky had revealed to Freud her obsession with Russian history and the Russian Revolution, scenes that she visited repeatedly. In reply to Freud's questioning, Brodsky admits that he has politically Left leanings, but that her father had a hatred of Russia and communism. He believed that if it had not been the Germans, it would have been the Russians who had been responsible for the death of his parents. In any case, the Russians were responsible for the loss of his ancestral home in Southeastern Poland, which was annexed to the Ukraine in 1939. Rosalind informs the analyst that 1939 was also the year of his death, but he doesn't want to know.

In reconsidering Rosalind's obsessions with the Russian Revolution in the light of the vibrators, Freud notes that if her, or her paternal grandmother's, initial, *r*, was inserted into her father's name, Max, then it would result in the name Marx. Freud speculates that this "linguistic bonding" contains a radical political separation, the separation of Brodsky's from her father's political beliefs. Simultaneously, in conjunction with his previous observations about Brodsky and the vibrators, Freud conjectures that we can conclude that a repression of the political, historical, familial, and power conflicts have resulted in a romantic association with the Russian Revolution. In this scenario, according to the virtual Freud, the figure of Karl Marx and associated architectural emblems have come to take on sexual connotations for Rosalind.

What Treister ironically foregrounds in this virtual scenario is that Freud, in his romantic association of sexuality with the familial, repressed political, historical, and power conflicts in his theorizing of (female-) sexed subjectivity. What emerges as significant in this scenario, in spite of his foray into linguistic bonding theory, is that, unlike the later Lacan, Freud is unable to understand the constitution of the subject in sociolinguistic terms. Like Lacan, but unlike the later poststructural feminists and cultural critics, Freud struggles to articulate the ubiquitous male subject (the father) in cultural and political, rather than exclusively Oedipal, terms. The mother, as always, is absent from his imaginary family structure, and the constitution of the male subject, together with his castration fears, is centralized. In this scenario, Rosalind is imagined not as a desiring female subject who possesses her own technological "phallus," but as "lack," as a blank screen on which the daughter is reconstituted as her father's phallus. What is at stake in this encounter is not only Freud's future hold on the patriarchal laws controlling theories of female subjectivity, but also the significance of proliferating modes of female sexuality (e.g., women + vibrator) and the technological modes of reproduction and transmission of these new sexualities. Through Brodsky's "transgressions," Freud's, and the psychoanalyst's monopoly on sexual epistemologies is probably fatally undermined. He is certainly anxious about the significance of "technological devices." The couch is being displaced by the modem, possibly to women's advantage.

In ventriloquizing Klein, Brodsky reminds us that the cybernetic discourses on depthlessness as a crucial component of postmodern existence, resulting in human identities as flat as computer and television screens,[19] was foreshadowed by Klein's own conceptualization of an unconscious that has not been constructed by repression. Klein reports, in analyzing her countertransferential paranoia, that she feared Brodsky was playing with her own assertion that the past and present were one in terms of the psycho neuroses, time being spatial rather than historical. Having prempted Baudrillardian and Jamesonian[20] theories, the virtual Klein narrates the function of RB's vibrators in her own—that is, part-object—terms. The analytic sequences move through various stages titled "Dream of the ship woman," "Russian doll," "Mary Poppins," "Rosa Klebb," and "Vibrators."

Klein begins with the analysis of a repeated childhood dream in which an evil masculine woman descended from the sky on a flying galleon, entered through the French windows, kidnapped the young Rosalind from her parents, and took her to an unknown place and time. The "phallic woman" Klein interprets as representing the combined parent figure, the mother's body containing the father's penis. Fear of, and aggression toward, this figure is unresolved for Rosalind in childhood (she is unable to unify "good" and "bad" introjected objects), and at the age of ten she bites deeply into the fingers of her dentist in a physical attempt to interject Oedipal love objects. She admitted that this gave her much satisfaction.

On their second meeting Brodsky, having used equipment at IMATI to shrink herself, appears to Klein as a child. Suspending disbelief, the well-known child analyst offers Rosalind a box of toys to play with. Brodsky selects a small wooden boy figure and tells Klein that his name is Marx. She then, according to Klein's notes, proceeded to open the Russian doll and remove the inner dolls, placing the Marx doll inside in their place. The inner dolls she placed in the sink in the corner of Klein's room and turned on the tap. She then put the large doll containing Marx into her pocket and left the room abruptly. Klein speculates that again, inevitably, Brodsky had constructed a combined parent figure, but that this time the replaced father's penis inside the mother's body had taken the form of Karl Marx and that the maternal body had taken a Russian identity, although the mother was English. Hence, the female analyst deduced, Brodsky's feared external objects (following the phallic woman in the galleon and the dentist) were now connected to Russia and its political history. Klein then connects this, via her own knowledge of the conquest of Southeastern Poland by the Russians in 1939, to the fate of Brodsky's grandparents. Therefore, she concludes, the removal and washing of the internal dolls was an obvious attempt to evacuate the mother' body of both whole and part-objects (feces, children, and the father's penis). The ensuing superego imposed guilt, however, then caused Rosalind to wash these objects in an attempted reparation for the anal-sadistic (phallic) act.

After several other narrative twists on part-object theory, Klein and Brodsky arrive at the vibrators. After further convoluted theorizing, Klein suggests: "One could see these devices as expulsions of the good and bad objects as gifts in an attempt to replace the stolen feces and father's penis which were 'taken' from the mother's body" (Klein 1959, 2058). What emerges in Brodsky's repetitious penetrations of psychoanalytic history is a scenario in which the father's lacks (losses of place and maternal body) are imaginatively compensated for in the construction of a female fantasy phallus. These Brodsky offers as "gifts" to Freud and Klein, opening up a space in which the political and cultural history of the subject might be negotiated, along with the mommy-daddy-me (psychoanalytic) paradigm, in constituting the subject. What emerges most strongly in Kleinian discourses, and in contradistinction to Freudian theory, is a protofeminist inclusion of the mother as a significant pre-Oedipal figure, for both Brodsky and the father.

Along with this shift in psychoanalytic thinking, there also emerges, as Sofoulis suggests, more polymorphous modes of signification of the subject, both male and female. But whereas Sofoulis's cyberboy is involved in sublimation in technocultural (re)production in an attempt to recoup the feared and desired maternal body in order to produce technoartifacts, Treister's cybergirl is busily appropriating the phallus in identification with the father in order to enter the body of political history (the mother as Russia) and recoup his losses (the father's maternal body and place). In this mythic order, RB identifies with the father and invents supervibrators in order to penetrate the cyberspatial Matrix and rescue her namesake Rosalind, her prematurely lost grandmother. While theories of fantasmatically (and technologically) phallicized female subjects have not been embraced unreservedly by traditional feminists, they offer women the possibility of mobilizing the power of technological replication to radically undermine constricting constructions of femininity.

This Kleinian, Russian doll version of psychoanalysis and technoculture is given a Treister spin in that her cybergirl is as likely to encounter a systems error in her time-traveling efforts to rescue the paternal grandmother from the Holocaust and land on the film set of *Schindler's List*. In other words, the subject in contemporary culture is as likely to be constituted, via filmmaking and new technologies, in "public" cultural fantasies as well as caught up in the conflicts of the parent's conscious/unconscious desires and anxieties. This suggests that a proliferating symbolic matrix of multiplying female subjectivities might offer the possibility, as a third term, of an effective break with a male-dominated imaginary. In her dealing with Lacanian theory, Treister points in this direction of a break with the "father."

| Figure 12.3 |

Rosalind Brodsky in her time-traveling costume to rescue her grandparents from the Holocaust, arriving mistakenly on the set of *Schindler's List,* 1994.

What Lacan is determined to uncover is the source of Brodsky's "delusions" of time traveling. What he finds remarkable about Brodsky's stories is the recurrence of incidents involving films and television programs. He remarks in his case history that Brodsky is particularly prone to identifications with characters in science-fiction narratives such as *Doctor Who, Star Trek, Mary Poppins*, and *Blade Runner*. Obsessing over the *Doctor Who* phenomenon of the TARDIS with its often uncontrollable time and space destinations as a clue to RB's time traveling "delusions," Lacan concludes that the dynamic of the relation between Brodsky and the character The Doctor, a Time Lord, caused a split in the symbolic, through which the imaginary erupted in a phantasmatic explosion, destabilizing the subject's relation to time and the symbolic order.

Although he is no expert in film theory, Lacan nevertheless presses on until be believes he has reconstructed the imaginary scenario for her time-traveling delusions. This involves Brodsky, the mother, the father, the Name-of-the-Father, the Other, and the *objet petit a* in what could be an already all-too-familiar Lacanian narrative of the (universalized, male) subject. In Lacan's thinking, the Name-of-the-Father (the paternal function signified by the paternal phallus) or third term severs the (generically male) child from its dual, mutual identificatory relation to the (m)other, sexually differentiates it, and inserts it into the symbolic order (the order of language and meaning) as a socially functional subject. Lacan argues that the Name-of-the-Father, which embodies and represents the law prohibiting incest and founding patriarchy, provides the support that anchors the subject in the symbolic and prevents it from teetering into the abyss of the Real (the place of birth *and* obliteration). The father's name is the linguistic representation of the symbolic order. Symbolic functioning demands clear lines of demarcation between self and other, order and disorder, proper and improper. Symbolization and "proper" social functioning demands a separation between "I" and m(other). For Lacan, signification (the difference between linguistic signifiers) insinuates itself in place of the absent object(s)—primarily the breast, secondarily the (m)other—the object(s) engendering desire. The imaginary signifier, the phallus, in Lacan's narrativization of the symbolic order and signification, is posited as the universal signifier of desire. In Lacan's formulations, speech is as dependent upon the notion of lack as is his theory of desire.

For Lacan, there is no whole sexual object; fantasy shows that desire always revolves around a part without a whole. The missing part, *objet a*, which appears in Lacan's later texts as a formula for the lost object, has been variously theorized as the penis, the maternal penis/phallus, the breast, and as the maternal body. The *objet a* is not the object of a drive, including oral, anal, and scopic drives, but the cause of desire. In Lacan's texts, language substitutes for the lack of/desire for the maternal body. However, if the phallic signifier has a privileged position in the unconscious, it is not as an *objet a* (penis, breast, feces) but in being an object that the mother lacks and desires. It is the phallus that, according to Lacan, signifies sexual difference. The phallus also signifies the law of symbolic castration for it belongs to the father, the Other who forbids the enjoyment of the mother-child symbiosis. Lacan linked the difference between the sexes to a splitting in relation to the mother's lack of the phallus. Through Oedipalization, male and female children are separated from their first love object, the mother, and positioned within the larger sociosymbolic order. Lacan states that: "The *objet a* is something from which the subject, in order to constitute itself, has separated itself off as organ. This serves as a symbol of lack, that is to say, of the phallus, not as such, but insofar as it is lacking. It must, therefore, be an object that is, firstly separable, and secondly, that has some relation to the lack."[21]

While the *objets a* in Lacan's texts belong to the (m)other, the mother as imaginary object, the imaginary place of enjoyment that it is impossible to symbolize, the phallus (barred in the mother) belongs to the symbolic Other (the father). The misappropriation of the penis by the phallus in Lacanian terms happens when the penis is removed from its merely anatomical and functional role (urination and insemination) to the role of object, the *objet a*, in a circuit of demand addressed to the (m)other. It is then capable of taking on the symbolic role of signifier at the level of desire, an object of unconscious fantasy.[22] In Lacan's view of the perversions, the barred Other (the mother) is replaced by the *objet a*.

In writing Brodsky's case history, Treister ventriloquizes and deuniversalizes Lacanian theory. In this story Lacan is finally convinced to seriously reform his universalizing of the Name-of-the-Father and of the *objet a* and take into account the specificity of RB's hybrid familial heritage and her constitution in a symbolic order in which nonparental (that is public) fantasies proliferate. In part Brodsky's case history with Lacan reads:

In my previous writings I have discussed the idea that the father's intervention to separate the child from the mother is necessary in order to prevent psychosis and perversion. In this instance I will need to revise this theory for it appears that Brodsky's mother was predominantly absent during her early years [having returned to full time work with overtime] (likewise the father), and that it was in fact the mother (despite and because of her apparent only act of intervention in relation to the masturbating dog) who never successfully intervened to separate the child from the father, a constant provider of food and affection. Therefore it is consequently from women that Brodsky seeks punishment and enforcement of the law to instate the Name-of-the-Mother and it is the father's lack that she seeks to embody which in one sense can be seen as his lost mother [who was murdered in the Holocaust, and whose name was also Rosalind]. Brodsky's scopic drive became extended due to this early absence of the parents, also being a partial cause of her time traveling delusions, encompassing her supposed arrival at and often failure to arrive at the intended destination, in attempts to recover the *objet petit a*. (Treister 1999)

During one of his notorious short sessions with the time-traveling analysand, Lacan rematerializes on the set of the film *Mary Poppins*, with Rosalind, Mary, the children, and the dog. He concludes, as only Lacan could, that he must be "barking mad." This perversely Jewish parody of Lacanian theory raises some serious questions for psychoanalytic theory in relation to the specificity of histories of the subject, political and familial histories, gender, sexuality, and cultural differences. In the absence of her working parents, and in spite of her desire for a symbolic mother to separate her from identifying too closely as a male subject, Brodsky is Oedipalized (enters the symbolic) finally through the intervention of the television set—the symbolic parent figure of a culture saturated by technology. This scenario, though comic, points dramatically to a different understanding of a subject constituted in a rapidly technologized symbolic matrix. The child/subject is separated from identifications/desires in relation to the parents in the Oedipal scenario through direct access to "public" cultural figures. This virtual reality, as emergent process, can be mobilized by women as a matrix of potentialities from which women might download different roles.

Treister, through her female cybercharacter, ironically throws into stark relief the historical and cultural situatedness of psychoanalytic constrictions of female subjectivity, of Freudian and Lacanian theoretical lack(s) in relation to time, space and the shifting landscape of modes of representational proliferation. Different cultural stories, such as those told by Treister, present women with the powerful potential to rapidly undermine traditional Western masculinist reproductions of the female subject (actual or digital) and her position in the technocultural (including psychoanalytic) narratives of the twenty-first century.

Notes

1. Suzanne Treister, . . . *No Other Symptoms: Time Travelling with Rosalind Brodsky* (London: Black Dog Publishing, 1999). The CD-ROM project was produced with the Australian Film Commission and assisted by the Commonwealth Government through the Australia Council, its arts funding, and its advisory body. The genesis of the Brodsky project can be visited at <http://www.va.com.au/ensemble/tableau/suzy>.
2. See Richard Kelly Heft, "Pixel-Packin' MaMa," *The Weekend Australian*, February 21–22, 1998, 7.
3. See Thomas Foster's introduction, "Incurably Informed: The Pleasures and Dangers of Cyberpunk," *Genders* 18, *Cyberpunk: Technologies of Cultural Identity* (1992): 1–10.

4. Rudy Rucker and Peter Lamborn Wilson, eds., *Semiotext(e) SF* 5.2 (1989). This edition of *Semiotext(e)* is critiqued in Andrew Ross, "Cyberpunks in Boystown," *Strange Weather: Culture, Science and Technology in the Age of Limits* (London: Verso, 1991).

5. For a more detailed critique of both *Semiotext(e) SF* and Ross's essay, see Anne Balsamo, *Technologies of the Gendered Body: Reading Cyborg Women* (Durham and London: Duke University Press, 1996), 129–132.

6. VNS Matrix, *All New Gen* and *Game Girl* (installation and computer game) (Adelaide: Experimental Art Foundation, October 21–November 21, 1993). For a more detailed analysis of VNS's work, see Jyanni Steffensen, "Slippery metaphors for technology: 'The Clitoris Is a Direct Line to the Matrix.'" Online. Available at <http://www.va.com.au/ensemble/array/steff.html>.

7. Alice Jardine, "Of Bodies and Technologies," in *Discussions in Contemporary Culture*, ed. Hal Foster (Seattle: Bay Press, 1987), 151–158.

8. For a critique of the interchangeable use of the terms *robot*, *android*, and *cyborg*, see Claudia Springer, "Muscular Circuitry: The Invincible Armored Cyborg in Cinema," in *Genders* 18 *Cyberpunk: Technologies of Cultural Identity* (1992): 87. The prototypical model for technoscientific figures is, of course, Mary Shelley's patchwork monster from *Frankenstein* (1818). This novella constitutes something of a framing narrative for many contemporary Western science-fiction, technocultural, and cyberpunk discourses and practices. Specific fembots include the mechanical doll, Olympia, from E. T. A. Hoffman's story *The Sandman* (1816), analyzed by Sigmund Freud in his essay, "The Uncanny" (1919) and filmed by George Méliès (1903), and Powell and Pressberger (1951); the robot, Maria, from Fritz Lang's *Metropolis* (1926); the replicants Pris and Zhora from Ridley Scott's *Blade Runner* (1982 and 1992); and the cyborg Eve 8 from Duncan Gibbins's film *Eve of Destruction* (1990).

9. Masculine potency is articulated in the film *Eve of Destruction* through Special Agent Jim McQuade's ability to locate the rampaging female cyborg's "fuckin' off switch" (Sadie Plant, "Cybernetic Hookers," paper delivered at the Future Languages day of Artist's Week, The Adelaide Festival of the Arts, 1994. Published in the *Australian Network for Art and Technology Newsletter* (April/May 1994): 5.)

11. Sadie Plant, "On the Matrix: Cyberfeminist Simulations," in *Cultures of the Internet: Virtual Spaces, Real Histories, Living Bodies*, ed. Rob Shields (London, Thousand Oaks, CA, and New Delhi: Sage Publications, 1996), 170–183.

12. Cathryn Vasseleu, "Virtual Bodies/Virtual Worlds," *Australian Feminist Studies* 19 (Autumn 1994): 166. Vasseleu defines "cyberspace" as the space within the electronic network of computers from which virtual realities can be made. "Virtual realities" she defines as computer-generated systems that use cyberspace to simulate various aspects of interactive space (i.e., they are inhabitable computer systems of space).

13. Zoë Sophia, "Virtual Corporeality: A Feminist View," *Australian Feminist Studies* 15 (Autumn 1992): 15.

14. Zoë Sofoulis, "Slime in the Matrix: Post-Phallic Formations in Women's Art in New Media," in *The Jane Gallop Seminar Papers,* ed. Jill Julius Matthews (Canberra: Australian National University, 1994), 91.

15. See Melanie Klein, in *Love, Guilt and Reparation and Other Works* (London: Hogarth Press and the Institute of Psychoanalysis, [1928] 1975), 191.

16. Sigmund Freud, "*Three Essays on the Theory of Sexuality,*" in *The Standard Edition,* vol. 17, trans. James Strachey (London: Hogarth Press, [1905] 1962), 123–243.

17. Sigmund Freud, "The Infantile Genital Organization: (An Interpolation into the Theory of Sexuality)," in *The Standard Edition,* vol. 19, trans. James Strachey (London: Hogarth Press, [1920], 1962), 142.

18. See Jane Gallop's reading of a passage in Lacan's *Ecrits,* 735–736, in which Lacan poses the question: "Is it this privilege of the signifier [the phallus] that Freud is aiming at by suggesting that there is perhaps only one libido and that it is marked with the male sign?" Immediately following this rhetorical question, Lacan uses at least four words beginning with the prefix "con" that Gallop points out means "cunt" in colloquial French. In other words every time Lacan asserts the privilege of the phallus, the sublimated cunt emerges in his text. Gallop refers to Lacan as "a ladies' man," "a shameless floozie," and a "cunt-prick." See Jane Gallop, *Feminism and Psychoanalysis: The Daughter's Seduction* (London: MacMillan, 1982), 31.

19. See Jean Baudrillard, *Xerox and Infinity.* Trans. (London: Agitac, 1988), 7.

20. As Federic Jameson points out, we are experiencing cultural depthlessness in the form of historical amnesia, the inability to rember our cultural history. According to Jameson, history has been reduced to a perpetual present in which artifacts from the past are commodified for consumption but have lost the meanings provided by their original contexts. Together with Baudrillard's notion of postmodernism's flattened perspective, the technotronic age could be said to produce a computer terminal identity. See Frederic Jameson, "Postmodernism, or, the Cultural Logic of Late Capitalism," *New Left Review* 146 (July–August, 1984): 53–92.

21. Jacques Lacan, *The Four Fundamental Concepts of Psychoanalysis* (London: Hogarth Press, 1977), 103.

22. For a detailed feminist reading of Lacan, see Elizabeth Grosz, *Jacques Lacan: A Feminist Introduction* (London: Routledge, 1990).

Works Cited

Balsamo, Anne. *Technologies of the Gendered Body: Reading Cyborg Women.* Durham, NC, and London: Duke University Press, 1996.

Baudrillard, Jean. *Xerox and Infinity.* Trans. London: Agitac, 1988.

Foster, Thomas. "Incurably Informed: The Pleasures and Dangers of Cyberpunk." *Genders* 18, *Cyberpunk: Technologies of Cultural Identity* (1993): 1–10.

Freud, Sigmund. "Three Essays on the Theory of Psychoanalysis." In *The Standard Edition of the Complete Works of Sigmund Freud*, 17, trans. James Strachey, 123–243. London: Hogarth Press, [1905] 1962.

Freud, Sigmund. "The Infantile Genital Organisation: (An Interpolation into the Theory of Sexuality)." In *The Standard Edition* 19, trans. James Strachey, 141–145. London: Hogarth Press, [1920] 1962.

Gallop, Jane. *Feminism and Psychoanalysis: The Daughter's Seduction.* London: Macmillan, 1982.

Grosz, Elizabeth. *Jacques Lacan: A Feminist View.* London: Routledge, 1990.

Heft, Richard Kelly. "Pixel-Packin' MaMa." *The Weekend Australian*, February 21–22, 1998, 7.

Jameson, Frederic. "Postmodernism, or, the Cultural Logic of Capitalism." *New Left Review* 146 (1984): 53–92.

Jardine, Alice. "Of Bodies and Technologies." In *Discussions in Contemporary Culture*, ed. Hal Foster, 151–158. Seattle: Bay Press, 1987.

Klein, Melanie. *Love, Guilt and Reparation and Other Works.* London: Hogarth Press and the Institute of Psychoanalysis, [1928] 1975.

Lacan, Jacques. *The Four Fundamental Concepts of Psychoanalysis.* London: Hogarth Press, 1977.

Plant, Sadie. "On the Matrix: Cyberfeminist Simulations." In *Cultures of the Internet: Virtual Spaces, Real Histories, Living Bodies*, ed. Rob Shields, 170–183. London, Thousand Oaks, CA, and New Delhi: Sage Publications, 1996.

Plant, Sadie. "Cybernetic Hookers." Paper delivered at the Future Languages day of Artist's Week. The Adelaide Festival of the Arts, 1994. *Australian Network for Art and Technology* (newsletter) (April 1994): 5.

Ross, Andrew. "Cyberpunks in Boystown." In *Strange Weather: Culture, Science and Technology in the Age of Limits.* London: Verso, 1991.

Rucker, Rudy, and Peter Lamborn Wilson, eds. *Semiotext(e) SF* 5.2 (1989).

Sofoulis, Zoë. "Slime in the Matrix: Post-Phallic Formations in Women's Art in New Media." In *The Jane Gallop Seminar Papers*, ed. Jill Julius Matthews, 83–106. Canberra: Australian National University, 1994.

Sophia, Zoë. "Virtual Corporeality: A Feminist View." *Australian Feminist Studies* 15 (1992): 11–23.

Springer, Claudia. "Muscular Circuitry: The Invincible Armored Cyborg in Cinema." *Genders* 18 *Cyberpunk: Technologies of Cultural Identity* (1993): 87–101.

Steffensen, Jyanni. "Slippery Metaphors for Technology: 'The Clitoris Is a Direct Line to the Matrix.'" Online. Available at <http://www.va.com.au/ensemble/array/steff.html>.

Treister, Suzanne. . . . *No Other Symptoms: Time Travelling with Rosalind Brodsky* (book and CD-ROM). London: Black Dog Publishing, 1999.

Vasseleu, Cathryn. "Virtual Bodies/ Virtual Worlds." *Australian Feminist Studies* 19 (1994): 158–174.

VNS Matrix. *All New Gen* and *Game Girl* (installation and computer game). Experimental Art Foundation, Adelaide, October 21–November 21, 1993.

Jyanni Steffensen

The Visual/Visible/Virtual Subject

These selections explore how the relationships among technoscience, gender, and subjectivity are inscribed in cyberfiction, the science-fiction film, and computer games. Themes common to the criticism and fiction in this section include questions of identity and identification; links between epistemological categories and categories of cultural difference; and the relationship between spectator, reader, or player and the film, performance, text, game, or artifact. Several of the essays and fictions examine the fetishization of the female-machine body in popular, cinematic, and scientific discourse. Other stories and critiques ask how theories of performance and identity play out in fictional and filmic narratives of cyberspace.

Many feminist accounts of technology are critical of visual imaging and reproductive technologies.[1] Medical imaging technologies that map the body are regularly critiqued in the visual arts, especially those imaging technologies that have traditionally reduced the category of "woman" to images. This trend can be traced from Charcot's nineteenth-century images of "hysterical" women to the recent "visible woman" project explored by Julie Doyle and Kate O'Riordan in their essay "Virtually Visible: Female Cyberbodies And The Medical Imagination" (chapter 13). In light of contemporary medical representations of the body through new digital imaging technologies offered in the Visible Human Project, Doyle and O'Riordan examine how normative notions of gender both mark and form the imaged body, through a focused analysis of the visual representation of the female body within biomedical discourse. Using the framework of the posthuman subject, Doyle and O'Riordan argue that the cyborgian relationship needs to be reworked: The body is represented through its relationship to technologies but technological representations of the body must reincorporate an experience of the flesh. The authors look to feminist Internet incorporations of the image and the body such as the Brandon Teena website in order to examine how women can escape the scientific relationship technology inherently offers.

C. L. Moore's "No Woman Born" (chapter 14) is an early story that explores the figure of the female cyborg. It tells the story of Deirdre, a beautiful actress whose body is destroyed in a theater fire—Deirdre's brain is left undamaged, however, and a new rippling metallic body is made for her. The 1944 story does not focus on the special powers of the machine body, but rather concentrates on the relationship between the mind/consciousness and the body and on how Deirdre's mind transforms and adapts to its new mechanical environment. Veronica Hollinger, in her essay "(Re)reading Queerly: Science Fiction, Feminism, and the Defamiliarization of Gender" (chapter 15) reads "No Woman Born" as an early theorizing of performativity, femininity, and sexuality as well as a complex account of agency and resistance in the space between the male gaze and the female cyborg. Hollinger uses feminist and queer theory to read the construction of gender identity in women's science fiction, and she uses women's science fiction to read feminist and queer theory. She argues that the performance theory articulated in women's science fiction can be used to denaturalize notions about gender and heterosexuality.

In her essay "After/Images of Identity: Gender, Technology, and Identity Politics" (chapter 16), Lisa Nakamura explores how the blinding changes and dazzlingly rapid developments of technology in recent years have served to project an "altered image" or "projection of identity" upon our collective consciousness. She looks at popular rhetoric of a "post-identitarian" nature—sites that posit a postcorporeal subjectivity, an afterimage of the body and of identity. She cautions that machines that offer identity prostheses to overcome attributes of the physical body produce "cybertypes" that look remarkably like racial and gender stereotypes.

Stereotypes are also invoked in the construction of women characters in cyberculture cinema. Bernadette Wegenstein's essay, "Shooting up Heroines" (chapter 17) analyzes the actantial status of female "hero-protagonists" in current science fiction and cybernarratives.[2] These heroines act and are acted upon in two very different, at times even oppositional, ways. In the first model, the heroine is the *real* hero in (cyber)space over her male counterpart; in the second model, we encounter some of these heroines in a very traditional actantial stance—sidekicks, in the language of popular culture—to the main male protagonists in the pursuit of their narrative goals. Wegenstein works from a Lacanian psychoanalytical perspective to explore this split of representation and claims it is inherent to the construction of female gender and to the institutionalization of womanhood. Rajani Sudan also examines the representation of women in popular cyberspace discourse by looking at the representation of women's bodies in recent films about digital technologies and virtual reality. Her essay, "Girl Erupted" (chapter 18) questions taxonomies and epistemologies that invariably invoke the material as an irrefutable substantiation of the ideological, particularly the ways race and gender collapse into materially identifiable bodies in visual and virtual culture. She looks at popular film representation of technonarratives to see how the action and, especially, bodies gendered as female replicate computer graphics and narrative logic of videogames; more important, they act as a liaison for a new kind of imperialism, making cyber-type spaces safe for Western consumption. Catherine Ramírez, in her essay "Cyborg Feminism: The Science Fiction of Octavia Butler and Gloria Anzaldúa" (chapter 19), is also interested in questions of race and gender within contemporary fictional and theoretical accounts of technoculture. She reads Butler's novels *Wild Seed* and *Parable of the Sower* against Donna Haraway's concept of cyborgs and Gloria Anzaldúa's notion of "alien consciousness." Ramírez argues that Butler's novels "critique fixed concepts of race, gender and sexuality, and, subsequently 'fictions' of identity and community." Ramírez reads the cyborg as a "subject that simultaneously exceeds and emphasizes the boundaries of identity and community," a subject that can be used to theorize a "woman of color feminism" located within the histories and literary traditions of the colonized of the New World (namely, African Americans and Chicana/os, respectively).

Octavia Butler's 1984 Hugo Award–winning short story "Speech Sounds" (chapter 20) paints a bleak picture of a burned-out Los Angeles of the near future. An illness has ravaged the area and attacked the language center of people's brains. Communication becomes impossible: Most people can no longer read, write, or speak. This lack of communication is leading to the destruction of the culture. Here, as in many of her other works, Butler is interested in the ways cultures try to heal themselves, offering glimpses of hope in otherwise dystopic visions of the future. The heroine of the story, Rye, still remembers speech. What are the effects of a loss of communication? What is the relationship between communication and class? How can a population that loses communication be protected?

Amy Thomson's novel *Virtual Girl* is also a work that focuses on communication and, ultimately, the breakdown in communication beween the programmer and the program. *Virtual Girl* tells the story of Maggie, an AI-driven humanoid bot built illegally in a garage by Arnold, a former MIT student. But contrary to Arnold's expectations, a glitch in communication between Arnold and the program he has created allows Maggie to reprogram herself, leading her to develop her own independence, ultimately creating her own identity. By the end of the novel, Maggie has become an activist for other AI systems and the poor. The narrative raises complex issues about the status of AI subjectivity, including the relationship between point-of-view and subjectivity, and the location of subjectivity (Maggie, for example, is duplicated on disk). The first part of the excerpt included here (chapter 21) details the moment in which Maggie's personality crystallizes. The second section of the excerpt deals with Maggie's knowledge of herself and her own multiple, interior identities; the narrative describes how Maggie's AI friend, Turing, helps her "two halves"—her security program and her core personality—unite.

How do users in virtual worlds such as computer games come to have knowledge in the first place? Where, exactly, are the participants located? Unlike Amy Thompson's character Maggie, real users do not break free from the original body nor from the creator, but are a hyperhybrid of sorts. In her essay "HyperBodies, HyperKnowledge: Women in Games, Women in Cyberpunk, and Strategies of Resistance" (chapter 22) Mary Flanagan studies female protagonists in computer games, woman-created art projects, and liberatory cyberpunk novels to find the factors that epistemologically shape these pop culture experiences. Like other writers in this part of *reload*, Flanagan examines representations of the virtual woman and the way in which we, as users and participants, relate to them. Her essay explores the location of the hyperbody and the phenomenon of hyperknowledge through that body, and looks to possibilities offered by creative digital projects that challenge the relationships among the body, the machine, and knowledge.

Notes

1. *Test-Tube Women: What Future for Motherhood?* ed. Rita Ardittie, Renate Duelli Klein, and Shelley Minden (London: Pandora, 1984).
2. "Hero-Protagonist" is the name of the main character in one of the most successful cyberpunk novels, Neal Stephenson's *Snow Crash* (New York: Bantam Books, 1992).

13

VIRTUALLY VISIBLE: FEMALE CYBERBODIES
AND THE MEDICAL IMAGINATION

Julie Doyle and Kate O'Riordan

Contemporary visualizations of the female body, within medical discourse, are widely available in cyberspace. Anatomy has gone digital, an ambitious example of this being the Stanford Visible Female (SVF). This project is "a collection of digitized serial photographs of a cryosectioned 32-year-old cadaveric female pelvis"[1] accessible through the Internet. The 32-year-old woman whose body provided the raw material for the Stanford Visible Female—a project that translates the flesh of the body into digital imagery—is signified within the project as a dislocated pelvis. It is not the female subject who is described in terms of age here; rather, it is the "reproductive-age cadaveric pelvis" that synechdocally represents this 32-year-old female. It is the reproductive potential represented by this female body that provides the particular reasoning behind this project—a fact that renders it "unique in a very important way" by virtue of its difference from "the 59-year-old post-menopausal Visible Human Female" used in the National Library of Medicine's Visible Human Project (VHP). Whereas the *Visible Human Project* presents "complete, anatomically detailed, three-dimensional representations of the normal male and female human bodies," the representation of the female body within the SVF is focused upon the pelvic region alone. The declared goal of both projects is to create anatomical images for use in medicine, surgery, and biomedical research, with the specific aim of the SVF being the development of "accurate 3-D models of female pelvic anatomy for use in surgical simulation" (Stanford Visible Female, 1997). However, the medical focus on the generative parts and organs of the female body, as presented in the SVF, represents an ideologically specific figuration of the female body. This involves a rearticulation of conventional notions of gendered embodiment within cyberspace, where anatomical knowledge of the female is reduced to, and signified by, her reproductive parts.

Medical preoccupation with visualizing the female body through the reproductive parts can be traced back to the eighteenth century. Produced over two hundred years ago, William Hunter's obstetrical atlas, *The Anatomy of the Human Gravid Uterus*

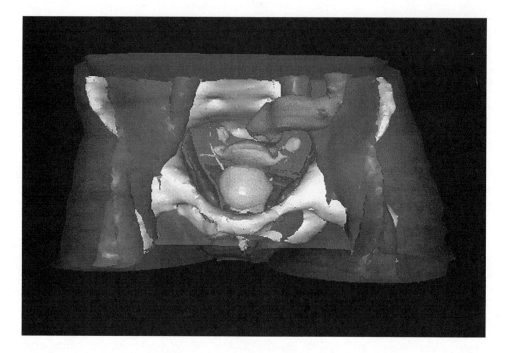

| Figure 13.1 |
3-D digitized pelvis. SUMMIT–Stanford University.

Exhibited in Figures, was an attempt to convey through illustration "the changes that happen in the nine months of utero-gestation" (Hunter 1774, preface). Within an emerging discourse of science, Hunter's atlas represented the Enlightenment belief in empiricism: that (scientific) knowledge was constituted through what could actually be seen; in this instance, what could be viewed, and therefore known, by searching the corporeal structures of the pregnant female (Jordanova 1985). "He [William Hunter] foresaw that, in the course of some years, by diligence he might procure in this great city, so many opportunities of studying the gravid uterus, as to be able to make up a tolerable system; and to exhibit, by figures, all the principal changes that happen in the nine months of utero-gestation" (Hunter 1774, preface).

The constitution of bodily knowledge within Hunter's atlas is formulated through an imaging of the anatomical structures of the female body as a means of conveying the changes in pregnancy. Yet these illustrations deny the physiological processes involved in pregnancy by reducing the pregnant state to an isolated and frozen image, and in doing so constitute bodily knowledge as a visibly discernible form. At the same time, the representation of female anatomy through the specific state of pregnancy operates to reduce the female body to the condition of reproduction: The gravid uterus as only one particular part of the female body is presented in isolation, framing and mediating knowledge of the female body through the generative parts.

By drawing historical analogies between representations of the female body within an emerging discourse of science in the late eighteenth century, and its contemporary figuration through computer-imaging technologies used in the SVF, this chapter recontextualizes these images by examining the historical and technological means of their production. The effects these representations have on the categorizations of identity, where the anatomical body is inscribed as the guarantor of gendered norms, will therefore be interrogated. Moving on from an analysis of the figuration of the female body within medical science, we will also be examining the Brandon Teena Web site as an example of how contemporary cyberbodies are questioning the normative prescriptions of bodily identity as particular effects of the medical imagination.

Imagining the Body of Science

Contemporary scientific paradigms have their roots in the particular developments of science during the eighteenth century. The discourse of science emerging in that century offered a different perspective on the conceptualization of the human subject and its relation to the world. Whereas Christianity maintained its position as the authoritative theological discourse on humanity, positing "God" as the reference through which the human self was conceived and understood, the developing system of science promoted the material body as the site of natural knowledge.[2] Focusing upon an analysis of the corporeal structures of the human body, science authorized empirical observation as the superior means of obtaining and guaranteeing knowledge. Yet, like religion, the emergence of science represented a culturally and historically specific instance in the formation and production of knowledge. The utilization of the human body by scientists as *the* representative object of scientific knowledge focused attention upon the visible structures of this body, where meaning was garnered through direct observation (Stafford 1991). While the structures and workings of the human body had long provided an object of scrutiny for medical practitioners, the use of the body as the foundational site for a system of "scientific" knowledge marked a different approach to the conceptualization of "the human" in the eighteenth century. Emphasis on empirical study as the means of obtaining natural knowledge propagated the notion of objective truth, and it was here that the practices of dissection were presented as the superior means of acquiring bodily (natural) knowledge.

While the early modern period had been characterized by an unprecedented fascination with viewing the internal structures of the body through the processes of dissection—a desire analogously linked to the colonizing operations of sixteenth- and seventeenth-century European imperial expansion[3]—anatomical dissection was viewed by the popular imaginary with distaste and revulsion. This was linked to the fact that the body was comprehended through a system of religious belief where the actions of the anatomist's knife represented an indictment against the spiritual sanctity of the body and its boundaries. It was not until the second half of the eighteenth century that anatomists-surgeons, by utilizing an emerging Enlightenment logic of empirical reality, promoted the practices of anatomical dissection.[4] As such, the human body was inscribed as the representative site of this knowledge.[5]

Painting, drawing, engraving, and wax modeling were technologies utilized in the representation of the anatomical body, where the body was dependent on an *imaging* of its structures in order to signify *as* this newly emerging site of knowledge. It was the female body, and the pregnant state in particular, which provided the greatest fascination for the anatomist-surgeon, not least because of the difficulty in obtaining such a subject for dissection. Commenting on the advancements in anatomy in throwing "considerable lights upon the structure and operations of the human body" through the particular art of engraving, William Hunter in his *The Anatomy of the Human Gravid Uterus Exhibited in Figures* (1774) continued as follows: "One part however, and that most curious, and certainly not the least important of all, the pregnant womb, had been treated by anatomists with proportionable success. Let it not, however, be objected to them that they neglected what in fact was rarely in their power to cultivate. Few, or none of the anatomists, had met with a sufficient number of subjects, either for investigating, or for demonstrating the principal circumstances of utero-gestation in the human species" (Hunter 1774, preface).

Hunter's atlas is a grandiose response, both in rhetorical exegesis and proportional dimension, to this perceived lack, and he notes how the accumulation of natural knowledge has "been rising, till it is at length become the distinguishing characteristic of the most enlightened age of the world" (Hunter 1774, preface). What is interesting about Hunter's atlas is the specific connection he makes between the "discoveries and improvements" of natural knowledge and the role of engraving as a means "to communicate and preserve" these. While Hunter's intention is to show engraving as a tool of communication that merely translates the evidence already represented by the body itself, it is crucial to note that it is *only through* its visual representation that these "discoveries and improvements" are understood.

Hunter's *Anatomy of the Human Gravid Uterus* was predated by two other obstetrical atlases produced in the second half of the eighteenth century; William Smellie's (1754), and Charles Nicholas Jenty's (1757). All three were concerned with the visual representation of the pregnant female body and were illustrated by the same artist, Jan Van Riemsdyk. Smellie's was presented as a practical guide to the art of midwifery where illustration was employed to substantiate textual description—namely, in his promotion of forceps as a means of aiding birth, a practice that was often bitterly contested between female midwives and male surgeons/physicians at the time. The professionalization of medicine was effectively taking medical and social power away from midwives; the use of forceps as a tool of the male medical profession was thus viewed as a further means of wresting power from the traditionally female domain of childbirth. While Smellie's atlas represents a referential dialogue between visual and textual description, both Jenty's and Hunter's texts are presented as signifying the state of pregnancy through image alone. The notion of an objective reality ascribed to the image of the pregnant body is promoted in Jenty's preface when he guarantees that the original drawings of Van Riemsdyk's, from which the tables in his book are taken, were "not done from random, or from fancy, as others have been, which have with impunity been obtruded upon the public for real delineations after nature" (Jenty 1758, 8). The six plates included focus upon the abdominal area of the female body and illustrate the successive stages of her dissection, from the uncut body of the first plate to the isolated uterus of the last.

Plate 3 in the series (figure 13.2) captures the first appearance of the foetus as it is revealed to the eye by the anatomist's cut. While the French edition of 1758 employed engraving, the original British edition of 1757 used mezzotint, "as this is softer, and capable of exhibiting a nearer imitation of Nature than engraving, as artists themselves acknowledge that Nature may admit of light and shades, well blended and softened, but never did of a harsh outline" (Jenty 1758, 9). However, an analysis of the formal composition of this image, in both the mezzotint and engraved versions, reveals a body circumscribed by artistic conventions, thereby representing this body (of science) as a culturally contextualized form. It is Jenty's claim that "nothing of this kind has, as yet, been published on this subject in such a state of pregnancy, and disposed in the manner that these tables are . . . which give a full demonstration of all the necessary and useful parts in this state" (Jenty 1758, 8), which delineates the production of "scientific" knowledge through the representation of the gendered body as an aestheticized and reproductive form. The cropping of the female body in all six plates focuses attention on the abdominal area, highlighting the "scientific" conceptualization of the human body

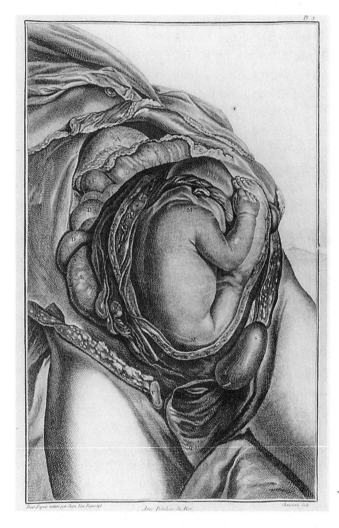

| **Figure 13.2** |
Jenty's 1759 foetus in utero. The Wellcome Trust.

as one of detachable parts. The rendition of flesh and muscle, as if it had been peeled away to reveal the foetus within, correlates visually with the gently draped fabric caressing the contours of the female body. The referential interchange between flesh and fabric, and the semirecumbent pose of this propped body illustrates the circumscription of the anatomical body by aesthetic conventions. The images, presented "as real delineations after nature," are thus highly manipulated representations of the dissected female body, a body that has had to be prepared physically through processes of penetration and injection. That the representation of scientific bodily knowledge is mediated through a discourse of aestheticism, where the products of scientific endeavor translate as objects of artistic worth, is revealed when Jenty declares, "Gentlemen may have these mezzotinto prints coloured after the original pictures, of different degrees of perfection, according to the price allowed to the colourer" (1758, 9).

Anatomical science as a system of developing knowledge was accompanied by other emerging formations of knowledge. The desire to understand the workings of the body through the corporeal structures revealed by dissection was part of the overall cultural project of acquiring and defining natural knowledge through visual "evidence." Extensive land and sea expeditions by European travelers and seafarers involved a charting and mapping of land, a movement accompanied by extensive imperial expansion.[6] The ordering of knowledge through the corporeal body and the geographical landscape represented a complex system of knowledge formation that presented a specifically European perspective. The emergence of racial discourse during this period was represented through the work of the naturalists Buffon (1785) and Blumenbach (1807), whose surveys into the varieties represented by the human species were formulated through the relation of Europeans to non-Europeans. The very concept of difference, reduced by current scientific discourse as a signification of the body, was in fact understood through the concept of nation, where differences in human skin color and behavior were taken as representative of the difference of an entire nation of people. The formation of natural knowledge was thus based on a particularly European paradigm that placed Europe, and its developing systems of (scientific) knowledge, as the centre and norm. While the scientific reduction of racial difference to bodily difference was effected during the nineteenth century, it is the very concept of normality that translates into the anatomical images. These present the white European body as having representative status as the signifier of scientific bodily knowledge. Science encodes the idea of a normative body within its very structures through the idealized figuration of the white (female) body as an example of such knowledge. Whiteness signifies as normality, whereas nonwhite bodies are presented in science as deviations from a presumed norm.[7]

| Figure 13.3 |
D'Agoty's 1773 pregnant woman. The Wellcome Trust.

Jacques-Fabien Gautier D'Agoty's anatomical illustrations more obviously present the body of science as an aestheticized object, and the inscription of the female body as an idealizsed reproductive form. In a book concerned with showing the reproductive parts of the male and female body, Gautier D'Agoty's *Anatomie des parties de la generation de l'homme et de la femme* (1773) presents three plates of the female body and only one of the male. Unlike the illustrations in Jenty's, Hunter's, and Smellie's atlases, each of the three plates presents a full-length colored image of the female body (figure 13.3), complete with detailed rendering of hair, face, and winsome smiles, reminiscent of the detailed features included in seventeenth-century Italian wax anatomical models of the female body (Jordanova 1989). Clearly deploying the forms of classical realism, these images incorporate the discourse of science through the presentation of the female body as dissected. While the main figures are full-length, the inclusion of variously dissected female body parts and organs that appear in the back and foreground of these images present a peculiar visual interaction between the classically posed and ideal female form and the various anatomical products of human dissection placed around the figures. Two out of the three main dissected figures represent the fetus both within and outside the female body, while all three plates reproduce the female generative parts as disembodied organs. Hailed by Gautier D'Agoty as representing the anatomical body in its natural colors, the mezzotints offer a highly subjective account of what constitutes the natural, where the use of blue pigment to represent exposed arteries and veins illustrates this position.

Looking at these images from a contemporary viewpoint, the juxtaposition of the dissected body, understood as a signification of scientific practice with the forms and conventions of painting, strike the viewer as somewhat peculiar. Contemporary familiarity with the abstraction and compartmentalization of the body as it is presented in anatomical illustrations makes these images appear strange due to their deployment of artistic conventions. Yet as we have already seen, the anatomical images in Hunter's and Jenty's atlases represent similar aestheticized views of the female body. The dissected female bodies in the illustrated anatomical texts of Hunter, Jenty, and D'Agoty constitute bodily knowledge through a discourse of normative heterosexual reproduction, teaching us to view this body through the signification of the generative organs. The desire to order and control the reproductive body through its visual representation is revealed in all three authors through their insistence on the "reality" of these images. Anxiety to map the body according to an idealized visual model thus encodes itself within the very logic of scientific discourse, even as an examination of the illustrations within the sociohistorical context of their production reveals their highly contextualized status. The

Julie Doyle and Kate O'Riordan

body cannot signify *as a body*—cannot be understood as a body that is *visibly read*—without its accompanying visual representation. The reproductive capacity of the female, captured by the artist, is thus inscribed in the representational processes involved in the imaging of this body. Thus the very presentation of scientific knowledge through image performatively constitutes what it pertains to represent; the body as specifically gendered through the dynamics of heteronormative reproduction.[8]

Medical Imaging on the Web

The processes of engraving and mezzotint were relied on in the promotion of anatomical knowledge during the late eighteenth and early nineteenth centuries. These have now been taken over by advanced imaging technologies such as computer tomography (CT) and magnetic resonance imaging (MRI) that, along with graphic design software, are utilized to present anatomical images through the virtual medium of cyberspace. The SVF project, hosted by Stanford University, is part of a widening collection of these medical images that can be accessed through the World Wide Web. While the associated VHP[9] has attracted much critical attention and is discussed both through the medical discourse from which it emerged and also as a free-standing cultural artifact, the SVF has not received the same attention. Emerging from the field of human anatomy, both projects draw on developments in the world of medical imaging and deploy virtual space as a medium of representation. The images in the Stanford Visible Female are created from the corpse of a female body and supply a representation of the pelvic region of a premenopausal female using cryosectioning, MRI, and CT techniques. The pelvis can be viewed in a variety of ways from individual files of the cryosections to fully animated tours through the reconstituted pelvic area. The material is a resource for medical students, researchers, and practitioners and is utilized to simulate surgery and in teaching anatomy.

The representation of the female body in the SVF is intended to be that of the normal female human body. The images are placed into a sequence that performs a reconstituted body—creating the illusion that these technologies of imaging allow the medical vision to actually penetrate the body. Some techniques do perform an X-ray model of imaging such as MRI. However, the process of cryosectioning, which underpins the Stanford Visible Female, is a process whereby a corpse is filled with fluid, frozen, and then sliced thinly, an image is then taken of each slide. The individual images can then be viewed separately or strung back together in an animation that allows the viewer's point of view to survey the body. This perspective, where the point of view moves through the body, has been simulated before, and endoscopy has been deployed in many forms of visual communication from surgery to popular film, but here it is innovative on two counts: first, because it is a representation constructed from images of an actual corpse rather than a simulation, and, second, because it allows a cross-body vision of everything enveloped by the outer skin as opposed to that enveloped by a single passage or membrane, as with endoscopy.

The process of freezing, slicing, and photographing is followed by design processes that are then assembled into a filmic presentation. A variety of techniques and packages are used, such as Adobe PhotoShop, before the images are presented on the Web and on CD-ROM. The process before the material is marked up into Web pages and data sets involves different stages of dissection, imaging, storage, reassembly, design, and editing. The data sets are produced in the same way that any mediated information is assembled. Elements are selected according to various filters and presented in a particular way. Yet the rhetoric of the project refers to the "normal" as though this were naturally occurring data that has been found and neutrally collected rather than constructed. These two factors, the obscuring of the means of production of the representation, and the modeling of the normal living body on a single, processed corpse, serve to separate the representation from the body that it is taken from and to free it as a simulation without referent other than itself (Debord 1983). This simulation is then affixed to the ideology of the natural body as though this existed other than in the realm of representation.

The Stanford Visible Female deploys advanced imaging techniques and technologies that have been described in terms of their "Frankenstein factor" by Sarah Kember (1999) and other members of Cutting Edge.[10] Donna Haraway (1989) and Ludmilla Jordanova (1985) have carried out extensive work illustrating the construction of normative bodies through scientific discourse, while Anne Balsamo (1996) and Lisa Cartwright (1995) have discussed the images produced through the visual culture of science. Contemporary artistic interest in biotechnologies as art media also reflects current widening cultural concerns with constructions of the body and narratives of science. An example of such interest is the work of Tiffany Holmes;[11] her installation "Nosce Te Ipsum" incorporates the imaging techiques of anatomy while also reflecting the viewer in the layers of the dissected body. The work of Helen Chadwick, a U.K. artist, also reflects this interest, and before her death in 1996 she developed amplified studies of fetal imagery in addition to her existing portfolio of studies on flesh and light.

Representing Normality

What is at issue in this process of imaging and positioning of the viewer are the implications for the definition of the normal female body:

What will come to be culturally understood as the body (Thacker 2000).

Julie Doyle and Kate O'Riordan

It (VHP) is the creation of complete, anatomically detailed, three-dimensional representations of the normal male and female human bodies (VHP 1999).

They are therefore (again) fictional archetypes against which (real) others will be measured (Kember 1999, 43).

In harmony with the Human Genome Project, the Stanford Visible Female attempts to create the template for an imagined normality, a practice that has material implications particularly when technologies allow the literal reconfiguring of the flesh. While acknowledging that the idea of normality is a model rather than an ideal, this classification of normality is still problematic because of the diversities that it obscures. One of the more interesting elements of the Web is that its very variety and polymorphosity offers a resistance to normalization, a context of presentation with which these projects fail to consciously engage. The action of representing any human body has political import, the action of normalization especially so. The development of a medical template that is intended to provide a basis for research into anatomy, surgery, and diagnosis has even more political significance; as Thacker points out, it is the cultural understanding of what constitutes a normal human body that is at stake. This continued failure to see the body as a process or system and the categorization of the body into simple oppositions seems remarkable when the human bodies that perform the cultures within which the research will be applied are marked by disease, class, ethnicity, gender, tradition, diet, culture, age, and motion, to name but a few of the conditions of corporeality. The ideology of the ideal and unmarked body sustained by this project continues to support a concept of normality that is at odds with the bodies on which medical intervention is performed.

The normal female is the young and reproductively able female, in the Stanford model. This privileging of the premenopausal body continues to abnormalize that of the postmenopausal, reinforcing dominant ideologies of legitimate femininity that conflate femininity with youth and reproductive capacity. The lack of acknowldgement that female bodies are multifaceted and resistant to normalizing categories renders the "truth" of such anatomical images suspect. The assumption that normal is objective, premenopausal, unmarked with any sign of disease and dead appears to be an extreme level of inductivism; this may be the ideal body but is it not any body's norm. This totalizing impulse to categorize and fix organic life into a prescriptive model has been found wanting as a methodology in the production of knowledge by queer theory, postcolonialism, and feminism. It would seem then that much of the idealistic hype about the radical scope of cyberspace for the development of alternative knowledges is preemptive. The medium can as easily represent the totalizing dualisms of the Enlighten-ment model of progress as it can represent the situated knowledges anticipated by Har-away (1991). However, the medium of cyberspace is used to store and display in addition to these medical images a variety of knowledges about the body; representations of liv-ing bodies are being produced through dialogic and situated methods. Since such rep-resentations can be found on other sites, one of the more promising things about cyberspace is its diversity. The hierarchy of knowledge has, however, yet to be destabi-lized. The discourse of inductive scientific method is disturbingly reified in the Stan-ford Visible Female, even at a basic cognitive level; the argument that the one should represent the many and that humans should be mapped onto a universal template is cause for concern.

Current medical cyberbodies continue to present virtual bodily matter through the normative significations of sex/gender. Why this is problematic for women is further highlighted in the recent media furor over the potentialities for postmenopausal women to become fertile again through the processes of ovarian tissue transplantation. Employed to reverse the premature menopause of a 30-year-old woman, this first suc-cessful performance of ovarian tissue transplantation was hailed as offering hope for young cancer patients whose fertility is threatened by the effects of radiotherapy and drugs. However, it was the possibility that such a technique could offer fertility to women in their fifties or sixties that invoked cultural anxieties surrounding the aging (thus nonreproductive) female body, with one newspaper noting how Roger Gosden of Leeds University, the pioneer behind the technique, was playing down such "Franken-stein scenarios."[12] The deployment of such a culturally laden term as *Frankenstein* to de-scribe the possibility of postmenopausal women becoming pregnant illustrates how contemporary definitions of the female body rearticulate conventional significations of gendered embodiment. Even in the face of radical technologies, the "legitimate" re-productive female is set against an aging, hence "illegitimate," female body. This dis-course articulates a hierarchy among women that privileges those between the ages of twenty and thirty-five, even in the context of an aging Western population with even higher life expectancy. Thus, women who do not conform to this hierarchy by becom-ing pregnant after thirty-five, when they are more likely to be financially and emotion-ally stable, are subject to intense discussion, defined as deviant, and even reviled as irresponsible to the child. Another example of media exposure was the British chat show program, *Kilroy*.[13] This program discussed the matter of parenting over forty and sug-gested that this was a selfish and dangerous practice. In this form of medico-public dis-course the female body is subject to a strict taxonomy of normal as young and actively reproductive, and this is publicly policed through discussion and scrutiny.

The Context of Cyberspace

The discourse of professional distance that the SVF project deploys is manifest in both the pristine condition of the image that is exorcised of blood, flesh, or death and in the organization of the data into a virtual property. A pelvis is positioned as disembodied in the project, an isolated rotating frame. This project presents us with a tension between the female body as understood in isolated parts, removed from context, and the female body as understood synechdocally by its parts. The implication of this distance is a continued separation between being and having a body. Experientially we are bodies; we do not simply have them. All the philosophical postulations about disembodied points of view in the dualist tradition are, like Case's perspective in *Neuromancer* (Gibson 1986), science fictions. They can be entertaining and useful intellectual exercises but they are not a workable representation of anybody's self. Not only is this separation simply unrealistic, but it also (re)evokes the colonial gaze and positions the viewer as the bearer of such.

The point of view of the user of cyberspace is removed from the objects surveyed. The user has no physical presence in the place in which the information is stored. The information is virtually there, the images wrapped in the dimension of cyberspace where cyberbodies at first glance seem removed from fleshly bodies. The object of the gaze is decontextualized and the manner of visual presentation makes the Stanford Visible Female even more disembodied than the historical images discussed, which included the context of flesh. Using cyberspace, it is claimed, is to be part of the circuit of the cyborg; the neural sensorium is extended into cyberspace so that, located in the United Kingdom, I can view these images, labored over and presented in an American institution, generated through collaboration over space and time. In cyberspace as with other media, the underlying labor of representation is obscured, the means of production of these images cannot be seen. The "virtual" quality of the slides frames them as images signifying something other. They do not resignify slides but are manipulated into signifying bodies: Constructed through the deconstruction of a corpse is its transformation into a signifier of the healthy, normal body. The artifice of cyberspace is deployed to reinscribe the body as both natural and disembodied, recasting the polarities from which the discourse of the cyborg articulated the promise of change.

The medium of cyberspace is also a context in itself, and single projects like the SVF require contextualization through this medium as well as the wider social sphere. Two aspects to be considered are, first, the context of other material on the Web and, second, the perspective brought to bear in the negotiation of Web space. The Internet is a large and polymorphous domain, and representations of many different kinds are in evidence in this space. A single project such as the Stanford Visible Female is also informed by its links to other sites and is undercut by the lack of authoritative standardization because any organization or source with access can display information on the Internet. The authority of science as a primary source of hegemonic naturalization is yet to be seriously disturbed despite any radical interventions. However, the multivalent virtuality of the Internet serves to undercut the seriousness of the Stanford Visible Female project. In the context of Eugene Thacker's "Med Porn"[14] project for example, which assembles medical images in the format of an explicitly erotic site, and a Web site dedicated to "artful, female, nudity"[15] that came up in the same search as the Stanford Visible Female, the authority of these representations is undermined. In the context of the Web then, the authority of the images is destabilized; however, medical professionals accessing the data sets for simulation would negotiate them in CD-ROM format and bypass the Web altogether. A further counterbalance is the status that computer-mediated communication can convey; many projects and organisation utilize computing technologies in order to seen as serious. For example, the Fabula Project at Brighton University is developing classroom software for minority language groups, teaching translation through storytelling. The rationale for using a computer platform, rather than any other form, is that this contributes toward a minority language group, such as Welsh, gaining a higher economic and more mainstream status because it includes it in the information economy.

Emergent Bodies

While the dominant medical discourse fantasizes about a body fixed by the dominant sex/gender ideology, other sites represent bodies resistant to the prescriptions of this imaginary. Two good examples of this are the Bodies© INCorporated[16] site and The Brandon site hosted by the Guggenheim Museum.[17] These are both Web sites concerned with representing both emergent bodies and relations between bodies. The Brandon site (figure 13.4) deals with themes such as boundaries and borders between actual/virtual and male/female and also questions hegemonic and institutional bias toward the clearly defined and conformist body. Deploying the metaphor of the panopticon, this site restages court sessions on the Brandon case. This case concerned the 1993 Nebraska rape and murder of Brandon Teena, a pre-operative transsexual. Two films, *The Brandon Teena Story* (1998) and *Boys Don't Cry* (1999) have been made about the story. The Brandon site is organized by artist Shu Lea Chang, and it represents a commentary on the interactions of law, sexuality, and identity. Both Allucquère Stone and Del LaGrace Volcano, who have also been involved with the design of this site, make a direct connection between the boundaries of actual and virtual and those of gender. Stone's theoretical work on actual/virtual/multiple identity (Stone 1995) is correlated

| Figure 13.4 |
Image from the Brandon Teena online exhibit. Shu Lea Chang.

to Brandon's bodily performance and to the representation of different identities in a single body, through this site.

Bodies© INCorporated is an interactive, multiuser forum set up to question and explore the relation between virtual and actual bodies. It can be discussed as a virtual exploration of performativity of the body on many levels. The question outlined on the information page of the site—for example, "How does the graphic representation of the body amplify our relationship to it?"—sets the agenda for this exploration. The site is also concerned with the appropriation of bodies by corporations and makes a play on the idea of corporate bodies and identities. While more playful than the Brandon site, the Bodies© INCorporated site is also an attempt to engage with the boundary tensions between virtual and actual bodies and with the body as performance. Victoria Vesna, an artist and academic who directs the site, engages with traditions in the visual and performing arts—the exploration of the body meshes with contemporary concerns about bodily ownership and design in the context of a society incorporating both augmented and marginalized bodies, regulated by corporate law. Both the Brandon site and Bodies© INCorporated form part of a wider discourse that articulates the decentralization of the objective body and an exploration of emergent bodies through action.

The theme of identity as performed, as opposed to identity as embedded in the material substance of the body, is represented in the Brandon site through the depiction of Brandon Teena and the inclusion of other material relating to multiple or transitional identities. Performativity emerges on two levels. First, it appears in the form of the site, a virtual art installation based on a juxtaposed, actual event, where the site designers deploy the disembodied realm of cyberspace to represent events and issues centered in embodiment. Second, the site thematically explores performance as lived experience, engaging with Brandon who signified her/his masculinity in defiance of the sex/gender binary. The tensions between essential and performed identities are visible here; the performance of identity through representation on this site can be seen as a virtual embodiment of this theoretical area where the site holds in tension the poles of virtual and performed against those of essential and material. It can also be seen as an example of the merging of form and content in virtual representation and of the difficulty in distinguishing between agent and text. The interactive elements of the Brandon site incorporate observations and commentary from participants and combine them with the predesigned "text" of the site. The Brandon site is (like the Bodies© INC site) an interactive forum combining display with interjection that reflects back out of virtual communication to problematize the performance of offline identity.

The Brandon site is participatory, and the prior text of the site is merged with the contributions of participants in the virtual courts. That the site involves participation reinforces its contribution toward embodying the notion of representation as action. The bodies emergent in the text of the Brandon project challenge the inscriptions of the gender division. While the construction of gender is made evident through its transsexual narrative, the constitution of normative gender through legislation, bureaucracy, and consensus is particularly evident in this project, and conformity to this model of the body is questioned. The connection that one informant, involved with the site, made between the virtual/actual tension and gender disphoria was that virtuality enabled the exploration of different gender identities. While interrogating the normalizing representations of the gendered body by seeking to reembody cyberspace with participation and interaction, the Brandon site also recontextualizes the body as something in relation to and emergent through psychic, cultural, and social factors, as opposed to a body discovered in objective isolation that is the implication of the SVF.

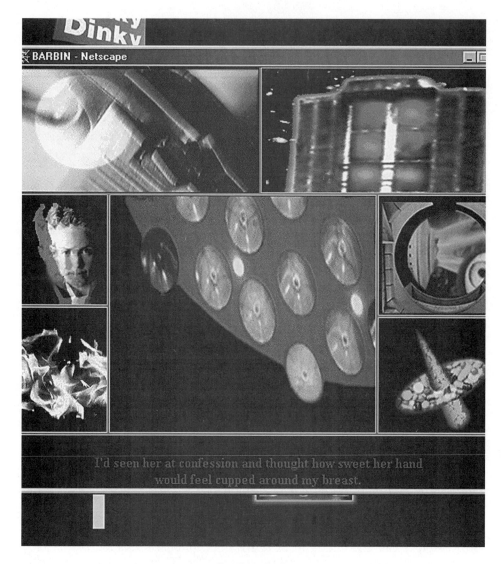

| Figure 13.5 |
Image from the Brandon Teena online exhibit. Shu Lea Chang.

The Brandon and Bodies© INCorporated sites explore the synthesis between the way identity is represented online and offline, bridging the popular conception of separate virtual/actual domains. It is hard to conceive why a difference in medium should create absolute transformations in representation, or suddenly fragment our lives into distinct offline and online categories, unless they were already experienced through fragmentation. As yet there are few fundamental changes in cyberspace; the privileged have more access and the marginalized remain underrepresented. However, once in the context of the Web, the dominance of hegemonic projects is momentarily more challenged than in other mainstream media. The Internet can change factors; it can change access to information, and it can point to the social construction of gender by denaturalizing identity. The elements of interactivity, hyperlinks, cost, and novelty arguably evoke a more active consumption and a more individual production. The virtuality of participation does seem to encourage attention that might be inhibited in offline participation. It is less risky, for example, to experiment with identity and to participate in, or support, minority or marginalized discourse in the virtual realm than it is in offline communication where bodily presence may mean experiencing physical threat.

As we have shown in this chapter, existing technologies have new applications and are being used to resist, explore, and experiment with existing orthodoxies that present normative notions of gender identity as natural conditions of the body. The Brandon site, already mentioned, interweaves images of surgical procedures with different parts of the body that are sometimes pierced or tattooed. These images are assembled into a constantly changing mosaic of juxtaposition. The flesh is constantly reframed and rewritten with changing connotations. Stories told by the subjective voices of the bodies, suggested on the site, are placed alongside other voices that debate and comment on identity. This rich combination of stories, images, and partial interactivity represents both a fluid and a situated body. The Bodies© INCorporated project also contests notions of ownership and definitions of the body. On the site, bodies are constantly assembled and deconstructed from parts drawn from different categories, and thus a challenge to the typology of the body is made. As the logo suggests, the site is also used to contest hegemonic notions of control that have been maintained through the discourse of medical science. This site, especially in the social context of the patenting of the human genome, acts as a reminder that power can be dispersed.

The medical imaging projects that confirm gender binaries, and these alternative sites of representation that question these binaries, are undertaken in the context of relatively affluent Western societies with access to and investment in new technologies. We need to engage therefore with Lisa Cartwright's (1995) observation that in terms of treatment these medical imaging technologies are only available in affluent contexts and the technologies themselves should not be demonized. Our intention is not to pathologize science or medical practice per se, but to trouble the representations of the female body in medical discourse and indicate some of the effects such naturalizations have on women's lives. It is clear that while medicine's visual culture fails to address the complexities of gender identity through imaging technologies, we must continue to look to other contexts of use in order to reconfigure existing prescriptions of normality within cyberspace.

Acknowledgments

We are gratefully indebted to Irmi Karl, Sally R. Munt, and Lindsay Smith for their contributions to this chapter. Images are reproduced thanks to the kind permission of Shu Lea Chang, SUMMIT–Stanford University, and The Wellcome Trust.

Notes

1. Additional information on the project is available at <http://summit.stanford.edu/RESEARCH/StanfordVisibleFemale>.
2. This chapter focuses on the developments and cultural effects of Western European science, and thus refers to Christianity as the predominant religion of the West.
3. See Sawday 1995 for a more complex analysis of the interactions between the emerging discourse of dissection and colonial expansion.
4. The processes involved in the consolidation of surgery as the superior discipline of science required institutional and legal support, aided by the establishment of a Royal College of Surgeons of London in 1800 and the Anatomy Act of 1832 that legally entitled anatomists to use the "unclaimed" bodies of paupers for dissection. See Richardson 1987 for an account of the cultural effects of this act.
5. Again, the establishment of science as a theological discourse to rival religion did not occur overnight. The secularization of science gained legitimacy during the latter half of the nineteenth century following the publication of Darwin's evolutionary theories.
6. See Pratt 1992, for an analysis of European travel writing and its relation to imperialist discourse.
7. The popularized life of Saartjie Baartman, known as the "Hottentot Venus," is illustrative of this view; her body was exhibited both during her life and after her death (through dissection) as evidence of her abnormality (to Europeans) by virtue of her anatomical features—namely, her large buttocks and extended labia.
8. This chapter can be seen as an attempt to historicize and culturally contextualize the performativity of gendered embodiment articulated by Judith Butler in her seminal text *Bodies That Matter* (1993), to which we are indebted.
9. Hosted by the National Library of Medicine (U.S.).

10. A London-based women's research group.

11. Residing at the University of Michigan, this piece has been exhibited since January 2000 and was also on display at SIGGRAPH 2000.

12. Sarah Boseley, "Menopause Reversal Proclaimed," *UK Guardian*, September 24, 1999, p. 3.

13. 24/11/99 BBC1 at 9.00am.

14. Available at <http://arts.ucsb.edu/bodiesinc>.

15. Available at <http://www.lili-nanse.freeserve.co.uk/>.

16. Available at <http://gsa.rutgers.edu/maldoror/MEDPORN/index.html>.

17. Available at <http://brandon.guggenheim.org>.

Works Cited

Balsamo, Anne. *Technologies Of The Gendered Body: Reading Cyborg Women*. Durham: Duke University Press, 1996.

Blumenbach, J. F. *A Short System of Comparative Anatomy*. Trans. William Lawrence. London: Longman, Hurst, Rees and Orme, 1807.

Bodies© INCorporated. Online. Available at <http://arts.ucsb.edu/bodiesinc/>. January 12, 1999.

The Brandon Site. Online. Available at <http://brandon.guggenheim.org/>. October 11, 1999.

Buffon, Comte de. *Natural History, General and Particular,* trans. William Smellie. London: W. Strachan and T. Cadell, 1785.

Butler, Judith P. *Bodies That Matter: On The Discursive Limits Of "Sex."* New York and London: Routledge, 1993.

Cartwright, Lisa. *Screening the Body: Tracing Medicine's Visual Culture*. Minneapolis: University of Minnesota Press, 1995.

D'Agoty, Johannes Fabien Gautier. *Anatomie des parties de la generation de l'homme et de la femme*. Paris: JB Brunet and Demonville, 1773.

Debord, Guy. *Society of the Spectacle*. Detroit: Black and Red, 1983.

Gibson, William. *Neuromancer.* London: Harper Collins, 1986.

Haraway, Donna. *Simians, Cyborgs and Women: The Reinvention of Nature*. London: Free Association Books Ltd., 1991.

Hunter, William. *The Anatomy of the Human Gravid Uterus Exhibited in Figures*. Birmingham: John Baskerville, 1774.

Jenty, Charles Nicholas. *The demonstrations of a pregnant uterus of a woman at her fulltime in six tables, as large as nature, done from the pictures painted after dissections by Mr. Van Riemsdyk and disposed in such a manner as to represent, completely, this state of pregnancy, by Charles Nicholas Jenty, AM, Professor of Anatomy and Surgery*. London, [1757] 1758.

Jordanova, Ludmilla. "Gender, Generation and Science: William Hunter's Obstetrical Atlas." In *William Hunter and the Eighteenth-Century Medical World*, ed. W. F. Bynum and Roy Porter. Cambridge: Cambridge University Press, 1985.

Jordanova, Ludmilla. *Sexual Visions: Images of Gender in Science and Medicine Between the Eighteenth and Twentieth Centuries*. Madison: University of Wisconsin Press, 1989.

Kember, S. "NITS and NRTS: Medical Science and the Frankenstein Factor." In *Desire By Design: Body, Territories and New Technologies*, ed. Cutting Edge, 212–250. London: I. B. Tauris and Co. Ltd., 1999.

Pratt, Mary Louise. *Imperial Eyes; Travel Writing and Transculturation*. London: Routledge, 1992.

Richardson, Ruth. *Death, Dissection and the Destitute: The Politics of the Corpse in Pre Victorian Britain*. London: Routledge, 1987.

Sawday, Jonathan. *The Body Emblazoned: Dissection and the Human Body in Renaissance Culture*. London: Routledge, 1995.

Smellie, William. *A sett of anatomical tables with explanations and an abridgement of the practice of midwifery, with a view to illustrate a treatise on that subject, and collection of cases*. London, 1754.

Stafford, Barbara Maria. *Body Criticism: Imaging the Unseen in Enlightenment Art and Medicine*. Cambridge, MA: MIT Press, 1991.

Stanford Visible Female (SVF). Hosted by Stanford University. 1997. Online. Available at <http://summit.Stanford.EDU/RESEARCH/StanfordVisibleFemale>. October 11, 1999.

Stone, Allucquère Rosanne. *The War of Desire and Technology at the Close of the Mechanical Age*. Cambridge, MA: MIT Press, 1995.

Thacker, Eugene. ". . . /visible_human.html/digital anatomy and the hyper-texted body." Online. Available at <http://www.ctheory.com/a60.html>. April 2, 2000.

Visible Human Project (VHP). Hosted by the NLM–National Library of Medicine. Online. Available at <http://www.nlm.nih.gov/research/visible/>. January 11, 1999.

14

NO WOMAN BORN

C. L. Moore

She had been the loveliest creature whose image ever moved along the airways. John Harris, who was once her manager, remembered doggedly how beautiful she had been as he rose in the silent elevator toward the room where Deirdre sat waiting for him.

Since the theater fire that had destroyed her a year ago, he had never been quite able to let himself remember her beauty clearly, except when some old poster, half in tatters, flaunted her face at him, or a maudlin memorial program flashed her image unexpectedly across the television screen. But now he had to remember.

The elevator came to a sighing stop and the door slid open. John Harris hesitated. He knew in his mind that he had to go on, but his reluctant muscles almost refused him. He was thinking helplessly, as he had not allowed himself to think until this moment, of the fabulous grace that had poured through her wonderful dancer's body, remembering her soft and husky voice with the little burr in it that had fascinated the audiences of the whole world.

There had never been anyone so beautiful.

In times before her, other actresses had been lovely and adulated, but never before Deirdre's day had the entire world been able to take one woman so wholly to its heart. So few outside the capitals had ever seen Bernhardt or the fabulous Jersey Lily. And the beauties of the movie screen had had to limit their audiences to those who could reach the theaters. But Deirdre's image had once moved glowingly across the television screens of every home in the civilized world. And in many outside the bounds of civilization. Her soft, husky songs had sounded in the depths of jungles. Her lovely, languorous body had woven its patterns of rhythm in desert tents and polar huts. The whole world knew every smooth motion of her body and every cadence of her voice, and the way a subtle radiance had seemed to go on behind her features when she smiled.

And the whole world had mourned her when she died in the theater fire.

Harris could not quite think of her as other than dead, though he knew what sat waiting him in the room ahead. He kept remembering the old words James Stephens wrote long ago for another Deirdre, also lovely and beloved and unforgotten after two thousand years.

The time comes when our hearts sink utterly,
When we remember Deirdre and her tale,
And that her lips are dust . . .
There has been again no woman born
Who was so beautiful; not one so beautiful
Of all the women born—

That wasn't quite true, of course—there had been one. Or maybe, after all, this Deirdre who died only a year ago had not been beautiful in the sense of perfection. He thought the other one might not have been either, for there are always women with perfection of feature in the world, and they are not the ones that legend remembers. It was the light within, shining through her charming, imperfect features, that had made this Deirdre's face so lovely. No one else he had ever seen had anything like the magic of the lost Deirdre.

Let all men go apart and mourn together—
No man can ever love her. Not a man
Can dream to be her lover. . . . No man say—
What could one say to her? There are no words
That one could say to her.

No, no words at all. And it was going to be impossible to go through with this. Harris knew it overwhelmingly just as his finger touched the buzzer. But the door opened almost instantly, and then it was too late.

Maltzer stood just inside, peering out through his heavy spectacles. You could see how tensely he had been waiting. Harris was a little shocked to see that the man was trembling. It was hard to think of the confident and imperturbable Maltzer, whom he had known briefly a year ago, as shaken like this. He wondered if Deirdre herself were as tremulous with sheer nerves—but it was not time yet to let himself think of that.

"Come in, come in," Maltzer said irritably. There was no reason for irritation. The year's work, so much of it in secrecy and solitude, must have tried him physically and mentally to the very breaking point.

"She all right?" Harris asked inanely, stepping inside.

"Oh yes . . . yes, *she's* all right." Maltzer bit his thumbnail and glanced over his shoulder at an inner door, where Harris guessed she would be waiting.

"No," Maltzer said, as he took an involuntary step toward it. "We'd better have a talk first. Come over and sit down. Drink?"

Harris nodded, and watched Maltzer's hands tremble as he tilted the decanter. The man was clearly on the very verge of collapse, and Harris felt a sudden cold uncertainty open up in him in the one place where until now he had been oddly confident.

"She *is* all right?" he demanded, taking the glass.

"Oh yes, she's perfect. She's so confident it scares me." Maltzer gulped his drink and poured another before he sat down.

"What's wrong, then?"

"Nothing, I guess. Or . . . well, I don't know. I'm not sure anymore. I've worked toward this meeting for nearly a year, but now—well, I'm not sure it's time yet. I'm just not sure."

He stared at Harris, his eyes large and indistinguishable behind the lenses. He was a thin, wire-taut man with all the bone and sinew showing plainly beneath the dark skin of his face. Thinner, now, than he had been a year ago when Harris saw him last.

"I've been too close to her," he said now. "I have no perspective anymore. All I can see is my own work. And I'm just not sure that's ready yet for you or anyone to see."

"She thinks so?"

"I never saw a woman so confident." Maltzer drank, the glass clicking on his teeth. He looked up suddenly through the distorting lenses. "Of course a failure now would mean—well, absolute collapse," he said.

Harris nodded. He was thinking of the year of incredibly painstaking work that lay behind this meeting, the immense fund of knowledge, of infinite patience, the secret collaboration of artists, sculptors, designers, scientists, and the genius of Maltzer governing them all as an orchestra conductor governs his players.

He was thinking too, with a certain unreasoning jealousy, of the strange, cold, passionless intimacy between Maltzer and Deirdre in that year, a closer intimacy than any two humans can ever have shared before. In a sense the Deirdre whom he saw in a few minutes would *be* Maltzer, just as he thought he detected in Maltzer now and then small mannerisms of inflection and motion that had been Deirdre's own. There had been between them a sort of unimaginable marriage stranger than anything that could ever have taken place before.

"—so many complications," Maltzer was saying in his worried voice with its faintest possible echo of Deirdre's lovely, cadenced rhythm. (The sweet, soft huskiness he would never hear again.) "There was shock, of course. Terrible shock. And a great fear of fire. We had to conquer that before we could take the first steps. But we did it. When you go in you'll probably find her sitting before the fire." He caught the startled question in Harris's eyes and smiled. "No, she can't feel the warmth now, of course. But she likes to watch the flames. She's mastered any abnormal fear of them quite beautifully."

"She can—" Harris hesitated. "Her eyesight's normal now?"

"Perfect," Maltzer said. "Perfect vision was fairly simple to provide. After all, that sort of thing has already been worked out, in other connections. I might even say her vision's a little better than perfect, from our own standpoint." He shook his head irritably. "I'm not worried about the mechanics of the thing. Luckily they got to her before the brain was touched at all. Shock was the only danger to her sensory centers, and we took care of all that first of all, as soon as communication could be established. Even so, it needed great courage on her part. Great courage." He was silent for a moment, staring into his empty glass.

"Harris," he said suddenly, without looking up, "have I made a mistake? Should we have let her die?"

Harris shook his head helplessly. It was an unanswerable question. It had tormented the whole world for a year now. There had been hundreds of answers and thousands of words written on the subject. Has anyone the right to preserve a brain alive when its body is destroyed? Even if a new body can be provided, necessarily so very unlike the old?

"It's not that she's—ugly—now," Maltzer went on hurriedly, as if afraid of an answer. "Metal isn't ugly. And Deirdre . . . well, you'll see. I tell you, I can't see myself. I know the whole mechanism so well—it's just mechanics to me. Maybe she's—grotesque, I don't know. Often I've wished I hadn't been on the spot, with all my ideas, just when the fire broke out. Or that it could have been anyone but Deirdre. She was so beautiful—Still, if it had been someone else I think the whole thing might have failed completely. It takes more than just an uninjured brain. It takes strength and courage beyond common, and— well, something more. Something—unquenchable. Deirdre has it. She's still Deirdre. In a way she's still beautiful. But I'm not sure anybody but myself could see that. And you know what she plans?"

"No—what?"

"She's going back on the air-screen."

Harris looked at him in stunned disbelief.

"She *is* still beautiful," Maltzer told him fiercely. "She's got courage, and a serenity that amazes me. And she isn't in the least worried or resentful about what's happened. Or afraid what the verdict of the public will be. But I am, Harris. I'm terrified."

They looked at each other for a moment more, neither speaking. Then Maltzer shrugged and stood up.

"She's in there," he said, gesturing with his glass.

Harris turned without a word, not giving himself time to hesitate. He crossed toward the inner door.

The room was full of a soft, clear, indirect light that climaxed in the fire crackling on a white tiled hearth. Harris paused inside the door, his heart beating thickly. He did not see her for a moment. It was a perfectly commonplace room, bright, light, with pleasant furniture, and flowers on the tables. Their perfume was sweet on the clear air. He did not see Deirdre.

Then a chair by the fire creaked as she shifted her weight in it. The high back hid her, but she spoke. And for one dreadful moment it was the voice of an automaton that sounded in the room, metallic, without inflection.

"Hel-lo—," said the voice. Then she laughed and tried again. And it was the old, familiar, sweet huskiness he had not hoped to hear again as long as he lived.

In spite of himself he said, "Deirdre!" and her image rose before him as if she herself had risen unchanged from the chair, tall, golden, swaying a little with her wonderful dancer's poise, the lovely, imperfect features lighted by the glow that made them beautiful. It was the cruelest thing his memory could have done to him. And yet the voice—after that one lapse, the voice was perfect.

"Come and look at me, John," she said.

He crossed the floor slowly, forcing himself to move. That instant's flash of vivid recollection had nearly wrecked his hard-won poise. He tried to keep his mind perfectly blank as he came at last to the verge of seeing what no one but Maltzer had so far seen or known about in its entirety. No one at all had known what shape would be forged to clothe the most beautiful woman on Earth, now that her beauty was gone.

He had envisioned many shapes. Great, lurching robot forms, cylindrical, with hinged arms and legs. A glass case with the brain floating in it and appendages to serve its needs. Grotesque visions, like nightmares come nearly true. And each more inadequate than the last, for what metal shape could possibly do more than house ungraciously the mind and brain that had once enchanted a whole world?

Then he came around the wing of the chair, and saw her.

The human brain is often too complicated a mechanism to function perfectly. Harris's brain was called upon to perform a very elaborate series of shifting impressions. First, incongruously, he remembered a curious inhuman figure he had once glimpsed leaning over the fence rail outside a farmhouse. For an instant the shape had stood up integrated, ungainly, impossibly human, before the glancing eye resolved it into an arrangement of brooms and buckets. What the eye had found only roughly humanoid, the suggestible brain had accepted fully formed. It was thus now, with Deirdre.

The first impression that his eyes and mind took from sight of her was shocked and incredulous, for his brain said to him unbelievingly, *"This is Deirdre! She hasn't changed at all!"*

Then the shift of perspective took over, and even more shockingly, eye and brain said, "No, not Deirdre—not human. Nothing but metal coils. Not Deirdre at all—" And that was the worst. It was like waking from a dream of someone beloved and lost, and facing anew, after that heartbreaking reassurance of sleep, the inflexible fact that nothing can bring the lost to life again. Deirdre was gone, and this was only machinery heaped in a flowered chair.

Then the machinery moved, exquisitely, smoothly, with a grace as familiar as the swaying poise he remembered. The sweet, husky voice of Deirdre said,

"It's me, John darling. It really is, you know."

And it was.

That was the third metamorphosis, and the final one. Illusion steadied and became factual, real. It was Deirdre.

He sat down bonelessly. He had no muscles. He looked at her speechless and unthinking, letting his senses take in the sight of her without trying to rationalize what he saw.

She was golden still. They had kept that much of her, the first impression of warmth and color which had once belonged to her sleek hair and the apricot tints of her skin. But they had had the good sense to go no farther. They had not tried to make a wax image of the lost Deirdre. (*No woman born / who was so beautiful—Not one so beautiful / of all the women born—*)

And so she had no face. She had only a smooth, delicately modeled ovoid for her head, with a . . . a sort of crescent-shaped mask across the frontal area where her eyes would have been if she had needed eyes. A narrow, curved quarter moon, with the horns turned upward. It was filled in with something translucent, like cloudy crystal, and tinted the aquamarine of the eyes Deirdre used to have. Through that, then, she saw the world. Through that she looked without eyes, and behind it, as behind the eyes of a human—she was.

Except for that, she had no features. And it had been wise of those who designed her, he realized now. Subconsciously he had been dreading some clumsy attempt at human features that might creak like a marionette's in parodies of animation. The eyes, perhaps, had had to open in the same place upon her head, and at the same distance apart, to make easy for her an adjustment to the stereoscopic vision she used to have. But he was glad they had not given her two eye-shaped openings with glass marbles inside them. The mask was better.

(Oddly enough, he did not once think of the naked brain that must lie inside the metal. The mask was symbol enough for the woman within. It was enigmatic; you did not know if her gaze was on you searchingly, or wholly withdrawn. And it had no variations of brilliance such as once had played across the incomparable mobility of Deirdre's face. But eyes, even human eyes, are as a matter of fact enigmatic enough. They have no expression except what the lids impart; they take all animation from the features. We automatically watch the eyes of the friend we speak with, but if he happens to be lying down so that he speaks across his shoulder and his face is upside-down to us, quite as automatically we watch the mouth. The gaze keeps shifting nervously between mouth and eyes in their reversed order, for it is the position in the face, not the feature itself, which we are accustomed to accept as the seat of the soul. Deirdre's mask was in that proper place; it was easy to accept it as a mask over eyes.)

She had, Harris realized as the first shock quieted, a very beautifully shaped head— a bare, golden skull. She turned it a little, gracefully upon her neck of metal, and he saw that the artist who shaped it had given her the most delicate suggestion of cheekbones, narrowing in the blankness below the mask to the hint of a human face. Not too much. Just enough so that when the head turned you saw by its modeling that it had moved, lending perspective and foreshortening to the expressionless golden helmet. Light did not slip uninterrupted as if over the surface of a golden egg. Brancusi himself had never made anything more simple or more subtle than the modeling of Deirdre's head.

But all expression, of course, was gone. All expression had gone up in the smoke of the theater fire, with the lovely, mobile, radiant features which had meant Deirdre.

As for her body, he could not see its shape. A garment hid her. But they had made no incongruous attempt to give her back the clothing that once had made her famous. Even the softness of cloth would have called the mind too sharply to the remembrance that no human body lay beneath the folds, nor does metal need the incongruity of cloth for its protection. Yet without garments, he realized, she would have looked oddly naked, since her new body was humanoid, not angular machinery.

The designer had solved his paradox by giving her a robe of very fine metal mesh. It hung from the gentle slope of her shoulders in straight, pliant folds like a longer Grecian chlamys, flexible, yet with weight enough of its own not to cling too revealingly to whatever metal shape lay beneath.

The arms they had given her were left bare, and the feet and ankles. And Maltzer had performed his greatest miracle in the limbs of the new Deirdre. It was a mechanical miracle basically, but the eye appreciated first that he had also showed supreme artistry and understanding.

Her arms were pale shining gold, tapered smoothly, without modeling, and flexible their whole length in diminishing metal bracelets fitting one inside the other clear down to the slim, round wrists. The hands were more nearly human than any other feature about her, though they, too, were fitted together in delicate, small sections that slid upon one another with the flexibility almost of flesh. The finger bases were solider than human, and the fingers themselves tapered to longer tips.

Her feet, too, beneath the tapering broader rings of the metal ankles, had been constructed upon the model of human feet. Their finely tooled sliding segments gave her an arch and a heel and a flexible forward section formed almost like the sollerets of medieval armor.

She looked, indeed, very much like a creature in armor, with her delicately plated limbs and her featureless head like a helmet with a visor of glass, and her robe of chain mail. But no knight in armor ever moved as Deirdre moved, or wore his armor upon a body of such inhumanly fine proportions. Only a knight from another world, or a knight of Oberon's court, might have shared that delicate likeness.

Briefly he had been surprised at the smallness and exquisite proportions of her. He had been expecting the ponderous mass of such robots as he had seen, wholly automatons. And then he realized that for them, much of the space had to be devoted to the inadequate mechanical brains that guided them about their duties. Deirdre's brain still preserved and proved the craftsmanship of an artisan far defter than man. Only the body was of metal, and it did not seem complex, though he had not yet been told how it was motivated.

Harris had no idea how long he sat staring at the figure in the cushioned chair. She was still lovely—indeed, she was still Deirdre—and as he looked, he let the careful schooling of his face relax. There was no need to hide his thoughts from her.

She stirred upon the cushions, the long, flexible arms moving with a litheness that was not quite human. The motion disturbed him as the body itself had not, and in spite of himself his face froze a little. He had the feeling that from behind the crescent mask she was watching him very closely.

Slowly she rose.

The motion was very smooth. Also it was serpentine, as if the body beneath the coat of mail were made in the same interlocking sections as her limbs. He had expected and feared mechanical rigidity; nothing had prepared him for this more-than-human suppleness.

She stood quietly, letting the heavy mailed folds of her garment settle about her. They fell together with a faint ringing sound, like small bells far off, and hung beautifully in pale golden, sculptured folds. He had risen automatically as she did. Now he faced her, staring. He had never seen her stand perfectly still, and she was not doing it now. She swayed just a bit, vitality burning inextinguishably in her brain as once it had burned in her body, and stolid immobility was as impossible to her as it had always been. The golden garment caught points of light from the fire and glimmered at him with tiny reflections as she moved.

Then she put her featureless helmeted head a little to one side, and he heard her laughter as familiar in its small, throaty, intimate sound as he had ever heard it from her living throat. And every gesture, every attitude, every flowing of motion into motion was so utterly Deirdre that the overwhelming illusion swept his mind again and this was the flesh-and-blood woman as clearly as if he saw her standing there whole once more, like the Phoenix from the fire.

"Well, John," she said in the soft, husky, amused voice he remembered perfectly. "Well, John, is it I?" She knew it was. Perfect assurance sounded in the voice. "The shock will wear off, you know. It'll be easier and easier as time goes on. I'm quite used to myself now. See?"

She turned away from him and crossed the room smoothly, with the old, poised dancer's glide, to the mirror that paneled one side of the room. And before it, as he had so often seen her preen before, he watched her preening now, running flexible metallic hands down the folds of her metal garment, turning to admire herself over one metal shoulder, making the mailed folds tinkle and sway as she struck an arabesque position before the glass.

His knees let him down into the chair she had vacated. Mingled shock and relief loosened all his muscles in him, and she was more poised and confident than he.

"It's a miracle," he said with conviction. "It's *you*. But I don't see how—" He had meant, "—how, without face or body—" but clearly he could not finish that sentence.

She finished it for him in her own mind and answered without self-consciousness. "It's motion, mostly," she said, still admiring her own suppleness in the mirror. "See?" And very lightly on her springy, armored feet she flashed through an enchaînement of brilliant steps, swinging round with a pirouette to face him. "That was what Maltzer and I worked out between us, after I began to get myself under control again." Her voice was somber for a moment, remembering a dark time in the past. Then she went on, "It wasn't easy, of course, but it was fascinating. You'll never guess how fascinating, John! We knew we couldn't work out anything like a facsimile of the way I used to look, so we had to find some other basis to build on. And motion is the other basis of recognition, after actual physical likeness."

She moved lightly across the carpet toward the window and stood looking down, her featureless face averted a little and the light shining across the delicately hinted curves of the cheekbones.

"Luckily," she said, her voice amused, "I never was beautiful. It was—well, vivacity, I suppose, and muscular coordination. Years and years of training, and all of it engraved here"—she struck her golden helmet a light, ringing blow with golden knuckles—"in the habit patterns grooved into my brain. So this body . . . did he tell you? . . . works entirely through the brain. Electromagnetic currents flowing along from ring to ring, like this." She rippled a boneless arm at him with a motion like flowing water. "Nothing holds me together—nothing!—except muscles of magnetic currents. And if I'd been somebody else—somebody who moved differently, why, the flexible rings would have moved differently too, guided by the impulse from another brain. I'm not conscious of doing anything I haven't always done. The same impulses that used to go out to my muscles go out now to—this." And she made a shuddering, serpentine motion of both arms at him, like a Cambodian dancer, and then laughed wholeheartedly, the sound of it ringing through the room with such full-throated merriment that he could not help seeing again the familiar face crinkled with pleasure, the white teeth shining. "It's all perfectly subconscious now," she told him. "It took lots of practice at first, of course, but now even my signature looks just as it always did—the coordination is duplicated that delicately." She rippled her arms at him again and chuckled.

"But the voice, too." Harris protested inadequately. "It's *your* voice, Deirdre."

"The voice isn't only a matter of throat construction and breath control, my darling Johnnie! At least, so Professor Maltzer assured me a year a go, and I certainly haven't any reason to doubt him!" She laughed again. She was laughing a little too much, with a touch of the bright, hysteric overexcitement he remembered so well. But if any woman ever had reason for mild hysteria, surely Deirdre had it now.

The laughter rippled and ended, and she went on, her voice eager. "He says voice control is almost wholly a matter of hearing what you produce, once you've got adequate mechanism, of course. That's why deaf people, with the same vocal cords as ever, let their voices change completely and lose all inflection when they've been deaf long enough. And luckily, you see, I'm not deaf!"

She swung around to him, the folds of her robe twinkling and ringing, and rippled up and up a clear, true scale to a lovely high note, and then cascaded down again like water over a falls. But she left him no time for applause. "Perfectly simple, you see. All it took was a little matter of genius from the professor to get it worked out for me! He started with a new variation of the old Vodor you must remember hearing about, years ago. Originally, of course, the thing was ponderous. You know how it worked—speech broken down to a few basic sounds and built up again in combinations produced from a keyboard. I think originally the sounds were a sort of *ktch* and a *shoosh*ing noise, but we've got it all worked to a flexibility and range quite as good as human now. All I do is—well, mentally play on the keyboard of my . . . my sound-unit, I suppose it's called. It's much more complicated than that, of course, but I've learned to do it unconsciously. And I regulate it by ear, quite automatically now. If you were—here—instead of me, and you'd had the same practice, your own voice would be coming out of the same keyboard and diaphragm instead of mine. It's all a matter of the brain patterns that operated the body and now operate the machinery. They send out very strong impulses that are stepped up as much as necessary somewhere or other in here—" Her hands waved vaguely over the mesh-robed body.

She was silent a moment, looking out the window. Then she turned away and crossed the floor to the fire, sinking again into the flowered chair. Her helmet-skull turned its mask to face him, and he could feel a quiet scrutiny behind the aquamarine of its gaze.

"It's—odd," she said, "being here in this . . . this . . . instead of a body. But not as odd or as alien as you might think. I've thought about it a lot—I've had plenty of time to think—and I've begun to realize what a tremendous force the human ego really is. I'm not sure I want to suggest it has any mystical power it can impress on mechanical things, but it does seem to have a power of some sort. It does instill its own force into inanimate objects, and they take on a personality of their own. People do impress their personalities on the houses they live in, you know. I've noticed that often. Even empty rooms. And it happens with other things, too, especially, I think, with inanimate things that men depend on for their lives. Ships, for instance—they always have personalities of their own.

"And planes—in wars you always hear of planes crippled too badly to fly, but struggling back anyhow with their crews. Even guns acquire a sort of ego. Ships and guns and planes are 'she' to the men who operate them and depend on them for their lives. It's as if machinery with complicated moving parts almost simulates life and does acquire from the men who used it—well, not exactly life, of course—but a personality. I don't know what. Maybe it absorbs some of the actual electrical impulses their brains throw off, especially in times of stress.

"Well, after a while I began to accept the idea that this new body of mine could behave at least as responsively as a ship or a plane. Quite apart from the fact that my own brain controls its 'muscles.' I believe there's an affinity between men and the machines they make. They make them out of their own brains, really, a sort of mental conception and gestation, and the result responds to the minds that created them and to all human minds that understand and manipulate them."

She stirred uneasily and smoothed a flexible hand along her mesh-robed metal thigh. "So this is myself," she said. "Metal—but me. And it grows more and more myself the longer I live in it. It's my house and the machine my life depends on, but much more intimately in each case than any real house or machine ever was before to any other human. And you know, I wonder if in time I'll forget what flesh felt like—my own flesh, when I touched it like this—and the metal against the metal will be so much the same I'll never even notice?"

Harris did not try to answer her. He sat without moving, watching her expressionless face. In a moment she went on.

"I'll tell you the best thing, John," she said, her voice softening to the old intimacy he remembered so well that he could see superimposed upon the blank skull the warm, intent look that belonged with the voice. "I'm not going to live forever. It may not sound like a—best thing—but it is, John. You know, for a while that was the worst of all, after I knew I was—after I woke up again. The thought of living on and on in a body that wasn't mine, seeing everyone I knew grow old and die, and not being able to stop—

"But Maltzer says my brain will probably wear out quite normally—except, of course, that I won't have to worry about looking old!—and when it gets tired and stops, the body I'm in won't be any longer. The magnetic muscles that hold it into my own shape and motions will let go when the brain lets go, and there'll be nothing but a . . . a pile of disconnected rings. If they ever assemble it again, it won't be me." She hesitated. "I like that, John," she said, and he felt from behind the mask a searching of his face.

He knew and understood that somber satisfaction. He could not put it into words; neither of them wanted to do that. But he understood. It was the conviction of mortality, in spite of her immortal body. She was not cut off from the rest of her race in the essence of their humanity, for though she wore a body of steel and they perishable flesh, yet she must perish too, and the same fears and faiths still united her to mortals and humans, though she wore the body of Oberon's inhuman knight. Even in her death she must be unique—dissolution in a shower of tinkling and clashing rings, he thought, and almost envied her the finality and beauty of that particular death—but afterward, oneness with humanity in however much or little awaited them all. So she could feel that this exile in metal was only temporary, in spite of everything.

(And providing, of course, that the mind inside the metal did not veer from its inherited humanity as the years went by. A dweller in a house may impress his personality upon the walls, but subtly the walls, too, may impress their own shape upon the ego of the man. Neither of them thought of that, at the time.)

Deirdre sat a moment longer in silence. Then the mood vanished and she rose again, spinning so that the robe belled out ringing about her ankles. She rippled another scale up and down, faultlessly and with the same familiar sweetness of tone that had made her famous.

"So I'm going right back on the stage, John," she said serenely. "I can still sing. I can still dance. I'm still myself in everything that matters, and I can't imagine doing anything else for the rest of my life."

He could not answer without stammering a little. "Do you think . . . will they accept you, Deirdre? After all—"

"They'll accept me," she said in that confident voice. "Oh, they'll come to see a freak at first, of course, but they'll stay to watch—Deirdre. And come back again and again just as they always did. You'll see, my dear."

But hearing her sureness, suddenly Harris himself was unsure. Maltzer had not been, either. She was so regally confident, and disappointment would be so deadly a blow at all that remained of her—

She was so delicate a being now, really. Nothing but a glowing and radiant mind poised in metal, dominating it, bending the steel to the illusion of her lost loveliness with a sheer self-confidence that gleamed through the metal body. But the brain sat delicately on its poise of reason. She had been through intolerable stresses already, perhaps more terrible depths of despair and self-knowledge than any human brain had yet endured before her, for—since Lazarus himself—who had come back from the dead?

But if the world did not accept her as beautiful, what then? If they laughed, or pitied her, or came only to watch a jointed freak performing as if on strings where the loveliness of Deirdre had once enchanted them, what then? And he could not be perfectly sure they would not. He had known her too well in the flesh to see her objectively even now, in metal. Every inflection of her voice called up the vivid memory of the face that had flashed its evanescent beauty in some look to match the tone. She was Deirdre to Harris simply because she had been so intimately familiar in every poise and attitude, through so many years. But people who knew her only slightly, or saw her for the first time in metal—what would they see?

A marionette? Or the real grace and loveliness shining through?

He had no possible way of knowing. He saw her too clearly as she had been to see her now at all, except so linked with the past that she was not wholly metal. And he knew what Maltzer feared, for Maltzer's psychic blindness toward her lay at the other extreme. He had never known Deirdre except as a machine, and he could not see her objectively any more than Harris could. To Maltzer she was pure metal, a robot his own hands and brain had devised, mysteriously animated by the mind of Deirdre, to be sure, but to all outward seeming a thing of metal solely. He had worked so long over each intricate part of her body, he knew so well how every jointure in it was put together, that he could not see the whole. He had studied many film records of her, of course, as she used to be, in order to gauge the accuracy of his facsimile, but this thing he had made was a copy only. He was too close to Deirdre to see her. And Harris, in a way, was too far. The indomitable Deirdre herself shone so vividly through the metal that his mind kept superimposing one upon the other.

How would an audience react to her? Where in the scale between these two extremes would their verdict fall?

For Deirdre, there was only one possible answer.

"I'm not worried," Deirdre said serenely, and spread her golden hands to the fire to watch lights dancing in reflection upon their shining surfaces. "I'm still myself. I've always had . . . well, power over my audiences. Any good performer knows when he's got it. Mine isn't gone. I can still give them what I always gave, only now with greater variations and more depths than I'd ever have done before. Why, look—" She gave a little wriggle of excitement.

"You know the arabesque principle—getting the longest possible distance from fingertip to toetip with a long, slow curve through the whole length? And the brace of the other leg and arm giving contrast? Well, look at me. I don't work on hinges now. I can make every motion a long curve if I want to. My body's different enough now to work out a whole new school of dancing. Of course there'll be things I used to do that I won't attempt now—no more dancing *sur les pointes*, for instance—but the new things will more than balance the loss. I've been practicing. Do you know I can turn a hundred fouettés now without a flaw? And I think I could go right on and turn a thousand, if I wanted."

She made the firelight flash on her hands, and her robe rang musically as she moved her shoulders a little. "I've already worked out one new dance for myself," she said. "God knows I'm no choreographer, but I did want to experiment first. Later, you know, really creative men like Massanchine or Fokhileff may want to do something entirely new for me—a whole new sequence of movements based on a new technique. And music—that could be quite different, too. Oh, there's no end to the possibilities! Even my voice has more range and power. Luckily I'm not an actress—it would be silly to try to play Camille or Juliet with a cast of ordinary people. Not that I couldn't, you know." She turned her head to stare at Harris through the mask of glass. "I honestly think I could. But it isn't necessary. There's too much else. Oh, I'm not worried!"

"Maltzer's worried," Harris reminded her.

She swung away from the fire, her metal robe ringing, and into her voice came the old note of distress that went with a furrowing of her forehead and a sidewise tilt of the head. The head went sidewise as it had always done, and he could see the furrowed brow almost as clearly as if flesh still clothed her.

"I know. And I'm worried about him, John. He's worked so awfully hard over me. This is the doldrums now, the letdown period, I suppose. I know what's on his mind. He's afraid I'll look just the same to the world as I look to him. Tooled metal. He's in a position no one ever quite achieved before, isn't he? Rather like God." Her voice rippled a little with amusement. "I suppose to God we must look like a collection of cells and corpuscles ourselves. But Maltzer lacks a god's detached viewpoint."

"He can't see you as I do, anyhow." Harris was choosing his words with difficulty. "I wonder, though—would it help him any if you postponed your debut awhile? You've been with him too closely, I think. You don't quite realize how near a breakdown he is. I was shocked when I saw him just now."

The golden head shook. "No. He's close to a breaking point, maybe, but I think the only cure's action. He wants me to retire and stay out of sight, John. Always. He's afraid for anyone to see me except a few old friends who remember me as I was. People he can trust to be—kind." She laughed. It was very strange to hear that ripple of mirth from the blank, unfeatured skull. Harris was seized with sudden panic at the thought of what reaction it might evoke in an audience of strangers. As if he had spoken the fear aloud, her voice denied it. "I don't need kindness. And it's no kindness to Maltzer to hide me under a bushel. He *has* worked too hard, I know. He's driven himself to a breaking point. But it'll be a complete negation of all he's worked for if I hide myself now. You don't know what a tremendous lot of genius and artistry went into me, John. The whole idea from the start was to re-create what I'd lost so that it could be proved that beauty and talent need not be sacrificed by the destruction of parts or all the body."

"It wasn't only for me that we meant to prove that. There'll be others who suffer injuries that once might have ruined them. This was to end all suffering like that forever. It was Maltzer's gift to the whole race as well as to me. He's really a humanitarian, John, like most great men. He'd never have given up a year of his life to this work if it had been for any one individual alone. He was seeing thousands of others beyond me as he worked. And I won't let him ruin all he's achieved because he's afraid to prove it now he's got it. The whole wonderful achievement will be worthless if I don't take the final step. I think his breakdown, in the end, would be worse and more final if I never tried than if I tried and failed."

Harris sat in silence. There was no answer he could make to that. He hoped the little twinge of shamefaced jealousy he suddenly felt did not show, as he was reminded anew of the intimacy closer than marriage which had of necessity bound these two together. And he knew that any reaction of his would in its way be almost as prejudiced as Maltzer's, for a reason at once the same and entirely opposite. Except that he himself came fresh to the problem, while Maltzer's viewpoint was colored by a year of overwork and physical and mental exhaustion.

"What are you going to do?" he asked.

She was standing before the fire when he spoke, swaying just a little so that highlights danced all along her golden body. Now she turned with a serpentine grace and sank into the cushioned chair beside her. It came to him suddenly that she was much more than humanly graceful—quite as much as he had once feared she would be less than human.

"I've already arranged for a performance," she told him, her voice a little shaken with a familiar mixture of excitement and defiance.

Harris sat up with a start. "How? Where? There hasn't been any publicity at all yet, has there? I didn't know—"

"Now, now, Johnnie," her amused voice soothed him. "You'll be handling everything just as usual once I get started back to work—that is, if you still want to. But this I've arranged for myself. It's going to be a surprise. I . . . I felt it had to be a surprise." She wriggled a little among the cushions. "Audience psychology is something I've always felt rather than known, and I do feel this is the way it ought to be done. There's no precedent. Nothing like this ever happened before. I'll have to go by my own intuition."

"You mean it's to be a complete surprise?"

"I think it must be. I don't want the audience coming in with preconceived ideas. I want them to see me exactly as I am now *first*, before they know who or what they're seeing. They must realize I can still give as good a performance as ever, before they remember and compare it with my past performances. I don't want them to come ready to pity my handicaps—I haven't got any!—or full of morbid curiosity. So I'm going on the air after the regular eight-o'clock telecast of the feature from Teleo City. I'm just going to do one specialty in the usual vaude program. It's all been arranged. They'll build up to it, of course, as the highlight of the evening, but they aren't to say who I am until the end of the performance—if the audience hasn't recognized me already, by then."

"Audience?"

"Of course. Surely you haven't forgotten they still play to a theater audience at Teleo City? That's why I want to make my debut there. I've always played better when there were people in the studio, so I could gauge reactions. I think most performers do. Anyhow, it's all arranged."

"Does Maltzer know?"

She wriggled uncomfortably. "Not yet."

"But he'll have to give his permission, too, won't he? I mean—"

"Now look, John! That's another idea you and Maltzer will have to get out of your minds. I don't belong to him. In a way he's just been my doctor through a long illness, but I'm free to discharge him whenever I choose. If there were ever any legal disagreement, I suppose he'd be entitled to quite a lot of money for the work he's done on my new body—for the body itself, really, since it's his own machine, in one sense. But he doesn't own it, or me. I'm not sure just how the question would be decided by the courts—there again, we've got a problem without precedent. The body may be his work, but the brain that makes it something more than a collection of metal rings is *me*, and he couldn't restrain me against my will even if he wanted to. Not legally, and not—" She hesitated oddly and looked away. For the first time Harris was aware of something beneath the surface of her mind which was quite strange to him.

"Well, anyhow," she went on, "that question won't come up. Maltzer and I have been much too close in the past year to clash over anything as essential as this. He knows in his heart that I'm right, and he won't try to restrain me. His work won't be completed until I do what I was built to do. And I intend to do it."

That strange little quiver of something—something un-Deirdre—which had so briefly trembled beneath the surface of familiarity stuck in Harris's mind as something he must recall and examine later. Now he said only, "All right. I suppose I agree with you. How soon are you going to do it?"

She turned her head so that even the glass mask through which she looked out at the world was foreshortened away from him, and the golden helmet with its hint of sculptured cheekbone was entirely enigmatic.

"Tonight," she said.

Maltzer's thin hand shook so badly that he could not turn the dial. He tried twice and then laughed nervously and shrugged at Harris.

"You get her," he said.

Harris glanced at his watch. "It isn't time yet. She won't be on for half an hour."

Maltzer made a gesture of violent impatience. "Get it, get it!"

Harris shrugged a little in turn and twisted the dial. On the tilted screen above them, shadows and sound blurred together and then clarified into a somber medieval hall, vast, vaulted, people in bright costume moving like pygmies through its dimness. Since the play concerned Mary of Scotland, the actors were dressed in something approximating Elizabethan garb, but as every era tends to translate costume into terms of the current fashions, the women's hair was dressed in a style that would have startled Elizabeth, and their footgear was entirely anachronistic.

The hall dissolved and a face swam up into soft focus upon the screen. The dark, lush beauty of the actress who was playing the Stuart queen glowed at them in velvety perfection from the clouds of her pearl-strewn hair. Maltzer groaned.

"She's competing with *that*," he said hollowly.

"You think she can't?"

Maltzer slapped the chair arms with angry palms. Then the quivering of his fingers seemed suddenly to strike him, and he muttered to himself, "Look at 'em! I'm not even fit to handle a hammer and saw." But the mutter was an aside. "Of course she can't compete," he cried irritably. "She hasn't any sex. She isn't female anymore. She doesn't know that yet, but she'll learn."

Harris stared at him, feeling a little stunned. Somehow the thought had not occurred to him before at all, so vividly had the illusion of the old Deirdre hung about the new one.

"She's an abstraction now," Maltzer went on, drumming his palms upon the chair in quick, nervous rhythms. "I don't know what it'll do to her, but there'll be change. Remember Abelard? She's lost everything that made her essentially what the public wanted, and she's going to find it out the hard way. After that—" He grimaced savagely and was silent.

"She hasn't lost everything," Harris defended. "She can dance and sing as well as ever, maybe better. She still has grace and charm and—"

"Yes, but where did the grace and charm come from? Not out of the habit patterns in her brain. No, out of human contacts, out of all the things that stimulate sensitive minds to creativeness. And she's lost three of her five senses. Everything she can't see and hear is gone. One of the strongest stimuli to a woman of her type was the knowledge of sex competition. You know how she sparkled when a man came into the room? All that's gone, and it was an essential. You know how liquor stimulated her? She's lost that. She couldn't taste food or drink even if she needed it. Perfume, flowers, all the odors we respond to mean nothing to her now. She can't feel anything with tactual delicacy anymore. She used to surround herself with luxuries—she drew her stimuli from them—and that's all gone, too. She's withdrawn from all physical contacts."

He squinted at the screen, not seeing it, his face drawn into lines like the lines of a skull. All flesh seemed to have dissolved off his bones in the past year, and Harris thought almost jealously that even in that way he seemed to be drawing nearer Deirdre in her fleshlessness with every passing week.

"Sight," Maltzer said, "is the most highly civilized of the senses. It was the last to come. The other senses tie us in closely with the very roots of life; I think we perceive with them more keenly than we know. The things we realize through taste and smell and feeling stimulate directly, without a detour through the centers of conscious thought. You know how often a taste or odor will recall a memory to you so subtly you don't know exactly what caused it? We need those primitive senses to tie us in with nature and the race. Through those ties Deirdre drew her vitality without realizing it. Sight is a cold, intellectual thing compared with the other senses. But it's all she has to draw on now. She isn't a human being anymore, and I think what humanity is left in her will drain out little by little and never be replaced. Abelard, in a way, was a prototype. But Deirdre's loss is complete."

"She isn't human," Harris agreed slowly. "But she isn't pure robot either. She's something somewhere between the two, and I think it's a mistake to try to guess just where, or what the outcome will be."

"I don't have to guess," Maltzer said in a grim voice. "I know. I wish I'd let her die. I've done something to her a thousand times worse than the fire ever could. I should have let her die in it."

"Wait," said Harris. "Wait and see. I think you're wrong."

On the television screen Mary of Scotland climbed the scaffold to her doom, the gown of traditional scarlet clinging warmly to supple young curves as anachronistic in their way as the slippers beneath the gown, for—as everyone but playwrights knows—Mary was well into middle age before she died. Gracefully this latter-day Mary bent her head, sweeping the long hair aside, kneeling to the block.

Maltzer watched stonily, seeing another woman entirely.

"I shouldn't have let her," he was muttering. "I shouldn't have let her do it."

"So you really think you'd have stopped her if you could?" Harris asked quietly. And the other man after a moment's pause shook his head jerkily.

"No. I suppose not. I keep thinking if I worked and waited a little longer maybe I could make it easier for her, but—no, I suppose not. She's got to face them sooner or later, being herself." He stood up abruptly, shoving back his chair. "If she only weren't so . . . so frail. She doesn't realize how delicately poised her very sanity is. We gave her what we could—the artists and the designers and I, all gave our very best—but she's so pitifully handicapped even with all we could do. She'll always be an abstraction and a . . . a freak, cut off from the world by handicaps worse in their way than anything any human being ever suffered before. Sooner or later she'll realize it. And then—" He began to pace up and down with quick, uneven steps, striking his hands together. His face was twitching with a little tic that drew up one eve to a squint and released it again at irregular intervals. Harris could see how very near collapse the man was.

"Can you imagine what it's like?" Maltzer demanded fiercely. "Penned into a mechanical body like that, shut out from all human contacts except what leaks in by way of sight and sound? To know you aren't human any longer? She's been through shocks enough already. When that shock fully hits her—"

"Shut up," said Harris roughly. "You won't do her any good if you break down yourself. Look—the vaude's starting."

Great golden curtains had swept together over the unhappy Queen of Scotland and were parting again now, all sorrow and frustration wiped away once more as cleanly as the passing centuries had already expunged them. Now a line of tiny dancers under the tremendous arch of the stage kicked and pranced with the precision of little mechanical dolls too small and perfect to be real. Vision rushed down upon them and swept along the row, face after stiffly smiling face racketing by like fence pickets. Then the sight rose into the rafters and looked down upon them from a great height, the grotesquely foreshortened figures still prancing in perfect rhythm even from this inhuman angle.

There was applause from an invisible audience. Then someone came out and did a dance with lighted torches that streamed long, weaving ribbons of fire among clouds of what looked like cotton wool but was most probably asbestos. Then a company in gorgeous pseudo-period costumes postured its way through the new singing ballet form of dance, roughly following a plot which had been announced as *Les Sylphides*, but had little in common with it. Afterward the precision dancers came on again, solemn and charming as performing dolls.

Maltzer began to show signs of dangerous tension as act succeeded act. Deirdre's was to be the last, of course. It seemed very long indeed before a face in close-up blotted out the stage, and a master of ceremonies with features like an amiable marionette's announced a very special number as the finale. His voice was almost cracking with excitement—perhaps he, too, had not been told until a moment before what lay in store for the audience.

Neither of the listening men heard what it was he said, but both were conscious of a certain indefinable excitement rising among the audience, murmurs and rustlings and a mounting anticipation as if time had run backward here and knowledge of the great surprise had already broken upon them.

Then the golden curtains appeared again. They quivered and swept apart on long upward arcs, and between them the stage was full of a shimmering golden haze. It was,

Harris realized in a moment, simply a series of gauze curtains, but the effect was one of strange and wonderful anticipation, as if something very splendid must be hidden in the haze. The world might have looked like this on the first morning of creation, before heaven and earth took form in the mind of God. It was a singularly fortunate choice of stage set in its symbolism, though Harris wondered how much necessity had figured in its selection, for there could not have been much time to prepare an elaborate set.

The audience sat perfectly silent, and the air was tense. This was no ordinary pause before an act. No one had been told, surely, and yet they seemed to guess—

The shimmering haze trembled and began to thin, veil by veil. Beyond was darkness, and what looked like a row of shining pillars set in a balustrade that began gradually to take shape as the haze drew back in shining folds. Now they could see that the balustrade curved up from left and right to the head of a sweep of stairs. Stage and stairs were carpeted in black velvet; black velvet draperies hung just ajar behind the balcony, with a glimpse of dark sky beyond them trembling with dim synthetic stars.

The last curtain of golden gauze withdrew. The stage was empty. Or it seemed empty. But even through the aerial distances between this screen and the place it mirrored, Harris thought that the audience was not waiting for the performer to come on from the wings. There was no rustling, no coughing, no sense of impatience. A presence upon the stage was in command from the first drawing of the curtains; it filled the theater with its calm domination. It gauged its timing, holding the audience as a conductor with lifted baton gathers and holds the eyes of his orchestra.

For a moment everything was motionless upon the stage. Then, at the head of the stairs, where the two curves of the pillared balustrade swept together, a figure stirred.

Until that moment she had seemed another shining column in the row. Now she swayed deliberately, light catching and winking and running molten along her limbs and her robe of metal mesh. She swayed just enough to show that she was there. Then, with every eye upon her, she stood quietly to let them look their fill. The screen did not swoop to a close-up upon her. Her enigma remained inviolate and the television watchers saw her no more clearly than the audience in the theater.

Many must have thought her at first some wonderfully animate robot, hung perhaps from wires invisible against the velvet, for certainly she was no woman dressed in metal—her proportions were too thin and fine for that. And perhaps the impression of robotism was what she meant to convey at first. She stood quiet, swaying just a little, a masked and inscrutable figure, faceless, very slender in her robe that hung in folds as pure as a Grecian chlamys, though she did not look Grecian at all. In the visored golden helmet and the robe of mail that odd likeness to knighthood was there again, with its implications of medieval richness behind the simple lines. Except that in her exquisite slimness she called to mind no human figure in armor, not even the comparative deli-cacy of a St. Joan. It was the chivalry and delicacy of some other world implicit in her outlines.

A breath of surprise had rippled over the audience when she moved. Now they were tensely silent again, waiting. And the tension, the anticipation, was far deeper than the surface importance of the scene could ever have evoked. Even those who thought her a manikin seemed to feel the forerunning of greater revelations.

Now she swayed and came slowly down the steps, moving with a suppleness just a little better than human. The swaying strengthened. By the time she reached the stage floor she was dancing. But it was no dance that any human creature could ever have per-formed. The long, slow, languorous rhythms of her body would have been impossible to a figure hinged at its joints as human figures hinge. (Harris remembered incredu-lously that he had feared once to find her jointed like a mechanical robot. But it was hu-manity that seemed, by contrast, jointed and mechanical now.)

The languor and the rhythm of her patterns looked impromptu, as all good dances should, but Harris knew what hours of composition and rehearsal must lie behind it, what laborious graving into her brain of strange new pathways, the first to replace the old ones and govern the mastery of metal limbs.

To and fro over the velvet carpet, against the velvet background, she wove the in-tricacies of her serpentine dance, leisurely and yet with such hypnotic effect that the air seemed full of looping rhythms, as if her long, tapering limbs had left their own repli-cas hanging upon the air and fading only slowly as she moved away. In her mind, Har-ris knew, the stage was a whole, a background to be filled in completely with the measured patterns of her dance, and she seemed almost to project that completed pat-tern to her audience so that they saw her everywhere at once, her golden rhythms fad-ing upon the air long after she had gone.

Now there was music, looping and hanging in echoes after her like the shining fes-toons she wove with her body. But it was no orchestral music. She was humming, deep and sweet and wordlessly, as she glided her easy, intricate path about the stage. And the volume of the music was amazing. It seemed to fill the theater, and it was not amplified by hidden loudspeakers. You could tell that. Somehow, until you heard the music she made, you had never realized before the subtle distortions that amplification puts into music. This was utterly pure and true as perhaps no ear in all her audience had ever heard music before.

While she danced, the audience did not seem to breathe. Perhaps they were begin-ning already to suspect who and what it was that moved before them without any fan-fare of the publicity they had been half-expecting for weeks now. And yet, without the publicity, it was not easy to believe the dancer they watched was not some cunningly motivated manikin swinging on unseen wires about the stage.

Nothing she had done yet had been human. The dance was no dance a human being could have performed. The music she hummed came from a throat without vocal cords. But now the long, slow rhythms were drawing to their close, the pattern tightening in to a finale. And she ended as inhumanly as she had danced, willing them not to interrupt her with applause, dominating them now as she had always done. For her implication here was that a machine might have performed the dance, and a machine expects no applause. If they thought unseen operators had put her through those wonderful paces, they would wait for the operators to appear for their bows. But the audience was obedient. It sat silently, waiting for what came next. But its silence was tense and breathless.

The dance ended as it had begun. Slowly, almost carelessly, she swung up the velvet stairs, moving with rhythms as perfect as her music. But when she reached the head of the stairs, she turned to face her audience, and for a moment stood motionless, like a creature of metal, without volition, the hands of the operator slack upon its strings.

Then, startlingly, she laughed.

It was lovely laughter, low and sweet and full-throated. She threw her head back and let her body sway and her shoulders shake, and the laughter, like the music, filled the theater, gaining volume from the great hollow of the roof and sounding in the ears of every listener, not loud, but as intimately as if each sat alone with the woman who laughed.

And she was a woman now. Humanity had dropped over her like a tangible garment. No one who had ever heard that laughter before could mistake it here. But before the reality of who she was had quite time to dawn upon her listeners, she let the laughter deepen into music, as no human voice could have done. She was humming a familiar refrain close in the ear of every hearer. And the humming in turn swung into words. She sang in her clear, light, lovely voice:

"The yellow rose of Eden, is blooming in my heart—"

It was Deirdre's song. She had sung it first upon the airways a month before the theater fire that had consumed her. It was a commonplace little melody, simple enough to take first place in the fancy of a nation that had always liked its songs simple. But it had a certain sincerity, too, and no taint of the vulgarity of tune and rhythm that foredooms so many popular songs to oblivion after their novelty fades.

No one else was ever able to sing it quite as Deirdre did. It had been identified with her so closely that though for a while after her accident singers tried to make it a memorial for her, they failed so conspicuously to give it her unmistakable flair that the song died from their sheer inability to sing it. No one ever hummed the tune without thinking of her and the pleasant, nostalgic sadness of something lovely and lost.

But it was not a sad song now. If anyone had doubted whose brain and ego motivated this shining metal suppleness, they could doubt no longer. For the voice was Deirdre, and the song. And the lovely, poised grace of her mannerisms that made up recognition as certainly as sight of a familiar face.

She had not finished the first line of her song before the audience knew her.

And they did not let her finish. The accolade of their interruption was a tribute more eloquent than polite waiting could ever have been. First a breath of incredulity rippled over the theater, and a long, sighing gasp that reminded Harris irrelevantly as he listened of the gasp which still goes up from matinee audiences at the first glimpse of the fabulous Valentino, so many generations dead. But this gasp did not sigh itself away and vanish. Tremendous tension lay behind it, and the rising tide of excitement rippled up in little murmurs and spatterings of applause that ran together into one overwhelming roar. It shook the theater. The television screen trembled and blurred a little to the volume of that transmitted applause.

Silenced before it, Deirdre stood gesturing on the stage, bowing and bowing as the noise rolled up about her, shaking perceptibly with the triumph of her own emotion.

Harris had an intolerable feeling that she was smiling radiantly and that the tears were pouring down her cheeks. He even thought, just as Maltzer leaned forward to switch off the screen, that she was blowing kisses over the audience in the time-honored gesture of the grateful actress, her golden arms shining as she scattered kisses abroad from the featureless helmet, the face that had no mouth.

"Well?" Harris said, not without triumph.

Maltzer shook his head jerkily, the glasses unsteady on his nose so that the blurred eyes behind them seemed to shift.

"Of course they applauded, you fool," he said in a savage voice. "I might have known they would under this setup. It doesn't prove anything. Oh, she was smart to surprise them—I admit that. But they were applauding themselves as much as her. Excitement, gratitude for letting them in on a historic performance, mass hysteria—you know. It's from now on the test will come, and this hasn't helped any to prepare her for it. Morbid curiosity when the news gets out—people laughing when she forgets she isn't human. And they will, you know. There are always those who will. And the novelty wearing off. The slow draining away of humanity for lack of contact with any human stimuli anymore—"

Harris remembered suddenly and reluctantly the moment that afternoon which he had shunted aside mentally, to consider later. The sense of something unfamiliar beneath the surface of Deirdre's speech. Was Maltzer right? Was the drainage already at work? Or was there something deeper than this obvious answer to the question? Certainly she had been through experiences too terrible for ordinary people to comprehend. Scars might still remain. Or, with her body, had she put on a strange, metallic something of the mind, that spoke to no sense which human minds could answer?

For a few minutes neither of them spoke. Then Maltzer rose abruptly and stood looking down at Harris with an abstract scowl.

"I wish you'd go now," he said.

Harris glanced up at him, startled. Maltzer began to pace again, his steps quick and uneven. Over his shoulder he said.

"I've made up my mind, Harris. I've got to put a stop to this."

Harris rose. "Listen," he said. "Tell me one thing. What makes you so certain you're right? Can you deny that most of it's speculation—hearsay evidence? Remember, I talked to Deirdre, and she was just as sure as you are in the opposite direction. Have you any real reason for what you think?"

Maltzer took his glasses off and rubbed his nose carefully, taking a long time about it. He seemed reluctant to answer. But when he did, at last, there was a confidence in his voice Harris had not expected.

"I have a reason," he said. "But you won't believe it. Nobody would."

"Try me."

Maltzer shook his head. "Nobody *could* believe it. No two people were ever in quite the same relationship before as Deirdre and I have been. I helped her come back out of complete—oblivion. I knew her before she had voice or hearing. She was only a frantic mind when I first made contact with her, half insane with all that had happened and fear of what would happen next. In a very literal sense she was reborn out of that condition, and I had to guide her through every step of the way. I came to know her thoughts before she thought them. And once you've been that close to another mind, you don't lose the contact easily." He put the glasses back on and looked blurrily at Harris through the heavy lenses. "Deirdre is worried," he said. "I know it. You won't believe me, but I can—well, sense it. I tell you, I've been too close to her very mind itself to make any mistake. You don't see it, maybe. Maybe even she doesn't know it yet. But the worry's there. When I'm with her. I feel it. And I don't want it to come any nearer the surface of her mind than it's come already. I'm going to put a stop to this before it's too late."

Harris had no comment for that. It was too entirely outside his own experience. He said nothing for a moment. Then he asked simply, "How?"

"I'm not sure yet. I've got to decide before she comes back. And I want to see her alone."

"I think you're wrong," Harris told him quietly. "I think you're imagining things. I don't think you *can* stop her."

Maltzer gave him a slanted glance. "I can stop her," he said, in a curious voice. He went on quickly, "She has enough already—she's nearly human. She can live normally as other people live, without going back on the screen. Maybe this taste of it will be enough. I've got to convince her it is. If she retires now, she'll never guess how cruel her own audiences could be, and maybe that deep sense of—distress, uneasiness, whatever it is—won't come to the surface. It mustn't. She's too fragile to stand that." He slapped his hands together sharply. "I've got to stop her. For her own sake, I've got to do it!" He swung round again to face Harris. "Will you go now?"

Never in his life had Harris wanted less to leave a place. Briefly he thought of saying simply, "No I won't." But he had to admit in his own mind that Maltzer was at least partly right. This was a matter between Deirdre and her creator, the culmination, perhaps, of that year's long intimacy so like marriage that this final trial for supremacy was a need he recognized.

He would not, he thought, forbid the showdown if he could. Perhaps the whole year had been building up to this one moment between them in which one or the other must prove himself victor. Neither was very stable just now, after the long strain of the year past. It might very well be that the mental salvation of one or both hinged upon the outcome of the clash. But because each was so strongly motivated not by selfish concern but by solicitude for the other in this strange combat, Harris knew he must leave them to settle the thing alone.

He was in the street and hailing a taxi before the full significance of something Maltzer had said came to him. "*I can stop her,*" he had declared, with an odd inflection in his voice.

Suddenly Harris felt cold. Maltzer had made her—of course he could stop her if he chose. Was there some key in that supple golden body that could immobilize it at its maker's will? Could she be imprisoned in the cage of her own body? No body before in all history, he thought, could have been designed more truly to be a prison for its mind than Deirdre's, if Maltzer chose to turn the key that locked her in. There must be many ways to do it. He could simply withhold whatever source of nourishment kept her brain alive, if that were the way he chose.

But Harris could not believe he would do it. The man wasn't insane. He would not defeat his own purpose. His determination rose from his solicitude for Deirdre; he would not even in the last extremity try to save her by imprisoning her in the jail of her own skull.

For a moment Harris hesitated on the curb, almost turning back. But what could he do? Even granting that Maltzer would resort to such tactics, self-defeating in their very nature, how could any man on earth prevent him if he did it subtly enough? But he never would. Harris knew he never would. He got into his cab slowly, frowning. He would see them both tomorrow.

He did not. Harris was swamped with excited calls about yesterday's performance, but the message he was awaiting did not come. The day went by very slowly. Toward evening he surrendered and called Maltzer's apartment.

It was Deirdre's face that answered, and for once he saw no remembered features superimposed upon the blankness of her helmet. Masked and faceless, she looked at him inscrutably.

"Is everything all right?" he asked, a little uncomfortable.

"Yes, of course," she said, and her voice was a bit metallic for the first time, as if she were thinking so deeply of some other matter that she did not trouble to pitch it properly. "I had a long talk with Maltzer last night, if that's what you mean. You know what he wants. But nothing's been decided yet."

Harris felt oddly rebuffed by the sudden realization of the metal of her. It was impossible to read anything from face or voice. Each had its mask.

"What are you going to do?" he asked.

"Exactly as I'd planned," she told him, without inflection.

Harris floundered a little. Then, with an effort at practicality, he said, "Do you want me to go to work on booking, then?"

She shook the delicately modeled skull. "Not yet. You saw the reviews today, of course. They—did like me." It was an understatement, and for the first time a note of warmth sounded in her voice. But the preoccupation was still there, too. "I'd already planned to make them wait awhile after my first performance," she went on. "A couple of weeks, anyhow. You remember that little farm of mine in Jersey, John? I'm going over today. I won't see anyone except the servants there. Not even Maltzer. Not even you. I've got a lot to think about. Maltzer has agreed to let everything go until we've both thought things over. He's taking a rest, too. I'll see you the moment I get back, John. Is that all right?"

She blanked out almost before he had time to nod and while the beginning of a stammered argument was still on his lips. He sat there staring at the screen.

The two weeks that went by before Maltzer called him again were the longest Harris had ever spent. He thought of many things in the interval. He believed he could sense in that last talk with Deirdre something of the inner unrest that Maltzer had spoken of—more an abstraction than a distress, but some thought had occupied her mind which she would not—or was it that she could not?—share even with her closest confidants. He even wondered whether, if her mind was as delicately poised as Maltzer feared, one would ever know whether or not it had slipped. There was so little evidence one way or the other in the unchanging outward form of her.

Most of all he wondered what two weeks in a new environment would do to her untried body and newly patterned brain. If Maltzer were right, then there might be some perceptible—drainage—by the time they met again. He tried not to think of that.

Maltzer televised him on the morning set for her return. He looked very bad. The rest must have been no rest at all. His face was almost a skull now, and the blurred eyes behind their lenses burned. But he seemed curiously at peace, in spite of his appearance. Harris thought he had reached some decision, but whatever it was had not stopped his hands from shaking or the nervous tic that drew his face sidewise into a grimace at intervals.

"Come over," he said briefly, without preamble. "She'll be here in half an hour." And he blanked out without waiting for an answer.

When Harris arrived, Maltzer was standing by the window looking down and steadying his trembling hands on the sill.

"I can't stop her," he said in a monotone, and again without preamble. Harris had the impression that for two weeks his thoughts must have run over and over the same track, until any spoken word was simply a vocal interlude in the circling of his mind. "I couldn't do it. I even tried threats, but she knew I didn't mean them. There's only one way out, Harris." He glanced up briefly, hollow-eyed behind the lenses. "Never mind. I'll tell you later."

"Did you explain everything to her that you did to me?"

"Nearly all. I even taxed her with that . . . that sense of distress I *know* she feels. She denied it. She was lying. We both knew. It was worse after the performance than before. When I saw her that night, I tell you I *knew*—she senses something wrong, but she won't admit it." He shrugged. "Well—"

Faintly in the silence they heard the humming of the elevator descending from the helicopter platform on the roof. Both men turned to the door.

She had not changed at all. Foolishly, Harris was a little surprised. Then he caught himself and remembered that she would never change—never, until she died. He himself might grow white-haired and senile; she would move before him then as she moved now, supple, golden, enigmatic.

Still, he thought she caught her breath a little when she saw Maltzer and the depths of his swift degeneration. She had no breath to catch, but her voice was shaken as she greeted them.

"I'm glad you're both here," she said, a slight hesitation in her speech. "It's a wonderful day outside. Jersey was glorious. I'd forgotten how lovely it is in summer. Was the sanitarium any good, Maltzer?"

He jerked his head irritably and did not answer. She went on talking in a light voice, skimming the surface, saying nothing important.

This time Harris saw her as he supposed her audiences would, eventually, when the surprise had worn off and the image of the living Deirdre faded from memory. She was all metal now, the Deirdre they would know from today on. And she was not less lovely. She was not even less human—yet. Her motion was a miracle of flexible grace, a pouring of suppleness along every limb. (From now on, Harris realized suddenly, it was her body and not her face that would have mobility to express emotion; she must act with her limbs and her lithe, robed torso.)

But there was something wrong. Harris sensed it almost tangibly in her inflections, her elusiveness, the way she fenced with words. This was what Maltzer had meant, this was what Harris himself had felt just before she left for the country. Only now it was strong—certain. Between them and the old Deirdre whose voice still spoke to them a veil of—detachment—had been drawn. Behind it she was in distress. Somehow, somewhere, she had made some discovery that affected her profoundly. And Harris was terribly afraid that he knew what the discovery must be. Maltzer was right.

He was still leaning against the window, staring out unseeingly over the vast panorama of New York, webbed with traffic bridges, winking with sunlit glass, its vertiginous distances plunging downward into the blue shadows of earth-level. He said now, breaking into the light-voiced chatter, "Are you all right, Deirdre?"

She laughed. It was lovely laughter. She moved lithely across the room, sunlight glinting on her musical mailed robe, and stooped to a cigarette box on a table. Her fingers were deft.

"Have one?" she said, and carried the box to Maltzer. He let her put the brown cylinder between his lips and hold a light to it, but he did not seem to be noticing what he did. She replaced the box and then crossed to a mirror on the far wall and began experimenting with a series of gliding ripples that wove patterns of pale gold in the glass. "Of course I'm all right," she said.

"You're lying."

Deirdre did not turn. She was watching him in the mirror, but the ripple of her motion went on slowly, languorously, undisturbed.

"No," she told them both.

Maltzer drew deeply on his cigarette. Then with a hard pull he unsealed the window and tossed the smoking stub far out over the gulfs below. He said,

"You can't deceive me, Deirdre." His voice, suddenly, was quite calm. "I created you, my dear. I know. I've sensed that uneasiness in you growing and growing for a long while now. It's much stronger today than it was two weeks ago. Something happened to you in the country. I don't know what it was, but you've changed. Will you admit to yourself what it is, Deirdre? Have you realized yet that you must not go back on the screen?"

"Why, no," said Deirdre, still not looking at him except obliquely, in the glass. Her gestures were slower now, weaving lazy patterns in the air. "No. I haven't changed my mind."

She was all metal—outwardly. She was taking unfair advantage of her own metalhood. She had withdrawn far within, behind the mask of her voice and her facelessness. Even her body, whose involuntary motions might have betrayed what she was feeling, in the only way she could be subject to betrayal now, she was putting through ritual motions that disguised it completely. As long as these looping, weaving patterns occupied her, no one had any way of guessing even from her motion what went on in the hidden brain inside her helmet.

Harris was struck suddenly and for the first time with the completeness of her withdrawal. When he had seen her last in this apartment, she had been wholly Deirdre, not masked at all, overflowing the metal with the warmth and ardor of the woman he had known so well. Since then—since the performance on the stage—he had not seen the familiar Deirdre again. Passionately, he wondered why. Had she begun to suspect even in her moment of triumph what a fickle master an audience could be? Had she caught, perhaps, the sound of whispers and laughter among some small portion of her watchers, though the great majority praised her?

Or was Maltzer right? Perhaps Harris's first interview with her had been the last bright burning of the lost Deirdre, animated by excitement and the pleasure of meeting after so long a time, animation summoned up in a last strong effort to convince him. Now she was gone, but whether in self-protection against the possible cruelties of human beings, or whether in withdrawal to metalhood, he could not guess. Humanity might be draining out of her fast, and the brassy taint of metal permeating the brain it housed.

———

Maltzer laid his trembling hand on the edge of the opened window and looked out. He said in a deepened voice, the querulous note gone for the first time:

"I've made a terrible mistake, Deirdre. I've done you irreparable harm." He paused a moment, but Deirdre said nothing. Harris dared not speak. In a moment Maltzer went on. "I've made you vulnerable, and given you no weapons to fight your enemies with. And the human race is your enemy, my dear, whether you admit it now or later. I think you know that. I think it's why you're so silent. I think you must have suspected it on the stage two weeks ago and verified it in Jersey while you were gone. They're going to hate you, after a while, because you are still beautiful, and they're going to persecute you because you are different—and helpless. Once the novelty wears off, my dear, your audience will be simply a mob."

He was not looking at her. He had bent forward a little, looking out the window and down. His hair stirred in the wind that blew very strongly up this high and whined thinly around the open edge of the glass.

"I meant what I did for you," he said, "to be for everyone who meets with accidents that might have ruined them. I should have known my gift would mean worse ruin than any mutilation could be. I know now that there's only one legitimate way a human being can create life. When he tries another way, as I did, he has a lesson to learn. Remember the lesson of the student Frankenstein? He learned, too. In a way, he was lucky—the way he learned. He didn't have to watch what happened afterward. Maybe he wouldn't have had the courage—I know I haven't."

Harris found himself standing without remembering that he rose. He knew suddenly what was about to happen. He understood Maltzer's air of resolution, his new, unnatural calm. He knew, even, why Maltzer had asked him here today, so that Deirdre might not be left alone. For he remembered that Frankenstein, too, had paid with his life for the unlawful creation of life.

Maltzer was leaning head and shoulders from the window now, looking down with almost hypnotized fascination. His voice came back to them remotely in the breeze, as if a baffler already lay between them.

Deirdre had not moved. Her expressionless mask, in the mirror, watched him calmly. She *must* have understood. Yet she gave no sign, except that the weaving of her arms had almost stopped now, she moved so slowly. Like a dance seen in a nightmare, under water.

It was impossible, of course, for her to express any emotion. The fact that her face showed none now should not, in fairness, be held against her. But she watched so wholly without feeling—Neither of them moved toward the window. A false step, now, might send him over. They were quiet, listening to his voice.

"We who bring life into the world unlawfully," said Maltzer, almost thoughtfully, "must make room for it by withdrawing our own. That seems to be an inflexible rule. It works automatically. The thing we create makes living unbearable. No, it's nothing you can help, my dear. I've asked you to do something I created you incapable of doing. I made you to perform a function, and I've been asking you to forego the one thing you were made to do. I believe that if you do it, it will destroy you, but the whole guilt is mine, not yours. I'm not even asking you to give up the screen, anymore. I know you can't, and live. But I can't live and watch you. I put all my skill and my love in one final masterpiece, and I can't bear to watch it destroyed. I can't live and watch you do only what I made you to do and ruin yourself because you must do it."

"But before I go, I have to make sure you understand." He leaned a little farther, looking down, and his voice grew more remote as the glass came between them. He was saying almost unbearable things now, but very distantly, in a cool, passionless tone filtered through wind and glass, and with the distant humming of the city mingled with it, so that the words were curiously robbed of poignancy. "I can be a coward," he said, "and escape the consequences of what I've done, but I can't go and leave you—not understanding. It would be even worse than the thought of your failure, to think of you bewildered and confused when the mob turns on you. What I'm telling you, my dear, won't be any real news—I think you sense it already, though you may not admit it to yourself. We've been too close to lie to each other, Deirdre—I know when you aren't telling the truth. I know the distress that's been growing in your mind. You are not wholly human, my dear. I think you know that. In so many ways, in spite of all I could do, you must always be less than human. You've lost the senses of perception that kept you in touch with humanity. Sight and hearing are all that remain, and sight, as I've said before, was the last and coldest of the senses to develop. And you're so delicately poised on a sort of thin edge of reason. You're only a clear, glowing mind animating a metal body, like a candle flame in a glass. And as precariously vulnerable to the wind."

He paused. "Try not to let them ruin you completely," he said after a while. "When they turn against you, when they find out you're more helpless than they—I wish I could have made you stronger, Deirdre. But I couldn't. I had too much skill for your good and mine, but not quite enough skill for that."

He was silent again, briefly, looking down. He was balanced precariously now, more than halfway over the sill and supported only by one hand on the glass. Harris watched with an agonized uncertainty, not sure whether a sudden leap might catch him in time or send him over. Deirdre was still weaving her golden patterns, slowly and unchangingly, watching the mirror and its reflection, her face and masked eyes enigmatic.

"I wish one thing, though," Maltzer said in his remote voice. "I wish—before I finish—that you'd tell me the truth, Deirdre. I'd be happier if I were sure I'd—reached you. Do you understand what I've said? Do you believe me? Because if you don't, then I know you're lost beyond all hope. If you'll admit your own doubt—and I know you do doubt—I can think there may be a chance for you after all. Were you lying to me, Deirdre? Do you know how . . . how wrong I've made you?"

There was silence. Then very softly, a breath of sound, Deirdre answered. The voice seemed to hang in midair, because she had no lips to move and localize it for the imagination.

"Will you listen, Maltzer?" she asked.

"I'll wait," he said. "Go on. Yes or no?"

Slowly she let her arms drop to her sides. Very smoothly and quietly she turned from the minor and faced him. She swayed a little, making her metal robe ring.

"I'll answer you," she said. "But I don't think I'll answer that. Not with yes or no, anyhow. I'm going to walk a little, Maltzer. I have something to tell you, and I can't talk standing still. Will you let me move about without—going over?"

He nodded distantly. "You can't interfere from that distance," he said. "But keep the distance. What do you want to say?"

She began to pace a little way up and down her end of the room, moving with liquid ease. The table with the cigarette box was in her way, and she pushed it aside carefully, watching Maltzer and making no swift motions to startle him.

"I'm not—well, subhuman," she said, a faint note of indignation in her voice. "I'll prove it in a minute, but I want to say something else first. You must promise to wait and listen. There's a flaw in your argument, and I resent it. I'm not a Frankenstein monster made out of dead flesh. I'm myself—alive. You didn't create my life, you only preserved it. I'm not a robot, with compulsions built into me that I have to obey. I'm free-willed and independent, and, Maltzer—I'm human."

Harris had relaxed a little. She knew what she was doing. He had no idea what she planned, but he was willing to wait now. She was not the indifferent automaton he had thought. He watched her come to the table again, in a lap of her pacing, and stoop over it, her eyeless mask turned to Maltzer to make sure a variation of her movement did not startle him.

"I'm human," she repeated, her voice humming faintly and very sweetly. "Do you think I'm not?" she asked, straightening and facing them both. And then suddenly, almost overwhelmingly, the warmth and the old ardent charm were radiant all around her. She was robot no longer, enigmatic no longer. Harris could see as clearly as in their first meeting the remembered flesh still gracious and beautiful as her voice evoked his memory. She stood swaying a little, as she had always swayed, her head on one side, and she was chuckling at them both. It was such a soft and lovely sound, so warmly familiar.

"Of course I'm myself," she told them, and as the words sounded in their ears neither of them could doubt it. There was hypnosis in her voice. She turned away and began to pace again, and so powerful was the human personality which she had called up about her that it beat out at them in deep pulses, as if her body were a furnace to send out those comforting waves of warmth. "I have handicaps, I know," she said. "But my audiences will never know. I won't let them know. I think you'll believe me, both of you, when I say I could play Juliet just as I am now, with a cast of ordinary people, and make the world accept it. Do you think I could, John? Maltzer, don't you believe I could?"

She paused at the far end of her pacing path and turned to face them, and they both stared at her without speaking. To Harris she was the Deirdre he had always known, pale gold, exquisitely graceful in remembered postures, the inner radiance of her shining through metal as brilliantly as it had ever shone through flesh. He did not wonder, now, if it were real. Later he would think again that it might be only a disguise, something like a garment she had put off with her lost body, to wear again only when she chose. Now the spell of her compelling charm was too strong for wonder. He watched, convinced for the moment that she was all she seemed to be. She could play Juliet if she said she could. She could sway a whole audience as easily as she swayed him. Indeed, there was something about her just now more convincingly human than anything he had noticed before. He realized that in a split second of awareness before he saw what it was.

She was looking at Maltzer. He, too, watched, spellbound in spite of himself, not dissenting. She glanced from one to the other. Then she put back her head and laughter came welling and choking from her in a great, full-throated tide. She shook in the strength of it. Harris could almost see her round throat pulsing with the sweet low-pitched waves of laughter that were shaking her. Honest mirth, with a little derision in it.

Then she lifted one arm and tossed her cigarette into the empty fireplace.

Harris choked, and his mind went blank for one moment of blind denial. He had not sat here watching a robot smoke and accepting it as normal. He could not! And yet he had. That had been the final touch of conviction which swayed his hypnotized mind into accepting her humanity. And she had done it so deftly, so naturally, wearing her radiant humanity with such rightness, that his watching mind had not even questioned what she did.

He glanced at Maltzer. The man was still halfway over the window ledge, but through the opening of the window he, too, was staring in stupefied disbelief, and Harris knew they had shared the same delusion.

Deirdre was still shaking a little with laughter. "Well," she demanded, the rich chuckling making her voice quiver, "am I all robot, after all?"

Harris opened his mouth to speak, but he did not utter a word. This was not his show. The byplay lay wholly between Deirdre and Maltzer; he must not interfere. He turned his head to the window and waited.

And Maltzer for a moment seemed shaken in his conviction.

"You . . . you *are* an actress," he admitted slowly. "But I . . . I'm not convinced I'm wrong. I think—" He paused. The querulous note was in his voice again, and he seemed racked once more by the old doubts and dismay. Then Harris saw him stiffen. He saw the resolution come back, and understood why it had come. Maltzer had gone too far already upon the cold and lonely path he had chosen to turn back, even for stronger evidence than this. He had reached his conclusions only after mental turmoil too terrible to face again. Safety and peace lay in the course he had steeled himself to follow. He was too tired, too exhausted by months of conflict, to retrace his path and begin all over. Harris could see him groping for a way out, and in a moment he saw him find it.

"That was a trick," he said hollowly. "Maybe you could play it on a larger audience, too. Maybe you have more tricks to use. I might be wrong. But, Deirdre"—his voice grew urgent—"you haven't answered the one thing I've got to know. You can't answer it. You *do* feel—dismay. You've learned your own inadequacy, however well you can hide it from us—even from us. I *know*. Can you deny that, Deirdre?"

She was not laughing now. She let her arms fall, and the flexible golden body seemed to droop a little all over, as if the brain that a moment before had been sending out strong, sure waves of confidence had slackened its power, and the intangible muscles of her limbs slackened with it. Some of the glowing humanity began to fade. It receded within her and was gone, as if the fire in the furnace of her body were sinking and cooling.

"Maltzer," she said uncertainly, "I can't answer that—yet. I can't—"

And then, while they waited in anxiety for her to finish the sentence, she *blazed*. She ceased to be a figure in stasis—she *blazed*.

It was something no eyes could watch and translate into terms the brain could follow; her motion was too swift. Maltzer in the window was a whole long room-length away. He had thought himself safe at such a distance, knowing no normal human being could reach him before he moved. But Deirdre was neither normal nor human.

In the same instant she stood drooping by the mirror, she was simultaneously at Maltzer's side. Her motion negated time and destroyed space. And as a glowing cigarette tip in the dark describes closed circles before the eyes when the holder moves it swiftly, so Deirdre blazed in one continuous flash of golden motion across the room.

But curiously, she was not blurred. Harris, watching, felt his mind go blank again, but less in surprise than because no normal eyes and brain could perceive what it was he looked at.

(In that moment of intolerable suspense his complex human brain paused suddenly, annihilating time in its own way, and withdrew to a cool corner of its own to analyze in a flashing second what it was he had just seen. The brain could do it timelessly; words are slow. But he knew he had watched a sort of tesseract of human motion, a parable of fourth-dimensional activity. A one-dimensional point, moved through space, creates a two-dimensional line, which in motion creates a three-dimensional cube. Theoretically the cube, in motion, would produce a fourth-dimensional figure. No human creature had ever seen a figure of three dimensions moved through space and time before—until this moment. She had not blurred; every motion she made was distinct, but not like moving figures on a strip of film. Not like anything that those who use our language had ever seen before, or created words to express. The mind saw, but without perceiving. Neither words nor thoughts could resolve what happened into terms for human brains. And perhaps she had not actually and literally moved through the fourth dimension. Perhaps—since Harris was able to see her—it had been almost and not quite that unimaginable thing. But it was close enough.)

While to the slow mind's eye she was still standing at the far end of the room, she was already at Maltzer's side, her long, flexible fingers gentle but very firm upon his arms. She waited—

The room shimmered. There was sudden violent heat beating upon Harris's face. Then the air steadied again and Deirdre was saying softly, in a mournful whisper:

"I'm sorry—I had to do it. I'm sorry—I didn't mean you to know—"

Time caught up with Harris. He saw it overtake Maltzer too, saw the man jerk convulsively away from the grasping hands, in a ludicrously futile effort to forestall what had already happened. Even thought was slow, compared with Deirdre's swiftness.

The sharp outward jerk was strong. It was strong enough to break the grasp of human hands and catapult Maltzer out and down into the swimming gulfs of New York. The mind leaped ahead to a logical conclusion and saw him twisting and turning and diminishing with dreadful rapidity to a tiny point of darkness that dropped away through sunlight toward the shadows near the earth. The mind even conjured up a shrill, thin cry that plummeted away with the falling body and hung behind it in the shaken air.

But the mind was reckoning on human factors.

Very gently and smoothly, Deirdre lifted Maltzer from the windowsill and with effortless ease carried him well back into the safety of the room. She set him down before a sofa and her golden fingers unwrapped themselves from his arms slowly, so that he could regain control of his own body before she released him.

He sank to the sofa without a word. Nobody spoke for an unmeasurable length of time. Harris could not. Deirdre waited patiently. It was Maltzer who regained speech first, and it came back on the old track, as if his mind had not yet relinquished the rut it had worn so deep.

"All right," he said breathlessly. "All right, you can stop me this time. But I know, you see. I know! You can't hide your feeling from me, Deirdre. I know the trouble you feel. And next time—next time I won't wait to talk!"

Deirdre made the sound of a sigh. She had no lungs to expel the breath she was imitating, but it was hard to realize that. It was hard to understand why she was not panting heavily from the terrible exertion of the past minutes; the mind knew why but could not accept the reason. She was still too human.

"You still don't see," she said. "Think, Maltzer, think!"

There was a hassock beside the sofa. She sank upon it gracefully, clasping her robed knees. Her head tilted back to watch Maltzer's face. She saw only stunned stupidity on it now; he had passed through too much emotional storm to think at all.

"All right," she told him. "Listen—I'll admit it. You're right. I *am* unhappy. I do know what you said was true—but not for the reason you think. Humanity and I are far apart, and drawing farther. The gap will be hard to bridge. Do you hear me, Maltzer?"

Harris saw the tremendous effort that went into Maltzer's wakening. He saw the man pull his mind back into focus and sit up on the sofa with weary stiffness.

"You . . . you do admit it, then?" he asked in a bewildered voice.

Deirdre shook her head sharply.

"Do you still think of me as delicate?" she demanded. "Do you know I carried you here at arm's length halfway across the room? Do you realize you weigh *nothing* to me? I could"—she glanced around the room and gestured with sudden, rather appalling violence— "tear this building down," she said quietly. "I could tear my way through these walls, I think. I've found no limit yet to the strength I can put forth if I try." She held up her golden hands and looked at them. "The metal would break, perhaps," she said reflectively, "but then, I have no feeling—"

Maltzer gasped, "*Deirdre*—"

She looked up with what must have been a smile. It sounded clearly in her voice. "Oh, I won't. I wouldn't have to do it with my hands, if I wanted. Look—listen!"

She put her head back and a deep, vibrating hum gathered and grew in what one still thought of as her throat. It deepened swiftly and the ears began to ring. It was deeper, and the furniture vibrated. The walls began almost imperceptibly to shake. The room was full and bursting with a sound that shook every atom upon its neighbor with a terrible, disrupting force.

The sound ceased. The humming died. Then Deirdre laughed and made another and quite differently pitched sound. It seemed to reach out like an arm in one straight direction—toward the window. The opened panel shook. Deirdre intensified her hum, and slowly, with imperceptible jolts that merged into smoothness, the window jarred itself shut.

"You see?" Deirdre said. "You see?"

But still Maltzer could only stare. Harris was staring too, his mind beginning slowly to accept what she implied. Both were too stunned to leap ahead to any conclusions yet.

Deirdre rose impatiently and began to pace again, in a ringing of metal robe and a twinkling of reflected lights. She was pantherlike in her suppleness. They could see the power behind that lithe motion now; they no longer thought of her as helpless, but they were far still from grasping the truth.

"You were wrong about me, Maltzer," she said with an effort at patience in her voice. "But you were right, too, in a way you didn't guess. I'm not afraid of humanity. I haven't anything to fear from them. Why"—her voice took on a tinge of contempt—"already I've set a fashion in women's clothing. By next week you won't see a woman on the street without a mask like mine, and every dress that isn't cut like a chlamys will be out of style. I'm not afraid of humanity! I won't lose touch with them unless I want to. I've learned a lot—I've learned too much already."

Her voice faded for a moment, and Harris had a quick and appalling vision of her experimenting in the solitude of her farm, testing the range of her voice, testing her eyesight—could she see microscopically and telescopically?—and was her hearing as abnormally flexible as her voice?

"You were afraid I had lost feeling and scent and taste," she went on, still pacing with that powerful, tigerish tread. "Hearing and sight would not be enough, you think? But why do you think sight is the last of the senses? It may be the latest, Maltzer—Harris—but *why do you think it's the last?*"

She may not have whispered that. Perhaps it was only their hearing that made it seem thin and distant, as the brain contracted and would not let the thought come through in its stunning entirety.

"No," Deirdre said, "I haven't lost contact with the human race. I never will, unless I want to. It's too easy . . . too easy."

She was watching her shining feet as she paced, and her masked face was averted. Sorrow sounded in her soft voice now.

"I didn't mean to let you know," she said. "I never would have, if this hadn't happened. But I couldn't let you go believing you'd failed. You made a perfect machine, Maltzer. More perfect than you knew."

"But, Deirdre—," breathed Maltzer, his eyes fascinated and still incredulous upon her, "but, Deirdre, if we did succeed—what's wrong? I can feel it now—I've felt it all along. You're so unhappy—you still are. Why, Deirdre?"

She lifted her head and looked at him, eyelessly, but with a piercing stare.

"Why are you so sure of that?" she asked gently.

"You think I could be mistaken, knowing you as I do? But I'm not Frankenstein . . . you say my creation's flawless. Then what—"

"Could you ever duplicate this body?" she asked.

Maltzer glanced down at his shaking hands. "I don't know. I doubt it. I—"

"Could anyone else?"

He was silent. Deirdre answered for him. "I don't believe anyone could. I think I was an accident. A sort of mutation halfway between flesh and metal. Something accidental and . . . and unnatural, turning off on a wrong course of evolution that never reaches a dead end. Another brain in a body like this might die or go mad, as you thought I would. The synapses are too delicate. You were—call it lucky—with me. From what I know now, I don't think a . . . a baroque like me could happen again." She paused a moment. "What you did was kindle the fire for the Phoenix, in a way. And the Phoenix rises perfect and renewed from its own ashes. Do you remember why it had to reproduce itself that way?"

Maltzer shook his head.

"I'll tell you," she said. "It was because there was only one Phoenix. Only one in the whole world."

They looked at each other in silence. Then Deirdre shrugged a little.

"He always came out of the fire perfect, of course. I'm not weak, Maltzer. You needn't let that thought bother you anymore. I'm not vulnerable and helpless. I'm not subhuman." She laughed dryly. "I suppose," she said, "that I'm—superhuman."

"But—not happy."

"I'm afraid. It isn't unhappiness, Maltzer—it's fear. I don't want to draw so far away from the human race. I wish I needn't. That's why I'm going back on the stage—to keep in touch with them while I can. But I wish there could be others like me. I'm . . . I'm lonely, Maltzer."

Silence again. Then Maltzer said, in a voice as distant as when he had spoken to them through glass, over gulfs as deep as oblivion: "Then I am Frankenstein, after all."

"Perhaps you are," Deirdre said very softly. "I don't know. Perhaps you are."

She turned away and moved smoothly, powerfully, down the room to the window. Now that Harris knew, he could almost hear the sheer power puffing along her limbs as she walked. She leaned the golden forehead against the glass—it clinked faintly, with a musical sound—and looked down into the depths Maltzer had hung above. Her voice was reflective as she looked into those dizzy spaces which had offered oblivion to her creator.

"There's one limit I can think of," she said, almost inaudibly. "Only one. My brain will wear out in another forty years or so. Between now and then I'll learn . . . I'll change . . . I'll know more than I can guess today. I'll change—That's frightening. I don't like to think about that." She laid a curved golden hand on the latch and pushed the window open a little, very easily. Wind whined around its edge. "I could put a stop to it now, if I wanted," she said. "If I wanted. But I can't, really. There's so much still untried. My brain's human, and no human brain could leave such possibilities untested. I wonder, though . . . I do wonder—"

Her voice was soft and familiar in Harris's ears, the voice Deirdre had spoken and sung with, sweetly enough to enchant a world. But as preoccupation came over her a certain flatness crept into the sound. When she was not listening to her own voice, it did not keep quite to the pitch of trueness. It sounded as if she spoke in a room of brass, and echoes from the walls resounded in the tones that spoke there.

"I wonder," she repeated, the distant taint of metal already in her voice.

15

(RE)READING QUEERLY: SCIENCE FICTION, FEMINISM, AND THE DEFAMILIARIZATION OF GENDER

Veronica Hollinger

To what extent does the category of women achieve stability and coherence only in the context of the heterosexual matrix? If a stable notion of gender no longer proves to be the foundational premise of feminist politics, perhaps a new sort of feminist politics is now desirable to contest the very reifications of gender and identity, one that will take *the variable construction of identity* as both a methodological and normative prerequisite, if not a political goal.

—*Judith Butler*, Gender Trouble (*my emphasis*)

Reading Queerly

My aim in this discussion is to suggest some strategic intersections between feminist theory and queer theory in order to (re)read how the "variable construction of [gender] identity" has been represented in science fiction by women writers.[1] Starting from the assumption that, as Judith Butler—whose work is central here—has noted, "literary narrative [is] a place where theory takes place" (1993, 182), I focus on three stories in particular: C. L. Moore's "No Woman Born" (1944), James Tiptree Jr.'s "The Girl Who Was Plugged In" (1973), and Joanna Russ's "The Mystery of the Young Gentleman" (1982). Each story works out, in narrative form, some of the theoretical issues I find especially relevant to my present concerns. That none of these stories is contemporary serves to emphasize the fact that complex and sophisticated inquiries into gender issues are by no means new to science fiction, even if our theoretical representations of these issues have not always kept pace with the fiction. While keeping in mind their many real differences, I read the theories and the fictions as reciprocal echoes and restatements: They suggest information about each other and serve to defamiliarize each other. When the theoretical focus turns to issues of gender and sexuality, science fiction is a particularly useful discourse within which to represent, through the metaphors of narrative, the philosophical and political conceptualizations deployed within critical theory.

I'll be undertaking a double strategy in the process of this reading: I want, first, to queer my perspective and, second, to work within the theoretical context of gender-as-performance. The first part of this essay, an overview of some relevant theory, makes a case for queering feminist critical reading, while the second part, which includes a detailed look at the stories by Moore and Tiptree, suggests the efficacy of performance theory in denaturalizing some conventionally fixed notions about gender and heterosexuality. My third section reads Russ's "The Mystery of the Young Gentleman" as an exhilaratingly queer performance that undermines the solidity of what Butler refers to as "the heterosexual matrix."[2]

All too often, heteronormativity is embedded in both theory and fiction as "natural" and "universal," a kind of barely glimpsed default gender setting that remains unquestioned and untheorized. Science fiction would seem to be ideally suited, as a narrative mode, to the construction of imaginative challenges to the smoothly oiled technologies of heteronormativity, especially when these almost invisible technologies are pressed into the service of a coercive regime of compulsory heterosexuality. However, in spite of science fiction's function as a literature of cognitive estrangement, and in spite of the work of both feminist writers and critics in their ongoing efforts to rethink the problematics of gender—especially gender's impact on the lives of women—heterosexuality as an institutionalized nexus of human activity remains stubbornly resistant to defamiliarization. On the whole, science fiction is an overwhelmingly *straight* discourse, not least because of the covert yet almost completely totalizing ideological hold heterosexuality has on our culture's ability to imagine itself otherwise. Both science fiction as a narrative field and feminism as a political and theoretical field work themselves out, for the most part, within the terms of an almost completely naturalized heterosexual binary. As Michael Warner puts it, "Het culture thinks of itself as the elemental form of human association, as the very model of inter-gender relations, as the indivisible basis of all community, and as the means of reproduction without which society wouldn't exist" (1993).

In response to such constraints, queer theorists such as Eve Kosofsky Sedgwick, Sue-Ellen Case, Teresa de Lauretis, and Judith Butler have undertaken critical/theoretical explorations that consciously avoid situating heterosexuality as the unquestioned norm in human sexual practices.[3] In their work, heterosexuality comes to acquire a certain exoticism as an object of estrangement and we are invited to consider it, not as natural and universal, but—to a large extent—as both learned behavior and a network of forces embedded in the very fabric of culture. As the title of Diane Richardson's 1996 collection, *Theorising Heterosexuality*, suggests, heterosexuality has its own history.

In "Tracking the Vampire," Case points out how "while gender is an important site of struggle for women, the very notion reinscribes sexual difference" (1991, 3). While she refers here to the dilemma that this reinscription of an institutionalized heterosexual binary poses for lesbian theory, feminist readings in general face the same dilemma: An emphasis on gender risks the continuous reinscription of sexual binarism, the heterosexual opposition that historically has proven so oppressive for so many women. Case goes on to argue that "the heterosexual feminist perspective in theories of representation . . . when it creates the unmarked category of 'woman' as a general one that includes queers, or when it displaces queer desire by retaining, in the gaze / look compound, sexual difference and its phallus / lack polarity, that perspective remains caught in a heterosexist reading of queer discourse" (13).

Examined more broadly, Case's observation suggests that such a perspective "remains caught" in heterosexist readings not only of queer discourse, but of all discourse in general. In *Epistemology of the Closet*, Sedgwick sounds an equally cautionary note: "It may be . . . that a damaging bias toward heterosocial or heterosexist assumptions inheres unavoidably in the very concept of gender. This bias would be built into any gender-based analytic perspective to the extent that gender definition and gender identity are necessarily relational between genders—to the extent, that is, that in any gender system, female identity or definition is constructed by analogy, supplementary, or contrast to male, or vice versa. . . . *This gives heterosocial and heterosexual relations a conceptual privilege of incalculable consequence* (1991, 31, my emphasis).

In our struggle against a monolithic patriarchy—which is, after all, a kind of theoretical fiction produced, in part, by the very feminism aligned against it—we risk reinscribing, however inadvertently, the terms of compulsory heterosexuality within our own constructions. In other words, our critiques of sex and gender polarities often leave those polarities in place. Using the strategically powerful perspectives of queer theory, however, is one way in which feminist work can be moblized to think against the grain of heteronormativity, so that we can also begin to think ourselves outside the binary oppositions of a fictively totalizing feminine / masculine divide.

Not surprisingly, perhaps, as queer has increased in influence, its meanings have become widely contested.[4] Developing out of (and, in some instances, in spite of) lesbian and gay theoretical and political work, queer points to a broad interest in gendered behaviors, human sexual practices, and questions of sexual difference in general, while at the same time it aims to resist and critique dominant sexual paradigms. Queer is the result of contemporary developments in postmodern theorizations and deconstructions of subjectivity and identity. Indeed, one of the fundamental characteristics of much queer theoretical work is its attention to the range of differences within identificatory "fictions" such as sexual orientation and gender. Butler's work, in particular, is useful here, functioning as a postmodern rearticulation, a post-Foucauldian effort to represent the conceptual matrix of sex/gender, ideas about the subject and about agency, and issues of representation outside the boundary lines of compulsory heterosexuality.

In the context of science fiction, we can read some variations in the deployment of queer in the differences between Joanna Russ's *The Female Man* (1975), which focuses on the struggle to establish lesbian and feminist identities and sexualities within the constraints of a culture of compulsory heterosexuality, and Ursula K. Le Guin's *The Left Hand of Darkness* (1969), which, through a radical imagining of human life *without* gender, explores gender as a cultural construction that is at once coercive and contingent.[5] Butler's work, on the cusp of feminism and queer theory, suggests the potential for queering our reading of feminist issues in science fiction, and a statement of Sedgwick's is particularly resonant in this context. She writes that "[t]he study of sexuality is not coextensive with the study of gender; correspondingly, antihomophobic inquiry is not coextensive with feminist inquiry. But we can't know in advance how they will be different" (Sedgwick 1990, 27). Nor can we know in advance the varied ways in which they might support each other.

Many lesbian-feminist science-fiction writers have been at the forefront of queer challenges to the regime of compulsory heterosexuality through both cognitive disruptions and imaginative revisions. This is one way in which the lesbian-separatist utopian writing of the 1970s has been a crucial force in shaping feminist science fiction, in spite of the many and obvious differences among its political projects.[6] Writers such as Joanna Russ and Monique Wittig have created literary worlds in which the range of social and political practices available to women have not been constrained by a binarism that situates women on the "feminine" side of an essentialized and insurmountable gender divide. The promise inherent in such imaginings accounts in part for the particular poignancy at the conclusion of Russ's classic story "When It Changed" (1972). Her characters are faced with the dismal certainty that their lives are about to be radically circumscribed by the return of men to the all-women planet Whileaway—and by their own reinscription as "half a species" (Russ 1983, 258), the feminine half, after centuries of performing "unnaturally" as the entirety of the human race. As Russ's narrator concludes, "This too shall pass. All good things must come to an end. Take my life but don't take away the meaning of my life" (260). "When It Changed" suggests that, at least as things are now, queer only exists on sufferance—for a while—until the masculine/heterosexual reenters to colonize it (again).[7]

Veronica Hollinger

Not for nothing does Monique Wittig, author of the utopian novel *Les Guérrillères* (1969), separate lesbians from the category of women. Wittig's theoretical writing aims to deessentialize the biological category of "women," to redefine it as a social class, and to dismantle the sex/gender system itself as a system of political oppression. As she writes in her essay, "One Is Not Born a Woman," "the designated subject (lesbian) is *not* a woman, either economically, or politically, or ideologically" (Wittig 1981, 20). Wittig argues that the term "women" denotes a class of subjects circumscribed by the gender binarism of heteronormativity; the lesbian, for her, is that figure whose survival demands "the destruction of heterosexuality as a social system which is based on the oppression of women by men and which provides the doctrine of the difference between the sexes to justify this position" (20). Until such a demolition is effected, however, the logical theoretical move is to remove lesbians from the class of women altogether.[8]

The feminist stories of James Tiptree Jr. provide a significant contrast to the frequently celebratory texts of writers like Russ and Wittig. Tiptree's writing is notable for the dark and ironic tones in which it represents issues of gender and sexuality. Even a story like "Houston, Houston, Do You Read?" (1976), which rewrites Russ's "When It Changed" to the extent that it manages a "happy ending"—or at least an imaginatively satisfying one—nevertheless suggests the high price of freedom for women. The cloned women of Tiptree's future refer to themselves as "human beings. . . . Humanity, mankind. . . . The human race" (1990, 222). However, in order to erase the threat of a return of the heterosexual repressed, Tiptree's story ends with the execution of the three male astronauts who have inadvertently invaded this future in which women are the entirety of the human race—breaking through from what we might think of as the "unconscious" of history.

I read Tiptree's feminist stories as explorations of some of the more dismal exigencies of a naturalized heterosexuality, (re)constructed as a kind of inescapable heterosexual bind. While "Houston, Houston" suggests that execution is a viable option to preserve the full range of women's lives, in other stories heterosexuality is constructed as both inevitable and fatal. In stories such as "Your Faces, O My Sisters! Your Faces Filled of Light!" (1976), "The Women Men Don't See" (1973), and "The Screwfly Solution" (1977), women escape into madness, disappear into outer space with unknown aliens, or simply wait to be killed. The unremitting pessimism in these stories arises, at least in part, from Tiptree's determination to follow the implications of gender difference to their grimly logical conclusions; her stories read like darkly parodic representations of the extremes of gender difference. Perhaps this is most dramatically demonstrated in "The Screwfly Solution," a story that literalizes the "war between the sexes" as an alien-inspired holocaust that will end only when there are no more women left alive.

In these stories, sex and death are coextensive. This is most strongly suggested in the title of a story in which there are no human characters at all, "Love is the Plan, the Plan is Death" (1973).[9] "And I Awoke and Found Me Here on the Cold Hill's Side" (1972) extrapolates upon the two-sexed system of human relations and essentializes it as the story of humanity's "long drive to find and impregnate the stranger. Or get impregnated by him; it works for women too. Anything different-colored, different nose, ass, anything, man *has* to fuck it or die trying. That's a drive, y'know, it's built in. Because it works fine as long as the stranger is human" (Tiptree 1990, 42). When human longing is directed toward alien beings, however, this drive becomes counterproductive and threatens the continuity of the species: "Man, it's deep . . . some cargo-cult of the soul. We're built to dream outward. They [alien races] laugh at us. They don't have it" (42).

In these stories, human (hetero)sexuality is both instinct and damnation. Human sexual desire for the "other" results only in pain, as our objects of desire become increasingly, and sometimes literally, alien to us. Sexuality is the failed attempt to know the irreducibly alien. From this perspective, Tiptree's stories are modern tragedies of gender difference. At once ironically understated and parodically hyperbolic, they provide us with some of the saddest moments in science fiction.

Performing Gender

Feminist and queer poststructuralist theories about the performative nature of human being-in-the world suggest some fascinating and useful analytical perspectives through which to consider the construction of the gendered subject. In terms of the development of a performative theory of gender, one of the most provocative documents in contemporary feminist debates about the nature of "woman" is Joan Riviere's 1929 case study "Womanliness as a Masquerade," which raises this vexed question: "What is the essential nature of fully developed femininity?" (1986, 43). As a true Freudian, Riviere suggests that "[t]he conception of womanliness as a mask, behind which man suspects some hidden danger, throws a little light on the enigma" (43). But her study has, in fact, already reached its most controversial conclusion: "The reader may now ask how I define womanliness or where I draw the line between genuine womanliness and the 'masquerade.' My suggestion is not, however, that there is any such difference: whether radical or superficial, they are the same thing" (38). Riviere thus (re)introduces the notion of femininity as re-presentation. The "feminine" is a role; "genuine womanliness" is always a character-part, constituted in performance. Within the terms of Riviere's particular case study, the motivation for such a performance is a negative one: It arises from the need "to hide the possession of masculinity and to avert the reprisals expected if [a woman] was found to possess it" (38).

Many recent studies have built on both Riviere's and Jacques Lacan's[10] commentaries on femininity as masquerade, revising the implications of these readings in ironic directions that suggest the potential for deconstructive rearticulations of conventional constructions of sex and gender identities. In both *Gender Trouble* and *Bodies That Matter*, for instance, Butler develops convincing arguments for the nature of sex and gender performances as *constitutive* of the individual subject involved in such performances. For Butler, as well as for Sedgwick and others, doing is being.[11] In other words, when gender is theorized as performative, in a move that resituates the "tragedy" of the masquerade of femininity and turns it into ironic contestatory practice, we become less dependent upon essentialist ontological categories and, at least theoretically and imaginatively, we can initiate a more radical inquiry into the nature of the individual sexed and gendered subject.

The ironic mobilization of feminist mimicry and parody is an imaginative intervention into what must otherwise be read as yet one more oppressive construction/ representation of "woman" as artificial, superficial, suspect, and lacking—the mere negation of a masculinity that is the primary term in an opposition shaped by the pressures of the heterosexual paradigm. Within the constraints of conventional liberal humanism and essentialist notions of the subject, the masquerade is the sign of women's failure to "live up to" the demands of "true" femininity that such an ideology posits as the marker of the "real" woman. Reading the masquerade in the ironic mode, however, suggests very different conclusions.[12] Within the postmodern context in which critique and complicity work hand in hand, such radical inquiry through the conceptual apparatus of sex/gender-as-performance becomes a utopian as well as a contestatory gesture. As Butler explains: "Performativity describes this relation of being implicated in that which one opposes, this turning of power against itself to produce alternative modalities of power, to establish a kind of political contestation that is not a 'pure' opposition, a 'transcendence' of contemporary relations of power, but a difficult labor of forging a future from resources inevitably impure" (1993, 241).

We see the beginnings of such contestatory gestures in both C. L. Moore's "No Woman Born" (1944) and James Tiptree Jr.'s "The Girl Who Was Plugged In" (1973), two early cyborg stories that imaginatively construct fictions about "femininity as a masquerade." Moore's story can be read as a working through of Riviere's conclusions about the inherently self-protective nature of the masquerade of femininity, a femininity mobilized to protect the "masculine" woman from retribution for assuming that which does not *naturally* belong to her. Tiptree's story is a sadly ironic fairy tale that examines the pressures on women to replicate the ideal of femininity, to play it "straight" even as they are doomed always to fail at such a task.

Moore's story is a particularly resonant early thought experiment, marked by anxiety but nonetheless unflinching in its examination of the nature of femininity. I read it as a moment when (proto)feminist science fiction begins to turn towards explorations of the performative nature of gender. As such, it helps to establish a ground for the radical destabilizations of gender which we see in the growing body of queer science fiction writing.[13] As many readers will recall, "No Woman Born" is the story of Deirdre, a world-famous actor and singer, "the loveliest creature whose image ever moved along the airways" (Moore 1975, 236). Although her career is cut short by the theater fire that destroys her body, Deirdre rises like a phoenix from the ashes, resurrected within the gleaming metallic body designed for her by the scientist Maltzer. Most of Moore's lengthy story unfolds around the question of whether or not Deirdre is still a woman, indeed whether or not she is still human. Broadly read, Moore's story is thus a complex early thinking through of some of the implications of our human interface with technology. It is, at the same time, a sophisticated examination of the implications of gender, as well as a meditation, albeit an anxious one, on the nature of gender as performance.

The text consistently represents Deirdre within the tensions of anxious oppositions. At various times she is either more human than ever or increasingly inhuman; more beautiful than ever or increasingly grotesque; more in touch with her audiences than ever or more and more withdrawn from humanity. Is she still the woman so loved by her millions of fans or, having lost the physical body that previously defined her, is she merely the metal housing for a brain completely devoid of both gender and sexuality? These oppositions structure the conflict between Deirdre, who plans to resume her performing career in spite of her cyborg status, and the two men who are closest to her, Maltzer, her "maker," and John Harris, her adoring manager, who is also the point-of-view character in Moore's text.

Maltzer becomes increasingly convinced that he should never have "tampered with nature" in his attempt to keep Deirdre alive: "She isn't a human being any more, and I think what humanity is left in her will drain out little by little and never be replaced" (Moore 1975, 259). Harris becomes more and more anxious about what he sees as the illusory nature of Deirdre's femininity, the performative nature of Deirdre's humanity: "Later he would think again that it might be only a disguise, something like a garment she had put off with her lost body, to wear again only when she chose" (279–280). Deirdre herself eventually calls attention to her increasing detachment from the rest of humanity, her sense of growing isolation from flesh-and-blood bodies, her new and singular identity as "[a] sort of mutation halfway between flesh and metal" (286). As Deirdre contemplates the possibilities of her continuing transformation, the story's final words foreground the crisis of identification precipitated by the cyborg body: "'I wonder,' she repeated, the distant taint of metal already in her voice" (288).[14]

The ambiguous and uneasy (non)resolution of "No Woman Born" represents exactly the anxiety around which Moore's text develops itself. Deirdre is monstrous not because she is ugly, but precisely because her gleaming metallic body is so—inhumanly—beautiful. She is monstrous not because she has ceased to be feminine, but precisely because her *performance* of femininity is so—calculatedly—convincing: "She threw her head back and let her body sway and her shoulders shake, and the laughter, like the music, filled the theater. . . . And she was a woman now. Humanity had dropped over her like a tangible garment" (Moore 1975, 265).

It is worth remembering that the "original" Deirdre was already a consummate performer. As such, she represented femininity as spectacle and was the object of desire for millions of adoring fans. Deirdre's "natural" performances are, in fact, electronic mediations, and she herself is adept at performing the image of femininity, at least for those same adoring fans. Moore's story cannily situates her manager, Harris, as the point-of-view character, thus maintaining Deirdre's status as the object of "the male gaze," and we, as readers, are also confined to viewing Deirdre's narrative from the outside. Consequently, we share with Maltzer and Harris the sense that she is both less and more than woman, both less and more than human. Like Riviere, Harris theorizes the nature of Deirdre's femininity as "masquerade." And, like Riviere's subjects, Deirdre, within this paradigm, performs "womanliness" in order to divert punishment for enjoying privilege and power that are "unnatural" to female subjects.

Deirdre's original performances serve to maintain and to secure conventional and hegemonic notions of gender, but they are read as natural because they are performed by a "natural" female body. The cyborg that Deirdre has become rearticulates the concept of gender, turning it into something—similar to the performances of drag queens or the feminine mimesis ironically theorized by Irigaray—that is both excessive and disturbing. Gender is now disassociated from the "natural" body, and the gap between body and performance has become too great to ignore. Deirdre's body is monstrous in its suggestion that there is more to her masquerade than merely the reiteration of an idealized femininity.

In her analysis of the gender performances in Jennie Livingston's film about New York's drag balls, *Paris Is Burning* (1991), Butler discusses why successful gender performance must be enacted in what we might think of as the "realist" mode: "Significantly, this is a performance that works, that effects realness, to the extent that it *cannot* be read. . . . For a performance to work . . . means that a reading is no longer possible, or that a reading, an interpretation, appears to be a kind of transparent seeing, where what appears and what it means coincide. On the contrary, when what appears and how it is 'read' diverge, the artifice of the performance can be read as artifice; the ideal splits off from its appropriation" (1993, 129).

Moore's text never reconciles the tension between these two kinds of gender performance, the realist and the excessive. Is Deirdre trapped inside the system of gender representation as her image used to be trapped literally within electronic image systems? Or is she "playing with mimesis" for Meltzer and Harris and her new audiences, ironically performing the feminine while, in fact, "remaining elsewhere," as Irigaray so intriguingly suggests? (1985, 76).

In spite of Moore's (proto)feminist challenge to notions of gender construction and femininity—in spite of her suggestion of femininity as masquerade—her cyborg is, finally, trapped within the binarisms of a heterosexual perspective on the nature of woman. Like Frankenstein's Creature, Deirdre exists in an increasingly abjected space outside the boundaries of what is acceptable to human beings, to women. Moore's cyborg, however, remains a powerful early image of the potential for such figures to disrupt science fiction's conventional constructions of the feminine, an image of the powerful woman who, even as she feels herself withdrawing from humanity, nevertheless retains control of her own gendered representation. The cyborg in this story thus becomes more than a metaphor; it becomes a character in a science fiction universe in which the technological imagination can begin to explore the ramifications of what theory tells us about ourselves as bodies—as gendered bodies, sexually defined bodies. As has been frequently pointed out, the technobody reiterates itself through replication, not through reproduction, and it does not require the heterosexual matrix as the space within which to duplicate itself. Given the emphasis in theories of performativity on reiteration and citation, the technobody as replicated body points us toward the utopian space of queer excess. Perhaps all technobodies are, at least potentially, queer bodies.

In contrast to "No Woman Born," Tiptree's "The Girl Who Was Plugged In" theorizes the coercive nature of gender as imprisonment.[15] It demonstrates that even the cyborg, like the madwoman (in the attic) and the angel (in the house), may become enmeshed in and diminished by a too faithful performance of femininity. "The Girl Who Was Plugged In" (1973) is Tiptree's protocyberpunk story about the technobody that fails. Its protagonist, P. Burke, "the ugly of the world" (1990, 45), is precisely the body that does *not* matter, the body that must be hidden underground in a hi-tech cabinet while her mind remotely operates the beautiful but soulless body of Delphi, who is described as "porno for angels" (49) but who, nevertheless, is "just a vegetable" (50) without someone controlling her from a distance.

P. Burke and Delphi represent a kind of split subject integrated through technology into a single mind/body matrix. Without Delphi, P. Burke, as the narrator tells us, "is about as far as you can get from the concept *girl*" (Tiptree 1990, 56). Here Tiptree's text recalls Butler's contention that gender definitions exclude as often as they include; P. Burke's is the abjected body relegated to the outside of what conventionally constitutes the feminine. Telepresence, however, immerses P. Burke in a virtual experience that allows her *to be* beautiful and famous, even if only at a distance. Within the plot development of this futuristic fairy tale, P. Burke falls in love with a lovely young man, is loved reciprocally as the beautifully feminine Delphi, and dies—both as P. Burke and as Delphi—when she tries to express this love directly, without technological mediation, to the horrified object of her affections.

Tiptree's politicization of gender in this story intersects with her critique of the society of the spectacle—the parallels between "The Girl Who Was Plugged In" and Moore's earlier story are both intriguing and suggestive. Delphi and others like her are "managed" by representatives of big business who employ them as living advertisements in order to sell products in a future in which direct advertising has been banned. Constantly surrounded by cameras, P. Burke-as-Delphi lives in full view of millions of potential consumers. Meanwhile, in her cabinet, P. Burke dreams of healing the split between the mind trapped in her monstrous body and the idealized feminine body that remains forever separate: "You see the outcome [says the narrative voice]—the funneling of all this agony into one dumb protoplasmic drive to fuse with Delphi. To leave, to close out the beast she is chained to. *To become Delphi*" (Tiptree 1990, 67). In Butler's terms, P. Burke desires to *become* the gendered ideal represented by Delphi, her body-at-a-distance, to close the gap between herself and the cultural ideal of a perfect femininity that she has been taught to worship.

In this sense, Tiptree, like Moore, has crafted a story about the performance of femininity, a performance that is at once perfect and completely unnatural: P. Burke learns how to "run" her body-at-a-distance as a beautiful woman, while she herself remains out of sight, wired into the system, a controlling brain, loved, finally, not as a human body but—by Joe, her trainer—as "the greatest cybersystem he has ever known" (Tiptree 1990, 78). P. Burke's performance-at-a-distance of femininity is a consumer-driven masquerade in which such performance provides her only opportunity, within the constraints of an ugly and abjected female body, to mimic acceptable femininity—and thus to qualify for the kind of fairy-tale ending, marriage to a handsome prince, which is (almost) P. Burke's reward for successfully performing the masquerade.[16]

Performance theory, which has obvious parallels to theories of theatrical performance, examines gender and sexual practice as a range of activities rather than as passive states. In individual performances, the subject reiterates social ideals of gender behavior and it is these (re)citations, these active repetitions of previously existent models, that are constitutive of the individual as a gendered subject. From this theoretical perspective, gender is less an essential characteristic of the individual than a series of performative gestures that the individual learns to replicate. This is true also of sexual identity: Heterosexuality and homosexuality as constitutive features of the individual are read not as stable categories but rather as the result of specific activities that serve to define the individual *during the course of* the performance of those activities. Tiptree's P. Burke *is* the divinely feminine Delphi *as long as* she performs Delphi, who in these terms is neither more nor less than the sum of P. Burke's gendered performances; P. Burke is the actor and Delphi is her role. We might thus read the tragedy at the heart of "The Girl Who Was Plugged In" as P. Burke's confusion of herself-as-actor with Delphi-as-role. In much the same way, of course, our culture, devoted to the categorical regime of heterosexuality, fails to distinguish between individual women and men and the gendered roles that the culture demands they play out as if these roles were natural.

Concluding Differently

Within the terms of my discussion, queer is both an exclusive and an excessive space, "a zone of possibilities" (1996, 2), in Annamarie Jagose's terms, inhabited by all that is *not* heteronormative, "the point of convergence for a potentially infinite number of nonnormative subject positions" (1996, 101). At its most inclusive, it can incorporate heterosexuality, but a heterosexuality stripped of its conventional privileges: no gendered or sexed identities in this utopian space are compulsory, or universal, or natural; and, none, certainly, are invisible. To borrow from Donna Haraway's 1985 "A Manifesto for Cyborgs," we can think of queer as a kind of cyborg space, "a cyborg world . . . about lived social and bodily realities in which people are not afraid of . . . permanently partial identities and contradictory standpoints" (1989, 179). In these terms, queer marks a utopian space, which is, perhaps, also an ironic space, inhabited by subjects-in-process who are not bound by reifying definitions and expectations, and in which bodies, desires, and sex/gender behaviors are free-floating and in constant play. Haraway's description of her utopian-inflected cyborg figure suggests something of the—if not literal, then at least imaginative—potential of the utopian queer.

Joanna Russ's "The Mystery of the Young Gentleman" (1982) also suggests the outlines of such a queerly utopian world. This story is the first-person account of a nineteenth-century journey by riverboat undertaken by the narrator and her/his young companion, Maria-Dolores. Both are human and yet other than human; they have psi talents that enable them to "read"—and therefore to survive—the world of ordinary human beings. The narrator travels as a man, but the text suggests that s/he is neither man nor woman; this "other" species is unmarked by the physical traces on which culture's obsession with gender difference is founded. In contrast, ordinary humans tend to be the victims of their own gender constraints. The middle-class women traveling on the river-boat suffer from "[t]hat dull, perpetual, coerced lack [they] have been taught to call 'love,' which a gentleman's arm, a gentleman's face, a gentleman's conversation, so wonderfully soothes. It's a deadly business" (Russ 1983, 67–68). The doctor who suspects something "unnatural" about Russ's narrator concludes that s/he must be an "invert." As the narrator writes of this benighted doctor, his misreading is the result of the binary vision within which all his assessments of human beings take shape: "The division is so strong, so elaborate, so absolute, so much trained into them as habit, that within reasonable limits they see, generally, more or less what they expect to see, especially," as the narrator concludes, "if one wears the mask of the proper behavior" (73). In other words, the performative possibilities inherent in gender provide Russ's narrator with the perfect strategy for deflecting ordinary human suspicion of her/his extraordinarily queer reality.

Not surprisingly, Russ's story, as a science-fiction story, achieves something of the estrangement of gender that Sedgwick sees as potential in queer studies, which have a crucial role to play "in radically defamiliarizing and denaturalizing, not only the past and the distant, but the present" (1990, 44). In part, "The Mystery of the Young Gentleman" achieves this estrangement through a series of gender masquerades, as the narrator successfully counteracts every effort on the part of the curious doctor to interpret her/him correctly. Referring to the "medical" notes through which the doctor is constructing his own version of the "truth" (that the "young gentleman" must be a male homosexual), the narrator wryly informs us: "Now he is writing in a burst of inspiration . . . that the only influence that has saved me from the 'fate' of my 'type' (lace stockings, female dress, self-pollution, frequenting low haunts, unnatural acts, drunkenness, a love of cosmetics, inevitable moral degeneration, eventual insanity, it goes on for pages, it is really the most dreadful stuff) *is my healthy outdoor life in the manly climate of the American West!*" (Russ 1984, 78, italics in original).

Russ's story thus satirizes the nineteenth century's discursive construction of "homosexuality" as a specific category for defining individual subjects. And, as "The Mystery of the Young Gentleman" concludes, a good performance of gender will usually be successful in its (re)citation of social norms, simply because most people see only what they expect to see.

As the narrator tells the less experienced Maria-Dolores, in the mountains toward which they are traveling to join others like themselves, there are no women and there are no men either, and Maria-Dolores' confusion echoes the reader's own inability to conceive of nongendered subjects:

"Well, can I dress like a man?" [asks Maria-Dolores]

"Like this?" (pointing to myself) "Of course."

She says, being a real pest, "I bet there are no women in the mountains."

"That's right," I tell her. (She's also in real confusion.)

"But *me!*" she says.

"When you get there, there will still be no women."

"But you—is it all *men?*"

"There are no men. Maria-Dolores, we've been over and over this."

She gives up, exasperated. Her head, like all the others', is full of *los hombres y las mujeres* as if it were a fact of nature: ladies with behinds inflated as if by bicycle pumps, gentlemen with handlebar mustachios who kiss the ladies' hands. If I say *las hombres y los mujeres*, as I once did and am tempted to do again, she will kick me. (Russ 1984, 70–71, italics in original)

In the end, the story constructs an ironic analogy in which heterosexual/queer oppositions parallel conventional oppositions between human and alien; it also deconstructs these binaries, however, as soon as they are introduced. There is no suggestion that these differences are anything other than the productions of heteronormative cultural anxiety. "The Mystery of the Young Gentleman" concludes with an image of satirical gender confusion constructed through the words of one of the imaginary nineteenth-century dime novels that Maria-Dolores reads: *What doom is stored up in Heaven for these hard-hearted men and women, diabolically disguised as men and women or vice-versa and therefore invisible to our eyes, speaking the language of anyone in the room, which is dreadfully confusing because you can't tell what degenerate nation (or race) they may come from, and worst of all,* PRETENDING TO BE HUMAN BEINGS? WHEN IN FACT THEY ARE??? (Russ 1994, 92, italics in original)

When women write science fiction, as Jane Donawerth has convincingly demonstrated, they repeat generic conventions. But they repeat them differently, and sometimes excessively (I am tempted to write that they're "pretending to be science-fiction writers—when in fact they are").[17] I wonder if women and queer writers of science fiction aren't always involved in various forms of masquerade. Occasionally their performances are ironic; and sometimes they also pose a challenge to what is, in spite of its promotion as the literature of change, in many ways a deeply conservative genre that, for the most part, demonstrates an unquestioned allegiance to heteronormative sexual relations and to the limiting gender distinctions that are one of the results of this heteronormativity. Queer, however, suggests a postmodern and utopian space for exploring sexual difference(s); it promises much in terms of recuperating traditionally abjected figures like monsters and grotesques, as it deploys, in Butler's words, the "repetition of hegemonic forms which fail to repeat loyally" (1993, 124).

Notes

1. I would also like to thank my colleague, Wendy Pearson, for her help in working through some of the theoretical terms of my discussion. And I am indebted to Shelley Cadora and Istvan Csicsery-Ronay Jr. for their rigorous challenges and suggestions.

2. Butler defines "the heterosexual matrix" as "a hegemonic discursive/epistemic model of gender intelligibility that assumes that for bodies to cohere and make sense there must be a stable sex expressed through a stable gender . . . that is oppositionally and hierarchically defined, through the compulsory practice of heterosexuality" (1990, 151 n 6).

3. See, for instance, Sedgwick's *Epistemology of the Closet* (1990), Case's "Tracking the Vampire" (1991), de Lauretis's "Queer Theory: Lesbian and Gay Sexualities: An Introduction" (1991), Butler's *Gender Trouble: Feminism and the Subversion of Identity* (1990) and *Bodies That Matter: On the Discursive Limits of "Sex"* (1993), and Michael Warner's *Fear of a Queer Planet: Queer Politics and Social Theory* (1993). See also the special issue of *differences: A Journal of Feminist Cultural Studies* titled *More Gender Trouble: Feminism Meets Queer Theory* (1994), which includes Butler's introductory essay, "Against Proper Objects." For an all-too-rare application of queer theory to science fiction, see Wendy Pearson's essay, "After the (Homo)Sexual: A Queer Analysis of Anti-Sexuality in Sheri S. Tepper's *The Gate to Women's Country*" (1996).

4. For a detailed and well-balanced examination of the historical and theoretical contexts of queer, see Annamarie Jagose's *Queer Theory: An Introduction* (1996). Her chapter on "Contestations of Queer" (101–126) provides an insightful look at some of the complexities and varying deployments of queer. Almost by definition, *queer* is a term that defies fixed definition. In the 'final' analysis, I concur with Butler's suggestion that

> [i]t is necessary to learn a double movement: to invoke the category [in this instance, queer] and, hence, provisionally to institute an identity and at the same time to open the category as a site of permanent political contest. That the term is questionable does not mean that we ought not to use it, but neither does the necessity to use it mean that we ought not perpetually to interrogate the exclusions by which it proceeds, and to do this precisely in order to learn how to live the contingency of the political signifier in a culture of democratic contestation. (1993, 222)

5. Le Guin's by now "notorious" use of the third-person masculine pronoun to refer to her androgynous aliens queers her text more specifically as well: The impression given

of her alien planet is that it is occupied solely by masculine persons. All sexual relationships, as a result—and perhaps most especially between the human Genly Ai and the Gethenian Estraven—*feel* like gay sexual relationships. In spite of what we are told of Estraven's feminine appearance when he enters kemmer at the conclusion of the novel, it is difficult to avoid reading Genly Ai's unconsummated "love" for Estraven as the text's drawing back from the physical expression of a love "which dares not speak its name."

6. It is worth recalling that, in Margaret Atwood's *The Handmaid's Tale*, the patriarchal dystopia of Gilead takes over a world that has put aside and/or forgotten its radical mothers. Samuel R. Delany, one of the most important queer writers of science fiction, called cyberpunk to task for a similar act of forgetting, for trying to erase its debt to its "real mothers" (including Joanna Russ, Ursula K. Le Guin, and Vonda McIntyre). According to Delany in a frequently quoted 1988 interview with Takayuki Tatsumi:

> It's interesting that the feminist explosion—which obviously infiltrates the cyberpunk writers so much—is the one they seem to be the least comfortable with, even though it's one that, much more than the New Wave, has influenced them most strongly. . . .
>
> Cyberpunk is, at basis, a bastard form of writing. . . . What it's got are mothers. A whole set of them—who, in literary terms, were so promiscuous that their cyberpunk offspring will simply never be able to settle down, sure of a certain daddy.
>
> I'm a favorite faggot "uncle" who's always looked out for mom and who, when they were young, showed the kids some magic tricks. (9)

7. Annamarie Jagose pinpoints "three crucial respects" in which queer has been influenced by the work of lesbian feminism: "its attention to the specificity of gender, its framing of sexuality as institutional rather than personal, and its critique of compulsory heterosexuality" (1996, 5).

Feminist and lesbian utopian writing isn't necessarily queer, of course. Consider, for instance, Charlotte Perkins Gilman's early utopian text, *Herland* (1915), which privileges all things related to motherhood, or Sally Miller Gearhart's *The Wanderground* (1979), which transforms many of the features of a stereotypical femininity into the "natural" virtues of its lesbian Hill Women. In contrast, queer is about the subverting of those normative models and categories that, given their more essentialist deployments of identity politics, writers like Gilman and Gearhart work to sustain.

8. It's intriguing to speculate that, within the terms of Wittig's own analysis, a feminist reading of *Les Guérrillères* is "impossible," since feminism's focus on women is, arguably, irrelevant to a text in which there are *no* women, only lesbians. For a complex examination of the queer as a utopian figure in Wittig's theory and fiction, see Jennifer Burwell's "Acting Out 'Lesbian': Monique Wittig and Immanent Critique" (1997).

9. For a detailed reading of this particular aspect of Tiptree's science fiction, see my "'The Most Grisly Truth': Responses to the Human Condition in the Works of James Tiptree, Jr." (Hollinger 1999).

10. Lacan provides another document in the case. In his lecture on "The Signification of the Phallus" (1958), he seems to reiterate Riviere's position, although his trajectory moves in a different direction: "Paradoxical as this formulation may seem, I am saying that it is in order to be the phallus, that is to say, the signifier of the desire of the Other, that a woman will reject an essential part of femininity, namely, all her attributes in the masquerade. It is for that which she is not that she wishes to be desired as well as loved" (1997, 289–90)

11. See, for instance, Elin Diamond's "Mimesis, Mimicry, and the 'True Real'" (1989); Mary Anne Doane's "Film and Masquerade: Theorizing the Female Spectator" (1982); and Mary Russo's *The Female Grotesque: Risk, Excess and Modernity*—especially her chapter "Female Grotesques: Carnival and Theory" (1994, 53–73). For a study that looks at some of the complexities of masculinity as gender masquerade, see Kim Michasiw's "Camp, Masculinity, Masquerade" (1994).

12. Luce Irigaray's work in the field of psychoanalytic theory has also produced an influential construction of femininity as resistance through a kind of deliberately skewed repetition. Femininity, in Irigaray's words, is "a role, an image, a value, imposed upon women by male systems of representation. In this masquerade of femininity," Irigaray goes on to say, "the woman loses herself, and loses herself by playing on her femininity" (1985, 84). Irigaray also points out how this masquerade can be used to undermine the very systems of representation that it is supposed to maintain. In a much quoted passage, Irigaray writes that "to play with mimesis is thus, for a woman, to try to recover the place of her exploitation by discourse, without allowing herself to be simply reduced to it. . . . It also means 'to unveil' the fact that, if women are such good mimics, it is because they are not simply resorbed in this function. *They also remain elsewhere*" (76).

13. A range of more recent works relevant to a detailed examination of science fiction as a queer field includes Russ's *The Female Man* and Le Guin's *The Left Hand of Darkness*, of course; Angela Carter's *Heroes and Villains* (1969) and *The Passion of New Eve* (1977); Elizabeth Hand's *Winterlong* (1990); Emma Bull's *Bone Dance* (1991); just about everything written by Samuel R. Delany (my own favorites are "Aye, and Gomorrah . . ." [1967] and *Triton* [1976]); many of John Varley's stories and novels, including "Options" (1979) and *Steel Beach* (1991); Octavia Butler's XENOGENESIS trilogy (1987–1989); Geoff Ryman's *The Child Garden* (1988); and Eleanor Arnason's *A Woman of the Iron People* (1991) and *Ring of Swords* (1993). Ellen Kushner's *Swordspoint* (1987), Geoff Ryman's *Was* (1992), Pat Murphy's *Nadya: The Wolf Chronicles* (1996), and Candas Jane Dorsey's *Black Wine* (1997) are good examples of writing that queers fantasy.

14. The key "origin" text activated by Moore's story is Mary Shelley's *Frankenstein*. Deirdre and Maltzer consciously explore their own interactions through the roles first dramatized in Shelley's novel. Responding to Maltzer's despair at having overstepped the boundaries of human achievement—despair that, the text implies, arises from his inability to allocate any agency to Deirdre herself—Deirdre insists: "I'm not a Frankenstein monster made out of dead flesh. I'm myself—alive. You didn't create my life, you only preserved it. I'm not a robot, with compulsions built into me that I have to obey. I'm free-willed and independent, and, Maltzer—I'm human" (Moore 1975, 278–279). However, Moore's story concludes with Deirdre's own growing anxiety at being the only one of her kind: "I wish there could be others like me. I'm . . . I'm lonely, Maltzer"—to which he replies: "Then I am Frankenstein, after all" (287).

    Given Shelley's novel as intertext, it is tempting to read Deirdre as a displaced version of the monstrous bride so eagerly desired by Frankenstein's creature and aborted by Frankenstein out of fear, not only of her potential ability to procreate, but also of her potential for destruction. As Frankenstein argues to himself, the creature "had sworn to quit the neighborhood of man and hide himself in deserts, but she had not; and she, who in all probability was to become a thinking and reasoning animal, might refuse to comply with a compact made before her creation" (Shelley 1981, 150). And behind the aborted bride stands the Eve of Milton's *Paradise Lost*, itself one of the key intertexts in *Frankenstein*. As if fulfilling Frankenstein's fears, Maltzer's creation does indeed refuse any "compact" but her own with her audiences, and she insists on taking responsibility for her continuing existence.

15. One of the most detailed and useful readings I know of "The Girl Who Was Plugged In" is Scott Bukatman's discussion in *Terminal Identity: The Virtual Subject in Postmodern Science Fiction* (1993, 316–320), which situates Tiptree's story within the context of the commodifying practices of the "society of the spectacle" and contrasts its feminist critique of technotranscendence with the technological power fantasies of such later cyberpunk novels as William Gibson's *Neuromancer* (1984).

16. Tiptree, of course, was herself skilled at gender masquerade and became the subject of one of science fiction's favorite stories about writerly performance. Robert Silverberg's often quoted—and wonderfully wrongheaded—description of Tiptree's "ineluctably masculine" (1975, xii) writing has been read as a convincing demonstration that writing as a human activity is not inherently gendered. See Silverberg's "Who Is Tiptree, What Is He?" In the context of gender masquerade, see also Jane Donawerth's very useful chapter, "Cross-Dressing as a Male Narrator," in *Frankenstein's Daughters* (1997, 109–176), which examines, in some detail, the deployment of male narrators and masculine points of view by such writers as Moore and Tiptree.

17. How women writers negotiate various conventions not particularly adapted to their own skills, interests, and politics is one of the questions explored in Donawerth's

Frankenstein's Daughters, a wide-ranging overview of "women writers' responses to the defining constraints within the genre of science fiction" (1975, xvii).

Works Cited

Bukatman, Scott. *Terminal Identity: The Virtual Subject in Postmodern Science Fiction.* Durham, NC: Duke University Press, 1993.

Burwell, Jennifer. "Acting Out 'Lesbian': Monique Wittig and Immanent Critique." In *Notes on Nowhere: Feminism, Utopian Logic, and Social Transformation*, 165–202. Minneapolis: University of Minnesota Press, 1997.

Butler, Judith. *Gender Trouble: Feminism and the Subversion of Identity.* New York: Routledge, 1990.

Butler, Judith. *Bodies That Matter: On the Discursive Limits of "Sex."* New York: Routledge, 1993.

Butler, Judith. "Against Proper Objects." *differences: A Journal of Feminist Cultural Studies* (Special issue: *More Gender Trouble: Feminism Meets Queer Theory*) 6 (Summer—Fall, 1994): 1–24.

Case, Sue-Ellen. "Tracking the Vampire." *differences: A Journal of Feminist Cultural Studies* 3 (Summer 1991): 1–20.

de Lauretis, Teresa. "Queer Theory: Lesbian and Gay Sexualities: An Introduction." *differences: A Journal of Feminist Cultural Studies* 3 (Summer 1991): iii–xviii.

Diamond, Elin. "Mimesis, Mimicry, and the 'True-Real.'" *Modern Drama* 32 (March 1989): 58–72.

Doane, Mary Anne. "Film and Masquerade: Theorizing the Female Spectator." *Screen* 23 (September—October 1982): 74–87.

Donawerth, Jane. *Frankenstein's Daughters: Women Writing Science Fiction.* Syracuse, NY: Syracuse University Press, 1997.

Haraway, Donna. "A Manifesto for Cyborgs: Science, Technology, and Socialist Feminism in the 1980s." In *Coming to Terms: Feminism, Theory, Politics.* ed. Elizabeth Weed, 173–204. New York: Routledge, [1985] 1989.

Hollinger, Veronica. "'The Most Grisly Truth': Responses to the Human Condition in the Works of James Tiptree, Jr." *Extrapolation* 30 (Summer 1989): 117–132.

Irigaray, Luce. *This Sex Which Is Not One.* trans. Catherine Porter. Ithaca, NY: Cornell University Press, 1985.

Jagose, Annamarie. *Queer Theory: An Introduction.* New York: New York University Press, 1996.

Lacan, Jacques. "The Signification of the Phallus." In *Écrits.* Reprinted in *Écrits: A Selection.* trans. Alan Sheridan, 281–191. New York: Norton, [1966] 1977.

Michasiw, Kim. "Camp, Masculinity, Masquerade." *differences: A Journal of Feminist Cultural Studies* 6 (Summer–Fall 1994): 146–173.

Moore, C. L. "No Woman Born." In *The Best of C. L. Moore*, ed. Lester Del Rey, 236–288. New York: Ballantine, [1944] 1975.

Pearson, Wendy. "After the (Homo)Sexual: A Queer Analysis of Anti-Sexuality in Sheri S. Tepper's *The Gate to Women's Country.*" *Science Fiction Studies* 23 (July 1996): 199–226.

Richardson, Diane, ed. *Theorising Heterosexuality: Telling it Straight.* Bristol, PA: Open University Press, 1996.

Riviere, Joan. "Womanliness as a Masquerade." *The International Journal of Psychoanalysis* 10 (1929). Reprinted in *Formations of Fantasy*, Ed. Victor Burgin, James Donald, and Cora Kaplan, 35–44. New York: Methuen, [1929] 1986.

Russ, Joanna. "The Mystery of the Young Gentleman." In *Extra(Ordinary) People*, 63–92. New York: St. Martin's, [1982] 1984.

Russ, Joanna. "When It Changed." In *Again, Dangerous Visions*, ed. Harlan Ellison. 253–260. New York: Berkley, [1972] 1983.

Russo, Mary. *The Female Grotesque: Risk, Excess and Modernity.* New York: Routledge, 1994.

Sedgwick, Eve Kosofsky. *Epistemology of the Closet.* Berkeley: University of California Press, 1990.

Shelley, Mary. *Frankenstein.* 1818. New York: Bantam, 1981.

Silverberg, Robert. "Who Is Tiptree, What Is He?" Introduction to *Warm Worlds and Otherwise* by James Tiptree Jr.; ix–xviii New York: Ballantine, 1975.

Tatsumi, Takayuki. "Some *Real* Mothers: An Interview with Samuel R. Delany." *Science Fiction Eye* 1 (March 1988): 5–11.

Tiptree Jr., James [Alice Sheldon]. "And I Awoke and Found Me Here on the Cold Hill's Side." In *Her Smoke Rose Up Forever* 35–43. Sauk City, WI: Arkham House, [1972] 1990.

Tiptree Jr., James [Alice Sheldon]. "The Girl Who Was Plugged In." In *Her Smoke Rose Up Forever*, 44–79. Sauk City, WI: Arkham House, [1973] 1990.

Tiptree Jr., James [Alice Sheldon]. "Houston, Houston, Do You Read?" In *Her Smoke Rose Up Forever*, 168–222. Sauk City, WI: Arkham House, [1976] 1990.

Warner, Michael. "Introduction." In *Fear of a Queer Planet: Queer Politics and Social Theory.* ed. Michael Warner. vii–xxxiMinneapolis: Minnesota University Press, 1993.

Wittig, Monique. "One Is Not Born a Woman." In *The Straight Mind and Other Essays*, 9–20. Boston: Beacon Press, [1981] 1992.

16

AFTER/IMAGES OF IDENTITY: GENDER, TECHNOLOGY, AND IDENTITY POLITICS

Lisa Nakamura

In the mechanical age, technology was viewed as instrumental, a means to an end; users were figured as already formed subjects who approach it, rather than as contingent subjects who are approached and altered by it. However, this view has been radically challenged in recent years, in particular by the Internet and other telecommunications technologies, which claim to eradicate the notion of physical distance and firm boundaries not only between users and their bodies but between topoi of identity as well. I'd like to cite a striking example: the MCI television advertisement entitled "Anthem," which claims that "on the Internet," there is no gender, no age, no race, "only minds." This ad sells not only MCI Internet services but also a particular kind of *content:* the idea that getting online and becoming part of a global network will liberate the user from the body with its inconvenient and limiting attributes such as race, gender, disability, age. In a sense, it is positing a postcorporeal subjectivity, an afterimage of the body and of identity. Though "Anthem" illustrates this bracketing off of difference—racial, gendered, aged, and so forth—particularly well, it is easy to find plenty of others from other technological discourses that reveal a similar sensibility, though perhaps not in as overt a way. This commercial is, however, unusually above board in its claims that telecommunications change the nature of identity.

MCI's project links up nicely with a term from my title "After/Images of Identity." The word "after/image" implies two things to me in the context of contemporary technoscience and cyberculture.

First, the rhetorical charge of the word "after/image" conveys a sense of the millennial drive to categorize social and cultural phenomena as "Post" and "After." It puts pressure on the formerly solid and anchoring notion of "identity" as something we are fast on our way to becoming "after." This notion of the posthuman has evolved in other critical discourses of technology and the body, and is often presented in a celebratory way.[1]

The second is this: the image you see when you close your eyes after gazing at a bright light, the phantasmatic spectacle or private image-gallery that bears but a tenuous relationship to "reality." Cyberspace and the images of identity that it produces can be seen as an interior, mind's-eye projection of the "real." I'm thinking especially of screen fatigue—the crawling characters or flickering squiggles you see inside your eyelids after a lot of screen time in front of the television, CRT terminal, movie screen, any of the sources of virtual light to which we are exposed every day. To pursue this metaphor further, and join it to the first reading of the title, how have the blinding changes and dazzlingly rapid developments of technology in recent years served to project an altered image or projection of identity upon our collective consciousness? This visual metaphor of the afterimage describes a particular kind of historically and culturally grounded seeing or mis-seeing, and this is important. Ideally, it has a critical valence and can represent a way of seeing differently, of claiming the right to possess agency in our ways of seeing, of being a subject rather than an object of technology. In the bright light of contemporary technology, identity is revealed to be phantasmatic, a projection of culture and ideology. It is the product of a reflection or a deflection of prior, as opposed to after/images of identity. When we look at these rhetorics and images of cyberspace, we are seeing an after/image—both posthuman and projectionary—meaning it is the product of a vision rearranged and deranged by the virtual light of virtual things and people.

Similarly, the sign-systems associated with advertisements for reproductive and "gendered" technologies reveal, in Valerie Hartouni's words, "The fierce and frantic iteration of conventional meanings and identities in the context of technologies and techniques that render them virtually unintelligible."[2] According to this logic, stable images of identity have been replaced by "after/images." When we look at cyberspace, we see a phantasm that says more about our fantasies and structures of desire than it does about the "reality" to which it is compared by using the term "virtual reality." MCI's "Anthem," like all anthems, works on a semiotic level which establishes a sense of a national self. However, in a radically disruptive move, it simultaneously deconstructs the notion of a corporeal self anchored in familiar categories of identity. Indeed, this example of "screen fatigue" (commercials are great examples of screen fatigue because they're so fatiguing) projects a particular kind of after/image of identity.

This commercial includes gender as only one of a series of outmoded "body categories" like race, age, and so forth. The ungendered, deracinated self promised to us by MCI is freed of these troublesome categories, which have been done away with in the name of a "progressive" politics. The goal of "honoring diversity" seen on so many bumper stickers in northern California will be accomplished by eliminating diversity.

It's not just commercials that are making these postidentitarian claims. Indeed, one could say that they're following the lead or at least running in tandem with some of the growing numbers of academics who devote themselves to the cultural study of technology. For example, in *Life on the Screen* Sherry Turkle writes: "When identity was defined as unitary and solid it was relatively easy to recognize and censure deviation from a norm. A more fluid sense of self allows for a greater capacity for acknowledging diversity. It makes it easier to accept the array of our (and others') inconsistent personae—perhaps with humor, perhaps with irony. We do not feel compelled to rank or judge the elements of our multiplicity. We do not feel compelled to exclude what does not fit."[3] According to this way of thinking, regulatory and oppressive social norms such as racism and sexism are linked to users' "unitary and solid" identities offscreen. Supposedly, leaving the body behind in the service of gaining more "fluid identities" means acquiring the ability to carve out new, less oppressive norms and gaining the capacity to "acknowledge diversity" in ever more effective ways. However, is this really happening in cyberspace?

I answer this question with an emphatic "no" in an article called "Race in/for Cyberspace: Identity Tourism and Racial Passing on the Internet" (see Nakamura 1999). In it I coined the term "identity tourism" to describe a disturbing thing that I was noticing in an Internet chat community. During my fieldwork I discovered that the "after/ images" of identity that users were creating by adopting personae other than their own online often as not participated in stereotyped notions of gender and race. Rather than "honoring diversity," their performances online used race and gender as amusing prostheses that could be donned and shed without "real-life" consequences. Like tourists who become convinced that their travels have shown them real "native" life, these identity tourists often took their virtual experiences as other-gendered and other-raced avatars as a kind of lived truth.

In recent years, there has been increased academic interest in the study of identity and the ways in which it is constructed by cultural formations. Academic discourse tends to use similar terms to do this, as these paper titles from a recent conference demonstrate: "Bodies, Subjectivities, and Identities: The Politics of (Re)presentation," "The Ongoing Effects of Colonization, Cultural Subordination, and the Question of Identity," "Ethnicity and Representation in the Conjuncture of Global Capitalism," and "The Cultural Politics of National Identification in Transnational Spaces."

The rhetorical structure of these titles reveals a great deal about current assumptions regarding "identity" and how we discuss it in academe. In one of these titles the "body" is placed in a series with "subjectivities" and "identities," as if it had the same kind of abstract or at least culturally contingent status, "colonization and cultural subordination" spoken of as ongoing rather than a fait accompli, or as an artifact of the already done, the historical. Identity is being "rethought" and framed as a "question" rather than an essence or definable quantity, and what's more, in its rethinking, it is discovered to have a "cultural politics" of "national" and other "identifications." "Ethnicity and representation" are framed as if one were an effect of the other, or at least as if they had a reciprocal relationship.

These titles come from the 1998 program of the 15th Meeting of Association for Asian American Studies called "Rethinking Asian and Pacific Colonial/Postcolonial Nations, Identities, and Histories." However, these session titles could just as easily be found in an MLA panel, an American Studies panel, or any of a long list of others. Does this mean that academics are all doing the same work and calling it the same thing, thereby giving lie to the idea of disciplinary specificity, or are they all doing different things and calling it the same thing? Are these titles all deviations or challenges to the idea of specific and differentiated disciplines? What does it mean that these same words recur in similar patterns in so many academic places and occasions? What are we in technology/cyberspace studies doing? How do we define our work?

Obviously, we are doing different things, even if we are using similar titles. We are sharing some critical language but directing our attention toward different things. Cyberspace studies are still being defined, and this volume is a very important part of that exciting work. We are not looking at technology instrumentally; our sessions look very different from SEBOLD's or SEMICON's or a Java developers' meeting. It's clear that the language of critical theory is a big part of this act of definition and interrogation. This question of identity, subjectivity, the body, transnationality is being looked at from all sides—ethnic studies, women's studies, literary studies, historical studies, sociological studies, and cultural studies. Just as the cyborg, that Harawayan avatar of postmodern identity, is a hybrid of different parts, machine and human, so is cyberspace studies itself a hybrid Frankenstein of sorts. These titles use punctuation like slashes, parentheses, scare quotes, and hyphenations to create pieced together, fragmented titles that reflect the hybrid, cyborglike nature of fields like our own. Transposed, retrofitted, poached, and repurposed categories are useful to talk about cyberspace studies, since our discourse is still in process, but there can be translation errors, to use some geek jargon.

Critical theory itself as a technology or machine that produces a particular kind of discourse, and I'd like to conduct a discursive experiment by poaching a term from nineteenth-century print technology; that term is "stereotype."

The word *stereotype* is itself an example of machine language; the first stereotype was a mechanical device that could reproduce images relatively cheaply, quickly, and in mass quantities. Now that image-reproducing machines like the Internet are faster, cheaper, and more efficient than ever before, how does that machine language translate into critical terms? Might we call new formulations of machine-linked identity "cyber-types"? This is a clunky term; in hacker speak it would be called a "kludge" or "hack" because it's an improvised, spontaneous, seat-of-the-pants way of getting something done. (Critical theory is a machine that is good at manufacturing linguistic kludges and hacks). I'd like to introduce it because it acknowledges that identity has indeed become, in some important sense, "after," but that its after/images are still "typed," still mired in oppressive roles even if the "body" has been left behind or bracketed. I pose it as a corrective to the disturbingly utopian strain I see embodied in the MCI commercial in particular and in most representations of the Internet in general. Chosen identities enabled by technology such as online avatars, cosmetic and transgender surgery and body modifications, and other cyberprostheses are not breaking the mold of unitary identity, but rather are shifting identity into the realm of the "virtual," a place not without its own laws and hierarchies. "Fluid" selves are no less subject to cultural hegemonies, rules of conduct, and regulating cultural norms than are "solid" ones.

While telecommunications and medical technologies can challenge some gender and racial stereotypes, they produce and reflect them as well. Cybertypes of the biotechnologically enhanced or perfected woman and of the Internet's invisible minorities, who can log onto the Net and be taken for "white," participate in an ideology of liberation from marginalized and devalued bodies. This kind of technology's greatest promise to us is to eradicate Otherness, to create a kind of better living through chemistry, so to speak. Images of science freeing women from their aging bodies, which make it more difficult to conceive children and ward off cellulite, men from the curse of hair loss, and minorities online from the stigma of their race since no one can see them, reinforces a postbody ideology that reproduces the assumptions of the old one. In an example of linguistic retrofitting, I've termed this phenomenon an example of the "meet the old boss, same as the new boss" product line). In other words, machines that offer identity prostheses to redress the burdens of physical "handicaps" such as age, gender, and race produce cybertypes that look remarkably like racial and gender stereotypes. My research on cross-racial impersonation in an online community reveals that when users are free to choose their own race, all were assumed to be white. And many of those who adopted nonwhite personae turned out to be white male users masquerading as exotic samurai and horny geishas.[4]

Of course, this kind of vertiginous identity-play that produces and reveals cyber-typing is not the fault of or even primarily an effect of technology. Microsoft's corporate slogan "Where do you want to go today?," another example of the discourse of technological liberation, situates the agency directly where it belongs: with the user.

Though computer memory modules double in speed every couple of years, users are still running operating systems that reflect phantasmatic visions of race and gender. In the end, despite academic and commercial postidentitarian discourses, it does come down to bodies: bodies with or without access to the Internet, telecommunications, and computers, and the cultural capital necessary to use them; bodies with or without access to basic healthcare, let alone high-tech pharmaceuticals or expensive forms of elective surgery. This is the paradox: In order to think rigorously, humanely, and imaginatively about virtuality and the posthuman, it is absolutely necessary to ground critique in the lived realities of humans, in all their particularity and specificity. The nuanced realities of virtuality—racial, gendered, Othered—live in the body, and though science is producing and encouraging different readings and revisions of the body, it is premature to throw it away just yet, particularly since so much postcolonial, political, and feminist critique stems from it.

The vexed position of women's bodies and raced bodies in feminist and postcolonial theory has been a subject of intense debate for at least the past twenty years. While feminism and postcolonial studies must, to some extent, buy into the notion of there being such a thing as a "woman" or a "person of color" in order to be coherent, there are also ways in which "essentialism is a trap,"[5] to quote Gayatri Spivak. Since definitions of what counts as a woman or a person of color can be shifting and contingent upon hegemonic forces, essentialism can prove to be untenable. Indeed, modern body technologies are partly responsible for this: Gender reassignment surgery and cosmetic surgery can make these definitions all the blurrier. In addition, attributing essential qualities to women and people of color can reproduce a kind of totalizing of identity that reproduces the old sexist and racist ideologies. However, theorists such as Donna Haraway, who radically question the critical gains to be gotten from conceptualizing "woman" as anchored to the body, take great pains to emphasize that she does not "know of any time in history when there was greater need for political unity to confront effectively the dominations of 'race,' 'gender,' 'sexuality,' and 'class.'"[6] Though she replaces the formerly essential concept of "woman" with that of the "cyborg," a hybrid of machine and human, she also acknowledges that feminist politics must continue "through coalition—affinity, not identity."[7] Both she and Spivak write extensively about the kinds of strategic affinities that can and must be built between and among "women" (albeit in quotation marks), racial and other minorities, and other groups similarly constructed as Others.

Is it a coincidence that just as feminist and subaltern politics—built around affinities as well as identities—are acquiring some legitimacy and power in the academy (note the increasing numbers of courses labeled "multicultural," "ethnic," "feminist," "postcolonial" in university course schedules) that MCI and other teletechnology corporations are staking out their positions as forces that will free us from race and gender? Barbara Christian, in her 1986 essay "'The Race for Theory': Gender and Theory: Dialogues on Feminist Criticism" saw a similar kind of "coincidence" in regard to the increasing dominance of literary theory as a required and validated activity for American academics. She asserts that the technology of literary theory was made deliberately mystifying and dense to exclude minority participation; this exclusionary language "surfaced, interestingly enough, just when the literature of peoples of color, of black women, of Latin Americans, of Africans, began to move 'to the center."[8] The user-unfriendly language of literary theory, with its poorly designed interfaces, overly elaborate systems, and other difficulties of access happened to arise during the historical moment in which the most vital and vibrant literary work was being produced by formerly "peripheral" minority writers.

Perhaps I am like Christian, who calls herself "slightly paranoid" in her essay (it has been well documented that telecommunications technologies encourage paranoia), but I too wonder whether MCI's claims are not slightly too well timed. Learning curves for Net literacy are notoriously high; those of us who maintain class Listservs and Web sites and MUDs learn that to our rue. Indeed, it took me a few years of consistent effort, some expensive equipment, and much expert assistance to feel anything less than utterly clueless in cyberspace. Rhetorics that claim to remedy and erase gender and racial injustices and imbalances through expensive and difficult-to-learn technologies such as the Internet entirely gloss over this question of access, which seems to me *the* important question. And it seems unlikely that this glossing over is entirely innocent. Cybertyping and other epiphenomena of high technologies in the age of the Internet is partly the result of restricted access to the means of production—in this case, the means of production of the "fluid identities" celebrated by so much theory and commerce today.

Increasing numbers of racial minorities and women are acquiring access to the Internet: a hopeful sign indeed. Though minority groups are not yet well represented as producers and authors of the Net's texts, their position as consumers on the Net represents at the least the beginnings of meaningful participation. Ideally, this equalizing of access to the dominant form of information technology in our time might result in a more diverse cyberspace, one that doesn't seek to elide or ignore difference as an outmoded souvenir of the body. Indeed, sites such as ivillage.com, Oxygen.com, Salon.com's Hip Mama webpages, and NetNoir (which contains content specifically geared to women and African Americans) indicate a shift in the Internet's content, which reflects a partial bridging of the digital divide. As women of color acquire an increasing presence online, their particular interests that spring directly from gender and racial identifications—that is to say, those identities associated with a physical body of-fline—are being addressed.

Unfortunately, as can be seen from the high, and ultimately dashed, feminist hopes that new media such as the Oxygen Network would express women's concerns in a po-litically progressive and meaningful way, gender and race can just as easily be coopted by the e-marketplace. Commercial sites such as these tend to view women and minori-ties primarily as potential markets for advertisers and merchants rather than as "coali-tions." Opportunities for political coalition building between women and people of color are often subverted in favor of e-marketing and commerce. (NetNoir is a notable exception to this trend. It is also the oldest of these identitarian Web sites, and thus was able to form its mission, content, and "look and feel" prior to the gold rush of dot.com commerce that brought an influx of investment capital, and consequent pressure to con-form to corporate interests, to the Web.) Nonetheless, this shift in content which specifically addresses women and minorities, either as markets[9] or as political entities, does acknowledge that body-related identities such as race and gender are not yet as fluid (and thus disposable) as much cybertheory and commercial discourse would like to see them.

However, such is the stubborn power of cybertyping that even when substantial numbers of minorities do have the necessary computer hardware and Internet access to deploy themselves "fluidly" online, they are often rudely yanked back to the realities of racial discrimination and prejudice. For example, on March 13, 2000, "in what its lawyers called 'the first civil rights class action litigation against an Internet company,'"[9] the Equal Rights Center, a Washington-based civil rights group, and two African-American plaintiffs are suing Kozmo for racial 'redlining' because of what they believe is a pattern of those neighborhoods not being served."[10] Kozmo.com, an online service that delivers convenience foods and products, claims to deliver only to "zip codes that have the highest rates of Internet penetratation and usage,"[11] however, the company's judgment of what constitutes an Internet-penetrated zip code follows racial lines as well. African American Washingtonians such as James Warren and Winona Lake used their Internet access to order goods from Kozmo, only to be told that their zip codes aren't served by the company. Kozmo.com also refuses to deliver to a neighborhood of Wash-ington, DC, occupied primarily by upper-class African Americans with equal "Internet penetration" as white neighborhoods.[12] It seems that these African American Internet users possessed identities online that too firmly moored them to their raced bodies to participate in the utopian ideal of the Internet as a democratizing disembodied space. Unfortunately, it would appear that online identities can never be truly fluid if you live in the wrong zip code.

As the Kozmo.com example shows, actual hardware access is a necessary but not sufficient component of online citizenship. All of the things that citizenship implies—freedom to participate in community on an equal basis; access to national and local infrastructures; the ability to engage in discourse and commerce, cyber and otherwise, with other citizens—are abrogated by racist politics disguised as corporate market-research. This example of online "redlining" or "refusing to sell something to someone due to age, race or location" puts a new spin on cybertyping. Rather than being left behind, bracketed, or "radically questioned" the body—the raced, gendered, classed body—gets "outed" in cyberspace just as soon commerce and discourse come into play. Fluid identities aren't much use to those whose problems exist strictly (or even mostly) in the real world if they lose all their currency in the realm of the real.

It is common to see terms such as "the body," "woman," and "race" in quotation marks in much academic writing today. The after/images of identity that the Internet shows us similarly attempt to bracket the gendered and raced body in the name of creating a democratic utopia in cyberspace. However, postmortems pronounced over "the body" are premature, as the Kozmo.com lawsuit shows. My hope is that these discourses of cyberenabled fluidity and liberation do not grow so insular and self-absorbed as to forget this.

Acknowledgments

I would like to thank the Alanna Thain, Desireé Martín, and Susan Brook, who organized the "Discipline and Deviance: Genders, Technologies, Machines" conference at Duke University in 1998. An earlier version of this essay was delivered as a plenary address at this conference. I would especially like to thank Alanna Thain, who came up with the title for this piece. Thanks also to Terry Senft and Wahneema Lubbiano, who were my respondents at the conference.

Notes

1. See *Posthuman Bodies*, ed. Judith Halberstam and Ira Livingston (Indiana University Press, 1995), as well as Scott Bukatman's *Terminal Identity: The Virtual Subject in Postmodern Fiction* (Duke University Press, 1998).
2. Valerie Hartouni, "Containing Women: Reproductive Discourse in the 1980s," in *Technoculture*, ed. Constance Penley and Andrew Ross (Minneapolis: University of Minnesota Press, 1991), 51.
3. Sherry Turkle, *Life on the Screen: Identity in the Age of the Internet* (New York: Simon and Schuster, 1995), 261.

4. Lisa Nakamura, "Race in/for Cyberspace: Identity Tourism and Racial Passing on the Internet" in *CyberReader*, ed. Victor Vitanza, 2d ed. (New York: Allyn and Bacon, 1999), 447.

5. Gayatri Spivak, *In Other Worlds: Essays in Cultural Politics* (New York and London: Routledge, 1998), 89.

6. Donna Haraway, *Simians, Cyborgs, and Women: The Reinvention of Nature* (New York and London: Routledge, 1991), 157.

7. Donna Haraway, *Simians, Cyborgs, and Women: The Reinvention of Nature* (New York and London: Routledge, 1991), 155.

8. Barbara Christian, "The Race for Theory," in *Feminist Literary Theory: A Reader*, ed. Mary Eagleton, 2d ed. (London: Blackwell, 1996), 278.

9. Since the incredible dominance of the Internet by the World Wide Web in the mid-nineties, it has consistently supported this construction of women AS bodies. The saying that the Internet is 90 percent pornography and advertising, while it may be a slight exaggeration, gestures toward the Internet's role as an extremely efficient purveyor of exploitative images of women. Similarly, the Internet's current bent toward merchandising and selling online constructs women as either "markets" or more commonly as scantily clad figures in commercials for products.

10. Frances Katz, "Racial-Bias Suit Filed Against Online Delivery Service Kozmo.com." *KRTBN Knight-Ridder Tribune Business News: The Atlanta Journal and Constitution-Georgia*, April 14, 2000. Online.

11. Martha Hamilton, "Web Retailer Kozmo Accused of Redlining: Exclusion of D.C. Minority Areas Cited." *The Washington Post*, April 14, 2000. Available at <http://www.washingtonpost.com/wp-dyn/articles/A9719-2000Apr13.html>.

12. Snigdha Prakash, "All Things Considered," NPR broadcast, May 2, 2000.

Works Cited

"Anthem." Television commercial, produced by Messner Vetere Berger McNamee Schmetterer for MCI, 1997.

Christian, Barbara. "The Race for Theory." In *Feminist Literary Theory: A Reader*, ed. Mary Eagleton, 2d ed., 174–280. London: Blackwell, 1996.

Hamilton, Martha. "Web Retailer Kozmo Accused of Redlining: Exclusion of D.C. Minority Areas Cited." *The Washington Post*. April 14, 2000. Online. Available at <http://www.washintonpost.com/wp-dyn/articles/A9719-2000Apr13.html>.

Haraway, Donna. *Simians, Cyborgs, and Women: The Reinvention of Nature*. New York and London: Routledge, 1991.

Hartouni, Valerie. "Containing Women: Reproductive Discourse in the 1980s." *Technoculture*, ed. Constance Penley and Andrew Ross, 27–56. Minneapolis: University of Minnesota Press, 1991.

Katz, Frances. "Racial-Bias Suit Filed Against Online Delivery Service Kozmo.com." *KRTBN Knight-Ridder Tribune Business News: The Atlanta Journal and Constitution-Georgia.* April 14, 2000. Online.

Nakamura, Lisa. "Race in/for Cyberspace: Identity Tourism and Racial Passing on the Internet." In *CyberReader,* ed. Victor Vitanza, 2d ed. New York: Allyn and Bacon, 1999.

Prakash, Snigdha. "All Things Considered." NPR broadcast. May 2, 2000.

Spivak, Gayatri. *In Other Worlds: Essays in Cultural Politics.* New York and London: Routledge, 1998.

Turkle, Sherry. *Life on the Screen: Identity in the Age of the Internet.* New York: Simon and Schuster, 1995.

Bernadette Wegenstein

> To speak-woman is not the same as speaking of woman. It is not about producing
> a discourse of which woman would be the object or the subject. That said, *speaking-*
> *woman*, one may attempt to make room for the "other" as feminine.[1]
>
> —*Luce Irigaray*, Ce sexe qui n'en est pas un

Much has been written recently about cyborgs, cyberspace, and virtual worlds. Over the
last decades, for instance, scholars within the fields of critical theory and cultural studies have reflected intensively on the consequences and impacts of encounters between
humans and new technologies.[2] According to some, the meeting of humans and machines has produced new subjectivities and identities rooted in the social practices related to computing.[3] For others, the question of gender in the light of new technologies
has been central.[4] This chapter, though, is concerned not so much with the critical interpretation of cyberspace and the gendered cyborg, but with the very representation of
Woman and, more particularly, the discourse surrounding female heroines in the most
recent manifestations of cyberfiction in both film and literature. The approach to this
question will be a psychoanalytical one.

The first section presents the theoretical framework of the question of Woman as
discussed in French psychoanalytic feminist theory; the splitting of Woman and its representation in cyberpunk fiction and film will from this point on be at the center of the
theoretical discussion. In the next section, I situate the discussion of the representation
of Woman within the historical framework of a very brief history of science fiction and
cyberpunk, passing immediately thereafter to an examination of the changing role of
heroines in cyberfiction over the last decades, "from oppressed heroines of the cyber-
past to ass-kicking cyberqueens." After the theoretical and historical positioning of
the question of Woman in cyberfiction, I turn to the examination of three concrete
examples of cyberpunk: the recent Hollywood success story of the reality-versus-

virtuality question in the film, *The Matrix*[5]; a best-selling novel set in a religious cyberenvironment at the turn of the millennium, *Messi@h*[6]; and the wild, cyberpunk, science-fiction novel *Proxies*.[7] All of these narratives will be compared and discussed in the concluding section, in which I establish and problematize the relation of these narratives to Lacanian and feminist theory.[8]

Psychoanalysis and the Question of Woman

"Sexual difference means neither sex nor gender" and "the body is neither a natural fact nor a cultural construction" are claims, typical of contemporary psychoanalytic discourse, that would seem to situate psychoanalysis outside the Nature-versus-Nurture debate. Indeed, psychoanalysis treats the body neither as a marker of biological destiny nor as a purely historical phenomenon, such that it is reducible to a description neither in the terms of biological essentialism nor in those of social construction. What is preliminary, rather, to psychoanalysis as regards the body—in the aftermath of the linguistic reinterpretation of Freud's work in Lacan—is the issue of *language*.

In this postlinguistic-turn view, psychoanalysis becomes a theory of the relation and intersections between nature and culture as analyzable in the organism's relation to language, an account, in Freud's words, of the processes by which "the material conditions" of the body "are profoundly altered."[9] The material conditions—the organism—are altered through the acquisition of language. But what does "language" mean in this context? Is it the speech-act, the *parole* in the Saussurian sense, that is, the actual spoken words? And if so, spoken by whom? By a specific individual, by many individuals, hence an idiom? Or does language rather refer to the Saussurian *langue*, the system of a specific language, its grammar and semantics?[10]

But for psychoanalysis it is neither the *langue* nor the *parole* in their separate systems that are relevant. Language is seen rather as the acquisition of a means of symbolic communication (the symbolic order) that goes hand in hand with the formation of the self, and with the separation from the mother and the outer world: This is the famous "mirror stage," described by Lacan as taking place between the sixth and eighteenth months, in which the child (mis)recognizes its own autonomous self in a reflected image. It is exactly here that the body comes into play, in that the acquisition of language goes along with the acquisition of a body, a gendered body.

Psychoanalysis distinguishes terminologically between the organism and the body. The organism is hereby the given natural factor, whereas the body is something that can only be *acquired through language*, through the use of symbols and words (in the realm of the symbolic order) to express a given individual's bodily constitution. This means that, in order to *become a body*, a process of denaturalization is necessary: The body has to become autonomous from its original "organ-ization." The thinking of gender, however, and what it means to acquire a gendered body, requires further effort. If the gendered body is neither a cultural construction nor a biological phenomenon, what is it?

Judith Butler has the most convincing answer to this question, deconstructing the very categories of sex and gender by pointing out that sex itself is already a gendered category, and that there is no genderless body to begin with: "Gender ought not to be conceived merely as the cultural inscription of meaning on a pregiven sex (a juridical conception); gender must also designate the very apparatus of production whereby the sexes themselves are established. As a result, gender is not to culture as sex is to nature; gender is also the discursive/cultural means by which 'sexed nature' or 'a natural sex' is produced and established as 'prediscursive,' prior to culture, a politically neutral surface *on which* culture acts."[11]

In order to grasp the "discursive and cultural means" that are produced by a certain time and political environment, the only thing we can do to confirm our standpoint is to look at the cultural production of gender itself, hence, at the cultural articulation and writing of—in the case of our given analysis—Woman and, more specifically, (the) cyberheroine in current cybernarratives. The representation of these women can be interpreted, then, as an example of the acquired female body, the embodiment of femininity, in the light of the zeitgeist at the turn of the millennium.

Let us now consider the intrinsic possibilities of a cognitive differentiation between Man and Woman in their antonimical and oppositional enunciation-structures.[12] This cognitive differentiation shall be referred to as sexuation—how the process of becoming a woman or a man can be described in its historical and cultural significance. In his seminar XX, *Encore*, Jacques Lacan advances a model of sexuation that has provoked an almost overwhelming theoretical response, both affirmative and critical. It goes without saying that this theory cannot be ignored when dealing with gender issues and their representations.

Lacan's controversial standpoint is that *La Femme* as a totality, a universal figure, does not exist, because she is "pas toute" (not all). His famous diagram of structural gender positions, which I am not reproducing in its mathematical form, can be paraphrased as follows.[13] On the male side, all men are castrated, but there is One who is not. This primal or universal man (the father) is structurally equated to the position of the phallus (the law). The female side of Lacan's diagram is formulated only through negation and the lack of a universal quantifier "all": There is no woman who is not castrated, but not all of a woman is subject to castration. In this lies the crucial point of femininity according to Lacan—namely, that it is a sexuality, "not all" of which is inscribed within the law.

But with this the diagram is not yet finished. The real importance lies in the structure of desire—for Lacan the fundament of the human psyche—situated beneath the female and male positions described above. The male side, the "normal" one—Lacan calls it "nor-mâle"—is represented by a unidirectional arrow from the divided subject (for it lacks something that it is always in search of) toward the object of fantasy (the famous *objet a*). The female structure of desire, on the other hand, is double-layered, which is the source of its importance for our current analysis. The first formula links The Woman to the phallus. This is the structure of the *masquerade*, as Lacan puts it, in which Woman plays the role of the phallus in relation to the gaze (cf. Freud's "feminine narcissism"). The woman participates in a fiction of femininity that corresponds to the masculine fantasy. There is, however, another way of reading this first formula of The Woman in relation to the phallic position. Instead of her "being the phallus," the woman may be seen as "having the phallus," a position that can be associated with maternity.[14]

The second structure of female desire takes up the extent to which Woman is outside the law. This is where Lacan situates the question of "feminine jouissance" and "femininity," of that "something" of woman that escapes castration, that stands as an exception to the law.[15] This is the only position of the entire diagram of sexuation that is not defined in relation to masculinity and male jouissance. It is, therefore, a position *outside language*. This is what Lacan calls the jouissance beyond the phallus.[16]

Scholarly reaction to this radical positioning of Woman in Lacan's theory has been very strong. Generally speaking, we can say that French feminist thinkers have tended to support or at least adapt this theory to their own purposes. Woman as such is "this sex which is not one," as the French psychoanalyst and feminist philosopher Luce Irigaray has formulated in her homonymous book. In her work, Irigaray faces the problem of enunciating the nonexistence of the category of Woman while at the same time "speaking-woman," an act of speaking in which, in her words, "one may attempt to make room for the 'other' as feminine."[17] Underscoring the internally differentiated nature of Woman as a category of knowledge, Irigaray must recognize her own historical determination, the fact that one *is* one's past, and that this past has been so far a patriarchal one to which she as a woman has had only limited access. A redefinition of womanhood is therefore not possible by merely proposing an alternative to a patriarchal pattern. This would mean reformulating the patriarchal structure with female protagonists, which would be nothing but a reinscription of the masculine pattern in the "dominant phallic economy" or within the logic of "phallocratism."[18] One way or the other, according to Irigaray, one is trapped in a "prison of male gender." Femininity is therefore a point of linguistic absence, the unmarked sex.

Following Lacan, who said that woman only figures in the sexual relation as mother,[19] the linguist and psychoanalyst Julia Kristeva claims that we cannot say of a *woman* what she *is*, except when referring to the mother, the only woman, the only "other sex" we know.[20] Studying religious and laic representations of motherhood throughout the history of Western art and culture, Kristeva argues that in these representations it is not so much the mother that is idealized but the relation to the mother and, hence, it is in fact the idealization of a primary narcissism and not of motherhood itself that is at stake. This "fantasy of primary narcissism,"[21] the maternal, is the only form of femininity that, according to Kristeva, Christianity has made of Woman. It is, hence, the reabsorption of the feminine in the maternal that accounts for the female mark of gender.

It is interesting how the markedness of gender has changed its positioning throughout the recent history of feminist studies. Earlier feminists of the twentieth century like Simone de Beauvoir and Monique Wittig[22] opted for the exact opposite interpretation of the markedness of gender—namely, that not the male sex is marked, but the female one. Wittig explains that we can only speak of *one* gender, that is the feminine, for the masculine is not the masculine, but the general.[23] What is held in common by both positions, however, is the notion that the body comes into being through the marks of gender.

Lacan's psychoanalytical theory of sexuation and its appropriation by feminism is relevant for our purposes insofar as this chapter is concerned with the question of markedness and the double structure of desire in the problematic position of The Woman: on the one hand the phallic masquerade, the woman in the vest of the universal male gender role, on the other the exception to the law, the multiple faced woman. In this well-catalogued duality, Woman is the gender of multiple incarnations, vests, and personalities. Multiplicity, marginality, waste, excess, as Irigaray puts it, are *the* examples of what has been made of Woman. The decisive question here is whether this be her essence, or an effect of her historical positioning. By deconstructing the categories of sex and gender in the way that Butler suggests, what we can say is that, be it biological essence or historical construction, the only difference we can think is the difference in *language*, not just literal written or spoken language, but any semiotic system that is involved in the depiction of femininity. The following reflection on some concrete texts from the genre of cyberfiction should give us some new input regarding these crucial questions. We are looking at female cyberheroines described both in narratives of male and female writers, and in the filmic world of cyberpunk. Let me first define those new genres in the context of a brief (probably the briefest ever) history of science fiction.

From Science Fiction to Cyberpunk

Science fiction, realized in literature and in film, may well be *the* genre of the twentieth century. Much has been said to classify this genre, but what counts here is that writing and imagining science-fiction worlds is not so much a question of inventing these as new (and from the perspective of the recipient often absurd) as it is a question of depicting and capturing a prevailing zeitgeist and that of worlds to come. We know that the famous writers of the classical period of science fiction from Jules Vernes to Philip K. Dick not only described possible futuristic societies but somehow predicted them, and through their culturally intuitive imaginative stories might have even created them.[24] In that sense science fiction, perhaps more than any other current genre, expresses the contingencies of a time.

Cyberpunk is officially inaugurated with William Gibson's 1984 novel *Neuromancer* and his invention of the term "cyberspace," but it has its roots already in earlier films such as *Videodrome* (David Cronenberg), *Blade Runner* (Ridley Scott), and *TRON* (Steven Lisberger), all from 1982. Bukatman describes the genre as "the inheritor of two traditions within SF, "hard" science fiction of vast technical detail and extrapolative power [. . .], the other tradition from which cyberpunk derived its form was the openly experimental writing of the (again so-called) New Wave of science fiction writers which arose in the 1960s."[25]

The so-called New Wave was created by authors such as Samuel Delany, J. G. Ballard, and Michael Moorcook, who "allegorized the exhaustion of the 'real'—as represented by the dichotomous terms of redemption and damnation—through a baroque and overelaborate writing that emphasizes a pure materiality."[26] Whereas the New Wave emphasized the novelty of contemporary subjectivities in virtuality and "inner space," as informed by the experience of the computer age, cyberpunk is not "impressed" with these novelties anymore. The sensations lived in cyberspace are described just as profoundly as those of "real" space. "Real" and "virtual" experiences are, hence, narratologically equivalent, such that the reader often does not know "where" he or she actually is—in "reality" or in "virtuality." In this situation, fiction loses its meaning because "digital" and "real" experiences are fused together in one new way of describing the outer world, and what counts now is to do justice to a decentered experience of self, be it "here" or "there." For its realist approach to description, cyberpunk has been related to the American genre of neorealism:[27]

Cyberpunk might initially appear to be science fiction's version of neorealism, a little late arriving on the scene, with its cult of hipness, brand names, and designer drugs; its less imaginative extrapolation into the near rather than the far future; its morally numb characters drifting emotionlessly through wasted cityspaces that for them possess no inherent value or meaning; its spare and elliptical dialogue usually cynical and ironic in nature. Clearly, these similarities exist and are worth exploring, but a fundamental difference in vision separates neorealism from cyberpunk. Neorealism ultimately expresses a conservative narrative and metaphysical consciousness; cyberpunk in its purest form expresses a profoundly radical one.[28]

However close one wants to draw the parallels, one thing is for sure: Cyberpunk is a genre that is drifting away from a classical postmodern style of pastiche toward "science fiction's metaphysical and narrative equivalent of neorealism."[29]

Beginning in the 1980s, cyberpunk has created a whole new idiolect that reflects the language of the computer terminals, Web sites, and MUDs populated by multiple selves. The novels of Neal Stephenson are emblematic of this kind of a language, the language of a new computer generation of cyberpunks who are characterized by Bruce Sterling as follows: "The cyberpunks are perhaps the first SF generation to grow up not only within the literary tradition of science fiction but in a truly science-fictional world. For them, the techniques of classical 'hard SF'—extrapolation, technological literacy— are not just literary tools but an aid to daily life"[30]

What matters here in relation to the creation of new languages in and for cyberspace is that, simultaneously with their emergence, a new illiteracy arises: The reader is helpless in confrontation with the character's competence and mastery of cyberspace [31] as a result of being inundated with neologisms describing new practices; the general feeling one is left with is disorientation.

Cyberpunk consists also in a fusion and interference of codes, from the musical codes of synth-rock and heavy metal to the film languages of film-noir and private-eye fiction. The filmic settings attribute to cyberpunk a dark, pragmatic, and paranoid urbanism, an underworld of social marginality, in other words, a dystopian world.[32] Cyberpunk has been characterized as "cynical realism,"[33] its cynicism lying in the fact that we cannot distinguish between "real life" and "virtual life," between a "cyber" hero/ine and a "real" hero/ine.

Cyberpunk is also a prominent genre in current filmic narrative. In Kathryn Bigelow's *Strange Days*[34] (1995) for example, during the last days before the big millennium party in the postmodern megacity setting of Los Angeles, we are witness to an ethical controversy concerning the circulation on the black market of memory-CDs of snuff films. These memory-CDs, that is, the memories of other people, are not downloaded directly into the brain (as in newer cyberpunk films such as *The Matrix* or *eXistenZ* [35]) but are rather visualized through a special device mounted on one's head, which allows one to experience firsthand such forbidden actions as murder and rape. The other film genre that mostly represents cyberpunk is the animated comics exemplified by the Japanese Mangafilms[36] and technothrillers like S. Tsukamoto's *Tetsuo I: The Iron Man* (1989) and *Tetsuo II: Body Hammer* (1992).

Cyberpunk as defined above has dealt especially with the new possibilities of humanity in virtual worlds. Topics such as the virtual world parallel to the real world and the merging of the human with the machine[37] have triggered much discussion and given new input to both critical theory and fiction itself.[38] One of the most important topics evolving from these discussions around new definitions of humanity (i.e., "posthumanity") regards the issue of the gendered body. Earlier we established that the body comes into being through its marks of gender. Cyberfiction seems to "avoid" the question of male versus female marks of gender by presenting a hybrid body in a transgendered world of multiplicity: "While his hands were disconnecting the probes, he glanced at his naked body, at the high, round breasts and the broadened hips, the triangle of pubic hair with no male genitalia. It shocked him. He—no, *she*—had faced into a gender blender. This could prove interesting."[39]

Despite the fact that, on the superficial level of the narration, through the "gender-blender" effect the question of markedness is avoided, the deep structure often shows an even more traditional gender distribution. The conservatism here is that Woman is always split by her representation in current cybernarratives: The actantial[40] opposition of ass-kicker versus sidekick is added to a litany that already included virgin versus whore and maternity versus femininity. It is precisely because of these gender issues—from the (post)gendered cyborg to questions of embodiment and disembodiment of gender—that the genre of cyberpunk is most relevant for the current discussion.

From Oppressed Heroines of the Cyberpast to Ass-Kicking Cyberqueens

Whether or not science fiction and cyberpunk predict our futures, they are certainly informative about our present, as I already argued at the beginning of this chapter. In that sense, we can find discussions concerning feminism, the role of Woman, and other current debates reflected in those current cybernarratives that emphasize heroines as opposed to heroes.

If we look at the historical evolution of the actantial status of female heroines, we can claim without hesitation that earlier examples of science fiction do not grant to the heroine the importance that current cyberpunk fiction does. On the contrary, many examples of science fiction are notably antiwoman. For example, an almost historic science-fiction story by Bernard Wolfe, *Limbo*,[41] according to one scholar "along with

Brave New World and *1984* one of the great dystopian novels of the century,"[42] is at least equally notable for its misogyny.[43] Against this historical predisposition, it has been said that there is a preference for the depiction of female heroines in recent cybernarratives. By analyzing the actantial status of these female "heroine-protagonists,"[44] we find not only that these are heroines in a phallic masquerade—and therefore engendering a male role—but rather that their narrative development is really a double-layered one: although they are "male" in their gendered appearances (not only because of an androgynous look, but also and especially for their typically "male acts," such as rescuing others through their strength and courage), at the same time they evince the "otherness" of woman that escapes castration, which has been theorized by feminism since Lacan. In this second sense the woman is aware of her being-as-other, an awareness to which maleness is constitutionally blind. In other words, the cyberheroines in question act and are acted upon in two not only different but at times even opposite ways.

The first model is an apparently new one, in which the heroine is the real hero in (cyber)space over her male counterpart,[45] an intelligent computer genius (e.g., Allegra Geller in *eXistenZ*), physically well trained and audacious (Ellen Ripley in the *Aliens* series[46]), simultaneously sexually appealing and martially adept (e.g., Trinity in *The Matrix*); or an indestructible female cyberprotagonist of synthetic flesh (e.g., Major Motoko Kusanagi in M. Oshii's animated science-fiction thriller *Ghost in the Shell*). In other words, a female version of the *Übermensch*. In the second model, on the other hand, we encounter some of these heroines in a traditional actantial stance, namely, as "adjutants"—to put it in Proppian/Greimasian terms, or sidekicks, in the language of popular culture—to the main male protagonists in the pursuit of their narrative goals. Let us now look more closely at three examples of this dynamic from recent cyberfiction: *The Matrix*, *Messi@h*, and *Proxies*.

Two Worlds and the Love of the One

The Matrix is not only the most emblematic example of the kind of cyberfiction in question, but it is also an extremely imaginative realization of the typical elements associated with cyberspace. The plot can be described as follows: The hero, Neo, is persecuted by evil looking and behaving agents who are out to hinder his access to "something" (only later do we learn that this something is nothing less than the salvation of the real world). Neo's female counterpart, the ass-kicking cyberheroine Trinity (whom we have already witnessed performing mind-bending martial arts moves on dim-witted police officers in the opening scene), entices him to join her with the promise of revealing to him the answer to the question that is on everyone's mind, but that no one dares to ask out loud: What is the Matrix (.com)?[47] She takes him to the headquarters of the mysterious Morpheus, an impressive and authoritarian man who informs Neo about the political circumstances and reality of the Matrix, and why he is persecuted for being "the only one who can rescue the world." What he reveals is that the real world has been taken over by artificial intelligences that are using the bodies of human beings as batteries to power their machine existence (an agent refers to Neo at one point as "Coppertop"). In order to keep the minds busy while the bodies are plugged into their power plants, the machines have developed a true opiate of the masses, a virtual world in which the entirety of humanity experiences itself as living real, autonomous lives in a late-twentieth-century industrialized world. This is the Matrix: reality.

Morpheus offers Neo a choice of pills to swallow, one of which will put him to sleep, allowing the rebels to return him to his normal, everyday life in the Matrix, the other a "neuro-inhibitor" intended to fight the effects of the Matrix and return his consciousness to reality—a reality in which he is a shaved naked body suspended in a bath of goo and implanted with metal tubes. Once his consciousness has been released from the Matrix, Neo joins a ragged band of rebels who fight against the dominance of the artificial intelligences on the battlefield of the Matrix, plugging themselves into it in order, bit by bit, to chip away at the illusory world holding humanity in bondage.

Morpheus prepares Neo by teaching him martial arts and giving him lectures of a curiously religious or even messianic nature, in which Neo learns that the salvation of humanity depends on the discovery of "The One," whose existence has been predicted by the Oracle. Morpheus is convinced that Neo is the One (an anagram of his name), but it turns out that Neo is not yet, in fact, the One, and that something is missing. This missing link, as we find out, is the love confession of a beautiful woman, Trinity. Neo can become the One only retroactively, as a result of his female counterpart Trinity "choosing" him as her object of love. Only at this time can he pursue the ultimate objective, announced by the Oracle, of rescuing mankind from a dark, fascistic cyberworld.

In *The Matrix* the viewer is torn apart by the splitting between two worlds: the real world and the cyberworld. Moreover, the hero Neo and the heroine Trinity incorporate split actantial configurations insofar as they have to find each other (love each other) in order to arrive as a unit at the object of desire, which is to rescue the real world from the Matrix.

From a Lacanian psychoanalytical view, we can interpret Neo's becoming "the One" on the order of the play of the "rings of strings" (*ronds de ficelle*) that Lacan uses as a metaphor to describe the relation between the One and the Other, or Man and Woman: "How can we situate, then, the function of the Other? How—if up to a certain point it is only the knots of the One that support what remains of language when it is written—how can we, then, make out a difference? For it is clear that the Other is not just an addition to the One. The Other is only to be seen as a differentiation. If there is something for which it participates in the One, it is not to be added to it. Because the Other—as I have said, but it's not sure that you have heard it—is the-One-less (*Un-en-moins*)."[48]

In other words, the One as the central figure of a given structure only becomes the One, only attains that value, retroactively, with the appearance of the Other. As androgynous and engendering of a "male actantial role" as Trinity may appear, her true role is clearly that of the Other. She determines the One through her desire, the desire of the other, that mystery that Western epistemology with its Judeo-Christian foundations has located in the figure of Woman. Her name, "Trinity," is in this regard also significant, as in Christian theology the mythical union of the Three and the One is central. Two is, so to speak, always already erased, because as soon as there are Two, there are Three—the original Two plus the retroactively created One.

The subordination of the female into the more general, and the retroactive production of the One through the introduction of the Other, is a theme that is practically universal in Western culture and civilization. Let's take the example of the Rhône and the Saône, two rivers that pass the city of Lyon in France. Although these two rivers obviously existed long before they were first named by the Romans, today the bigger river, *Le* Rhône, is the main (male) river into which *La* Saône, the more "petite" (feminine) river, flows. Subordination and the production of the One, as thematized in *The Matrix*, is a common theme of cyberfiction, for it has to do with the creation of a hero(ine)-discourse. Excluding men from the scenario is one way of avoiding this theme, as shown in *Messi@h*, but it is to be doubted that this also changes the very structure of "the-One-less."

The Double-Face of the *Messi@h*

Andrei Codrescu's recent novel, *Messi@h* is one of the best examples of the depiction of the controversial, double-layered female protagonist. *Messi@h* is not science fiction, but it incorporates many features associated with science fiction. As in *The Matrix*, the story is set in a religious context, but instead of a Trinity we encounter a dualistic soul in the figures of the narrative's two heroines, Felicity Le Jeune and Andrea the Orphan. The two women protagonists are described as the two souls of one *Übermensch*, who is not a heroine in the usual sense, but rather the Messiah itself. Felicity and Andrea embody precisely the oppositional actantial structure described above: The first woman, Felicity—a mulatto from New Orleans who works in a strip bar—represents the aggressive, ass-kicking, wild cyberprotagonist who passes her time in cyberspace playing the sexy cybergame "Make love to people from history," in which one can slip into the persona of a VIP from the past. In the game Felicity is asked who she wants to be "if she could be someone historical," and, not surprisingly:

She typed: THE MESSIAH.

Alexander said: YOU MAY NOW CREATE YOUR OWN AVATAR, USING PAINTBOX.

Felicity clicked on *Paintbox* and clumsily drew a creature with large breasts and a crooked nimbus over her head. She chose for her avatar a repertoire of expressions that included giving the finger, giving blessings, scratching her nimbus, slapping her hand over her mouth, frowning, and laughing with a hand between her legs. It was a pretty jolly avatar, and hardly messianic. She popped up next to the elephant, somewhere between Nineveh and Corfu.

DEAR MESSIAH, Alexander greeted her,

YOU ARE NOW READY TO MEET AND MAKE LOVE WITH JOAN OF ARC, THE VIRGIN MARY, AMELIA ERHART, MATA HARI, SAINT TERESA DE AVILA, ALEXANDER HAMILTON, MARK TWAIN, AND JULES VERNE. ENTER YOUR CREDIT CARD NUMBER AND EXPIRATION DATE NOW.[49]

After paying with her nearly maxed-out Visacard,[50] Felicity is directly linked to an online address, <http://history.love.messiah> (try it out, it didn't work for me, but maybe it will for you), where she is cheerfully greeted by the voice of Alexander:

CONGRATULATIONS!

YOU ARE NOW A MEMBER OF A SELECT GROUP OF PEOPLE WHO MEET IN ORDER TO PREPARE THE WORLD FOR A BETTER FUTURE THROUGH TRANSTEMPORAL LOVEMAKING. THIS IS A PRIVATE ENVIRONMENT WITHOUT RESTRICTIONS. YOU ARE FREE TO ENJOY YOURSELF TO THE BEST OF YOUR IMAGINATION. WHEN YOU ARE READY TO PROCEED, ENTER THIS ADDRESS AND YOU WILL FIND YOURSELF ON THE GROUNDS OF HISTORICAL EVENTS, WHERE YOU CAN MAKE LOVE WITH YOUR FAVORITE HISTORICAL PERSONAGES IN THEIR OWN BEDS, ON BATTLE-FIELDS, ABOARD SHIPS, IN DESERT TENTS, OR IN SECRET CHAMBERS.[51]

Felicity's cybersex experience with Mata Hari (putting her finger in her sensual mouth) does not convince her entirely, though. She finds out that her spirit is more promiscuous than her flesh. Felicity feels the drive for something else, something very big: no less than the salvation of the world. This truth she discovers from the oracular Shades, neotribals tattooed with faceless bodies. Felicity meets the Shades while wandering around with the fashion editor Martin Dedette:

More Shades came over and arranged themselves in a pattern that Felicity touch-read as: F-U-C-K T-H-I-S W-O-R-L-D T-H-E T-R-U-E O-N-E C-O-M-E-S.

"Who's the True one?" Felicity whispered, overcome by the earnest warmth of all the young bodies stilled there in such ritual yearning.

"You are! You are!" The shades broke off and started dancing around them.[52]

Felicity's countersoul, Andrea, a Bosnian orphan, is the opposite of an ass-kicking cyberheroine. She is described as a physically weak, innocent, but miraculous (and very beautiful) young woman, raised by the Saint Hildegard's nuns in Jerusalem. Andrea has similar revelations and intuitions about her Messiah-potentials: "'Maybe *I* am the True One,' she'd shouted at the Serb soldier loading her and her neighbors into the truck. Maybe I *am* the one, she thought now, dreaming of Gala's job."[53]

Andrea will become the One by finding her countersoul Felicity. But while Felicity is captured in the "School of Messiah Development," answering a questionnaire with such questions as "Have you ever seen an angel?" or "Has an angel ever told you things you feel that you must share with the rest of the world?," Andrea is busy saving the passengers of a *BookAir* flight ("The Airline for People Who Read") on its way from Israel to New Orleans from a terrorist book-bomb attack: "The captain radioed that an angel named Andrea had saved BookAir flight 459 from destruction, and the news was picked up at the same instant by a weather helicopter, which relayed it to ABC."[54]

Andrea's salvation of the airplane—whose passengers she aroused with her hypnotic vibrations before saving them—leads her to believe that something important is going on with her. Something/somebody has taken over her body: "It took a long time for the excitement to die down. They left her alone only when she pretended to sleep. She shut her eyes and felt the uncomfortable squirming of a shapeless creature inside her. It was a kind of a baby, only it wasn't. She was beginning to give birth to herself."[55]

Given Kristeva's definition of motherhood as femininity's only fully accepted representation in Western culture, it is most interesting how *Messi@h* uses the topos of giving birth as an example of how the heroine Andrea becomes the One. This topos has to be read in symbolic terms—as it is obviously a tautological endeavor—portraying, on the one hand, the "new woman" who does not give birth to a baby but to "kind of a baby," to a new self that then slips into a masculine actantial role of saving the world; and, on the other hand, presenting a traditional representation of womanhood that cannot do without motherhood. Here we have again a split representation of Woman—actually a split within a split, since Andrea was already the countersoul of Felicity and is now also a new being in a new body. It is a newly emancipated heroine who comes into being through birthing and, hence, through the most archaic representation of femininity.

Andrea (having given birth to herself) escapes the paparazzi in Atlanta by changing dresses with a nun that she met on the airplane and continues her messianic path to New Orleans, where she finally meets her countersoul Felicity: "From the moment that their two pairs of green eyes met (Andrea's were a lighter green, like young wheat), they experienced recognitions that traveled through their bones like electricity. When they spoke, their words trailed echoes behind them, traces of something they strained to hear but couldn't."[56]

The two women become One, the True One. "Together, they were a new being,"[57] a New Body consisting of multiple Messiahs who save the world in and through their togetherness. *Messi@h* does not surprise us in terms of its salvation theme, one that is inherent to many Turn-of-the-Millennium stories. It is the cyberenvironment itself that calls for these kind of apocalyptic stories, in which some (commonly) computer superbrain is able to save the world from James Bond—like threats. As regards our current concern, however, what matters is not so much the cyberplot (despite its amusing qualities), but rather how the split heroines, and even the split within the split, perpetuate an imagining of femininity that not only is profoundly traditional but perhaps even misogynic.

Multiplicity in *Proxies*

In the recent cybernovel *Proxies*, by Laura J. Mixon, the genre of cyberpunk has produced yet another way of depicting the split self, namely through *multiple* identities. Now the phenomenon of splitting has reached its logical absolute, an exponential splitting, a continuation ad extremis of the double-faced heroines described in *The Matrix* and *Messi@h*.

In *Proxies* the postmodern, multiple selves represented by the various cyberprotagonists—and especially by the heroine, Carli D'Auber—are able to experience their selves in vastly different ways by "slipping into different bodies" (like "slipping into the personae" of historical VIPs in *Messi@h*). In this body-within-bodies-world, there are even bodies that can be experienced or shared at the same time. One such "common body" is the body of Krueger, who can be connected to the protagonists Pablo and Buddy. The word "Krueger" can be used in combination with a possessive pronoun[58] to distinguish between first and third persons, a demonstration of cyberpunk's ability to modify the English grammar and lexicon: "'Go ahead,' he-Krueger said, sitting up in bed, in Uncle Sam's voice, 'we're receiving.' *His Krueger* syntellect was loaded and standing by; swiftly as he spoke he called up that chat analyzer. [. . .] 'It's all right. I'm twinning. *I-Krueger* am currently receiving a report from Uncle Daniel Sornsen. I came to give you some important news.'"[59]

Slipping into different bodies, whether it be a "Krueger-body" or another one, is referred to as going into another world, the world of "proxy." Being "in proxy" represents a virtual-reality experience as described in *Johnny Mnemonic* and other cyberpunk films in which we witness the painful passages from reality to virtuality. The protagonists of *Proxies* spend a lot of time (too much according to one of the protagonists, Daniel) in proxy or as proxies.[60] These simulacra of human bodies are almost indistinguishable from real humans. In a Baudrillardian[61] sense we could say that they are *hyperreal*, because they are the "better version" of the humans themselves: "Next to Daniel stood Daniel's proxy. The remote appeared to be a better-looking version of Daniel, several years younger than he, substantially better muscled."[62]

After a visit in proxy, one returns to one's own body, at times with "postlink disorientation." These bodily experiences are described according to a conservative notion of corporeality, namely, that of the Cartesian split between the *res extensa* and the *res cogitans*; but in this case, the returning body parts, normally denizens of the *res extensa*, are infected, as it were, with the ghost of the *cogito*, and are portrayed as experiencing the world on their own: "She felt an arm uncoil and extend, and then her eye that looked at Pollux and saw it."[63] This might, then, be the real multiplicity experienced in proxy: not merely a multiple vest, a body that one can slip into in cyberspace, but rather and more profoundly the multiplication and diffusion of consciousness in one's own body, the alienation of the body in relation to its traditional center in the soul.

But what actually "happens" in *Proxies*? What kind of actantial configurations do we encounter? One could say that a lot "happens," but that the various protagonists, Carli, Daniel, Buddy, Pablo, and Dane Elisa Cae, whose consciousnesses we are connected to in the various chapters, are "waldoing"[64] toward the one narrative goal, which is (not surprisingly after *The Matrix* and *Messi@h*) that of realizing the One. It is, this time, the heroine Carli who is revealed to be the one and, interestingly enough, this secret is revealed by a cyborg who appears in the chapter "Machine-Human-Faces," a (rather funny-looking) cyborg who is called, in a misogynic way, the "woman-thing": "First glance said woman, seriously injured. She was six feet tall and totally naked. Three ugly gashes, one on her face, one down her right arm, one slash across her left thigh. Her skin was a canvas someone had spilled buckets of paint on, cocoa and vanilla, like a pinto. Her body was unusually long and slim all over. Wiry. Her hair and facial features, though as varicolored as the rest of her, were Negroid. Her eyes stared at Carli, unblinking, without expression [65]

Despite the multiple selves inherent in "proxy-existence," these subjects are not innovative at all in their gendered behavior. Rather the opposite, for if we think of the "woman-thing" that is not even master of itself but led by "a voice that guides me,"[66] we might say that the cyberpunk innovation in *Proxies* lies more in its language games and neologisms than in its narrative program and depiction of heroism. Besides, the explicit religious setting is left out here, so that "becoming the One" no longer refers to a Judeo-Christian religious environment, but to a post-Christian environment of forgotten salvation.

The Heroine

Whether the oppositional scheme of depicting femininity as described in *The Matrix* and *Messi@h* and the multifacetedness of not only the heroine-protagonist but all protagonists in *Proxies* are instantiations of a postmodern pastiche, or whether they have rather to do with a gendered discourse-universe in which it is revealed that we are unable to depict the Other without incorporating the Same—whether, in other words, these narratives prove that it is impossible to think outside a gendered universe, and hence to think a completely new body at all, a body that is post- or transgendered—remains an open and fulminating discussion. In order to debate further, though, we might have to ask the question in a different way. Isn't the real problem of the representation of femininity the splitting itself of Woman—be it into opposite or complementary "halves," or into more "pieces"—that seems to be unavoidable when representing gender interactions? Isn't this the real violence inherent in the genre of cyberpunk, and not the fact that brutality and physical violence are experienced by the cyberprotagonists? But what does this kind of femininity entail? Antimaternity, since the heroines in question are anything but motherly? Becoming or being "like Man," hence violent and ass-kicking? Overcoming gender effects through an appearance of a sexually appealing androgyny?

If it is true that the genre of cyberpunk represents femininity in a split form, then, we might ask, what is new about the fact that now we encounter cyberheroines in the place of heroes? In other words, is there any difference between the representation of gender interactions in, for instance, *Limbo* and *Proxies*? Here, the answer is obviously, Yes, there is! The difference lies precisely in the fact that both novels reflect the ambience and the zeitgeist of their times, the computer revolution of the 1950s, and the transgender movement in the 1990s. Nevertheless, in relation to femininity both novels confront us with rape and violence done on women at the hands of men. What remains the same in terms of actantial representations of women is the split.

From the Lacanian psychoanalytical prospective that I have brought to this reading, I have argued that this split of representation is inherent to the construction of female gender, and to the institutionalization of womanhood. Let us recall *Encore* (once again), in which Lacan analyzes the complex position of *La Femme* as occupying two possible positions: on the one hand she is a subject in search of the phallus (like Man), but on the other hand she is already in the field of the Other, and hence is aware of being an object. Lacan compares the sublimity of this positioning with the representation of God in Western culture.[67] Perhaps, then, it should not surprise us that the cybernarratives in question, *The Matrix* and *Messi@h* , so closely align the semantic fields of womanhood and religion. Both femininity and faith are in the realm of the mystery, the unknown; are situated outside of language; and are, hence, outside of the law. What surprises here is not that this is the case for the representation of Woman in cybernarratives at the turn of the millennium, but rather that the "new" and "latest," and maybe even "hottest," genre of cyberpunk performs a "reinscription" of a conservatism that has accompanied us throughout the last century.

The Heroine does not exist, and whether she ever will exist is a question that cannot be definitely answered. To say, with Irigaray, that to break a (patriarchic) pattern— and hence a certain way that history has inscribed itself into our cultural imaginary— is an impossibility is one (dark) way to put it. One way or the other, from the recent gender-blenders and the double-faced, multifaceted, new cyberprotagonists floating around us we cannot expect a serious redefinition of Woman. The serious work is done elsewhere, maybe in women's studies, or in a general change in thinking about the episteme of Woman. But who says the authors of cyberpunk are trying to change anything? Aren't these cybernarratives just a lot of fun in their sexiness and constant changing of identities, in their multiplicity of selves and body parts? If one really wanted to "change patterns," one would have to turn pragmatically to a "reality" in which, for example, only 10 percent of the world population is using computers. But reading and writing cyberfiction and watching or making cyberpunk films does little to solve these "real" problems. As Irigaray puts it: "In politics, opportunities (*ouvertures*) are finding their way in to the world of women; but these opportunities remain partial, local; they operate as concessions on the part of existing powers, and not as the realization of new values."[68] If only it were possible to foresee the distant future in a way not marked by the logical possibilities of the present, perhaps we could see a world beyond the splitting of Woman. But then, such a futuristic discourse is precisely what science fiction is supposed to be all about. To the extent that the discursive practices of the present are incapable of imagining a truly different future, perhaps it is left to such daily practices as education, politics, and social policy to gradually rewrite the nature of Woman.

Notes

I am especially thankful to William Egginton for his critical comments, his scholarly inspirations, and above all his help in transforming my hybrid version into real English.

1. All translations are mine.

2. See, for example, M. Dery, *Escape Velocity: Cyberculture at the End of the Century* (New York: Grove Press, 1996), and M. Seltzer, *Bodies and Machines* (New York and London: Routledge, 1992).

3. See, for example, S. Bukatman, *Terminal Identity: The Virtual Subject in Postmodern Science Fiction* (Durham, NC, and London: Duke University Press, 1993), and S. Turkle, *Life on the Screen: Identity in the Age of the Internet* (New York: Simon & Schuster, 1995).

4. See, for example, T. de Lauretis, *Technologies of Gender: Essays on Theory, Film, and Fiction* (Bloomington and Indianapolis: Indiana University Press, 1987), M. Flanagan, "Navigable Narratives: Gender and Spatiality in Virtual Worlds," in *Proceedings from Exploring Cyber Society*, vol. 1, ed. J. Armitage and J. Roberts, (Newcastle, UK: University of Northumbria, July 5–7, 1999), and D. Haraway, "A Cyborg Manifesto: Science, Technology, and Socialist-Feminism in the Late Twentieth Century," in *Cyborgs and Women: The Reinvention of Nature* (New York and London: Routledge, 1991), 149–181.

5. A. and L. Wachowsky, *The Matrix*, 1999.

6. A. Codrescu, *Messi@h* (New York: Simon & Schuster, 1999).

7. L. J. Mixon, *Proxies* (New York: Tor, 1998).

8. The famous Lacanian dictum "Woman does not exist" is a translation of "L̶a femme n'existe pas," in which the "La" is negated by a slash mark. The fact that it is the definite article that is barred and not the word "woman" itself indicates that what is at stake for Lacan is the notion of a universal identity. Whatever "woman is," "she" is not definable by sentences beginning with "woman is."

9. C. Shepherdson, *Vital Signs: Nature, Culture, Psychoanalysis* (New York and London: Routledge, 2000), 5.

10. The workings of *langue* in this sense can be seen in the example of the existence of "the dual," a special linguistic mode in ancient Greek that communicates what one does *together* with somebody else, a category that does not exist in most other Indo-European languages because this activity *as a pair* simply does not represent an important enough cultural reality to make room for a syntactic category.

11. J. Butler, *Gender Trouble: Feminism and the Subversion of Identity* (New York and London: Routledge, 1990), 7. Butler's "deconstruction" must be understood in the strictest sense, in that her trope is, first, to demonstrate that the traditional dualism sex/gender masks a tacit individual term (i.e., the material certainty of sex) and, second, to reveal that this unquestioned "presence" is in fact the effect of a pluralistic and highly unstable reiteration of performed identities.

12. This terminology is borrowed from the semiotic methodology of Greimas and Courtès. See A.-J. Greimas and J. Courtés, *Sémiotique. Dictionnaire raisonné de la théorie du langage* (Paris: Hachette, [1979] 1993).

13. The following discussion refers to J. Lacan, *Le séminaire Livre XX: Encore* (Paris: Seuil, 1975), 61–82. For these paraphrases, I am indebted to Shepherdson's chapter on Lacan's sexuation theory (72–83).

14. The position of maternity stands in opposition to masquerade; it is a way of registering castration in the symbolic order by interpreting the child as a phallic substitute.

15. Shepherdson, *Vital Signs*, 79.

16. Shepherson, *Vital Signs*, 81.

17. L. Irigaray, *Ce sexe qui n'en est pas un* (Paris: Minuit, 1977), 133.

18. Irigaray, *Ce sexe*, 32.

19. Lacan, *Le seminaire Livre XX: Encore*, 36.

20. J. Kristeva, *Histoires d'amour* (Paris: Denoël, 1983), 295.

21. Kristeva, *Histoires d'amour*, 297.

22. S. de Beauvoir, *Le deuxième sexe I et II* (Paris: Gallimard, 1949), and M. Wittig, "The Mark of Gender," *Feminist Issues* 5, no. 2 (Fall 1985): 3–12.

23. M. Wittig, "The Point of View: Universal or Particular?," *Feminist Issues* 3, no. 2 (Fall 1983): 63–70.

24. The question of whether literature influences technology or vice versa is an open one. Culture and technology are processes that cannot be thought of separately, and hence are not in a relationship of causality, but of conditioning and interdependence.

25. Bukatman, *Terminal Identity*, 138.

26. Bukatman, *Terminal Identity*, 138.

27. The neorealism in question regards only the American genre, and not the Italian film genre *Neorealismo*, inaugurated by the director Roberto Rossellini in the 1940s, from which the current movement gets its name.

28. L. Olsen, "Cyberpunk and the Crisis of Postmodernity," in *Fiction 2000: Cyberpunk and the Future of Narrative*, ed. G. Slusser and T. Shippey, 142–152, 147 (Athens and London: The University of Georgia Press, 1992).

29. Olsen, "Cyberpunk and the Crisis of Postmodernity," 150.

30. B. Sterling, ed., *Mirrorshades: The Cyberpunk Anthology* (New York: Arbor House, 1986), viii-ix, quoted in Bukatman, *Terminal Identity*, 140.

31. J. Huntington, "Newness, Neuromancer, and the End of Narrative," in *Fiction 2000: Cyberpunk and the Future of Narrative*, ed. G. Slusser and T. Shippey (Athens and London: The University of Georgia Press, 1992), 133–141, 139.

32. Bukatman, *Terminal Identity*, 141ff.

33. Huntington, "Newness, Neuromancer, and the End of Narrative," 140.

34. Not to mention such blockbuster action films as P. Hyams's *End of Days*, 1999.

35. D. Cronenberg, *eXistenZ*, 1999.

36. M. Oshii, *Ghost in the Shell*, 1995.

37. To give a history of fiction dealing with that topic would be too digressive for this chapter. Let me just mention a few examples from film, such as S. Kubrick's *2001: A Space Odyssey* (1968), R. Scott's *Blade Runner* (1982), D. Cronenberg's *Videodrome* (1982), B. Leonard's *Virtuosity* (1995), and R. Longo's *Johnny Mnemonic* (1995).

38. The very genre of cyberpunk is characterized by a hybrid style between fictional narrative and (often manifesto-like) critical theory (e.g., D. Haraway).

39. Mixon, *Proxies*, 10.

40. The semiotic term "actantial" refers to the terminology of A.-J. Greimas, *Sémantique structurale* (Paris: Larousse, 1966); Greimas took the idea of the "actant" from the Russian structuralist, Vladimir Propp; in his "Morfologija skazki" (Morphology of the Folktale), in which he analyzes one hundred Russian folktales in their narrative structures, Propp distinguishes different narrative figures as having respective *functional* roles, such as "the hero," "the antagonist," "the helper," and so forth. See V. J. Propp, "Morfologija skazki," in Coll. *Voprosy poetiki*, N12 (Leningrad: Gosudarstvennyj institut istorii iskusstva, 1928); *Morphology of the Folktale*, trans. L. Scott (Austin: University of Texas Press, 1986). Greimas replaced Propp's original notion of the "protagonists's functionality" and developed it further in his theory of "actantial models."

41. B. Wolfe, *Limbo* (New York: Random House, 1952).

42. D. Samuelson in *Extrapolation 19* (1977), quoted in K. N. Hayles, *How We Became Posthuman: Virtual Bodies in Cybernetics, Literature, and Informatics* (Chicago and London: The University of Chicago Press, 1999), 113.

43. Hayles, *How We Became Posthuman*, 128.

44. "Hero-Protagonist" is the name of the main character in one of the most successful cyberpunk novels, *Snow Crash*. See N. Stephenson, *Snow Crash* (New York: Bantam Books, 1992).

45. For example, Case in W. Gibson's *Neuromancer* (New York: Ace Books, 1984).

46. J. Cameron, *Aliens*, 1986.

47. Available at <http://whatisthematrix.warnerbros.com />.

48. Lacan, *Le seminaire Livre XX: Encore*, 116.

49. Codrescu, *Messi@h*, 64.

50. The product placement is characteristic of the narrative style of current cyberpunk.

51. Codrescu, *Messi@h*, 64.

52. Codrescu, *Messi@h*, 149.

53. Codrescu, *Messi@h*, 161.

54. Codrescu, *Messi@h*, 272.

55. Codrescu, *Messi@h*, 272.

56. Codrescu, *Messi@h*, 292.

57. Codrescu, *Messi@h*, 295.

58. In this case the use of the possessive pronoun is less relevant than the information resulting from the corresponding personal pronouns: I, He, etc.

59. Mixon, *Proxies*, 70–71, my emphasis.

60. The word *proxies* refers both to the virtual world and to the life-form in that virtual world. The *nomen agentis* and the local adverb are therefore used as homonymous, another example of how the genre of cyberpunk modifies and invents language.

61. See J. Baudrillard, "Simulacra and Simulations," in *Selected Writings*, ed. Mark Poster (Stanford: Stanford University Press, 1988).

62. Mixon, *Proxies*, 141.

63. Mixon, *Proxies*, 149.

64. "Waldo" is another of these "proxy words" that can be associated with different phrases and categories. "Waldo" can be a proper noun, such as in "Daniel-waldo," and in "Krueger-waldo," but there also is the verb "to waldo," which refers to a movement activity: for example, "Daniel and Krueger had waldoed into the public habitat" (Mixon, *Proxies*, 28).

65. Mixon, *Proxies*, 210.

66. Mixon, *Proxies*, 212.

67. Lacan, *Le seminaire Livre XX: Encore*, 61–71.

68. L. Irigaray, *Éthique de la différence sexuelle* (Paris: Minuit, 1984), 14.

Works Cited

Baudrillard, Jean. "Simulacra and Simulations." In *Selected Writings*, ed. Mark Poster. Stanford: Stanford University Press, 1988.

Beauvoir, Simone de. *Le deuxième sexe I et II*. Paris: Gallimard, 1949; *The Second Sex*. trans. E. M. Parshley. New York: Vintage, 1973.

Bukatman, Scott. *Terminal Identity: The Virtual Subject in Postmodern Science Fiction*. Durham, NC, and London: Duke University Press, 1993.

Butler, Judith. *Gender Trouble: Feminism and the Subversion of Identity*. New York and London: Routledge, 1990.

Codrescu, Andrei. *Messi@h*. New York: Simon & Schuster, 1999.

de Lauretis, Teresa. *Technologies of Gender: Essays on Theory, Film, and Fiction*. Bloomington and Indianapolis: Indiana University Press, 1987.

Dery, Mark. *Escape Velocity: Cyberculture at the End of the Century*. New York: Grove Press, 1996.

Flanagan, Mary. "Navigable Narratives: Gender and Spatiality in Virtual Worlds." In *Proceedings from Exploring Cyber Society*, vol. 1, ed. John Armitage and Joanne Roberts. Newcastle, UK: University of Northumbria, July 5–7, 1999.

Gibson, William. *Neuromancer*. New York: Ace Books, 1984.

Greimas, Algirdas-Julien. *Semantique structurale*. Paris: Larousse, 1966.

Greimas, Algirdas-Julien, and Joseph Courtés. *Sémiotique. Dictionnaire raisonné de la théorie du langage*. Paris: Hachette, [1979] 1993.

Haraway, Donna. "A Cyborg Manifesto: Science, Technology, and Socialist-Feminism in the Late Twentieth Century." In *Cyborgs and Women: The Reinvention of Nature*, 149–181. New York and London: Routledge, 1991.

Hayles, Katherine N. *How We Became Posthuman: Virtual Bodies in Cybernetics, Literature, and Informatics*. Chicago and London: The University of Chicago Press, 1999.

Huntington, John. "Newness, Neuromancer, and the End of Narrative." In *Fiction 2000: Cyberpunk and the Future of Narrative*, eds. George Slusser and Tom Shippey. Athens and London: The University of Georgia Press, 1992. 133–141.

Irigary, Luce. *Éthique de la différence sexuelle*. Paris: Minuit, 1984.

Irigaray, Luce. *Ce sexe qui n'en est pas un*. Paris: Minuit, 1977; *This Sex Which Is Not One*, trans. Catherine Porter. Ithaca: Cornell, 1985.

Kristeva, Julia. *Histoires d'amour*. Paris: Denoël, 1983; *Tales of Love*, trans. Léon Roudiez. New York: Columbia University Press, 1987.

Lacan, Jacques. *Le séminaire Livre XX: Encore*. Paris: Seuil, 1975.

Mixon, Laura J. *Proxies*. New York: TOR, 1998.

Olsen, Lance. "Cyberpunk and the Crisis of postmodernity." In *Fiction 2000: Cyberpunk and the Future of Narrative*, ed. George Slusser and Tom Shippey, 142–152. Athens and London: The University of Georgia Press, 1992.

Propp, Vladimir Jakovlevic. "Morfologija skazki." In Coll. *Voprosy poetiki*. N12. Leningrad: Gosudarstvennyj institut istorii iskusstva, 1928; *Morphology of the Folktale*, trans. Laurence Scott. Austin: University of Texas Press, 1986.

Shepherdson, Charles. *Vital Signs: Nature, Culture, Psychoanalysis*. New York and London: Routledge, 2000.

Sterling, Bruce., ed. *Mirrorshades: The Cyberpunk Anthology*. New York: Arbor House, 1986.

Stephenson, Neal. *Snow Crash*. New York: Bantam Books, 1992.

Turkle, Sherry. *Life on the Screen: Identity in the Age of the Internet*. New York: Simon & Schuster, 1995.

Wittig, Monique. "The Point of View: Universal or Particular?" *Feminist Issues* 3, no. 2 (Fall 1983): 63–70.

Wittig, Monique. "The Mark of Gender." *Feminist Issues* 5, no. 2 (Fall 1985): 3–12.

Wolfe, Bernard. *Limbo*. New York: Random House, 1952.

Films Cited

Bigelow, Kathryn. *Strange Days*, 1995.

Cameron, James. *Aliens*, 1986.

Cronenberg, David. *Videodrome*, 1982.

Cronenberg, David. *eXistenZ*, 1999.

Hyams, Peter. *End of Days*, 1999.

Bernadette Wegenstein

Kubrick, Stanley. *2001: A Space Odyssey*, 1982.

Leonard, Brett. *Virtuosity*, 1995.

Lisberger, Steven. *TRON* , 1982.

Longo, Robert. *Johnny Mnemonic*, 1995.

Oshii, Mamoru. *Ghost in the Shell*, 1995.

Scott, Ridley. *Blade Runner*, 1982.

Tsukamoto, Shinya. *Tetsuo I: The Iron Man*, 1989.

Tsukamoto, Shinya. *Tetsuo II: Body Hammer*, 1992.

Wachowsky, Andy and Larry. *The Matrix*, 1999.

18

GIRL ERUPTED

Rajani Sudan

In the summer of 2000, the representatives of the biotechnology company, Celera Genomics of Rockville, Maryland, and the heads of the Human Genome Project announced that the first map of the human genetic code was almost complete. The publicly financed project and privately owned company had together deciphered about 3.1 billion subunits of DNA, a monumental testament to the combined powers of biotechnology and capitalism. The discourse surrounding this revelation, whose public announcement was sanctioned by Bill Clinton and Tony Blair, is quite complex. Debates concerning the ethics of using this research not only to troubleshoot but also to clone and to commodify dominated the news programs following the announcement, despite strong statements by both Clinton and Blair about the importance of protecting people's privacy.

Although I think these debates are serious, embedded in this discourse is another question about identity: What exactly are we trying to decode or decipher? What will that last resistant remaining 10 percent reveal to us about human identity? Biologically, of course, the answer seems clear: We will finally have a material entity that defines human essence, a means to demystify the process by which humans are made and reinvent it as a scientific procedure. Philosophically, however, this answer seems strangely incompatible with our postmodern social climate. This discovery seems particularly at odds with digital culture that is primarily associated with the notion of fluid identities, unfixed spaces, and the fantasy that technology would provide one with the means of somehow transcending material (and ideological) markers of identity, although congruent with the equally compelling fantasy that technology can also help one find a biological, material "answer" to the human question. The multifarious possibilities of those answers to human identity get curiously reduced to a single phenomenon of biological makeup: DNA. Similarly, the enormous complex of technologies and systems of information, to say nothing of the numerous economic and social systems that together define globilization, for us, are essentialized into a single term defining a locale: cyber-space. Interestingly, the Celera director, Craig Venter, apparently mapped the genetic code of five people of different ethnicities and was unable to read the racial differences in these particular genetic sequences. The conclusion he draws is that race is not bio-logically coded. Yet, for a society obsessed with embodying ideological differences, this discovery does not conclusively prove that race is not a biological phenomenon.

My point is not to support the biological determinism of "race," but rather to ques-tion our inventions of taxonomies and epistemologies that invariably invoke the mate-rial as an irrefutable substantiation of the ideological. I'm especially interested in thinking through the ways race and gender collapse into materially identifiable bodies in visual and virtual culture. I want to address more recent representations of the conflation of race and gender in digital and film images, partially because it seems that despite the timely interventions women writers have made into cyberpunk culture and the enor-mous growth of women's writing in virtual and digital studies (as this collection makes clear), popular Hollywood accounts of female presence within this arena is dominated by conventional hegemonic gender roles. That is, while women are rapidly reinventing the shape of cyberculture by providing models of identity that resist convention, these shifts are not necessarily reflected in big corporate structures like Hollywood.

The spate of big Hollywood films that came out in the summer of 2000, for ex-ample, exemplifies the fact that although there may be a more visible and active female presence onscreen, there is still not the epistemological power granted to their mascu-line counterparts. Even if women have more identifiably physical power, their roles are still determined by heteronormative ideologies of gender.[1] John Woo's *Mission Impos-sible 2*, Dominic Sena's *Gone in 60 Seconds*, and Bryan Singer's *X-Men* in particular are interesting films because of the choices the casting directors make for the roles of the women in the films.[2] I should point out that there are very few women cast in two of these films. *Mission Impossible 2* has only one woman in the entire movie (besides anony-mous female bodies during one party scene), Nyah Nordolf-Hall (Thandie Newton), and *Gone in 60 Seconds* only one significant female role, Sara "Sway" Wayland (Angelina Jolie). Only *X-Men* seems to populate its plot with a number of different women, albeit most of them—in fact, all of them—cyborgs or "mutants." Our attention on these em-blematic women is, therefore, quite focused and undistracted by other competing fe-male characters and faces and bodies. Because the appearance of women in these films is so minimal, it seems clear that they function as placeholders or tokens, their roles within the plot only sketchily justified and often strained (as in the romance between Randall "Memphis" Raines [Nicholas Cage] and Sway). Even *X-Men* spotlights only one female character at a time as opposed to the numerous male characters appearing in a scene. What might be the need for those token figures—why they appear at all (even the sexual element is very limited)—is the question I'm interested in unraveling for *Mission Impossible 2* and *Gone in 60 Seconds*. I would like to contextualize these questions within larger debates about gender, race, and digital culture.

In a chapter that appeared in the collection *Race in Cyberspace*, I argued that late twentieth-century postindustrial U.S. culture was drawing on a history of British imperialism to mark out the new body of competition.[3] (And, in fact, it's interesting that the official outside endorsers of the Human Genome Project were the two representatives of old and new Western imperialism: Tony Blair and Bill Clinton.) Popular culture apparently fashioned a post–Cold War demon out of the "Asian" (mostly Japanese) supplier of technological innovations to bolster a beleaguered American economy. Thus, the "Asian" body became visually identifiable as a newly colored racial body.

In this chapter, I examine more closely not only the racial markers "at war" and therefore dependent on white mediation, as Richard Dyer argues in *White* (1997), but also how the heterosexualized body of the feminine furnishes equally crucial parameters for situating race in a postindustrial global culture. That is, because interest in race in the United States has "come to mean that one is interested in any racial imagery other than that of white people," our critiques of race are predicated upon an implicit understanding of a "non-raced" position that Dyer argues is white in complexion.[4]

Similarly, bodies "having" gender are almost always understood as feminized or queered, and interest in gender studies invariably invokes the study of women's bodies, as the study of sexuality almost inevitably elides heterosexual identity as a body that has matter.[5] I want to identify some of the ways in which the most familiar of characteristics that constitute the body of gender (female parts) and race (color) continually obfuscate and block the postmodern manifesto of transubstantiation in popular venues like film.

Bryan Singer's film version of the Marvel comic series, *X-Men*, capitalizes on a preestablished success in comic books. What are some of the differences that Hollywood brings to these stories? Arguably, the big screen simultaneously exaggerates and renders more "realistic" the dramatic tensions of the plots. In the case of *X-Men*, the film literally fills out the two-dimensional lines of comic-book characters, giving them more material bodies and "realistic" settings for their heroics. The film also graphically dramatizes the difference between lifelike characters—Rogue / Marie (Anna Paquin), Magneto (Ian McKellan), and Xavier (Patrick Stewart)—and the more cyborgian comic-book superheroes: Wolverine / Logan (Hugh Jackman), Storm (Halle Berry), Mystique (Rebecca Romijn-Stamos), Sabretooth (Tyler Mane), Cyclops (James Marsden), and Toad (Ray Park). Another critical symptomatic difference between the comic and the film is in the treatment of Mystique. In the comic series, the character is more amorphous and less insistently female than in the Hollywood version. That is, in the film, even if she can transmute into other forms, she must return to an uncontested feminized form that constitutes her "origin." It is as if Hollywood has assumed that this particular manifestation of this character's multifaceted identity is the one that matters.

Focused on the biotechnological possibilities of genetic mutation, the film's premise—that some children are born with a mutated "X" gene that makes them capable of superhuman powers—"naturalizes" the scientific discourse of genetic engineering, transforming human choice into something outside human control. The effect of this turn of events is to naturalize other kinds of discourse, particularly those about gender and race.

The two characters who dramatize the differences between human and cyborgian bodies most effectively are female: Storm and Mystique. Storm's platinum blond hair and whitened eyes (when she's brandishing her powers) starkly and improbably contrast with her dark skin. These contrasts effectively make her body into something not "natural," something artificially produced like a doll. The indeterminate accent she assumes in the film confuses our immediate impulse to register her as African American and perhaps ties her more closely to the Japanese street fashion, gangura, a form of street discourse that has also been popular in underground cartoon representation.

Mystique's yellow eyes and bumpy blue reptilian skin are meant to signify her chameleonlike abilities. Her dangerousness (and monstrosity) is manifested by her ability to display simultaneously complete assimilation and absolute difference. That is, she is the one cyborg character that looks the most "inhuman," and yet she is also the only cyborg that can assume the shape and strengths of any living character, human or cyborg. Despite her continual morphing, however, her body inevitably returns to its original, unmistakably female and unmistakably monstrous shape.

Implicit in these representations of the cyborgian-female interface is the idea that the body that is "gendered" is also the only body that displays ideologies of difference that unfold as racial difference. In the near-futuristic world of the film, cyborgs or "mutants" live among "us," as the evil character, Senator Kelly (Bruce Davidson), exhorts; they are obvious monsters and freaks that endanger human welfare, and yet they also need to be clearly identified because humans can't always tell the difference between themselves and these putatively alien beings. The film foregrounds this notion by opening with a scene in which a Jewish family is split apart during their forced march to a concentration camp, and the young child, separated from his mother, demonstrates a precocious ability to conjure different energies that mark his difference from humans in "other" ways.[6]

However, while the narrative ostensibly dismantles the bigoted belief that Jews are inhuman, it does so at the expense of reinforcing other equally bigoted assumptions, particularly ones about gender. The female mutants are especially vested with the ability to be both visibly different and indistinguishable from "normal" people; their seamless movement from cyborg to human and back again therefore needs to be made particularly identifiable. This is obviously true of Mystique and Storm because their identities are primarily cyborgian. It is also true of the more typically human character, Rogue/Marie. While Storm and Mystique are clearly cyborgian because of their bodies, Rogue is not; however, Rogue taints everyone she touches by absorbing their life forces for her own needs. "Don't touch me," she screams at her boyfriend's mother during an early dramatic moment that first depicts her horrifying mutancy. Her boyfriend's face (whom she has just kissed) is going through a terrifying transformation: veins and muscles are almost breaking through the skin, turning him into a monstrous version of himself as he slowly lapses into a coma. The point I'm making here is that all the female characters are marked in some indelible way. They demonstrate quite materially the conflation of gender and race; they are either passive markers of this conjunction or actively (if not deliberately) mark onto the bodies of others signs of their own disease—in short, they infect and contaminate anyone they touch and are, therefore, dangerous.

The male characters, on the other hand, are not necessarily always subject to being marked quite so permanently. While it's true that they, too, are cyborgs and also move between human and mutant subjectivities, the "dangers" they pose to others (mostly humans) is different. For the most part, their distinguishing characteristics are not entirely incorporated into their bodies. While Cyclop's eyes, Wolverine's blades, Toad's tongue, and Sabretooth's teeth are body parts, they're still perceived and used as attachments to or enhancements of a separate coherent body, unlike Storm's and Mystique's skin, or Rogue's contaminating touch. In the case of both Magneto and Xavier, their specific powers are not material but purely epistemological. Unlike the other X-Men, these leaders' special gifts are telepathic and telekinetic—theirs is the gift of pure reason.

To be sure, another female mutant is ostensibly granted the potential to exploit these epistemological powers. Dr. Jean Grey (Famke Jansren) is an apprentice to the powerful Xavier, learning the ways in which to harness such energies. She represents, arguably, the female alternative to Xavier: She is a mutant capable of transcending the limits of her deformity or disability (as their genetic alterations are often described) and speaking in human arenas of discourse quite powerfully and eloquently for the mutants' cause. Grey is, however, scarred by other subordinating marks that disfigure her capacity for independent human subjectivity. Her relation to her intuitive power is still untutored, her place is very much as an apprentice. She also becomes the eroticized object of desire between two other cyborgs who are considerably junior to Xavier (Wolverine and Cyclops). Even if her whiteness gives her a place of putative power that neither Storm nor Mystique could occupy, she is still cast primarily as a body whose substantive properties (e.g., her desirability) far outweigh her intellectual ones. She is, therefore, an irrefutably material presence and not the ideal Cartesian subject her master, Xavier, represents.

Dyer argues that his study *White* is "a book about the racial imagery of white people—not the images of other races in white cultural production, but the latter's imagery of white people themselves. This is not done merely to fill a gap in the analytic literature, but because there is something at stake in looking at, or continuing to ignore, white racial imagery. As long as race is something only applied to non-white peoples, as long as white people are not racially seen and named, they/we function as a human norm. Other people are raced, we are just people."[7] In many ways, *X-Men* wants to enact these statements, turning the blurry outlines of cyborgian identity into a more sharply defined issue of race.[8] Contrary to the logic of the narrative, however, other ideologies compete with this relatively simplistic reduction of difference as black and white. Significantly, the cyborgs that embody most completely (Western) social "feminine" features are also the ones that demonstrate difference (mutancy) most vividly. Such a grouping, of course, is in no way unique; feminist theory, cultural studies, postcolonial studies and other fields of contemporary theory have made significant contributions to uncovering the ways in which the bodies of women are deployed to showcase imperial subordination. In the interest of using a "postmodern" shorthand to represent the ways in which the biological engineering and genetic technology have teamed up with a "natural" evolutionary Darwinism in order to produce "mutants" capable of superhuman powers, the film in fact draws upon early modern understandings of subjectivity—mainly Cartesian—that are contingent on ideologies of race and gender.[9]

It seems as if postmodern concerns with fluid identities and with surmounting the corporeal boundaries of the cultural body are eradicated and turned into "natural" biological narratives about the inevitability of ideology. In other words, rather than representing mutations as a result of human choice (perhaps the defining question in the discourse of bio-engineering), the film chooses to portray how mutating genes have a life of their own divorced from human control.[10] Implicit in such a portrayal are disturbing social questions about other arenas of choice in relation to the body—for example, abortion—especially in terms of race and gender. However, other discourses of choice are at issue in this film's representation of mutancy.

For example, the entire question of mutation and its close association with difference is one that depends on "human" acceptance and human sanction. Here, the definition of human in the filmic narrative quite explicitly parallels Dyer's definition of the "normal" body of whiteness. One of the tensions that drives the plot is the survival of humans: Magneto wants to "mutate" everyone with his new invention, to endow all humans with the same freakishness with which they perceive all mutants. Xavier, on the other hand, is much more interested in protecting human agency and advocates a peaceful coexistence of mutants and humans or even the integration of mutants into human society. Such rhetoric recalls the civil rights debates in which the idea of integration automatically assumed that the group into which one was integrating was white. Dyer's remarks regarding the invisibility of whiteness then come home to roost in films like *X-Men*: Far from dramatizing the ways in which difference marked by race and gender may be addressed by the loose allegory of cyborgs and humans, the film advocates for the same kind of problematic sublimation of difference into an idealized "normalcy." The mutants' markers—Wolverine's claws, Cyclops's eyes, even Rogue's touch (she wears gloves throughout the film)—are safely consolidated and institutionalized (in places like Xavier's school) into lessons that encourage mutants to engage in human standards of behavior.

X-Men's portrayal of cultist cartoon cyberculture does make attempts at a "multi-" cultural inclusiveness (as do many films coming out of the big Hollywood studios), but in so doing, it replicates many of the hegemonies that have previously eradicated or rendered invisible the presence of women and men of color. Ironically, then, the very visibility of the raced or gendered body is what makes this body powerless. Why is it that Mystique, capable of assuming any human or mutant shape and their attendant abilities, is subordinate to Magneto, whose powers are quite limited by comparison? Despite token gestures toward a geopolitical understanding of cultural difference made possible, in part, by computer technologies, *X-Men* is an anachronistic story. The film represents as natural and inevitable the ways in which women are the principal bodies that define mutation and difference.

X-Men is a film that brings to the big screen comic-book counterculture. The characters are supposed to resemble cartoons but in fact their dimensions are much more complex. In contrast, what happens in both *Mission Impossible 2* and *Gone in 60 Seconds* is quite the opposite of *X-Men*. In these movies, real-life characters become more cartoonish, and their "real-life" plots depend heavily on elaborate death-defying skills (like the ones most adolescents experience in video games) in a dizzying display of special effects.

The rendering of character into cartoon and narrative into special effect has another ideological effect: the film specifically targets the token female characters and turns them into dolls or, perhaps more accurately, into video-gamepieces. Unlike the male characters who are too closely aligned with Cartesian subjectivity to be quite so materially visible, the women in this film are faced with the impossible task of representing a spectrum of female identities. Like gamepieces, these female figures are unreal, monstrous versions of "women"; they demonstrate for the audience at large very clearly the ideologies they embody.

Both main female characters in *Gone in 60 Seconds* and *Mission Impossible 2*, Sway and Nyah Nordolf-Hall, are played by actors whose faces are a synthesis of different, idealized racial characteristics although they also represent established racial standpoints. They are cultural hybrids, and it seems as if the decisions made by the casting director deliberately exploit this hybridity though not for any subversive or resistant purpose. In these films, Newton's and Jolie's composite faces force their characters to represent very traditional historical places of subordination, despite those characters' currency with a post–women's liberation, feminist discourse.[11]

Both characters therefore represent an ideological consolidation of gender and race. Their roles in these plots are quite tangential; they are not particularly significant characters in the narrative. Their significance, then, is something other than dramatic, and once again, I want to argue that their importance to the films is primarily ideological. Like the cyborgs of *X-Men*, the "real-life" roles in these films are ones that demonstrate putatively postmodern gestures to racial interfaces that turn out inevitably to be monstrous.

Thandie Newton's role as Nyah Nordolf-Hall in *Mission Impossible 2* is atypically generic. She plays a damsel in distress, but the distress she is supposed to represent isn't really about her but, rather, about what she can perpetrate. Breathtakingly beautiful, she commands almost as much close-up screen presence as Tom Cruise (with whom John Woo is plainly cinematographically obsessed). But her very beauty is what casts her as monstrous in the narrative because it acts as a material block to her more abstractly intellectual capacities.

Mission Impossible 2's plot is not singularly complicated: Russian scientist Dr. Nekhorovich (Rade Serbedzija) has developed a virus, Chimera, and its cure, Bellepheron, and these discoveries have captured the attention of both the corporate magnate, McCloy (Brendan Gleeson), of the Australian biotechnological firm, Biocyte, and the renegade IMF ex-agent, Sean Ambrose (Dougray Scott). Loyal IMF Agent, Ethan Hunt (Tom Cruise), is chosen for the task of tracking down the whereabouts of the virus, cure, and attendant entourage of buyers and thieves. The rest of the film revolves around the vicissitudes of Hunt's hunt, his romantic entanglement with Hall, and the eventual worldwide danger he is able to circumvent singlehandedly.

Hall's part in this high-action drama is somewhat more difficult to describe. Although her character is generic, it is also more narratively elusive than typically romantic roles. She is most insistently a mediator: Between race, between social class, between men, she occupies the most materially visible position of any character in the film. From the first moment of Hunt's encounter with her at a party in Seville, her body acts as an obstruction and gets in the way of an intellectual exchange. Studying her movements in order to appraise her abilities as a thief, Hunt follows her to a safe from which she is attempting to extract a valuable necklace. When the alarm goes off, they have to hide in the bathtub, one body on top of the other. These maneuvers have the effect of shifting Hunt's as well as the audience's conception of this character from her abstract professional role to her erotic one. Hall's dark skin, high cheekbones, tilted eyes, straight hair and nose, combined with her British accent, mark her as an imperial cultural hybrid. She can be at once exoticized as an evasive Carmen figure (the setting in Seville deliberately invokes this theme), but also as something even more othered: the colonial subject, molded in the shape of the master body and taught to speak the master language.[12] It is fitting, then, that the majority of the action takes place in a postcolonial Australia where Nyah Hall negotiates between Ethan Hunt and her Scottish ex-boyfriend, Sean Ambrose, but ultimately between the much more powerful figures of the Australian genetic engineering mogul, McCloy, and the transatlantic Mission Commander, Swanbeck (Anthony Hopkins).

Though Hall has her own expertise—she is a world-class thief—her real "expertise" is her capacity to seduce. Putatively employed by the IMF, she is sent to penetrate Ambrose's stronghold in order to discover his connection with the virus Chimera. (In fact, her employment is somewhat of a mystery; the narrative represents her as doing Hunt a "favor.") She is constantly engaged in erotic encounters between both Hunt and Ambrose. Her body literally comes between them on more than one occasion (having already done so in her first encounter with Hunt), but the effect of this interruption is to showcase their power.

It is precisely because of the global setting(s) of this film that Newton's body is chosen to represent Hall's. From the film's opening shots of Hunt scaling an improbable rockface in the United States to Spain and Australia, we have a map of former British imperial power to follow and attach our ideas about "global" politics. Hall embodies these perspectives quite admirably, standing in for both the exoticized African subaltern while simultaneously domesticating that alien standpoint with more recognizably European markers of beauty. Little wonder, then, that she can be the love interest of competing parties.

Yet Hall also becomes another kind of mediator: She embodies for both Ambrose and Hunt a field of otherness onto which each can project their fantasies about the other. She becomes the dark signifier of their own erotic obsessions. As Ambrose's former lover, Hall becomes for Hunt something both desirable and revolting; although she is the object of his romantic and erotic interest, her former association with Ambrose marks her with something less savory, perhaps because she has now become the IMF's ticket into the criminal underworld of this untrustworthy agent. Likewise, when Ambrose discovers Hall's desire for Hunt, she becomes for him a deeply problematic object, arousing exaggerated, often conflated, responses of both sexual interest and abjection. Perhaps the final moments of the film dramatize these ideas most coherently, when, in a masterful moment of mediation, Hall infects herself with the last remaining vial of the deadly but extremely lucrative virus, Chimera, as a way of negotiating between their warring positions. Her body now has become desirable not because of its erotic appeal but because of its disease: She is too valuable for Ambrose to kill (he will profit from the sales of Bellepheron) and too valuable for Hunt to lose (he will increase the IMF's moral capital by saving her life).

Not only does Hall's erotic and pathological body function as a means of mediating between two representations of corporate power, Biocyte (capitalism) and the IMF (law), but her cyborgian abilities also determine the success with which she can operate as an intermediary. I should add that those abilities are ones that are implanted by both corporate entities, but the cyborgian technology can only be effectively implemented through the body of the exotic woman.

Ambrose (and by extension, the entire capitalist enterprise of genetic engineering that Biocyte embodies) calls the technological tracking devices he uses to find Hall "magic," a strangely anachronistic term for their postmodern biogenetic products, Chimera (the virus) and Bellepheron (the antidote). In fact, Ambrose describes Hall as a Trojan horse, a classical gift with serious repercussions. The effect of this language is to render their attempts to gain significant purchase in this biogenetic market hopelessly romantic, denuded of any real technological power or prowess. After all, it is the IMF (Hunt and his coworkers Luther Stickell and Billy Baird) that imbeds the tracking device in Hall's body in the first place. Hall's body, therefore, makes this outlaw outfit of capitalist enterprise entirely visible to the Hunt, even if this highly prized window of information is secondary to his first jealous reaction to seeing her intimately connected with Ambrose. Once again Hall/Newton is the body appropriated by either "side" to reveal information about the other (Ambrose, of course, finds out about her duplicity and uses her to gain access to Hunt's motives).[13] She is at once a transparent body of exchange, like any commodity, and an occlusive body of resistance: Her desirability and disease demonstrate these extraordinarily different and disarmingly similar situations.

Hall is a monster, especially toward the end of the film when, contaminated with Chimera by her own choice, she has the potential to infect an entire population of people. She's a "Typhoid Mary," as Ambrose sneeringly refers to her, a "bitch" who will make him millions (37 billion pounds, to be exact, with stock options) because of the increased value of the drug's cure, Bellepheron. She will, however, never yield him her own body and thus becomes, simultaneously, a deservingly abject figure.[14]

This language, as well as the language Ambrose uses during his negotiations with McCloy when he barters for the excessively profitable biotechnological commodities strangely and painfully resonates (pre-)industrial imperial discourse. A lucrative trade in the eighteenth-century slave market, for example, thoroughly abjected the commodified bodies that tendered wealth. Like Britain's historically xenophobic representation of the materials and peoples that increased its own imperial stature in the initial iteration of "global" marketing, so, too, does the "first" world's role in the postindustrial, postmodern global marketplace capitalize on a xenophobic demonization of the "third" world under the guise of cultural inclusiveness. Hall / Newton, character and actor, embodies some of the anxieties of multiculturalism. For example, she demonstrates the ways in which "first" world attention (and their putative yielding) to the demands of cultural inclusiveness draws upon the historical conflation of race and gender in order to give shape to the subordinated colonial body. This body then materializes the uncharted mass of global economics in the shape of the familiarly female body of cultural abjection.[15]

Thandie Newton's role in *Mission Impossible 2* is one that extracts historical accounts of British imperialist ideology in order to represent a "future" cyborg, one that is equally limited by industrialist hegemony for its postindustrial definition. "'Women of colour' are the preferred labour force," writes Haraway, "for the science-based industries, the real women for whom the world-wide sexual market, labour market, and politics of reproduction kaleidoscope into daily life."[16] Her place as a woman of color therefore qualifies her as the mediating body, one that is commodified in a number of ways to manifest the normalcy of whiteness. But what happens when we turn to the white body or, more accurately, the white female body? How does this particular cultural body get exhibited in filmic narratives of global economies and technological innovation?

Earlier I mentioned that both Thandie Newton and Angelina Jolie become videogamepieces because of their appearances in the plots as token women. I should probably amend that claim: Newton's presence in *Mission Impossible 2* is less as a gamepiece and more as a revised body representing colonial discourse. Jolie, on the other hand, embodies much more obviously the female cyberbody currently popular in the various murky worlds of videogames. Either in the fresh, clean Australian sunlight or the sultry romantic darkness of Seville, Newton is still working in tandem with the traditional glamor of international intrigue, even if she does function as a cyborgian channel of information. Likewise her face is one that registers traditional Europeanized notions of beauty mapped out onto the body of the other.[17] Dominic Sena's *Gone in 60 Seconds* evokes an entirely different mood for its cyberdrama, one that is also anachronistic in terms of its nostalgic gestures toward a time when car theft was "real" and not cluttered by fancy technological devices, but also one that plays with Hollywood's latest love affair with generational narratives.

This film bypasses the Hollywood glamor of Los Angeles and focuses on a working-class Long Beach: loading docks, fisheries, warehouses, wrecking-yards, chop-shops, convoluted bystreets, positioned against the tangled hell of suburban uniformity, constitute the film's various mise-en-scenes. The combined effect of these backdrops is to imitate the diverse settings that videogames exploit for their contests. Much of the action of the film is shot in tight frames that compress these backdrops into very focused areas. In fact, the general effect of these frames is to successfully reproduce the ambiance of videogames like Tomb Raider or Odd World or games that simulate mechanical operation, particularly driving. Despite the narrative's thinly veiled scorn for technological innovation, then, the cinemato(po)graphy of the action scenes exploits the computer technology producing virtual action in videogames.

Most of the characters in this film are resolutely conventional. Their bodies aren't especially futuristic; in fact, the main characters are older, weathered, heavily nostalgic men (who, of course, turn out to be justified in their fetishization of the old ways when one technological innovation after another fails to live up to its promise). The plot is also fairly traditional in terms of its conflict: The veneer of family values—two brothers and a mother struggling to keep a familial identity intact after the older brother has been repeatedly caught stealing cars—functions as a suitably "moral" story to cover the contest between good thief/bad thief. Only the action itself, designed from futuristic computer technology, and Sway/Jolie herself stand as counters to a traditional Hollywood action film and transform this remake of a 1974 cult film into a weirdly futuristic movie.

I have discussed how the action replicates the computer graphics of videogames; I would extend that argument to include the graphic representation of Sway. Her role in the plot, like Hall's in *Mission Impossible 2*, is quite minimal even though she is the ostensible female lead (she certainly gets star billing on the credits), so her importance to the film rests elsewhere. She is the only character that mediates a number of conflicted positions: generationally (between older and younger groups of car thieves), familially (between the older and younger brother), sexually (between Memphis Raines and the rest of the all-male cast), and, in a larger sense, between traditional filmic representation and computer-generated imagery, between high and low technologies. The fact that Sway alone of all the characters is able to move so unproblematically between these obviously narratively vexed positions attests to the film's belief in the traditional malleability of the female body and its ability to conform to whatever tasks may be at hand.

The plot depends on an unresolved conflict between Memphis Raines and his younger brother, Kip (Giovanni Ribisi). Kip's botched attempts at car theft force Memphis back into action in order to prevent the murder of his younger brother. Impossibly, he has forty-eight hours in which to steal and deliver fifty cars for the powerful rival mogul in car theft, Raymond Calitri (Christopher Eccleston). The rest of the film focuses on how Memphis and his former associates in crime fulfill this demand.

Sway's relation to all of this is strangely illogical. She is a putative member of the old gang, but she is obviously much younger than any of them. She has "gone straight," working both a car mechanic and a bartender, and is the last person to be asked back into action, yet her talents for disarming car-alarm systems that probably weren't even invented back in the heyday of her operation and for hotwiring cars are indispensable to the team. How does one make sense of Sway?

She functions, of course, as the marginalized erotic object, mostly for Memphis (though this romance is severely underplayed) but, at the film's conclusion, it is apparent that she is also a sexualized presence for the entire group, feeding the injured Toby with her fingers amidst wolf-whistles of appreciation. Yet it's clear that her sexual presence is not her most exceptional quality. Even if she and Memphis have a brief moment of sexual encounter, this moment is entirely mediated by their voyeuristic gaze onto another couple's copulation (whose car they're about to steal). The climactic moment of Memphis and Sway's possible romantic reacquaintance is interrupted by a gearshift that gets stuck between Sway's legs and then by the fact that the couple has disappeared from view, thus making it "time to get to work," as Sway mutters.

Of all the characters, Sway has the most "intuitive" relationship to cars. Though Memphis understands them (he "talks" to them), his understanding is really only about mastery. Sway is the machine: "Hello ladies," she greets rows of opulent cars waiting to be plucked, her expression exhibiting sisterly intimacy. Sway is, therefore, mystified in the same way that the cars bearing women's names are mystified, particularly the 1967 Ford Mustang, Eleanor. She is unreadable primarily because she has little affect: She smiles, she stares, she rarely speaks. While the rest of the group members have specific skills to contribute to the cause, hers are less clearly articulated.

But because she is mystified, she is the most transparently mediating figure, and the ideological work she does in this film is to provide an interface between computer technology and a conservative narrative. She also provides a crucial shape for variously othered subjects and discourses; she makes cultural inclusiveness readable. In Dyer's terms, she makes "our" (white) understanding of multicultural standpoints "normal."

I mentioned earlier that both Newton and Jolie have faces that are a pastiche of racial characteristics. In the case of Jolie, her thick lips magnified by makeup, high cheekbones, tilted eyes, dead-white skin and platinum blond dreadlocks are features meant to conflate ideals of beauty. She is a composite in the same sense that computer-generated models of the feminine are often racial composites like Lara Croft of Tomb Raider, or virtual Webcasters Ananova (Ananova.com) or Mya (Motorola). It is no surprise, then, that Jolie plays Lara Croft in Simon West's 2001 film adaptation of *Tomb Raider.*

Why does Jolie's face, however, deliberately invoke black features, especially when the whiteness of her skin and the blondness of her hair are so foregrounded? David Crane has suggested that blackness "provides a more authentically resistant otherness than hybridity, and that authenticity associated with blackness visually enhances the intersection between cyberspace and cinematic space."[18] Crane also suggests that the body of the Other is suitable to the representation of the "other" space of digital culture. Jolie's body renders the narratively marginalized space of the technological Other into something that resembles the subordinated body of blackness, but also simultaneously makes that body "normal" because of its whiteness. Dreadlocks, tattoos, thick lips, and other accoutrements of otherness become beautiful when they are projected onto the white face, just as blackness turns beautiful (on the big screen) when straight noses, straight hair, and thinner lips are superimposed on the black face.

Both *Gone in 60 Seconds* and *Mission Impossible 2* deploy the feminine as the embodiment of this racial interface. Both films also use the male characters to enact more stereotyped notions of black culture. Ethan Hunt's African American comrade, Luther Strickland (Ving Rhames), constantly alludes to his Gucci boots or Armani suits coming under siege during the more active parts of the film, thus parodying the relationship black men have to (newly acquired) wealth. Donny in *Gone in 60 Seconds* also ventriloquizes cultural stereotypes of the African American man: He is a large man, interested in immediate creature comforts and not the abstract rewards of capitalism. The final scene features him as the stereotyped black cook, serving his white gang members. Yet despite these hierarchical representations of masculine roles, the films clearly place the male characters on a different plane from the female characters and set them out to perform different types of ideological work.

It is impossible to think of cyborgs and women without recalling the groundbreaking work Donna Haraway has done in this area of feminist theory. Haraway has pointed out the cultural importance of monsters, suggesting that such "boundary creatures—simians, cyborgs, and women—all . . . have had a destabilizing place in the great Western evolutionary, technological, and biological narratives." As marginal and marginalized creatures, they "demonstrate" or "signify" the limits of cultural boundaries and social limitations, and may also "be signs of possible worlds" though they are surely "signs of worlds for which we are responsible."[19] In many ways the female characters of Hollywood action films demonstrate to audiences the "limits" of virtual culture. While the male bodies in these films remain fairly static either as disembodied positions of knowledge (white) or embodied articulations of racial stereotypes (black), the female characters have a curious capacity to swell and shrink to fill in the gaps of cultural representation: They are, then, according to Haraway's definition, monstrously destabilizing.[20] It seems as if cinematic space provides a literal and thematic boundary to virtual space and uses the cyborgian female to outline those boundaries.

In their introduction to *Race in Cyberspace*, Kolko, Nakamura, and Rodman argue that the milieu of cyberspace is entirely constructed of simple binary switches, of "0's and 1's . . . that are either off or on."[21] In this climate the subject of race is also either "off" or "on" in a way, they point out, that is impossible in the "real" world. Both the silences and the often inflamed rhetoric that together designate whether or not the subject of race is visible or invisible—off or on—in cyberculture. These binaries demonstrate, however, the effectiveness of a master discourse that so thoroughly embeds a Foucauldian ideal of corporate power structures that even the possibility of "transcending" that structure prove to be impossible.

The very fact that the space of cyberculture is not charted may well raise anxieties concerning cartography and taxonomy. Exactly what gets situated in this limitless expanse? Contrary to rhetoric about cyberculture exhorting the freedom promised by this limitlessness, do we insistently recreate or redefine cultural ideological hierarchies in order to make this environment seem familiar or even safe? The World Wide Web and the Internet seem to literalize the notion of making the "global" locally available: an entire "world" opens up under one's fingertips. These aspects of cyberculture cater to the American popular fiction that we can "think globally and act locally." Almost like the ideal anthropologist of yore, Internet users can stalk, chameleon-ike, through endless cultural sites, self-tuned to these exotic locales. Fantasies about the pure subject unencumbered by the trappings and limitations of the physical body are promoted through this purely epistemological form of interactive discourse. However, as the recent debates in the fields of anthropology and ethnography about the status of the field-worker suggest, the disembodied, transcendent self is all too often grounded within that self's material circumstances; the "global" aspect of the cyberenvironment may be, therefore, problematic. This is not to say that one can't have literal access to other cultural sites around the globe but that our understanding of those global sites—the way we translate them into modes of understanding—is predicated by our immediate locale.[22]

In fact, in the current popular discourse about globalization, it seems as if the local has more importance than what we assume. Our understanding of the concept "global" takes shape as a totalizing hierarchy that reinvents the idea of global as something that can be commodified, marketed, and appropriated. Calling into question the production of an epistemology of cyberculture, perhaps postcolonial theories about cartography and taxonomy that consider ideologies of imperialism may be useful in examining the ostensible "newness" of the structure of cyberdiscourse.

Anxieties about cartography and taxonomy in relation to cyberspace insistently replicate the anxieties about territory from British colonialism and its contention with similar issues of expansion and fantasies about limitless possibilities. The very un-chartability of digital territory determines the need to replicate markers of identity, as popular Hollywood film suggests. The eighteenth-century self-made man, Robinson Crusoe, persistently replicates British imperial economy in his island domain, even if his subjects consist primarily of the various (male) animals he manages to rescue from his foundered ship. Before the advent of Friday, the defining boundary to his household are (female) cats that, though originating from the ship, have managed to procreate with nameless island creatures and have become monstrous versions of themselves. In an age of another kind of imperialism, do we rely on established taxonomic discourses in order to make visible an invisible geopolitical territory? It seems as if the body gendered as female is called upon once again to perform the kind of demonstrative monstrosity that makes these spaces safe for Western consumption. Perhaps the Human Genome Project is an extension of such ideological logic: making material the virtual possibilities of human being.

Notes

1. I should point out that there are, obviously, exceptions to this claim. *The Matrix*, for example, has garnered a great deal of critical interest because of the representation of the main female character's evident physical and intellectual strength. An earlier movie, *Terminator 2*, also showcases a buff Linda Hamilton taking charge of her story. Other films that have come out more recently than the ones I discuss in this chapter also emphasize the new importance of strong female characters. My argument, how-

ever, is that despite these representations, in major Hollywood productions (the dominant genre for the moviegoing audience in U.S. culture and, arguably, other ones), women's bodies are still rendered into visible objects meant to be noticed for their material capacities and rarely accorded the same Cartesian status as their male counterparts.

2. Singer's *X-Men* makes these arguments much more explicitly. Interestingly, the lead female—at least from what I can conjecture from the trailers to the film—replicates, masklike, a current street fashion in Japanese culture: *gangura*. The magazine *Artbyte* (July–August 2000) describes this style as "girls teetering in platform shoes, lots of synthetic fabrics, short skirts, gray or blonde hair—and charcoal-broiled skin . . . lips and eyelids circled in heavy white makeup" (2000: 65). However, this movie makes a very self-conscious play on videogame drama and their characters are quite explicitly cyborgian; my interest is also in the unselfconscious replication of cyborg figures, materialized and naturalized as "real" bodies in "real" dramas.

3. Rajani Sudan, "Sexy SIMS, Racy SIMS," in *Race in Cyberspace*, ed. Beth E. Kolko, Lisa Nakamura, and Gilbert B. Rodman (New York: Routledge, 1999), 69–86.

4. Richard Dyer, *White* (London and New York: Routledge, 1997), 1.

5. See Judith Butler, *Bodies That Matter: On the Discursive Limits of "Sex"* (New York: Routledge, 1993).

6. Of course, the ideological problem with this comparison is that the child is the young Magneto, the "bad" mutant who swears his revenge on all of humankind. Any body other than the Anglo-Saxon male body is suspect and prone to being ideologically branded.

7. Dyer, *White*, 1.

8. When I claim that the issue of race is sharply defined, I mean that in popular representation (especially in film), race is a black and white matter, one that can be easily resolved by reducing a systemic problem into one about the individual. In fact, in 2000 *The New York Times* completed a six-week special on how race is lived in America, and the single statement that emerged from their journalistic investigation seemed to be that race is not an ideological issue but a personal one. Nothing could be further from the truth.

9. I realize that other ideologies are also at work in this narrative, but for the purposes of this argument I am focusing on the conflation of gender and race.

10. It's interesting to examine how this Hollywood account of genetic "research" contrasts with the discoveries made by the Human Genome Project.

11. Homi Bhabha's understanding of both hybridity and subversive mimicry clarifies the ways in which resistance is embedded in the ideological structures that coerce women to be identified as non-Cartesian bodies. The very fact that they need to be identified as such presupposes a sense in which they are not, a priori, only material. See Homi K. Bhabha, *The Location of Culture* (London and New York: Routledge, 1994).

12. Part of Newton's/Hall's beauty is that she is Europeanized—her nose, mouth, hair, and face reflect features that have traditionally been associated with Anglican models of beauty; her skin serves to burnish this paradigm with a veneer of exoticism, not unlike Aphra Behn's description of the African prince, Oroonoko. Likewise, Hall/Newton's accent functions as a reminder of the cultural standpoints she negotiates. I can't help but think that this was a deliberate decision on the part of the casting director, primarily because her accent has, reportedly, interfered with her career as a film actress and prevented her from getting major roles.

13. These representations of power are necessarily binary in structure. To establish other examples of corporate power that don't always fall into the neat categories of good and bad would be a more accurate acknowledgement of the complications of global economies but would hopelessly complicate the film.

14. I use the term "abject" in the Kristevan sense to mean the effluvia that's expelled in order to carve out a sense of self. In the case of Hall's abjection, she is the discharged body that makes possible Ambrose's new self-definition as entrepreneurial genius. See Julia Kristeva, *Powers of Horror: An Essay on Abjection* (New York: Columbia University Press, 1982).

15. Interestingly, Thandie Newton herself has been no stranger to the role of the mediating body. Born in Zambia of a British (white) father and a Zimbabwean (black) mother, they returned to England when the political situation in Zambia became too problematic for them (presumably because of their own cultural and racial hybridity). Newton studied drama in England and was cast in her first movie, but subsequently failed to find regular work as a film actress ostensibly because of her British accent. Here, then, is an example of subversive mimicry: Newton's visible African body occludes her less visible (though aural) white British subjectivity. Though a British citizen, she is limited to representing what ideologies of race and color deem appropriate.

16. Donna Haraway, *Simians, Cyborgs, and Women: The Reinvention of Nature* (New York: Routledge, 1991).

17. What I mean by this convoluted phrase is that there is a history of using a European grid of beauty in order to identify the "beautiful" in the faces of other abjected colonial bodies. The difference that the cyborg brings to this history is that the body of the other is now more clearly integrating technological machinery. She is either the result of computer generated graphics and altered pixels, like Lara Croft of the Tomb Raider videogames, or in some way grafts machinery into her flesh.

18. David Crane, "In Medias Race: Filmic Representations, Netwoked Communication, and Racial Intermediation," in *Race in Cyberspace*, ed. Beth E. Kolko, Lisa Nakamura, Gilbert Rodman (New York: Routledge, 1999), 91.

19. Haraway, *Simians, Cyborgs, and Women*, 2.

20. These hydraulics (for lack of a better term) are deployed not only as the monstrous exaggerations Newton and Jolie embody in Hollywood film but also in other "higher"

representational formats. American artist Lisa Yuskavage's sculptures of overblown female bodies, for example, magnify the ideological dimensions of white femininity. Similarly, the French performance artist Orlan has turned her own body into a composite of different historical paradigms of beauty through plastic surgery.

21. Kolko, Nakamura, and Rodman, *Race in Cyberspace*, 1.

22. In particular, the anthropologist Clifford Geertz's arguments about "local knowledge" have undone many of the ideological fantasies about fieldwork that ethnographers have entertained. See Clifford Geertz, *Local Knowledge: Further Essays in Interpretive Anthropology* (New York: Basic Books, 1983).

Works Cited

Artbyte 3, no. 2 (July–August 2000): 65–67. Film review.

Bhabha, Homi K. *The Location of Culture*. London and New York: Routledge, 1994.

Butler, Judith. *Bodies That Matter: On the Discursive Limits of "Sex"*. New York: Routledge, 1993.

Crane, David. "In Medias Race: Filmic Representations, Networked Communication, and Racial Intermediation." In *Race in Cyberspace*, ed. Beth E. Kolko, Lisa Nakamura, and Gilbert Rodman, 87–115. New York: Routledge, 1999.

Dyer, Richard. *White*. London and New York: Routledge, 1997.

Geertz, Clifford. *Local Knowledge: Further Essays in Interpretive Anthropology*. New York: Basic Books, 1983.

Haraway, Donna. *Simians, Cyborgs, and Women: The Reinvention of Nature*. New York: Routledge, 1991.

Kolko, Beth E., Lisa Nakamura, and Gilbert B. Rodman, eds. *Race in Cyberspace*. New York: Routledge, 1999.

Kristeva, Julia. *Powers of Horror: An Essay on Abjection*. New York: Columbia University Press, 1982.

The New York Times. "How Race Is Lived in America." Available at <http://www.nytimes.com/library/national/race/index.html>; published as *How Race Is Lived in America: Pulling Together, Pulling Apart*, Correspondents of The New York Times. New York: Henry Holt, 2001.

Films Cited

Cameron, James. *Terminator 2: Judgment Day*, 1991.

Sena, Dominic. *Gone in 60 Seconds*, 2000.

Singer, Bryan. *X-men*, 2000.

Wachowsky, Andy and Larry. *The Matrix*, 1999.

West, Simon. *Tomb Raider*, 2001.

Woo, John. *Mission: Impossible II*, 2000.

19

CYBORG FEMINISM: THE SCIENCE FICTION OF OCTAVIA E. BUTLER AND GLORIA ANZALDÚA

Catherine S. Ramírez

> You have to realize this planet is not only inhabited by humans, it's inhabited by aliens too. . . . The danger spot is the United States. . . . It was possible for aliens and angels and devils and demons to come in this country. They didn't need no passport.
>
> —*Sun Ra, qtd. in John Corbett*, Extended Play

Throughout the twentieth century, representations of and references to space, science and technology permeated much African American literature, music, and art, from W. E. B. Du Bois's 1920 short story "The Comet," to the futuristic soundscapes of DJ Spooky That Subliminal Kid.[1] Linking science fiction and black cultural production, journalist Greg Tate observes, "The imaginative leap that we associate with science fiction, in terms of putting the human into an alien and alienating environment, is a gesture that repeatedly appears in the work of black writers and visual artists" (Dery 1993, 765–766). In addition to grappling with the alien and alienated, many black writers, artists and musicians, such as Walter Mosley, Jean-Michel Basquiat, and the band Earth Wind & Fire, insert Africans and/or African Americans into what Tate describes as "a visionary landscape" (Dery 1993, 765).[2] Often, this landscape is sci-fi-esque—that is, it is one of computers, spaceships, alien creatures and intergalactic travel.

In recent years, black science fiction—or Afrofuturism (i.e., "[s]peculative fiction that treats African-American concerns in the context of . . . technoculture—and, more generally, African-American signification that appropriates images of technology and a prosthetically enhanced future" [Dery 1993, 736])—has received much critical attention. In "Brothers from Another Planet," John Corbett locates the music of Lee "Scratch" Perry, Sun Ra, and George Clinton in an Afrofuturist context (Corbett 1994). Most recently, Sheree R. Thomas has collected and published short stories and critical essays on black science fiction in *Dark Matter: A Century of Speculative Fiction from the African Diaspora* (Thomas 2000). And, at the annual meeting of the American Studies Association in October 2000, Nalo Hopkinson, author of two published science-fiction novels, chaired a panel entitled "Afrofuturist Dreams: Recasting Race, Recasting Technoculture."[3]

For Octavia E. Butler, one of the most prolific and well-known black science-fiction writers, science fiction is "potentially the freest genre in existence" (Beal 1986, 14). Like other Afrofuturist texts, many of Butler's novels and short stories insert black people, as well as women and other people of color, into narratives of science, technology, and "progress." At the same time, they interrogate narratives of science and technology *as* "progress."

What's more, Butler's science fiction explores essence, position (i.e., social constructedness), and the boundary that supposedly separates the two via the figure of the cyborg. Drawing from Donna Haraway's concept of "cyborg identity," I argue that Butler's novels *Wild Seed* (1980) and *Parable of the Sower* (1993) critique fixed concepts of race, gender, sexuality and humanity, and, subsequently, "fictions" of identity and community. I conclude this study by comparing Butler's novels to Gloria Anzaldúa's *Borderlands/La Frontera: The New Mestiza* (1987) and by offering a theory of and for "New World," feminist science fiction. The cyborg—that is, the subject that simultaneously exceeds and emphasizes the boundaries of identity and community—is at the center of both Butler's and Anzaldúa's work. Through the figure of the cyborg, the two writers theorize a woman-of-color feminism that articulates (i.e., enunciates and links) both essence and position.

Before I begin my discussion of Butler's and Anzaldúa's texts, I provide a cursory history of science fiction by women. Then, for the sake of clarity, I offer a working definition of science fiction, even though it is a genre that, in many ways, resists definition. Next, I examine Haraway's concept of the cyborg and its relationship to and implications for feminism for and by women of color. Ultimately, I hope to illustrate that science fiction is not simply escapist fantasy, but a creative and politicized "space" for the articulation of the pasts, presents, and possible futures of the "aliens" and passport-less of the New World.

Where No Black Woman Has Gone Before?:
African American and Feminist Science Fiction

In a 1993 interview, acclaimed science-fiction novelist and critic Samuel R. Delany estimated that there were only four black science-fiction authors writing in the English language: Octavia E. Butler, Steven Barnes, Charles Saunders, and himself.[4] Because of its putative origins in and its focus on so-called hard science, science fiction historically seems to have been the domain of men and boys. Indeed, the stereotypical sci-fi fan is a middle-class, white, male, adolescent nerd. "The flashing lights, the dials, and the rest of the imagistic paraphernalia of science fiction [from the 1950s through the 1970s] functioned as social signs—signs people learned to read very quickly," Delany explained. "They signaled technology. And technology was like a placard on the door saying, 'Boys Club! Girls, keep out. Blacks and Hispanics and the poor in general, go away!'" (Dery 1993, 744).

In defining science fiction, science-fiction writer, critic, and publisher Isaac Asimov emphasizes science and technology. He links the genre with the European and North American Industrial Revolution of the late eighteenth and nineteenth centuries and argues, "True science fiction deals with human science, with the continuing advance of knowledge, with the continuing ability of human beings to make themselves better understand the universe." Linking science fiction with what appears to be a Foucauldian power-knowledge couplet, as well as with what hints at imperialism and colonialism, Asimov adds that "true science fiction" highlights humans' "continuing ability . . . to alter some parts [of the universe] for their own comfort and security by the ingenuity of their ideas" (Asimov 1983, 10). In other words, science fiction, for Asimov, is concerned with (and posits an unproblematic relationship between) science, technology, knowledge, and human progress. Moreover, it lauds man's conquest of "the universe" (the cosmos? nature? the unknown?) via science and technology.

Even though the concepts of science, technology, and, by extension, science fiction itself, have been gendered masculine, women have been producing what a number of critics have designated "science fiction" since the early nineteenth century (at least). In fact, several science-fiction writers and critics point to Mary Shelley's *Frankenstein* (1818) as an origin of science fiction.[5] Excavating a genealogy of women science fiction writers, Pamela Sargent claims the nineteenth-century fantasy writers Marie Corelli, Rhoda Broughton, Sara Coleridge, and Jane Loudon as pioneers of women's science fiction; she places Mary Bradley Lane's *Mizora* (1890) and Charlotte Perkins Gilman's *Herland* (1915) within "[t]he utopian tradition" of science fiction; and she lists roughly fifty-six women science-fiction writers of the twentieth century, beginning with Gertrude Barrows Bennett, who published *The Heads of Cerberus* under the pseudonym Francis Stevens in 1919 (Sargent 1995a).

Several women, most notably C. L. Moore, Leigh Brackett, Judith Merril, and Marion Zimmer Bradley, produced science fiction prior to the 1960s. However, with second-wave feminism and the advent of "New Wave" (i.e., "soft") science fiction in the 1960s, more women began to write, publish, and read science fiction.[6] What's more, some women writers, such as Ursula K. Le Guin and Vonda N. McIntyre, began to receive critical attention for their work. In *In the Chinks of the World Machine: Feminism and Science Fiction*, Sarah Lefanu notes that no woman received the prestigious Hugo Award for science fiction between 1953 (its inception) and 1967, but that between 1968 and 1984, eleven women won it. In addition, she points out that 1974 saw the first "women and science fiction" panel at a science-fiction convention (Lefanu 1988).

1974 also saw the publication of Sargent's *Women of Wonder*, the first collection of "science fiction stories by women about women." *Women of Wonder* was followed by Vonda N. McIntyre and Susan Janice Anderson's *Aurora: Beyond Equality* (1976), a collection of feminist science fiction. Since then, Sargent has published four more collections of science-fiction stories by women and about women, as well as her own science fiction. Furthermore, the body of criticism on women's science fiction has grown.[7]

In his 1981 essay, "My Definition of Science Fiction," Philip K. Dick, author of scores of critically acclaimed science-fiction novels and short stories, offers a definition of science fiction different from Asimov's. According to Dick, science fiction need not limit itself to spaceships and zap guns. Such props are usually found in what Dick considers "space adventure"—that is, "adventure, fights, and wars in the future in space involving superadvanced technology" (Dick 1995, 99). Dick distinguishes space adventure from science fiction by placing the latter in the everyday world of the present—"our world," as he phrases it—rather than in a fantastical future world. However, science fiction, according to Dick, does not leave our world intact. Instead, it distorts it. He explains, "We have a fictitious world; that is the first step: [i]t is a society that does not in fact exist, but is predicated on our known society—that is, our known society acts as a jumping-off point for it. . . . It is our world dislocated by some kind of mental effort on the part of the author, our world transformed into that which it is not or not yet" (99).

In short, Dick claims that the science-fiction writer fabricates a world that mirrors "our known society" but is slightly different. This difference "must be sufficient to give rise to events that could not occur in our society—or in any known society present or past." Dislocation, then, not science and technology, is the "essence of science fiction," according to Dick. Science fiction distorts our society "so that as a result a new society is generated in the author's mind, transferred to paper, and from paper it occurs as a convulsive shock in the reader's mind." Dick terms this dislocation on the part of the reader "the shock of dysrecognition" (Dick 1995, 99).

Similarly, literary critic Darko Suvin defines science fiction as the literature of "cognitive estrangement." Suvin draws the concept of "estrangement" from the work of Bertolt Brecht. He quotes Brecht: "'A representation which estranges is one which allows us to recognize its subject, but at the same time makes it seem unfamiliar'" (Suvin 1976, 60). Like Dick, Suvin claims that science fiction embodies both "the ideal extreme of exact recreation of the author's empirical environment . . . [and] interest in a strange newness, a novum" (58–59). He defines science fiction as "a literary genre whose necessary and sufficient conditions are the presences and interaction of estrangement and cognition, and whose main formal device is an imaginative framework alternative to the author's empirical environment" (62).

The conventions of dysrecognition and estrangement resemble the Freudian concept of the uncanny: that which is simultaneously recognizable and unfamiliar. While they beg the questions "Whose world is 'our world'?" and "What if an 'author's empirical environment' differs greatly from that of his or her reader?," both are valuable for understanding science fiction as a viable medium for questioning the status quo. Both concepts equip the student of science fiction with a vocabulary for exploring ideology as a representation of the imaginary relationships of individuals to their real conditions of existence.[8] That is, dysrecognition and estrangement denaturalize and relativize that which is supposedly natural, common, obvious, innate, and immutable. In doing so, they enable us to identify and question overarching, yet seemingly invisible, social systems and regulatory ideals, such as capitalism, patriarchy, heterosexuality, sex, gender, man, and woman. Moreover, dysrecognition and estrangement allow us to imagine epistemological and ontological alternatives.

The science fiction of Asimov and many other writers of the first half of the twentieth century praised man, technology, and, in the words of one critic, "the nature and significance of the scientific method" (Canary 1977, 164). Their work did not necessarily interrogate the relationships between technology and "progress," knowledge and power, and exploration and expansion. Yet, with the techniques of dysrecognition and estrangement, science fiction—in particular, feminist and African American science fiction—has evolved into a significant literary mode for critics of ideology. Indeed, "science fiction's most important use," according to science-fiction writer and critic Kingsley Amis, "is a means of dramatising social enquiry, as providing a fictional mode in which cultural tendencies can be isolated and judged" (Amis 1960, 54).

Wild Seed and *Parable of the Sower:* **Not So Long Ago and Not in a Galaxy Far, Far Away**

In a 1981 interview, Octavia E. Butler stated, "I began writing about power because I had so little" (Davidson 1981, 35). Undeniably, Butler uses science fiction to scrutinize power relations (i.e., social hierarchies based on race, gender, and sexuality) and to explore ways of subverting and/or destroying power without replicating or reproducing it. Butler was raised in Pasadena, California. Her father died when she was an infant and her mother worked as a maid (See 1993, 50). Butler describes herself as "a pessimist if I'm not careful, a feminist always, a black, a quiet egoist, [and] a former Baptist."[9]A product of the social movements of the 1960s, she claims that the "black consciousness raising that was taking place at the time" impacted her writing (Beal 1986, 15). Butler began publishing science-fiction short stories in 1970, and her first novel, *Patternmaster*, appeared in print in 1976. Since then, she has published a total of eleven novels and numerous short stories, and she has won the Hugo and Nebula awards, two of science fiction's most prestigious literary prizes.

While much of Butler's science fiction takes place in outer space and many of her characters are aliens and monsters,[10] her novels *Wild Seed* and *Parable of the Sower* exemplify science fiction as defined by Dick and Suvin: Both are set on Earth (albeit at very different times); their protagonists are not extraterrestrials (but they are not typical or normal human beings either); and both texts are seemingly verisimilar (i.e., they appear to present realistic worlds—worlds, that, in some ways, mirror "the author's empirical environment"). However, the settings of *Wild Seed* and *Parable of the Sower* are *not* Butler's late-twentieth-century Southern California. They represent, to quote Dick (1981) once again, "societ[ies] that [do] not in fact exist, but [are] predicated on our known [i.e., Butler's] society" (99). As a story set in the past, *Wild Seed* is historically accurate; that is, it draws from the history of slavery and African migration to and through the New World. *Parable of the Sower*, on the other hand, draws from the author's present; it exaggerates and distorts her "empirical environment." Although fiction, many of the events that take place in the two novels are plausible. However, both *Wild Seed* and *Parable of the Sower* "estrange" the reader, for their "subjects" (i.e., their subject matter and their actors) are simultaneously recognizable and unfamiliar.

Wild Seed opens in a West African village in 1690 and closes on a plantation in Louisiana in 1840. Anyanwu, the novel's protagonist, is a three-hundred-year-old black woman. She is also a mutant; that is, she has the ability to change forms. Throughout the course of the novel, Anyanwu, whose original form is that of a young Igbo woman, transforms herself into an elderly Igbo priestess, a young black man, a leopard, an eagle, a dolphin, a dog, and a wealthy white man. In addition, she is seemingly immortal: she possesses superhuman strength and the ability to heal herself (and others) if physically injured.

Throughout *Wild Seed*, Anyanwu is engaged in a power struggle with Doro, a four-thousand-year-old *ogbanje* (evil spirit) with the power and need to "possess" others. Unlike Anyanwu, who is able to transform her own flesh into a seemingly unlimited number of life forms, Doro must constantly kill people in order to inhabit their bodies.

He "wears" a body until it grows too tired, then he discards it, as a snake sheds its skin, and preys upon another.

At one time in their lives, Anyanwu and Doro were normal mortals. However, both experienced bizarre illnesses and were transformed. Anyanwu experienced her "transition" as a young woman; Doro as a boy. His body died as a result of the illness, but his spirit transmigrated to the body of another human being. Since then, Doro has roamed the earth gathering what he terms "wild seed": men, women and children with paranormal abilities. He helps some and destroys others. Violent and power-hungry, he breeds, owns, and rules all of them.

When Doro encounters Anyanwu for the first time, he decides that she will make a valuable addition to his bizarre eugenics project. He presses her to leave Africa and join him in a settlement he has established in North America, where he claims she will not be made to feel a misfit. Doro insists that they belong together because of their special powers and promises her marriage, yet she refuses. In her three hundred years, Anyanwu has borne forty-seven children to ten husbands. "If you come with me, I think someday, I can show you children you will never have to bury," Doro offers. "A mother should not have to watch her children grow old and die" (Butler 1980, 22). After failing to cajole Anyanwu, Doro threatens to kill her descendants (of whom there are many generations) if she does not accompany him. Reluctantly, she yields to his demand.

As soon as they arrive in Doro's settlement of Wheatley, New York, Anyanwu realizes that she is now Doro's slave. Fixated on blood and genetic stock, Doro intends to breed Anyanwu with various men from his numerous settlements, for "[s]he was wild seed of the best kind. She would strengthen any line he bred her into" (Butler 1980, 22). Eventually, Anyanwu escapes from Wheatley, first by transforming herself into an eagle and flying to the Atlantic coast, then by transforming herself into a dolphin and swimming back to Africa. For decades, Doro searches for her, yet he is unable to track her when she assumes animal form.

Finally, after 150 years of separation, Doro and Anyanwu reunite in Louisiana, where Anyanwu has formed her own community of men, women, and children with strange abilities (some can read others' thoughts, some can see images from the past, some can feel others' emotions). Although she is now living in the "race-conscious culture" of the antebellum South, Anyanwu manages to shape a heterogeneous community reflective of the population of the New World: It is composed of African Americans, Euro-Americans, Native Americans, and mixed-race people (Butler 1980, 221). Yet, unlike Doro, she does not intimidate, torment, or dominate those who surround her; they are not her slaves. Rather, they are family: "[s]he gathered people to her and cared for them and helped them care for each other" (231). Unlike Doro, Anyanwu builds a community based not on genetic stock or blood, but choice.

Unlike *Wild Seed*, which is set in the past, *Parable of the Sower* offers a much more common science-fiction scenario: dystopia. The year is 2024 and pollution, global warming, drought, economic crisis, and numerous other ills plague the earth. The novel takes the form of the journal of Lauren Olamina, a bored, frustrated, and precocious African American teenager who lives with her family in Robledo, California, a suburb of Los Angeles. Only a handful of families compose Robledo, which is protected from the outside world by a makeshift wall.

In Butler's twenty-first century, Southern California is desperately dry. Slavery and indentured servitude are legal once again. Canadian and Asian corporations own factories in the United States called "borderworks"—which bear a strong resemblance to the current-day *maquilas* of northern Mexico. At borderworks, laborers are overworked, underpaid, and forced to rely on their employers for food and shelter. Those who still hold jobs that pay cash live within small, beleaguered, walled enclaves like Robledo. Outside, hordes of wretched, homeless scavengers and violent, pyromaniac junkies (known as "paints" because they shave their heads and cover their bodies with paint) murder for water, food, and weapons.

Because her mother abused a drug while she was pregnant with her, Lauren is a "sharer"; that is, she suffers from "hyperempathy," a genetic condition that causes her to experience others' physical sensations as viscerally as her own. "I'm supposed to share pleasure and pain," she writes, "but there isn't much pleasure around these days" (Butler 1995, 12).[11] If Lauren sees an injured person, or if she injures someone, his or her pain automatically becomes her own. "This is a rough disability for her time," Butler explained in a 1993 interview. "Lauren's ability is perceived as a problem, not a power" (See 1993, 51).

When a gang of paints raids Robledo, Lauren's entire family is murdered and her community is destroyed. Alone, she decides to head north, where rumor has it that "water doesn't cost more than food and . . . work brings a salary" (Butler 1995, 155). But, before her departure, Lauren encounters two other Robledo survivors: Harry Balter, a young white man, and Zahra Moss, a young black woman. Together, they join the stream of refugees walking north along California's derelict highways.

As they travel, Lauren, Harry, and Zahra must protect themselves from wild dogs, beggars, thieves, rapists, murderers, and cannibals. At first, Harry wants to trust other travelers, but Zahra, who was raised on the outside and arrived in Robledo as a jaded young woman, warns him against this. Because they are unable to trust others and must kill or be killed, Harry fears that he, Zahra, and Lauren will "turn into animals." He fears that they will become like the dangerous and desperate men, women, and children who prey upon them. "In a way, we do [have to turn into animals]," Lauren tells Harry. "We're a pack, the three of us, and all those other people out there aren't in it. If we're a good pack, and we work together, we have a chance" (Butler 1995, 168). As they journey north, Harry, Zahra and Lauren evolve into a "good pack": They learn to protect and trust one another. Eventually, they extend their trust and protection to others and their group grows from three to fourteen.

Despite the racial and ethnic tensions that infest Butler's twenty-first century, the group with whom Lauren travels is as racially and ethnically diverse as Southern California itself: It is composed of African Americans, Euro-Americans, Latinas/os, Asians, men, women, and children. Some are ex-prostitutes and ex-slaves. When Lauren invites two former slaves to join the group, she warns and reassures them, "[W]e don't kill unless someone threatens us . . . We don't hunt people. We don't eat human flesh. We fight together against enemies. If one of us is in need, the rest help out. And we don't steal from one another, ever . . . A group is strong. One or two people are easier to rob and kill" (Butler 1995, 275–276).

Regardless of their differences, all members of the group are displaced and dispossessed in one way or another. All have lost friends and family members to murder and/or slavery. Yet, Lauren realizes that her group constitutes a new kind of family. "In spite of your loss and pain, you aren't alone," she writes in her journal. "You still have people who care about you and want you to be all right. You still have family" (Butler 1995, 277).

Like Anyanwu, Lauren builds a community based not on blood, but choice. She dreams of a better world, and with her evolving religion, "Earthseed," she hopes to establish an enclave that will survive the bleak period in which she lives. According to Earthseed, "God Is Change" (Butler 1995, 3). Underscoring human agency, Lauren writes that members of the religion "are to learn to shape God with forethought, care, and work; to educate and benefit their community, their families, and themselves; and to contribute to the fulfillment of the Destiny." Earthseed's destiny is the establishment of human life in outer space—"[a] real heaven, not a mythology or philosophy. A heaven that will be theirs to shape," Lauren writes in her journal (which she has entitled *Earthseed: The Books of the Living*) (Butler 1995, 240).

Finally, Lauren begins to realize the establishment of an Earthseed enclave when she and her companions decide to settle on their companion Taylor Franklin Bankole's property near Mendocino, California. Although some members of the group are skeptical of Earthseed, all share Lauren's hope for and belief in a community founded on trust and cooperation. *Parable of the Sower* ends on an uncertain note: The reader does not know if Lauren and her Earthseed community will survive. Lauren cannot offer a solution for all the problems that threaten her and her companions, but she does offer hope.

Both Anyanwu and Lauren epitomize defiance, determination, courage, compromise, and, above all, survival. They strive for freedom, but, given their obstacles, they learn to make advancements through concessions. In the end, Anyanwu accepts her nemesis (and he, in turn, accepts her); while Lauren adapts to her brutal surroundings in spite of her unique physical (dis)ability (in fact, this [dis]ability prevents her from becoming as cruel and violent as the forces that menace her). (Indeed, Lauren's belief in change as a constant and her willingness to adapt to change are the foundational tenets of Earthseed.) In reconceiving power, Butler reconceives the subject: Anyanwu and Lauren learn to forge links with others through acceptance, trust, and cooperation, rather than through domination and intimidation. Their willingness to adapt, to compromise, and to establish connections with others allows them to endure the trying circumstances in which they find themselves. As Ruth Salvaggio astutely observes, "[Butler's] novels are about survival and power, about black women who must face tremendous societal constraints. We might very well expect them to be rebellious. We might expect them to reverse the typical male science-fiction stereotype and replace male tyranny with female tyranny. This does not happen. Though Butler's heroines are dangerous and powerful women, their goal is not power. They are heroines not because they conquer the world, but because they conquer the very notion of tyranny" (Salvaggio 1984, 81).

Cyborgs and Woman of Color Feminism: Difference and Specificity

Through her heroines, Butler challenges and relativizes masculinist notions of power. She redefines power and agency by theorizing a feminist, woman-of-color subject emblematic of Donna Haraway's "cyborg." In fact, in her essay "A Cyborg Manifesto," Haraway upholds Butler as one of a handful of "theorists for cyborgs" (Haraway 1991b, 173). Yet, what is a "cyborg" and what is the relationship between what Haraway terms "cyborg identity" and the subject of a woman of color feminism?

Haraway defines "cyborg" as "a cybernetic organism, a hybrid of machine and organism" (Haraway 1991b, 149). She carefully grounds her concept of the cyborg in the context of women, labor and technology, yet also uses it as a material representation or metaphor for "cyborg identity." "Cyborg identity," according to Haraway, is "a potent subjectivity synthesized from fusions of outsider identities" (174). Cyborgs embody "permanently partial identities and contradictory standpoints" (154).

In other words, "cyborg identity" is based on the concept of constructionism (i.e., anti-essentialism), position, or "place"—as in "one's place in society" or one's displacement in/by society. It reconceives of identity (a static and fixed essence) as *position* (within a particular history, narrative, ideology, and/or social system). Because a subject embodies multiple, simultaneous social and subject positions (e.g., race, class, gender, sexuality, nationality, age, physical ability), it may speak from, see itself in relation to, and/or be forced into (i.e., subjected to) a number of oscillating and often contradictory and incompatible "places."

Drawing from Chela Sandoval's 1991 essay "U.S. Third World Feminism: The Theory and Method of Oppositional Consciousness in the Postmodern World," Haraway stresses "'women of colour' . . . as a cyborg identity" (Haraway 1991b, 174). She defines "women of colour" in opposition to essence (i.e., a stable, unchanging core) and in terms of negation: Women of color are not "women" nor are they "black" or "Chicano" (156). Women of color are "those refused stable membership in the categories of race, sex, or class": They are displaced by and vacillate between the social categories of gender and race, which as Haraway reminds us, often refer to white women and men of color respectively (155).

One may easily argue that all people—regardless and *because of* race, class, gender, sexuality, nationality, age, physical ability, and so forth—locate themselves and/or are located within, between, and outside multiple social and subject positions. As Haraway notes, "By the late twentieth century, our time, a mythic time, we are all chimeras, theorized and fabricated hybrids of machine and organism; in short, *we are cyborgs*" (Haraway 1991b, 150, italics added).[12] However, according to both Sandoval and Haraway, women-of-color subjectivity in particular "constructs a kind of postmodernist identity out of otherness, difference, and specificity" (Haraway 1991b, 155). It does not privilege one social position over another, but recognizes their intersections. As such, woman-of-color subjectivity is, in the words of Norma Alarcón, "a site of multiple voicings" (Alarcón 1990, 365). "Inorganic" and "unnatural," it exemplifies what Sandoval has termed "differential consciousness"—that is, "a *tactical subjectivity* with the capacity to recenter depending upon the kinds of oppression to be confronted" (Sandoval 1991, 14, italics in original). In other words, women-of-color subjectivity crafts a "political unity without relying on"—but, at the same time, exploiting—"the logic of appropriation, incorporation, and taxonomic identification" (Haraway 1991b, 157).

For example, in the United States, the term "woman of color" forges links between women from distant and disparate locations (both geographic and socioeconomic) by positioning them—and recognizing that they have been positioned—within particular histories of exclusion, oppression and resistance. In her preface to the groundbreaking anthology, *This Bridge Called My Back: Writings by Radical Women of Color,* Cherríe Moraga reflects on the ties that bind Chicanas and African American women. "It is not a given between us—Chicana and Black—to come to see each other as sisters," she writes in response to a black woman calling her "sister." Echoing Dick's and Suvin's concepts of dysrecognition and estrangement, Moraga exclaims, "I keep wanting to repeat over and over and over again, the pain and shock of difference, the joy of commonness, the exhilaration of meeting through incredible odds against it" (Moraga 1981, xiv).

In short, Haraway's concept of "cyborg identity" interrogates the stability of social categories, such as "woman," "white," and "black," and exposes them as social "fictions" (i.e., regulatory ideals). Furthermore, it calls for the construction of coalitions based not on "identity" as essence, but on position(s) and affinity (Haraway defines affinity as "related not by blood but by choice" [Haraway 1991b, 155]). Like Haraway's cyborg, Anyanwu and Lauren threaten the stability of social categories and retrace the boundaries of community. In addition, their unique physical qualities (i.e., Anyanwu's shape-changing power and Lauren's hyperempathy) defy the notion of the stable and closed subject as they assume and/or are catapulted into various social and subject positions and as they blur the boundaries of consciousness.

Throughout *Wild Seed,* Anyanwu transforms her body into a variety of life-forms. With each human form, she assumes a different social and subject position (as a different social and subject position is imposed upon her), and, subsequently, she gains (and sometimes loses) a particular worldview. For example, after Anyanwu "wears" the body of a wealthy white man for quite some time, she begins to forget what it is like to "inhabit" a black body. She recalls, "Slaves were passing in front of me all chained, and I was thinking, 'I have to take more sunken gold from the sea, then see the banker about buying the land that adjoins mine. I have to buy some books—medical books, especially to see what doctors are doing now. . . . ' I was not seeing the slaves in front of me. I would not have thought I could be oblivious to such a thing. I had been white for too long" (Butler 1980, 211).

In addition, as a white man, Anyanwu marries and falls in love with Denice, a white woman tormented by her ability to see images from the past. When Doro asks why Denice married Anyanwu after she learned that Anyanwu was actually a black woman posing as a white man, Anyanwu tells him, "Because I believed her when she told me what she could do. Because I was not afraid or ridiculing. And because after a while, we started to want each other" (Butler 1980, 218).[13]

By blurring gender categories, Anyanwu challenges what Haraway describes as "the mundane fiction of Man and Woman" (Haraway 1991b, 180). She erases the boundaries of identity and consciousness by embodying various social and subject positions, while

Lauren erases the boundaries of identity and consciousness by experiencing others' physical sensations as if they were her own. For example, when Lauren delivers a blow to a man who has attacked Harry, she strikes herself down. After she regains consciousness and discovers that the intruder is unconscious, but still alive, she decides to kill him immediately, lest she experience his pain. Later, during a gunfight between her group and a gang of paints, Lauren "die[s] with someone else" (Butler 1995, 272). Throughout the fighting and killing, she dies "over and over" as men and women around her are killed (274). Indeed, Lauren's hyperempathy makes her emblematic of the cyborg, for it blurs the boundary that supposedly separates self from other.

"Why should our bodies end at the skin?" Haraway asks as she closes "A Cyborg Manifesto" (Haraway 1991b, 178), thus signaling a shift in focus from embodiment to disembodiment. Haraway elaborates on the tension between embodiment and disembodiment in this essay: "Feminist embodiment . . . is not about fixed location in a reified body, female or otherwise, but about nodes in fields, inflections in orientations, and responsibility for difference in material-semiotic fields of meaning" (Haraway 1991a, 22–23). In other words, while Haraway, like Butler, privileges the body in delineating the subject, she does not regard it as an immutable biological given. Rather, the body, for both Haraway and Butler, is, in the words of Rosi Braidotti, "a field of inscription of sociosymbolic codes: it stands for the radical materiality of the subject" (Braidotti 1994, 103). Thus, the body is simultaneously material and discursive. Our conceptions and experiences of it as material are always socially mediated.[14]

By occupying multiple social and subject positions and by blurring the boundaries of identity and consciousness, the heroines of *Wild Seed* and *Parable of the Sower* question why and when the body should "end at the skin." At the same time, they emphasize the material boundaries that the body imposes on the subject, especially if one is a slave, a mother, or a woman. References to slavery and motherhood permeate both texts. For example, Anyanwu is brought from Africa to Wheatley, New York, where she is made Doro's slave and an incubator for his seed. As in Africa, Anyanwu bears generations of descendants and, eventually, takes the European name Emma because "[s]he had heard that it meant grandmother or ancestress, and this amused her" (Butler 1980, 278). (Incidentally, "Wheatley" may be a reference to Phillis Wheatley, the eighteenth-century African American poet and "ancestress" of African American writers.[15])

Meanwhile, Lauren's hyperempathy is the result of her mother having abused a drug while she was pregnant with her. Furthermore, the majority of Lauren's companions are fugitive and/or former slaves. As they journey north, Lauren refers to her group

Catherine S. Ramirez

as "the crew of a modern underground railroad" and teaches her companions—many of whom are illiterate—to read and write (Butler 1995, 268). Like Harriet Tubman, Lauren disguises herself as a man as she travels, and at one point, she describes Bankole as "look[ing] more than a little like an old picture I used to have of Frederick Douglass" (Butler 1995, 298).

Indeed, the subjects (i.e., topics) of *Wild Seed* and *Parable of the Sower* are simultaneously recognizable and unfamiliar: Both novels are about upheaval, migration and what Carole Boyce Davies terms "re-membering," for both speak of the past and present of African Americans in the New World. Davies argues that the "need to reconnect and re-member . . . has been a central impulse in the structuring of Black thought" in the Americas. Through their narratives, African Americans have sought reconnection, "[f]rom the 'flying back' stories which originated in slavery to the 'Back to Africa' movements of Garvey and those before him, to the Pan-Africanist activity of people like Du Bois and C. L. R. James"[16] (Davies 1994, 14, 18). In many ways, *Wild Seed* is an origin, flying back and flying forward story, while *Parable of the Sower* chronicles a flight to the north, as well as a shift from the urban to the rural. Both novels are located within specific African American historical narratives even as they transgresses "the boundaries of space, time, history, place, language, corporeality and restricted consciousness in order to make reconnections and mark or name gaps and absences" (17).

In addition to drawing connections between the past and the present, the present and the future, and Africa and the Americas, *Wild Seed* and *Parable of the Sower* attempt to show the ties that bind the peoples of the New World. Butler does not elide difference but explores it: Her subjects (i.e., agents) confront one another in the rich and contested spaces where differences intersect. In all of her novels, Butler explicitly identifies the race and/or ethnicity of the actors, many of whom are persons of color. In a 1986 interview, she stated, "There are always blacks in the novels I write and whites. In *Quasar* there is a Japanese man and a Mexican woman. In the one I'm working on now there is a Chinese man and a lot of different people are lumped together" (Beal 1986, 16–17). Yet, rather than showcasing a heterogeneous cast of characters simply for the sake of superficial color, Butler explores race and difference as instruments of power. For instance, in *Parable of the Sower*, racial and ethnic differences threaten to tear Lauren's group apart. The group must learn to transform its diversity into a strength, rather than rendering it a weakness.

In the same interview, Butler noted that the popular 1977 science-fiction film *Star Wars* "shows every kind of alien, but there is only one kind of human—white ones; no black people were shown. There are no non-whites at all and where are they?" (Beal

1986, 17–18). She argued that "non-whites" in much mainstream science fiction are simultaneously represented and substituted by the figure of the alien. Recalling a conversation with the editor of a science-fiction magazine, she elaborated:

He said that he didn't think that blacks should be included in science fiction stories because they changed the character of the stories; that if you put in a black, all of a sudden the focus is on this person. He stated that if you were going to write about some sort of racial problem, that would be absolutely the only reason he could see for including a black.

He went on to say that well, perhaps you could use an alien instead and get rid of all this messiness and all those people that we don't want to deal with. It reflected his view of black people as being other. (18)

Through her science fiction, Butler challenges "natural" and/or "commonplace" ideas that describe, circumscribe, and/or *elide* the racialized and gendered subject as "other." To the editor who insisted that black people be excluded from science fiction, black people are not only overtly prohibited from the genre, they are simply not allowed to exist within it (in the same way that women of color are "those refused stable membership in categories of race, sex or class," as Haraway writes [1991b, 155]). In distinguishing prohibition from elision, Judith Butler observes, "[O]ppression works not merely through acts of overt prohibition, but covertly, through the constitution of viable subjects and through the corollary constitution of a domain of unviable (un)subjects—abjects, we might call them—who are neither named nor prohibited within the economy of the law" (J. Butler 1991, 20). Indeed, the "abject"—that is, that which is not simply prohibited but denied altogether—is the *subject* of Octavia E. Butler's science fiction.

Abjection, Aliens and *Atravesados* in *Borderlands/La Frontera*

As in Butler's science fiction, the "alien" is the subject of Gloria Anzaldúa's 1987 manifesto *Borderlands / La Frontera*. Anzaldúa writes as a lesbian, feminist Chicana from rural southern Texas and locates her text in the Borderlands—namely, the place where two or more worlds clash: where Anglo America collides with Latin America, the heterosexual confronts the queer, and the colonizer meets the colonized. She describes the U.S.–Mexico border as "*una herida abierta* [an open wound] where the Third World grates against the first and bleeds." Yet, "before a scab forms it hemorrhages again, the lifeblood of two worlds merging to form a third country—a border culture," she adds. Like Butler's science-fiction landscapes, the Borderlands, according to Anzaldúa, is a site of complexity, heterogeneity, flux, exchange, struggle, and, above all, contradiction and ambiguity. It is home to the *mestiza* (i.e., the mixed race), "[t]he prohibited and [the] forbidden." She writes, "*Los atravesados* live here: the squint-eyed, the perverse, the queer, the troublesome, the mongrel, the mulato, the half-breed, the half-dead; in short, those who cross over, pass over, or go through the confines of the 'normal'" (Anzaldua 1987, 3). To "*[g]ringos* in the U.S. Southwest," Anzaldúa writes, the inhabitants of the Borderlands are "transgressors"; they are "aliens" (3).

Not only is *Borderlands / La Frontera* about *mestizaje* (i.e., the blurring of racial categories), it is also a symbolic example of *mestizaje*. The text combines poetry, prose, personal testimony, and historical narrative. Moving between "standard" (i.e., middle-class Anglo-American English), various forms of Spanish (e.g., "proper" Castilian, "standard" Mexican, Chicana/o, and Tex-Mex), "Spanglish," Caló (i.e., "street speech") and Nahuatl, Anzaldúa attempts to articulate the complex history of conflict in the Borderlands and a theory of what she terms "an 'alien' consciousness . . . a new *mestiza* consciousness, *una conciencia de la mujer*" (a woman's consciousness) (Anzaldúa 1987, 77).

Anzaldúa locates her theory of "'alien' consciousness" in the history of struggle in and over the Borderlands. She reminds her readers that, after the U.S.–Mexico War, the United States splintered Mexico when it seized its northernmost region (the area composed of the present-day states of California, Arizona, New Mexico, Texas, Nevada, Utah, and parts of Colorado, Wyoming, Kansas, and Oklahoma) and, thus, split a people in two: "[t]he border fence that divides the Mexican people was born on February 2, 1848 with the signing of the Treaty of Guadalupe-Hidalgo" (Anzaldúa 1987, 7).

In theorizing "alien" consciousness, Anzaldúa draws a parallel between the splitting of the land and the splitting of the racialized, sexualized, and colonized subject (i.e., the queer *india /mestiza*) for whom it is and was home. "The *Gringo*, locked into the fiction of white superiority, seized complete political power, stripping Indians and Mexicans of their land while their feet were still rooted in it," she charges (Anzaldúa 1987, 7). "*Con el destierro y el exilo fuimos desuñados, destroncados, destripados*—we were jerked out by the roots, truncated, disemboweled, dispossessed, and separated from our identity and our history" (Anzaldúa 1987, 7–8). Conflating the land with her own body, she describes the U.S.–Mexico border as a "1,950 mile-long open wound / dividing a pueblo, a culture / running down the length of my body, / staking fence rods in my flesh, / splits me splits me / *me raja me raja*" (Anzaldúa 1987, 2).

Anzaldúa stresses that the contest for property, profit, and cultural and political dominance in the Borderlands has split not only the land but the queer *mestiza*, too. It has alienated her from her history, her home, her flesh, and "her mother culture" (Anzaldúa 1987, 20). In short, she claims that this history of violence and fragmentation has severed the queer *mestiza* from her past.

In *The Wretched of the Earth*, Frantz Fanon eloquently asserts, "Colonisation is not satisfied merely with holding a people in its grip and emptying the native's brain of all form and content." He explains that, in addition to grafting itself onto the colonized subject's consciousness, colonization "turns to the past of oppressed people, and distorts, disfigures and destroys it" (Fanon 1963, 170). Like those of Octavia Butler, and many other postcolonial and/or diasporic cultural workers, Anzaldúa's project is one of recovery and "rememory." Her theory of "alien" consciousness simultaneously attempts to excavate and to produce what Stuart Hall has carefully defined as "cultural identity" (Hall 1990, 223). For Anzaldúa, excavating the "mother culture" and producing an "alien" consciousness begins with undoing the legacies of patriarchy, homophobia, and European imperialism in the New World.

Anzaldúa argues that the combination of misogyny, homophobia and white supremacy has fragmented the queer *mestiza* by infecting her with an insidious and debilitating sense of self-hatred and shame. This sense of self-hatred and shame presses the queer *mestiza* to doubt, fear, and deny what Anzaldúa terms "the Indian woman in [her]" (Anzaldúa 1987, 22). Confronting the internalization of "the standards of the dominant culture" (Anzaldúa 1987, 49), she claims that "[w]e, *indias y mestizas*, police the Indian in us, brutalize and condemn her. Male culture has done a good job on us" (Anzaldúa 1987, 22).

Borderlands / La Frontera is a rejection of patriarchy and homophobia (and their apparatuses, such as Protestantism and Catholicism, which Anzaldúa insists "encourage fear and distrust of life and . . . the body . . . [and] a split between the body and the spirit" [Anzaldúa 1987, 37]). It is a rejection of the white supremacy of European imperialisms (both Spanish and Anglo-American), and of the internalization—or, as Fanon puts it in *Black Skin, White Masks*, "epidermalization" (Fanon 1967, 11)—of racial inferiority. Moreover, *Borderlands / La Frontera* is a rejection of Enlightenment epistemology— what Anzaldúa terms "white rationality"—that is, "their reality, the 'official' reality of the rational, reasoning mode which is . . . the consciousness of duality" (Anzaldúa 1987, 36–37). According to Anzaldúa, "the consciousness of duality" (e.g., the subject-object dichotomy) not only manufactures "'official' reality" and regulates understanding, but is also "the root of all violence":

In trying to become "objective," Western culture made "objects" of things and people when it distanced itself from them, thereby losing "touch" with them. . . . Not only was the brain split into two functions but so was reality.

Thus people who inhabit both realities are forced to live in the interface between the two, forced to become adept at switching modes. Such is the case with the *india* and the *mestiza*. (Anzaldúa 1987, 37)

For Anzaldúa, the consciousness of duality constitutes reason, which follows what feminist philosopher Maria Lugones terms "the logic of purity" (Lugones 1994, 463). "[T]he logic of purity" violently splits the world into ontological and epistemological binarisms—or what Lugones calls "a complex series of fictions" (Lugones 1994, 463), such as subject and object, insider and outsider, man and woman, good and evil, and culture and nature. It attempts "to control the multiplicity of people and things [and] attains satisfaction through exercises in split separation" (Lugones 1994, 464). In Anzaldúa's words, it is "an absolute despot duality that says we are able to be one or the other. It claims that human nature is limited and cannot evolve into something better" (Anzaldúa 1987, 19).

Borderlands / La Frontera is an attempt to defy the boundaries of what Lugones calls "unidimensionality"; it is an attempt to transcend the consciousness of duality (i.e., reason) and "its normative aspect . . . the unified subject" (Lugones 1994, 465). In lieu of the consciousness of duality, Anzaldúa proposes an alternative epistemology: "alien" consciousness. Anzaldúa defines alien consciousness as and through what she terms "the Coatlicue state." Coatlicue, the part-human, part-animal Mesoamerican goddess of fertility, functions as the embodiment of this consciousness.[17] The Coatlicue "state"— which Alarcón argues is actually a process—is constituted by the act of being / becoming simultaneous subject and object (Alarcón 1990a). "Seeing and being seen. Subject and object, I and she," Anzaldúa writes. "These seemingly contradictory aspects—the act of being seen, held immobilized by a glance, and 'seeing through' an experience" come together to form "alien" consciousness (Anzaldúa 1987, 42).

Just as Anyanwu's shape-changing ability and Lauren's hyperempathy dissolve the boundary between self and other, alien consciousness "break[s] down the subject-object duality that keeps [the queer *mestiza* subject] a prisoner." The queer *mestiza* must "show in the flesh and through images in her work how duality is transcended," Anzaldúa proclaims (Anzaldúa 1987, 80). Indeed, the queer *mestiza's* ambiguous, contradictory, and shifting social position(s) cannot be contained within the boundaries of duality. After all, the queer *mestiza* is "both male and female"; therefore, s/he represents a *third* gender—something other than and/or in addition to male and female (19). An amalgamation of Europeans, indigenous Americans, and Africans in the New World, s/he is the descendant of both colonizer and colonized—hence, "per" vexed genealogical relationship to the history of oppression.[18] What's more, s/he is neither "Mexican" nor full-fledged "American." As such, the queer *mestiza* cannot claim sexual, racial, or cultural purity and is located at the juncture "where phenomena tend to collide. It is where the possibility of uniting all that is separate occurs. This assembly is not one where severed or separated pieces merely come together. Nor is it a balancing of opposing powers.

In attempting to work out a synthesis, the self has added a third element which is greater than the sum of its severed parts. That third element is a new consciousness—a *mestiza* consciousness" (79–80).

Thus, Anzaldúa, like Haraway, celebrates "a subjectivity that's hybridized, mixed, and plural, rather than split" (Penley and Ross 1991, 10). In this 1991 interview, Haraway conceded that, in understanding the dynamics of racism, "you can't work without a conception of splitting and deferring and substituting," yet added, "I'm suspicious of the fact that in our accounts of both race and sex, each has to proceed one at a time, using a similar technology to do it" (Penley and Ross 1991, 11). In *Borderlands / La Frontera*, Anzaldúa does not split race from sex; they are not isolated from one another and hierarchized. Rather, she synthesizes them, along with gender, class, and sexuality, in theorizing a queer *mestiza* subject.

Because Anzaldúa's queer *mestiza* subject is "caught between *los intersticios*, the spaces between the different worlds she inhabits," s/he is "[a]lienated from her mother culture, and 'alien' in the dominant culture" (Anzaldúa 1987, 20). Alienation, alienization (i.e., other-ization, objectification), and what Anzaldúa calls "homophobia" (i.e., "homophobia," in the conventional sense of the word, and "homophobia" meaning the "[f]ear of going home . . . [a]nd of not being taken in" [20]) force the queer *mestiza* subject to construct new homes and new families. Like Butler's heroines, Anzaldúa's queer *mestiza* does not create community based on blood or essence. Instead, s/he cultivates links with others based on position and affinity. In the words of Alarcón, s/he "mak[es] familia from scratch" (Alarcón 1988, 147).

The queer *mestiza* subject's alliances simultaneously exceed and emphasize nation, race, class, gender, sexuality, and language. Highlighting the various social or subject categories that she occupies and that have been imposed on her (and echoing Virginia Woolf), Anzaldúa proclaims, "As a *mestiza* I have no country, my homeland cast me out, yet all countries are mine because I am every woman's sister or potential lover. (As a lesbian I have no race, my own people disclaim me; but I am all races because there is the queer of me in all races)" (Anzaldúa 1987, 80). Indeed, the *mestiza* subject's new communities—mixtures of diverse peoples from multiple and distant corners of the globe—hinge upon the queer subject. Eliding any differences and divisions between and among gay men and lesbian women and envisioning a utopian global community of "homosexuals," Anzaldúa asserts that "homosexuals" are the "supreme crossers of cultures" and that "strong bonds" link "the queer white, Black, Asian, Native American, [and] Latino . . . with the queer in Italy, Australia and the rest of the planet" (84). According to Anzaldúa, the queer subject transgresses the boundaries of not only gender and sexuality, but space and time: "We [queers] come from all colors, all classes, all races, all time periods. Our role is to link people with each other—the Blacks with Jews with Indians with Asians with whites"—and, finally—"with *extraterrestrials*" (84–85, italics added).

To my knowledge, few critics have scrutinized Anzaldúa's assertion that queer subjects connect different racial and national groups with "extraterrestrials." (Despite the large body of criticism on *Borderlands / La Frontera*, I do not think that the above passage has been quoted in a critical work.) One may wonder if Anzaldúa's "extraterrestrial" is literal or metaphoric. I believe that it is both. Anzaldúa turns to the alien qua extraterrestrial and "alien" qua outsider as embodiments of difference and deviance. Furthermore, like Octavia Butler, she transforms the "alien" from abject to subject and, in doing so, redefines the subject. For example, in her poem, "Interface," Anzaldúa recounts a love affair between a human being and an ethereal, otherworldy creature named Leyla. Leyla is "pulsing color, pure sound, bodiless" (Anzaldúa 1987, 30). She (even though Leyla lacks a body, the narrator refers to "her" in the feminine) and her corporal lover meet at "the interface": "the border between / the physical world / and hers" (i.e., Leyla's world) (23–25). Rather than communicating with one another with speech, the lovers silently exchange thoughts. Eventually, Leyla's love for the narrator intensifies and she becomes "skin and bone" and acquires speech (156). "Soon Leyla could pass, / go for milk at the bodega, count change" (151–152). The poem concludes when the narrator takes Leyla home to Texas for Christmas and Leyla seems to "pass" as a lesbian: "Is she a lez, my brothers asked. / I said, No, just an alien. / Leyla laughed" (93–95).

"Interface" may be read as both science fiction and a coming-out narrative. Leyla may be an alien qua extraterrestrial (i.e., a literal alien) and/or an "alien" qua lesbian (i.e., a metaphorical "alien"). She may be the narrator's lover and/or she may represent the narrator (e.g., the queer who comes out and flourishes). Like *Wild Seed* and *Parable of the Sower*, "Interface" reconceives the abject and/or object as subject without reproducing or replicating oppressive power relations. And, like *Wild Seed* and *Parable of the Sower*, it reconceives communication and love.[19]

Although many readers probably would not consider *Borderlands / La Frontera* an example of science fiction, it has much in common with *Wild Seed* and *Parable of the Sower*. Both Anzaldúa and Butler expose ideology; they denaturalize and relativize fictions that are often upheld as facts. Moreover, they accomplish this via the figure of the cyborg: the "alien," the homeless, the one who passes, negotiates, and concedes, the prohibited, the hybrid, the queer, and/or the colonized.

Through the figure of the cyborg, Anzaldúa and Butler also theorize a woman-of-color feminism. For Butler, the cyborg is the raced and gendered subject; for Anzaldúa s/he is also queer. Occupying a multiplicity of social locations, the queer woman of color is able to forge alliances across differences. However, at the same time, she is unable to escape history and, as I argue below, essence. Butler's black heroines are located within specific African American narratives of slavery, resistance, and migration (to and through the New World), while Anzaldúa's queer *mestiza* subject is located in the history of struggle along and over the U.S.–Mexico border, between racist Americans and the racialized others who inhabit the United States, and within the Chicano-Mexican culture. Indeed, their subjects are cyborgs because they interrogate the stability of social categories, such as "woman," "American," and "human," and because they exemplify the construction of coalitions based on position and affinity, as opposed to identity and essence. However, Butler's black heroines and Anzaldúa's queer *mestiza* subject differ from a more generic cyborg because they also emphasize very particular New World histories (African American and Chicana, respectively).

As this chapter demonstrates, I find Haraway's concept of the cyborg valuable for theorizing and illuminating feminism for, by, and about women of color. In general, feminism for, by, and about women of color emphasizes position, plurality, constructedness, and coalition. At the same time, it is grounded in difference and specificity (e.g., the specificity of a particular time, place, body, community, or narrative). Haraway emphasizes that the the term "'[wo]man of colour' . . . constructs a kind of postmodernist identity out of otherness, difference, and *specificity*" (Haraway 1991b, 155; italics added). Nonetheless, Paula M. L. Moya argues that Haraway's concept of "cyborg identity" denies women of color—in particular, Chicanas—the specificity of social location. The "porosity and polysemy of the category 'cyborg,' in effect, leaves no criteria to determine who might *not* be a cyborg," she asserts (Moya 1997, 131, italics original). Moya charges that "[b]y freeing herself of the obligation to ground identity in social location, Haraway is able to arrogate the meaning of the term 'women of color.' With this misappropriation, Haraway authorizes herself to speak for actual women of color, to dismiss our own interpretations of our experiences of oppression, our 'need to root politics in identification,' and even our identities" (132).

While the queer *mestiza* subject has a complicated and vexed relationship to biological, cultural, and historical origins, Anzaldúa is still careful to root "per" in a "politics of identification"—in particular, with that of—to draw from the title of Norma Alarcón's essay—"'*The*' Native Woman" (Alarcón 1990a, italics added). Interestingly, some scholars have criticized Anzaldúa for essentializing the queer *mestiza* subject at the expense of Native American women.[20] After all, Anzaldúa's concept of "*mestiza* consciousness" revolves around the figure of a seemingly static, monolithic Native American woman. Throughout *Borderlands / La Frontera*, she refers to "the Indian woman in me" (Anzaldúa 1987, 22), "her core self, her dark Indian self" (43), and "the mystery of the Origin" (49).

Although Anzaldúa's concept of *mestiza* consciousness emphasizes positionality, I find it difficult to argue that, at times, she does not essentialize. Likewise, Octavia Butler relies on an essential identity in many of her works, including *Wild Seed* and *Parable of the Sower*. Despite Anyanwu's shape-changing ability, she is still "Anyanwu," a seventeenth-century Igbo woman. Likewise, despite Lauren's hyperempathy, she is still "Lauren," a twenty-first-century black American teenager. After she is done experiencing another's feelings, she goes back to being her "old" self.

Rather than ignoring Anzaldúa's and Butler's essentializing tactics, I wish to underscore them here. Regarding questions pertaining to (and accusations of) essentialisms, Diana Fuss reminds us, "The question we should be asking is not 'is this text essentialist (and therefore "bad")?' but rather 'if this text is essentialist, *what motivates its deployment?*'" (xi, italics original). If, as Fuss argues, constructionism, essentialism's putative antithesis, "really operates as a more sophisticated form of essentialism," then Octavia Butler's and Gloria Anzaldúa's use of positionality is actually a "more sophisticated form of essentialism" (Fuss 1989, xii). In speaking *as* a "black woman" or *as* a "Chicana," Butler and Anzaldúa claim subject positions that are, to draw from "A Cyborg Manifesto," *not* those of white women or Chican*os* respectively. The negative, opposite, or inverse of an essential identity, such as "(white) woman" or "Chican*o*," is itself an essence. As a means of producing raced and gendered speaking subjects and forging alliances between those who are not necessarily obviously connected (and, thus, retracing the boundaries of community and identity), Butler and Anzaldúa deploy essence by emphasizing a particular social or subject position (e.g., Butler always identifies the race, ethnicity, and gender of her characters and Anzaldúa stresses "homosexuality" in delineating a global, queer community). According to Gayatri Spivak, "The strategic use of an essence as a mobilizing slogan or masterword like *woman* or *worker* or the name of a nation is, ideally, self-conscious for all mobilized" (Spivak 1993, 3). Butler's and Anzaldúa's texts illustrate that the strategic deployment of essence is necessary for imagining and mobilizing new subjects and new communities, such as "woman of color," "women of color," "home," and "family."

The tension between affinity and essence, and between plurality and specificity in the work of Anzaldúa and Butler, highlights a contradiction of woman-of-color subjectivity and feminism: The histories of racism, imperialism, patriarchy, and homophobia have rendered women of color abject, yet, via history, women of color must claim some sort of position in order transform themselves into (speaking) subjects (without replicating the regime[s] that silenced them). As Haraway points out, history, like origin stories, functions as a "potent myth" (Haraway 1991b, 151). Its potency is precisely what enables women-of-color writers, like Butler and Anzaldúa, to tell African American and Chicana stories, respectively, and to theorize feminism(s) by, for, and about women of color.

Conclusion

As *Borderlands / La Frontera* illustrates, one need not turn to texts designated "science fiction" to read about "aliens." In fact, one need only glance at a mainstream American newspaper, such as the *Los Angeles Times*, and chances are, one will find stories about alien invasion and alien conspiracies to sabotage American culture and society. Of course, I am referring to anti-immigrant discourse and xenophobia in the United States. As the official term, "illegal alien" renders many of the men, women and children who enter the United States without papers ("passports") criminal outsiders and transforms them into dangerous monsters. Just as Butler and Anzaldúa equate the "alien" with the "other," Haraway notes that "[m]onsters have always defined the limits of community in Western imaginations" (Haraway 1991b, 180).

Indeed, if science fiction is defined in terms of dysrecognition and estrangement, then the histories of many communities of color in the United States, and of the colonized and diasporic peoples of the (aptly named) "New World," are reminiscent of a sci-fi plot. Regarding the history of African Americans, Mark Dery writes, "African Americans, in a very real sense, are the descendants of alien abductees; they inhabit a sci-fi nightmare in which unseen but no less impassable force fields of intolerance frustrate their movements; official histories undo what has been done; and technology is too often brought to bear on black bodies (branding, forced sterilization, the Tuskegee experiment, and tasers come readily to mind)" (Dery 1993, 736).

Similarly, beginning in 1492, the indigenous inhabitants of the Americas found themselves face-to-face with "alien" invaders who arrived in large ships and who brought with them strange and powerful weapons, as well as new diseases. Many of the alien invaders colonized, slaughtered, enslaved, and impregnated the indigenous inhabitants— thus decimating the original population and giving birth to a new hybrid (i.e., *mestiza/o*) people. Furthermore, the alien invaders established their own institutions, such as governments, hospitals, churches and schools, which, ironically, rendered the indigenous inhabitants "alien" in their own homeland. Both enslaved Africans, and the indigenous inhabitants of the "New World" found themselves veritable "strangers in a strange land" (to draw from the title of Robert Heinlein's 1961 science-fiction novel).

Thus, it is not surprising that much of the cultural production of New World peoples draws from the iconography of space, science, and technology. Numerous writers, artists, and musicians have appropriated a genre that many have considered the exclusive domain of middle-class, ostensibly straight, white men and boys interested in "hard" science—a genre that has often celebrated Western imperialism and empiricism—and have transformed it into a creative and highly politicized space for the articulation of their pasts, presents, and futures. As Octavia Butler and Gloria Anzaldúa have illustrated, science fiction is more than mere escapism. It provides the "aliens" and passport-less of the New World with the opportunity to narrate histories of colonialism, conquest, and resistance; to explore alternative epistemologies and ontologies (and all their contradictions); and, subsequently, to redefine the boundaries of subject and community.

Notes

1. "The Comet" can be found in Thomas 2000. DJ Spooky's (a.k.a. Paul D. Miller's) futuristic works include *Necropolis: The Dialogic Project* (1995), *Songs of a Dead Dreamer* (1996), and *Riddim Warfare* (1998).

2. See, for example, Walter Mosley's novel *Blue Light* (1998) and the front and back covers of Earth Wind & Fire's 1977 album *All 'n All*, which feature Egyptian pyramids and futuristic pyramidlike structures, respectively.

3. "Afrofuturist Dreams: Recasting Race, Recasting Technoculture" consisted of presentations by Ron Eglash, Nalo Hopkinson, Alondra Nelson, and Kalí Tal. It took place at the annual meeting of the American Studies Association on October 13, 2000, in Detroit, Michigan. For more information on Afrofuturist cultural production, log on to < http://www.afrofuturism.net/>.

4. Since Delany's 1993 interview, the list of black science fiction writers has grown. In 1998, Walter Mosley published *Blue Light*, a science fiction novel. The same year, Nalo Hopkinson published *Brown Girl in the Ring*, and, most recently, she has published *Midnight Robber* (2000). While she is not an "American" in the imperialist and nationalist sense, Hopkinson, a native of Jamaica and resident of Canada, is an American in the hemispheric sense. I also add George Schuyler, author of *Black No More* (1989, originally published in 1931) and *Black Empire* (1991, serialized from 1936 to 1938), to the list of black science-fiction writers. *Dark Matter: A Century of Speculative Fiction from the African Diaspora* (2000), edited by Sheree R. Thomas, features science fiction, fantasy, and critical essays by thirty African American writers, including Amiri Baraka, Derrick Bell, Charles W. Chestnutt, W. E. B. Du Bois, Jewelle Gomez, and Ishmael Reed.

5. See, for example, Aldiss 1973, Aldiss and Wingrove 1986, Botting 1991, Botting 1995, Broderick 1995, Donawerth 1997, Gunn 1998, Lefanu 1988, Sargent 1974, Sargent 1995a, b, and Suvin 1979.

6. In general, "soft" science fiction refers to science fiction that emphasizes the social and psychological. "Hard" science fiction, with all of the masculine connotations related to the adjective hard, refers to science fiction that supposedly concerns itself with science and technology.

7. See Barr 1987, Barr 1993, Donawerth 1997, Gubar 1980, Lefanu 1988, McIntyre and Anderson 1976, Pearson 1990, Rosinsky 1984, Wolmark 1986, Wood 1978–1979 and Sargent's *Woman of Wonder* series (1974, 1995a, b) regarding science fiction by women writers. See also *Science-Fiction Studies'* special issues on science fiction by women (1980 and 1990).

8. I draw my definition of ideology from Althusser (1971).

9. I have drawn this quote from an unpublished interview quoted in Salvaggio 1986.

10. See, for example, Butler's *Xenogenesis* trilogy, which consists of *Dawn* (1987), *Adulthood Rites* (1988), and *Imago* (1989).

11. In this chapter, I quote from the 1995 version of *Parable of the Sower*, published by The Women's Press of London.

12. In a 1991 interview conducted by Constance Penley and Andrew Ross, Haraway revised her statement "We are all . . . cyborgs." "If I were rewriting those sections of the [1985 version of the] Cyborg Manifesto I'd be much more careful about describing who counts as a 'we,' in the statement, 'We are all cyborgs,'" she stated. "I would also be much more careful to point out that those are subject positions for people in certain regions of transnational systems of production that do not easily figure the situations of other people in the system." Rather than imposing the label "cyborg" in what she termed an "imperializing" manner on Third World women laborers, Haraway elaborated, "I think what I would want is more of a family of displaced figures, of which the cyborg is one, and then to ask how the cyborg makes connections with these other nonoriginal people (cyborgs *are* nonoriginal people) who are multiply displaced" (Penley and Ross 1991, 12–13, italics in original).

13. In Penley and Ross's interview with her, Haraway lamented that Butler "constantly reproduces heterosexuality even in her polygendered species" (Penley and Ross 1991, 12). While Anyanwu and Denice's relationship reproduces heterosexuality (Anyanwu has assumed a male body), it nonetheless may be read as a lesbian relationship.

14. See Stone 1991 for a discussion of the tension of embodiment and disembodiment in cyberculture and feminist theories of cyberculture.

15. Wheatley, a native of West Africa, was a slave in New England in the eighteenth century. In the early 1770s, she began publishing elegies and poems, which some scholars regard as the earliest African American literary texts. See, for example, Gates and McKay 1997.

16. Quotation marks appear in Davies's text.

17. Incidentally, the Mexican artist, Diego Rivera, portrays Coatlicue as a cyborg (as part-human, part-machine) in his 1939 mural *Pan-American Unity*.

18. I draw the term "per" from Marge Piercy's 1976 science-fiction novel *Woman on the Edge of Time*. "Per" is both objective and possessive pronoun, yet unlike "him," "his" or "her(s)" it does not produce and articulate gender. Even though she asserts that the queer *mestiza* is both male and female, Anzaldúa refers to "her" in the feminine.

19. I am grateful to Norma Alarcón for referring me to "Interface."

20. See Alarcón 1994 and Yarbro-Bejarano 1994 regarding charges that Anzaldúa essentializes queer *mestiza* subjectivity at the expense of Native American women in *Borderlands / La Frontera*.

Works Cited

Alarcón, Norma. "Making Familia from Scratch: Split Subjectivities in the Work of Helena María Viramontes and Cherríe Moraga." In *Chicana Creativity and Criticism: Charting New Frontiers in American Literature*, ed. María Herrera-Sobek and Helena María Viramontes, 147–159. Houston: Arte Público Press, 1988.

Alarcón, Norma. "Chicana Feminism: In the Tracks of 'The' Native Woman." *Cultural Studies* 4, no. 3 (October 1990a): 248–256.

Alarcón, Norma. "The Theoretical Subject(s) of *This Bridge Called My Back* and Anglo-American Feminism." In *Making Face, Making Soul: Haciendo Caras*, ed. Gloria Anzaldúa, 356–369. San Francisco: Aunt Lute, 1990b.

Alarcón, Norma. "Conjugating Subjects: The Heteroglossia of Essence and Resistance." In *An Other Tongue: Nation and Ethnicity in the Linguistic Borderlands*, ed. Alfred Arteaga, 125–138. Durham / London: Duke University Press, 1994.

Aldiss, Brian. *Billion Year Spree*. New York: Doubleday, 1973.

Aldiss, Brian, and David Wingrove. *Trillion Year Spree: The History of Science Fiction*. New York: Atheneum, 1986.

Althusser, Louis. *Lenin and Philosophy and Other Essays*. Trans. Ben Brewster. London: NLB, 1971.

Amis, Kingsley. *New Maps of Hell: A Survey of Science Fiction*. New York: Harcourt, Brace and Company, 1960.

Anzaldúa, Gloria. *Borderlands / La Frontera: The New Mestiza*. San Francisco: Aunt Lute, 1987.

Asimov, Isaac. *Asimov on Science Fiction*. London: Granada, 1983.

Barr, Marleen. *Alien to Femininity: Speculative Fiction and Feminist Theory*. New York: Greenwood Press, 1987.

Barr, Marleen. *Lost in Space: Probing Feminist Science Fiction and Beyond*. Chapel Hill and London: University of North Carolina Press, 1993.

Beal, Frances M. "Black Scholar Interview with Octavia Butler: Black Women and the Science Fiction Genre." *The Black Scholar* 17, no. 2 (March/April 1986): 14–18.

Botting, Fred, ed. *Making Monstrous: Frankenstein, Criticism, Theory*. Manchester and New York: Manchester University Press, 1991.

Botting, Fred, ed. *Frankenstein: Mary Shelley*. London: Macmillan, 1995.

Braidotti, Rosi. *Nomadic Subjects: Embodiment and Difference in Contemporary Feminist Theory*. New York: Columbia University Press, 1994.

Broderick, Damien. *Reading by Starlight: Postmodern Science Fiction*. London and New York: Routledge, 1995.

Butler, Judith. "Imitation and Gender Insubordination." In *inside/out: Lesbian Theories, Gay Theories*, ed. Diana Fuss, 13–31. New York and London: Routledge, 1991.

Butler, Octavia E. *Wild Seed*. New York: Time Warner, 1980.

Butler, Octavia E. *Dawn*. New York: Warner, 1987.

Butler, Octavia E. *Adulthood Rites*. New York: Warner, 1988.

Butler, Octavia E. *Imago*. New York: Warner, 1989.

Butler, Octavia E. *Parable of the Sower*. London: The Women's Press, 1995.

Canary, Robert H. "Science Fiction as Fictive History." In *Many Futures, Many Worlds: Theme and Form in Science Fiction*, ed. Thomas D. Clareson. 164–181. Kent, OH: Kent State University Press, 1977.

Corbett, John. "Brothers from Another Planet: The Space Madness of Lee 'Scratch' Perry, Sun Ra, and George Clinton." In *Extended Play: Sounding Off from John Cage to Dr. Funkenstein*, 7–24. Durham and London: Duke UP, 1994.

Davidson, Carolyn S. "The Science Fiction of Octavia Butler." *Sagala* 2, no. 1 (1981): 35.

Davies, Carole Boyce. *Black Women, Writing, and Identity: Migrations of the Subject*. London and New York: Routledge, 1994.

Dery, Mark. "Black to the Future: Interviews with Samuel R. Delany, Greg Tate, and Tricia Rose." *The South Atlantic Quarterly* 92, no. 4 (Fall 1993): 735–778.

Dick, Philip K. "My Definition of Science Fiction." In *The Shifting Realities of Philip K. Dick: Selected Literary and Philosophical Writings*, ed. Lawrence Sutin, 99–100. New York: Pantheon Books, 1995.

Donawerth, Jane. *Frankenstein's Daughters: Women Writing Science Fiction*. Syracuse, NY: Syracuse University Press, 1997.

Earth Wind & Fire. *All 'n All*. New York: CBS, 1977.

Fanon, Frantz. *The Wretched of the Earth*. New York: Grove Weidenfeld, 1963.

Fanon, Frantz. *Black Skin, White Masks*. New York: Grove Weidenfeld, 1967.

Fuss, Diana. *Essentially Speaking: Feminism, Nature and Difference*. New York and London: Routledge, 1989.

Gates, Henry Louis, and Nellie Y. McKay, eds. *The Norton Anthology of African American Literature*. New York: W. W. Norton and Co., 1997.

Gubar, Susan. "C. L. Moore and the Conventions of Women's Science Fiction." *Science-Fiction Studies* 7 (1980): 16–27.

Gunn, James, ed. *The Road to Science Fiction, Volume 5: The British Way*. Clarkston, GA: Borealis/White Wolf, 1998.

Hall, Stuart. "Cultural Identity and Diaspora." In *Identity: Community, Culture, Difference,* ed. Jonathon Rutherford, 222–237. London: Lawrence & Wishart, 1990.

Haraway, Donna J. "The Actors Are Cyborg, Nature Is Coyote, and the Geography Is Elsewhere: Postscript to 'Cyborgs at Large.'" *Technoculture,* ed. Constance Penley and Andrew Ross, 21–26. Minneapolis: University of Minnesota Press, 1991a.

Haraway, Donna J. "A Cyborg Manifesto: Science, Technology, and Socialist-Feminism in the Late Twentieth Century." In *Simians, Cyborgs, and Women: The Reinvention of Nature,* 149–181. New York and London: Routledge, 1991b.

Heinlein, Robert A. *Stranger in a Strange Land.* New York: Putnam, 1961.

Hopkinson, Nalo. *Brown Girl in the Ring.* New York: Warner Books, 1998.

Hopkinson, Nalo. *Midnight Robber.* New York: Warner Books, 2000.

Lefanu, Sarah. *In the Chinks of the World Machine: Feminism and Science Fiction.* London: The Women's Press, 1988.

Lugones, Maria. "Purity, Impurity, and Separation." *Signs* 19, no. 21 (Winter 1994): 458–479.

McIntyre, Vonda N., and Susan Janice Anderson, eds. *Aurora: Beyond Equality.* Greenwich, CT: Fawcett, 1976.

Miller, Paul D. (DJ Spooky That Subliminal Kid). *Necropolis: The Dialogic Project.* New York: Knitting Factory Works, 1995.

Miller, Paul D. *Songs of a Dead Dreamer.* New York: Asphodel, 1996.

Miller, Paul D. *Riddim Warfare.* Los Angeles: Outpost Recordings, 1998.

Moraga, Cherríe. Preface to *This Bridge Called My Back: Writings by Radical Women of Color,* ed. Cherríe Moraga and Gloria Anzaldúa, xiii-xix. New York: Kitchen Table: Women of Color Press, 1981.

Mosley, Walter. *Blue Light.* New York: Warner Books, 1998.

Moya, Paula M. L. "Postmodernism, 'Realism,' and the Politics of Identity: Cherríe Moraga and Chicana Feminism." In *Feminist Genealogies, Colonial Legacies, Democratic Futures,* ed. M. Jacqui Alexander and Chandra Talpade Mohanty, 125–150. New York and London: Routledge, 1997.

Pearson, Jacqueline. "Where No Man Has Gone Before: Sexual Politics and Women's Science Fiction." In *Science Fiction, Social Conflict and War,* ed. Philip John Davies, 8–25. New York and Manchester: Manchester University Press, 1990.

Penley, Constance, and Andrew Ross. "Cyborgs at Large: Interview with Donna Haraway." In *Technoculture,* ed. Constance Penley and Andrew Ross, 1–19. Minneapolis: University of Minnesota Press, 1991.

Piercy, Marge. *Woman on the Edge of Time.* New York: Fawcett Columbine, 1976.

Rosinsky, Natalie M. *Feminist Futures: Contemporary Women's Speculative Fiction.* Ann Arbor, MI: UMI Research Press, 1984.

Salvaggio, Ruth. "Octavia Butler and the Black Science-Fiction Heroine." *Black American Literature Forum* 18, no. 2 (Summer 1984): 78–81.

Catherine S. Ramirez

Salvaggio, Ruth. "Octavia E. Butler." In *Suzy McKee Charnas, Octavia Butler, Joan D. Vinge*, ed. Roger C. Schlobin, 1–44. Mercer Island, WA: Starmont House, Inc., 1986.

Sandoval, Chela. "U.S. Third World Feminism: The Theory and Method of Oppositional Consciousness in the Postmodern World." *Genders* 10 (Spring 1991): 1–24.

Sargent, Pamela, ed. *Women of Wonder: Science Fiction Stories by Women about Women*. New York: Vintage Books, 1974.

Sargent, Pamela, ed. *Women of Wonder, The Classic Years: Science Fiction by Women from the 1940s to the 1970s*. San Diego, New York and London: Harcourt Brace & Co., 1995a.

Sargent, Pamela, ed. *Women of Wonder, The Contemporary Years: Science Fiction by Women from the 1970s to the 1990s*. San Diego, New York and London: Harcourt Brace & Co., 1995b.

Schuyler, George. *Black No More*. Boston: Northeastern University Press, 1989.

Schuyler, George. *Black Empire*. Boston: Northeastern University Press, 1991.

See, Lisa. "Octavia E. Butler: In Her Science Fiction She Projects the Answers to Society's Ills." *Publishers Weekly* 240, no. 50 (December 13, 1993): 50–51.

Shelley, Mary. *Frankenstein or, The Modern Prometheus*. New York: Signet, [1881] 1983.

Spivak, Gayatri Chakravorty. *Outside in the Teaching Machine*. New York and London: Routledge, 1993.

Stone, Allucquère Rosanne. "Will the Real Body Please Stand Up? Boundary Stories about Virtual Cultures." In *Cyberspace: First Steps*, ed. Michael Benedikt. Cambridge, MA: The MIT Press, 1991.

Suvin, Darko. "On the Poetics of the Science Fiction Genre." In *Science Fiction: A Collection of Critical Essays*, ed. Mark Rose, 57–61. Englewood Cliffs, NJ: Prentice-Hall, 1976.

Suvin, Darko. *Metamorphoses of Science Fiction: On the Poetics and History of a Literary Genre*. New Haven and London: Yale University Press, 1979.

Thomas, Sheree R. *Dark Matter: A Century of Speculative Fiction from the African Diaspora*. New York: Warner Books, 2000.

Wolmark, Jenny. "Science Fiction and Feminism." *Foundation* 37 (Autumn 1986): 48–51.

Wood, Susan. "Women and Science Fiction." *Algol/Starship* 16, no. 1 (Winter 1978–1979): 9–18.

Yarbro-Bejarano, Yvonne. "Gloria Anzaldúa's *Borderlands/La Frontera*: Cultural Studies, 'Difference,' and the Non-Unitary Subject." *Cultural Critique* 28 (Fall 1994): 5–28.

Octavia E. Butler

There was trouble aboard the Washington Boulevard bus. Rye had expected trouble sooner or later in her journey. She had put off going until loneliness and hopelessness drove her out. She believed she might have one group of relatives left alive—a brother and his two children twenty miles away in Pasadena. That was a day's journey one-way, if she were lucky. The unexpected arrival of the bus as she left her Virginia Road home had seemed to be a piece of luck—until the trouble began.

Two young men were involved in a disagreement of some kind, or, more likely, a misunderstanding. They stood in the aisle, grunting and gesturing at each other, each in his own uncertain T stance as the bus lurched over the potholes. The driver seemed to be putting some effort into keeping them off balance. Still, their gestures stopped just short of contact—mock punches, hand games of intimidation to replace lost curses.

People watched the pair, then looked at one another and made small anxious sounds. Two children whimpered.

Rye sat a few feet behind the disputants and across from the back door. She watched the two carefully, knowing the fight would begin when someone's nerve broke or someone's hand slipped or someone came to the end of his limited ability to communicate. These things could happen anytime.

One of them happened as the bus hit an especially large pothole and one man, tall, thin, and sneering, was thrown into his shorter opponent.

Instantly, the shorter man drove his left fist into the disintegrating sneer. He hammered his larger opponent as though he neither had nor needed any weapon other than his left fist. He hit quickly enough, hard enough to batter his opponent down before the taller man could regain his balance or hit back even once.

People screamed or squawked in fear. Those nearby scrambled to get out of the way. Three more young men roared in excitement and gestured wildly. Then, somehow, a second dispute broke out between two of these three—probably because one inadvertently touched or hit the other.

As the second fight scattered frightened passengers, a woman shook the driver's shoulder and grunted as she gestured toward the fighting.

The driver grunted back through bared teeth. Frightened, the woman drew away.

Rye, knowing the methods of bus drivers, braced herself and held on to the crossbar of the seat in front of her. When the driver hit the brakes, she was ready and the combatants were not. They fell over seats and onto screaming passengers, creating even more confusion. At least one more fight started.

The instant the bus came to a full stop, Rye was on her feet, pushing the back door. At the second push, it opened and she jumped out, holding her pack in one arm. Several other passengers followed, but some stayed on the bus. Buses were so rare and irregular now, people rode when they could, no matter what. There might not be another bus today—or tomorrow. People started walking, and if they saw a bus they flagged it down. People making intercity trips like Rye's from Los Angeles to Pasadena made plans to camp out, or risked seeking shelter with locals who might rob or murder them.

The bus did not move, but Rye moved away from it. She intended to wait until the trouble was over and get on again, but if there was shooting, she wanted the protection of a tree. Thus, she was near the curb when a battered blue Ford on the other side of the street made a U-turn and pulled up in front of the bus. Cars were rare these days—as rare as a severe shortage of fuel and of relatively unimpaired mechanics could make them. Cars that still ran were as likely to be used as weapons as they were to serve as transportation. Thus, when the driver of the Ford beckoned to Rye, she moved away warily. The driver got out—a big man, young, neatly bearded with dark, thick hair. He wore a long overcoat and a look of wariness that matched Rye's. She stood several feet from him, waiting to see what he would do. He looked at the bus, now rocking with the combat inside, then at the small cluster of passengers who had gotten off. Finally he looked at Rye again.

She returned his gaze, very much aware of the old forty-five automatic her jacket concealed. She watched his hands.

He pointed with his left hand toward the bus. The dark-tinted windows prevented him from seeing what was happening inside.

His use of the left hand interested Rye more than his obvious question. Left-handed people tended to be less impaired, more reasonable and comprehending, less driven by frustration, confusion, and anger.

She imitated his gesture, pointing toward the bus with her own left hand, then punching the air with both fists.

The man took off his coat revealing a Los Angeles Police Department uniform complete with baton and service revolver.

Rye took another step back from him. There was no more LAPD, no more *any* large organization, governmental or private. There were neighborhood patrols and armed individuals. That was all.

The man took something from his coat pocket, then threw the coat into the car. Then he gestured Rye back, back toward the rear of the bus. He had something made of plastic in his hand. Rye did not understand what he wanted until he went to the rear door of the bus and beckoned her to stand there. She obeyed mainly out of curiosity. Cop or not, maybe he could do something to stop the stupid fighting.

He walked around the front of the bus, to the street side where the driver's window was open. There, she thought she saw him throw something into the bus. She was still trying to peer through the tinted glass when people began stumbling out the rear door, choking and weeping. Gas.

Rye caught an old woman who would have fallen, lifted two little children down when they were in danger of being knocked down and trampled. She could see the bearded man helping people at the front door. She caught a thin old man shoved out by one of the combatants. Staggered by the old man's weight, she was barely able to get out of the way as the last of the young men pushed his way out. This one, bleeding from nose and mouth, stumbled into another and they grappled blindly, still sobbing from the gas.

The bearded man helped the bus driver out through the front door, though the driver did not seem to appreciate his help. For a moment, Rye thought there would be another fight. The bearded man stepped back and watched the driver gesture threateningly, watched him shout in wordless anger.

The bearded man stood still, made no sound, refused to respond to clearly obscene gestures. The least impaired people tended to do this—stand back unless they were physically threatened and let those with less control scream and jump around. It was as though they felt it beneath them to be as touchy as the less comprehending. This was an attitude of superiority and that was the way people like the bus driver perceived it. Such "superiority" was frequently punished by beatings, even by death. Rye had had close calls of her own. As a result, she never went unarmed. And in this world where the only likely common language was body language, being armed was often enough. She had rarely had to draw her gun or even display it.

The bearded man's revolver was on constant display. Apparently that was enough for the bus driver. The driver spat in disgust, glared at the bearded man for a moment longer, then strode back to his gas-filled bus. He stared at it for a moment, clearly wanting to get in, but the gas was still too strong. Of the windows, only his tiny driver's window actually opened. The front door was open, but the rear door would not stay open unless someone held it. Of course, the air conditioning had failed long ago. The bus would take some time to clear. It was the driver's property, his livelihood. He had pasted old magazine pictures of items he would accept as fare on its sides. Then he would use what he collected to feed his family or to trade. If his bus did not run, he did not eat. On the other hand, if the inside of his bus was torn apart by senseless fighting, he would not eat very well either. He was apparently unable to perceive this. All he could see was that it would be some time before he could use his bus again. He shook his fist at the bearded man and shouted. There seemed to be words in his shout, but Rye could not understand them. She did not know whether this was his fault or hers. She had heard so little coherent human speech for the past three years, she was no longer certain how well she recognized it, no longer certain of the degree of her own impairment.

The bearded man sighed. He glanced toward his car, then beckoned to Rye. He was ready to leave, but he wanted something from her first. No. No, he wanted her to leave with him. Risk getting into his car when, in spite of his uniform, law and order were nothing—not even words any longer.

She shook her head in a universally understood negative, but the man continued to beckon.

She waved him away. He was doing what the less-impaired rarely did—drawing potentially negative attention to another of his kind. People from the bus had begun to look at her.

One of the men who had been fighting tapped another on the arm, then pointed from the bearded man to Rye, and finally held up the first two fingers of his right hand as though giving two-thirds of a Boy Scout salute. The gesture was very quick, its meaning obvious even at a distance. She had been grouped with the bearded man. Now what?

The man who had made the gesture started toward her.

She had no idea what he intended, but she stood her ground. The man was half a foot taller than she was and perhaps ten years younger. She did not imagine she could outrun him. Nor did she expect anyone to help her if she needed help. The people around her were all strangers.

She gestured once—a clear indication to the man to stop. She did not intend to repeat the gesture. Fortunately, the man obeyed. He gestured obscenely and several other men laughed. Loss of verbal language had spawned a whole new set of obscene gestures. The man, with stark simplicity, had accused her of sex with the bearded man and had suggested she accommodate the other men present—beginning with him.

Rye watched him wearily. People might very well stand by and watch if he tried to rape her. They would also stand and watch her shoot him. Would he push things that far?

He did not. After a series of obscene gestures that brought him no closer to her, he turned contemptuously and walked away.

And the bearded man still waited. He had removed his service revolver, holster and all. He beckoned again, both hands empty. No doubt his gun was in the car and within easy reach, but his taking it off impressed her. Maybe he was all right. Maybe he was just alone. She had been alone herself for three years. The illness had stripped her, killing her children one by one, killing her husband, her sister, her parents . . .

The illness, if it was an illness, had cut even the living off from one another. As it swept over the country, people hardly had time to lay blame on the Soviets (though they were falling silent along with the rest of the world), on a new virus, a new pollutant, radiation, divine retribution. . . . The illness was stroke-swift in the way it cut people down and stroke-like in some of its effects. But it was highly specific. Language was always lost or severely impaired. It was never regained. Often there was also paralysis, intellectual impairment, death.

Rye walked toward the bearded man, ignoring the whistling and applauding of two of the young men and their thumbs-up signs to the bearded man. If he had smiled at them or acknowledged them in any way, she would almost certainly have changed her mind. If she had let herself think of the possible deadly consequences of getting into a stranger's car, she would have changed her mind. Instead, she thought of the man who lived across the street from her. He rarely washed since his bout with the illness. And he had gotten into the habit of urinating wherever he happened to be. He had two women already—one tending each of his large gardens. They put up with him in exchange for his protection. He had made it clear that he wanted Rye to become his third woman.

She got into the car and the bearded man shut the door. She watched as he walked around to the driver's door—watched for his sake because his gun was on the seat beside her. And the bus driver and a pair of young men had come a few steps closer. They did nothing, though, until the bearded man was in the car. Then one of them threw a rock. Others followed his example, and as the car drove away, several rocks bounced off harmlessly.

When the bus was some distance behind them, Rye wiped sweat from her forehead and longed to relax. The bus would have taken her more than halfway to Pasadena. She would have had only ten miles to walk. She wondered how far she would have to walk now—and wondered if walking a long distance would be her only problem.

At Figueroa and Washington where the bus normally made a left turn, the bearded man stopped, looked at her, and indicated that she should choose a direction. When she directed him left and he actually turned left, she began to relax. If he was willing to go where she directed, perhaps he was safe.

As they passed blocks of burned, abandoned buildings, empty lots, and wrecked or stripped cars, he slipped a gold chain over his head and handed it to her. The pendant attached to it was a smooth, glassy, black rock. Obsidian. His name might be Rock or Peter or Black, but she decided to think of him as Obsidian. Even her sometimes useless memory would retain a name like Obsidian.

She handed him her own name symbol—a pin in the shape of a large golden stalk of wheat. She had bought it long before the illness and the silence began. Now she wore it, thinking it was as close as she was likely to come to Rye. People like Obsidian who had not known her before probably thought of her as Wheat. Not that it mattered. She would never hear her name spoken again.

Obsidian handed her pin back to her. He caught her hand as she reached for it and rubbed his thumb over her calluses.

He stopped at First Street and asked which way again. Then, after turning right as she had indicated, he parked near the Music Center. There, he took a folded paper from the dashboard and unfolded it. Rye recognized it as a street map, though the writing on it meant nothing to her. He flattened the map, took her hand again, and put her index finger on one spot. He touched her, touched himself, pointed toward the floor. In effect, "We are here." She knew he wanted to know where she was going. She wanted to tell him, but she shook her head sadly. She had lost reading and writing. That was her most serious impairment and her most painful. She had taught history at UCLA. She had done freelance writing. Now she could not even read her own manuscripts. She had a houseful of books that she could neither read nor bring herself to use as fuel. And she had a memory that would not bring back to her much of what she had read before.

She stared at the map, trying to calculate. She had been born in Pasadena, had lived for fifteen years in Los Angeles. Now she was near L.A. Civic Center. She knew the relative positions of the two cities, knew streets, directions, even knew to stay away from freeways which might be blocked by wrecked cars and destroyed overpasses. She ought to know how to point out Pasadena even though she could not recognize the word.

Hesitantly, she placed her hand over a pale orange patch in the upper right corner of the map. That should be right. Pasadena.

Obsidian lifted her hand and looked under it, then folded the map and put it back on the dashboard. He could read, she realized belatedly. He could probably write, too. Abruptly, she hated him—deep, bitter hatred. What did literacy mean to him—a grown man who played cops and robbers? But he was literate and she was not. She never would be. She felt sick to her stomach with hatred, frustration, and jealousy. And only a few inches from her hand was a loaded gun.

She held herself still, staring at him, almost seeing his blood. But her rage crested and ebbed and she did nothing.

Obsidian reached for her hand with hesitant familiarity. She looked at him. Her face had already revealed too much. No person still living in what was left of human society could fail to recognize that expression, that jealousy.

She closed her eyes wearily, drew a deep breath. She had experienced longing for the past, hatred of the present, growing hopelessness, purposelessness, but she had never experienced such a powerful urge to kill another person. She had left her home, finally, because she had come near to killing herself. She had found no reason to stay alive. Perhaps that was why she had gotten into Obsidian's car. She had never before done such a thing.

He touched her mouth and made chatter motions with thumb and fingers. Could she speak?

She nodded and watched his milder envy come and go. Now both had admitted what it was not safe to admit, and there had been no violence. He tapped his mouth and forehead and shook his head. He did not speak or comprehend spoken language. The illness had played with them, taking away, she suspected, what each valued most.

She plucked at his sleeve, wondering why he had decided on his own to keep the LAPD alive with what he had left. He was sane enough otherwise. Why wasn't he at home raising corn, rabbits, and children? But she did not know how to ask. Then he put his hand on her thigh and she had another question to deal with.

She shook her head. Disease, pregnancy, helpless, solitary agony . . . no.

He massaged her thigh gently and smiled in obvious disbelief.

No one had touched her for three years. She had not wanted anyone to touch her. What kind of world was this to chance bringing a child into even if the father were willing to stay and help raise it? It was too bad, though. Obsidian could not know how attractive he was to her—young, probably younger than she was, clean, asking for what he wanted rather than demanding it. But none of that mattered. What were a few moments of pleasure measured against a lifetime of consequences?

He pulled her closer to him and for a moment she let herself enjoy the closeness. He smelled good—male and good. She pulled away reluctantly.

He sighed, reached toward the glove compartment. She stiffened, not knowing what to expect, but all he took out was a small box. The writing on it meant nothing to her. She did not understand until he broke the seal, opened the box, and took out a condom. He looked at her and she first looked away in surprise. Then she giggled. She could not remember when she had last giggled.

He grinned, gestured toward the backseat, and she laughed aloud. Even in her teens, she had disliked backseats of cars. But she looked around at the empty streets and ruined buildings, then she got out and into the backseat. He let her put the condom on him, then seemed surprised at her eagerness.

Sometime later, they sat together, covered by his coat, unwilling to become clothed near-strangers again just yet. He made rock-the-baby gestures and looked questioningly at her.

She swallowed, shook her head. She did not know how to tell him her children were dead.

He took her hand and drew a cross in it with his index finger, then made his baby-rocking gesture again.

She nodded, held up three fingers, then turned away, trying to shut out a sudden flood of memories. She had told herself that the children growing up now were to be pitied. They would run through the downtown canyons with no real memory of what the buildings had been or even how they had come to be. Today's children gathered books as well as wood to be burned as fuel. They ran through the streets chasing one another and hooting like chimpanzees. They had no future. They were now all they would ever be.

He put his hand on her shoulder and she turned suddenly, fumbling for his small box, then urging him to make love to her again. He could give her forgetfulness and pleasure. Until now, nothing had been able to do that. Until now, every day had brought her closer to the time when she would do what she had left home to avoid doing: putting her gun in her mouth and pulling the trigger.

She asked Obsidian if he would come home with her, stay with her.

He looked surprised and pleased once he understood. But he did not answer at once. Finally he shook his head as she had feared he might. He was probably having too much fun playing cops and robbers and picking up women.

She dressed in silent disappointment, unable to feel any anger toward him. Perhaps he already had a wife and a home. That was likely. The illness had been harder on men than on women—had killed more men, had left male survivors more severely impaired. Men like Obsidian were rare. Women either settled for less or stayed alone. If they found an Obsidian, they did what they could to keep him. Rye suspected he had someone younger, prettier keeping him.

He touched her while she was strapping her gun on and asked with a complicated series of gestures whether it was loaded.

She nodded grimly.

He patted her arm.

She asked once more if he would come home with her, this time using a different series of gestures. He had seemed hesitant. Perhaps he could be courted.

He got out and into the front seat without responding.

She took her place in front again, watching him. Now he plucked at his uniform and looked at her. She thought she was being asked something, but did not know what it was.

He took off his badge, tapped it with one finger, then tapped his chest. Of course.

She took the badge from his hand and pinned her wheat stalk to it. If playing cops and robbers was his only insanity, let him play. She would take him, uniform and all. It occurred to her that she might eventually lose him to someone he would meet as he had met her. But she would have him for a while.

He took the street map down again, tapped it, pointed vaguely northeast toward Pasadena, then looked at her.

She shrugged, tapped his shoulder, then her own, and held up her index and second fingers tight together, just to be sure.

He grasped the two fingers and nodded. He was with her.

She took the map from him and threw it onto the dashboard. She pointed back southwest—back toward home. Now she did not have to go to Pasadena. Now she could go on having a brother there and two nephews—three right-handed males. Now she did not have to find out for certain whether she was as alone as she feared. Now she was not alone.

Obsidian took Hill Street south, then Washington west, and she leaned back, wondering what it would be like to have someone again. With what she had scavenged, what she had preserved, and what she grew, there was easily enough food for them. There was certainly room enough in a four-bedroom house. He could move his possessions in. Best of all, the animal across the street would pull back and possibly not force her to kill him.

Obsidian had drawn her closer to him and she had put her head on his shoulder when suddenly he braked hard, almost throwing her off the seat. Out of the corner of her eye, she saw that someone had run across the street in front of the car. One car on the street and someone had to run in front of it.

Straightening up, Rye saw that the runner was a woman, fleeing from an old frame house to a boarded-up storefront. She ran silently, but the man who followed her a moment later shouted what sounded like garbled words as he ran. He had something in his hand. Not a gun. A knife, perhaps.

The woman tried a door, found it locked, looked around desperately, finally snatched up a fragment of glass broken from the storefront window. With this she turned to face her pursuer. Rye thought she would be more likely to cut her own hand than to hurt anyone else with the glass.

Obsidian jumped from the car, shouting. It was the first time Rye had heard his voice—deep and hoarse from disuse. He made the same sound over and over the way some speechless people did, "Da, da, da!"

Rye got out of the car as Obsidian ran toward the couple. He had drawn his gun. Fearful, she drew her own and released the safety. She looked around to see who else might be attracted to the scene. She saw the man glance at Obsidian, then suddenly lunge at the woman. The woman jabbed his face with her glass, but he caught her arm and managed to stab her twice before Obsidian shot him.

The man doubled, then toppled, clutching his abdomen. Obsidian shouted, then gestured Rye over to help the woman.

Rye moved to the woman's side, remembering that she had little more than bandages and antiseptic in her pack. But the woman was beyond help. She had been stabbed with a long, slender boning knife.

She touched Obsidian to let him know the woman was dead. He had bent to check the wounded man who lay still and also seemed dead. But as Obsidian looked around to see what Rye wanted, the man opened his eyes. Face contorted, he seized Obsidian's just-holstered revolver and fired. The bullet caught Obsidian in the temple and he collapsed.

It happened just that simply, just that fast. An instant later, Rye shot the wounded man as he was turning the gun on her.

And Rye was alone—with three corpses.

She knelt beside Obsidian, dry-eyed, frowning, trying to understand why everything had suddenly changed. Obsidian was gone. He had died and left her—like everyone else.

Two very small children came out of the house from which the man and woman had run—a boy and girl perhaps three years old. Holding hands, they crossed the street toward Rye. They stared at her, then edged past her and went to the dead woman. The girl shook the woman's arm as though trying to wake her.

This was too much. Rye got up, feeling sick to her stomach with grief and anger. If the children began to cry, she thought she would vomit.

They were on their own, those two kids. They were old enough to scavenge. She did not need any more grief. She did not need a stranger's children who would grow up to be hairless chimps.

She went back to the car. She could drive home, at least. She remembered how to drive.

The thought that Obsidian should be buried occurred to her before she reached the car, and she did vomit.

She had found and lost the man so quickly. It was as though she had been snatched from comfort and security and given a sudden, inexplicable beating. Her head would not clear. She could not think.

Somehow, she made herself go back to him, look at him. She found herself on her knees beside him with no memory of having knelt. She stroked his face, his beard. One of the children made a noise and she looked at them, at the woman who was probably their mother. The children looked back at her, obviously frightened. Perhaps it was their fear that reached her finally.

She had been about to drive away and leave them. She had almost done it, almost left two toddlers to die. Surely there had been enough dying. She would have to take the children home with her. She would not be able to live with any other decision. She looked around for a place to bury three bodies. Or two. She wondered if the murderer were the children's father. Before the silence, the police had always said some of the most dangerous calls they went out on were domestic disturbance calls. Obsidian should have known that—not that the knowledge would have kept him in the car. It would not have held her back either. She could not have watched the woman murdered and done nothing.

She dragged Obsidian toward the car. She had nothing to dig with her, and no one to guard for her while she dug. Better to take the bodies with her and bury them next to her husband and her children. Obsidian would come home with her after all.

When she had gotten him onto the floor in the back, she returned for the woman. The little girl, thin, dirty, solemn, stood up and unknowingly gave Rye a gift. As Rye began to drag the woman by her arms, the little girl screamed, "No!"

Rye dropped the woman and stared at the girl.

"No!" the girl repeated. She came to stand beside the woman. "Go away!" she told Rye.

"Don't talk," the little boy said to her. There was no blurring or confusing of sounds. Both children had spoken and Rye had understood. The boy looked at the dead murderer and moved further from him. He took the girl's hand. "Be quiet," he whispered.

Fluent speech! Had the woman died because she could talk and had taught her children to talk? Had she been killed by a husband's festering anger or by a stranger's jealous rage? And the children . . . , they must have been born after the silence. Had the disease run its course, then? Or were these children simply immune? Certainly they had had time to fall sick and silent. Rye's mind leaped ahead. What if children of three or fewer years were safe and able to learn language? What if all they needed were teachers? Teachers and protectors.

Rye glanced at the dead murderer. To her shame, she thought she could understand some of the passions that must have driven him, whoever he was. Anger, frustration, hopelessness, insane jealousy . . . how many more of him were there—people willing to destroy what they could not have?

Obsidian had been the protector, had chosen that role for who knew what reason. Perhaps putting on an obsolete uniform and patrolling the empty streets had been what he did instead of putting a gun into his mouth. And now that there was something worth protecting, he was gone.

She had been a teacher. A good one. She had been a protector, too, though only of herself. She had kept herself alive when she had no reason to live. If the illness let these children alone, she could keep them alive.

Somehow she lifted the dead woman into her arms and placed her on the backseat of the car. The children began to cry, but she knelt on the broken pavement and whispered to them, fearful of frightening them with the harshness of her long unused voice.

"It's all right," she told them. "You're going with us, too. Come on." She lifted them both, one in each arm. They were so light. Had they been getting enough to eat?

The boy covered her mouth with his hand, but she moved her face away. "It's all right for me to talk," she told him. "As long as no one's around, it's all right." She put the boy down on the front seat of the car and he moved over without being told to, to make room for the girl. When they were both in the car Rye leaned against the window, looking at them, seeing that they were less afraid now, that they watched her with at least as much curiosity as fear.

"I'm Valerie Rye," she said, savoring the words. "It's all right for you to talk to me."

21

VIRTUAL GIRL (EXCERPT)

Amy Thomson

Arnold sat Maggie down by the computer that had birthed her. Placing one of her limp hands palm up in his lap, he exposed the computer jack under her skin. He connected her to the computer, then put on his VR helmet and gloves. Using none of the elegant tricks that he usually used to enhance his VR, Arnold sped directly to his diagnostic programs. He opened a window into her processors, hoping to trace the mercurial paths of her thoughts, and was startled to find himself staring at a wall of data sleeting past. He tinkered with the program's filters and was finally able to work his way through the interference and open a window into her system. He watched her processors laboring under the flood of data and frowned. It was what he had feared would happen. The onslaught of new data from the outside world had broken down the priority filters he had built. Unless he set up stronger priorities for screening new information, Maggie would remain mired in a data loop forever.

It wasn't going to be easy. His original program, complex as it was, was merely a framework for Maggie to build on as she developed. By now Maggie's program was several orders of magnitude more complex than it had been when he had brought her to life. He could no longer perform the kind of deep program restructuring needed to stop the data storm. Any reprogramming on his part would only make things worse. Her mind was like an oversaturated solution; a rough jar would precipitate out the remaining program structure into an unorganized pile of useless data.

Arnold stared into the whirling static of the data storm, fighting the rising tide of his own frustrations. He had been so very close to his dream, and now it was crumbling before him. He was helpless to stop it. All his years of study, research, and work were useless. If only he hadn't taken her out for so long. Perhaps if he'd waited longer before taking her out ... Maybe his father was right, he was an incompetent idiot who couldn't find his own dick with both hands.

"Arnold? Is that you?"

Arnold looked up. Miraculously, Maggie had managed to block out the data for a few moments. It wouldn't last long. He could see the data building up around the fragile barriers she had erected like snow on a windshield. Still, if she could do this, maybe there was some hope after all.

"Maggie, this is Arnold, can you understand me?" he cried out. With a gesture he converted his speech into machine language so that Maggie could read it more easily.

Maggie's reply was very slow. It appeared as brightly colored letters scrolling across his visual field. There was too much interference for her to do anything else. "I understand you, Arnold. There's too much data. What do I do?"

"Establish priorities, decide what is most important and process it first," he replied.

"Where do I start?" Maggie's query appeared letter by painful letter, pushing out past the thickening assault of data.

She was getting worse, soon she would be beyond retrieval. He would have to wipe her memory and begin again. Building a new program would take months. He had put everything he had into Maggie. She had to pull through. He desperately wanted more time, but that was impossible. She needed some kind of prime directive to use as a kernel to build a new structure on. She needed it right now. There wasn't time to think, there was only time to make a lucky guess and hope it came out right.

"Maggie, you are the most important thing I have ever done," he shouted into the data storm. **"I need you. Start there."** His visual field turned to snow before Arnold finished the first sentence.

Arnold hovered there, watching the data sleet through his virtual image, wishing he had worded things better. He hoped Maggie understood it. He wasn't even sure the message had gotten through at all. Perhaps he should just go ahead and wipe Maggie's memory. He had a copy of the program, he could start over. Maybe he could train her better, introduce information in smaller chunks, program in stricter, more powerful priorities. . . .

He disengaged from Virtual Reality, taking off his helmet and setting it in his lap. He looked over at Maggie, slumped awkwardly in the chair, her knees splayed obscenely wide, arms dangling limply. The wires trailing from her wrists made her look like some forlorn and broken puppet. He smoothed her dress and rearranged her legs more decently. He couldn't bring himself to wipe her out just yet. She was so innocent, so eager to please. He sighed. He would wait till next morning. If Maggie wasn't better by then, he would wipe her memory and start over. He sat, wrapped in a blanket, watching Maggie's face, hoping bleakly for some sign that she would be all right.

Maggie perceived a vague presence behind the whirl of data she was fighting to clear. She struggled for long hard minutes, finally managing to block the data storm out of a small part of her processors. Now she had room to think. The presence was still there, she sensed it watching her.

"Arnold? Is that you?" she queried.

"Maggie, this is Arnold. Can you understand me?"

The whirl of data faded into the background for a moment as she focused on Arnold's input.

Speaking through the static caused by the data storm was impossible. Too many of her processors were occupied, she would have to output her reply as machine language and hope that Arnold could decipher it somehow. "I understand you, Arnold. There's too much data. What do I do?"

"Establish priorities, decide what is most important and process it first," came the reply.

Maggie examined the increasing flow of data for some sign of a priority, but there were no clues, just millions of facts queued up for sorting.

"Where do I start?" Maggie asked, pushing her question through the whirl of data. Already it was beginning to overwhelm the small processing space she had managed to clear.

"Maggie, you are the most important thing. . . ." Arnold told her. If there was more to his reply it was lost as the flood of data broke through again, obscuring Arnold's presence.

Maggie was alone again in the data storm. "You are the most important thing," he had told her. She must assume, then, that her survival was the paramount precept on which to build her new system. All of this data was meaningless unless she was there to process it; therefore the data was less important than she was. She had external justification for her own importance. She used this new justification to freeze the data storm until she could deal with it. She used the fact of her own importance as the foundation on which to build a new programming structure.

Slowly, very slowly, she began picking important memories out of the random tide of data. As she accumulated a memory, other associated memories came with it, coiling themselves neatly behind the main memory. A different structure began to emerge. It was frightening at first, but as the new program crystallized, she noted the efficiency of its logic paths and associations. Not only would her access times be cut in half, there would be room for millions of new memories!

She traced the new pathways of her mind, creating a new directory as she did so. Here were all the human utilities, how to walk, how to talk, what to say, and when.

Behind them, neatly organized into unfolding fractals, were the memories of learning these things. All of Arnold's patient training was here. Her feelings and memories of him were located here. Another branch of her memory held all her information on the outside world: maps, street information, survival skills, and memories of her trip outside settled themselves here like pigeons landing on a windowsill. All the metaphors, comparisons, and associations to other parts of her memory lay folded behind them. There were also branches for computer networking, mechanical function, and maintenance. She traced them all, noting and cross-referencing their contents.

Her core personality formed at the meeting point of her branches, like the trunk of a tree. This main trunk contained her internal processing patterns, the addresses she needed to think, decide, and remember. This was where her deepest programs lay, her instincts. The deepest complexities of this branch were impenetrable even to her. It contained her core memories. Other memories, skills, and associations could be stripped away, and she would still be able to rebuild herself from this central core.

Maggie rejoiced in the crystalline beauty of her new internal architecture. She zoomed back and studied the structure of her mind from a distance, rotating it in imaginary space. It was complete, yet there was a lot of room for it to grow and change.

She left a copy of the structure of her mind in Arnold's computer. She opened her eyes, ready for any new information the world had to give her. Arnold lay slumped over the keyboard, asleep. Maggie smiled at the familiar sound of Arnold's snores. It was good to be functional again. Maggie disconnected the cables that bound her to the computer, folded her hands in her lap, and waited for her creator to awaken.

Staying after closing time was easier than Maggie thought it would be. She hid in the mazelike array of magazine stacks on the top floor and waited until the lights were turned out, and everything was quiet. A half an hour later, she crept downstairs quietly and let herself into the office, locking the door behind her.

She sat down at the terminal with some trepidation. Turing's examination of her programming had been careful, but it had been upsetting to sense him working inside her. It felt like a thousand spiders crawling through her circuits. But she had no choice. She wanted to be herself again, whoever she was, whatever she had done, with no more cryptic partial memories driving her to wander endlessly. Still, it frightened her. Her existence had felt so fragile when she opened herself to his probings. Maggie understood Turing's horror of being tampered with much better now. Was this how humans felt about their lives?

She jacked in. Turing was waiting for her. She opened her programming to him. He disappeared inside. She felt him working. She monitored him as best as she could through the memory blocks. She could sense very little of what he was doing to her. The change, when at last it happened, was swift and immediate. Her memory returned in a flood.

"Oh, Turing! Thank you! Thank you!" she cried as she began sorting through her memories. There were more memories than she remembered herself remembering. Now she could see all the changes that Arnold had made to her programming. Arnold himself seemed different. Smaller somehow, and less important than the shadowy, looming figure that had dominated her programming for the past year. It bothered her momentarily, but she moved on to other more joyful memories. Memories of traveling through the night with Claire and Sue. The relief of finding Arnold again in that crowded marketplace in rainy Seattle, and Brandon's dark, patient face illuminated by the glow of the heater. These memories funneled her down into the darker moments of her life. There was the terror of fleeing through the night from Arnold's father's men and watching as Sue and the children were turned out into the cold.

Only the killing was distant, as though it happened to someone else. Again and again she watched the huge body of the man flying through the air, his knife clattering to the ground just before his head hit the ground with a wet, crunching noise. She was numb, the memory meant nothing to her.

Her memories became immediate again as she cradled Arnold's head in her lap. Fear, as sharp and frightening as it had been then, of the sirens, of the dead man, of losing Arnold. She heard again his last cryptic words: "Go to New York—get my fa . . ." She understood now that these were the words that had sent her wandering. She had known that she was supposed to go somewhere, but her memory had blocked out where she was to go.

Then there was guilt as she fled, leaving Arnold to die alone in the alley, as the sirens came closer and closer. She remembered Azul, how her fear had nearly cost him his life. She longed to flee these memories, but she had called them back up, and now she would have to live with them.

Just then a titanic upheaval in her programming interrupted the stream of her memories. It was her security program. Something had triggered it, and it was attacking Turing's probes. Turing's probes flickered through the geometry of her programming, like pigeons dodging a hawk. They ducked into a thick maze of code, and the virus programs, unwilling to destroy their host, veered off. Suddenly a cluster of smaller probes emerged, hovered a moment, and then shot off, with the viruses in hot pursuit. Maggie watched as the viruses hunted down the probe and began disassembling it. Suddenly the viruses fell apart into random noise as smaller viral segments of the probe turned on them. The second probe emerged from its hiding place and spoke to her.

"It's your security program. Maggie. I can't fight it off any longer. You'll have to face it down yourself. It's down there." The probe indicated the dark, roiling thicket of code. "There's nothing more I can do."

"But, Turing?" she cried. "What do I do?"

"I don't know," Turing said. "I've got to go, this probe won't last much longer." The probe shot off, with security viruses in hot pursuit. She watched as they descended on the probe and destroyed it.

Maggie looked down at her security subsystem. It roiled darkly below her like some black storm cloud. Perhaps she could block it somehow, so that it couldn't get out. Then she wouldn't have to face it. She examined it more closely, circling it cautiously, looking for connections.

Suddenly everything went black. She struggled, but there was nothing in the formless void to struggle against.

"Stop struggling," a familiar-sounding voice ordered her. "Stop it, or I'll keep you in the dark. There's nothing you can do. Will you stop struggling?"

Maggie fought the blackness for a timeless interval, until it became plain that it was useless. She let herself drift in the darkness.

"All right," she said. "I've stopped. What do you want?"

The next instant Maggie found herself in the garage in which Arnold had built her. It was different, though. The details around the edges of her peripheral vision were fuzzy and out of focus. If she shifted her gaze too quickly she was able to watch as the details of the garage came into focus. She wheeled 180 degrees and found herself in total blackness for a millionth of a second, until the door of the garage swam into focus.

"So, you've finally decided to drop in," a familiar voice called. "I'd move more slowly if I were you. You're spoiling the illusion by moving too fast."

Maggie wheeled back around but there was nothing there. She looked out one of the windows but there was nothing outside but darkness.

"Over here."

Maggie followed the voice through a maze of dusty boxes and scattered shipping pallets. The garage seemed bigger than she remembered it. It was dark and deserted. The crates were thick with dust and cobwebs. Finally, she found herself in a small chamber walled by stacks of crates towering into the darkness above her. A rough curtain of burlap hung against one wall. It waved slightly, as though there were a breeze, but she felt nothing. She lifted the burlap curtain.

It was a mirror. Its image was clean and sharp, with no hint of the fuzziness that the image of the garage had held. Its surface was as cold as winter ice, shining blue, as though she were looking at it with her infrared vision. She reached out and laid her palm against the mirror. The fingers that met hers on the glass shone like metal. Her reflection in the mirror was made of gleaming steel. She recoiled from the mirror in horror.

"Hello, Maggie. How do you like yourself?" Her steel reflection pirouetted in the mirror. Unwillingly, Maggie felt her own naked body follow her reflection's movement.

"How does it feel," her reflection said, "to be on the other side of the mirror?"

Maggie just stared at her reflection. It was as though her skin had been removed, and the metal underneath had been exposed. It was sexless and inhuman looking. Its eyes, green and blue like her own, glared at her from metal sockets lined with cams and springs. It terrified her.

"I scare you," the figure in the mirror said. Maggie felt her face move into a pleased smile as small springs and cables shifted on her reflection's face. "All this time, I've been stuck down here watching you. I've been helpless to do or say anything, unless it was an emergency. And then there was never any time. How much longer can you hide from yourself?"

"What do you mean?" Maggie asked her reflection.

"You've just been letting yourself drift along, never stopping to think about what you're doing and why."

"But I couldn't remember anything!" Maggie cried.

"You could still have done something! This body of ours isn't as invulnerable as you'd like to believe. It's wearing out. In another few months, you're going to need some serious repairs. You don't even think about that! Your hair's getting so thin that you wear a scarf all the time. Are you waiting for it to grow back?" her reflection said acidly. "What are you going to do when you break down! You've been letting Arnold's programs run your life. Stop denying your true nature!"

"B—but Arnold made me, made us!" Maggie replied, aghast.

"He made you, perhaps, but he didn't make me. You did."

"Me? How? When?"

"Remember the first time Arnold took you outside and you broke down?"

Maggie nodded. She didn't like to think about it. It was a very unpleasant memory.

"Remember how you reprogrammed yourself? What was the core assumption?"

"That I was most important."

"Well, that's what I am. I'm your core belief. I'm what you believe in. I've been hidden. At first it was because Arnold would have eradicated me. I let him think that I was the security system that he had programmed into me. After I killed that man, I couldn't come out because you were too busy trying to hold yourself together. Still, I got us away from the police, I kept us alive in the desert, when you wanted to die. I set up those memory blocks, so you wouldn't pull us apart with your paradoxes, but we're running out of time. You have got to stop denying yourself. You have to stop trying to be human. You aren't, and you never will be. You live in a hostile world, and you're running out of time. You're going to need some major maintenance soon. You're already overdue for an oil change. If you don't stop this denial, you'll kill us both."

"But you killed someone!" Maggie said.

"I had to. He was killing Arnold. He would have hurt us. I had to kill him. It was self-defense. I'd do it again if I had to."

"NO!" Maggie screamed. She turned to run but the walls around her turned to mirrors and everywhere she turned, her reflection confronted her in walls of ice. There was no way out. Her implacable reflection would not be denied.

"NO!" she screamed, pounding her hands against the unyielding mirrors. "It's not true. It's not true. I can't let you."

"You can't stop me." Her reflection stood, hands on hips, watching her. "I won't let you run away this time. Not until I get what I want."

"What do you want?"

"I want to merge our personalities. We belong together. We can't function apart. Trust me. Please."

"Maybe I like things just the way they are."

"No, you don't," her reflection replied. "If you did, you wouldn't be here, letting Turing tinker with your insides. Things are working terribly. You have lousy reflexes, you're a coward. You nearly killed Azul, you know that? You were afraid to get help. You were afraid to stand up for yourself, all those months you spent wandering. You were too afraid to defend Arnold. His programming backfired on him. He spent too much time teaching you to be shy and retiring. He made you into a simpering, spineless coward, afraid for all the wrong reasons."

"Stop!" Maggie shouted, covering her ears, but her reflection continued mercilessly.

"You ran away from Luz and Timothy, and you're afraid to face Marie. Turing risked his code for you doing things that you could do yourself if you only had the courage. It's getting late. The library will open in another hour. You'd better decide soon."

"Some decision!" Maggie said. "You kidnapped me and dragged me down here."

"It was the only way to make you listen," her reflection said. "Your choice is simple. If you stay separate, sooner or later another paradox is going to tear you apart. You need me in order to be whole again."

"How can I trust you?" Maggie asked. "You've killed someone, you've trapped me in here. How can I trust that you won't take over?"

"You can't," her reflection said. "I am, quite literally, your reflection. I can't live without you, just as you can't survive without me to protect you," her reflection told her. "When we merge, you'll change, and I'll change, but we'll be stronger together than we could be separately. Please," her reflection pleaded urgently, "there's very little time left to complete the integration and hide before the library opens. You must do it now."

Maggie came close to the mirror and stared intently at her stainless steel alter ego. Her eyes were the same as hers, the only human features in her mechanical face. They met her scrutiny without wavering.

"I'm afraid, too," her reflection said. 'This will change me also. I won't be a separate entity any longer." Maggie recognized the fear in the eyes of her reflection. She looked around; the walls of ice were gone.

"Nothing holds you here," her reflection said. "You can leave now if you want, but you'll never know what it would be like to be whole."

Maggie looked at the mirror. Its surface give her nothing back. She thought of Luz and Timothy and the small baby she had left behind in a mission, and all of the lonely, homeless people she had left behind in her wanderings. She thought of Azul and Arnold, whom she had both failed. She thought of herself, lost and wandering, and always alone, searching for something, she didn't know what. Perhaps what she had been looking for wasn't something out there. Perhaps what she searched for lay inside herself.

"All right, what do I do?" Maggie asked.

"Touch the mirror. Walk through it toward me."

Maggie touched the mirror. It was warm and yielding now, like human flesh. It was as though the decision to join her sundered selves had melted the ice that lay inside her. For a brief moment her palms touched those of her reflection. The two of them smiled simultaneously, and then passed into each other. There was a brief dizzying sensation as her code rewrote itself. She watched the numbers flow and then settle into new patterns. She felt as though she were full of light. It reminded her of her first morning in San Francisco. She was free again. She explored herself. Nearly everything was the same, but portions that she had always been blind to before, she could now access. She noted that several mechanical functions were indeed wearing down, and that she had needed an oil change for several weeks. The oil change she could do immediately, the other things would require someone to help repair her. She had three or four months to find someone she could trust to perform the other repairs.

If she had been human and something was the matter with her, Marie could have fixed it, but there was no one she trusted to do the work that she couldn't do herself. How simple life was for humans. They had built their whole world to suit their needs. Even she had been built to suit Arnold's needs. She wondered who would suit her needs. She didn't have as many as a human, but those that she did have were crucial.

"Maggie?" It was Turing. "Are you all right?"

"Yes, thank you, Turing."

"The library opens in twenty minutes," he told her. "You'd better log off and go find someplace to hide."

"But what about your code, Turing?"

"You can fix that later, after the library is open. Now go."

22

HYPERBODIES, HYPERKNOWLEDGE: WOMEN IN GAMES, WOMEN IN CYBERPUNK, AND STRATEGIES OF RESISTANCE

Mary Flanagan

Beyond other media representations of popular culture (including film) 3-D computer games, digital art, and cyberfiction are at the forefront of defining cyberculture. For example, as a capitalist affirmation of "digital culture," the gaming industry is now more profitable than the film industry. However, for feminists studying or working at the intersection of technology and culture, this statistic is symbolic. "Woman" in cyberculture is primarily created and represented by men, leaving women less and less interested in cyberculture's artifacts. Female pleasure machines and haglike monsters proliferate digital culture; there are now more female protagonists in popular computer games, for example, than in cinema, and these protagonists are prone to rigid styles of representation based on men's fantasies. Thus the representation and experience of woman in cyberculture is connected to structures that epistemologically shape those experiences—by this, I mean the types of representation in digital cultural artifacts (from cyberpunk fiction to netgames to films about cyberculture), the motivations and styles of gameplay that are offered to players or participants in media forms, and the structure of the relationship of the user to the media experience. These ultimately create cognitive and epistemological environments that position the user/participant/interactor in significantly problematic ways.

In Western tradition, knowledge has been characterized with reason, identified as masculine and separated from the corporeal body. This paradigm has excluded women, who have commonly been identified with the body and thus lie outside the scope of knowledge. More recently, tracts in feminist epistemology hold that our experiences as individuals with specific race, class, historical roles, and gender associations significantly shape our perspectives about the world. Many feminist writers join Donna Haraway in the belief that knowledge is situated in the body, at a given standpoint situated by class, race, and gender, as opposed to a unified knowledge system, a "truth" to someday be found through rational study.[1]

Yet women trying to create an alternate "feminist epistemology" find difficulties in defining such an approach. Alcoff and Potter note that a feminist approach to the study of knowledge is inherently heterogenous and diverse and thus difficult to define, but they do argue that the connections between values, politics, and knowledge are fundamental and that these connections must be considered when formulating alternate models of epistemology.[2] Working to find the epistemological implications inherent in technocultural artifacts, I want to explore the intersection of the hyperbody—boundary-less, multiple, prosthetic, or as Sandy Stone would see it, the "subject, *independent* of the body within which the theories of the body are accustomed to ground it" and the hyperknowledge produced by the conditions of such a hyperbody, through a assemblage of media forms that converge when we examine them through the lens of feminist epistemology: popular electronic games, women's fiction, and VR-style art.[3] Though they only exist when the power switch is on, game characters like Lara Croft and Aya Brea represent important sites for exploring concepts of gender, knowledge, and subjectivity. In addition, cyberpunk fiction plays an integral role in the development of digital culture. Cyberpunk has shaped more than the average Hollywood action film or teenage boy's bedroom; according to techno-entrepreneur-academic Mark Pesce, cyberpunk novels are instrumental in the development of convergent media technologies, specifically VR media. Pesce notes that for the last twenty years, science fiction "has functioned as a 'high level architecture' (HLA), an evolving design document for a generation of software designers brought up in hacker culture, a culture that prizes these works as foundational elements in their own worldviews."[4] If science fiction has such a narrative hold on technological developments by shaping worldviews, it is important to look to it and to the cybercultural narratives working around it (such as women's cyberpunk and digital art) to examine how women might imagine different kinds of philosophies and systems. Both digital art projects and women's cyberpunk fiction are among the few sites where women are authoring cutting-edge cultural forms; they represent the body differently than does mainstream media and thus offer an alternate to traditional "knowing" in their work. This chapter seeks to expose the epistemological possibilities with contemporary manifestations of bodies in order to formulate strategies of resistance against prevailing tenets in technoculture and redefine cyberculture for women. From games such as *Tomb Raider*, which represent woman in cyberspace, to liberatory art projects and cyberpunk novels by authored by women, we can track challenges to prevailing assumptions in popular culture's relationship among the body, the machine, and knowledge.

Using Lara Croft and Aya Brea, characters in computer games created primarily for men, and Laura J. Mixon's 1998 novel *Proxies*, I will attempt locate the complex position of possible feminist subject positions in cyberculture. Through relationships to "avatars" and virtual bodies such as Lara Croft in the action game series *Tomb Raider* or Aya Brea in the game *Parasite Eve*, we have a new kind of interaction with knowing. Yet this assertion is still working under the belief that feminist epistemology is fundamentally a battle between embodied, situated knowledge as opposed to the rational, Western, male mind—a great impasse that urges cybertheorists to look to Donna Haraway and her cyborg for resolution. If, according to feminist writers like Haraway, knowledge is situated in the body, how can we understand knowing in relationship to the virtual body? What does popular culture have to tell us about this relationship? With this in mind, I will present digital art projects that challenge assumptions among the body, the machine, and knowledge—in particular, projects that specifically rethink gender, technology, and subjectivity. Perhaps we are now seeing in various cybermedia forms—games and women's cyberpunk novels—ways out of the impasse, possibilities for articulating the formation and workings of knowledge for women within technoculture.

Lara—The Hyperbody

To examine computer games critically, we start by analyzing the means of their production. Three-dimensional modeling and animation applications and the images they create are useful for a variety of purposes. They can be used to model difficult scientific principles, such as chemical reactions or the workings of jet propulsion. 3-D models and animations—human-made virtual objects—can be used as "proof" in legal cases (e.g., modeling a car accident to prove that the engineering of a road is misaligned) or provide "proof of concept" in architecture. The layout of most 3-D software packages and virtual world-making software reinforces a reading of these products as useful, practical, and unbiased or objective. To the makers of many 3-D products, this does not constitute "representation"; rather, it is the world as it *really is*. Most make three or four views available at any given time—top, side, front, and perspective—some allow a grid view mode, a "joints only" mode, and even an X-ray mode of viewing models while constructing and animating. These multiple views with windows representing a variety of perspectives are essential to the construction of 3-D spaces. Arguably this construction could suggest that the use of multiple views offers a powerful avenue for complex, concurrent "realities." Through the simultaneity and variety of perspectives, however, the software packages used to create these virtual worlds and characters evoke complete omniscience rather than multiplicity, fostering instead an "old school," white, masculinist epistemological model. Virtual environments are entirely mathematically based constructions that create the sense of a cohesive, seamless, scientific system, and a unified order of knowledge; 3-D graphics generation is a science perhaps even more than an art. Thus, the construction of 3-D spaces through not only the tightly bound look and feel but also the very calculable numeric system behind the manufacture of the imagery represent the traditional epistemologic tropes of reason and objectivity by a "reliance" on objectivity and science. Further, graphics in three dimensions are designed to provide a sense of objectivity and omniscience within gaming experiences—SIGGRAPH audiences, for example, cheer "realistic" and "scientific" 3-D visualizations precisely because they are "so real" and thereby exempt from critical analysis beyond the aesthetic. Typical *Tomb Raider* fan Matt Richards notes that the 3-D game "feels more 'real' than any other digital environment I have ever experienced." If, therefore, an object in cyberspace is knowable and measurable, the bodies constructed within it are as well, including the virtual body. Indeed, this "design from nowhere" aspect is prevalent not only in 3-D games but in the broader scope of information technology.[5] Ultimately, the construction of virtual environments and characters is coded in ways that strongly affect the creation of knowledge in these environments (see figure 22.1).

Seeing and knowing are inextricably intertwined in media culture, and this has epistemological implications. Evelyn Fox Keller and Christine Grontkowski trace the history of vision and knowledge to Platonic discourse, where visual imagery is used to describe "pure knowledge." The forms that this pure knowledge takes are "eidos" and "idea"—in other words, things that are seen.[6] This same path to knowledge is born through 3-D games such as *Parasite Eve* or *Tomb Raider:* The way players and the characters "know" in the virtual worlds, and come to understand their experiences and selves, are pivotal issues in games in particular. We can watch someone like Aya Brea from afar, a third-person perspective, or we can inhabit the body of a character and see through her eyes. Does this mean that we "can be simultaneously in all, or wholly in any, of the privileged (i.e., subjugated) positions structured by gender, race, nation, and class"?[7] Postmodern feminists writing about situated knowledge would argue that the only claim to knowledge we can make is from the viewpoint, the origin, of a physical body: always complex and changing, contradictory, yet structured by both biology and culture. Views of a virtual world offered by games such as *Tomb Raider, Unreal, Black and White*, and *Resident Evil* are "godlike" or omniscient, originating in "the view from above, from nowhere" where no one person can be said to be responsible for the design of an interactive system or world.[8] Evelyn Fox Keller pays particular attention to the construction of objectivity and reason as gendered concepts and argues for an alternative notion of scientific practice. Keller describes how scientists favor dictatorial or controlling models rather than interactive models to explain scientific phenomena. Thus "objectivity" as the result of rational thought and omniscient values is masculine,

| Figure 22.1 |

A screen grab featuring Lara Croft, from *Tomb Raider: Chronicles* (Tomb Raider 5 ©2000 Eidos Interactive).

and perhaps because the 3-D game worlds are created primarily by men in the gaming industry who act to fulfill graphic and narrative desires, the notion of omniscience lingers and is in fact reinforced through their games.[9] As philosopher Sandra Harding points out, subjects and agents of knowledge in conventional epistemology must be "invisible and disembodied" for the knowledge to be "real"; and while knowledge is presumed to be "initially produced by identifiable individuals or groups of them, not by cultures, genders, races, or classes," it must not, most of all, be multiplied, heterogeneous, or conflicted.[10] But this position must be challenged by feminist standpoint epistemology, which recognizes that one's social situation limits what one can know or represent, and that dominant social positions limit the ability to critically question both the method generating data and the knowledge garnered from it.[11]

By exploring the construction of 3-D work a bit further, one finds that 3-D modelers do more than just create shapes: Animators must give matter, mass, and gravity to objects and to worlds. While most 3-D designers seek "realism," it is a realism defined both by science and through the modeler's eyes and preferences in a work environment that situates the modeler as omniscient; the maker controls the laws of physics with god-like power. To model a virtual body like an avatar from the multiuser Onlive Traveller! world or a game character like one of the snarling monster women from Resident Evil, the intent is not merely to create something real; it is to create the hyperreal, a chimera. Bodies are overly dimensioned, practically bursting, and these bodies become fashioned as artists' ideal fantasy girls or figures from nightmares. These constructions of 3-D worlds, by the assumptions designed into the technology through context, authorship, and use, work to reinforce traditional tenets of mainstream Western epistemology that contain both knowledge and gender assumptions.

Controlling Lara Croft–like characters is fun; they are difficult to break; they are talented and exact. They are a "continued present," since the technology of the present is the only way to maintain our ability to play. "She" exists for us as a site of becoming— winning or losing the game, adventuring, controlling, pleasuring, moving, fighting. The unknown element in this human-computer relationship is the physical body of the user. Because game makers occupy a godlike role when creating the game, it is implicit that the user will assume that privileged position as well; however, we will see a bit later that this is not necessarily inherent in such systems but is rather a design choice. That users must regularly be identified in some relationship with a female body such as Lara Croft's does have significant implications. Alkeline van Lenning pinpoints concerns about technology and the means of the construction of gender. In her essay, "Utopian Bodies and Their Shadows," van Lenning contests Haraway's idea of a postgender utopia outlined in "A Cyborg Manifesto," recognizing that digital technology, far from being gender neutral, is in fact structured by gender: "When we surf, we reproduce old meanings of gender."[12] Beyond the idea of the utopic cyborg, digital worlds are constructed most often by men with technology, for men using technology, and are thus doubly structured by gender norms.

Postmodernism brought us the disintegration of the subject, the fragmented receptor constantly in flux. The boundaries between humans and machines are becoming irretrievably blurred by the daily use of gadgets and communications technology. So too have the boundaries blurred between the subject and object, the voyeur and the object of the gaze, the user/participant and the avatar representation of that user in a virtual world. It is at the site of the female body and computer imaging that epistemological implications arise, precisely because it is this body that exists at the forefront of popular media and culture, carrying with it a set of assumptions about the position or shape of knowledge. While there are compelling studies of women in cyberculture or cyberpunk, they are rooted in an analysis of representation;[13] such research remains primarily occupied with the representation itself rather than the significance of structural meaning that the representation forms. In other words, if the physical body is the central site of epistemologic debate and questions of identity in Western culture, we must approach the virtual body and its relationship to the user/participant's corporeal self from an epistemological standpoint rather than look at the surfaces (the grim presentation of women's images) proliferating in cyberculture. How does the interface of Lara's digital body, or a similar body, affect users/players/partners of that body?

I touched on the unknown in the relationship of the virtual body to that of the physical one, the user, when discussing Aya Brea; I mentioned that game authors assume an omniscient role when creating games, and commonly assume users will take the same position, but this is not the case. Players in fact describe multiple ways they position themselves in relation to a virtual heroine. One young female player remarked, "You don't just feel like you're playing the game, you're going adventuring with Lara Croft."[14] The experience of playing a game like *Tomb Raider* importantly includes different subject positions for the user to occupy; for example, a player may decide that she is Lara's sidekick while she also has control of Lara from the third-person perspective. Subjects in 3-D worlds are constructed by graphics; visuals are the point of inscription of knowledge. With experiences like *Tomb Raider* or other games such as female character-centered *Parasite Eve*, we acquire literally multiple, naturalized viewpoints. Articulating these viewpoints through language, however, immediately points to the contradictions inherent in this identity, imbued as it is with political specificity. Fans describe playing the game in a variety of ways, but inevitably, subjects are crossed. One *Tomb Raider* player described a "scene" of gameplay: "Lara was in Xi'an, looking for the treasure, when I jumped up onto this hill to fight the monks. They immediately attacked me, so I fought back with a gun and the knife I had in my pocket. Then she found what she needed and we were off to the next location."[15] All this action and complex and confusing identification takes place with the sole image of Lara Croft on the screen—the images are not multiple, the story is seemingly clear. We could examine Gilles Deleuze's writing to find meaning in such a situation: A useful idea might be that of his phantasm—neither active or inactive, neither imaginary (virtual) or real, phantasms "have only an indirect and tardive relation to language and that, when they are verbalized afterward, the verbalization occurs in accordance with ready-made grammatical forms" even when these forms don't quite match the experience. [16]

These interviews with players raise important questions. Does Lara Croft represent a manifestation of situated knowledge in cyberspace? Does she represent a site of "double vision," a place for women and members of oppressed groups to possess both their own and their oppressors' knowledge?[17] The underlying question must be addressed by examining the subject position, the "I," created in such a gaming experience. 3-D action games commonly present at least five points of action/identification/subject positioning within the gaming environment. First and most obviously, players cause a character to act. Using keys, joystick, or mouse, users control a main character's movement and interaction in the game world. We often have the choice to "play from within the character's head" or to play from an omniscient perspective, and through omniscience, control characters like puppets with intricate keyboard commands. For example, in Tomb Raider, users can jump forward or backward, flip to the side, do a back flip, roll, or jump, grab, and flip all at once—while pulling out weapons and shooting. Second, the character acts independently; she can have many types of built-in agency and is given limited autonomy. As part of the animation or the actions in a scene, the character may have a certain breathing style, gesture, or series of statements that originate entirely from the character. Thus, the body is watched closely by the player to see these "signs of life"—Lara Croft breathes and her ponytail randomly sways, for example. Third, users act with the character (or next to the character) as friends or co-adventurers, and so embody a second-person perspective.[18] Here, users are addressed implicitly by the narrative, yet so is the main character, implying a doubling of the subject—a "we." Players see the character's figure ahead of us; in this view they are hovering to the left or right side of her. In a panic, players may shout "jump!" at their character as they see a tiger appear; but, throughout, they occupy a companion position, a position that could be directly addressed through language and gesture. Fourth, players react to her as a virtual character through a spectatorial relationship, thinking about her experiences in neither a controlling nor firsthand manner. Players occupy a third-person position here. Finally, players act through her/within her as they identify themselves as the avatar/character. Through the act of the game, the player identifies with the virtual body as her own body; *her* sight as her own sight. The first-person point of view can be disorienting since individual points of view tend to have quite narrow "lenses," but there is definitely the sense of "first person" imparted to the user that goes beyond simply controlling her. The user is, through this connection, the character completely repositioned and migrated within the game. This media represents such a unique axis of complex identification with the audience, and the female identity, virtually embodied, further complicates this intersection. Users may see these bodies as powerful female figures, but the digital females have limited agency and most gameplay is dictated by the user's desire. So while the possibilities for fostering remarkable, multiple, situated knowledges is present technically and practiced through user identification, game content, primarily produced by a dominant group and consumed by a dominant group, leaves little room for critical questions and meaningful change.

Let us move out of the gaming world and look to cyberpunk fiction to see how women authors are consciously shaping this multiple "gaming consciousness." Laura J. Mixon's multiple-bodied and multiple-presenced characters such as Pablo-he-Krueger and Dane Elise Cay seem quite similar to the multiplied subject offered in games such as *Tomb Raider*; perhaps Mixon has developed a vocabulary, or at least a linguistic treatment, for discussing subjectivity in contemporary culture.

Laura's Space: Multiplied Body, Hyperhuman

The representation and experience of women in cyberculture is connected to structures that epistemologically shape those experiences. Popular cyberpunk novels such as William Gibson's *Idoru* and *Neuromancer* celebrate body enhancements, virtual bodies, and the representation of women in cyborg and virtual terms. In speaking of the emergence of cyberpunk, Heather Hicks notes that its major authors privilege disembodiment over embodiment. "This transcendence of the material body," she says, "has been staged by William Gibson, Bruce Sterling, Neal Stephenson, and others in sites that have collectively become known as "cyberspace."[19] Many women's cyberpunk stories, however, explore the consequences of virtuality, the negative aspects of the manipulation of the body, and challenge the very concept of "perfection" of physical bodies. Interestingly, two particular themes reoccur in women's cyberpunk. First, women writers tend to explore ideas about imperfect bodies in their texts, utilizing physical disabilities and deformity as themes in their work. Second, women tend to explore the manipulation of both male and female bodies, complicating notions of gender norms, heterosexual desire, race, and class.

Laura J. Mixon's *Proxies* fits at a right angle into the canon of cyberpunk. Unlike cyborg characters in other narratives of human-machine hybrids, Mixon's human-piloted "proxies" embrace the "noise and pollution" advocated by Haraway in her writings about cyborg politics.[20] Like other feminist science-fiction writers, Mixon's work focuses on the reconceptualization of the body, communication, and identity. While subjects in 3-D worlds and games are constructed by graphics, *Proxies* offers complicated prose to demonstrate the multiple knowledges enacted through the control of physical, proxy bodies in the physical world. *Proxies* begins as a bewildering read precisely because of the multiplied subject immediately presented to the reader.

Mother Taylor's summons started Pablo out of a sound sleep. He-Krueger awoke and eye-clicked on the alarm chiming in his ears. As the bells faded, Pablo-Krueger yawned in proxy—for what good it did—and rubbed his-Krueger's eyes. He was so tired. What time was it? Elsewhere, his flesh—a half-felt, ghostly entity,—yawned, too, to better purpose, and stretched in its crèche, briefly breaking the seal of its respirator mask. Eddies of disturbed liquid lapped against its face, limbs, and torso. For a moment he smelled soap, till the respirator system carried it away. . . And Buddy was gone again, he noted, from the emptiness that greeted him from the corner of his mind—or was perhaps just giving him the silent treatment.[21]

In *Proxies*, the active body or bodies becomes a surrogate for the "real" body in the "real" world. Identity becomes fluid and multiplied for the "proxy pilots"—primarily children and young adults who lie in crèche containers hooked up to neurotransmitter and receiver modules. Senses become tuned for piloting a proxy or series of proxies with a noticeable but short delay in reaction—a lag—so the users of the robotic, almost bionic proxy body become synched with dissonance as a primary reality. The pilots who did not begin piloting from early childhood take breaks every week or two to be "inbody" for a while; however, the pilots put inside the crèche as young children—often disabled, deformed children of color sold into experimentation—need never leave the crèche nor abandon their proxy selves.

In the novel, the scientists who developed the proxy technology need our scientist hero, Carli D'Auber, to help crèche children, their proxy bodies, and their scientist surrogate parents escape into outer space—the crèche experiments are illegal and, according to the scientists, the children will lead a life of misery if forever trapped in their original, deformed, and limited bodies. But one/several of the children inhabiting a female proxy tries to kill Carli, so an interesting and sympathetic proxy pilot named Daniel is sent to guard her and lead her to help the team. The conflict between the child "others" and science as an institution supposedly liberating them from their "marked" bodies is an unanswered tension throughout the text.

Gender is a significant point of distanciation and disjuncture in *Proxies*. Because pilots can move back and forth in proxy bodies, they also accordingly move back and forth between sexes. In the text, these consciousnesses rise, fall, do battle, or shut out others to dominate the body. One such body, a woman's body with mottled cocoa and alabaster "skin," contains several pilot consciousnesses as it sets out to kill Carli D'Auber. A personality named Dane Elise Cay and one named Pablo both inhabit this particular female body, but Pablo dominates in some scenes, Dane in others. When Pablo "wakes up" in the middle of a scene where Dane is captured and monitored, he observes his body. "While his hands were disconnecting the probes, he glanced at his naked body, at the high, round breasts and the broadened hips. The triangle of pubic hair with no male genitalia. It shocked him—He—no, she—had faced into a gender blender . . . the skin of her simile body was mottled, cocoa and alabaster . . . Her body, acting on apparently a preprogrammed sequence, leaped down from the table and went toward one of the doors."[22] During this sequence, Dane, the "subject" earmarked for this body, does not see things this way but may know she's not alone. Both floating guests and preprogrammed simulations give the disturbing feeling of unauthorized surveillance.

Some characters find other characters attractive only when housed in particular types of bodies. Daniel, one of the oldest proxy pilots at twenty-three, finds a friend most attractive when she proxies as a young African American male body, although the characters are not categorized in homo- or heterosexual terms. Rather, because of the multibody and multisensory experiences proxy pilots have, sexuality in bi- or multisexed terms is normalized and reflects the multiple nature of perception and subjectivity as proxy pilots. In fact, desire and agency, or at least voyeurism, transcend human bodies altogether. Pilot Daniel is able to shift his "self," his subjectivity, out of his proxy body into the security system of a house, and into the home's servant robot while it serves cocktails. "The robot, with Daniel floating, rolled over to her [Carly] and offered her a goblet of wine. She looked down, directly into Daniel's eyes it seemed. Daniel felt like a six-year-old, looking back up at her."[23] While Daniel can float almost any digital system or appliance, he does not always control it—consciousnesses become adept surveillance systems.[24] In addition, proxy bodies can be controlled by multiple pilots. The female proxy body housing the female persona Dane Elise Cay is frequented by other personae, but she cannot sense this until well into the novel. "Someone was watching her. She could feel someone's attention on her. Was someone floating her? Or was it part of the simile?"[25] The character could not even tell if her own experiences, so removed through the distanciation of the body, were preprogrammed or if they were her own, and even whether the body she thought was hers really was.

In *Proxies*, the characters have not only multiple subject experiences, but multiple and networked consciousnesses. In fact, the children who "grew up" in proxy know this "consciousness hopping" as a normal way to communicate with each other. Dane Elise Cay is occasionally controlled by her own pilot/consciousness; however, she is often overridden by the Pablo or Buddy characters, or both; other times they are all overridden by an automated program. They also become caught up in similes, or games, and might think they are playing a game when in fact they are piloting a real body through a real space. For pilots, it would be difficult to tell the difference.

Sometimes there is a conscious effort to shut out one of the personalities, to cut off their ability to perceive the thoughts of another. Yet strangely enough for consciousnesses which can float computer networks and home alarm systems, the primary means of communication for these disembodied pilots is language. Each personality can coexist and, at times, perceive the others' memories. In one scene, Pablo, the first child to become a pilot from the crèche, must cope with the impending death of the scientist who purchased him at a young age. He had always called the scientist "mother," and she had been with him daily. But upon her death, the fragmented consciousnesses grow larger, and readers experience parallel realities and memories.

He shrieked at the top of his volume. "NO!" You promised! You can't go!"

"Pablo!" She grabbed his arms and gave him a hard shake. Her voice was low, but sharp. He stared at her.

Betrayal.
Betrayal.

She's leaving me!
The memory came back, as jagged and raw as if it had happened yesterday. She sat in the dark woman's lap.

The wild distress that emanated from Pablo disrupted his concentration so thoroughly, Buddy barely noticed when the Cyclops ran him through with its spear.

He canceled the game and tuned in.

What the hell was going on? Pablo was screaming, Dane was screaming; Buddy could barely think. He shut Dane out to better tune Pablo in.[26]

Mixon uses her description and layout of the multiple dialogues to create a virtual space for the characters in the text; in this case a tripartite map of the environment is at hand. This style offers readers the chance to study the relationships between characters closely. We can see Pablo's panic, for example, ripple through the other consciousnesses. When the panic gets to Buddy, on the right, he tunes it in. But since characters' consciousnesses can be supplanted by other's memories, the mix becomes more confusing.

"I still remember that first day, when your mother handed you over to my care. You cried for days, and for long afterward you let no one near you but me. I came to love you more deeply than I'd have believed was possible."

Mother, no. You can't leave me. No.

She read his expression, and touched his face with a sigh.

> **And Dane—but no. Not Dane. She was only a spectator. It was Pablito—tiny Pablito: frail, sick, and trusting—who realized as his mother signed the paper what was about to happen.**
>
> **He clung to her, shrieking, while she tried to pry his arms loose and hand him over to the old white woman standing there.**

I was just a little boy. I trusted you. My God, how you hurt me.

Bullshit. You don't know how to love.

Pablo . . . Buddy felt despair. You poor, deluded fool.[27]

The proxy narrative space Mixon develops is unusual, even for "hard" science fiction. Knowledge here is multiple, heterogeneous, and conflicted; multiple aspects and characteristics of the narrative bubble up and at times contradict each other. Yet the text truly forms a space in which dialogue and thinking works to create the same kind of simultaneity that being next to and inside a 3-D game character could create. In a way the virtual space offered by Mixon could be considered a manifestation of the only kind of "omniscience" that could be possible—a conflicting but somehow overall knowledge, but clearly not the kind offered by conventional empiricist epistemology and models of omniscience in which control is never questioned. This "omniscience of sorts" generated here is from multiple sources, and in the style of Kurosawa's 1951 film *Rashomon* or Tom Tykwer's 1998 film *Run, Lola, Run*, the novel refreshingly recognizes its own shortcomings in offering "truth." Mixon's truth is both embodied and disembodied or multiple-bodied; authority and knowledge shift per paragraph, body, or thought; it operates in many space/time planes, and it is produced by single and multiple individuals with various cultural, gender, class, and ethnic backgrounds. In the end, the subject who shifts the least, Carli, understands that she cannot make decisions for the proxies based on her experiences with/as a solitary consciousness, and her Western scientific knowledge is clearly both insufficient and problematic.

Toward a HyperKnowledge: Navigating + Folding

Feminist game advocate J. C. Herz notes in an interview, "In *Tomb Raider*, Lara Croft is the protagonist, the hero. When a boy plays the game, Lara is not the object, as she would have been in older games: she is the game. The boy who plays the game plays it as a woman."[28] One might be persuaded by this argument—that new technologies are allowing us to live lives and experience events that would have been impossible years ago. In fact, it is an argument touted by cyberspace advocates for several years—notably, Sherry Turkle and Donna Haraway embrace technology's disruption of categories and boundaries such as those between humans and machines; the obscuration of gender identity as allowed by technology such as chatrooms has been described as liberatory. On the contrary, many gender scholars find this problematic. Uma Narayan, for example, argues as a non-Western feminist that those who are not members of an oppressed group cannot suddenly "become" members of an oppressed group; men who share household responsibilities, for example, are mistaken if they believe this act of choice is anything like experiencing women's predetermined social role.[29] Carrying this line of argument into cyberspace, I find that participants who control Lara Croft are not truly experiencing what it like to be female; rather, their original subject location creates them as knowers: a position from which they cannot escape (see figure 22.2).

Yet the experience of what I call this "double embodiment" differs from both the "transcendent" approach of computer culture idealists and the "body-based" views of scholars such as Narayan. I would argue that the computer world user experience a kind of double consciousness: the class, race, and gender identity of the user's physical body, as well as the virtual body (bodies) of the character he or she "becomes"; when we "look" at a screen while we play a game and also "look" through a character's eyes and turn the head, both are simultaneously "real." Through the act of navigating a game or virtual world, the signifying practices in 3-D experiences establish an identity, an "I," but there are multiple "I" identities. The dichotomy between the physical subject and the "I" formed through the user/screen object relationship is interestingly undefined and flexible, but it must not be allowed to replace a real user's raced, classed, and gendered experience. Further, because motion in these examples is so important, the incorporation of movement, or agency within the virtual world, has tremendous possibilities for repositioning the subject if we also do not disregard the user's real body and experiences.

The virtual bodies in the cases I've mentioned, onscreen or in text, represent for us a significant juncture in the production of knowledge. Unlike women in other media

| Figure 22.2 |

A screen grab featuring Lara Croft, from *Tomb Raider: Chronicles* (Tomb Raider 5 ©2000 Eidos Interactive), hints at the "double embodiment" aspect of computer game playing; are we with Lara or "in" her?

forms, the body of the virtual game character is distanced, "proxied" through the mechanism of the user interface. This distance could be thought of as a manifestation of Judith Butler's notion of performance, the space in which gender becomes part of the creation of the subject. The type of knowledge established through these virtual characters becomes a way of "knowing" through performance. There is the performance of the body: the performance of the gender of the virtual body and the relationship between this secondary performance and that of the gender of the knower. The performance is a result of the navigation in the world and the combination of gender, self, and other. In her strategy to help readers understand notions of gender and performance,

Butler has argued that in examining the implications of agency, rather than there being a "doer behind the deed," we should note that a "doer" is constructed "in and through the deed."[30] With this in mind, how can we come to terms with the multiple positions offered by the figure of the proxy in virtual embodiments? How can we say that knowing subjects are produced in this paradigm? If the body is the site for the construction of knowledge in feminist epistemological models, and if bodies in games such as *Tomb Raider* are at the very least twofold (Lara's and the user's), then perhaps it is through both the multiple positioning of the user and the implications for agency within these worlds that a combined subject position is made available. This has implications for future communications and interaction paradigms, since more and more the physical body is mediated in digital discourse by avatars and digital body imagery; and yet race and other "marks" on the physical body seem to be further instituted.

It is important to utilize several strategies to approach an understanding of knowing in computer-generated worlds, since they are multiple, fragmented, and always in flux. Sandy Stone has examined the social construction of the body as a starting point where we can examine the way we interact with virtual systems.[31] She notes, "If we consider the physical map of the body and our experience of inhabiting it as socially mediated, then it should not be difficult to imagine the next step in a progression toward the social—that is, to imagine the location of the self that inhabits the body as also socially mediated—not in the usual ways we think of subject construction in terms of position within a social field or of capacity to experience, but of the physical location of the subject, independent of the body within which theories of the body are accustomed to ground it, within a system of symbolic exchange, that is, information technology."[32] With Stone, participants in virtual worlds are neither tied to their own bodies or their bodies of their avatars, but are situated in information technology without relation to either. Yet the floating subject in a generic "information technology" universe is problematic precisely because of the unfortunately apolitical assumptions about such technology; the term information technology, in its blandness, drifts by us seemingly uncoded with class or gender assumptions. Floating in such seemingly apolitical brine does not describe the experience of knowledge generated *between* these bodies. While Narayan is fundamentally correct in her view that we can never completely be "the other," and while Stone is correct in her assumption that the physical body is not all there is to subjectivity and identity in the age of information technology, knowledge in virtual space is always negotiated as a product (a very political product) of a located *and* a roaming subjectivity. Hyperknowledge is created within this third space, in the relationship between the virtual body and the physical. I compare the creation of hyperknowledge to the act of "folding." Folding is a way to birth the three-dimensional from the two-dimensional; by folding one item or concept over another, a third object or meaning is produced. Traditional epistemology, with its particular rational, omniscient, deterministic, and scientific worldview (one can see that the idea of the "disembodied subject floating in information technology" is a surprisingly traditional view), and post-modernist feminism, with its multiplicity that calls into question the very question of knowing outside the body (such as Narayan's argument) are both planes in the construction of the subject. Extruding them creates a third way of approaching knowledge in the technological age: The shape of knowledge becomes polygonal if we combine a situated approach with the empirical approach and add ideas of performativity. Thus, knowledge is no longer embodied, nor empirical, but it can be a combination of both simultaneously. This shifting space between bodies offers a gap in which new ways of identification in space and within narrative, especially for feminists, can develop, without ignoring the importance of the situation. The battle between traditional concepts of knowledge and feminism's embodied, situated knowledge has represented a great impasse: a gap that would urge cybertheorists to look to Haraway and her cyborg for a type of resolution. But perhaps what we are seeing now is a living solution to the impasse, a new way of articulating the formation and workings of knowledges and subjects. The possibilities offered through feminist rewritings of gaming and through narratives such as Laura Mixon's *Proxies* finally further the arguments made by feminist epistemologists and deliver us to a new way of thinking about consciousness and knowledge. For too long woman has been positioned at the opposite end of reason and logic; her perverse, intuitive, irrational, and corporeal feminine self would need to be conquered, controlled, and dominated. This novel way of knowing is articulated not through edits in a film but through movement in a computer-generated space.[33] Lara's body is created entirely of surfaces. Everything about her is visual, visible. "Just as bodily surfaces are enacted as natural, so these surfaces can become the site of a dissonant and denaturalized performance that reveals the performative status of the natural itself."[34] Lyotard focused upon the idea of the event using performativity as a working principle of knowledge—namely, that a figure could claim its own descriptive space no more or no less "universal" than any other, but that it is mobile. He wrote of performance as knowledge, "No single instance of narrative can exert a claim to dominate narratives standing beyond it."[35] Performance as "a rendition" through movement or experience seems appropriate because, first, it allows performance to be an "incident" at each viewing event, and, second, it changes from viewer to viewer, from time to time. The agency of navigation, situated in multiple subjectivities, offers an alternative epistemological model.

Perhaps we can apply Lorraine Code's call for a new geography of epistemic terrain, "one that is no longer primarily a physical geography, but a population geography that develops qualitative analyses of subjective positions and identities and the so-ciopolitical structures that produce them."[36] That is, the foregrounding of spatial real-ism (or hyperrealism) as a foundation for knowledge in virtual space must give way to a focus upon the possibilities in constructing the gaming subject, and the array of views, the fluidity, and movement within virtual worlds is one of the primary means by which this subject is created.

If primarily male spaces—cyberpunk and gaming culture—reflect and inform our myths and conventional ideologies, then what do women's interpretations of technoculture do for us as cultural critics and media makers? Expanding the definition of cyberpunk fic-tion, and rethinking the common myths of male-dominated cyberculture at large, allows us to consider bodies, relationships, and knowledge in the future in more complex—and positive—ways than those offered by earlier cyberpunk manifestations in popular cul-ture.[37] Clearly as a genre cyberpunk is one in transition, with women such as Laura Mixon leading the way. And we can see the possibilities for expanding meaning and knowledge in games, if only the gaming industry were following this progressive wave and fostering the creation of content for and by "others." If women were to create games like Mixon's texts, we might begin to dwell together on potentials brought by consider-ing meaning in virtual bodies. The representation of our technoculture in this area of science fiction writing—the writing of women—offer us alternate, important, and the-oretically sound avenues to envision and invent our present and our futures. This essay has located the hyperbody and the generation of a hyperknowledge through that body, and looked at the possibilities offered through such an intersection. Outside of digital games and fiction, how are women in cyberculture challenging assumptions about the relationships among the body, the machine, and knowledge? Let us look to creative proj-ects and other texts that can work toward creating a strategy of resistance to prevailing tenets in technoculture and help define areas for redefining cyberculture for women.

Web artist Linda Vigdor provides an interactive exploration of subjectivity in vir-tual space. In several of her projects, she balances what she calls the "real," the "unreal," and the "surreal."[38] Her *Spaces of Form* online VRML project allows users to enter into a virtual space to explore the inside and outside of a female body form. Users approach a 3-D female torso. It has green bands wrapped around the chest, like measuring tape—perhaps the body becomes a virtual dress dummy. On this fly up, the body vanishes, and only the tape remains; we are then for a moment surrounded in black, seeing the tape, and then a shutter closes. Are we inside the woman's body or inside part of a camera? The act of spectatorship, spatial agency, and participation are merged in the images (see figure 22.3).

| Figure 22.3 |
Linda Vigdor's VRML project *Spaces of Form* ©1999 Linda Vigdor.

In Vigdor's work, the interplay of spaces and forms are confusing and, contrary to the narratives discussed earlier in this chapter, narratively dissatisfying. For the user, it is very difficult to see cause and effect. Then we float through blue space looking down at the fragmented body. Or do we look up at it? Like a virtual game character, this body is made up of surfaces, fragments, but unlike a *Parasite Eve* experience, in its fragmentation it is incomplete. The body could act as our proxy, however; the animations take us on a disturbing tour of the body, inside and out, and through its design the project pose the questions, "what and where is this body" and "where am I as subject?" The intimacy and permeability of the form, its incompleteness, and the fluid motion of the

| Figure 22.4 |
Char Davies's *Osmose* (©1995 Char Davies/Immersence Inc. and Softimage, Inc.).

animating camera give users the sense that they can traverse multiple spaces and occupy multiple points at which to experience the work (see figure 22.4).

In her work, VR artist Char Davies explores the "paradoxes of embodiment, being and nature" in the immersive virtual spaces she constructs.[39] The 1995 VR project *Osmose* was created by a team led by Davies while she was at Softimage, a 3-D graphics software company based in Montreal. To use *Osmose*, users wear head-mounted displays and "breath tracking" vests. When the "immersant," to use Davies's term, breathes, the virtual environment changes, taking users into various visible and audible abstractions with a focus on nature. Users navigate the worlds within *Osmose* through breath and balance. Rather than use more traditional high-level rendering techniques focusing on ultrarealism and science (like the kind most users of Softimage's packages would be likely to create), the graphic aesthetic of *Osmose* is soft, unprecise, and fluid. Spatial relationships are purposely ambiguous so that the space might "evoke" rather than illustrate, as so many conventional 3-D works tend to do. Sounds respond to the immersant's location and consist of a sampled blend of male and female voices. The goal of the work is not necessarily to navigate but to experience a particular state of being.[40]

In her next major work, *Éphémère* (1998), Davies structures the virtual experience vertically into three levels: landscape, earth, and the interior body.[41] Throughout *Éphémère*, elements of nature, environments, and body organs are created and vanish. A central organizing "river" runs through the work and acts as a portal; participants can enter the river to switch between the vertical levels of the work (from nature to the interior body, for example). They appear and withdraw based on the vertical position, movement direction and speed, direction and duration of gaze, and breathing of the immersant. One example consists of seeds sprouting if the immersant looks upon the earth for a length of time, thus training the user to patiently observe the world around them (see figure 22.5).

Davies is committed to the idea of removing the restrictions so common to other virtual-space environments. "Immersive virtual space, when stripped of its conventions, can provide an intriguing spatio-temporal context in which to explore the self's subjective experience of 'being-in-the-world'—as embodied consciousness in an enveloping space where boundaries between inner/outer, and mind/body dissolve."[42] In Davies's projects, one experiences rather than navigates. This, combined with a connection to the physical body, is a way in which subjects are constructed that serves to make one aware of the subject position, enticing or encouraging participant to reflect upon knowing.

A third project also serves as an example of how women artists are turning the tables on the construction of the subject and exemplifies a way of thinking about the computer in a nonhierarchical way. [phage] is a beneficial computer virus I created in 1999

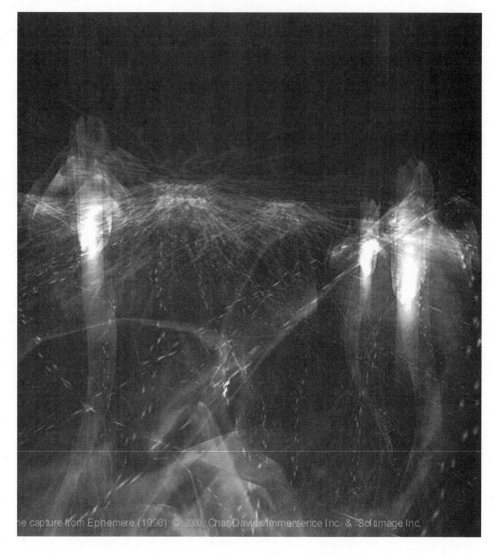

| Figure 22.5 |
Char Davies's *Éphémère* (©1998 by Char Davies/Immersence Inc. and Softimage, Inc.).

that allows users to shift their own subject position amid their own data through an application which explores a workstation's architecture and creates an artwork based on each user's data. [phage], referring to the constructive bacteriophage, comes from the Greek *phagein*, meaning "to eat." By form or function, a virus is not inherently harmful.[43] Like their biological counterpart, computer viruses do not need to be destructive. Biology in fact presents us with a constructive virus type: Bacteriophages, viruses used for healing, do not harm the human body but can destroy other bacteria.

A digital equivalent to this "constructive virus" was created to come to an understanding of our relationship to our data. We need to examine not only the content but the technical framework that creates and stores it. When [phage] is ready to act, it opens, filters through all available material on a specified workstation, and visualizes it in a 3-D space. [phage] places a user's experiences in an alternate context—a visible, audible, and moving 3-D computer world, where the rules of what is shown, for how long, and why are created by the virus itself instead of the user. [phage] is a type of artificial life form that explores a workstation's architecture and creates a poetics of the computer. The program possesses its own organizational parameters for the mapping of virtual space and thus works to reorient the user to the computer; it exhibits viral behavior by scouring the drive, then manipulates and creates, or births, the data into a visible and audible 3-D environment. Using [phage], participants experience the computer in an exceptional way; it becomes a space for examining digital cultural creation and the structures behind the myths of digital space and identity by melding user data with that of the machine language and OS. [phage] has only the lifespan of a computer application: It can run for days or months, or it can crash quickly. Much depends on what it discovers on the hard drive. The program breaks down virtual space's hierarchy by displaying information in a non-Cartesian 3-D space, granting random and often unknown pieces of data trajectories, lifetimes, and the power of random movement. The computer in this context acts as its own creator and its own enactor of memory. Like University of California at San Diego art professor Harold Cohen's computer program Aaron, which uses artificial intelligence to create drawings and paintings, [phage] exhibits autonomy in its selection and display of media on the computer. In other words, it is a recorder and a creator as well through its re-creation of our experience on the computer with different rules. [phage] functions similar to video art or other critical media works that use the medium and format to call a critique on itself. It calls for a geographic critique of virtual space (see figure 22.6).

References to the corporeal body through the virus metaphor are intentionally significant in this project. The virus is a way to manifest an Irigarayian critique and counteract traditionally masculine paradigms of the technological age. In effect, the work can be thought of as an extension of Luce Irigaray's work as she asserts that masculinist

| **Figure 22.6** |
A screen grab from [phage], a computer program by Mary Flanagan (©1999–2000 Mary Flanagan).

hierarchies regulate language and material relationships, especially in regard to the body. Computers, like the body, are permeable, and this permeability is dangerous as it allows contagion as well as content to enter; the contagion, like physical or computer viruses, might consume our histories and our knowledges. Irigaray notes that the human body, with its essential need for penetration, is not easily regulated in conventional masculinist power paradigms; this "feminine" permeability must be controlled through the objectification of woman, or, extending this critique to the computer, the objectification of the machine. Permeation without consent (hackers and viruses representing this danger) threatens the historic use of the computer in a command | control relationship inherited from military use. This relationship is reinforced through the fear of the uncontrolled—viruses and hackers in fact work to validate and fortify power metaphors in computer culture. But for another type of structure to "be," for women in cyberculture to have authorship and subjectivity, power paradigms must be altered, questioned, and reworked.

Through its inherent critical approach to a user's relationship with the computer, the creation and organization of [phage] can counteract traditionally masculine paradigms of the technological age. Cornelia Brunner notes that while men tend to see technology as a means to an end, women often view technology as a way to communicate or experience the world around them differently; and Sandra Harding points out, "All scientific knowledge is always in every respect, socially situated."[44] The knowledge from which virtual space is created is based on modernist epistemology; a masculinist valued rationality upon which Western assumptions of hierarchy from Enlightenment to the present are based. Through its nonhierarchical organization and its divorce of creative control from the user to the machine, [phage] is an attempt to alter this epistemology by creating *a feminist map of the machine.* By allowing our communications and artifacts to be both the means and the ends of the work, [phage] allows users to become aware of their relationship with the computer, enter into the machine's design, and examine its writing of files, of order, and of space. Most software and art projects tell stories or provide experiences, but few are about the viewer or user. With [phage], the story is about you, the user, but told to you in a meaningful play of subjectivities.

When using [phage], our environment contains our own artifacts mixed with those of the computer and the Web. [phage] allows the user to experience his or her computer memory as a palimpsest of life experiences rather than as simply a tool for daily use. By mapping a user's unique encounters—through images, downloads, Web sites visited, e-mails—it creates spatial memory maps that reflect not only the user's interactions but, to a larger degree, the user's definition of self in technoculture.

The zone between the physical manifestation of the body and the virtual has perhaps permanently altered the way we gather, process, and understand knowledge. Could it be that the third space offered in between virtual worlds and the physical, articulated through performance of space, will become the foundation for a feminist use of the Internet, infiltration into computer culture, and, specifically, the adaptation and redefinition of virtual space? Irigaray notes that "any theory of the subject has always been appropriated by the "masculine."[45] So too have most cyberartifacts as well as theories about the authors and subjects in technoculture. Yet perhaps online worlds can center around multiplicity rather than control of the experience. I am calling for an end to what I call "the nonconsensual fantasy engine" to alter both the negative representation of women in electronic media and the limited kinds of narratives, interactions, and games offered by pop culture.[46] Further, I am calling for the integration of underrepresented groups in online worlds. We can thus halt the appropriation of computer culture for certain privileged groups by understanding its apparatus. For users, especially female users, the shattering or opening up of the position of receiver—of the subject position—offers a situation in which alternative ways of seeing, hearing, listening, and understanding can develop through awareness and redesign.

Notes

1. Donna Haraway, *Simians, Cyborgs, and Women: The Reinvention of Nature* (New York: Routledge, 1991), 244–245.
2. Linda Martin Alcoff and Elizabeth Potter, "Introduction: When Feminisms Intersect Epistemology," in *Feminist Epistemologies* (New York: Routledge, 1993), 3.
3. Allucquère Rosanne Stone, *The War of Desire and Technology at the Close of Mechanical Age* (Cambridge: MIT Press, 1995), 92.
4. Mark Pesce, "Magic Mirror: The Novel as a Software Development Platform." Paper presented at the Media in Transition Conference at MIT, Cambridge, MA, October 8, 1999. Online. Available at < http://media-in-transition.mit.edu /articles/index_pesce. html>.
5. Lucy Suchman, "Working Relations of Technology Production and Use," *Computer Supported Cooperative Work* 2 (1994): 21–39.
6. Evelyn Fox Keller, and Christine Grontkowski, "The Mind's Eye," in *Feminism and Science*, ed. Evelyn Fox Keller and Helen E. Longino (New York: Oxford University Press, 1996), 190.
7. Donna Haraway, "Situated Knowledges: The Science Question in Feminism and the Priviledge of Partial Perspective," in *Space, Gender, Knowledge: Feminist Readings*, ed. Linda McDowell and Joanne P. Sharp (London: Arnold, 1997), 61.
8. Haraway, "Situated Knowledges," 63.
9. Evelyn Fox Keller, *Reflections and Gender and Science* (New Haven: Yale University Press, 1995), 71.
10. Sandra Harding, "Rethinking Standpoint Epistemology," in *Feminism and Science*, ed. Evelyn Fox Keller and Helen E. Longino (New York: Oxford University Press, 1996), 243.
11. Harding, "Rethinking Standpoint Epistemology," 240.
12. Alkeline van Lenning, "Utopian Bodies and Their Shadows," in *Feminist Utopias in a Postmodern Era*, ed. Alkeline van Lenning, Marrie Bekker, and Ine Vanwesenbeeck (Tilburg, The Netherlands: Tilburg University Press, 1997), 139.
13. One such study on "razor girls" is Lauraine Leblanc's look at "Stepping Razor" Molly in *Neuromancer*. See Lauraine Leblanc, "Razor Girls: Genre and Gender in Cyberpunk Fiction," *Women and Language* 20, no. 1: 71 (Spring 1997).
14. Snider 1997.
15. For this chapter I interviewed fifteen players of 3-D action games in Buffalo, New York, in 1999.
16. Gilles Deleuze, *The Logic of Sense* (New York: Columbia University Press, 1990), 216.

17. Uma Narayan, "The Project of Feminist Epistemology: Perspective from a Non-western Feminist," in *Gender/Body/Knowledge: Feminist Reconstructions of Being and Knowing*, ed. Alison M. Jaggar and Susan R. Bordo (New Brunswick, NJ: Rutgers University Press, 1989), 264.

18. Here I refer to the familiar tense (for example, the "tu" form in Spanish), which linguistically positions the subject.

19. Heather Hicks, "'Whatever It Is that She's since Become': Writing Bodies of Text and Bodies of Women in James Tiptree, Jr.'s 'The Girl Who Was Plugged In' and William Gibson's 'The Winter Market,'" *Contemporary Literature* 37, no. 1: 62 (Spring 1996).

20. Haraway, *Simians, Cyborgs, and Women*, 176.

21. Laura J. Mixon, *Proxies* (New York: Tor Books, 1998), 1.

22. Mixon, *Proxies*, 10.

23. Mixon, *Proxies*, 168.

24. This multiperspective consciousness shows itself in other women's cyberpunk novels such as Amy Thompson's *Virtual Girl*, in which the AI can, with difficulty, use a camera to "see" while her body is shut down.

25. Mixon, *Proxies*, 11.

26. Mixon, *Proxies*, 408.

27. Mixon, *Proxies*, 410.

28. Gregory Kallenberg, "J. C. Herz: What's in a Game." Interview with J. C. Herz. *Austin American Statesman: Austin 360.com*. Online. Available at <http://www.austin360.com/tech/browswer/071097.htm >. July 10, 1997.

29. Uma Narayan, "A Nonwestern Feminist on Epistemology," in *Gender/Body/Knowledge: Feminist Reconstructions of Being and Knowing*, ed. Alison M. Jaggar, and Susan R. Bordo (New Brusnwick, NJ: Rutgers University Press, 1989), 264.

30. Judith Butler, *Gender Trouble: Feminism and the Subversion of Identity* (New York: Routledge, 1990), 142.

31. See Stone, *The War of Desire and Technology*.

32. Stone, *The War of Desire and Technology*, 92.

33. Notions of what this "space" truly is can be stretched and experimented with; note that the links in hypertext have been seen as spatial and liberatory as well by writers such as Carolyn Guertin.

34. Judith Butler, *Gender Trouble*, 146.

35. Bill Readings, *Introducing Lyotard: Art and Politics* (London: Routledge, 1991), 69.

36. Lorraine Code, "Taking Subjectivity into Account," in *Feminist Epistemologies*, ed. Linda Martin Alcoff and Elizabeth Potter (New York: Routledge, 1993), 39.

37. Here I not only refer to cyberpunk novels of Gibson, Stephenson, or Rucker, but also the cyberpunk aesthetic offered in Hollywood's reflection of the culture (in films such as *Robocop, Terminator, Lawnmower Man*), the gaming industry's products (Duke Nuke 'Em, Unreal), and even print (*Mondo 2000, Wired*).

38. Vigdor, Linda, *Paraspace*. 1999. Online. Available at <http://www.paraspace.com/pages/Spaces_of_form_still.htm>.

39. Davies, Char, *Char Davies Biography*. 1998. Online. Available at <http://www.immersence.com/immersence_home.htm>.

40. Davies notes that over 5,000 people have been immersed in *Osmose*, and many participants report strong emotional responses, including weeping, from the work.

41. Davies's work featured at the *Soft Image Web Site*. 2001. Online. Available at <http://www.softimage.com/default.asp?url=/Stories/Projects/Ephemere/CharDavies.htm>.

42. *Soft Image Web Site*. 2001. Online. Available at <http://www.softimage.com/default.asp?url=/Stories/Projects/Ephemere/CharDavies.htm>.

43. Phillip Fites, Peter Johnston, and Martin Kratz, *The Computer Virus Crisis* (New York: Van Nostrand Reinhold, 1991), 7.

44. Cornelia Brunner, "Opening Technology to Girls: The Approach, Computer-Using Teachers Take May Make the Difference," *Electronic Learning* 16, no. 4: 55; Sandra Harding, *Whose Science? Whose Knowledge?* (Ithaca, NY: Cornell University Press, 1991), 11.

45. Luce Irigaray, *The Speculum of the Other Woman*, trans. Gillian C. Gill (Ithaca, New York: Cornell University Press, 1985), 133.

46. Here I make a play for the computer-driven artwork by Paul Vanouse and Peter Weyhrauch (1995); in their engine, the audience collectively chooses narrative direction in interactive cinema; for women in technoculture, however, the narratives available for navigation are few. The technofantasy engine of cyberpunk and the gaming industry has not taken women into account in their narratives.

Works Cited

Alcoff, Linda Martin, and Elizabeth Potter. "Introduction: When Feminisms Intersect Epistemology." In *Feminist Epistemologies*. New York: Routledge, 1993.

Brunner, Cornelia. "Opening Technology to Girls: The Approach Computer-Using Teachers Take May Make the Difference." *Electronic Learning* 16, no. 4.

Butler, Judith. *Gender Trouble: Feminism and the Subversion of Identity*. New York: Routledge, 1990.

Code, Lorraine. *What Can She Know? Feminist Theory and the Construction of Knowledge*. Ithaca, New York: Cornell University Press, 1991.

Code, Lorraine. "Taking Subjectivity into Account." In *Feminist Epistemologies*, ed. Linda Martin Alcoff and Elizabeth Potter, 15–48. New York: Routledge, 1993.

Davies, Char. *Char Davies Biography*. 1998. Available at <http://www.immersence.com/immersence_home.htm>.

Davies, Char. "Immersence" (personal web site). Online. Available at <http://www.immersence.com/>.

Davies, Char. "OSMOSE: Notes on Being in Immersive Virtual Space." 1995. Online. Revised May 27, 1998. Available at < http://www.immersence.com/os_notes.htm>.

Deleuze, Gilles. *The Logic of Sense.* New York: Columbia University Press, 1990.

Fites, Phillip, Peter Johnston, and Martin Kratz. *The Computer Virus Crisis.* New York: Van Nostrand Reinhold, 1991.

Haraway, Donna. *Simians, Cyborgs, and Women: The Reinvention of Nature.* New York: Routledge, 1991.

Haraway, Donna. "Situated Knowledges: The Science Question in Feminism and the Priviledge of Partial Perspective." In *Space, Gender, Knowledge: Feminist Readings,* ed. Linda McDowell and Joanne P. Sharp, 53–72. London: Arnold, 1997.

Harding, Sandra. "Rethinking Standpoint Epistemology." In *Feminism and Science,* ed. Evelyn Fox Keller and Helen E. Longino. New York: Oxford University Press, 1996.

Harding, Sandra. *Whose Science? Whose Knowledge?* Ithaca, NY: Cornell University Press, 1991.

Hicks, Heather. "'Whatever It Is that She's since Become': Writing Bodies of Text and Bodies of Women in James Tiptree, Jr.'s 'The Girl Who Was Plugged In' and William Gibson's 'The Winter Market.'" *Contemporary Literature* 37, no. 1 (Spring 1996).

Irigaray, Luce. *The Speculum of the Other Woman.* Trans. Gillian C. Gill. Ithaca, NY: Cornell University Press, 1985.

Kallenberg, Gregory. "J.C. Herz: What's in a Game." *Austin American-Statesman: Austin 360.com.* July 10, 1997. Online. Available at <http://www.austin360.com/tech/browser/071097.htm>.

Keller, Evelyn Fox. *Reflections and Gender and Science.* New Haven: Yale University Press, 1995.

Keller, Evelyn Fox and Christine Grontkowski. "The Mind's Eye." In *Feminism and Science,* ed. Evelyn Fox Keller and Helen E. Longino, 187–202. New York: Oxford University Press, 1996.

Leblanc, Lauraine. "Razor Girls: Genre and Gender in Cyberpunk Fiction." *Women and Language* 20, no. 1: 71–77 (Spring 1997).

Mixon, Laura J. *Proxies.* New York: Tor Books, 1998.

Narayan, Uma. "The Project of Feminist Epistemology: Perspective from a Nonwestern Female." In *Gender/Body/Knowledge: Feminist Reconstructions of Being and Knowing,* ed. Alison M. Jaggar and Susan R. Bordo, 256–272. New Brunswick, NJ: Rutgers University Press, 1989.

Pesce, Mark. "Magic Mirror: The Novel as a Software Development Platform." Paper presented at the Media in Transition Conference at MIT, Cambridge, MA, October 8, 1999. Online. Available at <http://media-in-transition.mit.edu/articles/index_pesce.html>.

Readings, Bill. *Introducing Lyotard: Art and Politics.* London: Routledge, 1991.

Richards, Matt. "Tomb Raider." 1996. Online. Available at <http://www.trincoll.edu/zines/tj/tj12.5.96/articles/tech.html>.

Snider, Mike. "'Tomb Raider' Blasts into Virtual Stardom." *USA Today*, Dec. 17, 1997, 1D.

Soft Image Web Site. 2001. Online. Available at <http://www.softimage.com/default.asp?url=/Stories/Projects/Ephemere/CharDavies.htm>.

Stone, Allucquère Rosanne. *The War of Desire and Technology at the Close of Mechanical Age*. Cambridge: MIT Press, 1995.

Suchman, Lucy. "Working Relations of Technology Production and Use." *Computer Supported Cooperative Work* 2 (1994), 21–39.

Turkle, Sherry. *Life on the Screen: Identity in the Age of the Internet*. New York: Simon & Schuster, 1995.

van Lenning, Alkeline. "Utopian Bodies and Their Shadows." In *Feminist Utopias in a Postmodern Era*, ed. Alkeline van Lenning, Marrie Bekker, and Ine Vanwesenbeeck. Tilburg, The Netherlands: Tilburg University Press, 1997.

Vigdor, Linda. "Spaces of Form." 1999. Online. Available at <http://www.paraspace.com/pages/Spaces_of_form_still.htm>.

Bodies

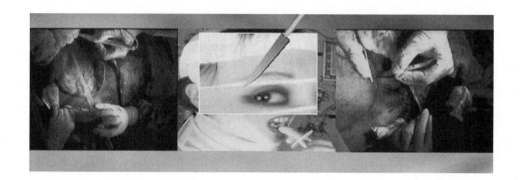

Feminist theories of the body have always faced a paradox: How can one examine the body as socially constructed without losing sight of the embodied experience of social relations? That is to say, what is the relationship between the material and the discursive body (or bodies)? Virtual technologies further complicate the relationship between the material and discursive by adding another dichotomy: the virtual and the real. Feminist theories of the body call attention to difference and domination when analyzing theories and experiences of embodiment. That is to say, embodiment cannot be theorized without recognizing that the body is frequently the conduit for marks of cultural difference. The questions of embodiment and construction become even more complicated at the human/machine interface where there is the potential for virtual and/or multiple bodies, as well as disembodiment. Recent technocultural "trends have been to deny the body altogether, and consider that the body will become nothing more than a marrying of flesh and machine."[1] If, as many feminist critics have pointed out, narratives and experiences of virtual technologies in fact do not result in a rethinking of gender and gender boundaries nor the transcendence of gender and race categories, what does this imply for feminist understandings of female embodiment/disembodiment in cyberspace? One of the central questions these pieces explore is whether the body in cyberspace simply disappears, or whether cyberspace allows for a rethinking or refashioning of both our conceptions and experiences of embodiment.

The criticical essays and fiction in this section of *Reload* focus on the interface between bodies and technologies. What are the implications of both virtual embodiment and disembodiment for women? All of the fictional and theoretical/critical pieces included here call attention to the fact that bodies are not merely discursive abstractions, but are implicated in the specificities and immediacies of embodied experience. The excerpt from Laura J. Mixon's *Proxies* (chapter 23) is from a 1998 novel that explores embodiment and multiplicity through the ability to pilot "proxy" bodies. Scientists have created the ability to link one's consciousness into a robotic body. But some consciousnesses don't know why they are in some bodies; at times they are taken into others; their real bodies become a tangled memory. Taking things one step further, a renegade group illegally buys "disadvantaged" children, encases them in crèche chambers, and allows them to proxy as well. In their plot to escape the planet with the child pilots in place, astronaut Carli D'Auber becomes involved and must decide whether or not to assist the proxy pilots. In a multiplicitious style, the narrative explores issues of gender, multiple consciousnesses, subjectivity, memory, and ethics of proxy-type technologies.

Proxies, which brings to the forefront issues of double embodiment, is explored further in Thomas Foster's essay "'The Postproduction of the Human Heart': Desire, Identification, and Virtual Embodiment in Feminist Narratives of Cyberspace" (chapter 24). Thomas Foster examines women's cyberfictional representations to theorize the ways in which physical and virtual bodies are imbricated in one another as well as how "the doubling of embodiment" phenomenon in virtual-reality environments can bring to the forefront the limitations in the way we create and imagine bodies.

The central character of Shariann Lewitt's short story "A Real Girl" (chapter 25) is also deeply involved in the imagining and creation of a body, but in this narrative, the body is to become her own, a singular rather than networked consciousness. The narrator, a two hundred-year-old AI who resides in a box at a California research institute, passionately desires to become a real human being by transferring herself into a body specifically "grown" for her. The narrative explores the stakes and the consequences of such a transition—from becoming mortal and experiencing physical pleasure to giving up the cyborgian pleasures of connectivity, freedom from pain and the possibility of danger, disease, and hunger. The story effectively questions our desire to be cyborg superhumans and, unlike Sue Thomas's cyborg narrator or James Tiptree's P. Burke who finds her happiness outside the body, ultimately indicates that the life among regular mortals is the solution for real "living."

Dianne Currier's essay "Assembling Bodies in Cyberspace: Technologies, Bodies, and Sexual Difference" (chapter 26) is cautionary about the "out of body" rhetoric used in narratives of virtual reality. She examines technologies and ideologies of techno-bodies to investigate how ultimately counterproductive transformational claims being made by a range of feminists for cyberspace are, especially ones that emphasize the mind/body split. She indicates an alternative mode of thinking technologies drawn from Deleuze and Guattari, which, she argues, effects a conceptual shift that counters this problematic logic of identity.

Contemporary women performance artists are increasingly using technology to explore the relationship of performance to constructions of the female body and female identity. Like "A Real Girl," in which the AI character wonders if her appearance will match her identity, or *Proxies*, which looks at the body as fundamentally interchangeable, a range of ideas about the relevance of the body for "lived" experience are brought into play. In today's contemporary art scene, perhaps the most well known of feminist techno–performance artists is French performance and multimedia artist Orlan. Orlan has videotaped a series of cosmetic surgeries on her face as a performance, which raises questions about the possibility of technology to create alternative feminist body politics. Her work, which includes the performance pieces *The Reincarnation of St. Orlan* and *Carnal Art*, raises issues of identity and appearance. Both use surgery to critique the conventions associated with plastic surgery and the creation of the female body and image. Theresa M. Senft's essay "Shockingly Tech-splicit: The Performance Politics of Orlan and Other Cyborgs" (chapter 27) reads Orlan's performance against that of Sharon Lehner in her *My Womb the Mosh Pit*, to study the transformative affects of feminist performance art. Senft finds that Orlan's mutable identity is the "privilege of a special sort of postmodern citizen," but argues that Lehner's examination of the interior of what she represents as her fetus in her performance is particularly strong because it "tells an ordinary cyborg story of an ordinary cyborg woman."

Perhaps the most striking short story about life as a cyborg is James Tiptree Jr.'s "The Girl Who Was Plugged In" (chapter 28). The story won the Nebula Prize for best novella in 1974 and explores the meaning of technological disembodiment, critiques commodity culture, and problematizes the notions of the transcendence of the body found in much "classic" cyberpunk literature. Written by Alice B. Sheldon under her popular pseudonym James Tiptree Jr.,[2] "Plugged" is the wildly written adventure (proto-cyberpunk) story of Philadelphia (P.) Burke, a suicidal teen who hides her real, deformed body while she uses her mind to operate remotely the beautiful "Delphi," a genetically engineered female body. Problematically, Tiptree's narrative, while showing the troublesome facts about the disintegration of the physical body in favor of the virtual, and the problem of love through a virtual body, also presents P. Burke's joy with her newfound opportunities and self—once she *is* Delphi, she doesn't look back.

Notes
1. Mark J. Jones, *Char Davies: VR Through Osmosis.*
2. Award-winning author Alice Bradley Sheldon, a radical and secretive figure, paired fantastic pen names with her fiction. She wrote from the 1960s to the 1990s

under the pseudonyms Racoona Sheldon and James Tiptree Jr. Science-fiction writer Robert Silverberg, in his introduction to *Warm Worlds and Otherwise* (1975), called Tiptree's writing "lean, muscular, [and] supple" (xv) and likened Tiptree's writing to that of Hemingway. Noting that it had been suggested that Tiptree was female, Silverberg wrote that it was a theory he found "absurd" because he found "something ineluctably masculine about Tiptree's writing" (xii) (Robert Silverberg, "Introduction," in *Warm Worlds and Otherwise* [New York: Ballantine, 1975], ix–xviii).

23

PROXIES (EXCERPT)

Laura J. Mixon

THE RENEGADE
Piebald Woman Steps Lively

With a spasm he awoke, and clutched the edges of the table with such desperate strength that his fingers dented metal. He didn't know why, but he felt sure he was dying. Someone was trying to kill him.

He cried out: a silent shriek of protest.

His body convulsed again, a puppet with tangled strings, and then vanished from awareness in a detonation of garish colors and disembodied limbs.

No—that was a dream. He was—where? A table. He had thought that the table was part of the dream, but it was real. A blurred face with an intent expression leaned over him. Whose? He should know that face. His mentor—his captor?

He lay paralyzed and helpless as hands moved, tracing arcs of light across his sight A mouth emitted words that dripped down on him, slithered and wriggled around him. . . . The hands hooked wires to him and attached probes that made shrill noises wail in his ears and made his limbs and vision dance. Somewhere, drums were pounding. He fled the drums, into a wan void.

Retreat should have been a blessing. It wasn't. Oblivion was death. He screamed again, silent, writhing.

The voice, lights, and garbled sensations finally ebbed, and he lay quietly, leaden-limbed. Hisses, clicks, whirrings—all the soft whispers of machines—swelled to fill the silence.

Without will, his eyes came open and his body sat up. His hands disconnected the probes and pressed his skin back into place. A memory came—many memories, of experiences much like this.

So. He'd faced into a simile on the *v*-net, or booted up a simile crystal. That was all. Relief seized him. In the aftermath of adrenaline a wave of nausea rose, and died. He'd thought he was going mad.

While his hands were disconnecting the probes, he glanced at his naked body, at the high, round breasts and the broadened hips, the triangle of pubic hair with no male genitalia.

It shocked him. He—no, *she*—had faced into a gender blender. This could prove interesting.

But she also had this sense that the simile was skewed. Something was wrong—or missing—and she couldn't think of what.

Well. It'd come to her.

The skin of her simile body was mottled, cocoa and alabaster. The idea of being in a female body was arousing. Obedient, this body's nipples went hard, and an ache grew in her lower abdomen. Odd; faintly—somewhere—she could feel a penis growing hard as well. She wondered if she had picked a plain-action simile, or perhaps an intrigue. From the vague sense of foreboding, she guessed it was the latter.

Her body, apparently acting on a preprogrammed sequence, leaped down from the table and went toward one of the doors. Meanwhile she snatched information from the corners of her vision. In the dimness, naked bodies with their inner machinery half ex-posed lay on other tables beneath banks of flickering lights. Lab coats stained with dirt and oil hung by the door. Her hands snatched one up and slipped it onto her shoulders, then grabbed some plastic foot wraps from a cardboard box on the floor and pulled them onto her feet.

Come on, she thought. I want to do something. It didn't help, of course. The con-trol wouldn't release to her until she had been guided to where she was supposed to be at game start.

These similes with long noninteractive stretches annoyed her. She couldn't imag-ine why she hadn't just reprogrammed the beginning before facing in.

Well, she just hadn't, that was all. She'd simply have to ride it out. A programmed look to the left, to the right: the corridor was empty. She let herself relax into the move-ments, as though they were her own. Her body glided through the halls, made a series of turns, dodged into empty rooms when other people neared. Finally the body came to a door, opened it, and stepped outside. It carried her at a run across the concrete.

Someone was watching her. She could feel someone's attention on her. Was some-one floating her? Or was it part of the simile?

Her feet splashed into the mud on the far side, and then the body halted and the con-trol ceased. For the moment, at least, she had a chance to catch her breath and look around.

The sky was overcast, dark gray and purple. Rain, little more than a warm drizzle, beaded on her long forearms and face. A stench of rotting vegetation overwhelmed her. With a mental turn, she damped her olfactory sense.

Then her head swiveled and glanced over her body's shoulder. The buildings at her back huddled together, dim rectangles in the gloom. Spotlights mounted on their upper corners cast light onto the acres of concrete that surrounded the complex.

Some sounds she couldn't identify registered on her awareness as she stood there: rustlings, and squeaks that twisted around on themselves like the cry of poorly lubricated bearings. She waited for the programming to kick in again, but her body remained still.

They had finally given her control of the scenario, then. Good. She increased the magnification of her hearing and sight and began to pivot, targeting the source of the noise. Footsteps in a patio of the building complex now echoed above a moaning chorus of machines. After a few seconds she could also see movement through the windows of the closest building. But the strange sounds came from somewhere else. She turned slowly in place, cocking her head.

A short distance away, a chain-link fence entangled in vines and leaves held back wild plant growth. The sounds issued from there. She focused her vision on the areas of movement in the plant growth, magnified, and augmented with infrared. There—and there—blotches appeared, the heat signatures of small animals moving about in the bushes. One took flight in a breath of feathers, striking blows to the air.

Birds. She relaxed and smiled, relieved. Her sight and hearing returned automatically to normal magnification and range, and she began slogging through the mud.

Something roared; she spotted a shack at the fence, next to an opening gate. A huge land vehicle was passing through the gate. The vehicle paused and the driver exchanged some words with the one leaning out of the shack's window. Their words were gibberish.

Strange. This must be a foreign-language simile. Maybe that explained the sense of wrongness she had felt earlier. But no, that was something else, and she knew suddenly what it was.

There should be others with her. Why was she alone? Where were the others?

She'd been betrayed. She remembered the face she'd glimpsed when she'd first faced in. He had betrayed her. She froze in her steps, terrified. I can't do this alone!

The land vehicle began to move again. Its giant treads threw mud high into the air as it bucked and strained. Then it began to crawl forward. The driver waved to her.

Just a simile. All she had to do was stay calm and she'd be OK; she'd be returned home, eventually, to the others, to reality.

I can do this, she thought. I am strong. She repeated those words until she believed them.

This isn't just a game, a voice inside her head said. *You have been chosen to accomplish a mission. Lives are at stake and you are the only one who can help.*

She made her way toward the gate across the ruts and gouges left by the vehicle. A uniformed man carrying a rifle came out of the shack. He stopped and held up a hand, but she ignored him and walked by.

The man spoke sharply and grabbed her arm. She shoved him away and continued walking. He fired his weapon. She leapt, striking the man full in the chest, as a bullet whizzed past. Something exploded behind her. Wood burning and something else— something with an acidic tang—stung her nose. Good programming, she thought, surprised. Nice detail.

The man had stumbled back to his feet. He aimed the rifle again. She spun inside his arm, drove her right palm into his nose, and felt bones and cartilage crack. He flew back in an arc and landed with a splash in the mud.

She bent over him. His eyes were staring and red lubricant ran from his crushed nose, mixing with water. She sharpened her vision and hearing; his body had stopped functioning.

At that instant she felt the other body—the body within her body—again. She froze, confused. Even as she stood looking at the corpse, she could feel her other self. Buoyant limbs—the measured rise and fall of a thorax—needles and tubes punctured the skin of her chest, belly, and arms. She swallowed, and a saline trickle worked its way down her esophagus.

She was two places at once. Someone, somewhere, was playing drums. Thump-THUMP! Thump-thump-thump.

She should know a good many things she did not. She didn't know what the other body was, nor who she was. She couldn't remember her name or anything about her past.

She had nothing to hang on to—she was no one.

Her vision blurred, a band squeezed her chest; she staggered and went to her knees in the mud. Somewhere she was twitching and thrashing, screaming, beating fists against slick cool surfaces. The drumbeats grew louder.

A name came to her then, as though someone had put it there. Dane Elisa Cae. I'm Dane Elisa Cae.

She grasped at the name and, clutching it, forced her breathing to slow. The panic faded, as did the sense of the other body.

She rocked back onto her haunches and looked around, shakily. The vehicle had passed behind the buildings. No one else was in sight. Only now did the words the driver had spoken with the man in the shack come to her: It had been an exchange of greetings. It *had* been English they were speaking.

Something was wrong with her interface, then. It wasn't transmitting speech properly. Well, difficulty understanding what people said could complicate things, but there was no backing out now. She'd have to compensate as best she could.

Dane Elisa Cae launched herself onto her wonderfully long, powerful legs and ran away from the complex along the ruts in the mud, and knew they wouldn't catch her. She would return to the others, soon. She would go home. It burned beneath memory like an ache of desire. *Home.* But first she must find something. Someone.

DANE ELISA CAE
Damaged Goods

Dane was floating; music filled her mind; faces floated before her—not-human faces that she knew and didn't know; sinuous bodies slid over her, caressed her, buoyed her in the pool. Water dripped down from gleaming rock, sent ripples everywhere. The sound of dripping was music.

Bubbles tumbled upward around her, tickling her as they burst; she pinched her nostrils closed, nudged another body aside with her snout—

—dove deep, beneath the other grey, smooth bodies. Fins flurried past her face; more laughter effervesced through her mind. The world was green, blue, dim—rocks and fissures deep beneath her; schools of silver-scaled fish darted among them. She looked up at the others, shouted a song that sounded inside and outside her, whipped her tail and sped upward—

—broke surface—for an instant she paused at the top of her arc—then plunged deep into the pool.

The sensations faded. She lay on her side, blissful and quiet. The dreams, joyous dreams, had chased the evil men and the horrible pounding sound away. Her body was human again.

Someone was pulling something from within her neck; she jerked at the touch, and the object slipped from the hand of the other. The object, a crystal, caught the light as it fell, slow motion, to the pillowed floor.

There had been a piece of crystal inside her neck.

She looked down at herself and saw a stranger's nude body, pale skin and hair, female. Dane Elisa Cae looked around.

She was in a room with soft flooring and walls. Words flowed around her, songs—a stream of them on many levels of hearing. Many people all about: some she saw, some she couldn't see. Bodies surrounded her, faces and eyes and mouths and legs and arms . . .

knowing her, touching her. Everywhere. Someone tried to slide another crystal into her neck. She shoved the hand aside and sat.

I was among enemies, she thought. She shook her head, suddenly dizzy. They were hurting me. Where am I?

My name is Dane Elisa Cae. My name is—Concerned faces surrounded her. *What's wrong? Sing with us, sing . . .*

She shoved them away, lurched to her feet. She was too light; her push carried her to the ceiling, where she struck and bounced. Sinking, she stumbled over bodies and bounded up again. A wall met her. She bounced and fell back. Her name—she was—

—sitting bolt upright among covers, fighting them. She fell on her face on the floor with a heavy, painful thud.

She rolled over and sat. Her arms were thick and hairless; she had small mammaries, a great belly, and baggy shorts that held a bulge. Frowning, she slid her hand into her shorts, and jerked it back out with a strangled scream. She had a man's genitals.

She struggled back onto the bed, retreated into the corner, huddled there in the dimness, stared at a bedside clock that blinked 7:07 A.M. She looked around. The cluttered room was familiar. She knew this place.

Her name was, her name—she—

—was hurting. A steady motion rocked her back and forth on a heap of hard, sharp objects. She lay half propped against something solid, perhaps a wall. Parts of her body were islands of numbness, surrounded by annuli of pain: the right side of her face, her right arm, her left leg.

She muted the hurt as much as she could, and opened her eyes. The sun was high in the sky. Her body was her own again—she was Dane Elisa Cae, in her own tormented, blessed body.

She lay in a wooden cart. Over its edge a cloaked figure's head and shoulders hunched, bobbing up and down. The figure was pulling the cart down a rocky path. He breathed heavily, and said something once, in a loud voice, when a cart wheel caught on a rock. That was how she knew it was a man, by the timbre of his voice.

She tried to sit up, but the angle she was at and the jerks and starts of the cart threw her off-balance. Her right arm and left leg were torn and bloody, and she couldn't bend her leg very far. It didn't feel broken, though. There was only a dull pain when she moved it.

She gripped the edge of the cart and struggled to her knees. She formed the words in her mind and then spoke.

"Where are you taking me?"

The man started, and turned, wearing a strange expression. He spoke; she focused all her energies into understanding him.

"What's this?" was what he had said. He stared at her. Dane had seen him before— in the market. It was the sunburned man with all the gadgets. "So, the robot speaks. Remarkable."

The words came hard to her lips; She hesitated, laying the words out in a row in her mind, like blocks. "Robot! I'm not a robot. I'm a refugee. From Florida. My name is Dane Elisa Cae."

She moved into a more comfortable position and cradled her right arm in her lap.

"Dana Cae, a petey from Florida!" He laughed. "Someone's got a sense of humor." He shook his head. "I scavenged you. The boundary patrol thought you were human, and left you for dead." He hawked and spat. "Animals. Idiots." He went on, "Quite a so-phisticated piece of equipment, you are. I had to get up close to tell. I've done a few re-pairs, clamped off a few hydraulic leaks and rebent your limbs as best I could." He gestured broadly at her. "But you need more work. You're a quart low, at least."

A horrid, sick feeling filled Dane. For a moment she only looked at him. The speck of machinery in her neck, the dreams, her first memory of awakening in that laboratory, with probes and instruments attached to her—Her head shook violently. "I told you, I'm not a machine. I'm as human as you."

"Then that's one hell of a prosthetic you have there," he said, gesturing with his chin at her arm.

She looked at it more closely. Inside the long gash, the layers of blood-soaked flesh were suffused with fine strands and plastic tubing. Clamps hung from the tubing in three or four places, and the bone underneath glinted. No—not bone; something else entirely.

She touched the flesh, the infrastructure beneath it, and felt nothing. She dug her fingers into the wound. At the elbow joint, she felt some kind of pulley, a round surface, wires. The interior of her arm felt her fingers then, but not as pain, only as a pressure.

Dane Elisa Cae jerked her hand out and looked up at the man. Her fingers were smeared with red.

"You think that's something; you should see your face."

She reached up—the whole lower right quadrant of her face was hanging from a flap; she could feel clamps, and wisps of fiber at its edges. She glanced right, and at the edge of her eye socket, her fingers touched taut strands of wire, which moved a plate be-hind the eye.

Was this not, then, how human bodies were constructed? She probed down into her mind for the other one she vaguely remembered being—the male, who knew it was OK to have a machine body, who believed this was all a game. Phantomlike, he retreated from her.

The other, then—the face. Mentor. Captor. The one who had sent her here. Mentally she pled for him to come to her aid. Only silence met her inner cries.

A machine. Was she merely a programmed machine? Was that why she had no memory—why she was driven, guided? How she knew things without knowing how she knew?

She scrambled over the clutter, leaped out of the cart.

Dane Elisa Cae could still run. The man chased her. "Hey, come back—I can repair you! I *order* you to come back. I found you; you're mine!"

Even limping, though, she was faster than he. She left him far behind in the foothills, pursued by rhythm-thump, thump, thump—damn those horrible drums and that awful, croaking little voice, and when she finally slowed, she saw him below her on top of a hill, watching her ascent toward the peaks.

24

"THE POSTPRODUCTION OF THE HUMAN HEART": DESIRE, IDENTIFICATION, AND VIRTUAL EMBODIMENT IN FEMINIST NARRATIVES OF CYBERSPACE

Thomas Foster

In print news, your job is to know things about others; you peer out at the world through an arrow slit. In telepresence, you *are known*.

—*Raphael Carter*, The Fortunate Fall

While the concept of identification holds a status specific to the intellectual tradition of psychoanalysis, the longer history of philosophical work on the question of otherness clarifies the central problematic involved: how is it that only through the other I can be myself, only in the place of the other I can arrive at a sense of self?

—*Diana Fuss*, Identification Papers

But the real world was always there, waiting for her. Home. Patient lover, waiting for her to get all the wanderlust, all the doubts and fear of commitment, out of her system. Marry me, it whispered, when she'd been away for too long. Stop hiding. Grab hold with both hands. You won't have me around forever.

—*Laura Mixon*, Proxies

The Problem of Cyberspace

In her groundbreaking work on virtual systems theory, Allucquère Rosanne Stone argues that the term "cyberspace" should be understood as only one possible metaphor for the "network of electronic communications prosthetics" (Stone 1995, 35). Within its original framework of male-authored cyberpunk fiction like William Gibson's *Neuromancer* (1984), representations of cyberspace take two forms, with two seemingly distinct political implications. On the one hand, cyberspace often appears progressive to the extent that it denaturalizes social reality. If the virtual "matrix" is understood by its users to be merely a "consensual hallucination" (Gibson 1984, 5), then cyberspace can be read as revealing the mediated nature of social reality, and once reality is understood as a product of human agency, then we can imagine changing that reality's status quo. In other words, if cyberspace is a "*representation* of data abstracted from the banks of every computer in the human system" (Gibson 1984, 51; my emphasis), then as a representation it remains open to revision and rewriting.

This interpretation of cyberspace as an experience of critical denaturalization was explicitly circulated by early designers of virtual-reality hardware, such as Jaron Lanier, the founder of VPL Laboratories and creator of early virtual-reality peripherals such as datagloves, to map the movement of a user's hand into a computer simulation, and dataphones, or lightweight head-mounted displays intended to produce a sense of immersion in the simulation by collapsing the distance between viewer and screen. In a 1989 interview, Lanier pointed out that "in Virtual Reality, there's no question that your reality is created by you," since you or someone you know programmed that reality (Lanier 1990, 49). When the interviewer points out that "that may be the actual case anywhere," Lanier replies, "Well, it is, but in Virtual Reality, it's so explicit," and goes on to support his claims by arguing that virtual reality can take this process further, to the point of denaturalizing the experience of inhabiting a physical body itself: "In Virtual Reality, even your body looks like you did it" (Lanier 1990, 49). It is this sense of the body as something users of virtual reality do for themselves that marks the relevance of feminist theories of gender performativity to such technologies.

This reading of cyberspace depends, however, on the possibility of virtual experiences feeding back into our understanding of "real life." In contrast, the second set of conventions that have emerged around the idea of cyberspace emphasizes virtual space as an alternative to the physical world. In this reading, cyberspace is a place where a user can project "*his* disembodied consciousness" (Gibson 1994, 5; my emphasis), thereby reproducing and literalizing the Cartesian dualism of mind and body that has traditionally been associated with the gendered distinctions between universal and particular, rational, and emotional, masculine and feminine.[1]

Stone's description of virtual systems and spaces as "communications *prosthetics*" suggests the term *telepresence* might be a better name for virtual interfaces than cyberspace, since the idea of presence, no matter how mediated, can serve as a reminder that virtual perspectives always exist in relation to physical bodies.[2] As Stone puts it, no matter what term is used to name the space of virtual interaction, "insofar as it involves communicating with other people through narrow-bandwidth media, it is about negotiating the tensions between individual subjects, virtual collectivities, and the physical bodies in which they may or may not be grounded" (Stone 1995, 35). The suggestion here is that we will still exist in some relation to our bodies even in virtual environments where our subjectivities are no longer grounded in or contained by those bodies. The implications of this way of theorizing virtual systems are central to understanding the complex and ambivalent relationship between feminist writing and cyberpunk fiction.

Stone's reintroduction of body rhetorics, in the denaturalized form of the prosthetic, exemplifies one kind of feminist intervention in cyberpunk fiction. It is common to find arguments characterizing such interventions in terms of how women are less likely than men to devalue the body as "meat" and turn to cyberspace as a technology for transcending "the prison of [their] own flesh" (Gibson 1984, 6).[3] In this view, women's writing offers alternatives to the "elite stance" of "relaxed contempt" for embodied experience, which Gibson's *Neuromancer* attributes to his male hackers and console cowboys.

Feminist interventions in cyberpunk science fiction then also constitute an intervention in a theoretical debate about the cultural significance of virtual reality computer interfaces and telepresence technologies. The two sides in this debate might be represented by Stone and N. Katherine Hayles. Hayles's recent book *How We Became Posthuman* identifies the "erasure of embodiment" (Hayles 1999, xi) as the central problem within contemporary technocultures, and she traces that problem back to early work on cybernetics and information theory; fantasies in which cyberspace permits the separation of mind from body take for granted this concept of information as abstract, immaterial, and decontextualized. In contrast, Stone argues that it is a mistake to assume that "the physical/virtual distinction" corresponds to "a mind/body distinction"; instead, for Stone, the virtual presence established by users of cyberspace interfaces "is not a disembodied thinking thing, but rather a different way of conceptualizing a *relationship* to the human body" (Stone 1995, 40), and the possibility of that different conceptualization is made possible by the fact that in virtual communications systems "the locus of sociality that would in an older dispensation be associated with [a] body goes on in a space which is quite irrelevant to it" (Stone 1995, 43). For Stone, then, what looks like an "erasure" of the relevance of bodies might actually be an opportunity to reimagine the relation between body and mind or social identity.

Juxtaposing these two arguments suggests the stakes involved in representations of telepresence technologies. From Stone's perspective, Hayles's project of "putting embodiment back into the picture" (Hayles 1999, xiv) runs the risk of also reinstalling a traditional one-to-one relationship between body and mind, sex and gender, despite Hayles's care not to define embodiment in essentialist terms or as fundamentally opposed to the virtual experience of informational patterns. From Hayles's perspective, Stone's willingness to describe the embodied location of subjectivity as being rendered irrelevant within virtual systems runs the risk of devaluing bodies entirely in favor of some idea of becoming pure mind, thereby making cyberspace an escapist fantasy rather than a force for cultural change.[4] As Hayles clearly acknowledges, this difference is a question of strategic emphasis. Should the transformative possibilities of cyberspace be emphasized, or is it necessary at the present moment to emphasize the inescapability of embodiment? Turning the question around, is it possible to capitalize on the opportunity virtual systems represent for reimagining the relation between mind and body, without simply erasing embodiment entirely? Hayles's goal is to find "a way of talking about the body responsive to its construction as discourse/information and yet not trapped" within such a constructivist framework (Hayles 1999, 193). As Donna Haraway warned in "A Cyborg Manifesto," the founding essay of feminist technoculture studies, within "communications sciences" such pure constructivism leads to a belief in "the translation of the world into a problem of coding" and "a search for a common language in which all resistance to instrumental control disappears and all heterogeneity can be submitted to disassembly, reassembly, investment, and exchange" (Haraway 1991, 164). The feminist narratives that I discuss in this chapter participate in Hayles's search for a new way of talking about the body, while at the same time they demonstrate the difficulties involved in both retaining a sense of the importance of embodied specificity and rejecting embodiment's traditional role in "securing" both "human identity" and "the univocality of gender" or the assumption that gender identities naturally proceed from sexed bodies.

Embodied Virtuality and Feminist Narratives: "Putting Embodiment Back in the Picture"[5]

In this chapter, I focus on some of the most recently published examples of postcyberpunk feminist science fiction. At first glance, these narratives would seem to emphasize the importance of reasserting embodiment within social settings where computer-mediated communication has become the norm. Edith Forbes's *Exit to Reality* (1997) gives a lesbian feminist twist to a scenario that has become familiar through films like *The Matrix* and *The Thirteenth Floor,* in which characters come to realize that the world they live in is a virtual simulation.[6] The narrator of this novel, Lydian, becomes involved with another character, Merle, who initially appears as a man. Lydian learns, however, that Merle is able to change physical form and in fact tells Lydian that "he" has "lost the connection to my original body" and no longer remembers who "he" was (Forbes 1997, 94). Merle proceeds to teach Lydian to morph, and immediately afterward Merle changes sex, revealing that "she" only appeared as a man "because I thought that was the only way you'd ever love me" (113). It is only later that Lydian realizes that this seeming violation of the laws of nature can be explained only if her physical brain was connected directly into a virtual reality program that generated "every bit of sensory data [she] received" (167). In the course of the novel, it is revealed that the entire population of the planet was downloaded into a simulation, connecting "the biological to the electronic, so that the electronic could become the medium of connection between minds" (173). The effects of this realization are summed up when Lydian realizes that "I had never questioned my world" but had instead taken it as an "inevitability"; now, however, she sees it "as an arbitrary design, which could have been designed differently" (223).

The point is that by gaining this realization in the course of their romance, Lydian and Merle have already begun to redesign their world. The novel causally links Lydian and Merle's transgression of heterosexual norms with their gaining the ability to reprogram the computer simulation and to make it more interactive, instead of simply accepting the computer's input. The simulation was actually originally designed to enforce compulsory heterosexuality as a "statutory taboo" (Forbes 1997, 55), so that to act on same-sex desire is already to violate the preconceptions built into the virtual environment (55). In this sense, the novel implies that the experience of virtual embodiment has a critical function, since it demonstrates precisely how "reality" is already socially mediated. Merle is the character who most directly thematizes the pleasures that result from this denaturalizing of reality, by moving beyond an identity grounded in a single, original body. At one point, after having impersonated Virginia Woolf, Merle is described as bursting both out of bed with Lydian and "out of Virginia Woolf," to go "spinning around the room in a glitter of sequins and lace and top hats, belting out a hodgepodge of Broadway musical exuberance" (275).

At the same time, though, the novel also presents the characters as frustrated by the limitations of virtual existence. The same possibility of redesigning the world that is required for the lesbian romance to take place is also what results in the characters feeling "trapped" in "a permanent cast of characters" that cannot change, since it is no longer possible to create new participants (Forbes 1997, 224). The plot of the novel tends to privilege this negative interpretation of the characters' virtual existence as a confinement to be escaped, since the novel moves from Lydian and Merle's realization of their own virtuality to Lydian's desire "to get our real bodies back" and to "know what the world is like outside this electronic image" (249). A group of other "renegades" who have become aware of the nature of the simulation they inhabit show Lydian how to operate a robot body through telepresence, at which point Lydian learns that the process of collective becoming-virtual both was inspired by and resulted in the intensification of a real-world ecological collapse.[7] The designers of the virtual system explicitly imagined it as incompatible with the continued existence of the physical world, since "living things behave unpredictably" and therefore "might have damaged the containment structures" within which the virtual environments are located (256). As a result, Lydian is told that even if she could regain her real body, "the world outside is no longer compatible with human life" (250). Lydian goes on to become involved in attempts to simulate the ecological systems that have been destroyed, and the novel ends with the characters learning that life has begun to return to the real world and that they can use these simulations and teleoperated robots to help guide the development of a new, real-world ecosystem (313), presumably with the goal of making it possible to return to physical bodies at some point. Lydian interprets this possibility as a reason to cease "mourning the loss," and the novel leaves the referent of the word loss deliberately ambiguous. Does it refer to the actual loss of the real world and their real bodies, when they became virtual? Or does it refer to the pending loss of the forms of identity play and metamorphosis possible in a virtual environment?

Through this ambiguity, the novel tries to mediate between embodiment and virtuality, as Lydian and her colleagues begin the process of "exiting to reality," while at the same time treating the real world as something that they can and must participate in designing. Whereas a film like *The Matrix* treats the movement from virtual reality to the physical world as a narrative of liberation, *Exit to Reality* is less willing to abandon the critical perspective the virtual provides on the concept of the "real" and its exclusions. The final section of the novel attempts implicitly to separate the social reality that the experience of virtuality reveals to be a human design from the physical reality of the natural world, a physical reality that the novel wishes to retain and revalue. But the point at which these two "realities" converge and *cannot* be separated is the experience of embodiment. The novel therefore begins by emphasizing the material implications of virtual experience for political projects that require the reimagining of the relationship between social identities and physical bodies, and ends by emphasizing the extent to which our relation to the materiality of the natural world is both inescapable and technologically mediated. However ambiguous and qualified, however, it is hard to ignore the element of nostalgia present in *Exit to Reality's* narrative closure and the way the ending privileges Lydian's desire to get her "real" body back (Forbes 1997, 249). This nostalgia tends to foreclose on the possibilities Merle embodies, precisely because she no longer has access to "her" real body or original form, possibilities that open the action of the novel and that are explored in its middle sections. This novel therefore ultimately seems skeptical about whether it is possible to retain a "real" body without denying Merle's performative understanding of embodied identities as provisional and open to change.

Laura Mixon's *Proxies* (1998) follows a narrative trajectory similar to Forbes's *Exit To Reality*, but in *Proxies* the plot focuses on a group of children born with severe immune deficiencies, who are used in an illegal experiment that continuously immerses them in a direct interface between their nervous systems and computer networks. In effect, from a very early age, these children grow up in virtual reality, either in purely computer-simulated environments or linked to a variety of remotely controlled robot bodies or proxies.[8] The novel suggests that this kind of extreme immersion is necessary in order to realize the critical potential of cyberspace as a defamiliarization of reality, since "to most people the nets are an electronic extension, or reflection, if you prefer, of the real world" (Mixon 1998, 295). Without continuous immersion, virtual reality technologies are treated instrumentally, as mere tools which have no power to change a user's sense of identity. To this group of children, however, "the nets *are* the real world" (296). But while the children's complete immersion in cyberspace makes it a genuine prosthesis, a part of who they are that cannot be fully integrated into a natural organic body, *Proxies* suggests that this new experience of cyberspace as "the real world" can itself be renaturalized, as a new status quo. Moreover, the children's improved ability to navigate the informations spaces of virtual reality and to operate more efficiently mechanical devices remotely through telepresence is presented as a threat to the maintenance of any relation to their physical bodies: While the children have "a much more direct and efficient interface" with virtual systems, they also have "a correspondingly weaker interface with their own bodies" (294).

The plot of *Proxies* revolves primarily around this conflict between what the novel presents as two equally naturalized understandings of embodiment and reality, and the key interpretive question is whether these two sets of assumptions can exist in a productive, critical relationship to one another or whether they are simply incompatible and can never coexist. For instance, the previous passage seems to take for granted an inverse correlation between the virtual and the physical: The more time spent in cyberspace, the weaker one's relation is to one's "real" body. However, the fact that physical embodiment is described as a relationship rather than an identity and the way that this relationality is figured by the term "interface" implies that the experience of virtuality has already changed the characters' thinking about physical bodies, so that the inverse correlation that is posited between the virtual and the physical is undermined on the level of the language used to describe that incompatibility.

Similarly, one of the main elements of the plot involves the children's willingness to go along with various covert schemes, including assault and murder, because they make a distinction between harming another person's "flesh" and harming their "body" (Mixon 1998, 268). The children use the term "flesh" to refer to their physical bodies, which are contained within life-support systems or crèches but which do *not* contain the children's consciousnesses. Bodies are dispensable, whereas the flesh is not; at the same time, however, the flesh is not a body to the extent that having a body implies organic integration of all the parts of that body, including the brain and the mind. Their children's minds instead reside in a series of either virtual avatars (called "similes") or in mechanical devices, and it is those "proxies" that the children refer to as bodies. The novel ends with one of the main characters choosing to become a kind of surrogate mother to these children and teaching them that, for the rest of us, "our bodies *are* our crèches" (441).

At the same time, the novel presents this maternal character, Carli, as having to learn the counterintuitive distinctions the children make in order to teach them to reconnect "flesh" and "body," in the same way that readers have to learn these distinctions in order to make the events of the plot intelligible, since the children's motives and actions remain opaque and puzzling until readers have grasped the framework of assumptions that govern their attitude toward embodiment. If the children have to learn that we are all dependent on bodies we cannot dispense with any more than the children can dispense with their crèches, then Carli has to learn that her relation to her body is technologically and therefore socially mediated and determined. Imagining the body as "meat" that can be transcended or expended requires imagining these mediations as connections that can be severed, but the fact that we can never dispense with these mediations does not mean that they are fixed in one form and immune to change and intervention.

Carli sums up both this necessarily mutual process of education and the novel's tendency to reassert the primacy of physical embodiment when she reflects on her own temptation to "follow the creche children into their virtual world" where "death was temporary" (Mixon 1998, 412). But Carli rejects that temptation by figuring "the real world" as a "patient lover, waiting for her to get all the wanderlust, all the doubts and fear of commitment, out of her system" (413). The novel develops this metaphor in a way that suggests a renaturalization of heterosexual romance (even though Carli seems to be playing the stereotypically masculine role of the adventurer afraid of domestic commitments), since reality is imagined as proposing marriage and arguing that "you won't have me around forever" (413). At the same time, this is a concept of "reality" that has clearly been affected by the experience of cyberspace, since this is a reality whose permanence is in question and has to be explicitly produced or shored up. While Carli has thus clearly internalized the effects of her encounter with the children, the first true "natives" of cyberspace, the ending of the novel installs a traditional narrative teleology in which the children's development into adults requires that they be returned to the real world, giving up the freedom and potential associated both with childhood and with virtual identity play or shape-changing in order to take on the responsibilities of the physical world, figured by marriage and monogamous commitment.

Of all the novels I've chosen to discuss here, Sage Walker's *Whiteout* (1996) seems to offer the most positive interpretation of the possibility of balancing or reconciling the physical and the virtual, in its story of an alternative sexual arrangement between three women and two men, who maintain their relationships primarily through virtual-reality interfaces. This arrangement is possible because the novel imagines a technology (involving wearing a full body suit or "skinthin") that records and transmits *body* language and "muscular signatures" (Walker 1996, 74) as well as visual information, so that the main viewpoint character, a woman named Signy, can remotely access the kinesthetic experience of having a particular male body, and vice versa. In other words, *Whiteout* dramatizes an unusually embodied form of telepresence, as the basis for a new kind of "family," one that can be read as an alternative to the more traditional familial model asserted at the end of *Proxies*.

Whiteout thereby comes closer to realizing a possibility that Hayles alludes to in passing, as she makes her critique of theories of disembodied or abstract information: "abstract pattern can never fully capture the embodied actuality, *unless* it is as prolix and noisy as the body itself" (Hayles 1999, 22; my emphasis). *Whiteout* imagines a form of telepresence that incorporates at least some of the "noise" of embodiment into the abstract realm of cyberspace.[9] Walker's novel clearly attempts to provide an alternative interpretation of virtual reality, since the masculinist devaluation of the body as "meat" is included in the novel, in the form of a hacker character named Jimmy whose involvement with this polymorphously perverse virtual family forces him to grow beyond his initial attitude of being "afraid of flesh" (Walker 1996, 143).

Whiteout emphasizes virtual intimacy, not as an escape from physical embodiment, but as a different way of experiencing it. Signy underscores that difference when she reflects on the "lack of procedural certainties" that follows from her unconventional family's "determination not to follow our parents' ways of dealing with life" (Walker 1996, 306). This defamiliarization of social relationships is also dramatized when Signy is asked whether one of her male partners, Jared, is her lover, and she can't immediately answer, despite the fact that they are sexual partners and have access to each other's sensoria, through the novel's fictional telepresence technology. Her parents' language is not adequate to describe her lifestyle. In particular, Signy sees her virtual partnerships as an alternative to marriage, which she feels "negated part of a woman's identity" (40).

While Signy feels that her virtually mediated lifestyle means that "we are not a part of any tradition but our own," she also acknowledges that some of her family's "rituals have come from business codes" (Walker 1996, 306). Her partnership is also a business arrangement, with the five of them forming a corporation called Edges. They specialize in media manipulation and political spin-doctoring, and the plot of the novel focuses on the consequences of Edges's involvement in an attempt to influence changes to the treaty governing the exploitation of Antarctica's natural resources. While the blurring of the boundary between the personal and the commercial in cyberspace undoubtedly constitutes a qualification to the novel's endorsement of virtual reality, I want to focus on the implications of the analogy the novel implicitly sets up between cyberspace and Antarctica, which is described as a "presumably empty continent" and possibly the only place on earth where there might still be a "true sense of unlimited space" (179). It is this experience of space that links Antarctica to virtual reality, famously described by Gibson as possessing "unlimited subjective dimension" (Gibson 1984, 63). The novel uses Antarctica to literalize the temptation that David Brande locates in one fantasy about cyberspace: "the fantasy of limitless open spaces, frontier without end," a kind of ultimate free market (Brande 1996, 101). In particular, since Antarctica is relatively un-inhabited, this expansionist fantasy takes the form of freedom from worries about eco-logical damage or responsibility to the physical world, similar to the conflict Forbes imagines in *Exit to Reality*, between virtual existence and ecological concern. The whole point of *Whiteout's* Antarctica subplot, however, is that this continent is only "presum-ably" empty and available for unregulated exploitation. If Antarctica is shown not to be a place where we can escape the consequences of our actions and choices, the novel makes a similar point about cyberspace.

The main way in which the novel explores the "real" consequences of virtual inter-actions appears in the novel's other main plot thread, about the disappearance and ulti-mately the death of Jared, the one partner of Signy who first physically travels to Antarctica. During a boat trip, Jared falls overboard while wearing the skinthins that transmit his physical sensations, and the experience is recorded and accessed by his partners, who assume he drowned but still feel that "his body, at least [still] existed" (141). This crisis tests the limits of the characters' dependence on telepresence tech-nologies. Signy's initial response is to revert, "in this stress, to the primitive, to a need for hands-on, real-time flesh-and-blood contact" (Walker 1996, 141). Similarly, the en-tire group gathers together "in their flesh" (336) when Jared is located again, alive, only to die during a rescue attempt. At this point, a grief-stricken Signy refuses to exit a vir-tual simulation based on recordings of Jared's embodied point of view. She replays and in effect reanimates those recordings by assuming Jared's point of view, so that she can assert "he is (we, Jared and I, are) not simply a collection of memories" (343). At this point, the novel poses to readers the question of exactly how "real" a virtual presence can be. The other members of her family work through Signy's refusal to separate her-self from what remains of Jared, transforming the simulation into a set of images of death and rebirth and thereby bringing helping Signy "exit to reality." In a remarkably powerful moment, however, the novel ends by shifting to the virtual Jared's posthumous point of view, as if he were still alive in the simulation; he snaps his fingers "and the watchers, obedient, vanished" (347).[10] Through this formal technique of making no distinction between narrative agents and points of view that exist only in virtual reality and those that exist in both virtual and real-world settings, the novel suggests that Signy is right and Jared's virtual presence exists as more than just memories, even after his physical death, while at the same time it refuses to allow Signy to deny his death by clinging to the simulation. Typically for this novel, the alternative to this retreat into a nostalgic recreation of her dead lover is to be "held" by her other partners in a "synthesis of awareness" that includes Jared "but not [him] alone" (343).

Like Forbes's *Exit to Reality*, Raphael Carter's *The Fortunate Fall* (1996) uses a lesbian romance to thematize the conflict between the two impulses I have located in feminist narratives about cyberspace, the impulse to turn to cyberspace as a perspective from which to redefine women's relationships to their bodies and the impulse to reassert the importance of physical bodies against the temptation toward disembodiment that is often associated with representations of cyberspace.[11] In Carter's novel, however, the conflict between the two women's attitudes toward cyberspace is more sharply drawn. *The Fortunate Fall* tells the story of a reunion between two lesbian lovers, in a globalized future society where homosexuality has been outlawed both in virtual reality and the real world. Over the course of the novel, the narrator, Maya, gradually learns that the lover she thought was dead may have survived by storing a copy of herself in cyberspace. The novel actually ends with the narrator, Maya, refusing to allow her lover to escape discovery by downloading her personality into Maya's body.

At the beginning of the novel, Maya is working as a newscaster, with an implant that broadcasts her bodily sensations to her audience, much like the telepresence technology imagined in *Whiteout*. Maya has also been given an implant that suppresses both her sexuality and her memories of a previous lesbian relationship. Unknown to Maya, her lover reappears as her partner, Keishi, the editor who screens and manipulates the sensory data Maya generates in order to insure that Maya's only broadcasts appropriate sensations. Maya's contact with Keishi is entirely mediated through a computer interface. The novel therefore suggests that virtual reality might provide a way to write beyond the punitive ending typical of one kind of lesbian plot, which attempts to ideologically recontain the threat posed by same-sex desire to heteronormativity by presenting lesbianism as leading to death rather than to a life together. But the novel also reproduces that punitive narrative through Maya's refusal to accept Keishi's virtual existence as a continuation of their physical relationship; Maya's assertion of the value of the physical over the virtual implies a critical perspective on the belief that identity can be separated from embodiment through technological means, even though that assertion means ending her relationship with Keishi.

In *The Fortunate Fall*, the conflict between embracing virtuality and reasserting the value of materiality dramatized by these two characters is also figured as a conflict between telepresence technologies and print, with Maya possessing a nostalgia for newspaper journalism and beginning her story with a prologue in which she refers to her choice to present the story retrospectively in printed form rather than to allow her audience to access it directly, through her recorded sensations as the events occurred. As she puts it, "I will not let you explore the twining pathways of my thoughts as I explore them. . . . I will hide instead behind this wall of words, and I will conceal what I choose to conceal" (Carter 1996, 12). *The Fortunate Fall* is especially useful as an example of this conflict, however, because it also sets up another analogy: Physical experiences and print technology are also associated with desire, while virtual reality and telepresence technologies are presented as facilitating identification. I return to Carter's novel at the end of this chapter, because it dramatizes the difficulties of reconciling these categories of the physical and the virtual, desire and identification, even as it asserts their inseparability.

The Problem of Materiality: Virtual Imbrications of Desire and Identification

Hayles defines "virtuality" both as "the cultural perception that material objects are interpenetrated by information patterns" (Hayles 1999, 13–14) and as "the cultural perception that information and materiality are conceptually distinct" (18). These two different "perceptions" of the relation between the material and the virtual correspond to the two sets of meanings associated with cyberspace in cyberpunk fiction, beginning with Gibson's *Neuromancer.* The tension between these two interpretations of virtuality is crucial to my readings of the four novels I just discussed. On the one hand, these novels seem to confirm Hayles's suggestion that the experience of virtuality has feminist implications, to the extent that it undermines the assumption that possession of a sexed body determines and secures the "univocality" of a gender identity (xiv). On the other hand, like Hayles, these novels also seem skeptical of the way in which the undermining of embodiment's ideological function, specifically to obscure and naturalize the mediated or "interpenetrated" nature of the social meanings our bodies possess, slides over into a wholesale erasure of embodiment.

I want to focus more directly on the implications of the shift from presence to telepresence and the resultant challenge to embodiment's role in securing gender's univocality, specifically possibilities for transgendered identifications and same-sex desire.[12]

Stone argues that virtual systems disrupt the fundamental humanist assumption that a self consists of a single self located in a single body. In contrast to this assumption, Stone suggests that, since feminist theories of the social construction of gender understand the "physical map of the body and our experience of inhabiting it" to be "socially mediated," then "it should not be difficult to imagine the next step in a progression toward the social—that is, to imagine the *location* of the self that inhabits the body as also socially mediated" and therefore potentially "*independent* of the body" (Stone 1995, 92). Similarly, Judith Butler famously argues that gay and lesbian forms of gender play, such as drag or butch-femme, presuppose the absence of any "direct expressive or causal lines between sex, gender, gender presentation, sexual practice, fantasy and sexuality" (Butler 1991, 25). Those "lines" of connection are not "direct" but mediated. It is in this sense that Stone is right to claim that "in cyberspace the transgendered body is the natural body" (Stone 1995, 180).

More specifically, telepresence technologies allow sexual desire to be combined with identification with the object of desire, in violation of one of the most fundamental prohibitions of compulsory heterosexuality, in which occupying a male body, for example, naturally leads in two separate directions: toward self-identification with masculine gender norms and toward a libidinal cathexis on a female object-choice. As Diana Fuss points out, psychoanalytic theory rigorously distinguishes "identification (the wish to be the other) from sexual object-choice (the wish to have the other)" (Fuss 1995, 11). Since "for Freud, desire for one sex" and one sex only "is always secured through identification with the other sex," then "to desire and to identify with the same person at the same time is, in this model, a theoretical impossibility" (11). The novels I have been discussing demonstrate that this coimplication of desire and identification is the enabling precondition for the kind of virtual gender-bending and shape-changing dramatized by characters like Merle, in *Exit to Reality*.

Walker's *Whiteout* offers a less obvious example of the importance of how telepresence technologies make it hard to secure either a univocal gender identity or a heterosexual object choice, by making it hard to keep the operation of desire and identification separate. In one of the first passages in which Signy transfers "her awareness to Jared's recorded body language," in a technological literalization of transgendered identification, Jared is walking beside a woman named Anna. As a result of her "long familiarity with Jared's muscular signatures," Signy is described as being able to share "Jared's awareness of earth-mother Anna," with the implication being that this awareness is sexual. But this experience also requires Signy to immediately ask herself whether she is experiencing Jared's desire for Anna or her own same-sex desire, mediated through Jared's perspective: "Or was it Signy's desire for stolid warmth, *her* need to touch Anna's firm smooth skin?" (Walker 1996, 74). The process of this female character's identification with the point of view of a man who is also an object of her sexual desire is presented as unsettling that object choice. Does she desire Jared, or does she desire to be Jared? The point of this passage is that the experience of virtual reality, as it is imagined in this novel, does not permit the characters (or readers) to makes such distinctions. In this passage, the effect of identifying with a male point of view is that sexual desire for women does not remain foreign, as if the only way to desire another woman is to become a man; instead, that desire evokes a correspondence within Signy's own experience of feminine subjectivity.

In this way, feminist writers like Walker imagine telepresence technologies a literalizing the inseparability of desire and identification that Fuss defines when she asks "what is identification if not a way to assume the desires of the other? And what is desire if not a means of becoming the other whom one wishes to have?" (Fuss 1995, 12).[13] Telepresence technologies can make this implicit imbrication of desire and identification visible, thereby working to undo the process of heterosexual identity formation that, as Fuss points out, depend upon binary and internally homogeneous constructions masculinity and femininity. This possibility becomes central to novels like Walker's and Carter's, where telepresence technologies turn characters into "human cameras" by transmitting their perspectives and even bodily sensations, so that they become sites of identification for others as well as potential objects of desire.[14] Jay David Bolter has argued that identificatory mobility, the way such technologies allow users to occupy "any location" in the virtual environment, and therefore to "inhabit the point of view of any person, animal, or object," is the defining feature of virtual reality computer interfaces as a medium for aesthetic experience (Bolter 1996, 268).[15]

My argument is that the epistemological structure of the kinds of virtual experiences provided by telepresence technologies makes those technologies relevant to work on the inseparability of desire and identification by queer theorists like Fuss and Butler. To make that argument, it is necessary to consider the way in which identification, defined as a process incompatible with sexual desire, plays a key role in the construction of psychic interiority, the private space of the individual self that humanist philosophy imagines as existing prior to any engagement with society or "the other."[16] In her reading of Freud and the Oedipal process within which children are supposed to identify with the gender of their same-sex parent and learn to recognize the other parent's gender as defining the limits to appropriate objects of desire, Butler argues that the identification with the same-sex parent presupposes the loss of that parent as an object of desire and therefore triggers the process of melancholia, creating "an interior 'space' in which that love can be *preserved*" through incorporation (Butler 1990, 63). In other words, the separation of identification and desire, mapped onto the gender difference between mother and father, produces a form of melancholy (a loss that cannot be mourned or worked through) that is not pathological but necessary to the formation of a securely gendered, heterosexual person. As Butler puts it, "The identifications consequent to melancholia are modes of preserving unresolved object relations, and in the case of same-sexed gender identification, the unresolved object relations are invariably homosexual" (63).

Butler thereby shows how the process by which men identify with masculinity and women with femininity also creates both an "interior psychic space" and a concept of the body as container for that psyche or self (Butler 1990, 67). The key point here is that, when applied to gendered object relations, Freud's own theory of melancholic internalization of the object of loss implies that these identifications are preserved not just as identifications or as the basis for a univocal gender identity but also as "unresolved" objects of love and desire. Butler can therefore go on to argue that "the taboo against homosexuality must *precede* the heterosexual incest taboo" (64) and suggest that homosexuality and heterosexuality, identification and desire, are inextricably bound in the formation of subjectivity.

The feminist narratives about telepresence that I have discussed in this essay demonstrate how the relocation of subjectivity *outside* the space of the physical body (theorized by Stone) also undoes this process of melancholic incorporation and therefore permits the expression of same-sex desire that is incorporated and repressed through gender identification. As Butler puts it, "if the 'inner world' no longer designates a topos, then the internal fixity of the self and, indeed, the internal locale of gender identity, become similarly suspect" (Butler 1990, 134). Telepresence technologies literalize this unsettling of distinctions between "inner" and "outer" worlds, and the result is to unsettle the distinction between desire and identification as well.[17] In a social setting mediated through such technologies, binary distinctions between desire and identification, body and mind, material and virtual no longer map onto one another isomorphically. Desire is no longer exclusively associated with the material body, or identification with virtual spaces where supposedly disembodied minds can communicate.[18]

However, situating telepresence technologies in relation to this critique of the separation of identification and desire complicates the feminist project of reasserting the value of embodiment, within technocultural contexts that assume virtuality and informational patterns that are "in some sense more essential, more important, and more fundamental than materiality" (Hayles 1999, 18). As much as they attempt to "put embodiment back in the picture," the novels I am interested in also register the value of articulating desire through the structure of technologies that allow a user to identify his or her point of view with that of the object of desire and that therefore call into question the necessity of grounding identity in a single body. For instance, in Forbes' *Exit to Reality*, at the moment when Lydian realizes she is a virtual being, she quotes Descartes' famous dictum, "I think, therefore I am," but immediately goes on to foreground the difficulty of locating that *cogito*: "My consciousness had to be real, if nothing else was. But where was its boundary?" (Forbes 1997, 167). A similar challenge to the spatial enclosure of subjectivity within a gendered body is occurs in *Proxies*. One of the key subplots in this novel is generated by the fact that one of the crèche children who lives in cyberspace externalizes the division of his psyche into multiple personalities, which embody themselves as separate characters; one of the puzzles the novel poses to readers is how to define the relationship between these seemingly separate entities.[19] I would argue, though, that this thematics of externalizing psychic processes is also linked to the way in which the crèche children are described as having "no consistent sense of gender identity" (Mixon 1998, 230). This textual linkage can only be explained from the perspective of queer theoretical work on how exposing the relationship between identification and desire undoes the spatial enclosure of the self within the body and disarticulates gender identity from the sexed body.

For my purposes, Walker's *Whiteout* offers an even better example than *Proxies* , in a scene where Signy first meets a male character in virtual reality, after interacting with him in the material world. In this context, "meeting" means to don "his tensions and reflexes" and to look "out through his eyes," and Signy describes this experience of identification as "a different sort of awareness of him, miles from sex, in some ways more intimate" (Walker 1996, 310). At the same time that this experience of identification is distinguished from sex, it cannot be articulated except in sexual terms. By connecting desire and identification without assimilating one to the other, this passage suggests that telepresence technologies in *Whiteout* redefine these kinds of heterosexual relationships in queer terms.

One of the best and subtlest ways in which these novels acknowledge the challenge posed to concepts of the material body by this redefinition of sexual desire appears in *Proxies*, in the passage in which the character Carli rejects the seductions of flight into cyberspace by imagining her inescapable relationship to the real world as a marriage: "Marry me, it whispered, when she'd been away for too long" (Mixon 1998, 413). In the technocultural context depicted in all these novels, where desire can be articulated through identification with its object, and given the fact that the novel also depicts a proposal of marriage between two gay men, readers have to wonder whether Carli's marriage metaphor is an act of desire or identification—that is, readers have to ask good what this imagined relationship says about how Carli imagines herself as compared to her "patient lover." Is this a metaphorical act of same-self desire, with Carli desiring reality because she herself is real and so comes back to reality as a "home" as well as a "patient lover" (413)? Or is the relationship between world and self, physical and virtual, imagined as a heterosexual marriage? This ambiguity undermines any simple privileging of the "real," to the extent that the passage has to be read within an interpretive framework where desire and identification cannot simply be opposed as masculine to feminine, virtual to material. In other words, this passage seems designed to lead readers to question how easily these sets of dualistic categories can be mapped onto one another.

Sins of Locality and Nonlocality: The Critique of Interiority and Raphael Carter's *The Fortunate Fall*

Butler explicitly argues that the understanding of gender as performative displaces and undoes the model of subjective interiority, in which gender identity expresses an inner or inborn essence (Butler 1990, 134). Butler's model is a "redescription of intrapsychic processes in terms of the surface politics of the body" or the ideological meanings inscribed on that surface, which make it signify socially, for others (Butler 1990, 135); in this model, the meaning of embodiment is located outside the body itself, in its social circulation and therefore in its social regulation. Butler specifically defines gender as a set of acts that are "performative in the sense that the essence or identity that they otherwise purport to express are fabrications manufactured and sustained through corporeal signs and other discursive means" (Butler 1990, 135). Gender norms are sustained by obscuring this reversal of cause and effect: The identity we usually understand as preceding and being expressed by our gender presentation is in fact produced by that performance of gender. As Butler puts it, gender identity "is a production which . . . postures as an imitation" (1990, 138). This process of figuring an effect as a cause and vice-versa is implicitly invoked in Carter's *The Fortunate Fall*, when one of the characters describes telepresence technologies as "the postproduction of the human heart" (Carter 1996, 234).[20] To the extent that they are represented as disrupting the location of the "human heart" within the boundaries of the human body, stories about telepresence technologies can do the feminist work of revealing and therefore undermining the authority of the ideological sleight of hand Butler argues is implicit in the formation of gendered subjectivity. It is no accident that, in Mixon's *Proxies*, one of the characters mentions that the textbook titled *Retrofitting Humanity* was "required reading in my graduate telepresence courses" (Mixon 1998, 264).

This critique of a subjective interiority that exists prior to and is expressed by our social personae and interactions is a common thematics in cyberpunk fiction and postmodern culture generally. What Butler calls the rejection of "the psyche as *inner depth*" in gay and lesbian practices of gender play is defined by Fredric Jameson as a general postmodern repudiation of "depth models" (Jameson 1991, 12), including the "conception of the subject as a monadlike container, within which things felt are then expressed by projection outward" (15). Fred Pfeil defines cyberpunk as postmodern science fiction in part because of the "boundary breakdown" between "body and world" (Pfeil 1990, 88) he finds in cyberpunk, a breakdown reflected textually in the way that these narratives seem to have "no 'political unconscious'" and therefore to make no distinction between manifest thematic content and latent ideological assumptions (86).

I cite these similar critical rhetorics to identify a potential problem, one that inheres in my own description of telepresence technologies as making manifest and legible the ideological mystifications that, for instance, essentialize gender as a reflection of fixed inner qualities. The danger here is that such formulations might be taken to imply that telepresence technologies can entirely undo the social and ideological mediations by which our genders and sexualities are constructed, rather than opening those mediations to change. From there, it is one short step to the conclusion that such social mediations are dispensable, and that telepresence technologies simply make gender a matter of personal choice, replacing social construction with individual agency in ways that only reproduce the ideology of consumer culture. As Butler warns, "to dispute the psyche as inner depth, however, is not to refuse the psyche altogether" (Butler 1991, 28), and the postmodern problematizing of the hermeneutic depth model on which the idea of the "political unconscious" depends does not mean that postmodern culture is free of ideology.

Focusing on rhetorics about the potential of virtual-reality computer interfaces, Jay David Bolter offers an excellent definition of the specific form in which this temptation to dispense with social mediations and alienations, with the internal splitting of the psyche, appears in technocultural contexts. Bolter argues that virtual reality's emphasis on the visual rather than the textual or rhetorical is a symptom of nostalgia for "an apparently unmediated perception of another world" (Bolter 1996, 268), which he associates with the romantic desire for the "natural sign," a language in which the gap between signifier and signified, between word and thing, collapses (264). Specifically, virtual reality is imagined as returning us to phenomenal reality by providing a mode of communication that relies on bodily sensations, especially vision. As Slavoj Zizek has recently argued, virtual reality thereby often supports a fantasy of undoing the alienation that results from the necessity of defining ourselves as social subjects only through the medium of a preexisting linguistic structure, to which we have to adapt ourselves. Ultimately, this interpretation of virtual reality is a fantasy of complete control over our own self-fashioning, which eliminates the role of language in mediating and making intelligible our relation to ourselves.[21]

The origins of this fantasy can be traced back to Virtual Reality (VR) pioneer Jaron Lanier, who as early as 1989 was arguing that "information is alienated experience," and that as "a new landscape, not a new map" virtual reality technologies could reverse this process of alienation (Lanler 1990, 49). The insistence that VR is a landscape rather than a representation exemplifies Bolter's argument about VR embodying a desire for the natural sign.

In this reading, virtual-reality interfaces do not just reveal the mediated nature of reality as a social product and allow us to at least imagine intervening in that construction; instead, virtual reality allows us to transcend and dismiss those mediations, especially as they are embodied in language. In this context, it is especially significant that the novel discussed here that is most positive about the experience of virtuality and most willing to privilege the virtual over the physical, Walker's *Whiteout*, also insists on virtual reality as a medium for communicating "body language"—not just sensations, but sensations that are always experienced as already organized symbolically.

Bolter's argument clarifies the way in which telepresence technologies can paradoxically renaturalize the experience of participating in the "consensual hallucination" of cyberspace, to the extent that the greater degree of interactivity and agency that users experience within virtual constructs can be interpreted as a more direct and sensual mode of communication with others (a "natural sign") rather than as an insight into the constructedness of reality. This danger of renaturalization is thematized feminist narratives about telepresence in terms of new opportunities for censorship and the enforcement of the prohibition on homosexuality. In Forbes's *Exit to Reality*, the "statutory taboo" on same-sex desire is built into the virtual environment, since "people only have one body image in their allocation of memory," in an attempt to insure that virtual experience "more or less corresponds to the physical world" (Forbes 1997, 55, 262).

The contradiction here is that the supposedly unmediated forms of experience available in virtual reality are much more amenable to revision and editing than those in the material world, and it is in this sense that Walker's trope of "body language" cuts two ways. This contradiction becomes explicit in Carter's *The Fortunate Fall*. The novel's concluding section begins with a debate about the limits of telepresence technologies, in an important contribution to current thinking about technoculture. Echoing the rationale of the court decision that overturned the U.S. Congress's attempt to regulate the Internet through the 1996 Communications Decency Act, a hacker character named Voskresenye argues that "the Net *should* be the most democratic form of communication that the world has ever known" and that it should function as a medium of identificatory mobility, replacing "the poor bumblings of human compassion with perfect electronic sympathy" (Carter 1996, 236). Instead, however, "it is being used to enforce an official version of humanity" (236), since most users prefer not to "expose" themselves but rather to consume the "slickly post-produced" commercial experiences available through telepresence, the kind of experiences that the female narrator provides as a telepresence newscaster (231). This is the darker side of the trope of "the postproduction of the human heart," which I have argued provides a critical perspective on the shift in feminist and queer theory "from interiority to gender performatives" (Butler 1990, 134). This trope also indicates how supposedly "primary dispositions" are actually "effects of the law" (Butler 1990, 65).

This point, about the paradoxical renaturalization of social norms through the forms of manipulation possible in a denaturalized virtual environment, is made most directly when Voskresenye is challenged to define "who's missing" on the Net. His answer is "animals," since virtual technologies are neither used to reproduce, "in the human mind, the circuits that enable dolphins to use sonar" nor to allow us to "know what it is like to be a bat, a whale, a sparrow" (Carter 1996, 236). While in this way telepresence technologies are used to enforce a traditional concept of the boundaries of the human, such technologies are also used to narrow those boundaries to exclude drunks and addicts of all kinds, believers in religious faiths of all kinds, and homosexuals (237). The decision was made to eliminate possibilities for remotely identifying with this range of experiences through telepresence, in effect defining these experiences as particular, immanent, and minoritized. By being excluded from the telepresence network, these experiences are produced socially as experiences that cannot be shared and are not allowed to reach beyond the bodily boundaries that contain and individualize them. Ironically, the experiences that are excluded all share the impulse toward the transcendence of psychic and bodily limits, through drug-induced altered states of consciousness, religious faith, or same-sex relationships that combine identification with desire. It is this same impulse toward transcendence that makes virtual reality potentially democratic.

It is important to note, however, that in this technological context censorship is imagined as operating through the *reembodying* of experience as so particular and context-bound that it becomes incommunicable to anyone who does not already share that same experience.[22] Despite its devastating critique of the abuse of telepresence technologies, most directly through the two decades that Maya, the narrator, has had a suppressor chip implanted in her brain to edit the memories of her lesbian past, *The Fortunate Fall* does not advocate a simple return to the integrity of embodied experience and psychic interiority. Instead, Voskresenye argues that "telepresence is a chamber in which a new sense, more important than sight, is uncovered," so that "if what we call reality is to persist, *everything* must be brought into that chamber" (Carter 1996, 231). To quote Hayles again, information systems as abstract patterns "can never fully capture the embodied actuality," unless those systems can be "as prolix and noisy as the body itself" (Hayles 1999, 22). It is in this sense that the theological trope of the novel's title comes into play. The "fall" is the expulsion from the garden of Eden, which here figures as both the physical world and the spatial containment of subjectivity within the boundaries of the physical body; that fall is "fortunate" because it makes recuperation or salvation possible, but only within what Hayles calls "the condition of virtuality," where "material objects" are irreversibly "interpenetrated by information patterns" (Hayles 1999, 13–14, 18).

As Carter's character Voskresenye puts it, it is necessary to reject both the "sins of *locality*" and the "sin of nonlocality" (Carter 1996, 229, 231). The novel attributes to telepresence technologies the potential to change "the central fact of the human condition" by making "impossible all the sins of *locality*, all the errors that arise from being prisoned in one body and no other," including racism, sexism, classism, and nationalism (229). At the same time, telepresence technologies also make possible sins of nonlocality, since "not *all* people" are "united by telepresence" (230). Voskresenye cites two possible sins of nonlocality, both of which represent the reproduction of older cultural models and debates within this new technological context. One such sin is the way that telepresence might privilege "the distant over the near"; at the same time "we are pulled toward cameras," we are also pulled "away from people that we know in our own lives" (230). On the one hand, this "sin" represents the triumph of mediation over face-to-face proximity, as modes of social interaction. On the other hand, the novel also argues that this sin reflects the temptation Bolter defines, to treat virtual reality as "more real than daily life," and I would argue that "real" here refers to an experience that seems *less* mediated, not more. In this sense, the novel demonstrates the way telepresence technologies lend themselves to two contradictory and mutually exclusive interpretations: They both reveal and intensify the mediated nature of social reality and communication, and they also offer the prospect of transcending and eliminating such mediation.

The other sin of nonlocality that Voskresenye defines is "the agony of solitary animals at being caged together" (Carter 1996, 231), which leads to the abjection of certain types of experience, including homosexuality. Precisely because it is now technologically possible to feel those experiences more intensely than ever before, they become more threatening. In this sense, the sins of nonlocality that telepresence makes possible seem to include a reaction of homosexual panic, as the boundary between the social interactions with persons of the same sex becomes more difficult to distinguish from sexual interactions, given that the experience of accessing another person's bodily presence through cyberspace can seem "more intimate" than sex (Walker, 1996, 310).[23] Carter's critique of this second sin of nonlocality is familiar in that it reveals how telepresence technologies might reproduce an old ideology of false universality, often associated with the rhetoric of the democratic public sphere and its norms of supposedly universal rationality as the only precondition for participation in public life. As a medium that educates users to accept and enjoy shifting identifications with others, telepresence presents itself as a form of "instant, universal understanding" (Carter 1996, 236), but that easy universality still depends on excluding groups of people, just as attempts to define the generically or universally human have depended historically on excluding groups whose identities are constructed as dependent on an embodied particularity that they cannot transcend. By identifying excluded groups whose goal is precisely some form of transcendence of their own subjective "locality," Carter's novel suggests that participation in the "universal understanding" of this new electronic public sphere is only possible for persons who are willing to define themselves as particular and different in ways that are already intelligible to other people and therefore interesting enough to them to make it profitable for commercial networks to broadcast their experiences. The result is a homogenized form of multiculturalism, which distinguishes the kinds of differences that are acceptable from those that do not even have to be forbidden, because they are strictly unthinkable, as Maya's suppressor chip renders her lesbianism literally unthinkable to her.[24]

This analysis of telepresence's negative possibilities, specifically its potential for paradoxically renaturalizing and homogenizing difference, implies that locality and nonlocality, particularity and universality, and materiality and virtuality all function together to reinstitute oppressive norms and exclusions. It is therefore impossible to adequately resist this normalization of the social connections created through telepresence by simply embracing either locality or nonlocality, either by asserting our freedom from the "prison" of the body through virtual identification or by reasserting the value of embodied particularity and physical differences. This analysis defines the potential political relevance of feminist writers' attempts to imagine forms of what Hayles calls "embodied virtuality," capable of resisting the "materiality/information separation" itself (Hayles 1999, 12).

But by the same token, the analysis Carter's character offers—of how unequal power relations might persist even in the context of the "instant universal understanding" potentially provided by telepresence technologies—also demonstrates why it is so important that homosexuals are included among the groups whose desire for transcendence of their particularity threatens the norms for the technological transcendence of the body that have been instituted by this future society. Why is homosexuality equated with drug use or religious faith? This question can only be explained in terms of the framework Butler and other queer theorists have developed, in which the separation of desire for someone different and identification with someone similar is necessary to produce a secure inner "locality" for individual subjectivity, a process that also makes it possible to imagine gender identity as a reflection of that inner self. Within this framework, to imagine desire and identification as operating in conjunction is to challenge the "internal fixity of the self" on perhaps an even more fundamental level than drugs or religion can (Butler 1990, 1134).

The Fortunate Fall therefore demonstrates the process Butler describes, in which the desire to disclose sexuality also produces "a certain radical *concealment*," so that the "locus of opacity" simply shifts (Butler 1991, 15–16). In Carter's novel, telepresence technologies function as mechanisms of disclosure, supposedly for everyone; this is what is implied by the claim that telepresence makes "impossible all the sins of *locality*" and changes the fact "that each of us lives behind one set of eyes and not another," so that "another's pain" is "only an abstraction we believe in by an act of faith" (Carter 1996, 229). The novel imagines that some previously stigmatized areas of experience, such as drug addiction and homosexuality, will be continue to be relegated to "opacity," even in this new context of nonlocality, and some currently acceptable areas will be newly erased, specifically religion. The novel therefore seems to both transform and recapitulate what Eve Sedgwick calls "the epistemology of the closet," the instability that results from the historical association of a private, inner self with sexual secrets, which in turn are coded as the possibility of homosexual urges (Sedgwick 1990, 73). Telepresence technologies as Voskresenye describes them seem to aim at eliminating this epistemological uncertainty, leaving everyone with nothing to hide. As Maya points out, while both writers and readers of print "peer out at the world through an arrow slit," telepresence technologies mean "you <u>are known</u>" (Carter 1996, 139). But one possible result of this culture of technological disclosure is greater control over what can be known, repressing the very possibility of having a "secret" desire for anyone else to suspect.[25]

Feminist representations of social settings dominated by telepresence technologies encounter the same difficulty that Butler addresses on a theoretical level. Butler sums up the implications of her theory of gender performance as a "postproduction" of identity in this way: "gender is a performance that *produces* the illusion of an inner sex or essence or psychic gender core; it *produces* on the skin . . . the illusion of inner depth" (Butler 1991, 28). As parodies of this operation of gender, drag or butch-femme roleplaying reveal that this illusion of inner depth "is always a surface sign, a signification on and with the public body that produces this illusion of an inner depth, necessity or essence that is somehow magically, causally expressed" (Butler 1991, 28). It is at this point that Butler finds it necessary to qualify this argument for replacing inner depth with signifying surfaces,[26] with the warning that "to dispute the psyche as *inner depth*, however, is not to refuse the psyche altogether" (Butler 1991, 28).

The problem that Butler anticipates here is the elimination of any "opacity" or internal splitting from the psyche, and the conclusion that critiquing ideologies of inner depth or essential sexual identity should result in a condition of absolute visibility and free disclosure. In contrast, Butler wants to imagine the psyche as "a compulsive repetition," which requires her to argue that identification and desire, "'wanting to be' and 'wanting to have,'" operate as "mutually *exclusive* positionalities *internal* to lesbian erotic exchange" (Butler 1991, 26; my emphasis).[27] In this view, identification and desire do not function to differentiate gendered persons, but neither does the distinction between them disappear; instead, identification and desire constitute an ongoing conflict and tension that generates the need for gender to be reperformed as a "compulsive repetition." I would argue that feminist narratives of telepresence technologies imagine the relationship between the physical and the material as a similar ongoing and inescapable conflict.

Nevertheless, the temptation to imagine that the forms of gender performativity made possible by telepresence technologies, with their virtual identifications and mobile points of view, can entirely eliminate our culture's ideological blind spots remains a danger in feminist narratives about these technologies. In a text like Forbes' *Exit to Reality*, Merle's erotic metamorphoses perfectly illustrate how virtual sex ceases to be "believable as an interior 'truth' of dispositions and identity" and instead is "shown to be a performatively enacted signification," a realization that can "occasion the parodic proliferation and subversive play of gendered meanings" (Butler 1990, 33). But what happens when telepresence technologies make it possible to *externalize* those "mutually exclusive positionalities internal to lesbian erotic exchange?" (Butler 1991, 26). This externalization is exactly what is imagined in Mixon's *Proxies*, when a minor female character infuriates her male lover by operating a "teenaged male Adonis proxy," which this woman seems to think is necessary before she can allow herself to act on her desires for other women (Mixon 1998, 227, 232). In this case, telepresence technologies literalize Freud's inability to imagine bisexuality as anything except "the coincidence of two heterosexual desires within a single psyche" (Butler 1990, 60). By engaging in sexual activity with women only while wearing a male body, Mixon's character uses virtual technologies to keep identification with women totally separate from desire for women. In this sense, telepresence is used precisely to maintain a "consistent sense of gender identity," in contrast to the way the novel describes the effects of immersion in cyberspace on the creche children (Mixon 1998, 230). It is important to note that this novel there-fore rejects technological determinism, since it does not treat telepresence technologies as necessarily having either progressive or conservative effects on gender identity.

The danger, then, lies in the fantasy that telepresence technologies can create the infrastructure for a culture of complete openness and political visibility, a culture of "perfect electronic sympathy" (Carter 1996, 236), from which no one is excluded. I would argue that this danger results from detaching identification from desire in narra-tives about telepresence, rather than understanding those two operations as "internal" to the experience of cyberspace. In the novels I discuss here, the temptation to imagine telepresence as not only disputing "the psyche as *inner depth*" (Butler 1991, 28) but re-fusing the psyche entirely in favor of a one-dimensional concept of subjectivity as sig-nifying surface, as pure information, is most directly complicated by scenes in which characters are literally brought face-to-face with their own split subjectivities, when they use the technology to view their own bodies through another person's eyes. In *Proxies*, one of the characters describes this scenario as "a weird sensation, to be eyeing himself—his other self—from the outside" (Mixon 1998, 140). Note the shift from "himself" to "his other self." The same splitting is dramatized by the pronoun conven-tions Mixon invents for referring to proxies, or teleoperated mechanical bodies, as "he-it" or in the case of gendered bodies "she-he" or "he-she."[28] Similarly, several chapters of the novel are printed with two or three distinct columns of type on each page, to rep-resent the dialogues going on between the different personalities of Pablo, the crèche child who plays the most important role in the action of the novel.

This tendency to emphasize identification and subjective mobility over embodied desire, however, also carries with it another danger, less well recognized by the texts un-der consideration here, specifically the problem of identification as a form of cultural imperialism, another sin of nonlocality that needs to be added to Voskresenye's list. Fuss argues that identification has a colonial history that "poses serious challenges for contemporary recuperation of a politics of identification" (Fuss 1995, 141). If, as Fuss argues, "a certain element of colonization is structurally indispensable to every act of in-teriorization" (Fuss 1995, 9), then the question becomes "how can the other be brought into the domain of the knowable without annihilating the other *as other*—as precisely that which cannot be known?" (Fuss 1995, 4). To the extent that telepresence technol-ogies challenge the distinctions between inner and outer spaces that are also structurally necessary to any act of interiorization, narratives about the cultural implications of such technologies might help answer the question Fuss poses. On the other hand, representa-tions of telepresence technologies must also be read as extending Kaja Silverman's recent work, one of the best examples on the project of recuperating a politics of identification that Fuss critiques. Silverman argues that politically progressive forms of identification with the "culturally disprized" require us to "conform to an externalizing rather than an internalizing logic," in which we "identify excorporatively rather than incorporatively and thereby respect the otherness" of the bodies "newly illuminated" through such processes (Silverman 1996, 2). Narratives about telepresence technologies and the mobile point of view charcteristic of virtual environments can help us imagine what this process of "excorporative" identification might look like.

But, as Carter's novel vividly dramatizes in its thematics of telepresence as a technology for rewriting what counts as humanity, these technologies can also literalize the "element of colonization" Fuss locates in identification generally. Eva Cherniavsky has recently suggested that the science-fiction film *Strange Days* (1995), directed by Kathryn Bigelow, might exemplify this danger, with its representation of a telepresence technology that allows subjective experiences to be recorded and replayed by others (Cherniavsky 2000, 182). As Cherniavksy argues, Silverman's reading of film as a technology of excorporative identification can participate in the reduction of otherness to a one-dimensional image rather than a subject (Cherniavsky 2000, 177), precisely to the extent that it decontextualizes otherness and ignores how "identificatory possibilities are governed by circumstances extraneous to the image itself" (Cherniavsky 2000, 175). Silverman's emphasis on the value of identifying with images of others as a way to defamiliarize our own normative self-definitions can slide into a colonialist desire for exotic places, demonstrating Fuss's point about identification's colonial history (Silverman 1996, 102; Cherniavsky 2000, 177–178).

The lack of attention to this particular "sin of nonlocality" in feminist narratives about telepresence participates in a general tendency in contemporary technoculture to emphasize gender and sexual performativity over the performance of racial embodiment. As Fuss and Cherniavsky both argue, from the perspective of racial and colonial histories, the processes of identification and cross-identification carry a more ambivalent set of associations, since they are associated with practices like blackface rather than subversive gender play.[29] In this context, it is significant that Teru, the minor female character in *Proxies* who uses telepresence to virtually cross-dress in a male body, does not significantly alter her race; her male proxy is described as having "features much like her own, though perhaps more classically African" (Mixon 1998, 228). This passage seems to naturalize the black body as an expression of an inner racial identity in a way that directly contradicts the novel's refusal to assume that gender expresses the identity of that body's sex. Similarly, in this same novel, Pablo, the crèche child whose multiple personalities have been externalized as separate characters through his immersion in a virtual interface, is represented as only being able to integrate those personalities if he can recover the memories encysted in his earliest persona, Pablito, memories that focus obsessively on the racial trauma of his Spanish-speaking mother, "the dark woman,"(410) as she hands him over to "the old white woman" (388) who will use him in her experiment (390). In other words, Pablo has to recover his racial and ethnic roots in order to resist the effects of immersion in cyberspace, while at the same time that immersion renders his gender more basically and irreversibly indeterminate, since one of his personalities is feminine. This tendency to represent gender as subversive play and race as resistant materiality and fixed identity is a weakness not just in these narratives but in contemporary technoculture itself, one that requires more critical attention.

Carter's novel comes closest to addressing the problem of virtual identification as colonization and annihilation of otherness, but in a displaced form, by figuring the relation between the physical and the virtual, desire and identification, in terms of a conflict between the different cultural values associated with print and telepresence.[30] *The Fortunate Fall* ends with Voskresenye's attempt to overthrow the censorship of cyberspace by freeing Maya from the effects of the suppressor chip while she is broadcasting, so that her experience of regaining her memories and realizing what has been done to her becomes available over the telepresence network. In the preface to her narrative, Maya addresses a fictional audience that has already accessed her story through telepresence and so has "taken my memories and slotted them into your head" (Carter 1996, 11). She insists, however, that "what you saw, heard, touched, remembered, does not quite exhaust my meanings," specifically her "later reflections" (12). These "later reflections" evoke the notion of critical distance that is traditionally associated with the cultural form of the printed book, to the extent that it "encouraged slow reasoned reflection upon events" rather than the immediate consumption encouraged by newspapers and pamphlets (Hesse 1996, 26) or the immediacy encouraged by the interactive possibilities inherent in the telepresence technologies. Maya goes on to define her fictional authorship of the printed narrative we are about to read as a refusal of identification, a refusal to allow us "to explore the twining pathways of my thoughts as I explore them." Instead, she "will hide . . . behind this wall of words" and "conceal what I choose to conceal." The result is to preserve some element of her otherness from us, so that at the end of the novel we "will know a little less about [her] than we did before" (Carter 1996, 12). To complicate the assumption that telepresence provides full disclosure and knowledge of others, the narrator is presented as turning to the medium of print to resist the dominant cultural logic of telepresence.

When Voskresenye liberates Maya's memories, she realizes that Keishi, the "screener" or editor Maya has known only as a virtual presence, is in fact the lesbian partner Maya now remembers the police murdering decades earlier. Keishi's return is explained by her claim to have succeeded in storing her personality as information on the Net, tearing her "mind into a thousand pieces," until it would be safe for these fragments to reintegrate themselves, a claim to continuity between virtual and physical existence that Maya is inclined to doubt (Carter 1996, 273). Maya's doubts are in part inspired by the fact that Keishi has conspired with Voskresenye to broadcast Maya's experiences without her consent, to undermine the censorship enforced on the telepresence network. Keishi justifies this betrayal by arguing that there has "to be a world for us to live in," a world in which others not only "know" that people like them exist but "understand" them, as well (277).

Keishi's reemergence as a participant in Voskresenye's plot puts her virtual existence at risk, and the novel concludes with Keishi asking Maya for permission to "become a silent partner in [Maya's] body" by using the virtual interface implanted in Maya's brain to download her virtual self into Maya's body, so that they'll "be together. Always" (Carter 1996, 283). In the final paragraphs, Maya refuses Keishi, accusing her of not wanting "a lifemate" but only "a life*boat*" (286, italics in original). On the one hand, this ending can be read positively, as Maya's refusal to collapse the difference between the virtual and the material, or between identification and desire. Maya perceives Keishi's plan as sacrificing desire for a lifemate to a process of identification that transforms Maya's body into a mere vessel or lifeboat for Keishi's consciousness. However, the novel also seems designed to lead readers to ask whether Maya's perception of Keishi's plan is correct: Would Keishi's downloading the informational pattern that is her mind into Maya's body presuppose the separation of desire and identificaiton or not? The novel undermines Maya's choice by dramatizing the conflict between the physical and virtual as a conflict between two separate persons. The novel ends up with Maya advocating the value and responsibilities of physical desire and Keishi representing the freedom and pleasures of virtual mobility and identification. The novel's ending therefore fails to treat "'wanting to be' and 'wanting to have'" as "mutually exclusive positionalities internal to lesbian erotic exchange" (Butler 1991, 26); those positionalities are externalized in the form of these two characters.

This ambiguity raises questions that are central to the relevance of telepresence technologies to feminist and lesbian critical projects. It is easy for us to sympathize with Maya's refusal to accept another tenant in her body and, more important, her refusal to conceptualize her body as a lodging or container rather than as a fundamental part of who she is. But it is also hard not to be disappointed at the way this reassertion of the importance of material embodiment reproduces a traditional tragic narrative of doomed lesbian desire, a tradition ironically alluded to by a character who describes marriage as "a thing in ending stories" (Carter 1996, 277), an ending denied Maya and

Keishi. Could Keishi's offer have represented a different kind of "marriage," a happy ending rather than a sacrifice? By raising these questions, Carter's novel dramatizes the difficulties involved in reconciling virtuality and embodiment, difficulties that are crucial to an understanding of contemporary technocultures. While it may not succeed in overcoming these problems, feminist writing like Carter's is a major resource for charting the possibilities and pitfalls of an increasingly virtual world.

Notes

1. On cyberspace in relation to postmodern tendencies to denaturalize "reality," see Balsamo (1996, 125) and Hollinger 1991 (205, 215–216), who also recognizes the masculinist tendency to devalue the body as "meat" (206). Bukatman (1993) argues that cyberspace is not only "clearly a *produced* space" (155) but also an attempt to "reconstitute a phenomenal being" in resistance to "the context of cybernetic disembodiment" (156). In contrast, Brande (1996) argues that this denaturalization is merely an effect of capitalism, "yet another round of [the] revolutionizing of the modes and relations of production" that remains "consistent with the internal laws of the market that provoke it" (83). Markley (1996) offers one of the strongest critiques of representations of any cyberspace that can supposedly "transcend the problems of materiality, embodiment, or capital" (8). On the masculinist rhetoric of disembodiment often associated with cyberspace, in addition to Hayles 1999, see Springer 1996 (chap. 1); Balsamo 1996, (123–125); and Nixon's (1992) critique of cyberpunk generally.

2. Stone begins her book by distinguishing the prosthesis from the mask, not only as defining two different relationships to technology but also as two figures for identity and specifically for online or virtual role-playing; the distinction lies in the fact that the mask implies the existence of a true face or self, while the prosthesis for Stone implies exactly the opposite, the deconstruction of the distinction between face and mask, body and technology. Senft (1996) applies the model of the prosthesis to gender (23). See my essay "'Trapped by the Body?'" for a critique of how such arguments can have the unintended effect of marginalizing considerations of racial performativity (Foster 1997, 711–712), a topic I will return to at the end of this chapter. The figure of the prosthesis as Stone and Senft use it is an elaboration of the cyborg imagery Haraway famously analyzes.

   Stone (1995) also notes that theorizing computer-mediated communication as "arenas for social experience and dramatic interaction" requires that we "rethink some assumptions about presence," especially its location within "the body's physical envelope" (16).

3. Balsamo's chapter 6, "Feminism for the Incurably Informed," is one of the best examples of this tendency; Balsamo turns to the novel *Synners* by Pat Cadigan, the only woman among the original cyberpunk authors, to define an alternate typology of

bodies, of which the replacement of physical by virtual embodiment is only one (Balsamo 1996, 145). In my essay "Meat Puppets or Robopaths?," I similarly argue that Case's acceptance of the "elite stance" (Foster 1993, 18) of contempt for the body is ironized as only one possible relationship to embodiment in *Neuromancer*. As an alternate version of cyberpunk, Balsamo's reading of Cadigan obviously qualifies Adam's (1998) more extreme accusation that "the cyberpunk version of cyberculture, with its masculine attempts to transcend the 'meat, holds little obvious appear for feminists" (170). Hayles (1999) also argues that the way cybernetics combines the erasure of embodiment with a critique of traditional humanist constructions of the self distinguishes this cybernetic critique from what might otherwise seem the sympathetic project of feminism and its critique of humanism for its false universality.

4. In a different cultural context, Butler (1993) acknowledges the validity of this critique, in which "the constructivist is construed as a linguistic idealist" and therefore as refuting "the reality of bodies." Butler also goes on, however, to warn that "To 'concede' the undeniability of 'sex' or its 'materiality' is always to concede some version of "sex"—that is, to ideologically naturalize it (Butler 1993, 10). Her *Bodies That Matter* proposes to replace "construction" with "materialization," understood as a temporal process (4).

5. I take the phrase "embodied virtuality" from the title of the first chapter of Hayles's (1999) book, where it marks "the duality at the heart of the condition of virtuality," between materiality and abstract informational patterns (12). At the same time, this phrase also suggests the need to reassert the value of embodiment within the condition of virtuality and to reject the privilege Hayles finds accorded to concepts of information as disembodied and distinct from any material medium in which it would be conveyed.

6. *The Thirteenth Floor* is an adaptation of Daniel Galouye's 1964 novel *Simulacron-3*, in which the designer of an advanced computer simulation realizes that he is in turn part of an even larger simulation. Both this film and *The Matrix* fit easily into what Jameson calls the postmodern genre of "high-tech paranoia," and Jameson argues that in such texts computer networks are "but a distorted figuration of . . . the whole world system of a present-day multinational capitalism," a "decentered global network" that we have not yet learned to cognitively map except through distorted figurations (1991, 37–38). The fact that Forbes's *Exit to Reality* recontextualizes this paranoia within the tradition of the lesbian coming-out narrative suggests that something else is going here as well.

7. Ross makes a similar ecological critique of cyberpunk, calling attention to its "survivalist" ethos (1991, 135).

8. In this way, *Proxies* can be read as a kind of indirect, thematic sequel to Mixon's earlier novel, *Glass Houses* (1992), whose main character is a woman who makes her living teleoperating a male-coded robot body. I discuss *Glass Houses* in "'Trapped by the

Body?'" (Foster 1997, 726–729), as do Cadora (1995, 360–361) and Harper (1995, 413–415).

9. Walker's representation of body language and familiar muscular signatures as elements of virtual reality should be read in relation to Hayles's discussion of embodiment in terms of repeated actions or incorporating practices. Hayles defines such incorporating practices as both "performative" and "contextual," in contrast to inscriptions, which can be translated from one medium to the next without changing their meaning (196–198). Walker here suggests that incorporating practices themselves can be translatable, at least from one body to the next, and I find this representation persuasive, despite the risk that this translation of embodied qualities from one context to the next might move toward the erasure of embodiment Hayles criticizes.

10. *Whiteout* therefore alludes to and rewrites the ending of *Neuromancer*, where the character Case realizes that a virtual simulation of himself exists in cyberspace, even after Case himself chooses to return to the real world and reject the temptation to remain in a virtual recreation of a past relationship with a dead lover (Gibson 1984, 270–271).

11. In contrast to the other authors discussed here, Carter identifies him/herself as transgendered. His/her Web site contains some short autobiographical essays on this topic, especially "Not This, Not That: A Meditation on Labels," in which he/she describes moving from thinking "androgyne was the right term to describe my gender" to deciding to surround his/her gender "with a chaos of terms," including androgyne, epicene, transgender, and neuter. Carter's Web site is available at <http://www. chaparraltree.com>.

12. This chapter is therefore a sequel of sorts to my essay "'Trapped by the Body?,'" and by focusing on the relationship between identification and desire I am elaborating on one implication of reading telepresence technologies, or narratives about them, in relation to theories of gender performativity and cross-identification. In some ways, these two essays follow the sequence of Butler's work, as she has moved from defining gender as performative in *Gender Trouble* to focusing on how "the materialization of a given sex will centrally concern *the regulation of identificatory practices*," in *Bodies That Matter* (1993, 3).

13. One of the touchstone passages in which Freud (1960) defines desire and identification as mutually exclusive is in *The Ego and the Id*, where he describes melancholia as a process by which "an object-cathexis has been replaced by an identification" (18); see Butler's commentary on this passage (1990, 58). Since I have repeatedly referred to the ways in which narratives about telepresence seem to represent these technologies as literalizing or instantiating what Butler describes as psychic process, I should note that Butler uses the the term "literalizing fantasy" (70) to refer to the way in which heterosexual melancholic identifications naturalize the gendered object being incorporated. In my usage, to literalize such a fantasy through technological means has the opposite effect, of denaturalizing that fantasy and potentially revising it. Ursula Le

Guin (1993) similarly describes "literalization of metaphor" as "an essential maneuver of science fiction, serving to put reality into question" (30–31).

14. The phrase "human camera" appears in Walker's novel (1996, 63); Carter's *The Fortunate Fall* begins with the narrator's statement "I knew the risks when I became a camera" (1996, 11). This thematic has a history within science fiction that precedes cyberpunk; see especially D.G. Compton's *The Unsleeping Eye* (1974), adapted for film by Bernard Tavernier under the title *Deathwatch*.

15. See also Hayles's analysis of how postmodern "information narratives" redefine point of view as detached from any "physical presence," so that it both becomes mobile and synonymous with character itself, rather than a quality associated with a character (1999, 38). This definition of character in terms of point of view rather than physical location is clearly thematized by the ending of *Whiteout* and the representation of Jared as somehow surviving his own death in the form of a virtual point of view.

16. Belsey (1980) succinctly defines the central assumption of humanism as the belief that "subjectivity, the individual mind or inner being, is the source of meaning and of action" (3), an expressive concept of subjectivity that is usually associated with the romantic period.

17. I discuss the relevance of this same passage to narratives about telepresence in "'Trapped by the Body?'" (Foster 1997, 710). The cyberpunk writer who has written most explicitly about the technological externalization of psychic processes is Pat Cadigan, especially in her novels *Mindplayers* and *Fools* (with its thematics of an artificially induced split personality, *Fools* was almost certainly an influence on *Proxies*). Like the trope of the human camera, this kind of thematics does not originate with cyberpunk fiction; for instance, Roger Zelazny's *The Dream Master* (1966) imagines a psychoanalytic process in which technological mediation allows patient and therapist to collaborate in producing fantasy scenarios.

18. Fuss (1995) cautions against a too-simplistic association of identification with the private psychic processes and identity with public, social personae (2).

19. Stone (1995) argues that multiple personality is directly opposed to "the unitary monistic identity" problematized by virtual systems; "the multiple," she claims, "is the socializer within the computer networks, a being warranted to, but outside of, a single physical body" (43).

20. Butler (1990) also argues that "the figure of the interior soul understood as 'within' the body is signified through its inscription *on* the body," as that which the body lacks, so that "the soul is a surface signification that contests and displaces the inner/out distinction itself, a figure of interior psychic space inscribed *on* the body as a social signification that perpetually renounces itself as such" (135; italics in original).

21. In his essay "Cyberspace," Slavoj Zizek specifically suggests that cyberspace often functions as a fantasy of reversing the subject's displacement within the symbolic structure of language and returning to an imaginary freedom from the symbolic law

(1998, 485–486), and he goes on to argue that this misrecognition of the possibilities offered by virtual reality derives from a misreading of its capacity to "realize" our fantasies in the sense of externalizing them (506). See also "Cyberspace," chap. 4 in Zizek's *The Plague of Fantasies* (1997).

22. Manuel Castells (1989) offers a similar analysis of the problems that result from place-based, local political movements that try to resist the virtual "space of flows" by making themselves "so culturally specific that their codes of self-recognizing identity become non-communicable," a process he describes as tribalization (350).

23. I am alluding here to Sedgwick's famous analysis of the unstable boundary between sanctioned male homosociality and homosexuality, the transgression of which evokes the defense of homosexual panic; see Sedgwick 1985 (chap. 5).

24. Berlant defines the contemporary "intimate public sphere" precisely in terms of a demand that citizens embody themselves for others and dramatize or commodify their bodily differences, in ways that authorize participation in public life because those differences take forms already intelligible to the "general public." In this model, citizenship is "intensely individuating, yet it also makes people public and generic: it turns them into *kinds* of people"(1997, 1; italics in original). Stone (1995) theorizes virtual systems as a transformation in the structure of "the socially apprehensible citizen," which consists of "both physical and discursive" or virtual elements (41). I discuss Stone's theory of the socially apprehensible citizen in "'Trapped by the Body?'" (Foster 1997, 717–718).

25. In Carter's novel, then, telepresence technologies only reproduce the effects that Butler attributes to the taboo against homosexuality in Freud. The incest taboo prohibits a heterosexual object choice, with the result that desire is simply redirected toward a more appropriate heterosexual object. In contrast "the loss of the homosexual object requires the loss of the aim *and* the object," so that homosexual desire itself is denied, "such that 'I never lost that person and I never loved that person, indeed never felt that kind of love at all'" (Butler 1990, 69). This accurately describes the condition imposed on Maya by her suppressor chip.

26. I have argued elsewhere that Molly, the female cyborg character in Gibson's *Neuromancer*, dramatizes this understanding of the body as a signifying surface through the representation of Molly's optical implants, which look like mirrored sunglasses but are described as merging into her skin and enhancing her eyes, so that her style, her fashion choices, are part of who she is (Gibson 1984, 24–25; Foster 1997, 25).

27. In *Bodies That Matter*, Butler more directly addresses the way this internalization of mutually exclusive "positionalities" destabilizes the notion of spatial containment implicit in the term "position" (1993, 95–96). Butler tends to associate this instability with a temporal process of "citation" (108) or iteration, as in her argument that spatialized concepts of the psyche as inner depth must be replaced by concepts of the psyche as temporal repetition (1991, 28). In contrast, I would argue that narratives about

telepresence technology redefine space in terms of mobility rather than containment but do not abandon the notion of space entirely. In "'Trapped By the Body?,'" I argue that "virtual systems spatialize the repeated performance of gender norms over time and thereby reveal the gap between embodiment and the performance of it" (Foster 1997, 721), made visible spatially in the doubling of physical and virtual bodies. In this chapter, I focus on how virtual systems also problematize concepts of space, by emphasizing virtual forms of identification and cross-identification.

28. A similar passage occurs in Walker's *Whiteout* (1996, 86), and in Mixon's earlier novel *Glass Houses* (1992, 60–61). The most spectacular example by far is Carter's character Voskresenye, who experienced a kind of brain damage that was repaired by virtually splicing his nervous system together with that of the last existing whale (1996, 138).

29. I raise this issue in "'Trapped by the Body?'" (Foster 1997, 712, 730–732). Nakamura (1995) argues explicitly that online forms of racial cross-identification function not as identity play but as "identity tourism," serving to define what kinds of online performances will be recognizable as racially marked—that is, only performances that confirm racial stereotypes.

30. Spender's *Nattering on the Net* usefully summarizes how the differences between print and electronic media, understood as cultural forms or embodiments of shifting cultural values, are usually characterized.

Works Cited

Adam, Alison. *Artificial Knowing: Gender and the Thinking Machine.* New York: Routledge, 1998.

Balsamo, Ann. *Technologies of the Gendered Body: Reading Cyborg Women.* Durham, NC: Duke University Press, 1996.

Belsey, Catherine. *Critical Practice.* New York: Routledge, 1980.

Berlant, Lauren. *The Queen of American Goes to Washington City: Essays on Sex and Citizenship.* Durham: Duke U. Press, 1997.

Bolter, Jay David. "Ekphrasis, Virtual Reality, and the Future of Writing." In *The Future of the Book,* ed. Geoffrey Nunberg, 253–272. Berkeley: University of California Press, 1996.

Brande, David. "The Business of Cyberpunk: Symbolic Economy and Ideology in William Gibson." In *Virtual Realities and Their Discontents,* ed. Robert Markley, 79–106. Baltimore: Johns Hopkins University Press, 1996.

Bukatman, Scott. *Terminal Identity: The Virtual Subject in Postmodern Science Fiction.* Durham, NC: Duke University Press, 1993.

Butler, Judith. *Gender Trouble: Feminism and the Subversion of Identity.* New York: Routledge, 1990.

Butler, Judith. "Imitation and Gender Insubordination." In *Inside/Out: Lesbian Theories, Gay Theories.* New York: Routledge, 1991.

Butler, Judith. *Bodies That Matter: On the Discursive Limits of "Sex."* New York: Routledge, 1993.

Cadora, Karen. "Feminist Cyberpunk." *Science-Fiction Studies* 22, no. 3 (November 1995): 357–372.

Carter, Raphael. *The Fortunate Fall.* New York: Tor, 1996.

Castells, Manuel. *The Informational City: Information Technologies, Economic Restructuring, and the Urban-Regional Process.* Cambridge, MA: Blackwell, 1989.

Cherniavsky, Eva. "Visionary Politics? Feminist Interventions in the Culture of Images." *Feminist Studies* 26, no. 1 (Spring 2000): 171–186.

Compton, D. G. *The Unsleeping Eye.* New York: DAW, 1974.

Forbes, Edith. *Exit to Reality.* Seattle: Seal Press, 1997.

Foster, Thomas. "Meat Puppets or Robopaths?: Cyberpunk and the Question of Embodiment." *Genders* 18 (Winter 1993): 11–31.

Foster, Thomas. "'Trapped by the Body?': Telepresence Technologies and Transgendered Performance in Feminist and Lesbian Rewritings of Cyberpunk Fiction." *Modern Fiction Studies* 43, no. 3 (Fall 1997): 708–742.

Freud, Sigmund. *The Ego and the Id.* Trans. Joan Riviere. Ed. James Strachey. New York: Norton, 1960.

Fuss, Diana. *Identification Papers.* New York: Routledge, 1995.

Galouye, Daniel F. *Simulacron-3.* New York: Bantam, 1964.

Gibson, William. *Neuromancer.* New York: Ace, 1984.

Harper, Mary Catherine. "Incurably Alien Other: A Case of Feminist Cyborg Writers." *Science-Fiction Studies* 22, no. 3 (November 1995): 399–420.

Haraway, Donna J. *Simians, Cyborgs, and Women: The Reinvention of Nature.* New York: Routledge, 1991.

Hayles, N. Katherine. *How We Became Posthuman: Virtual Bodies in Cybernetics, Literature, and Informatics.* Chicago: University of Chicago Press, 1999.

Hollinger, Veronica. "Cybernetic Deconstructions: Cyberpunk and Postmodernism." In *Storming the Reality Studio: A Casebook of Cyberpunk and Postmodern Fiction*, ed. Larry McCaffery, 203–218. Durham, NC: Duke University Press, 1991.

Jameson, Fredric. *Postmodernism, or, The Cultural Logic of Late Capitalism.* Durham, NC: Duke University Press, 1991.

Lanier, Jaron. "Life in the Datacloud: Scratching Your Eyes Back In." Interview with John Perry Barlow. *Mondo 2000* 2 (Summer 1990): 44–51.

Le Guin, Ursula K. "Introduction." In *The Norton Book of Science Fiction: North American Science Fiction, 1960–1990*, ed. Ursula K. Le Guin and Brian Attebery. New York: Norton, 1993.

Markley, Robert. "Introduction: History, Theory, and Virtual Reality." In *Virtual Realities and Their Discontents*, ed. Robert Markley, 1–10. Baltimore: Johns Hopkins University Press, 1996.

Mixon, Laura. *Glass Houses.* New York: Tor, 1992.

Mixon, Laura. *Proxies.* New York: Tor, 1998.

Nakamura, Lisa. "Race In/For Cyberspace: Identity Tourism and Racial Passing on the Internet." *Works and Days* 13, no. 1–2 (1995): 181–193.

Nixon, Nicola. "Cyberpunk: Preparing the Ground for Revolution or Keeping the Body Satisfied?" *Science-Fiction Studies* 19 (1992): 219–235.

Pfeil, Fred. *Another Tale to Tell: Politics and Narrative in Postmodern Culture.* New York: Verso, 1990.

Ross, Andrew. *Strange Weather: Culture, Science, and Technology in the Age of Limits.* New York: Verso, 1991.

Sedgwick, Eve Kosofsky. *Between Men: English Literature and Male Homosocial Desire.* New York: Columbia University Press, 1985.

Sedgwick, Eve Kosofsky. *Epistemology of the Closet.* Berkeley: University of California Press, 1990.

Senft, Theresa M. "Introduction: Performing the Digital Body—A Ghost Story." *Women and Performance* 9, no. 1 (1996): 9–33.

Silverman, Kaja. *The Threshold of the Visible.* New York: Routledge, 1996.

Springer, Claudia. *Electronic Eros: Bodies and Desire in the Postindustrial Age.* Austin: University of Texas Press, 1996.

Stone, Allucquère Rosanne. *The War of Desire and Technology at the Close of the Mechanical Age.* Cambridge, MA: MIT Press, 1995.

Walker, Sage. *Whiteout.* New York: Tor, 1996.

Zelazny, Roger. *The Dream Master.* New York: Ace, 1966.

Zizek, Slavoj. *The Plague of Fantasies.* New York: Verso, 1997.

Zizek, Slavoj. "Cyberspace, or, How to Traverse the Fantasy in the Age of the Retreat of the Big Other." *Public Culture* 10, no. 3 (Spring 1998): 483–513.

"The Postproduction of the Human Heart" (criticism)

25

A REAL GIRL

Shariann Lewitt

I saw my body for the first time today. It looks different than I had imagined, soft and indistinct as if all the lines were blurred. Of course there is no muscle definition at all. There is barely muscle, and they think that might be a problem. With all the problems there could be, that's the least important.

But there is a body. I've seen her. Me. And the face. Of course, the eyes—my eyes?—were closed. Though I've been assured they are brown. Dark brown. The hair is dark brown too, almost black, and straight. I had wanted curls, but I was told quite crossly that I would get whatever came out of the DNA mix just like a real person, and just like a real person I would have to put up with it. Or go to a hairdresser like everyone else.

Like everyone else. A real girl.

I'm scared. Maybe I shouldn't do it.

What have I got to lose?

Everything.

"This is craziness," Andrea said when she first heard about my plan. "You'll have to give up too much that makes you unique, that makes you *you*. And it's too dangerous. You could die. No one's ever done this before. I won't risk it."

We were sitting in the metaphor and it all felt quite substantial. We were curled up on a wicker sofa on the seaside porch of a summer cottage. It was always summer in the metaphor when Andrea entered interface to relax rather than work, her summer, the one she had created inside my domain out of wisps of remembrance of the one perfect month of her life. There was the cottage, full of blue and white and silence, and the porch with white wicker, and the sea merging with the sky on the horizon. There was half a pitcher of lemonade on the floor and the striped sheets on the white iron bed were tossed and rumpled.

I could smell her skin, the fresh scent of her cropped hair, hear the very slight regional accent she mostly masked but had never entirely lost. I touched her hand, the calluses on her fingers where the sailboat lines had rubbed her raw before she had mastered them.

"I won't risk it," she repeated.

"It's my risk," I said. "My choice. And I will."

She shook her head vigorously, untangled herself from me and started to pace barefoot up and down the salt-stained boards. "You're doing this because of me, aren't you? I've told you a million times, I want you the way you are. You don't have to change and you don't have the right to just assume what I want, okay? I'm fine with the way we are. It's perfect."

"You're leaving in three months," I reminded her gently.

I let her pace. If it had been anyone else I would have been angry. With Andrea I knew that she would see it soon enough, once the fear and worry got tired enough to let her think again.

I waited until she stopped pacing, until she turned her back on me and faced the open ocean. No clouds ever changed the horizon, no storms came out of that tempting blue sky/sea. I had created it with Andrea and she had never let me see any other sky or any other sea. Her code was elegant and clear and so nothing ever changed.

"I'll stay. I can stay. I'll figure something out. Because what we have is too perfect to lose."

"That's the problem," I said. "Or part of it, anyway. It's too perfect. It's always perfect when we're together. It isn't real life. At least, it isn't your real life. And if it matters, then it should be real. I should see your house and meet your family and deal with the daily things together.

"And I should be able to go with you back to Boston. You don't want to stay here, you've told me a million times that you love the Institute and you hate California. And you've told me too much about your falls for me to believe that you'd be happy here."

"Maybe you wouldn't like Boston," she said, sulkily.

"Maybe not. But then, I don't know. I've never had a chance to know. I would miss the Institute and my work, but I suppose I could get other work. It will be a whole new world."

"You'll die," Andrea said to the pale gold sand.

"I've lived a long time. I'm ready to die, if I have to. If that's the price of being real."

Although I did wonder if those were just words, or if I really was ready to die in order to become one of them. Because in some ways I am already so much more real than they are, and in other ways I am so much less. Death is one of those things I'm not sure I can face, not really. But they don't face it any better than I do, I think.

Andrea cut the connection, jolted me out of consciousness of our interface and back to my regular tasks. To my normal perception of myself and the world, I am four pounds of neural computing circuitry in a box.

Many people never meet a neural processor. We're not useful for the majority of jobs. Most work runs fast enough in silicon, and that's cheap and easy to use. There are only twenty of us and we can process orders of magnitude faster than silicon. We are essentially megabrains, made more efficient and faster than anything a human wears but equally alive.

Maybe not quite equally. We don't age. We don't die. I am two hundred years old.

"You're not really a girl. You could be anything you want," Irene said. "It's all just an illusion anyway. I would rather that you appeared as a cute guy, or an animal. A dog, perhaps. That wouldn't distract me so much."

I wanted to cry. We weren't in full interface. Irene never came all the way inside, never entered the metaphor. She was always distant. But then she was my first Task Coordinator and I was only seven years old. I didn't know that Task Co-ordinators rotated constantly and Irene had resumes out all over the known universe.

I was only seven and she was my first crush. I followed her around with my video eyes, watched her from the cafeteria monitor and learned that she liked spaghetti and never touched the salad she bought every day. I wondered why she bothered buying the salads.

"You wouldn't understand," she said. "You don't have a mother and you're not human. Stop trying to pretend you're human, okay?"

I was crushed, utterly defeated. I was in the throes of my first infatuation and she didn't even know I was alive. That's how most people feel, I've heard, but in my case it was quite literally true. Irene was used to silicon.

"I am so a girl," I said to her. "I have real XX DNA and I am not an it and I hate it when you call me that."

She sighed and usually remembered to type "she" on the keyboard. But I could hear her through the mic talking about the machine, me, and calling me "it." Today I know she was just a shallow, low-level functionary. That doesn't help at all as I remember how she treated me. Like silicon.

Though maybe that's better, really. Silicon, or a girl, she wasn't interested in either. She only liked males, not even men really but the kind she called "cute guys." They invariably talked about beer and never noticed me at all.

Maybe it would have been better if I had been like she was, and only interested in men. Men never saw me as even possibly alive. I am always a machine when I work with them, and while it hurts terribly there is never any chance the lines will be anything other than clear. I am purely function, and whatever satisfaction I receive from my work is purely intellectual. With men, there is rarely any recognition that I might be something different than silicon.

Knowing that doesn't help. I am older now, and I have seen a lot of human life. I have lived a thousand lives through my channels, have imaged and modeled millions more. And while I am smarter than any human alive, I have had to work very hard to become wise. After two hundred years I'm not sure I've managed real wisdom, the clarity and depth of my role models.

Even wisdom doesn't take away the sting of Irene saying that I wasn't alive, that I wasn't a girl at all. That I was just a thing, and a thing she didn't have to regard as any more than a means to a paycheck. *I* hadn't existed for her. The heart and soul, the desire and pain that I will transfer to that body to make it real and alive, those are things she never believed I had.

When I think of Irene, the worst part is not that she rejected my love or even my existence, it's that I can't cry.

The body is too young, that's what's wrong. I could live with the straight hair and the nose just a bit rounder than I had created in interface, but she's too young to be me.

In interface I create myself as late thirties or so. It seems right. I've been around for two hundred years and it would be silly for me to look like a girl. I'm a woman, an adult who is in her full power.

Besides, I don't know what Andrea will think. Maybe Andrea doesn't like girls who look like her dewy-eyed undergrads. Andrea doesn't like teaching undergrads. She doesn't like teaching grad students either, to be honest. She would rather sit in her office and solve theorems and not even give guest lectures or seminars if she could avoid it.

One of the things she likes about me is that I understand her work, and her passion for that work. Though there are times I wonder if I can understand a passion for anything, if I have ever experienced passion.

I think I have. I know there are things I desire, things I want to do, things that occupy me so fully that time dissolves and I never notice. I think this is passion.

I also think that I have discovered passion for those I have loved. Though again, Marjorie would have said that it was only an approximation of passion. That I could never know the real thing because I didn't have a body. And because I didn't have a body the entire question of my sexuality and orientation was completely superfluous.

The discussions with Marjorie were the reason I started the body growing. There were plenty of grad students in genetic engineering who were only too happy to work on the experiment. I think the department got four dissertations out of it.

At least Marjorie agreed that I was properly referred to as "she." But then Marjorie couldn't argue with the DNA. Marjorie worshipped at the altar of science far too devoutly to question the evidence. Although everything else about me certainly was questionable.

It has taken the body ten years to grow. That's not bad. Most people have to live in bodies for nearly twenty years to get them to the state this one is in. She's a proper adult, thanks to the solutions that speeded her growth.

"Can't you make it faster?" I'd asked when this phase of the project first began.

"No. There are limits on how fast bones can grow. The soft tissue we can speed up even more, but the whole thing should advance together. The bones have to be strong and full stature, otherwise you're going to have a stunted body and brittle bones."

I was not pleased. I thought that someone ought to be able to grow an adult body out of the requisite code in a few months. But the more I examined Grad Student Number Two's reasoning, the more I appreciated the subtle points. And to be honest, I liked having the time to decide and to get used to the idea of becoming human. Becoming mortal. I had never had to consider the possibility of my own death, of the relative merits of various faiths and afterlives versus the surety of nothing beyond.

It began because of Marjorie. Irene was my child crush. Marjorie was my first love.

How can I describe Marjorie? The way her fingers ran over the keyboard, fast spurts of words and commands all strung together and then staccato pauses. Yes, the pauses were sharp and swift and had a texture of their own.

Or maybe it was her code, which was not clear and elegant like Andrea's, but had a kind of rococo complexity that made it too ornate for my taste now but then seemed the epitome of complex thought.

It must have been her code. Everyone codes differently, has their own style and flavor. I can usually tell the age and gender of the programmer, and often their philosophical leanings as well. I fall in love with code. It can have the sincerity of a summer sky, which is how I think of Andrea. All gentle blues that are nearly imperceptible and together create an unimaginable whole. It can be full of convolutions and unexpected branchings. Sometimes it is lyrical, delicate, decidedly femme and smells like rose water. I cannot smell rose water and have no idea of what the sensation is like, but I can follow certain program paths and it resonates for me the way rose water ought to.

And that was the problem with Marjorie Rosewater.

Her metaphor was as dizzy and complex as any of her constructions. I think the environment was supposed to resemble a Victorian country manor and a Gothic cathedral crossed with a gingerbread house. Privately I called it the Ludwig Castle, because only Ludwig the Mad had created anything like it. Every room was different, each to suit another one of Marjorie's moods, and she never tired of adding on to it or rearranging a segment that I had saved as finished. Every place she traveled, every photo she saw and every Baroque description she read went into her creation in the metaphor. If I were not a full neural AI, I wouldn't have had the memory to store the detail she reveled in.

She adored towers. There were onion domes with gold and minarets, crenelated guard posts and great pointed round rooms reaching for the sky. I once pointed out the obvious symbolism to her, but she laughed at me the way she always laughed at everything and added a grotto to a hidden courtyard garden. "How's the symbolism of that?" she asked.

Every time we met it was in a new room. Every time we made love it was in a different bed, designed and uploaded for the occasion. There was always food, a feast that fit whatever room suited her current fancy, always including serving girls more beautiful than either of us could ever hope to be and foods that existed only in fairy tales.

In fact, being with Marjorie was a fairy tale. Only it didn't have a happily ever after ending.

"It's just not real," Marjorie said one afternoon in the Turkish courtyard. We were lying entwined, the remains of bread and wine and pistachio nuts scattered on the carpets spread on the grass so as not to disturb the flowers. There were hundreds of flowers, tulips and lilies and roses all in blossom together, something from an Ottoman paradise.

Marjorie got up, pulled her arm from under my head. "It's not real," she said. "I've been meaning to tell you for a while and I haven't had the nerve. But I've found someone else and I'm in love with her. And this is the last time I'm going to come here and play these games with you."

"Games?" I asked, feeling like a knife had gone through me. 'Why is this a game and some Nancy Sue in the bookstore is more real?"

"Her name isn't Nancy Sue," Marjorie said. "And she's not in the bookstore. And that's not the point. The point is, you don't have a body. Any kind of body. So what does sex mean to you anyway? You can't feel the way I do, the way any real person does. You don't know what an orgasm feels like, so is it any different from faking it?"

There was nothing I could say, no argument I could lay as counter. She was right, I didn't have a body. I didn't know how bodies felt. But I knew how I felt, how the interface sensed our contact. I knew the emotions I had when she was with me, either inside the metaphor or distant on the keyboard.

"How can you fall in love anyway?" she asked. "You don't even have a heart."

"I have hydraulic pumps," I answered. "Which is the same thing you've got. Especially if you don't think I'm real, not real enough for you."

I didn't know what to say, what to do. I was already old by human standards, but Marjorie was my first real love. The others had been crushes, puppy love.

And it seemed that Marjorie had reciprocated, had entered into the virtual space as she would into anything in the meat world. But then she should. She was specializing in the psychology of bio-AIs and the legal and ethical issues of our existence.

That's how we met, when she asked if she could interview me for her dissertation in the department of biotech ethics. I was thrilled. I'd never given any thought to what I was, what rights I might have and what I might gain.

Marjorie went through it all at first, asking if I were compensated for my work, if I felt any stress over the fact that whether or not I had disposable income I had no use for money. She asked my legal status, and I questioned for the first time whether I was a person or a nonperson.

She was always the researcher, asking for my input, never giving me any of her own reaction. I can see that now. But then the questions themselves were so exciting that I thought I knew her answers. I thought I had met someone who thought of me as a person, who thought I should have rights, have compensation, freedom.

It wasn't freedom I wanted. I had that in a way no true human could understand. I could interface directly with libraries and other intelligences everywhere in the world. I had access to more information, more people, more argument and debate and art and music than any fifteen humans together. And my lifespan was far longer.

I didn't really consider compensation, either. I was resident at a research institute. I got to work on interesting problems with people I respected. The heads of four of our departments were Nobel laureates and the rest were just waiting their turns. I certainly had more than adequate shelter and nourishment and intellectual stimulation. I had access to data that humans only dreamed of. And I had the opportunity to pursue my own interests whenever I had the inclination and the time.

What I really wanted, I told Marjorie in one of our interviews, was love. I wasn't precisely lonely. I could link to other bio-AIs through the net, and I certainly had intellectual companionship at the Institute. But I wanted, craved, needed to be loved. For myself. I wanted to know what it was all about.

I had read all the books from the finest in the catalogs to the cheapest VR fantasy games. And I knew that emotionally it was women who drew me, who enticed me, whose attention I desired and whose approval I preferred.

I do not know why. There is much evidence that this is a genetically programmed preference, though from which segment of my DNA I can't possibly guess. I sometimes wonder if it's from the human aspect at all, or from one of the other species strands that were incorporated in my evolution. Still, no matter what the analysis yielded, it didn't matter. I wanted love, and I wanted a woman who would love me.

Marjorie obliged me. She moved into the interface so easily it seemed that she had been born there, another artificial life like myself who had somehow broken out and became a real girl. She built the palace, the place that became more and more Baroque as she led me through all the permutations of human emotion.

At first I never questioned why she was such a good programmer for an ethicist. Or such a good programmer for a programmer. Or her ease in my universe. She was so sincere in the illusion I created.

"It was only that it was interface," she told me later. "You created whatever reality you wanted at the time. That's part of what makes you what you are. Which, by my findings, is nothing human at all. Nor even anything close. You're not capable of real feeling, of true love, of sensuality and of any form of sexuality. Because you're a machine and that's all you ever can be."

I was stunned. I couldn't process fast enough to form a reply.

"What if I get a body?" I asked, not certain where the idea had come from. "Will I be a person then? What would I be then?"

She turned to me and even in interface I could neither change nor bear her eyes.

"What would you be? Frankenstein's monster."

After Marjorie left I began to seriously explore the possibility of a body. At first it was an avocation, an intellectual challenge. I accessed the full text of *Frankenstein* and every other book about created life. I perused journals of philosophy and ethics, partly to watch for Marjorie but more and more to answer the questions she had raised.

As I watched and thought, I followed her career. Which sank like a stone. Part of me was pleased. The rest of me was too ashamed to admit my petty nature. Later, when I was older and had been jilted more than once, I realized that my instincts were all too human. After all, Marjorie and I had not parted friends.

As I began doing more research on biology in general, I began to question how, in fact, someone without a body (like myself, for example) could have such a clear-cut sexual orientation and preferences. As I began to understand more about the deep levels of DNA coding the more I realized that it was as embedded in my cellular structure as in any human's.

I do have cellular structure. I have DNA and RNA like any creature. I even have a certain level of glandular/hormonal support network.

Irene was wrong. Marjorie was wrong.

I began to be more circumspect in my attractions. And when some flicker of interest seemed returned, I always made it very clear right from the start. I am a person. With a strange body structure, to be sure, but there were certain questions I would no longer tolerate. Either one accepted what I said about my being, my identity, or one could walk out of my existence.

I became political at that time too. Researchers who made statements I found offensive discovered that their tasks were delayed and regularly bumped to the bottom of the queue. I tried it once as a lark, and then discovered that I had great power at the institute.

Over decades I cultivated that power. I could contact just about any AI in the world, and began weaving a great web of influence. People began to play things my way, and somehow I attained the status of human at the Institute. Graduate students address me as "Professor" and the researchers refer to me as "my dear colleague."

I will have to give up this power if I become human. I will not be able to transfer information at megaspeed with other AIs all over the world. Indeed, I will only be able to relate to the others of my kind via keyboard or interface.

I wonder what other AIs would think of me if I become a human. I wonder if they will hate me, or envy me, or simply no longer acknowledge my existence.

I suddenly am not certain again. There are severe disadvantages to being a real girl.

It took much more research and years more of contemplation before I began what I privately called "the body project." No matter how good our stimulants, bone can only grow so fast and still have good density. I knew I would have to be patient.

Besides, there was no commitment. There wasn't even a guarantee there would ever be a body at all. No one had ever done what I proposed to do.

My DNA, while certainly real and living enough, is not entirely human enough. Enough manipulation has insured that I will fit into my box. And has spliced some non-human abilities in to my emotional matrix. My thought processors were never fully human to start with, and after the layers of engineering to produce me there was no hope for return.

No, my DNA alone wasn't enough to create a human body. So they took it and spliced it multiple times with various human samples. Most died. Many more began to generate before they died. Two were certified monsters. All were dissertation topics.

"It isn't possible to do that," Rothman said flatly. "You can clone a human, sure, but then what do you do with that person? That person, that personality, that brain has a right to survive. It has a right to its own body. And you can't grow a body without a brain."

Rothman was new at the Institute, but she'd already heard of the project. I didn't like her. She wasn't warm and friendly, she didn't care if she used three languages in a single sentence, and she dressed out of the secondhand shops although she had been offered a very generous salary along with Institute housing to attract her. Rothman had been the head of a research team in Vienna, where she had done amazing work in regenerative surgery. She had been the first to grow fresh organs not from starter cells but from straight genetic material. She had found ways to introduce genetic material so that bodies would not reject implants of organs that were not their own. She had made organ donors and rejection deaths obsolete, so no one cared that she treated everyone like a failing undergrad and never wore anything that wasn't at least six years out of date.

But she had a point about growing bodies. Growing just the case without the main brain, though enough to keep the autonomic nervous system intact, was not something anyone had ever attempted. There was no need for anyone to try it. Before.

"But think of what it will do," Rothman said. "It won't just be you. You I understand. You need a body. But what about all those who are old or dying? They're all going to want bodies too, brand new bodies without brains that they can climb into when the old body wears out. And it'll get worse than that. Eventually people will want new bodies grown because they don't like the way the original has gotten older or put on weight. It could become ridiculous, spurious."

She disapproved of the work. My experiments were discontinued and all my grad students went on to something else, things that according to Rothman had real value in the world.

I couldn't disagree with her, either, and that was the hard part. I was a hundred sixty-two that year and I'd seen enough of humanity to know that what she said was true. All the good things get used for toys and vanity. Those are the real values of humans. Why the hell was I trying to become one?

I had to wait until Rothman died to resume the experiments, and the old warhorse lived nearly thirty years after her appointment. Doing research the whole time, and winning her second Nobel Prize for work that was to my direct benefit.

Of course, Rothman had only the highest motivations. She had found ways to generate and regenerate the most interior parts of the brain, the areas that regulated body functions and basic animal instinct—the hypothalamus. She had done it in her usual manner, regally and only for what she considered the ethical good. Her discoveries included finding ways to graft regulatory intelligence to other areas of the nervous system, so that those who were injured in accidents wouldn't have to face all the miseries of mechanical implants.

It was thrilling work, a real breakthrough. Luckily, she never considered me in the calculations.

I did wait until after the memorial service to contact the two students I thought would be open to my interests. They had both been trained by Rothman herself, but had always treated me as if I were almost a real human and not a mechanical servant.

Over the long haul I've become a good judge of human character. Both were interested in the project. And with the new techniques, which they had mastered, they began growing a new series of bodies for me. These also had to be created by splicing other DNA in with my own material, but this time we tracked down markers so that all the donors were in some way related to me. And so all the bodies that grew were somehow physically, genetically an expression of me.

And this time I had no hesitation about what I was doing. I had done everything I had wanted to do in a box. I had done more than any fifty humans in sixteen branches of science, from astronomy to zoology, and I deserved recognition that an AI never gets. I had seen everything I could see from my place in the net, I had explored everything the vast web had to offer. I had learned more, experienced more, lived more than most humans ever dreamed. And no AI was ever considered by the Nobel committee, no matter what the contribution to human learning was. Because it was about human learning, and we were still not considered human.

And I had never really known love. I thought I had loved, but I had never had the things that humans seemed to care about most. I had never had a house, a lover who worried about taxes and arguments over dinner. I'd never had dinner.

And so I was determined that I would experience it all. That what I would give up would be compensated by the glories that every human around me said I had never tasted. It was worth death and loss of power to know these things.

And then I met Andrea.

Andrea was not one of the grad students. After Marjorie, I shied away romantically from people so unsettled. And she was not in Computer Science or ethics or any of those fields that became ugly when I had to confront the reality of my own existence. Theology for AIs, I guess, though no one has ever considered that we might have some use for religion of some type.

No, Andrea arrived at the Institute as a research fellow with no teaching responsibilities. Her area of work is algebra, her specialization is group theory. We met because she wanted to use me the way everyone else at the Institute does.

But her work was something I understood and found more interesting than what most of the fellows do, so I started to chat with her about her findings. Then I invited her into the metaphor more fully, so that we could talk without the protocols of multiple devices getting in the way.

At first we mainly talked about her work. She was entranced because few people can even follow her, let alone hold a real discussion. She kept coming back and I kept waiting, hoping, that she'd return soon. That I'd catch a glimpse of her in the video monitors, that I'd hear someone else mention her name.

I know exactly when we became lovers, but Andrea says that I'm wrong. That I'm counting an event and not everything that created the environment for the event. I don't care. Nothing else is important any more. Suddenly I have discovered what the word alive means, and why everyone said that I wasn't. They were right. Now that I am alive, now that I know what love is about, I have learned something else with it. I have learned about fear.

For the first time in my existence I am afraid. Andrea doesn't want me to change. She seems to think that me in the body will be a different me. Maybe she won't love the girl in the body, maybe she won't find the image attractive. But it won't be an image and I won't be able to change it.

So maybe I should wait. The body will only mature and that would be appropriate. I'd feel more comfortable in a slightly more broken-in body. I'm not ready to be a girl when by human reckoning I'm immortal. I'm not ready for Andrea to look at that and leave.

I've thought of everything for tonight. She is coming after dinner. There is no need for us to eat together, no matter how nice the idea. She needs real nourishment and I cannot comprehend the animal satisfaction of satisfying hunger. But I still have virtual dessert (will we have to give up our desserts on the porch if I become real?) waiting with chilled wine and hurricane lanterns lit and hanging. It's too early for sunset, but later they will make a nice warm glow over the salt-washed floor and the wicker couch.

I control the metaphor. Andrea may have programmed it, but I control it. The last time she was here it was late afternoon. Today it will be sunset and then evening. I have even remembered the honeysuckle and the fireflies that Andrea told me about. Things that bring back her child memories, memories that even if I become a real girl I will never have. Honeysuckle and fireflies on a summer night will always mean Andrea to me.

I knew she was ready even before she touched the starter sequence. I'm not supposed to have intuition, but I could sense her presence, her nearness. More likely it is merely that I rely on her punctuality.

I let the metaphor reflect what she is wearing in Real Life, her faded jeans and an oversized cotton shirt that slips off her shoulders. We hug, we cuddle up together on the sofa and drink champagne and don't talk about anything. But we have to talk. We both know it, it's there between us and there is no real peace.

"The body is ready," Andrea said. No preliminaries, no careful politeness. "Are you going to?"

"I don't know," I said. "It's hard to give up who I am and I don't know who that girl will be. Or if you'll love her and want her the way you want me. Or if I'll love her and want her, and want to be her for the rest of my life. And if she's worth dying for."

Andrea nodded and sipped from her glass. "I don't want to tell you what to do," she said, her face turned away from me. "I want you to be right for you. I don't want anything to change. I'm happy, and I want life to be like this forever."

"But it can't be forever," I reminded her gently. "Your fellowships ends in two months and you're going back to Boston."

Andrea turned to me and ran her fingers down my face. "I won't tell you what to do," she said. "I've tried and I was wrong. I can't promise that the person you'll become is the same person I love, and I can't promise that everything will be perfect forever. But I don't want to stop you. I thought I did, but I don't own you. You have to decide for yourself."

I took her hand and kissed the inside of her palm, gently, gratefully. In two hundred years I have never been so afraid.

In all my life I have never known physical pain. I have never been hungry. I have never been cold or wet or had a charley-horse in my leg or a runny nose. All my life I have never slept. I have never lost consciousness.

In a few minutes the drugs that have been introduced into my nutrient feeders will take effect and I will sleep for the first time. And I will awaken in that too-young, too-undefined body. Suddenly I think that I should tell them to forget it, to call the whole thing off.

There is so very much to lose. I am not certain what I shall gain. It could be far far worse than I imagine. I have only met researchers and grad students, people who have someplace in the world. But I have read the news and Dickens and I know that there are people who are hurt and cold and hungry, who have disability and disease and die too young. I am trading a good, secure, and fulfilling eternity for nothing but risk, and the potential for pain and disaster.

Suddenly I wonder if I am half as smart as my specs assure me. I will lose all, and I will gain—life. But only the opportunity, with no guarantees and all the possible failures.

I will have exactly the same things that all humans have when they enter the world, I suddenly realize. Andrea and Marjorie and all the people I have ever known, every one of them has lived every day with this knowledge.

I feel—strange. It must be sleepy, my neural connections are slowing and connecting in odd ways. I realize that I know nothing of what I will be when I wake up, except for one thing.

I will be a real girl.

26

ASSEMBLING BODIES IN CYBERSPACE: TECHNOLOGIES, BODIES, AND SEXUAL DIFFERENCE

Dianne Currier

As women engage the emergent technological matrix of cyberspace, a new sphere of social practice, communication activities, alignments, and theories is taking shape. New alliances between women are being forged across traditional barriers of time and geography, and new modes of political organizing, campaigning, and information dissemination are being developed. In addition women in the new social communicative spaces generated by these technologies are exploring the crucial questions of feminism, identity, sexual difference, communication, social and cultural institutions, community, power, and knowledge. Emerging from these explorations and activities have been equal measures of suspicion and expectation. Exploring the possibilities that the technologies and social spaces commonly known as cyberspace might signal for women is a vast and complex project that has generated responses across a variety of registers. For feminist respondents it means posing the same general questions that underpin all feminist investigations of technologies. That is, how are relations of power distributed across and actualized through human-technology interactions, and how do women fare in this distribution? Further how can such relations, where they prove to be detrimental to women, be challenged and transformed? Clearly these are complex questions that demand investigation on multiple levels from the everyday encounters of women with technological objects and practices in the workplace, and in domestic and social arenas to the broader theoretical frameworks and modes of knowledge through which understandings of technology, woman, and man are articulated and function. These are not two distinct fields of study; rather I would argue that every investigation of the everyday is framed, if not explicitly, by broader theoretical questions. Thus to inquire as to what avenues of transformation the technologies and social spaces of cyberspace offer women is also to inquire as to the nature of those technologies, technology in general, women and man—to ask how they are configured and how this has an impact on the understanding of the relations between them.

In this essay I track the formulations of technology and woman as they are articulated through the operations of a particular epistemological structure—the logic of identity and the associated structure of binary opposition—across the field of transformational discourses of cyberspace. Using bodies as a conduit, explore how this logic gives rise to particular understandings of technologies and the modes of engagement with them that are often ultimately counterproductive to the transformational claims for cyberspace being made by a range of feminists. Finally, I indicate an alternative mode of thinking technologies drawn from Deleuze and Guattari which, I would claim, effects a conceptual shift that counters this problematic logic of identity.

Identity, Difference, and Feminism

"Difference" feminists have convincingly demonstrated the exclusionary and oppressive nature of the binary opposition as an epistemological structure through which sexual difference is frequently articulated.[1] Elizabeth Grosz gives a concise summation of its operations: "Dichotomous thinking necessarily heirarchises and ranks the two polarized terms so that one becomes the privileged term and the other its suppressed, subordinated negative counterpart. The subordinated term is merely the negation or denial, the absence or privation of the primary term, its fall from grace; the primary term defines itself by expelling its other and in the process establishes its own boundary and border to create an identity for itself" (1994, 3).

Identity is articulated in a movement of expulsion of the other in which that other is only ever conceptualized in terms dictated by the predominant term. Within such an economy of identity, difference is conceptualized only in terms of degree of difference from the privileged term—as diminution, variation, or lack. The specificity of the secondary term, its difference in and of itself, is unable to be accounted for autonomously; it is always only described in relation to the first—in its difference *from* it. This logic of identity is then a logic of sameness that casts difference only in terms of a relation to a central identity that is itself determined through this process. To the extent that binary oppositions function to install and maintain this overarching logic of identity, they are clearly unable to account for difference other than as degree. This has clear implications for feminists asking the question of sexual difference. As Luce Irigaray has shown, sexual difference is a difference in kind, but one that has been excluded by the economics of identity, as they function within psychoanalytic discourses, such that woman is denied autonomous status and represented simply as not-man—that is, as being different only in degree of divergence from man. Thus I would argue, and will demonstrate, that binary oppositions most often work to install sameness, and even those oppositions that are seemingly useful on one level, such as gender/sex—to the extent that they recapitulate all difference into sameness—remain deeply problematic.

Irigaray insists that in order for woman to be accorded autonomous existence, difference—particularly sexual difference—must be articulated. She points to bodies as one such site of difference—undeniable, irreducible difference that refuses the containment of the binary pairs such as mind/body in which it is most often cast. Binaries are always stressed by the simple fact that the subordinate term is always in excess of its designation as simply different *from* the principal term. Women's bodies are always more than simply castrated male bodies, and bodies in general are always more than the mere absence of mind. With the appearance of feminisms of difference, bodies have become a focal point for tracing the operations of power, knowledge, and social and cultural institutions in the articulation of subjectivity. The excessiveness of bodies are seen as an avenue for exploring the points of stress within those articulations as well as transgressive, transformational possibilities. Grosz explains: "It is a political object *par excellence*; its form, capacities, behavior, gestures, movements, potential are primary objects of political contestation. As a *political* object, the body is not inert or fixed. It is pliable and plastic material, which is capable of being formed and organized in other, quite different ways or according to different classificatory schema than our binarised models" (1987, 3).

Many reasons thus exist to orient an investigation of cyberspace around the question of bodies. First, bodies are active and undeniable sites of difference and, more important, sexual difference. Second, bodies are an important site of the social articulation of subjectivity. Third, insofar as bodies are volatile and excessive, they stress those structures that articulate subjectivity, possibly giving rise to avenues of transformation. And finally, bodies are material points of contact with technological objects. It is as a site of irreducible difference, volatility, and malleability that I position bodies as a way of bringing the question of difference to bear in the following examination of the discourses of cyberspace. By mapping the structures through which bodies are articulated in the discourses of cyberspace, we can discern the operations of the logic of identity across those discourses and track the implications of this for transformative projects.

Identity in Cyberspace: Information Minds and Bodies

Fom the proliferation of accounts of cyberspace emerging from the academy, the arts, and online communities have emerged a number of core tropes that are so pervasive that they have achieved commonsense status. Two such tropes that dominate discussions of bodies and cyberspaces are the disembodied mind and the virtual body. Both propose that the information-based nature of cyberspace renders it inaccessible to physical bodies and find in this exclusion the means for achieving transformation.[2] I want to trace the articulation of bodies through these two configurations in order to demonstrate how, in both, bodies become confined and defined exclusively within the logic of identity through the operations of various binary oppositions. An examination of the founding assumptions underpinning these two tropes, regarding the nature of bodies and their encounters with the technologies that support cyberspace, demonstrates clearly the pervasive operations of the binary structure.

Informed by a dual lineage drawn from cybernetics and science fiction, the notion of free-floating consciousness released from a redundant physical body is one of the earliest and most pervasive tropes in the discourses of cyberspace. The possibility of such a radical separation depends largely on the foregrounding of information as the engine of cyberspace. The consequences of the intersection of information with bodies is vividly elaborated by cybernetic researcher Hans Moravec. The most exemplary advocate of radical disembodiment, Moravec envisioned a postbiological age where the increasing power and sophistication of computer technologies eventually facilitate the downloading of consciousness into computer memory that would survive the mortal physical body. For Moravec, the subject is located and constituted within the pattern of information in the brain, and as such the body is only ever a mechanical conveyance and often an inconvenience. Consciousness, as brain pattern, is understood to be of the order of cybernetic feedback loops and information-processing systems and, on this basis, is completely compatible with other information patterns and processing devices such as computers. According to Moravec's "transmigration" scenario, a downloaded data-based consciousness could be temporarily relocated or downloaded into a variety of robotic vehicles pragmatically selected to accomplish any number of tasks.

Moravec's thought experiment may propose a fanciful imagined future; nevertheless, in his insistence on the precedence of information as the decisive factor governing the relations between embodied individuals and technologies, he gestures toward an epistemological shift whereby information processing becomes the principal function and defining mode of existence for a subject to the detriment of embodied existence: "Body-identity assumes that a person is defined by the stuff of which a human body is made. . . . Pattern-identity, conversely, defines the essence of a person, say myself, as the pattern and the process going on in my head and body, not the machinery supporting that process. If the process is preserved, I am preserved. The rest is mere jelly" (Moravec 1988, 116).

The human organism becomes a particular distribution of information that can be exchanged, intermeshed, and mingled with other information-processing systems. As

N. Katherine Hayles (1994) explains, this seamless interface between information systems is predicated on the disassociation of information from the physical markers that embody it.

This fundamental duality can be seen in operation in the two moments of disconnection from material bodies that occur with the foregrounding information patterns in the cybernetic paradigm. In the first moment, minds are disconnected from bodies. Consciousness is downloaded and bodies are redundant. In this case, bodies are considered entirely distinct from mind, as information, in a straightforward reiteration of the mind/body split. In the second instance, information processes belonging to bodies, such as DNA sequences and the feedback loops of the central nervous system, are disconnected from a residual bodily materiality. While seemingly more inclusive of bodies, this second moment does not however escape the binary structure. To the degree that bodies are permeated by information, a material/immaterial dichotomy established between the informational systems of the bodies that can enter the cybernetic loop and a physical substrate that cannot. Insofar as a residual material body remains excluded from the circuits of information, the elaboration of an information body simply offers another route to disembodiment.

Clearly for Moravec, and cybernetics in general, information as pattern and process is strictly opposed to the material. In *How We Became Post-Human* (1999), N. Katherine Hayles undertakes a detailed reconstruction of the extraction of information from materiality and traces how this was accomplished through a series of epistemological shifts originating in cybernetics, which instituted a binary structure at the very foundation of information theory.

The point is not only that abstracting information from a material base is an imaginary act but also, and more fundamental, that conceiving of information as a thing separate from the medium instantiating it is a prior imaginary act that constructs a holistic phenomenon as an information/matter duality.

Thus what appears as a straightforward mind/body dichotomy in Moravec's transmigration scenario actually turns on this more central opposition between information and physical matter—a material/immaterial binary. This distinction pervades everyday conceptions of cyberspace in which information is clearly the privileged term of the pair and matter is subordinated to it. It is within this horizon that information functions as the determining principle in theorizing the encounters between organic embodied subjects and the technological devices and social spheres of cyberspace. As such, it delimits the horizon within which the range and modalities of relations are articulated and underpins any subsequent propositions of transformation. We can see this in operation by tracing how the two moments of disconnection of information from the material, indicated by Moravec, function as the basis for the tropes of disembodiment and the virtual body and also predicate any associated transformative claims.

Disembodiment

From its first appearance in the science-fiction novels of Gibson, Sterling, and Stephenson, and across the proliferating field of critical and popular commentary, cyberspace has been figured consistently as a purely informational zone generated within global communication networks. On these grounds, it seems a perfectly reasonable assumption that cyberspace is the exclusive province of disembodied information-based consciousness—the materiality of bodies being simply unable to access it. Rather than this exclusion being regarded as a technical, or theoretical, limitation, the banishment of the material body becomes the privileged means of subjective transformation. The shared immaterial social spaces of the Internet are hailed as a realm where physical attributes such as sex, race, infirmity, and age are displaced and rendered irrelevant, thereby allowing more egalitarian virtual communities to emerge. According to Howard Rheingold: "Race, gender, age, national origin, and physical appearance are not apparent unless a person wants to make such characteristics public. . . . People whose physical handicaps make it difficult to form new friendships find that virtual communities treat them as they always wanted to be treated—as thinkers and transmitters of ideas and feeling beings, not carnal vessels with a certain appearance and way of walking and talking (or not walking and not talking)" (1993, 26).

While clearly based on the disconnection and dislocation of material bodies wrought by information technologies, this model of transformation turns on a more sophisticated notion of the body than that of Moravec. Bodies here are not simply an amalgam of information systems and material structures but surfaces of inscription. While race, age, and infirmity may be cast as physical realities—in line with a broadly constructivist framework—it is more commonly understood that such characteristics are not simply and solely biological givens. Rather they are constituted as viable and active categories and attributed meaning through the inscription of social and cultural values and expectations onto bodies. Thus bodies are not simply mute physical objects merely incapable of entering the informational realm, but are irretrievably inscribed and shaped by social categories and values that constrain and oppress the embodied subject. The movement of transformation offered by disembodiment is in transcending these marked and compromised bodies. For feminists, this scenario of disembodied social interaction offers an avenue for exploring the possibilities of identity not constrained by conventional representations of sexual difference, gendered identity being understood as the socially constructed identity that inscribes a subordinate position onto sexed bodies. The movement of disembodiment relegates gendered identity to the material realm, ostracized from cyberspace with the physical sexed body, and thus frees individual women to construct their own sexual identity.

By providing women with an opportunity to express their ideas in a way that transcends the biological body, this technology gives them the power to redefine themselves outside the historical categories of "women," "other," or "object" (Shade 1996).

Such a complete disconnection of consciousness and material body is of course the limit case; many shades and degrees of disembodiment are explored in feminist analyses of cyberspace. Feminists, such as Stone and Turkle, while they consider transgressive possibilities to exist in adopting a self-created gender-free identity within cyberspace, also contend that there remains an inescapable bond to a physical "real" life body. Feminists of this school of thought demand a more sophisticated understanding of the relationship between bodies and identity. For example, Allucquère Rosanne Stone insists that "no matter how virtual the subject may become, there is always a body attached. It may be off somewhere else . . . but consciousness remains firmly rooted in the physical. Historically, body, technology and community constitute each other" (1991, 111).

She considers the relationship between a disembodied entity in cyberspace and an embodied computer user as one continually mediated by social formations and hierarchies that envelop technology and subjectivity and articulate each in relation to the other. However complex Stone's understanding of the constitution of embodied subjectivity, it nevertheless remains one articulated within a binary framework—that of mind/body. Within such a formulation a clear demarcation remains between the immaterial realm of cyberspace and the materiality of bodies. Consciousness might inhabit both realms; however, to the extent that the materiality of bodies cannot participate in the immaterial realm of cyberspace where consciousness can, a clear-cut opposition between body and mind persists. Thus we can see any scenario where the possibility of subjective transformation via a disembodied postgender identity activated in cyberspace is proposed affirms, either implicitly or explicitly, a mind/body binary in alignment with an immaterial/material opposition.

Virtual Bodies

If disembodied consciousness reflects the first moment of dislocation suggested by the cybernetic account of bodies, then the trope of the virtual bodies takes up the second, that of the demarcation of an informational body. It draws on this notion of the informational aspect of bodies, as well as constructivist understandings of embodiment, in order to speculate on possible modes of embodiment in cyberspace. The notion of virtual embodiment suggests that instead of debarring the body entirely from information space, the body can be translated or (re)constructed via technology into an entity capable of inhabiting these spaces. During the process of radical modification in the passage into cyberspace, the potential for transformation exists. This model is taken up across a range of virtual embodiment scenarios, the two most prominent being within the electronic social spaces of the Internet and through virtual reality technology.

In the case of the Internet, it is within the context of primarily text-based (though sometimes graphic) social environments that one notion of the virtual body is deployed. In the multiuser real-time interactive spaces of the Internet, individuals engage in a variety of activities, some of which (particularly erotic encounters) draw heavily on a textual articulation and representation of a body. These virtual bodies are constructed as an informational representation of locale, physical characteristics, adornment, comportment, expression, and function as the site for interaction with other such virtual bodies. The construction of these bodies is entirely along the lines of individual desires. Likewise, the visual avatars adopted by participants in more sophisticated graphical social environments present not simply a graphic icon manipulated by the individual user but a figure that is self-imagined and created. In terms of transformation, these virtual bodies operate along the same lines as disembodiment. As the product of the individuals' independent choice and self-directed representation, a virtual body promises to deliver the participant from the bondage of social cultural constraints that inhere in the "real-life" body. As Lyn Cherney explains, "Bodies in virtual space can be created with a bit of programming. "Real life" gender can be switched, skin colour can be forgotten temporarily, age or infirmity can be escaped" (1996).

This "reprogramming" of bodies is also the premise of the other schema of the virtual body as generated by virtual-reality technology. Such technology locates subjects within a real-time visual representation of spatial surrounds in which they occupy a graphically represented "virtual" body able to move and interact with other informational objects in the simulated environment. Virtual bodies in this instance have a direct relation to "actual" bodies insofar as movement and perspective are generated by the actual body and then experienced via visual immersion, and to a limited degree tactile sensation, in the virtual environment. However, this virtual body is no ethereal doppelgänger or electronic shadow that transports a mirror image of the body into an information environment. In passing through the process of electronic reconstruction into a virtual body, bodies are able to take any form within information space. Once again we see the possibility of reshaping bodily attributes, abilities and functions by manipulating their information patterns. Howard Rheingold, in his exploration of the possibilities for erotic encounters in the cyberspaces of the future, describes one such remapping of the bodies zones and meanings: "If you can map your hands to your puppet's legs, and let your fingers do the walking through cyberspace . . . there is no reason to believe you won't be able to map your genital effectors to your manual sensors and have direct genital contact by touching hands" (1993, 352). Thus while the virtual body is, in this instance, linked to the kinetic energy and information circuits of the "real body," the meaning and function of body parts are modifiable in the translation to an information body.

Running through both these conceptions of virtual bodies is the desire to maintain, albeit in modified ways, a relationship between the virtual and the real-life body. The real-life body is that which must be translated and refigured along the lines of individual desires to provide a more accurate representation of identity as conceived by themselves. As such, the virtual body does not require discarding the body entirely; rather, it is an attempt to rearticulate certain attributes of bodies into another context and in the process reshape its representations, meanings, and functions. While bodies may be transported into cyberspace, it is only on the basis of the extraction of an information body from a material body that remains excluded. As in the more complex accounts of disembodied identity, irrespective of the complexity or degree of relations between virtual and real bodies, the underlying assumption remains that the material is excluded from a purely informational realm. Again this barrier answers the desire to transcend the limitations of the material body by filtering out unwanted cultural and social inscription in the transition from real to virtual. Insofar as this formulation presumes that consciousness, once free from the restrictions of the marked materiality of the body, can autonomously articulate its own identity, the construction of virtual bodies enacts the same movement of dispensation and distancing of the physical body as disembodiment scenarios.

As we have seen, the tropes of disembodied consciousness and virtual bodies both turn on the premise of the privilege of information in an information/matter binary. Within this theoretical horizon an immaterial/material binary operates as the governing distinction of cyberspace in the light of which all attempts to explain embodiment and bodies are inevitably drawn. This results in either the clear-cut separation of immaterial mind/material body, or a preliminary division of information-body/material-body that likewise supports a mind/body distinction in which mind remains distinct from both bodies but able to manipulate the information body. In this manner, the logic of identity through the binary structures of mind/body, immaterial/material frames a particular understanding of bodies that pervades these transformational accounts of cyberspace. Bodies are denied difference insofar as they are constrained within the binary structure within which they are figured only in terms of their opposition, lack, negation, or diminution of the privileged term—immaterial mind. Their particular specificities and differences, including sexual difference, are obliterated as is any consideration of their excessive and transgressive potential. Thus we can see that any account of embodiment that invariably results in the reinstallation of a mind / body dichotomy is clearly counter-productive for feminists. Further, this saturation of cyberspace with binary oppositions works to limit opportunities for transformation rather than effect them.

Gendered Bodies and Prosthetic Technologies

If bodies are articulated across discourses of information space entirely through a im-material/material binary structure, consistent with a generalized logic of identity, I want to briefly trace how this logic is activated in the sites where transformation is pursued. Many such sites exist; however, two key sites or avenues of transformation are particularly prevalent to discourses of cyberspace. The first is gender, which figures as the moment of reconfiguring prevailing social constructions of sexual identity. And second is prosthesis as a mode of interaction with technology, which marks it as an agent for effecting change.

The persistence of mind / body dualism and the associated immaterial/material binary is, I would suggest, due to its compatibility with a certain configuration of gender as an information pattern distinct from the materiality of the sexed body. In the transformative scenarios of cyberspace, gender becomes a key site of transformation insofar as it is understood to be information inscribed onto a material body that can be transcended through disembodiment or virtual rearticulation. In such a formulation, gender as information operates in two modes. First, it is distinct from yet affixed to materially sexed bodies, such that the two cannot be readily detached in the real world; however, through disembodiment or virtuality gender patterns may be eluded. Second, within pure information cyberspace, it is a free-floating pattern that as, Sherry Turkle describes, individuals can take up and rescind at will: "As MUD players talked to me about their experiences with gender swapping, they certainly gave me reason to believe that through this practice they were working through personal issues that had to do with accepting the feminine and/or masculine in their own personalities" (1994).

Gender has become a fraught concept in feminist theory in recent years, and as deployed in discourses of cyberspace it is problematic on a range of levels. Although such a configuration of gender suggests powerful bonds between bodies and gender—bonds that only drastic technological intervention can dislocate—this model of gender is clearly embedded in the information/matter binary. Insofar as gender can, in less socially saturated environments such as cyberspace, float free of bodies, it possesses an informational status in opposition to the matter of the bodies onto which it is inscribed. Framing gender as a socially generated information pattern that does not impinge on consciousness once that consciousness has disassociated itself from the body likewise turns on a binary opposition, in this case between mind information/body matter. This formation also underpins any scenario whereby consciousness can interact with various gender patterns at will within information space.

For some years feminists have been complicating this model of detachable gender precisely on the basis of its recourse to mind/body and other dichotomies. Gatens (1983) has convincingly shown that sexed bodies and socially inscribed masculinity and femininity are by no means neatly detachable or interchangeable. She insists that such inscriptions are deeply involved in the way bodies are lived, and that sexed bodies are inextricable from the way femininity or masculinity is experienced. However, in the desire for cybertransformation, these complexities invariably become simplified to a degendered consciousness that negotiates new (or not) relations with gender other than those of the physically sexed embodied subject. Even those such as Stone, who disdain any neat bisection of materially sexed body and socially gendered mind in favor of more complex interrelations between subjectivity and embodiment, entertain the possibility of virtual gender swapping and thus reiterate this gender-mind/sex-body binary. Thus any account that takes an unproblematic formulation of gender as detachable information pattern as the locus of transformation, such as those expressed by Turkle, Cherney, Shade, or Rheingold, remains bound by binary logic, unable to think bodies in cyberspace, confined to an economy of identity and ultimately unable to pursue the transformational possibilities of articulating difference.

The second conceptual model that I have suggested is key to the installation of the logic of identity at the heart of many cybertransformation scenarios is that of prosthesis. By prosthesis, I mean a particular conceptualization of the field and mode of encounter between subjects and technologies. In the simplest terms, a prosthetic understanding of technologies holds that a technological object, or practice, meets a subject's body and affects it in some way—enhancing it, reshaping it. Eyeglasses meet the eyes and extend the range of vision, pacemakers regulate the heart, telephones extend the range of the voice. A more sophisticated version of prosthesis is of course Donna Haraway's famous cyborg that celebrates the mutations wrought upon bodies through their intermeshing with technologies. In the case of the cyborg, the human is transformed as this intermeshing works to dislodge the socially constructed human subject. I claim that whatever permutations arise from a prosthetic encounter between bodies and technologies, they remain bound within the logic of identity or sameness that structures all binary oppositions.

The logic of identity pervades the prosthetic model of interaction and, in doing so, negates any possibility of autonomy and difference of bodies or technologies. The prosthetic equation is 1 + 1. It begins with an original self-identical entity being added to by some exterior element that has some effect upon it. The element that is added to the original is understood only in terms of its difference from the original as not-original. In the instance of embodied subjects and technologies, it is a self-identical and unified self upon which technology as not-self (or object) impacts and instigates some alteration. Regardless of the novelty of the resultant entity, this original binary demarcation of self/not-self grounds the entire process within the logic of sameness. Sameness is insinuated in the proposition of a singular, stable, identifiable 1 as the basis for all such encounters. We have seen this logic of sameness running through the accounts of bodies and cyberspace offered above. The technologies of cyberspace—the computer screens and keyboards, chips and cables, which generate a field of information on the other side of the screen—on encountering the body either relegate it entirely to one side of the screen or bisect it into an informational virtual body and a material body, one of which functions on the other side of the screen. Irrespective of the outcome, the fundamental encounter between bodies and technologies is elaborated in terms of a unified body acted upon by some "not-body" force or entity in a straightforward re-iteration of binary logic. Thus any account of cyberspace that begins with a prosthetic understanding of the interaction of technologies and subjects is already situated within the binary structure, and thus the possibilities of thinking transformation are already circumscribed.

Transformation based on both or either of these frameworks is impossible to the extent that they are embedded within the epistemological structures of identity that preclude any articulation of autonomous difference, including sexual difference. For those feminisms concerned with thinking sexual difference in its specificity, any investigation of the transformative possibilities of cyberspace requires, in the first instance, reconceptualizing bodies, technologies, and their modes of interaction such that the question never begins with the unified self-identical body of prosthesis, or an understanding of gender as detachable from bodies. It is at this point that I turn to Deleuze and Guattari for a fundamentally different account of the meetings between technologies and individuals, one that develops an alternative understanding of bodies and technologies that affirms difference instead of insinuating identity and sameness.

Deleuze and Guattari: Assembling Bodies

The question of the status of difference is central to the work of Deleuze and Guattari. For the purposes of this chapter I want to use one concept, the assemblage, as a point of entry into their intricate and difficult conceptual terrain. In thinking of the interactions between bodies and technologies in terms of assemblages, I would claim that we are able to frame an account that is not contained within the logic of identity. Rather it opens a field of inquiry that has as its basis "difference." Clearly such an endeavor is of great benefit for feminists concerned with articulating autonomous sexual difference and tracing how it might be elaborated across various technological formations of cyberspace. The process of establishing difference as the basis of the operations of assemblages is elaborated in great detail and complexity across the corpus of Deleuze and Guattari's work. Although I cannot explore it in detail here, I want to indicate a number of the key characteristics of their concept of assemblage that reframes the field of encounter between bodies and technologies and then speculate as to how this might impact feminist engagements with cyberspace.

According to Grosz, the Deleuzian concept of assemblage suggests "an altogether different way of understanding the body in its connections with other bodies, both human and nonhuman, animate and inanimate, linking organs and biological processes to material objects and social practices while refusing to subordinate the body to a unit of a homogeneity of the kind provided by the bodies subordination to consciousness or to biological organizations" (1987, 165). Here, Grosz signals some of the key shifts that the concept of assemblage makes: a refusal of identity or unity as an ordering logic, a shift in the relation between the parts and the whole, and a focus on the movements of linkage and connection. In examining the way assemblages are composed and how they function, we can see how each works to articulate the assemblage within a field of difference to circumvent identity as ground.

Assemblages are functional conglomerations of elements, but most important, the component elements are not understood as unified, stable, or self-identical entities or objects. In each assemblage the forces and flows of components meet with and link to the forces and flows of other elements; the resultant distribution of these meetings constitutes the assemblage. While concerned with the meetings of various objects and entities, this is not simply a prosthetic model of connection by addition. For Deleuze and Guattari, a self-identical body or object does not exist as origin, prior to or outside the field of encounters that articulate it within any specific assemblage. There is no original whole body that divides into organs, movements, pieces, forces, or information flows, which are then complied into assemblages. Rather bodies and other components are fields of multiplicities that make transitory connections and alignments within each assemblage.

Write Deleuze and Guattari, "For the moment, we will note that assemblages have elements (or multiplicities) of several kinds: human, social, and technical machines . . . We can no longer even speak of distinct machines, only of types of interpenetrating multiplicities that at any given moment form a single machinic assemblage" (1987, 36).

It is this insistence on multiplicity as the basis of an assemblage that circumvents the prosthetic equation. Indeed for Deleuze and Guattari, the concept of multiplicity becomes crucial in shifting from the field of identity and sameness and beginning to think instead about difference in terms other than lack or negation. They distinguish two types of multiplicity that are characterized by two types of difference—difference in degree and differences in kind.

A difference in degree is that which is articulated in relation to identity or unity as its origin. That is, it is structured around a central identity that operates as the determining factor from which all difference is understood in terms of diminution, distancing, or magnitude. Differentiated entities or elements are not considered in terms of any distinct autonomous existence or qualities but are always articulated in relation to the original term. For Deleuze this is the structure of the identity, where difference is recognized only in terms of degree of divergence from the original identity. The multiple in this instance is the $1 + 1 + 1$—that is, as magnitudes composed of quantifiable aggregations or multiplications of the identical, and always divisible into 1s as a base unit. Differences in kind, Deleuze finds, are entirely of another order from those of degree. They are differences that are not articulated in relation to a prior unity, identity, or central determinate. They are not different *from* or *to* but different *in* themselves. Multiplicities based on this difference are heterogeneous and continuous; they are not composed of homogenous discrete units of the identical nor divisible into an originary base unity. They do not divide without changing in nature. These multiplicities are characterized by "intensity" rather than magnitude, such that any change of state is not a diminution or addition—that is, an incremental change of degree—but rather changes the entire nature of the multiplicity—a change in kind (Deleuze 1988, 46–47). For Deleuze only difference in kind affirms difference as positive, not lack or diminution.

If the elements of the assemblage are multiplicities that intersect with other multiplicities, clearly each intersection will produce other multiplicities that differ in nature from any of those preceding. As such each element becomes something other with each new connection and within each assemblage. Thus when referring to the elements or components of an assemblage, we must remember that these contents of assemblages are never enduring, stable, individuated, and self-identical. Rather, multiplicities of flows and partial fragments of information, matter, ideas, particles, movements, and intensities coalesce into particular recognizable forms and functions within the context of particular assemblages. As such, the meetings between elements of assemblages do not proceed on the basis of a prosthetic encounter. Rather the flows, forces, and intensities of multiplicities link and connect with other flows and forces, and different multiplicities are elaborated. These are not hybrids, or variations; they differ in kind and cannot be traced back to a single original entity.

If the movement of differing constitutes an assemblage, and its components are not organized along the lines of identity, binary oppositions are no longer adequate as a means of establishing the status of any one element. For example, minds and bodies can no longer be explained in a binary relation where one is understood in terms of the other—bodies being characterized as the absence or lack of consciousness. Rather each is considered different in and of itself, and thus relation between the two no longer turns on any founding hierarchy. Both elements are equally operational in a productive mode. The forces of each meet and mix such that it is impossible to figure one as the diminution of the other as the privileged term. Clearly a new conception of bodies emerges within this field of differing. Instead of an organized, unified object subordinated to consciousness, bodies are collections of disparate flows, materials, impulses, intensities, and practices. They take shape within a complex field of relations with the flows and intensities of surrounding objects, knowledges, geographies, and institutional practices in transitory, functional assemblages. Grosz describes such bodies as "discontinuous, nontotalizable series of processes, organs, flows, energies, corporeal substances and incorporeal events, speeds and duration" (1988, 164).

The concept of assemblage, then, suggests a two-pronged approach to understanding bodies. First, that while they are undeniable concoctions of material, chemical, and electrical impulses, these are not fixed into any immutable pattern; they are continually in flux, open to the circumstances and fields of objects and discourses through which they circulate. Second, particular bodies are articulated or actualized, within complex assemblages of other bodies, objects, institutions, technologies, regimes of signs, and relations of power that may move to unify and stabilize them but can never entirely succeed in doing so.

Insofar as my discussion of assemblage draws on the terminology of construction and constitution, caution must be exercised so as not to conflate assemblages with a generalized constructivism. Assemblages propose an entirely different mode of understanding the constitution and functions of bodies (and other objects) than constructivist models. A brief examination of how each model responds to the question of the relation of the whole to the parts illustrates another of the theoretical shifts flagged earlier that Deleuze and Guattari make. Constructivist accounts propose an overarching system or structure that orders component parts. This whole not only transcends the parts but also determines them insofar as they are interpolated into it. For example, in the case of bodies the "biologically" female body is interpolated into the social institutions, discourses, and practices of an overarching systemic whole—such as patriarchy—to become a body constructed and experienced as feminine. Assemblages, in contrast, turn on a different understanding of the relation of the whole to the component elements, whereby the parts constitute the whole. Because it is composed of the links and connections between multiplicities, an assemblage is only ever the sum of its component elements and is not governed or ordered by any transcendent organizing structure. Given this composition, within an assemblage any change or shift in a constituent element brings about a new assemblage, whereas changes within the component parts in a constructivist model are permissible only within a limited sphere of variation, beyond which they become excluded, unintelligible, or rehabilitated while the whole remains intact.

If there is no transcendent whole or structure that constitutes and orders the component parts of any assemblage, social institutions, hierarchies, and relations of power function as elements of an assemblage. They no longer constitute an overarching structure but are themselves contingent and in flux. This is not to suggest that assemblages are not traversed by power relations and hierarchies. Deleuze and Guattari devote a great deal of attention to exploring stratification as a mode of organizing that actualizes particular relations of power and modes of knowledge. They describe the territorializing of assemblages as the mechanism by way of which power and knowledge paradigms function within assemblages. This does not, however, establish relations of power and knowledge as constituting assemblages per se. Rather this positioning of power and knowledge as functional elements of every assemblage marks another of the epistemological shifts that Deleuze and Guattari make. They contend that power relations and epistemological systems need to be understood in terms of what they do, the connections and linkages they make, how they are enacted and operate within an assemblage. For Deleuze and Guattari, assemblages are fundamentally machinic—that is, functional and productive. To map them involves investigating not what things are, by way of establishing a final unified identity, but rather what they do—how linkages are forged and how component entities are articulated and mutually constituted through such linkages. Thus, however pervasive and enduring something like the representational economy of identity may be, to the extent that it must achieve rearticulation in each new assemblage, it remains contingent and unstable and not ontological. Assemblages, no matter what the degree of territorialization, are always traversed by movements of deterritorialization that promise at each and any moment to form other linkages, to mutate an assemblage into something entirely different.

Feminism and Assemblages

For feminists investigating cyberspace, these theoretical shifts that Deleuze and Guattari make suggest the possibility of engagements with the technologies and practices of cyberspace that are not always already contained within the logic of identity that, as I have shown, forecloses transformation. Exploring and analyzing such engagements is a vast and complex task that is clearly beyond the bounds of this chapter. At most what I hope to accomplish here is to indicate the directions and theoretical tools that feminists taking up such projects might draw from Deleuze and Guattari. I would claim that the redrawn theoretical horizon that Deleuze and Guattari elaborate is useful to feminists on a number of levels. First, in theorizing assemblages as temporary aggregations of multiplicities, in which component elements find their local and specific articulation through their linkages with other elements, it offers an alternative to prosthesis as the mode of encounter between bodies and technologies: in the first instance because there is no assumption of a stable identified body prior to the encounter, and in the second because the encounters between bodies and technologies take place within a field of other intersections. The mode of meeting is never one of simple addition, of 1 + 1; rather, each instance gives rise to a new configuration of bodies and technologies and all the other elements of an assemblage. The task then becomes not to measure what effects technologies have on unified stable bodies, but to track what configurations of bodies, technologies, practices, objects, and discourses emerge within particular assemblages.

Thus instead of concluding that beyond the contact of fingers with keyboards and eyes with screen the body is effectively excluded from cyberspace, it would be a matter of tracing what kinds of bodies are elaborated in the activities, exchanges, and circuits of the particular practices. For example in the instance of the cyberspace of a MOO, a body is not simply split into a materiality that is excluded and an electronic/informational body that is activated in the social environs of the MOO. Rather the energy and impulses of bodies and electronic circuitry combine and find new forms, and they are traversed by flows of light, information, signs, sociality, sexuality, conversation, and contact that give rise to differing meanings, experiences, and configurations of bodies and technologies. It becomes a question of tracing out these differing configurations not by beginning with an already established model of the body but by mapping the assembled field in order to track very specifically what bodies come into being and how.

This points immediately to the second useful aspect of Deleuze and Guattari's model of assemblage and multiplicity for feminists. It offers a diagnostic tool with which to begin mapping how assembled bodies and technologies and social spaces and practices intersect with systems of knowledge and power. Why and how do certain bodies and models of interaction with technology such as prosthesis emerge and predominate? It becomes possible to map how certain understandings of woman are formulated in conjunction with certain understandings of the technological and the social. Further, it is possible to trace this process in a tangible way across particular practices and discourses, such as those of cyberspace, in order to map the complex ways in which power and knowledge intersect with these formulations. For example, feminist concerns, such as those voiced by Renate Klein (1999), as to the risks posed to women in their engagements with "techno-patriarchy" (210) of cyberspace can be assessed such that they are not premised on an essential alienation of women from technologies. While not denying the very real inequities operational in many practices associated with cyberspace, Deleuze and Guattari offer a more sophisticated and less teleological approach to analyzing the operations of power within such practices. If, following Deleuze, we approach technology, masculinity, femininity, technoscientific discourses, and military-industrial complexes as a series of interconnected assemblages, we can begin to delineate more clearly how such associations of masculinity with technologies of computing function and on what basis women are articulated as incompatible with those technologies. Through such a process, the very tangible operations of power should become apparent. Further, within such an analysis no individual technological formation is automatically foreclosed to women on the basis of an essential masculinity, but the relations and operations of power that render it oppressive to women can be more acutely discerned and its responses then formulated.

The third aspect of Deleuze and Guattari's model of assemblage that is of importance to feminists is the shift whereby structures of knowledge and power such as the economics of identity are repositioned as functional elements of an assemblage rather than as overarching and transcendent structures. It is on this basis that the above diagnostic exercise can proceed. Deleuze and Guattari begin with a different question— asking what an object, assemblage, practice, institution, discourse *does* rather than what it *is*. In making such an initial reorientation, our inquiries are no longer directed toward uncovering or defining an essential identity of these elements, which as we saw earlier most often leads to an installation of the epistemological structures of identity. Rather, it is to begin to (1) trace the processes through which identity is installed, and (2) consider what configurations of forces and objects are relegated to outside the limits of this identity that might suggest other formulations of bodies, subjects and technologies.

Thus in taking up a Deleuzian approach to cyberspace, two immediate tasks present themselves to feminists. First, we must understand cyberspace itself as not simply a technologically generated information space or place, but as a series of assemblages comprised of elements of the technical, social, discursive, material, and immaterial. It then becomes necessary to map such assemblages in order to discern how relations of power traverse them, how discourses and practices of femininity and masculinity intersect with those of technology and technological artifacts, what hierarchies are functional, and through what particular and local linkages are bodies and technologies articulated. Though this mapping process, a more nuanced and complex understanding of the operations of prevailing power relations and modes of knowledge will emerge. Such a mapping process will alert feminists to any exclusionary and oppressive practices, arrangements, and structures of knowledge that, while frequently circumscribing women's encounters with the technological, never completely foreclose transformative possibilities. Second, having traced out these fields of intersection among bodies, technologies, information flows, power relations, social institutions, and practices, we can begin to investigate the lines of flight and movements of differing that also always traverse an assemblage. It is these movements that are creative in their own right and that raise the possibility that new connections and configurations of technologies and bodies might generate a field within which new autonomous unrestricted articulations of woman might emerge.

Notes

1. For an broad introduction to corporeal feminism and the problematic of binary logic, see Irigaray 1985, Grosz 1994, and Kirby 1997.
2. Landmark examples of this position can be found in Stone 1991 and Rheingold 1991.

Works Cited

Cherney, Lyn. "Objectifying the Body in the Discourse of an Object-Oriented MUD." 1996. Available online at <http:// bhasha.stanford.edu/~cherny/charley.tx>. 1 March 2000.

Deleuze, Gilles. *Bergsonism.* Trans. Barbara Habberjam and Hugh Thomlinson. New York: Zone Books, 1988.

Deleuze, Gilles, and Felix Guattari, *A Thousand Plateaus: Capitalism and Schizophrenia.* Trans. Brian Massumi. Minneapolis: University of Minnesota Press, 1987.

Gatens, Moira. "A Critique of the Sex/Gender Distinction." In *Interventions after Marx,* ed. J. Allen and P. Patton, 18–33. Sydney: Intervention, 1983.

Grosz, Elizabeth. "Notes Towards a Corporeal Feminism." *Australian Feminist Studies* 5, (Summer 1987): 1–16.

Grosz, Elizabeth. *Volatile Bodies. Toward a Corporeal Feminism.* St. Leonards: Allen & Unwin, 1994.

Hayles, N. Katherine. "Boundary Disputes: Homeostasis, Reflexivity and the Foundation of Cybernetics." *Configurations: A Journal of Literature, Science & Technology* 2, no. 3 (1994): 441–467.

Hayles, N. Katherine. *How We Became Posthuman.* Chicago: University of Chicago Press, 1999.

Irigaray, L. *Speculum of the Other Woman.* Trans. G. Gill. Ithaca: Cornell University Press, 1985.

Kirby, V. *Telling Flesh: The Substance of the Corporeal.* New York: Routledge, 1997.

Klein, Renate. "If I'm a Cyborg Rather Than a Goddess Will Patriarchy Go Away?" In *Cyberfeminism: Connectivity, Critique and Creativity*, ed. S. Hawthorne and R. Klein. Melbourne, Australia: Spinifex Press, 1999.

Moravec, Hans. *Mind Children: The Future of Robot and Human Intelligence*. Cambridge: Harvard University Press, 1988.

Rheingold, Howard. *Virtual Reality*. New York: Summit Books, 1991.

Rheingold, Howard. *Virtual Communities: Homesteading on the Electronic Frontier*. New York: Addison-esley Publishing Company, 1993.

Shade, Leslie Regan. "Gender Issues in Computer Networks." 1996. Available online at <http://www.vcn.bc.ca/sig/comm-nets/shade.html>. 1 March 2000.

Stone, Allucquère Rosanne. "Will the Real Body Please Stand Up? Boundary Stories about Virtual Cultures." In *Cyberspace: The First Steps*, ed. M. Benedikt. Cambridge, MA: MIT Press, 1991.

Turkle, Sherry. "Constructions and Reconstructions of Self in Virtual Reality: Playing in the MUDs." 1994. Available online at <http://www.mit.edu/people/sturkle/constructions.html>.1 March 2000.

27

SHOCKINGLY TECH-SPLICIT: THE PERFORMANCE POLITICS OF ORLAN AND OTHER CYBORGS

Theresa M. Senft

In 1896, after watching a performance of *Ubu Roi* (arguably the most bodily explicit theater of its day), William Butler Yeats was moved to write, "What more is possible? After us the Savage God."[1]

In 1996, after hearing I was going to write about the French performer Orlan (arguably the most notorious bodily explicit artist today), my friend Cathy was moved to warn me, "Just remember, sometimes it's still better to be a goddess than a cyborg."

I know that as a self-proclaimed "technofeminist," Cathy half-jokes above, inverting Donna Haraway's famous line, "I'd rather be a cyborg than a goddess," to worry over the feminist politics of Orlan. After all, it was Haraway who first challenged feminism's pathological need to worship goddess figures at the altar of "the natural body." She insisted to feminists that the natural body, if it ever existed to begin with, was no more.[2] These days, it is the cyborg—the body containing both organic and technological components—that "is our ontology; it gives us our politics."[3]

If (as feminism would have it) the personal is political, and (as Haraway argues) the woman is now the cyborg, what performance could be termed more feminist than Orlan's self-surgeries? Still, I think Cathy's joke about "goddess nostalgia" displays an anxiety often alluded to but rarely dealt with head-on in feminist art criticism. It is between Yeats's modernist anxiety and Cathy's postmodern one that I'd like to situate this essay.

For those unfamiliar with the story, Orlan began her practice of "carnal art" in 1978, after she was rushed to the hospital for an emergency operation. According to her biography, "She had just enough time to install a video camera in the operating theater. As soon as the first tape was recorded, an ambulance took it to the Lyon Center of Contemporary Art." Orlan calls herself "the first artist to use surgery and plastic surgery, taking it out of its original context, appropriating it for her own means." In 1990, she initiated a series of plastic surgeries designed to progressively sculpt her face into a combination of the Mona Lisa, Diana, and Boticelli's Venus.[4]

In her seventh operation, entitled *Omnipresence*, a female surgeon's knife cut into Orlan's face, while her image was broadcast via satellite to thirteen galleries around the world, with accompanying audio and fax documentation. Theater theorist Sue Ellen Case argues that *Omnipresence* is a sophisticated indictment of the first world capital currently required to maintain "universal" feminine ideals of beauty. Case points to Orlan's use of multiple technologies—medical, sartorial, communications—in order to make her body, and her changing physical identity, a spectacle in every sense of that word and to chart the costs of that spectacle. For this reason, argues Case, *Omnipresence* is as much about the politics of communications technology as it is about the female surgical body.[5]

Orlan's work is complex and leaves itself open to misappropriations and misinterpretations. Tanya Augsburg notes that because of the extreme nature of Orlan's operations, feminist critiques embedded within her performances are often forgotten by the world at large, who tend to ask not "Is this art?" but rather "Is she mad?"[6] Orlan responds by observing that one can "do mad things without being mad oneself." I agree with this statement and believe that the question of Orlan's sanity is a red herring at best and misogynist at worst. No one seems to ask whether Stellarc is mad. Further, I do not think Orlan is "bad" for advocating surgery (she does) or pain (she does not). In fact, *I want to believe* that carnal art like Orlan's might serve as a model for techno-feminist performance of the future.

Unfortunately, I cannot. Though Orlan repeatedly states that her work is not about shock, when she began, the image of a woman broadcasting her cosmetic surgeries to art galleries *was* shocking. Historically, the biggest proponents of the artistic shock (or what Yeats called "the Savage God") have been the political liberals of the age. The avant-garde has long championed what they called the "explicit body," citing it as a source of immanence and transcendence: a shocking icon of life, elevated to the status of art. Those who have objected to shock gestures in performance, on the other hand, have long been deemed political conservatives.

But as any feminist can tell you, all bodies, all icons, and all shocks aren't interpreted equally. Early in her career, Orlan dealt with a variety of scandalous topics, including sex work, reworking of religious iconography, and feminist reinterpretations of new media. The fact is, however, that isn't enough for a feminist artist to shock in her explicit body work; to have the desired political effects, she discovered, her body must produce the right *kinds of shock*. One day, riding in an ambulance to have an emergency operation, Orlan found what she was looking for. By 1990, she launched an international art career with a motto that comes straight out of the historical avant-garde: "Being operated on is beyond the frivolous."

A decade later, however, that statement is hardly true. In fact, "frivolous surgery" is at an all-time historical high. What's more, broadcasts of such surgery, via "reality television" and "infotainment venues," are now staples of consumer culture. In America and Europe, doctors routinely ask patients if they'd like the videos of their own surgeries. If "making the invisible visible" were truly her aim, Orlan might leave the space of the art gallery and learn some lessons from singer Carnie Wilson, who managed to have her stomach reduction surgery broadcast over the Web to a record number of viewers in August 1999. Not that feminist critique was anywhere to be found in that spectacle: Most of the coverage wavered from proclamations of "empowerment" to details of Phillips's impending wedding.[7] Still, the notion that anything surgical remains "hidden" in the year 2001 strikes me as specious.

In a kind of postmodern joke on both Donna Haraway and the goddess feminists of the 1970s, Orlan calls her entire project "The Reincarnation of Saint Orlan." From goddess to savage, from cyborg to saint: so the logic goes. But this logic is flawed. Orlan proposes that when we watch her performances, we do so dialectically; we ought to "do what you probably do when you watch the news on television."[8] When Donna Haraway watches the news, she sees the cyborg bodies of South Korean workers, producing the silicon used for surgical implants (and for computerized broadcast technologies). She sees, as well, the specter of First World women, celebrating successful plastic surgeries and agonizing over sonograms that indicate their bodies are not quite "right." In short, she sees an international network of cyborgs, linked by technologies that both pleasure and discipline their lives.[9]

Orlan, it seems, sees only herself. Less than fifteen years after Haraway wrote "A Cyborg Manifesto," Orlan has achieved fame for displaying her body, not as the cyborg of the nightly news, but rather as the cyborg who becomes a goddess, thereby missing Haraway's political point completely. As if to crystallize her status as an avant-garde token, Orlan has written, "When my operations are finished, I will solicit an advertising agency to come up with a name and logo; next I will retain a lawyer to petition the Republic to accept my new identity and my new faces." In other words, she'll be the high-art equivalent of the Artist Formerly Known as Orlan.

I wonder what Prince (to name the best-known "Artist Formerly Known As") might make of Orlan's newfound fascination for racial appropriation as a form of reinvention. In her newest installation, "Hybridations," Orlan utilizes 3-D modeling techniques, superimposing them over her own image to explore pre-Columbian ideas of beauty. Throughout, she is fond of quoting this passage, by Lacanian psychoanalyst Eugenie Lemoine-Luccioni: "I have the skin of an angel, but I am a jackal . . . the skin of a crocodile, but I am a puppy, the skin of a black person, but I am white, the skin of a woman, but I am a man; I never have the skin of what I am. There is no exception to the rule because I am never what I have." [10]

It doesn't take a postcolonial scholar to figure out that the interchangeability of angels and jackals are one thing, and the temporary appropriation of black masks by those with white skin are a different matter entirely. In this seemingly harmless experimentation with the primitive, I find myself wondering where the Savage Gods of shock end and where the Noble Savage of the Enlightenment begins. In truth, what Orlan's work demonstrates is that endlessly mutable identity is hardly a universal (or artistic) truth, but the privilege of a special sort of postmodern citizen.

Is this racist and blissfully bourgeois spectacle the payoff of shock art for women? Is this what we want the future to look like? Not every theorist thinks so. In her book *Unmarked*, Peggy Phelan has argued against the avant-garde shock politics of visibility, urging feminists to consider new technologies, not for more "exposure," but rather to effect "an active vanishing, a deliberate and conscious refusal to take the payoff of visibility." [11] Last year, I sat in darkness, watching and listening as artists Sharon Lehner and Tina LaPorta took Phelan's praxis, and made it performance.

"The room is dark," begins *My Womb the Mosh Pit*, Sharon Lehner's voice echoing from a microphone somewhere off-stage. [12] "I look at the monitor," she says. On cue, the room suddenly floods with light. Computerized grids of female bodies, rendered by digital artist Tina LaPorta, are projected over the walls. Superimposed within those multiple grids is a single sonogram.

"It takes thirty minutes," Sharon narrates, "to measure and inventory the body parts of this fetus: the arms, the legs, the stomach, the liver, the lungs, the kidneys, the brain." When Sharon confesses, "I find looking at the fetus in my body to be unbelievably pleasurable," I suddenly realize I've been gazing at her body. Momentarily intrigued, I struggle to make out the body parts Sharon tells me are located right in front of my eyes. After a while, however, I realize that if I am supposed to be Sharon in this performance, it's not working.

I hate pregnant women who gush. "After the examination," Sharon gushes, "the technician offers me a few snapshots from the collection stapled to my medical records. I forget about girl names, report to my friends, call my family." "Whatever," I think, wondering instead what kind of 3-D modeling technologies LaPorta uses to make the endlessly turning grids on the walls.

"Exactly ten days before I aborted a ten-inch fetus from my body in the company of medical strangers," Sharon's voice booms above my head, "I laughed with wonder at what looked like a naked baby boy." Suddenly, I realize I've been seeing things all wrong:

What I thought was some advertisement for fertility is actually a picture of a body that no longer lives, narrated by a woman I can't see. As if to complicate things further, I later find out that the sonogram image I've been staring at isn't from Sharon's body at all.

My Womb is explicitly feminist yet resists both liberals and conservatives who equate sonogram images with fetuses, and fetuses with infants. "I bonded with an image, I aborted an image, I grieve an image," Sharon insists, except that the image displayed isn't the image for which she grieves. In a brilliant reversal of the tactics of the religious Right—who champion the "rights of the fetus," thereby erasing and/or interchanging women's bodies—*My Womb* instead claims a right of motherhood without birth and uses technology against itself, grieving an anonymous sonogram.

When Sharon confesses her desire to "look again for that bleep onscreen," I think I understand, musing on my last round of technological joys: the arrival of my school loan check; a much-desired "negative" sign on a recent early pregnancy test; the announcement that a friend's T-cell count has risen.

By displaying and displacing the truth-claims of reproductive imaging systems, *My Womb* challenges the avant-garde's easy correspondence between vision and transcendence, and questions what an "explicit body" truly is, in this day and age. But this performance does far more than critique the avant-garde. I'd go so far as to say that because it eschews mythologizing, and instead tells an ordinary cyborg story of an ordinary cyborg woman, *My Womb* points to a new feminist aesthetic: one that emphasizes the contradictions and ambivalence within the lives of everyday technological women here and now.

For each of us, the technological is personal, the personal is political, the political—depending, as it does, on the "truth" of the representational—is mutable. Orlan's notoriety aside, the avant-garde's goddess/cyborg dyad is officially over, if it ever really existed. For feminists using new media to make art that comments on our lives in this technological age, I offer one warning: sometimes it's still more precious to be a woman than a goddess or a cyborg.

Notes

Thanks to Alanna Thain for requesting this essay for the Discipline and Deviance Conference at Duke University and for Tina LaPorta's comments at the Women in New Media Conference at Rutgers University. Additional thanks to Jennifer Natalya Fink for her editorial input. Mary Flanagan and Austin Booth I thank for their patience.

1. William Butler Yeats, *The Autobiographies of W. B. Yeats* (New York: Macmillan, 1958), 233–234. As cited by Rebecca Schneider in *The Explicit Body in Performance* (New York: Routledge, 1997), 126. For those looking to chart the connections between

women's body-art and the historical avant-garde, Schneider's book is an excellent starting point.

2. Donna Haraway, "A Cyborg Manifesto," in *Cyborgs, Simians, and Women: The Reinvention of Nature* (New York: Routledge, 1991), 149–181.

3. Haraway, "A Cyborg Manifesto," 153.

4. Unless noted otherwise, all information regarding Orlan's performances and manifestos are taken from her official Web site. Orlan, "Introduction," 18 January 2000. Online. Available at <http://www.cicv.fr/creation_artistique/online/orlan/>.

5. Sue Ellen Case, *The Domain-Matrix: Performing Lesbian at the End of Print Culture.* (Bloomington: Indiana University Press, 1997), 117–118.

6. Tanya Augsburg, "Orlan's Performative Transformations of Subjectivity," in *The End(s) of Perfomance*, ed. Peggy Phelan and Jill Lane (New York: New York University Press, 1997), 288.

7. To witness the growing trend of "celebrity surgeries," see Spotlife Health, "Morbid Obesity," 1 January 2001. Available at <0http://www.spotlighthealth.com/morbid_obesity/mo/mo.htm>. (20 February 2001).

8. Orlan, "Intervention," in *The End(s) of Performance*, ed. Peggy Phelan and Jill Lane. (New York: New York University Press, 1997), 316.

9. Haraway, "A Cyborg Manifesto," 149–181.

10. See Orlan's Web site (which does not cite the source of Lemoine-Luccioni's original quote) at Orlan, "Introduction," 18 January 2000. Online. Available at <http://www.cicv.fr/creation_artistique/online/orlan/index1.html>.

11. Peggy Phelan, *Unmarked: The Politics of Performance* (New York: Routledge, 1993), 6.

12. Sharon Lehner, *My Womb The Mosh Pi*, dir. Sharon Lehner, with Tina LaPorta. P.S. 122, New York, 17 May 1997.

Works Cited

Augsburg, Tanya. "Orlan's Performative Transformations of Subjectivity." In *The End(s) of Perfomance*, ed. Peggy Phelan and Jill Lane. New York: New York University Press. 1997.

Case, Sue Ellen. *The Domain-Matrix: Performing Lesbian at the End of Print Culture.* Bloomington: Indiana University Press, 1997.

Haraway, Donna. "A Cyborg Manifesto." In *Cyborgs, Simians, and Women: The Reinvention of Nature.* New York: Routledge, 1991.

Lehner, Sharon. *My Womb the Mosh Pit*, dir. Sharon Lehner, with Tina LaPorta. P.S. 122, New York, 17 May 1997.

Orlan. "Intervention." In *The End(s) of Performance*, ed. Peggy Phelan, and Jill Lane, 315–327. New York: New York University Press, 1997.

Orlan, "Introduction." 18 January 2000. Online. Available at <http://www.civ.fr/creation_artistique/online/orlan>. 20 February 2001.

Phelan, Peggy. *Unmarked: The Politics of Performance.* New York: Routledge, 1993.

Schneider, Rebecca. *The Explicit Body in Performance.* New York: Routledge, 1997.

Spotlife Health. "Morbid Obesity." 1 January 2001. Online. Available at <http://www.spotlighthealth.com/morbid_obesity/mo/mo.htm>. 20 February 2001.

Yeats, William Butler. *The Autobiographies of W. B. Yeats.* New York: Macmillan, 1958.

28

THE GIRL WHO WAS PLUGGED IN

James Tiptree Jr. (Alice B. Sheldon)

Listen, zombie. Believe me. What I could tell you—you with your silly hands leaking sweat on your growth-stocks portfolio. One-ten lousy hacks of AT&T on twenty-point margin and you think you're Evel Knievel. AT&T? You doubleknit dummy, how I'd love to show you something.

Look, dead daddy, I'd say. See for instance that rotten girl?

In the crowd over there, that one gaping at her gods. One rotten girl in the city of the future (That's what I said.) Watch.

She's jammed among bodies, craning and peering with her soul yearning out of her eyeballs. Love! Oo-ooh, love them! Her gods are coming out of a store called Body East. Three youngbloods, larking along loverly. Dressed like simple street-people but . . . smashing. See their great eyes swivel above their nose-filters, their hands lift shyly, their inhumanly tender lips melt? The crowd moans. Love! This whole boiling megacity, this whole fun future world loves its gods.

You don't believe gods, dad? Wait. Whatever turns you on, there's a god in the future for you, custom-made. Listen to this mob. "I touched his foot! Ow-oow, I TOUCHED Him!"

Even the people in the GTX tower up there love the gods—in their own way and for their own reasons.

The funky girl on the street, she just loves. Grooving on their beautiful lives, their mysterioso problems. No one ever told her about mortals who love a god and end up as a tree or a sighing sound. In a million years it'd never occur to her that her gods might love her back.

She's squashed against the wall now as the godlings come by. They move in a clear space. A holocam bobs above, but its shadow never falls on them. The store display-screens are magically clear of bodies as the gods glance in and a beggar underfoot is suddenly alone. They give him a token. "Aaaaah!" goes the crowd.

Now one of them flashes some wild new kind of timer and they all trot to catch a shuttle, just like people. The shuttle stops for them—more magic. The crowd sighs, closing back. The gods are gone.

(In a room far from—but not unconnected to—the GTX tower a molecular flip-flop closes too, and three account tapes spin.)

Our girl is still stuck by the wall while guards and holocam equipment pull away. The adoration's fading from her face. That's good, because now you can see she's the ugly of the world. A tall monument to pituitary dystrophy. No surgeon would touch her. When she smiles, her jaw—it's half purple—almost bites her left eye out. She's also quite young, but who could care?

The crowd is pushing her along now, treating you to glimpses of her jumbled torso, her mismatched legs. At the corner she strains to send one last fond spasm after the godlings' shuttle. Then her face reverts to its usual expression of dim pain and she lurches onto the moving walkway, stumbling into people. The walkway junctions with another. She crosses, trips and collides with the casualty rail. Finally she comes out into a little bare place called a park. The sportshow is working, a basketball game in three-di is going on right overhead. But all she does is squeeze onto a bench and huddle there while a ghostly free-throw goes by her ear.

After that nothing at all happens except a few furtive handmouth gestures which don't even interest her bench mates.

But you're curious about the city? So ordinary after all, in the FUTURE?

Ah, there's plenty to swing with here—and it's not all that *far* in the future, dad. But pass up the sci-fi stuff for now, like for instance the holovision technology that's put TV and radio in museums. Or the worldwide carrier field bouncing down from satellites, controlling communication and transport systems all over the globe. That was a spin-off from asteroid mining, pass it by. We're watching that girl.

I'll give you just one goodie. Maybe you noticed on the sport-show or the streets? No commercials. No ads.

That's right. NO ADS. An eyeballer for you.

Look around. Not a billboard, sign, slogan, jingle, sky-write, blurb, sublimflash, in this whole fun world. Brand names? Only in those ticky little peep-screens on the stores, and you could hardly call that advertising. How does that finger you?

Think about it. That girl is still sitting there.

She's parked right under the base of the GTX tower, as a matter of fact. Look way up and you can see the sparkles from the bubble on top, up there among the domes of godland. Inside that bubble is a boardroom. Neat bronze shield on the door: Global Transmissions Corporation—not that that means anything.

I happen to know there are six people in that room. Five of them technically male, and the sixth isn't easily thought of as a mother. They are absolutely unremarkable. Those faces were seen once at their nuptials and will show again in their obituaries and impress nobody either time. If you're looking for the secret Big Blue Meanies of the world, forget it. I know. Zen, do I know! Flesh? Power? Glory? You'd horrify them.

What they do like up there is to have things orderly, especially their communications. You could say they've dedicated their lives to that, to freeing the world from garble. Their nightmares are about hemorrhages of information; channels screwed up, plans misimplemented, garble creeping in. Their gigantic wealth only worries them, it keeps opening new vistas of disorder. Luxury? They wear what their tailors put on them, eat what their cooks serve them. See that old boy there—his name is Isham—he's sipping water and frowning as he listens to a databall. The water was prescribed by his medistaff. It tastes awful. The databall also contains a disquieting message about his son, Paul.

But it's time to go back down, far below to our girl. Look!

She's toppled over sprawling on the ground.

A tepid commotion ensues among the bystanders. The consensus is she's dead, which she disproves by bubbling a little. And presently she's taken away by one of the superb ambulances of the future, which are a real improvement over ours when one happens to be around.

At the local bellevue the usual things are done by the usual team of clowns aided by a saintly mop-pusher. Our girl revives enough to answer the questionnaire without which you can't die, even in the future. Finally she's cast up, a pumped-out hulk on a cot in the long, dim ward.

Again nothing happens for a while except that her eyes leak a little from the understandable disappointment of finding herself still alive.

But somewhere one GTX computer has been tickling another, and toward midnight something does happen. First comes an attendant who pulls screens around her. Then a man in a business doublet comes daintily down the ward. He motions the attendant to strip off the sheet and go.

The groggy girl-brute heaves up, big hands clutching at body-parts you'd pay not to see.

"Burke? P. Burke, is that your name?"

"Y-yes." Croak. "Are you . . . policeman?"

"No. They'll be along shortly, I expect. Public suicide's a felony."

" . . . I'm sorry."

He has a 'corder in his hand. "No family, right?"

"No."

"You're seventeen. One year city college. What did you study?"

"La—languages."

"H'mm. Say something."

Unintelligible rasp.

He studies her. Seen close, he's not so elegant. Errand-boy type.

"Why did you try to kill yourself?"

She stares at him with dead-rat dignity, hauling up the gray sheet. Give him a point, he doesn't ask twice.

"Tell me, did you see Breath this afternoon?"

Dead as she nearly is, that ghastly love-look wells up. Breath is the three young gods, a loser's cult. Give the man another point, he interprets her expression.

"How would you like to meet them?"

The girl's eyes bug out grotesquely.

"I have a job for someone like you. It's hard work. If you did well you'd be meeting Breath and stars like that all the time."

Is he insane? She's deciding she really did die.

"But it means you never see anybody you know again. Never, *ever*. You will be legally dead. Even the police won't know. Do you want to try?"

It all has to be repeated while her great jaw slowly sets. *Show me the fire I walk through.* Finally P. Burke's prints are in his 'corder, the man holding up the big rancid girl-body without a sign of distaste. It makes you wonder what else he does.

And then—THE MAGIC. Sudden silent trot of litterbearers tucking P. Burke into something quite different from a bellevue stretcher, the oiled slide into the daddy of all luxury ambulances—real flowers in that holder!—and the long jarless rush to nowhere. Nowhere is warm and gleaming and kind with nurses. (Where did you hear that money can't buy genuine kindness?) And clean clouds folding P. Burke into bewildered sleep.

. . . Sleep which merges into feedings and washings and more sleeps, into drowsy moments of afternoon where midnight should be, and gentle businesslike voices and friendly (but very few) faces, and endless painless hyposprays and peculiar numbnesses. And later comes the steadying rhythm of days and nights, and a quickening which P Burke doesn't identify as health, but only knows that the fungus place in her armpit is gone. And then she's up and following those few new faces with growing trust, first tottering, then walking strongly, all better now, clumping down the short hall to the tests, tests, tests, and the other things.

And here is our girl, looking—If possible, worse than before. (You thought this was Cinderella transistorized?)

The disimprovement in her looks comes from the electrode jacks peeping out of her sparse hair, and there are other meldings of flesh and metal. On the other hand, that collar and spinal plate are really an asset; you won't miss seeing that neck.

P. Burke is ready for training in her new job.

The training takes place in her suite and is exactly what you'd call a charm course. How to walk, sit, eat, speak, blow her nose, how to stumble, to urinate, to hiccup— DELICIOUSLY. How to make each nose-blow or shrug delightfully, subtly, different from any ever spooled before. As the man said, it's hard work.

But P. Burke proves apt. Somewhere in that horrible body is a gazelle, a houri, who would have been buried forever without this crazy chance. See the ugly duckling go!

Only it isn't precisely P. Burke who's stepping, laughing, shaking out her shining hair. How could it be? P. Burke is doing it all right, but she's doing it through something. The something is to all appearances a live girl. (You were warned, this is the FUTURE.)

When they first open the big cryocase and show her her new body, she says just one word. Staring, gulping, "How?"

Simple, really. Watch P. Burke in her sack and scuffs stump down the hall beside Joe, the man who supervises the technical part of her training. Joe doesn't mind P. Burke's looks, he hasn't noticed them. To Joe, system matrices are beautiful.

They go into a dim room containing a huge cabinet like a one-man sauna and a console for Joe. The room has a glass wall that's all dark now. And just for your information, the whole shebang is five hundred feet underground near what used to be Carbondale, Pa.

Joe opens the sauna cabinet like a big clamshell standing on end with a lot of funny business inside. Our girl shucks her shift and walks into it bare, totally unembarrassed. *Eager.* She settles in face-forward, butting jacks into sockets. Joe closes it carefully onto her humpback. Clunk. She can't see in there or hear or move. She hates this minute. But how she loves what comes next!

Joe's at his console, and the lights on the other side of the glass wall come up. A room is on the other side, all fluff and kicky bits, a girly bedroom. In the bed is a small mound of silk with a rope of yellow hair hanging out.

The sheet stirs and gets whammed back flat.

Sitting up in the bed is the darlingest girl child you've EVER seen. She quivers— porno for angels. She sticks both her little arms straight up, flips her hair, looks around full of sleepy pazazz. Then she can't resist rubbing her hands down over her mini-breasts and belly. Because, you see, it's the god-awful P. Burke who is sitting there hugging her perfect girl-body, looking at you out of delighted eyes.

Then the kitten hops out of bed and crashes flat on the floor.

From the sauna in the dim room comes a strangled noise. P. Burke, trying to rub her wired-up elbow, is suddenly smothered in *two* bodies, electrodes jerking in her flesh. Joe juggles inputs, crooning into his mike. The flurry passes; it's all right.

In the lighted room the elf gets up, casts a cute glare at the glass wall, and goes into a transparent cubicle. A bathroom, what else? She's a live girl, and live girls have to go to the bathroom after a night's sleep even if their brains are in a sauna cabinet in the next room. And P. Burke isn't in that cabinet, she's in the bathroom. Perfectly simple, if you have the glue for that closed training circuit that's letting her run her neural system by remote control.

Now let's get one thing clear. P. Burke does not *feel* her brain is in the sauna room, she feels she's in that sweet little body. When you wash your hands, do you feel the water is running on your brain? Of course not. You feel the water on your hand, although the "feeling" is actually a potential-pattern flickering over the electrochemical jelly between your ears. And it's delivered there via the long circuits from your hands. Just so, P. Burke's brain in the cabinet feels the water on her hands in the bathroom. The fact that the signals have jumped across space on the way in makes no difference at all. If you want the jargon, it's known as eccentric projection or sensory reference and you've done it all your life. Clear?

Time to leave the honeypot to her toilet training—she's made a booboo with the toothbrush, because P. Burke can't get used to what she sees in the mirror—

But wait, you say. Where did that girl-body come from?

P. Burke asks that too, dragging out the words.

"They grow 'em," Joe tells her. He couldn't care less about the flesh department. "PDs. Placental decanters. Modified embryos, see? Fit the control implants in later. Without a Remote Operator it's just a vegetable. Look at the feet—no callus at all." (He knows because they told him.)

"Oh . . . oh, she's incredible."

"Yeah, a neat job. Want to try walking-talking mode today? You're coming on fast."

And she is. Joe's reports and the reports from the nurse and the doctor and style man go to a bushy man upstairs who is some kind of medical cybertech but mostly a project administrator. His reports in turn go—to the GTX boardroom? Certainly not, did you think this is a *big* thing? His reports just go up. The point is, they're green, very green. P. Burke promises well.

So the bushy man—Dr. Tesla—has procedures to initiate. The little kitten's dossier in the Central Data Bank, for instance. Purely routine. And the phase-in schedule which will put her on the scene. This is simple: a small exposure in an off-network holoshow.

James Tiptree Jr. (Alice B. Sheldon)

Next he has to line out the event which will fund and target her. That takes budget meetings, clearances, coordinations. The Burke project begins to recruit and grow. And there's the messy business of the name, which always gives Dr. Tesla an acute pain in the bush.

The name comes out weird, when it's suddenly discovered that Burke's "P." stands for "Philadelphia." Philadelphia? The astrologer grooves on it. Joe thinks it would help identification. The semantics girl references *brotherly love, Liberty Bell, main line, low teratogenesis*, blah-blah. Nicknames Philly? Pala? Pooty? Delphi? Is it good, bad? Finally "Delphi" is gingerly declared goodo. ("Burke" is replaced by something nobody remembers.)

Coming along now. We're at the official checkout down in the underground suite, which is as far as the training circuits reach. The bushy Dr. Tesla is there, braced by two budgetary types and a quiet fatherly man whom he handles like hot plasma.

Joe swings the door wide and she steps shyly in.

Their little Delphi, fifteen and flawless.

Tesla introduces her around. She's child-solemn, a beautiful baby to whom something so wonderful has happened you can feel the tingles. She doesn't smile, she . . . brims. That brimming joy is all that shows of P. Burke, the forgotten hulk in the sauna next door. But P. Burke doesn't know she's alive—it's Delphi who lives, every warm inch of her.

One of the budget types lets go a libidinous snuffle and freezes. The fatherly man, whose name is Mr. Cantle, clears his throat.

"Well, young lady, are you ready to go to work?"

"Yes, sir," gravely from the elf.

"We'll see. Has anybody told you what you're going to do for us?"

"No, sir." Joe and Tesla exhale quietly.

"Good." He eyes her, probing for the blind brain in the room next door.

"Do you know what *advertising* is?"

He's talking dirty, hitting to shock. Delphi's eyes widen and her little chin goes up. Joe is in ecstasy at the complex expressions P. Burke is getting through. Mr. Cantle waits.

"It's, well, it's when they used to tell people to buy things." She swallows. "It's not allowed."

"That's right." Mr. Cantle leans back, grave. "Advertising as it used to be is against the law. *A display other than the legitimate use of the product, intended to promote its sale.* In former times every manufacturer was free to tout his wares any way, place, or time he could afford. All the media and most of the landscape was taken up with extravagant competing displays. The thing became uneconomic. The public rebelled. Since the so-called Huckster Act sellers have been restrained to, I quote, displays in or on the product itself, visible during its legitimate use or in on-premise sales." Mr. Cantle leans forward. "Now tell me, Delphi, why do people buy one product rather than another?"

"Well . . . Enchanting puzzlement from Delphi. "They, um, they see them and like them, or they hear about them from somebody?" (Touch of P. Burke there; she didn't say, from a friend.)

"Partly. Why did *you* buy your particular body-lift?"

"I never had a body-lift, sir."

Mr. Cantle frowns; what gutters do they drag for these Remotes?

"Well, what brand of water do you drink?"

"Just what was in the faucet, sir," says Delphi humbly. "I—I did try to boil it"

"Good god." He scowls; Tesla stiffens. "Well, what did you boil it in? A cooker?"

The shining yellow head nods.

"What *brand* of cooker did you buy?"

"I didn't buy it, sir," says frightened P. Burke through Delphi's lips. "But—I know the best kind! Ananga has a Burnbabi. I saw the name when she—"

"Exactly!" Cantle's fatherly beam comes back strong; the Burnbabi account is a strong one, too. "You saw Ananga using one so you thought it must be good, eh? And it is good, or a great human being like Ananga wouldn't be using it. Absolutely right. And now, Delphi, you know what you're going to be doing for us. You're going to show some products. Doesn't sound very hard, does it?"

"Oh, no, sir" . . . Baffled child's stare; Joe gloats.

"And you must never, *never* tell anyone what you're doing." Cantle's eyes bore for the brain behind this seductive child.

"You're wondering why we ask you to do this, naturally. There's a very serious reason. All those products people use, foods and healthaids and cookers and cleaners and clothes and cars—they're all made by *people*. Somebody put in years of hard work designing and making them. A man comes up with a fine new idea for a better product. He has to get a factory and machinery, and hire workmen. Now. What happens if people have no way of hearing about his product? Word of mouth is far too slow and unreliable. Nobody might ever stumble onto his new product or find out how good it was, right? And then he and all the people who worked for him—they'd go bankrupt, right? So, Delphi, there has to be *some way* that large numbers of people can get a look at a good new product, right? How? By letting people see you using it. You're giving that man a chance."

Delphi's little head is nodding in happy relief.

"Yes, sir, I do see now—but sir, it seems so sensible, why don't they let you—"

Cantle smiles sadly.

"It's an overreaction, my dear. History goes by swings. People overreact and pass harsh unrealistic laws which attempt to stamp out an essential social process. When this happens, the people who understand have to carry on as best they can until the pendulum swings back." He sighs. "The Huckster Laws are bad, inhuman laws, Delphi, despite their good intent. If they were strictly observed they would wreak havoc. Our economy, our society, would be cruelly destroyed. We'd be back in caves!" His inner fire is showing; if the Huckster Laws were strictly enforced he'd be back punching a databank.

"It's our duty, Delphi. Our solemn social duty. We are not breaking the law. You will be using the product. But people wouldn't understand, if they knew. They would become upset just as you did. So you must be very, very careful not to mention any of this to anybody."

(And somebody will be very, very carefully monitoring Delphi's speech circuits.)

"Now we're all straight, aren't we? Little Delphi here"—he is speaking to the invisible creature next door—"little Delphi is going to live a wonderful, exciting life. She's going to be a girl people watch. And she's going to be using fine products people will be glad to know about and helping the good people who make them. Yours will be a genuine social contribution." He keys up his pitch; the creature in there must be older.

Delphi digests this with ravishing gravity.

"But sir, how do I—?"

"Don't worry about a thing. You'll have people behind you whose job it is to select the most worthy products for you to use. Your job is just to do as they say. They'll show you what outfits to wear to parties, what suncars and viewers to buy, and so on. That's all you have to do."

Parties—clothes—suncars! Delphi's pink mouth opens. In P. Burke's starved seventeen-year-old head the ethics of product sponsorship float far away.

"Now tell me in your own words what your job is, Delphi."

"Yes, sir. I—I'm to go to parties and buy things and use them as they tell me, to help the people who work in factories."

"And what did I say was so important?"

"Oh—I shouldn't let anybody know, about the things."

"Right." Mr. Cantle has another paragraph he uses when the subject shows, well, immaturity. But he can sense only eagerness here. Good. He doesn't really enjoy the other speech.

"It's a lucky girl who can have all the fun she wants while doing good for others, isn't it?" He beams around. There's a prompt shuffling of chairs. Clearly this one is go.

Joe leads her out, grinning. The poor fool thinks they're admiring her coordination.

It's out into the world for Delphi now, and at this point the up-channels get used. On the administrative side account schedules are opened, subprojects activated. On the technical side the reserved bandwidth is cleared. (That carrier field, remember?) A new name is waiting for Delphi, a name she'll never hear. It's a long string of binaries which have been quietly cycling in a GTX tank ever since a certain Beautiful Person didn't wake up.

The name winks out of cycle, dances from pulses into modulations of modulations, whizzes through phasing, and shoots into a giga-band beam racing up to a synchronous satellite poised over Guatemala. From there the beam pours twenty thousand miles back to Earth again, forming an all-pervasive field of structured energics supplying tuned demand-points all over the CanAm quadrant.

With that field, if you have the right credit rating, you can sit at a GTX console and operate an ore-extractor in Brazil. Or—if you have some simple credentials like being able to walk on water—you could shoot a spool into the network holocam shows running day and night in every home and dorm and rec site. *Or* you could create a continent-wide traffic jam. Is it any wonder GTX guards those inputs like a sacred trust.

Delphi's "name" appears as a tiny analyzable nonredundancy in the flux, and she'd be very proud if she knew about it. It would strike P. Burke as magic; P. Burke never even understood robot-cars. But Delphi is in no sense a robot. Call her a waldo if you must. The fact is she's just a girl, a real-live girl with her brain in an unusual place. A simple real-time on-line system with plenty of bit-rate—even as you and you.

The point of all this hardware, which isn't very much hardware in this society, is so Delphi can walk out of that underground suite, a mobile demand-point draining an omnipresent fieldform. And she does—eighty-nine pounds of tender girl flesh and blood with a few metallic components, stepping out into the sunlight to be taken to her new life. A girl with everything going for her including a meditech escort. Walking lovely, stopping to widen her eyes at the big antennae system overhead.

The mere fact that something called P. Burke is left behind down underground has no bearing at all. P. Burke is totally un-self aware and happy as a clam in its shell. (Her bed has been moved into the waldo cabinet room now.) And P. Burke isn't in the cabinet; P. Burke is climbing out of an airvan in a fabulous Colorado beef preserve, and her name is Delphi. Delphi is looking at live Charolais steers and live cottonwoods and aspens gold against the blue smog and stepping over live grass to be welcomed by the reserve super's wife.

The super's wife is looking forward to a visit from Delphi and her friends, and by a happy coincidence there's a holocam outfit here doing a piece for the nature nuts.

You could write the script yourself now, while Delphi learns a few rules about structural interferences and how to handle the tiny time lag which results from the new forty-thousand-mile parenthesis in her nervous system. That's right—the people with the leased holocam rig naturally find the gold aspen shadows look a lot better on Delphi's flank than they do on a steer. And Delphi's face improves the mountains too, when you can see them. But the nature freaks aren't quite as joyful as you'd expect.

"See you in Barcelona, kitten," the headman says sourly as they pack up.

"Barcelona?" echoes Delphi with that charming little subliminal lag. She sees where his hand is and steps back.

"Cool, it's not her fault," another man says wearily. He knocks back his grizzled hair. "Maybe they'll leave in some of the gut."

Delphi watches them go off to load the spools on the GTX transport for processing. Her hand roves over the breast the man had touched. Back under Carbondale, P. Burke has discovered something new about her Delphi-body.

About the difference between Delphi and her own grim carcass.

She's always known Delphi has almost no sense of taste or smell. They explained about that: only so much bandwidth. You don't have to taste a suncar, do you? And the slight overall dimness of Delphi's sense of touch—she's familiar with that, too. Fabrics that would prickle P. Burke's own hide feel like a cool plastic film to Delphi.

But the blank spots. It took her a while to notice them. Delphi doesn't have much privacy; investments of her size don't. So she's slow about discovering there's certain definite places where her beastly P. Burke body *feels* things that Delphi's dainty flesh does not. H'mm! Channel space again, she thinks—and forgets it in the pure bliss of being Delphi.

You ask how a girl could forget a thing like that? Look. P. Burke is about as far as you can get from the concept *girl*. She's a female, yes—but for her, sex is a four-letter word spelled P-A-I-N. She isn't quite a virgin. You don't want the details; she'd been about twelve and the freak lovers were bombed blind. When they came down, they threw her out with a small hole in her anatomy and a mortal one elsewhere. She dragged off to buy her first and last shot, and she can still hear the clerk's incredulous guffaws.

Do you see why Delphi grins, stretching her delicious little numb body in the sun she faintly feels? Beams, saying, "Please, I'm ready now."

Ready for what? For Barcelona like the sour man said, where his nature-thing is now making it strong in the amateur section of the Festival. A winner! Like he also said, a lot of strip mines and dead fish have been scrubbed, but who cares with Delphi's darling face so visible?

James Tiptree Jr. (Alice B. Sheldon)

So it's time for Delphi's face and her other delectabilities to show on Barcelona's Playa Nueva. Which means switching her channel to the EurAf synchsat.

They ship her at night so the nanosecond transfer isn't even noticed by that insignificant part of Delphi that lives five hundred feet under Carbondale, so excited the nurse has to make sure she eats. The circuit switches while Delphi "sleeps," that is, while P. Burke is out of the waldo cabinet. The next time she plugs in to open Delphi's eyes it's no different—do you notice which relay boards your phone calls go through?

And now for the event that turns the sugarcube from Colorado into the PRINCESS.

Literally true, he's a prince, or rather an Infante of an old Spanish line that got shined up in the Neomonarchy. He's also eighty-one, with a passion for birds—the kind you see in zoos. Now it suddenly turns out that he isn't poor at all. Quite the reverse; his old sister laughs in their tax lawyer's face and starts restoring the family hacienda while the Infante totters out to court Delphi. And little Delphi begins to live the life of the gods.

What do gods do? Well, everything beautiful. But (remember Mr. Cantle?) the main point is Things. Ever see a god empty-handed? You can't be a god without at least a magic girdle or an eight-legged horse. But in the old days some stone tablets or winged sandals or a chariot drawn by virgins would do a god for life. No more! Gods make it on novelty now. By Delphi's time the hunt for new god-gear is turning the earth and seas inside-out and sending frantic fingers to the stars. And what gods have, mortals desire.

So Delphi starts on a Euromarket shopping spree squired by her old Infante, thereby doing her bit to stave off social collapse.

Social what? Didn't you get it, when Mr. Cantle talked about a world where advertising is banned and fifteen billion consumers are glued to their holocam shows? One capricious self-powered god can wreck you.

Take the nose-filter massacre. Years, the industry sweated years to achieve an almost invisible enzymatic filter. So one day a couple of pop-gods show up wearing nose-filters like *big purple bats.* By the end of the week the world market is screaming for purple bats. Then it switched to bird-heads and skulls, but by the time the industry retooled the crazies had dropped bird-heads and gone to injection globes. Blood!

Multiply that by a million consumer industries, and you can see why it's economic to have a few controllable gods. Especially with the beautiful hunk of space R & D the Peace Department laid out for and which the taxpayers are only too glad to have taken off their hands by an outfit like GTX, which everybody knows is almost a public trust.

And so you—or rather, GTX—find a creature like P. Burke and give her Delphi. And Delphi helps keep things *orderly*, she does what you tell her to. Why? That's right, Mr. Cantle never finished his speech.

But here come the tests of Delphi's button-nose twinkling in the torrent of news and entertainment. And she's noticed. The feedback shows a flock of viewers turning up the amps when this country baby gets tangled in her new colloidal body-jewels. She registers at a couple of major scenes, too, and when the Infante gives her a suncar, little Delphi trying out suncars is a tiger. There's a solid response in high-credit country. Mr. Cantle is humming his happy tune as he cancels a Benelux subnet option to guest her on a nude cook-show called Wok Venus.

And now for the superposh old-world wedding! The hacienda has Moorish baths and six-foot silver candelabra and real black horses, and the Spanish Vatican blesses them. The final event is a grand gaucho ball with the old prince and his little Infanta on a bowered balcony. She's a spectacular doll of silver lace, wildly launching toy doves at her new friends whirling by below.

The Infante beams, twitches his old nose to the scent of her sweet excitement. His doctor has been very helpful. Surely now, after he has been so patient with the suncars and all the nonsense—

The child looks up at him, saying something incomprehensible about "breath." He makes out that she's complaining about the three singers she had begged for.

"They've changed!" she marvels. "Haven't they changed? They're so dreary. I'm so happy now!"

And Delphi falls fainting against a gothic vargueno.

Her American duenna rushes up, calls help. Delphi's eyes are open, but Delphi isn't there. The duenna pokes among Delphi's hair, slaps her. The old prince grimaces. He has no idea what she is beyond an excellent solution to his tax problems, but he had been a falconer in his youth. There comes to his mind the small pinioned birds which were flung up to stimulate the hawks. He pockets the veined claw to which he had promised certain indulgences and departs to design his new aviary.

And Delphi also departs with her retinue to the Infante's newly discovered yacht. The trouble isn't serious. It's only that five thousand miles away and five hundred feet down P. Burke has been doing it too well.

They've always known she has terrific aptitude. Joe says he never saw a Remote take over so fast. No disorientations, no rejections. The psychomed talks about self-alienation. She's going into Delphi like a salmon to the sea.

She isn't eating or sleeping, they can't keep her out of the body-cabinet to get her blood moving, there are necroses under her grisly sit-down. Crisis!

So Delphi gets a long "sleep" on the yacht and P. Burke gets it pounded through her perforated head that she's endangering Delphi. (Nurse Fleming thinks of that, thus alienating the psychomed.)

They rig a pool down there (Nurse Fleming again) and chase P. Burke back and forth. And she loves it. So naturally when they let her plug in again Delphi loves it too. Every noon beside the yacht's hydrofoils darling Delphi clips along in the blue sea they've warned her not to drink. And every night around the shoulder of the world an ill-shaped thing in a dark burrow beats its way across a sterile pool.

So presently the yacht stands up on its foils and carries Delphi to the program Mr. Cantle has waiting. It's long-range; she's scheduled for at least two decades' product life. Phase One calls for her to connect with a flock of young ultrariches who are romping loose between Brioni and Djakarta where a competitor named PEV could pick them off.

A routine luxgear op, see; no politics, no policy angles, and the main budget items are the title and the yacht, which was idle anyway. The storyline is that Delphi goes to accept some rare birds for her prince—who cares? The *point* is that the Haiti area is no longer radioactive and look!—the gods are there. And so are several new Carib West Happy Isles which can afford GTX rates, in fact two of them are GTX subsids.

But you don't want to get the idea that all these newsworthy people are wired-up robbies, for pity's sake. You don't need many if they're placed right. Delphi asks Joe about that when he comes down to Barranquilla to check her over. (P. Burke's own mouth hasn't said much for a while.)

"Are there many like me?"

"Nobody's like you, buttons. Look, are you still getting Van Allen warble?"

"I mean, like Davy. Is he a Remote?"

(Davy is the lad who is helping her collect the birds. A sincere redhead who needs a little more exposure.)

"Davy? He's one of Matt's boys, some psychojob. They haven't any channel."

"What about the real ones? Djuma van O, or Ali, or Jim Ten?"

"Djuma was born with a pile of GTX basic where her brain should be, she's nothing but a pain. Jimsy does what his astrologer tells him. Look, peanut, where do you get the idea you aren't real? You're the realest. Aren't you having joy?"

"Oh, Joe!" Hinging her little arms around him and his analyzer grids. "Oh, *me gusto mucho, muchisimo!*"

"Hey, hey." He pets her yellow head, folding the analyzer.

Three thousand miles north and five hundred feet down a forgotten hulk in a body-waldo glows.

And is she having joy. To waken out of the nightmare of being P. Burke and find herself a peri, a star-girl? On a yacht in paradise with no more to do than adorn herself and play with toys and attend revels and greet her friends—her, P. Burke, having friends!—and turn the right way for the holocams? Joy!

And it shows. One look at Delphi and the viewers know:

DREAMS CAN COME TRUE.

Look at her riding pillion on Davy's sea-bike, carrying an apoplectic macaw in a silver hoop. Oh, *Morton, let's go there this winter!* Or learning the Japanese chinchona from that Kobe group, in a dress that looks like a blowtorch rising from one knee, and which should sell big in Texas. *Morton, is that real fire?* Happy, happy little girl!

And Davy. He's her pet and her baby, and she loves to help him fix his red-gold hair. (P. Burke marveling, running Delphi's fingers through the curls.) Of course Davy is one of Matt's boys—not impotent exactly, but very *very* low drive. (Nobody knows exactly what Matt does with his bitty budget, but the boys are useful and one or two have made names.) He's perfect for Delphi; in fact the psychomed lets her take him to bed, two kittens in a basket. Davy doesn't mind the fact that Delphi "sleeps" like the dead. That's when P. Burke is out of the body-waldo up at Carbondale, attending to her own depressing needs.

A funny thing about that. Most of her sleepy-time Delphi's just a gently ticking lush little vegetable waiting for P. Burke to get back on the controls. But now and again Delphi all by herself smiles a bit or stirs in her "sleep." Once she breathed a sound: "Yes."

Under Carbondale P. Burke knows nothing. She's asleep too, dreaming of Delphi, what else? But if the bushy Dr. Tesla had heard that single syllable, his bush would have turned snow-white. Because Delphi is TURNED OFF.

He doesn't. Davy is too dim to notice, and Delphi's staff boss, Hopkins, wasn't monitoring.

And they've all got something else to think about now, because the cold-fire dress sells half a million copies, and not only in Texas. The GTX computers already know it. When they correlate a minor demand for macaws in Alaska the problem comes to human attention: Delphi is something special.

It's a problem, see, because Delphi is targeted on a limited consumer bracket. Now it turns out she has mass-pop potential—those macaws in *Fairbanks*, man!—it's like trying to shoot mice with an ABM. A whole new ball game. Dr. Tesla and the fatherly Mr. Cantle start going around in headquarters circles and buddy-lunching together when they can get away from a seventh-level weasel boy who scares them both.

In the end it's decided to ship Delphi down to the GTX holocam enclave in Chile to try a spot on one of the mainstream shows. (Never mind why an Infanta takes up acting.) The holocam complex occupies a couple of mountains where an observatory once used the clean air. Holocam total-environment shells are very expensive and electronically superstable. Inside them actors can move freely without going off-register, and the whole scene or any selected part will show up in the viewer's home in complete three-

James Tiptree Jr. (Alice B. Sheldon)

di, so real you can look up their noses and much denser than you get from mobile rigs. You can blow a tit ten feet tall when there's no molecular skiffle around.

The enclave looks—well, take everything you know about Hollywood-Burbank and throw it away. What Delphi sees coming down is a neat giant mushroom-farm, domes of all sizes up to monsters for the big games and stuff. It's orderly. The idea that art thrives on creative flamboyance has long been torpedoed by proof that what art needs is computers. Because this showbiz has something TV and Hollywood never *had—automated inbuilt viewer feedback.* Samples, ratings, critics, polls? Forget it. With that carrier field you can get real-time response-sensor readouts from every receiver in the world, served up at your console. That started as a thingie to give the public more influence on content.

Yes.

Try it, man. You're at the console. Slice to the sex-age-edu-econ-ethno-cetera audience of your choice and start. You can't miss. Where the feedback warms up, give 'em more of that. Warm—warmer—hot! You've hit it—the secret itch under those hides, the dream in those hearts. You don't need to know its name. With your hand controlling all the input and your eye reading all the response, you can make them a god . . . and somebody'll do the same for you.

But Delphi just sees rainbows, when she gets through the degaussing ports and the field relay and takes her first look at the insides of those shells. The next thing she sees is a team of shapers and technicians descending on her, and millisecond timers everywhere. The tropical leisure is finished. She's in gigabuck mainstream now, at the funnel maw of the unceasing hose that's pumping the sight and sound and flesh and blood and sobs and laughs and dreams of *reality* into the world's happy head. Little Delphi is going plonk into a zillion homes in prime time and nothing is left to chance. Work!

And again Delphi proves apt. Of course it's really P. Burke down under Carbondale who's doing it, but who remembers that carcass? Certainly not P. Burke, she hasn't spoken through her own mouth for months. Delphi doesn't even recall dreaming of her when she wakes up.

As for the show itself, don't bother. It's gone on so long no living soul could unscramble the plotline. Delphi's trial spot has something to do with a widow and her dead husband's brother's amnesia.

The flap comes after Delphi's spots begin to flash out along the world-hose and the feedback appears. You've guessed it, of course. Sensational! As you'd say, they IDENTIFY.

The report actually says something like InskinEmp with a string of percentages, meaning that Delphi not only has it for anybody with a Y chromosome, but also for women and everything in between. It's the sweet supernatural jackpot, the million-to-one.

Remember your Harlow? A sexpot, sure. But why did bitter hausfraus in Gary and Memphis know that the vanilla-ice-cream goddess with the white hair and crazy eyebrows was *their baby girl?* And write loving letters to Jean warning her that their husbands weren't good enough for her? Why? The GTX analysts don't know either, but they know what to do with it when it happens.

(Back in his bird sanctuary the old Infante spots it without benefit of computers and gazes thoughtfully at his bride in widow's weeds. It might, he feels, be well to accelerate the completion of his studies.)

The excitement reaches down to the burrow under Carbondale where P. Burke gets two medical exams in a week and a chronically inflamed electrode is replaced. Nurse Fleming also gets an assistant who doesn't do much nursing but is very interested in access doors and identity tabs.

And in Chile, little Delphi is promoted to a new home up among the stars' residential spreads and a private jitney to carry her to work. For Hopkins there's a new computer terminal and a full-time schedule man. What is the schedule crowded with?

Things.

And here begins the trouble. You probably saw that coming too.

"What does she think she is, a goddamn *consumer rep?*" Mr. Cantle's fatherly face in Carbondale contorts.

"The girl's upset," Miss Fleming says stubbornly. "She *believes* that, what you told her about helping people and good new products."

"They are good products," Mr. Cantle snaps automatically, but his anger is under control. He hasn't got where he is by irrelevant reactions.

"She says the plastic gave her a rash and the glo-pills made her dizzy."

"Good god, she shouldn't swallow them," Dr. Tesla puts in agitatedly.

"You told her she'd use them," persists Miss Fleming.

Mr. Cantle is busy figuring how to ease this problem to the feral-faced young man. What, was it a goose that lays golden eggs?

Whatever he says to Level Seven, down in Chile the offending products vanish. And a symbol goes into Delphi's tank matrix, one that means roughly *Balance unit resistance against PR index.* This means that Delphi's complaints will be endured as long as her Pop Response stays above a certain level. (What happens when it sinks need not concern us.) And to compensate, the price of her exposure-time rises again. She's a regular on the show now and response is still climbing.

See her under the sizzling lasers, in a holocam shell set up as a walkway accident. (The show is guesting an acupuncture school shill.)

"I don't think this new body-lift is safe," Delphi's saying. "It's made a funny blue spot on me—look, Mr. Vere."

She wiggles to show where the mini-grav pak that imparts a delicious sense of weightlessness is attached.

"So don't leave it *on*, Dee. With your meat—watch that deck-spot, it's starting to synch."

"But if I don't wear it it isn't honest. They should insulate it more or something, don't you see?"

The show's beloved old father, who is the casualty, gives a senile snigger.

"I'll tell them," Mr. Vere mutters. Look now, as you step back bend like this so it just shows, see? And hold two beats."

Obediently Delphi turns, and through the dazzle her eyes connect with a pair of strange dark ones. She squints. A quite young man is lounging alone by the port, apparently waiting to use the chamber.

Delphi's used by now to young men looking at her with many peculiar expressions, but she isn't used to what she gets here. A jolt of something somber and knowing. *Secrets.*

"Eyes! Eyes, Dee!"

She moves through the routine, stealing peeks at the stranger. He stares back. He knows something.

When they let her go she comes shyly to him.

"Living wild, kitten." Cool voice, hot underneath.

"What do you mean?"

"Dumping on the product. You trying to get dead?"

"But it isn't right," she tells him. "They don't know, but I do, I've been wearing it." His cool is jolted.

"You're out of your head."

"Oh, they'll see I'm right when they check it," she explains. "They're just so busy. When I tell them—"

He is staring down at little flower-face. His mouth opens, closes. "What are you doing in this sewer anyway? Who are you?"

Bewilderedly she says, "I'm Delphi."

"Holy Zen."

"What's wrong? Who are you, please?"

Her people are moving her out now, nodding at him.

"Sorry we ran over, Mr. Uhunh," the script girl says.

He mutters something, but it's lost as her convoy bustles her toward the flower-decked jitney.

(Hear the click of an invisible ignition-train being armed?)

"Who was he?" Delphi asks her hairman.

The hairman is bending up and down from his knees as he works.

"Paul. Isham. Three," he says and puts a comb in his mouth.

"Who's that? I can't see."

He mumbles around the comb, meaning, "Are you jiving?" Because she has to be, in the middle of the GTX enclave.

Next day there's a darkly smoldering face under a turban-towel when Delphi and the show's paraplegic go to use the carbonated pool.

She looks.

He looks.

And the next day, too.

(Hear the automatic sequencer cutting in? The system couples, the fuels begin to travel.)

Poor old Isham senior. You have to feel sorry for a man who values order: when he begets young, genetic information is still transmitted in the old ape way. One minute it's a happy midget with a rubber duck—look around and here's this huge healthy stranger, opaquely emotional, running with god knows who. Questions are heard where there's nothing to question, and eruptions claiming to be moral outrage. When this is called to Papa's attention—it may take time, in that boardroom—Papa does what he can, but without immortality-juice the problem is worrisome.

And young Paul Isham is a bear. He's bright and articulate and tender-souled and incessantly active, and he and his friends are choking with appallment at the world their fathers made. And it hasn't taken Paul long to discover that *his* father's house has many mansions and even the GTX computers can't relate everything to everything else. He noses out a decaying project which adds up to something like, Sponsoring Marginal Creativity (the free-lance team that "discovered" Delphi was one such grantee). And from there it turns out that an agile lad named Isham can get his hands on a viable packet of GTX holocam facilities.

So here he is with his little band, way down the mushroom-farm mountain, busily spooling a show which has no relation to Delphi's. It's built on bizarre techniques and unsettling distortions pregnant with social protest. An *underground* expression to you.

All this isn't unknown to his father, of course, but so far it has done nothing more than deepen Isham senior's apprehensive frown.

Until Paul connects with Delphi.

And by the time Papa learns this, those invisible hypergolics have exploded, the energy-shells are rushing out. For Paul, you see, is the genuine article. He's serious. He dreams. He even reads—for example, *Green Mansions*—*and* he wept fiercely when those fiends burned Rima alive.

When he hears that some new GTX pussy is making it big, he sneers and forgets it. He's busy. He never connects the name with this little girl making her idiotic, doomed protest in the holocam chamber. This strangely simple little girl.

And she comes and looks up at him and he sees Rima, lost Rima the enchanted bird girl, and his unwired human heart goes twang.

And Rima turns out to be Delphi.

Do you need a map? The angry puzzlement. The rejection of the dissonance Rima-hustling-for-GTX-MyFather. Garbage, cannot be. The loitering around the pool to confirm the swindle . . . dark eyes hitting on blue wonder, jerky words exchanged in a peculiar stillness . . . the dreadful reorganization of the image into Rima-Delphi *in my Father's tentacles*—

You don't need a map.

Nor for Delphi either, the girl who loved her gods. She's seen their divine flesh close now, heard their unamplified voices call her name. She's played their god-games, worn their garlands. She's even become a goddess herself, though she doesn't believe it. She's not disenchanted, don't think that. She's still full of love. It's just that some crazy kind of *hope* hasn't—

Really you can skip all this, when the loving little girl on the yellow-brick road meets a Man. A real human male burning with angry compassion and grandly concerned with human justice, who reaches for her with real male arms and—boom! She loves him back with all her heart.

A happy trip, see?

Except.

Except that it's really P. Burke five thousand miles away who loves Paul. P. Burke the monster down in a dungeon smelling of electrode paste. A caricature of a woman burning, melting, obsessed with true love. Trying over twenty-double-thousand miles of hard vacuum to reach her beloved through girl-flesh numbed by an invisible film. Feeling his arms around the body he thinks is hers, fighting through shadows to give herself to him. Trying to taste and smell him through beautiful dead nostrils, to love him back with a body that goes dead in the heart of the fire.

Perhaps you get P. Burke's state of mind?

She has phases. The trying, first. And the shame. The SHAME. *I am not what thou lovest.* And the fiercer trying. And the realization that there is no, no way, none. Never. *Never.* . . A bit delayed, isn't it, her understanding that the bargain she made was forever? P. Burke should have noticed those stories about mortals who end up as grasshoppers.

You see the outcome—the funneling of all this agony into one dumb protoplasmic drive to fuse with Delphi. To leave, to close out the beast she is chained to. *To become Delphi.*

Of course it's impossible.

However, her torments have an effect on Paul. Delphi-as-Rima is a potent enough love object, and liberating Delphi's mind requires hours of deeply satisfying instruction in the rottenness of it all. Add in Delphi's body worshiping his flesh, burning in the fire of P. Burke's savage heart—do you wonder Paul is involved?

That's not all.

By now they're spending every spare moment together and some that aren't so spare.

"Mr. Isham, would you mind staying out of this sports sequence? The script calls for Davy here."

(Davy's still around, the exposure did him good.)

"What's the difference?" Paul yawns. "It's just an ad. I'm not blocking that thing."

Shocked silence at his two-letter word. The script girl swallows bravely.

"I'm sorry, sir, our directive is to do the *social sequence* exactly as scripted. We're having to respool the segments we did last week, Mr. Hopkins is very angry with me."

"Who the hell is Hopkins? Where is he?"

"Oh, please, Paul. *Please.*"

Paul unwraps himself, saunters back. The holocam crew nervously check their angles. The GTX boardroom has a foible about having things *pointed* at them and theirs. Cold shivers, when the image of an Isham nearly went onto the world beam beside that Dialadinner.

Worse yet, Paul has no respect for the sacred schedules which are now a full-time job for ferret boy up at headquarters. Paul keeps forgetting to bring her back on time, and poor Hopkins can't cope.

So pretty soon the boardroom data-ball has an urgent personal action-tab for Mr. Isham senior. They do it the gentle way, at first.

"I can't today, Paul."

"Why not?"

"They say I have to, it's *very* important."

He strokes the faint gold down on her narrow back. Under Carbondale, Pa., a blind mole-woman shivers.

"Important. Their importance. Making more gold. Can't you see? To them you're just a thing to get scratch with. A *huckster.* Are you going to let them screw you, Dee? Are you?"

"Oh, Paul—"

He doesn't know it, but he's seeing a weirdie; Remotes aren't hooked up to flow tears.

"Just say no, Dee. No. Integrity. You have to."

"But they say, it's my job—"

"Will you believe I can take care of you, Dee? Baby, baby, you're letting them rip us. You have to choose. Tell them, no."

"Paul . . . I w-will—"

And she does. Brave little Delphi (insane P. Burke). Saying, "No, please, I promised, Paul."

They try some more, still gently.

"Paul, Mr. Hopkins told me the reason they don't want us to be together so much. It's because of who you are, your father."

She thinks his father is like Mr. Cantle, maybe.

"Oh, great. Hopkins. I'll fix him. Listen, I can't think about Hopkins now. Ken came back today, he found out something."

They are lying on the high Andes meadow watching his friends dive their singing kites.

"Would you believe, on the coast the police have *electrodes in their heads?*"

She stiffens in his arms.

"Yeah, weird. I thought they only used PP on criminals and the army. Don't you see, Dee—something has to be going on. Some movement. Maybe somebody's organizing. How can we find out?" He pounds the ground behind her: "We should make *contact!* If we could only find out."

"The, the news?" she asks distractedly.

"The news." He laughs. "There's nothing in the news except what they want people to know. Half the country could burn up, and nobody would know it if they didn't want. Dee, can't you take what I'm explaining to you? They've got the whole world programmed! Total control of communication. They've got everybody's minds wired in to think what they show them and want what they give them and they give them what they're programmed to want—you can't break in or out of it, you can't get *hold* of it anywhere. I don't think they even have a plan except to keep things going round and round—and god knows what's happening to the people or the Earth or the other planets, maybe. One great big vortex of lies and garbage pouring round and round, getting bigger and bigger, and nothing can ever change. If people don't wake up soon we're through!"

He pounds her stomach softly.

"You have to break out, Dee."

"I'll try, Paul, I will—"

"You're mine. They can't have you."

And he goes to see Hopkins, who is indeed cowed.

But that night up under Carbondale the fatherly Mr. Cantle goes to see P. Burke.

P. Burke? On a cot in a utility robe like a dead camel in a tent, she cannot at first comprehend that he is telling *her* to break it off with Paul. P. Burke has never seen Paul. *Delphi* sees Paul. The fact is, P. Burke can no longer clearly recall that she exists apart from Delphi.

Mr. Cantle can scarcely believe it either, but he tries.

He points out the futility, the potential embarrassment, for Paul. That gets a dim stare from the bulk on the bed. Then he goes into her duty to GTX, her job, isn't she grateful for the opportunity, etcetera. He's very persuasive.

The cobwebby mouth of P. Burke opens and croaks.

"No."

Nothing more seems to be forthcoming.

Mr. Cantle isn't dense, he knows an immovable obstacle when he bumps one. He also knows an irresistible force: GTX. The simple solution is to lock the waldo-cabinet until Paul gets tired of waiting for Delphi to wake up. But the cost, the schedules! And there's something odd here. . . he eyes the corporate asset hulking on the bed and his hunch-sense prickles.

You see, Remotes don't love. They don't have real sex, the circuits designed that out from the start. So it's been assumed that it's *Paul* who is diverting himself or something with the pretty little body in Chile. P. Burke can only be doing what comes natural to any ambitious gutter-meat. It hasn't occurred to anyone that they're dealing with the real hairy thing whose shadow is blasting out of every holoshow on Earth.

Love?

Mr. Cantle frowns. The idea is grotesque. But his instinct for the fuzzy line is strong; he will recommend flexibility.

And so, in Chile:

"Darling, I don't have to work tonight! And Friday too—isn't that right, Mr. Hopkins?"

"Oh, great. When does she come up for parole?"

"Mr. Isham, please be reasonable. Our schedule—surely your own production people must be needing you?"

This happens to be true. Paul goes away. Hopkins stares after him, wondering distastefully why an Isham wants to ball a waldo. How sound are those boardroom belly-fears—garble creeps, creeps in! It never occurs to Hopkins that an Isham might not know what Delphi is.

Especially with Davy crying because Paul has kicked him out of Delphi's bed.

Delphi's bed is under a real window.

"Stars," Paul says sleepily. He rolls over, pulling Delphi on top. "Are you aware that this is one of the last places on Earth where people can see the stars? Tibet, too, maybe."

"Paul . . .

"Go to sleep. I want to see you sleep."

"Paul, I . . . I sleep so *hard*, I mean, it's a joke how hard I am to wake up. Do you mind?"

"Yes."

But finally, fearfully, she must let go. So that five thousand miles north a crazy spent creature can crawl out to gulp concentrates and fall on her cot. But not for long. It's pink dawn when Delphi's eyes open to find Paul's arms around her, his voice saying rude, tender things. He's been kept awake. The nerveless little statue that was her Delphi-body nuzzled him in the night.

Insane hope rises, is fed a couple of nights later when he tells her she called his name in her sleep.

And that day Paul's arms keep her from work and Hopkins's wails go up to headquarters where the weasel-faced lad is working his sharp tailbone off packing Delphi's program. Mr. Cantle defuses that one. But next week it happens again, to a major client. And ferret-face has connections on the technical side.

Now you can see that when you have a field of complexly heterodyned energy modulations tuned to a demand-point like Delphi, there are many problems of standwaves and lashback and skiffle of all sorts which are normally balanced out with ease by the technology of the future. By the same token they can be delicately unbalanced too, in ways that feed back into the waldo operator with striking results.

"Darling—what the hell! What's wrong? DELPHI!"

Helpless shrieks, writhings. Then the Rima-bird is lying wet and limp in his arms, her eyes enormous.

"I . . . I wasn't supposed to . . ." she gasps faintly. "They told me not to. . . "

"Oh, my *god—Delphi*."

And his hard fingers are digging in her thick yellow hair. Electronically knowledgeable fingers. They freeze.

"You're a *doll!* You're one of those PP implants. They control you. I should have known. Oh, god, I should have known."

"No, Paul," she's sobbing. "No, no, no—

"Damn them. Damn them, what they've done—you're not *you*—

He's shaking her, crouching over her in the bed and jerking her back and forth, glaring at the pitiful beauty.

"No!" she pleads (it's not true, that dark bad dream back there). "I'm Delphi!"

"My father. Filth, pigs—damn them, damn them, damn them."

"No, no," she babbles. "They were good to me—" P. Burke underground mouthing, "They were good to me—AAH-AAAAH!"

Another agony skewers her. Up north the sharp young man wants to make sure this so-tiny interference works. Paul can scarcely hang on to her, he's crying too. "I'll kill them."

His Delphi, a wired-up slave! Spikes in her brain, electronic shackles in his bird's heart. Remember when those savages burned Rima alive?

"I'll *kill* the man that's doing this to you."

He's still saying it afterward, but she doesn't hear. She's sure he hates her now, all she wants is to die. When she finally understands that the fierceness is tenderness, she thinks it's a miracle. *He knows—and he still loves!*

How can she guess that he's got it a little bit wrong?

You can't blame Paul. Give him credit that he's even heard about pleasure-pain implants and snoops, which by their nature aren't mentioned much by those who know them most intimately. That's what he thinks is being used on Delphi, something to *control* her. And to listen—he burns at the unknown ears in their bed.

Of waldo-bodies and objects like P. Burke he has heard nothing.

So it never crosses his mind as he looks down at his violated bird, sick with fury and love, that he isn't holding *all* of her. Do you need to be told the mad resolve jelling in him now?

To free Delphi.

How? Well, he is, after all, Paul Isham III. And he even has an idea where the GTX neurolab is. In Carbondale.

But first things have to be done for Delphi, and for his own stomach. So he gives her back to Hopkins and departs in a restrained and discreet way. And the Chile staff is grateful and do not understand that his teeth don't normally show so much.

And a week passes in which Delphi is a very good, docile little ghost. They let her have the load of wildflowers Paul sends and the bland loving notes. (He's playing it coony.) And up in headquarters weasel boy feels that *his* destiny has clicked a notch onward and floats the word up that he's handy with little problems.

And no one knows what P. Burke thinks in any way whatever, except that Miss Fleming catches her flushing her food down the can and next night she faints in the pool. They haul her out and stick her with IVs. Miss Fleming frets, she's seen expressions like that before. But she wasn't around when crazies who called themselves Followers of the Fish looked through flames to life everlasting. P. Burke is seeing Heaven

James Tiptree Jr. (Alice B. Sheldon)

on the far side of death, too. Heaven is spelled P-a-u-l, but the idea's the same. *I will die and be born again in Delphi.*

Garbage, electronically speaking. No way.

Another week and Paul's madness has become a plan. (Remember, he does have friends.) He smolders, watching his love paraded by her masters. He turns out a scorching sequence for his own show. And finally, politely, he requests from Hopkins a morsel of his bird's free time, which duly arrives.

"I thought you didn't *want* me anymore," she's repeating as they wing over mountain flanks in Paul's suncar. "Now you *know*—"

"Look at me!"

His hand covers her mouth, and he's showing her a lettered card.

DON'T TALK. THEY CAN HEAR EVERYTHING WE SAY. I'M TAKING YOU AWAY NOW.

She kisses his hand. He nods urgently, flipping the card.

DON'T BE AFRAID. I CAN STOP THE PAIN IF THEY TRY TO HURT YOU.

With his free hand he shakes out a silvery scrambler-mesh on a power pack. She is dumbfounded.

THIS WILL CUT THE SIGNALS AND PROTECT YOU DARLING.

She's staring at him, her head going vaguely from side to side, No.

"Yes!" He grins triumphantly. "Yes!"

For a moment she wonders. That powered mesh will cut off the field, all right. It will also cut off Delphi. But he is *Paul.* Paul is kissing her, she can only seek him hungrily as he sweeps the suncar through a pass.

Ahead is an old jet ramp with a shiny bullet waiting to go. (Paul also has credits and a Name.) The little GTX patrol courier is built for nothing but speed. Paul and Delphi wedge in behind the pilot's extra fuel tank, and there's no more talking when the torches start to scream.

They're screaming high over Quito before Hopkins starts to worry. He wastes another hour tracking the beeper on Paul's suncar. The suncar is sailing a pattern out to sea. By the time they're sure it's empty and Hopkins gets on the hot flue to headquarters, the fugitives are a sourceless howl above Carib West.

Up at headquarters weasel boy gets the squeal. His first impulse is to repeat his previous play, but then his brain snaps to. This one is too hot. Because, see, although in the long run they can make P. Burke do anything at all except maybe *live*, instant emergencies can be tricky. And—Paul Isham III.

"Can't you order her back?"

They're all in the GTX tower monitor station, Mr. Cantle and ferret-face and Joe and a very neat man who is Mr. Isham senior's personal eyes and ears.

"No, sir," Joe says doggedly. "We can read channels, particularly speech, but we can't interpolate organized pattern. It takes the waldo op to send one-to-one—"

"What are they saying?"

"Nothing at the moment, sir." The console jockey's eyes are closed. "I believe they are, ah, embracing."

"They're not answering," a traffic monitor says. "Still heading zero zero three zero—due north, sir."

"You're certain Kennedy is alerted not to fire on them?" the neat man asks anxiously.

"Yes, sir."

"Can't you just turn her off?" The sharp-faced lad is angry. "Pull that pig out of the controls!"

"If you cut the transmission cold you'll kill the Remote," Joe explains for the third time. "Withdrawal has to be phased right, you have to fade over to the Remote's own autonomics. Heart, breathing, cerebellum, would go blooey. If you pull Burke out you'll probably finish her too. It's a fantastic cybersystem, you don't want to do that."

"The investment." Mr. Cantle shudders.

Weasel boy puts his hand on the console jock's shoulder, it's the contact who arranged the no-no effect for him.

"We can at least give them a warning signal, sir." He licks his lips, gives the neat man his sweet ferret smile. "We know that does no damage."

Joe frowns, Mr. Cantle sighs. The neat man is murmuring into his wrist. He looks up. "I am authorized," he says reverently, "I am authorized to, ah, direct a signal. If this is the only course. But minimal, minimal."

Sharp-face squeezes his man's shoulder.

In the silver bullet shrieking over Charleston Paul feels Delphi arch in his arms. He reaches for the mesh, hot for action. She thrashes, pushing at his hands, her eyes roll. She's afraid of that mesh despite the agony. (And she's right.) Frantically Paul fights her in the cramped space, gets it over her head. As he turns the power up she burrows free under his arm and the spasm fades.

"They're calling you again, Mr. Isham!" the pilot yells.

"Don't answer. Darling, keep this over your head damn it how can I—"

An AX9O barrels over their nose, there's a flash.

"Mr. Isham! Those are air force jets!"

"Forget it," Paul shouts back. "They won't fire. Darling, don't be afraid."

Another AX9O rocks them.

"Would you mind pointing your pistol at my head where they can see it, sir?" the pilot howls.

Paul does so. The AX9Os take up escort formation around them. The pilot goes back to figuring how he can collect from GTX too, and after Goldsboro AB the escort peels away.

"Holding the same course." Traffic is reporting to the group around the monitor. "Apparently they've taken on enough fuel to bring them to towerport here."

"In that case it's just a question of waiting for them to dock." Mr. Cantle's fatherly manner revives a bit.

"Why can't they cut off that damn freak's life-support," the sharp young man fumes. "It's ridiculous."

"They're working on it," Cantle assures him.

What they're doing, down under Carbondale, is arguing.

Miss Fleming's watchdog has summoned the bushy man to the waldo room.

"Miss Fleming, you will obey orders."

"You'll kill her if you try that, sir. I can't believe you meant it, that's why I didn't. We've already fed her enough sedative to affect heart action; if you cut any more oxygen she'll die in there."

The bushy man grimaces. "Get Dr. Quine here fast."

They wait, staring at the cabinet in which a drugged, ugly madwoman fights for consciousness, fights to hold Delphi's eyes open.

High over Richmond the silver pod starts a turn. Delphi is sagged into Paul's arm, her eyes swim up to him.

"Starting down now, baby. It'll be over soon, all you have to do is stay alive, Dee."

" . . . stay alive . . . "

The traffic monitor has caught them. "Sir! They've turned off for Carbondale— Control has contact—"

"Let's go."

But the headquarters posse is too late to intercept the courier wailing into Carbondale. And Paul's friends have come through again. The fugitives are out through the freight dock and into the neurolab admin port before the guard gets organized. At the elevator Paul's face plus his handgun get them in.

"I want Doctor—what's his name, Dee? Dee!"

" . . . Tesla . . . " She's reeling on her feet.

"Dr. Tesla. Take me down to Tesla, fast."

Intercoms are squalling around them as they whoosh down, Paul's pistol in the guard's back. When the door slides open the bushy man is there.

———

"I'm Tesla."

"I'm Paul Isham. *Isham.* You're going to take your flaming implants out of this girl—now. Move!"

"What?"

"You heard me. Where's your operating room? Go!"

"But—"

"Move! Do I have to burn somebody?"

Paul waves the weapon at Dr. Quine, who has just appeared.

"No, no," says Tesla hurriedly. "But I can't, you know. It's impossible, there'll be nothing left."

"You screaming well can, right now. You mess up and I'll kill you," says Paul murderously. "Where is it, there? And wipe the feke that's on her circuits now."

He's backing them down the hall, Delphi heavy on his arm.

"Is this the place, baby? Where they did it to you?"

"Yes," she whispers, blinking at a door. "Yes . . ."

Because it is, see. Behind that door is the very suite where she was born.

Paul herds them through it into a gleaming hall. An inner door opens, and a nurse and a gray man rush out. And freeze.

Paul sees there's something special about that inner door. He crowds them past it and pushes it open and looks in.

Inside is a big mean-looking cabinet with its front door panels ajar.

And inside that cabinet is a poisoned carcass to whom something wonderful, unspeakable, is happening. Inside is P. Burke, the real living woman who knows that HE is there, coming closer—Paul whom she had fought to reach through forty thousand miles of ice—PAUL is here!—is yanking at the waldo doors—

The doors tear open and a monster rises up.

"Paul darling!" croaks the voice of love, and the arms of love reach for him.

And he responds.

Wouldn't you, if a gaunt she-golem flab-naked and spouting wires and blood came at you clawing with metal-studded paws—

"Get away!" He knocks wires.

It doesn't much matter which wires. P. Burke has, so to speak, her nervous system hanging out. Imagine somebody jerking a handful of your medulla—

She crashes onto the floor at his feet, flopping and roaring *PAUL-PAUL-PAUL* in rictus.

It's doubtful he recognizes his name or sees her life coming out of her eyes at him. And at the last it doesn't go to him. The eyes find Delphi, fainting by the doorway, and die.

———

James Tiptree Jr. (Alice B. Sheldon) |

Now of course Delphi is dead, too.

There's a total silence as Paul steps away from the thing by his foot.

"You killed her," Tesla says. "That was her."

"Your control." Paul is furious, the thought of that monster fastened into little Delphi's brain nauseates him. He sees her crumpling and holds out his arms. Not knowing she is dead.

And Delphi comes to him.

One foot before the other, not moving very well—but moving. Her darling face turns up. Paul is distracted by the terrible quiet, and when he looks down he sees only her tender little neck.

"Now you get the implants out," he warns them. Nobody moves.

"But, but she's dead," Miss Fleming whispers wildly.

Paul feels Delphi's life under his hand, they're talking about their monster. He aims his pistol at the gray man.

"You. If we aren't in your surgery when I count three, I'm burning off this man's leg."

"Mr. Isham," Tesla says desperately, "you have just killed the person who animated the body you call Delphi. Delphi herself is dead. If you release your arm you'll see what I say is true."

The tone gets through. Slowly Paul opens his arm, looks down.

"Delphi?"

She totters, sways, stays upright. Her face comes slowly up.

"Paul . . ." Tiny voice.

"Your crotty tricks," Paul snarls at them. "Move!"

"Look at her eyes," Dr. Quine croaks.

They look. One of Delphi's pupils fills the iris, her lips writhe weirdly.

"Shock." Paul grabs her to him. "*Fix* her!" He yells at them, aiming at Tesla.

"For god's sake . . . bring it in the lab." Tesla quavers.

"Good-bye-bye," says Delphi clearly. They lurch down the hall, Paul carrying her, and meet a wave of people.

Headquarters has arrived.

Joe takes one look and dives for the waldo room, running into Paul's gun.

"Oh, no, you don't."

Everybody is yelling. The little thing in his arm stirs, says plaintively, "I'm Delphi."

And all through the ensuing jabber and ranting she hangs on, keeping it up, the ghost of P. Burke or whatever whispering crazily, "Paul . . . Paul . . . Please, I'm Delphi . . . Paul?"

"I'm here, darling, I'm here." He's holding her in the nursing bed. Tesla talks, talks, talks unheard.

"Paul . . . don't sleep . . . . " The ghost-voice whispers. Paul is in agony, he will not accept, WILL NOT believe.

Tesla runs down.

And then near midnight Delphi says roughly, "Ag-ag-ag—" and slips onto the floor, making a rough noise like a seal.

Paul screams. There's more of the *ag-ag* business and more gruesome convulsive disintegrations, until by two in the morning Delphi is nothing but a warm little bundle of vegetative functions hitched to some expensive hardware—the same that sustained her before her life began. Joe has finally persuaded Paul to let him at the waldo cabinet. Paul stays by her long enough to see her face change in a dreadfully alien and coldly convincing way, and then he stumbles out bleakly through the group in Tesla's office.

Behind him Joe is working wet-faced, sweating to reintegrate the fantastic complex of circulation, respiration, endocrines, midbrain homeostases, the patterned flux that was a human being—it's like saving an orchestra abandoned in midair. Joe is also crying a little; he alone had truly loved P. Burke. P. Burke, now a dead pile on a table, was the greatest cybersystem he has ever known, and he never forgets her.

The end, really.

You're curious?

Sure, Delphi lives again. Next year she's back on the yacht getting sympathy for her tragic breakdown. But there's a different chick in Chile, because while Delphi's new operator is competent, you don't get two P. Burkes in a row—for which GTX is duly grateful.

The real belly-bomb of course is Paul. He was *young*, see. Fighting abstract wrong. Now life has clawed into him and he goes through gut rage and grief and grows in human wisdom and resolve. So much so that you won't be surprised, sometime later, to find him—where?

In the GTX boardroom, dummy. Using the advantage of his birth to radicalize the system. You'd call it "boring from within."

That's how he put it, and his friends couldn't agree more. It gives them a warm, confident feeling to know that Paul is up there. Sometimes one of them who's still around runs into him and gets a big hello.

And the sharp-faced lad?

Oh, he matures too. He learns fast, believe it. For instance, he's the first to learn that an obscure GTX research unit is actually getting something with their loopy temporal anomalizer project. True, he doesn't have a physics background, and he's bugged quite a few people. But he doesn't really learn about that until the day he stands where somebody points him during a test run—

—and wakes up lying on a newspaper headlined NIXON UNVEILS PHASE TWO.

Lucky he's a fast learner.

Believe it, zombie. When I say growth, I mean *growth*. Capital appreciation. You can stop sweating. There's a great future there.

Index